The Life of Confucius

by Qu Chunli

Foreign Languages Press Beijing

First Edition 1996

The present volume is a translation of the first Chinese edition of
The Life of Confucius published in June 1990 by the Shandong
Friendship Press. The illustrations are drawn by Ma Ji specially for
the English edition of the book.

Translated by Sun Haichen

Hardback ISBN 7-119-01863-9
Paperback ISBN 7-119-01909-0

© Foreign Languages Press, Beijing, 1996
Published by Foreign Languages Press
24 Baiwanzhuang Road, Beijing 100037, China

Printed by Beijing Foreign Languages Printing House
19 Chegongzhuang Xilu, Beijing 100044, China

Distributed by China International Book Trading Corporation
35 Chegongzhuang Xilu, Beijing 100044, China
P.O. Box 399, Beijing 100044, China

Printed in the People's Republic of China

The portrait of Confucius

Preface to the Chinese Edition

Confucius was a great thinker, statesman and educationist in the late Spring and Autumn Period (770-476 B.C.) and founder of the Confucian school of thought in China. In this book Qu Chunli gives a detailed description of the life of Confucius by drawing on the vast compendium of historical data available. The arduous life journey of Confucius is placed against a broad background of feudal states competing for supremacy under the weakening authority of the Zhou Dynasty.

The contribution of Confucius in history is exceptional. He was the first private teacher in China. It is said that he taught a total of three thousand students in his lifetime, among whom seventy-two were well versed in the so-called six arts of rites, music, archery, charioteering, calligraphy, and arithmetic. He studied diligently and taught tirelessly all his life. His political and educational thought has influenced China for over two thousand years. He also contributed greatly to the preservation of ancient Chinese culture by expounding, collating and editing *The Book of Poetry*, *The Book of Rites*, *The Book of Music*, *The Book of Changes*, and *The Book of Documents* and composing *The Spring and Autumn Annals*. When he served as magistrate of Zhongdu and chief of justice in the state of Lu, he was able to prove the soundness of his political thought by making such great improvements in social moral standard that "people didn't have to lock their doors at night, and no one picked up the things others had lost." Unfortunately, wandering from state to state, he failed to find a ruler willing to commit himself to the moral reform he advocated. The author has based the plot of the story on historical facts and employed fictitious descriptions only as a complementary device. As a result, the book gives an objective, true-to-fact account of the great philosopher's life. Due to its compact structure, vivid story line, and fluent language, the book appeals to readers of various tastes.

I did not meet Qu Chunli until after the establishment of the China Confucian Foundation. He graduated from the Department of Chinese Literature at Shandong University in the 1960s. Subsequently he worked in Jining, the homeland of Confucius and Mencius, for over twenty years, which gave him a good opportunity to pursue his interests in Confucius. He studied a lot of historical data, met with a lot of people to collect legends about Confucius, and traveled over many rivers and hills in the footsteps of Confucius. He has already published *Folk Customs in the Homeland of Confucius and Mencius* and *Tales of Poetic Couplets and Inscribed Boards in the Confucius Residence.*

As *The Life of Confucius* is going to press, I have pleasure in writing this preface by way of congratulation.

Kuang Yaming
February 8, 1989 in Nanjing

Contents

CONTENTS

CONTENTS

Chapter One

Shuliang He Distinguishes Himself
in the Battlefield;
Yan Zhengzai Gives Birth to a Long-expected Son

In the Spring and Autumn period, China was torn asunder by intermittent wars among the vassal rulers. In autumn of 563 B.C. Duke Xiang, ruler of the state of Lu, dispatched his chief general Mengsun Mie with three hundred war chariots to attack the city of Biyang. The banner-strewn chariots raced along the main road, headed by the general's chariot flying a banner embroidered with an enormous character, "Lu."

The chariots reached the city and aligned themselves in preparation for attack. Mengsun Mie stood in his chariot and sized up the situation. He knitted his brows and stroked his grey beard. The city gate was wide open, and there were no soldiers to be seen. The firm and decisive general hesitated, fearing a trap.

His troops grew impatient. "General, let me lead an assault! Just give an order!" pleaded an officer. "General, let us charge into the city!" said another.

Mengsun Mie remained undecided despite these clamors for action. He rubbed his hands, trying hard to think, and finally stamped his foot and drew his sword, with which he made a decisive slicing motion in the air. "Charge!" he ordered.

More than twenty chariots rumbled forward. Each soldier carried a shield in the left hand and a broadsword in the right, and they rushed to the city gate amid deafening battle cries.

After eight chariots entered the city, enemy soldiers suddenly emerged on the city wall and started to lower a massive suspension gate. The men of Lu were taken by surprise.

At this critical moment the ninth chariot was just passing through the city gate. A tall driver leapt out and propped up the suspension gate with his hands, shouting, "There's ambush in the city! Withdraw quickly!"

Hearing this, the troops that had entered the city turned and rushed out.

1

The gate fell to the ground with a heavy thump as the soldier who had supported it stepped back nimbly. The men of Lu recognized him. It was Shuliang He, who had always showed great courage in combat.

Mie shouted his order, "The rear guard changes to vanguard! About face! Return to camp-site!" The battle chariots quickly retreated.

At this moment the enemy commander cried, "Shoot your arrows!" At his order, arrows fell from the city like rain, but the Lu army had already moved out of range.

When the army stopped for a rest, many soldiers jumped out of their chariots and crowded round Shuliang, hugging him. Those who had escaped from the city showed their gratitude by raising him aloft on their shoulders. Mie joined them, patted Shuliang on the shoulder, and said in a voice somewhat hoarse with excitement, "Excellent! What a hero! You have achieved great merits by saving our army from a heavy loss. I'll report this truthfully to the sovereign and ask for ample rewards on your behalf."

On their return to the capital of Lu, the troops were met by the residents of the city, who lined up along the main road to welcome their men returning from battle.

Still excited at what he had achieved in the battle, Shuliang headed home in bouncing steps. But his happy mood did not last when he was greeted by members of his family. His wife Shi had borne him nine daughters but no son. If he had no heir to continue the family line, how was he to face his own ancestors when he died?

Shuliang had an ancestral line reaching back to Cheng Tang, the sage king of the Shang Dynasty (c. 16th-11th century B.C.). After overthrowing the rule of Shang and setting up the Zhou Dynasty (11th century-256 B.C.), Ji Fa, or King Wu of Zhou, enfeoffed Wu Geng, the son of the last Shang king, to a place called Chaoge. When King Wu died, his teenaged son, Ji Song, succeeded to the throne. He was known as King Cheng of Zhou. The Duke of Zhou (Ji Dan), Ji Song's uncle, acted as the regent. Taking advantage of the situation, Wu Geng raised a revolt. The Duke of Zhou led an eastward expedition to Chaoge, subduing the revolt. King Cheng then designated Wei Ziqi, the elder brother of the last Shang king, as the legitimate heir of Cheng Tang, and endowed him with a fief called Song. Shuliang's grandfather of the fifth grade, Kong Fujia, decided to change the family name to Kong. Kong Fujia was later murdered together with the Duke of Song by a treacherous minister, and his son, Mu Jinfu, fled Song and took refuge in the state of Lu. The family settled down in Qufu, the capital of Lu. The state of Lu was the fief given to the Duke of Zhou by King Wu of Zhou. As he had to stay in the royal capital to help King Cheng govern the kingdom, the Duke of Zhou appointed his eldest son, Bo Qin, to rule Lu, and the dukedom was thus passed down generation after generation.

Mu Jinfu and his family lived on Queli Street in the city of Qufu. Mu Jinfu fathered Gao Yifu. Gao Yifu fathered Fang Shu. Fang Shu fathered Bo Xia. Bo Xia fathered Shuliang He.

Once back home, Shuliang He removed his army uniform and donned civilian clothes. Lady Shi helped him wash and served him a meal with a sumptuous variety of dishes. Shuliang sat down at the table and looked at his children. He was fond of his daughters, but could not help feeling depressed at the thought of having no male heir.

Though exhausted, Shuliang did not sleep well that night. He tossed and turned, kept awake until midnight by his obsessive desire for a healthy and clever son.

The next morning Mengsun Mie went to the court to report the events of the battle to Duke Xiang of Lu. "At the order of Your Lordship," he said, "I led troops to attack Biyang. After the vanguard entered the city, the enemy suddenly began to let down the gate. The troops in the city were able to retreat to safety only because Shuliang He held the gate back with his hands. I must be blamed for incompetent leadership, but I beg of Your Lordship to reward Shuliang and appoint him to an official post."

The duke asked with a smile, "Are you talking about the descendent of the sage king, Cheng Tang?"

"It is him," replied Mie.

"Excellent," said the duke. "I have thought about giving him an office before. What office do you think we shall give him?"

Mie was well prepared for that question. "How about the ministery of Zou?" he asked.

The duke looked at the civil and military officials gathered around him. "What do you think?" he asked.

The officials chanted in unison, "Your Lordship has made a wise decision!"

Thereupon the duke ordered Shuliang to be brought into the court.

As Queli Street was only two li from the palace, the messenger returned in a short time to report that Shuliang was waiting outside. The duke ordered, "Bring him in at once!"

Shuliang He came up to the gate, brushing off the dust from his clothes. Then he walked briskly into the palace until he was standing between rows of court officials. Lifting the hem of his dress and falling on his knees, he said, "Shuliang He salutes to Your Lordship!"

The duke stood up, took a close look at Shuliang, and bade him rise.

Thanking the duke, Shuliang got up on his feet and took his place at the end of the line of military officials.

The duke announced, "In view of your outstanding merits and heroic contribution, and also because you are the descendent of the sage king Cheng Tang, I endow you with two thousand taels of silver and appoint you Minister of Zou."

Shuliang He again walked up to the duke and knelt. "Your Lordship is thanked for his great favor!"

"Rise, my honored minister," said the duke.

Shuliang retreated to resume his place in the row of military officials.

On his return home, Shuliang was visited by many court officials who came to congratulate him on his promotion. Shuliang and Lady Shi were kept busy receiving the visitors until well after dark.

The family was just about to take a rest when Mie arrived looking very cheerful. When he was ushered into the room and took his seat, he sat politely, yet looking around. Taking the hint, Lady Shi led her daughters out of the room.

Without any preliminaries, Mie said bluntly, "Though you have attained high honor, there must be something you are still worrying about."

Astonished, Shuliang stared at Mie for a few moments and finally replied, "You are absolutely right. If there is someone who really knows me, it must be you."

"Since you are so worried about this problem," said Mie, "why not ask a matchmaker to find you a concubine?"

Shuliang replied, "We are an affectionate couple, Lady Shi and I. Though she has given me no son, I feel that taking a concubine would ..."

"It would be all right!" interposed Lady Shi, who had just bursted into the room. "Let's ask General Mengsun to find a concubine for you. If she gives the Kong family a male heir, I will regard her as my own sister."

Mie smiled, "Isn't it fortunate for your husband to have such a broad-minded wife as you! I'll talk to the matchmaker myself."

Mie was as good as his word. A few days later Shuliang took a concubine, the daughter of an ordinary family. She got on well with Lady Shi and her daughters, and the family lived together in harmony. Shortly afterward the family moved to Shuliang He's fief, Zou. In 557 B.C. the concubine was pronounced to be expecting a baby, and the whole family was in a happy mood. When the baby was born, Shuliang experienced both excitement and disappointment. He had a son at last, but the son was born lame. He named the son Mengpi, Meng meaning "elder," and in his heart hoped to have another son.

But things did not turn out as he wished. In the next two years his concubine did not conceive again. Shuliang He came to Mengsun Mie for advice. Mie said, "If you want to marry again, you'll have to divorce Lady Shi."

To enable her husband to fulfill his wish, Lady Shi left the family in great sorrow.

Mie sent his men to ask around, and received the news that Yan Xiang, a famous personage in Qufu, had three unmarried daughters. A matchmaker was dispatched.

The matchmaker found himself in front of a big courtyard. He knocked at the red gate.

Yan Xiang was reading in his studio when he heard the knocking. He put down the bamboo slips* and ushered the visitor into the drawing-room.

The matchmaker went straight to the point, explaining why he had come.

At this Yan Xiang said, "The name of Shuliang He is well-known, but he is more than twice my daughters' age. I have to ask them before I can give you a definite reply. Please wait a minute."

The matchmaker bowed and nodded his agreement.

Yan Xiang walked to the backroom and found to his satisfaction that all his three daughters were there reading or practicing calligraphy.

At the appearance of their father the three girls stood up to salute

---

* Used for writing on in ancient times.

him. They were all quiet in disposition and looked very attractive despite their plain clothes.

Yan Xiang said slowly and clearly, "A matchmaker has been sent by Shuliang He, Minister of Zou." He stroked his beard and looked at his daughters' reaction. "He is the descendent of the sage king Cheng Tang, and a hero whose name is known all over the kingdom. A marriage between our two families would be well-matched. However, he is already fifty-one, more than twice as old as any of you. Is anyone willing to marry him?"

The three girls remained silent for a while. At last the third daughter, Yan Zhengzai, hiding behind her second sister's back, said shyly, "According to ancient tradition, an unmarried daughter should obey her father. The father can make decision about his daughter's marriage himself. So why do you have to ask us?"

Hearing this, Yan Xiang realized that his third daughter was willing to marry Shuliang. He left the backroom to inform the matchmaker.

The matchmaker brought the news to Shuliang, who had some betrothal gifts prepared and sent to the Yan family. The wedding was held on an auspicious date. Yan Zhengzai took pity on Mengpi and treated him as her own son.

When Zhengzai did not become pregnant in two years, the couple began to worry. One day Zhengzai said to Shuliang, "Though I am still young, you are already over fifty. How can we go on like this? I have heard that the god of Mount Niqiu is very compassionate. Why don't we go and ask him to give us a son?" Shuliang agreed. They made ready for the trip that evening.

Early the next morning the couple set out for Mount Niqiu in a carriage. It was the spring of 552 B.C. The fine scenery made Zhengzai feel relaxed and lighthearted. Leaving behind the small lanes in the field, the carriage went up the northern bank of the Yishui River. Mount Changping on the southern bank and Mount Niqiu on the northern bank came into view in the morning light. Zhengzai became exhilarated. She had never seen such great natural beauty. Petals of peach blossoms floated in the breeze and landed on the river, joining the play of colors with the sunlight reflected on the water surface. Sometimes the petals fell on poplar trees to intermingle with the green leaves.

Mount Changping stretched from east to west, and Mount Niqiu from south to north. They looked like two giant flood-gates, allowing only a narrow passage for the Yishui River. A small lake was formed in front of the two mounts, where various aquatic birds were catching fish and shrimps. Zhengzai noticed that some birds did not eat their catches immediately but flew away with them. They must be hurrying to feed their youngsters, she thought. She wondered when she would be able to bring up her own son. Lost in thought, she took Shuliang's hand and placed it on her bosom, patting it softly and chanting a lullaby. She gave a little start when Shuliang drew away his hand. She looked up at him, blushing slightly, and he gave her a knowing smile.

The carriage passed around the southern foot of Mount Niqiu. Looking ahead, they saw that Mount Niqiu was connected to an undulating mountain range to the north. Here the Yishui River turned south. The mountain range on the eastern bank was reflected in the crystal-clear river surface. Zhengzai was so fascinated by the sight that she wanted to sing and chant poems.

The carriage stopped at the eastern foot of Mount Niqiu. Shuliang dismounted and helped Zhengzai down from the carriage.

They straightened their clothes and, taking the offerings, began to climb the steps. Here they saw luxuriant pines and cypresses, and dewdrops were still glittering on the leaves of the grass. They walked in high spirits and did not feel at all tired.

Halfway up the mountain, they arrived at the temple of the mountain god. They found themselves standing on a green meadow surrounded by wild flowers. Birds twittered in the trees and butterflies danced across the field. Zhengzai exclaimed, "Isn't it a fairyland, with all these birds and flowers!"

Shuliang smiled and, taking her by the arm, walked briskly to the temple.

Laying out their offerings, they knelt and prayed devoutly, asking the god to bless them with a son as soon as possible.

Having completed the sacrifice and prayer, they went down the mountain and returned home in the same carriage.

After the trip to the temple in the mountain, Zhengzai became much more cheerful than before. She had a better appetite, and her health improved greatly. In winter that year she fell pregnant. The prospect of being a mother made her feel happy and fulfilled. From time to time she was also worried for fear that she would give birth to a girl, or a handicapped boy like Mengpi. When she thought of this, she became more solicitous of Mengpi. The boy was then five years old, and she taught him to read and play games, making him live happily despite his handicap. Moved by this, Shuliang and Mengpi's mother sometimes prayed that her kindness would be repaid with good fortune. Zhengzai often went to visit Lady Shi to comfort and care for her. She knew that it had not been Lady Shi's fault that she had been removed from her home and felt that Lady Shi had been wronged. Considering her talents and virtue, it was unfair for Lady Shi to be divorced and whenever she thought of this, Zhengzai felt just a little cynical about the inequality between men and women.

Then came the time Zhengzai was about to give birth. Shuliang and Mengpi's mother became busy making preparations, and Lady Shi also came to lend a hand once in a while.

Because of the great disparity in age between Shuliang and Zhengzai when they got married, they were regarded as an "illegitimate couple" by their contemporaries. To shield herself from gossip and caustic comments, Zhengzai decided to rent a house near Mount Niqiu or Mount Changping for until after the baby was born. Shuliang had readily agreed and that same day rented a thatched house at the foot of Mount Niqiu. On the second day Zhengzai was brought there by carriage.

Zhengzai had a deep affection for the place. It was autumn, when golden chrysanthemums bloomed everywhere. She was so intoxicated with the beautiful sights around her that she was almost able to forget all the usual inconveniences of pregnancy.

The second day after their arrival at Mount Niqiu, or the 27th day of the eighth lunar month in 551 B.C., a philosopher was born.

The crying of the baby made Shuliang so happy that it took his breath away. He busily attended to both the baby and its mother. Taking up his son, who was dark-skinned and large-boned, he laughed softly to himself. "He takes after me, my precious son!" Suddenly, his eyes fell on the baby's head. The top of the baby's head was sunken, and there were some black bumps resembling small earth downs. "A blemish in an otherwise perfect jade!" he thought to himself, and his joy and excitement subsided.

Zhengzai was struck dumb with his reaction. She dared not think what might be wrong with the boy. She longed so much to look at her son, to kiss him, but she sensed something in Shuliang's eyes and withdrew her hands. She was so afraid that her son might be handicapped, just like Mengpi. After a stifling pause she plucked up her courage and said, "Let me have a look at the baby!"

Shuliang brought the baby before her in both hands, like someone offering a priceless gift to a king.

Zhengzai opened the swaddling clothes and, after examining the baby carefully, felt as if a heavy stone had been lifted off her chest. The baby had a square face, with large eyes and dark eyebrows. "Indeed, he takes after his father." This was what she thought, and she uttered the words without knowing it.

"It is a pity that he has those dirty things on top of his head," Shuliang responded, not without a touch of regret.

Stroking the baby gently, Zhengzai smiled, "This is not uncommon in newborn babies. I heard that a baby with such black bumps is more intelligent than others. Maybe our son will become a great scholar, or achieve great merits for our nation."

Shuliang could no longer contain his joy. He took the baby in his arms and kissed it gently on the head.

When Zhengzai saw the bright smiles on her husband's face, tears of joy welled up in her eyes. Wiping them away she said, "Let's find a name for the baby!"

"Right," said Shuliang. "... a name for our son." He stared at the top of his son's head and thought for a long time. "A year ago we came here to ask the god of Mount Niqiu to bless us with a son. Now our newborn baby has those black down-like bumps on his head, a sign of unusual intelligence, as you have told me. Let's make Qiu his name and Zhongni his styled name, shall we?"

Zhengzai replied, "It's fine with me."

Years later, as Confucius' given name the word Qiu became taboo, and Mount Niqiu had to be renamed.

There was no happier man than Shuliang after the birth of his son. When the baby was a month old, he gave a grand feast for his friends and relatives.

A spirited and lovable child, Kong Qiu became the favourite of the family. While taking care of Kong Qiu, Zhengzai did not stop teaching Mengpi. Actually, she treated Mengpi so well that people often mistook her for his natural mother.

Time passed quickly. Kong Qiu was now three years old. Exceptionally talented, he could recognize or pronounce a word after being taught only once. Shuliang and Zhengzai loved him dearly. At the same time they felt pity for Mengpi, deploring that heaven had treated the child unfairly. To make up for it, they took good care of him in every possible way. As the years rolled on, Mengpi came to regard Zhengzai as his own mother. The family lived together in great happiness and harmony.

However, the good days did not last long. One day Shuliang suddenly fell ill. His illness did not look serious at first, for Shuliang was a warrior with a very strong physique. He practiced a set of shadow boxing working up a great sweat, hoping thus to eliminate the illness. Instead of getting better, however, he became a little dizzy, and his health deteriorated day by day. At this the family became really worried, and a doctor was sent for. Zhengzai prepared the herbal medicine prescribed by the doctor and took care of her husband day and night. But Shuliang was beyond cure. Awaking from his delirium one night, he knew that he was going to die. He took Zhengzai by the hand and said in tears, "I am going to die, and life will be difficult for you and the children. Your son, Kong Qiu, is an extremely brilliant child. He has a bright future ahead of him if only he gets a good education. I am worried about Mengpi. He is not only slow in the head but also handicapped. If only for my sake, please take good care of him and teach him well."

Shuliang gasped for breath, his voice dwindling to a whisper. Placing her ear to his lips, Zhengzai could no longer hear anything. She quickly calmed herself and said with great sincerity, "Though Mengpi is not my own son, he is a member of the Kong family. I will care for him with all my heart. Please do not worry about it!" Hearing this, Mengpi's mother burst into tears.

Shuliang attempted to sit up in bed, but failed. Using all the strength he had left, he said, "If you can take good care of Mengpi, I will rest in peace in the afterworld." With this he took his last breath, his eyes remaining open.

Zhengzai sobbed, "You may leave in peace. I will keep my word to you." So saying, she gently closed his eyelids.

Shuliang's death was a catastrophe for the whole family. Zhengzai proved a stalwart woman. She wiped away her tears and took up the burden of the family, first arranging her husband's funeral in a burial ground on Fang Hill east of the city. After that, she began to think about how to run the household. By that time all Shuliang's nine daughters had married and left home, so that there were only four members in the family. Zhengzai knew that she must be frugal in order to bring up her sons with what little property they had. From then on, she became very thrifty and kept the household in good order.

Mengpi was now nine years old and went to school on clutches. Some naughty classmates often made fun of his lameness. On one occasion they hid his clutches so that he was unable to return home. He sat down at the stone steps of the school and wept. It was not until after dark that Zhengzai and his mother realized something was wrong and came to fetch him.

Afterward, Mengpi swore that he would never go to school again. Zhengzai and his mother tried to persuade him, but in vain.

Chapter Two

The Stepmother Brings Up Her Son;
The Grandfather Teaches His Grandson

Seeing Mengpi was adamant that he would not go to school anymore, Zhengzai said to his own mother with a sigh, "The boy is fatherless and handicapped. That must be too much for him to take. Well, let him stay at home. Starting from today, I will teach him myself."

Mengpi's mother was so moved she could not say a word. She almost fell on her knees to express her gratitude.

Born and brought up in a scholar's family, Zhengzai had received a very good education. She spent her days teaching Mengpi in addition to caring for Kong Qiu and doing household chores. Though Mengpi was not very clever, she taught him with great patience. Gradually, Mengpi began to make progress and his learning improved. Seeing the fruit of her efforts, Zhengzai found great comfort. She showed greater concern for him and helped him arrange his daily life and study in good order, never allowing him to be idle. She was not only a kindly mother but also a strict teacher.

Under Zhengzai's instruction Mengpi made continuous progress in his studies and felt very happy. He got on well with his younger brother, Kong Qiu, and often played games with him. He was also very filial to Zhengzai and called her "mother," which gave her great pleasure.

Shortly afterward the family moved back to the city of Qufu and settled down to life in a busy street. Their residence consisted of several thatched houses and a courtyard, unlike the magnificent houses of wealthy families. Though the street was busy and bustling, their house was quiet and peaceful, almost like a forsaken place. It was in such a place that a philosopher spent his childhood.

At six years old Kong Qiu had large, shining eyes and was unusually tall. Unwilling to be bounded by the domain of the few thatched houses and the small courtyard, he was always clamoring to go out and play in the street.

In the state of Lu the winter solstice was the time for a sacrificial ceremony in honor of heaven and earth in the capital. This sacrifice

was a very grand occasion for the state. Even the death of an important member of the ruling house, which might cause the sacrificial ceremonies in the ancestral temples to be delayed, was not allowed to interfere with the schedule of this sacrifice. No one in the state, not even the sovereign, dared discontinue the rituals of the sacrifice, which was held at the bank of the Yishui River outside the south gate of the capital.

One morning when Kong Qiu and Mengpi arose, Zhengzai said, "Qiu, you have been wanting to go out and play all these days, haven't you? Today the sacrificial ceremonies are to be held; you can go and watch with your elder brother."

Though he did not know anything about the sacrifice, Kong Qiu jumped with joy at his mother's permission to go out and play. "Oh!" he cried. "I am going out to watch the fun in the street!"

Zhengzai gave them a good meal and helped them dress up warmly. She cautioned them, saying, "Mengpi, you are the elder brother, so you should see to it that you and younger brother have a good time. Kong Qiu, your elder brother has some difficulty with his leg, so you should take good care of him and not just play by yourself."

Longing for the excitement of the street, Kong Qiu did not hear his mother's words clearly. He just nodded to whatever she said, eager to get out the door as soon as possible.

After Zhengzai had finished her exhortations, Kong Qiu jumped out of the gate like a bird flying out of its nest.

The state of Lu had a big capital, with eleven streets running from east to west and seven streets from south to north. The widest street was over sixty feet across. Stores and wineshops lined every street, which was busy with travelers, merchants and passing carriages. Kong Qiu looked around in excitement; there were too many things for the eye to take in. Everything looked so novel and strange to him. He rattled on while walking, "Elder brother, look at that pretty carriage, that high gate-tower, and that big horse...." He walked in bouncing steps, shouting and laughing, so that many passers-by looked at him curiously.

Unsociable in disposition and always afraid of other people ridiculing his handicap, Mengpi hobbled along behind his younger brother in silence. The gaze of other people made his heart thump and his face burn. Moving the clutches, he quickened his steps.

To prevent his younger brother from getting lost, Mengpi gave his left clutch to Kong Qiu and put his hand on Kong Qiu's shoulder. After a while, Kong Qiu became so tired that he broke out in a sweat all over his face. Mengpi took back his clutch and asked with concern, "Younger brother, you are tired, aren't you?"

Being a tough and stubborn boy, Kong Qiu threw out his chest and replied, "No, I am not tired at all!"

"Let's walk a little slowly, shall we?"

The tone was tentative, almost appealing. As a premature child, Kong Qiu was much more sensitive than most children of his age. He was touched by pangs of guilt, regretting that he had not shown enough concern for his elder brother. What should he say? Blinking his big eyes, he thought for a moment but could not come with a suitable remark, and ended up nodding his agreement.

The two brothers walked on, Mengpi on his two clutches, with Kong Qiu taking his arm, taking their time, walking among the crowds.

The capital of Lu had eleven gates in its city walls. Following the crowds, they left the city through the south gate and saw in the distance the platform for the sacrifice strewn with banners fluttering in the wind. Mengpi suddenly quickened his steps. Kong Qiu followed him closely, glancing from time to time at his elder brother's leg.

Arriving at the platform, they could see nothing but the banners fluttering in the northwest wind. A big crowd had gathered around the platform to watch the ceremony. Kong Qiu tried to squeeze his way into the crowd, but was soon pushed out because he was so small. He scratched his head with great anxiety. Suddenly he noticed a dike nearby to the south, which was much higher than the level of the ground. Without any explanation, he took Mengpi by the arm and pulled him toward the dike. Climbing up the bank, they turned back to face north and found they had a good view of the platform. On the platform were placed tables bearing sacrificial utensils, entire pigs and sheep and other offerings. Totally absorbed, Kong Qiu began to imitate the gestures of the master of ceremonies. He enjoyed himself so much that he felt a sense of loss when the ceremony was concluded and the crowd of onlookers dispersed. Supporting his elder brother by the hand, they too returned home.

Zhengzai and Mengpi's mother had been waiting for their sons at the gate for a long time. At the sight of the two brothers, they both felt relieved.

In vivid language Kong Qiu recounted all he had seen. Mengpi only replied to the questions put by his mother, snuggling up between his mother and Zhengzai. Feeling the coldness of his hands and seeing the sweat on his forehead, they hurriedly helped him into the room. After washing his head with warm water, Zhengzai washed his feet. When she took off his socks, she was astonished to see many blisters on his toes. Zhengzai's nose twitched, and she was on the brink of tears. She washed his feet quickly and bandaged them with soft strips of cloth.

After the outing Kong Qiu began to take a great interest in sacrificial ceremonies. Whenever a sacrifice was to be offered somewhere nearby, he would ask his elder brother to take him to watch it. Due to his handicap and his quiet disposition, Mengpi managed to force himself to accompany Kong Qiu twice, but refused to go a third time. So Kong Qiu went alone. In the capital of Lu there was an ancestral temple in commemoration of the Duke of Zhou, Ji Dan. The Duke of Zhou had been appointed by his elder brother, King Wu of Zhou, to be the first ruler of Lu. As the Duke of Zhou was the ancestor of the rulers of Lu, sacrificial ceremonies were often conducted in this temple. Kong Qiu watched every ceremony there, closely observing each gesture of the official in charge. After a few times, as he had a very good memory he had learned the procedure of the sacrificial rituals by heart.

One day, Kong Qiu brought home several miniature sacrificial vessels bought with his pocket money, placed them in the courtyard, and began to mimic the sacrificial rituals. He compelled Mengpi to join in the game. With the discomfort arising from his leg Mengpi soon lost interest and returned to Zhengzai's room to read. Kong Qiu continued to rehearse the ceremonies in great earnestness; again and again he practiced the rites, mimicking every word and gesture of the master of ceremonies.

Zhengzai did not pay much attention to his little games at first and let him play as he pleased. However, she began to feel he was much too absorbed for a boy so young, so she asked him seriously, "You are always playing with sacrificial vessels. Do you really want to learn the rites and become an official in charge of the Temple of the Duke of Zhou?"

Pouting, Kong Qiu replied, "You only teach my elder brother to read, but not me. What else can I do except play with these vessels?"

Zhengzai was very happy to hear that Kong Qiu wanted to learn to read. "If you want to read," she said, "I'll teach you, starting from tomorrow. However, from now on you should concentrate on reading and not idle away your time playing games."

Kong Qiu eagerly agreed to this and, gathering the vessels, he put them away in a corner of the courtyard.

Having finished household chores that evening, Zhengzai lit the oil lamp, placed several bundles of bamboo slips on the desk and carefully selected over three hundred characters that she planned to teach Kong Qiu in a month.

The following day she began to teach and to her amazement he memorized each character after learning it only once. At the end of the first day he had learned all the three hundred characters by heart. Filled with gladness, she remembered what she had said to her husband when Kong Qiu was born. She looked at her son and in her mind's eye saw him grown up, a tall and strong man just like his father. She felt a surge of unspeakable joy. She prayed silently, beseeching heaven to bless him, to make him a strong man, a pillar of the state.

"Mother, I have finished my studies," said Mengpi, interrupting her stream of thought.

Kong Qiu took her by the hand and pleaded, "Mother, I want to learn more."

For fear that he would get tired of too much study, Zhengzai replied, "Let's continue tomorrow. One cannot hope to grow fat by eating a big mouthful of food, you know."

Tilting his head, Kong Qiu said, "You teach elder brother all day, but stop after teaching me for only a short time. Do you prefer teaching him to me?"

Zhengzai smiled gently and said, "You have to review these three hundred characters today. I will test you tomorrow before we go on to learn new ones."

Kong Qiu nodded with great confidence.

That night Kong Qiu insisted that he sleep under the same quilt as his elder brother. Zhengzai disapproved at first, fearing that he would talk so much as to make Mengpi unable to get enough sleep. But when Mengpi's mother spoke up in Kong Qiu's favor, Zhengzai gave her reluctant consent. The two brothers slipped under the same quilt, warming each other's cold hands and feet. After their hands and feet got warm, Kong Qiu whispered, "Elder brother, mother is going to test me about the characters I have learned today. Let me write them out, and you can tell me if I make any mistakes."

"But it is dark in this room," said Mengpi. "How am I going to see?"

Kong Qiu had already worked that out. "I can write in your palm." Mengpi thought it a good idea and agreed.

Kong Qiu placed his brother's hand on his chest and began to write. After writing a character, he would read it out. "Heaven, earth, ancestor, kin, ..." He went on in this way, and his voice became inaudible after he had written about fifty. Only the even breaths of the two brothers could be heard. They fell sound sleep, Kong Qiu still holding his elder brother's hand.

Getting up early the next morning, they found the courtyard knee-deep in snow. It was still snowing heavily, but all the family came out to clear the paths. When Mengpi and Kong Qiu walked out the room, their eyes were almost blinded by the dazzling light of the snow-covered ground. They had great fun sweeping the snow. Putting away his clutches, Mengpi used the broom both to sweep the snow and support himself. Although the effort was great, they had a good time.

That was until Mengpi suddenly slipped and staggered. "Look out!" shouted Zhengzai and his mother, and they ran over to catch him. But it was too late. Mengpi had fallen sideways on his right foot, dislocating it. He was carried into the room, the pain producing beads of perspiration which rolled down his forehead. It was like frost plus snow—the injury on top of his handicap. At a loss, Mengpi's mother could do nothing but stand behind Zhengzai, looking at her son with tearful eyes. Zhengzai helped Mengpi into bed, covered him with the cotton quilt, and told him not to move, then went out to look for a doctor.

Out in the street everything was covered in ice and snow. Very few people were to be seen. The rows of thatched cottages looked strange under the snow. Zhengzai might have taken her time to enjoy the unusual scene but for the pressing urgency of Mengpi's injury. Burning with impatience, she wanted to find the doctor at once. She vaguely remembered having seen a "Fracture and Dislocation" sign somewhere on the north side of the street, but she could not see it now. She asked a passer-by and learned that she had walked past it. She turned back and, looking at each gate carefully, at last found the sign she had been looking for. Covered in snow, it had escaped her notice. She walked quickly to the gate and knocked on it.

The gate was opened by a grey-bearded man in his late sixties, who held himself straight as a ramrod. He asked politely, "Madam, is there an emergency, since you have braved heavy snow and violent wind to come here?"

Zhengzai at once felt a deep respect for the old man. "Greetings, venerable uncle!" she saluted.

Returning her salute, the old man ushered her into the room and pointed to the seat of honor, saying, "Please take this seat, madam."

Zhengzai was too anxious to sit down, and told the old man why she had come at once.

The old man did not delay a moment but hastily followed Zhengzai out of the room.

When Zhengzai returned home with the doctor, Mengpi's injured ankle had become badly swollen. The old doctor stroked the ankle with his hand and began to tell Mengpi the legend of Pan Gu, the god who created heaven and earth. Zhengzai and the others felt very puzzled. Suddenly Mengpi gave a cry, and the old doctor smiled, "It's over!" They looked at Mengpi and found his knitted brows smooth again.

They thanked the doctor, who took his leave after giving a few words of instruction.

Zhengzai and Mengpi's mother looked after Mengpi according to the doctor's instruction. Kong Qiu also kept himself busy tending for his elder brother, bringing him water and meals and carrying bed-pans for him.

Under such loving care, Mengpi recovered from the foot injury a few days later. Life in the household returned to normal. Mengpi continued his studies under Zhengzai's tutoring. As Kong Qiu complained he was not learning enough characters, Zhengzai changed her method and began to teach him various rituals and crafts in addition to reading, so that he would be able to understand affairs of the state as well as master some practical skills. Kong Qiu studied with great diligence. When asked to explain a passage, he always responded eloquently with the correct answer to Zhengzai's complete satisfaction. She encouraged Mengpi and Kong Qiu to ask each other questions and corrected the mistakes in their answers. Three years passed and Kong Qiu was nine years old. Fully engaged in teaching, Zhengzai had had no time for household tasks, which had to be taken up by Mengpi's mother. Due to over-exertion, Mengpi's mother had grown thinner and thinner; she had developed deep lines on her face and her eyes had become more and more sunken. Zhengzai was sorely distressed. "All these years she has stayed by my side supporting this family!" To improve the condition in the family, she decided that it was time to send Mengpi and Kong Qiu to a regular school, so that they could learn more and she could spend more time doing housework. She told her idea to Mengpi's mother, Mengpi and Kong Qiu, who all agreed readily. Kong Qiu had longed for such an opportunity.

Having talked with the master of a school near their house, Zhengzai took her two sons there the next morning. Mengpi was already fifteen and, with a brother by his side, no classmates dared make fun of him. Accompanied by his elder brother, Kong Qiu did not feel lonely in the new environment and devoted all his time to studies.

Three years later Kong Qiu asked his mother to find him a new place, for he was not learning enough in the school. Zhengzai could not find an ideal school for him, so after careful consideration, she announced, "You can go to study with your grandfather, who is a very erudite man. He taught me everything I know." Kong Qiu agreed. Mengpi decided that he would rather stay in the school as he liked what was taught there and he got along quite well with his classmates, so Zhengzai did not force him to go with his brother.

Yan Xiang lived in the northeast corner of the Lu capital. The following day Zhengzai took Kong Qiu to her father's house. Yan Xiang, over sixty, was dressed in a loose robe of coarse cloth; his hair and beard had turned grey. Having always doted on Kong Qiu, he was pleased to learn of his exceptional intelligence and eagerness to study and agreed to teach him without the least hesitation. He said, "Traditionally, there are six subjects to be studied: rites, music, archery, chariot driving, writing, and mathematics. These are referred to as "the six arts." I am familiar with only four of them, namely rites, music, writing and mathematics. As for archery and chariot driving, I know very little, as I have received no military training."

Kong Qiu said, "Mother has told me what the six arts refer to, but more than that I do not know."

Yan Xiang said with a smile, "They will be gradually explained to you."

"But I want to know about them this moment," said Kong Qiu

eagerly.

Zhengzai interposed, "Why are you so impatient? You will have plenty of time to study them."

Disappointed, Kong Qiu fell silent.

Yan Xiang was pleased with Kong Qiu's craving to learn. He pulled Kong Qiu to his side and said, "Let grandfather give you a general idea about them. I'll go into details later."

Breaking into a smile, Kong Qiu took Yan Xiang by the hand and said, "Grandpa, tell me!"

Yan Xiang sat down, cleared his throat, and began to speak. "The six arts include five rites, six types of music, five techniques of archery, five techniques of chariot driving, six types of handwriting, and nine methods of mathematics."

Kong Qiu asked, "What are the five rites?"

Yan Xiang replied, "The five rites include the auspicious rite for sacrifice, the inauspicious rite for funerals, the rite for welcoming guests, the military rite for regulating the troops, and the festival rite for initiation to adulthood and weddings.

Kong Qiu asked, "What are the six types of music then?"

Taking a deep breath, Yan Xiang replied, "These refer to six types of dance to the accompaniment of music. They are classified according to different historical periods. The music of the sage ruler Huangdi is called Yunmen, the music of Yao is called Xianchi, the music of Shun is called Dashao, the music of Yu is called Daxia, the music of Tang is called Dahuo, and the music of King Wu is called Dawu."

Hardly had Yan Xiang finished answering one question when Kong Qiu wanted to ask another one. Zhengzai stopped him, saying, "Let your grandfather have a rest!"

Yan Xiang said, "I'll explain everything to him! The five techniques of archery are called Baishi, Shenlian, Shanzhu, Xiangchi and Jingyi. The five techniques of chariot driving include Mingheluan, Zushuiqu, Guojunbiao, Wujiaoqu and Zuqinzuo. The six types of handwriting refer to six ways to form words, including self-explanatory characters, pictographic characters, pictophonetic characters, associative compounds, mutually explanatory characters, and phonetic loan characters. The nine techniques of mathematics refer to nine ways to calculate numbers, including Fangtian, Sumi, Chafen, Shaoguang, Shanggong, Junshu, Fangcheng, Yinbuzu and Pangyao. It is impossible to explain all these clearly in just a few words!"

"Yes!" agreed Zhengzai. She pulled her son to her side and exhorted him, "You have plenty of time ahead of you. Let grandfather teach these things to you one by one. Do not be too impatient."

Kong Qiu nodded and acknowledged to himself that there were so many words unknown to him. He had to spend quite some time studying them.

They went on to have a chat about family affairs. Yan Xiang watched his grandson closely. He had shown such an eagerness when asking questions, but now he looked so polite and well-mannered. The old man was filled with gladness.

After lunch Yan Xiang began to test Kong Qiu on his learning. He was surprised to find that Kong Qiu was conversant in knowledge that children of his age would find hard to comprehend. To every question he asked, Kong Qiu replied with great confidence and always gave the correct answer. This went on for four hours, and Yan Xiang did not feel the least tired. Instead, he grew more and more excited and satisfied. Finally he patted Kong Qiu on the shoulder and said to his daughter, "This is indeed a rare piece of jade waiting to be carved!"

Zhengzai said, "Father, you must not praise him like this. Be strict with him!"

Yan Xiang's eyes narrowed in a smile as he said, "Of course, of course."

Having entrusted her son to her father, Zhengzai felt assured that he would be all right. She stayed on for a few days watching her father, a patient teacher, and her son, a diligent pupil. Then she bade her father good-bye and returned home.

Back home, she did household chores and some handiwork during the day and helped Mengpi with his studies in the evening. Taught by the master in school and tutored by Zhengzai at home, Mengpi made remarkable progress in his studies.

Kong Qiu studied so hard that he often forgot to eat and sleep. Since early childhood he had been in the habit of getting to the bottom of everything. He would never switch his attention from a topic until he had learned all there was to know about it. The more questions he asked, the more pleased Yan Xiang felt, and the more detailed explanations he gave. Thus they passed six years together, during which time Yan Xiang taught Kong Qiu the knowledge he had accumulated in dozens of years, turning him into a great scholar conversant with things past and present.

Finding his grandson in possession of an exceptional memory and high aspirations, Yan Xiang began to teach him about the political thoughts of the ancient sage rulers and encouraged him to become a great man of both ability and integrity.

His grandfather's encouragement made Kong Qiu feel that there was so much for him to learn. Sometimes he even felt that his mind was empty so he studied more diligently than ever.

In the ninth lunar month of 533 B.C. Kong Qiu was eighteen years old. A day dawned when Yan Xiang suddenly felt tired physically as well as mentally. He realized that he was close to the end of his time, like an old silkworm that had spun its last thread of silk, or a lamp whose oil had dried up. He called Kong Qiu to him and said with great emotion, "For all the knowledge I have acquired, I have not had the opportunity to contribute my due to the nation. That is my lifelong regret. Fortunately I have taught you everything I know. I hope you will persevere in your studies with unmitigated efforts. Should there be a chance, you must try your best to serve in the government. Remember: to be a man you should work for a great cause, so that your name can be passed down in history as a good example for future generations. If you can do that, you will bring honor to your ancestors and pleasure to me even in the afterworld."

Being a staunch man, Kong Qiu seldom wept. At the last words of his grandfather, however, Kong Qiu's nose twitched, and tears rolled down his cheeks.

Though distressed, Yan Xiang managed to remain calm. His voice quivered a little but remained firm. He said, "Don't weep like this, it's unmanly. Be strong! The road of life is long and not always smooth. You must be prepared for hardships and must have the confidence to overcome them. Difficulties and heroes often go hand in hand. Furthermore, at my age, I have long had one foot in the grave."

Kong Qiu listened respectfully. He felt a surge of strength at first; at his grandfather's last remark, however, he could not help feeling deeply grieved and broke into a wail.

Yan Xiang said, "Quick, go and fetch your mother. I have something to tell her."

Kong Qiu tucked in the corner of the quilt and hurried home.

Hearing the news of her father's failing health, Zhengzai rushed to see him, choked with sobs.

Yan Xiang said, "Kong Qiu is already superior to me in learning. I think he will achieve great things in the future. I wish I could have lived to see him rapidly going up in the world, but heaven would not allow me. There's nothing to be done, for everyone's life span is predetermined. After my death, you must teach him well, so that his name can go down in history." With this he slowly closed his eyes.

Zhengzai sent Kong Qiu to go to the houses of her two sisters to report her father's death. When they arrived, the three sisters dressed their father in his burial-clothes.

Kong Qiu and his mother mourned his death for a hundred days and accompanied his coffin to the cemetery, in accordance with local customs. Then they returned home.

Soon afterward Mengpi got married. Zhengzai bustled about directing everything, while Kong Qiu helped with some odd jobs. The wedding was conducted smoothly, to the satisfaction of both the Kong's and the bride's family. Mengpi's mother sighed with great relief, "A load has been taken off my mind!"

By that time Kong Qiu had grown into a man. He was tall, broad-shouldered, square-faced, graceful in manners and elegant in his style of speech. An incessant stream of matchmakers visited the family in the hope of wooing the young man. One day Zhengzai said to her son gravely, "Listen, Qiu, I have something to discuss with you."

Chapter Three

Confucius Is Turned Away by a Powerful Man;
He Displays His Talents to the Lord
in a Discourse on State Affairs

"You are already grown up," Zhengzai continued. "I want to have your marriage arranged soon; this is something very much on my mind."

Adopting a respectful posture before his mother, Kong Qiu quoted the words of the ancients, "It has been a time-honored custom that men and women shall get married, and marriages should be arranged by parents. However, marriage is an important event in one's life and must not be arranged in haste. According to the rules set by the Duke of Zhou, a man gets married at the age of thirty. How can I go against ancient rules?"

The Duke of Zhou, named Ji Dan, was the son of Ji Chang, King Wen of Zhou. He had helped his brother, King Wu of Zhou, overthrow the rule of the last king of the Shang Dynasty and establish the Zhou Dynasty. He was said to have drafted all the regulations on rites and music of the Zhou court, and played a vital role in the founding and consolidation of the dynasty. After the death of King Wu, Ji Tong, later known as King Cheng, succeeded to the throne. As King Cheng was then a child, the Duke of Zhou did not leave for his fief, the state of Lu, but remained in Hao, the royal capital, to assist King Cheng. At first some people suspected that the Duke of Zhou wanted to usurp the throne. There arose many rumors and even slanders against him. When King Cheng grew up and began to attend to court affairs independently, the misunderstandings about the Duke of Zhou dissolved, and his loyalty to the king and to the dynasty was widely recognized. Thereafter he was praised and commended as the ideal minister who served the sovereign wholeheartedly.

The Duke of Zhou was one of the ancient figures Kong Qiu worshipped most. He regarded the Duke of Zhou as the noblest and the most learned of all men and took all his words as golden sayings. Thus he tried to dissuade his mother by quoting the matrimonial rules formulated by the Duke of Zhou.

Zhengzai had her own opinion. "It is good that you have studied hard and learned a lot about the rules of the ancients. However, you should not swallow ancient learning without digesting it. In other words, you should not accept the words and rules of the ancients as infallible law. As the saying goes, experience is the best teacher. Your father was advanced in years when he married me. As a result, I lost my husband when I was still young, and you lost your father when you were a child. You are now a strong and healthy young man. Getting married will do you no harm."

As a filial son, Kong Qiu felt deeply the hardships his mother endured in bringing him up. He wanted to fulfill his duties as a filial son and not cause her any displeasure, so standing with his hands at both sides he said softly, "I'll do as you say, mother."

Zhengzai was immensely pleased. She learned from a matchmaker that the Qiguan family in the state of Song had a daughter endowed with the four womanly virtues of morality, proper speech, modest manner and diligent work. The girl was the same age as Kong Qiu, and their dates of birth matched well. Zhengzai exchanged gifts with that family and made preparations for the wedding, which was conducted on an auspicious date.

After Kong Qiu got married, the family lived in peace and harmony. But still he cherished great aspirations. A young man of great learning, he did not want to remain forever in obscurity. He often thought of his grandfather, who had told him about the exploits of the ancient sage-kings. He was eager to explore the possibilities.

Kong Qiu wanted keenly to become acquainted with people with breadth of vision, achieve a status in society, get the chance to make use of his talents, so that he could contribute to the state and realize his political ideals. At that time officials were appointed on a hereditary basis. Despite his position as Minister of Zou, Kong Qiu's father, Shuliang He, did not enjoy much power in his life. People often curried favor with the powerful but seldom showed concern for those in distress. The aristocrats and court officials soon forgot about Shuliang He. While walking through the market, Kong Qiu would become enraged by the fraudulent behavior of the merchants. "If the general mood of the society does not improve, the state of Lu would have no future!" he said to himself, returning home in low spirits.

Kong Qiu began to suffer from insomnia, sometimes staying awake all night. In his mind he was devising a great plan to make Lu strong and powerful: Promulgate regulations, advocate kindness and righteousness, establish rites and put an end to despotism, so that there would be no theft, no cheating by the merchants, and the common people would be able to lead happy lives. Influenced by the practice adopted in Lu, the other states would follow suit, and the toppling Zhou Dynasty would become strong again. He knew all too well that his goal was a very big one. Where should he start? Unable to find a plan guaranteed to succeed, he could only encourage himself to search harder.

At that time the state of Lu was under the control of three powerful households known as the three Huans, and relating to this there was a long story. Formerly, Duke Huan of Lu married Wen Jiang, the younger sister of Duke Xiang of Qi. Before that, Wen Jiang and Duke Xiang had committed adultery. In the spring of 693 B.C. Wen Jiang accompanied Duke Huan of Lu on a visit to the state of Qi. Arriving at Qi, she took the chance to have rendezvous with Duke Xiang where they were exposed, and Duke Xiang had Duke Huan of Lu murdered. Duke Huan was succeeded by his son Jitong, who was known as Duke Zhuang. Duke Zhuang had three brothers, Qingfu, Shuya and Jiyou, all of whom enjoyed a certain power in Lu. After Duke Zhuang's death, Lu was ruled successively by five sovereigns: Duke Min, Duke Li, Duke Wen, Duke Xuan and Duke Cheng. When Duke Xiang of Lu died in 542 B.C., Duke Zhao became the ruler of Lu. During this period the houses of Qingfu, Shuya and Jiyou grew steadily powerful and came to be called the house of Zhongsun (later changed to Mengsun), the house of Shusun and the house of Jisun, known in history as the "three Huans." In 562 B.C. Chief Minister Jisun Su, in collaboration with the houses of Shusun and Mengsun, reorganized the troops of Lu into three armies, with each of the three houses leading one army. During the reign of Duke Zhao the three Huans grew increasingly powerful. In 537 B.C. Chief Minister Jisun Yiru reorganized the three armies into two armies, with himself leading one, and Shusun Chengzi and Mengsun Xizi jointly leading the other. At the same time he divided the land and people of Lu into four parts, with himself taking two parts and the other two houses taking one part each. In this way he not only usurped the authority of Duke Zhao but also weakened the other two houses. Unwilling to accept defeat, the houses of Shusun and Mengsun tried to fight back. Torn by the struggles among the three houses, Lu suffered steady decline.

A witness to all this, Kong Qiu wished he could stand out like a warrior, give a loud shout, and turn the tide even against all odds. Then he laughed at himself for being too naive. He was keenly aware that, in order to achieve a great ambition, he had to begin at the very beginning. After careful consideration he decided as the first step to go out and canvass the virtuous ministers and benevolent officials in the state of Lu.

While walking along the street one day, Kong Qiu happened to hear some people chatting.

"Chief Minister Jisun is seeking talents again."

"How do you know that?"

"He is giving a banquet for scholars and men of letters."

"He is only making a show."

"Maybe he is doing it in earnest."

Kong Qiu had heard this news before but did not take it too seriously. Now that it was confirmed by the conversation he just heard, he returned home in high spirits.

This was undoubtedly good news for Kong Qiu who, having long wanted to embark on an official career, decided to make use of the opportunity.

On the day of the banquet, Kong Qiu got up early in the morning, dressed himself neatly, and made for the chief minister's residence with great joy and anticipation.

The chief minister's residence looked very imposing with its high walls and enormous courtyard. Young men from big families dressed in showy clothes were seen swaggering in and out of the residence. Under the towering gate stood a burly man in his thirties. He wore a loose grey-blue robe, his face covered in ferocious-looking whiskers. To some people he bowed deeply and smiled obsequiously, while to others he frowned and even scowled.

Observing the man in a distance, Kong Qiu shuddered and said to himself, "What a petty man he is, currying favor with the powerful like that!" Taking a closer look, he recognized the man to be Yang Hu, Jisun Yiru's head steward.

The man was indeed Yang Hu. In the Spring and Autumn Period the position of ministers in the court of every vassal state was hereditary, and these ministers appointed stewards to run their houses.

At the sight of Yang Hu's repulsive appearance, Kong Qiu slowed his steps. He hesitated, thinking he might as well give up. But then he told himself that, for the sake of the nation, the people and his own ancestors, he must not let the opportunity slip. Throwing out his chest, he walked up to the gate and stopped to salute under the terrace.

Instead of returning the salute, Yang Hu asked with a sneer, "Who are you? Why do you come here?"

Kong Qiu bowed and replied respectfully, "My name is Kong Qiu. I have heard that the chief minister is giving a banquet to scholars and men of letters all over the state, so that ..."

"Hahaha!" Yang Hu bursted into a fit of laughter that made Kong Qiu's hair stand on end. "The chief minister only invites people of high honor and great fame. What does a poor man like you come here for? You certainly have a great opinion of yourself!"

Thus ridiculed, Kong Qiu looked up with indignation. He took a step forward, making ready for an argument.

Sensing his intention, Yang Hu stopped Kong Qiu before he could speak and, with a sweep of his wide sleeve, cried, "Go away at once! Don't stand in the way here!"

Though modest and unassuming in manners, Kong Qiu had a strong sense of pride. At the insult, his face was flushed with shame. He turned away and walked home feeling highly despondent.

After the humiliating episode Kong Qiu did not lose heart but learned something important: Life is a long and winding road. A man will not achieve great things unless he can endure hardships. Therefore never one to waste his time, he put more efforts into his studies of the six arts. While studying music, rites, writing and mathematics, he also practiced archery and chariot driving. Not far from his house there was a public garden called Juexiang, where people could practice archery. He went there to practice regularly. Duly rewarded for his hard work, he acquired great expertise in all the five techniques of archery. Whenever he arrived at Juexiang Garden to practice, many people would come to watch. He would be surrounded by a big crowd, which often greeted his performance with shouts of approval.

Kong Qiu became famous for his great learning and mastery of various skills. People began to visit him for instruction.

One day a sacrificial ceremony was conducted at the temple of the Duke of Zhou. Built on high ground a little north to the center of the capital of Lu, amid pines and cypresses, the temple could be seen from a distance.

It was autumn. In the three courtyards of the temple chrysanthemums were blooming, their golden colors intermingling beautifully with the green pines and red walls.

Before the ceremony began, a crowd had gathered in the temple. Kong Qiu stood among them, waiting anxiously. At the appointed hour, amid the sounding of bells and drums, the master of ceremonies, leading Duke Zhao and a team of musicians and dancers, ascended the altar. The altar was a rectangular platform aligned east-west in front of the Duke of Zhou's statue. The wall was made of stone slabs and the ground was covered in square stones. Duke Zhao offered some wine in sacrifice, read an eulogy to the Duke of Zhou's exploits, and retreated after kowtowing his respect. The musicians then gathered under the eaves of the hall, instruments in hand. The dancers arranged themselves in six lines, each line consisting of eight people. Holding a pheasant-feather in the left hand and a flute in the right, the dancers performed to the accompaniment of music played on instruments made of metal, stone, strings, bamboo, gourds, earth, fur and wood. The dance was characterized by an air of serenity, deliberate postures and smooth, flowing movements. Watching intently, Kong Qiu began to move his hands and hum the tune without knowing it.

When the music stopped, the dancers retreated from the altar in an orderly procession. The master of ceremonies announced that the sacrifice was concluded.

Kong Qiu felt as if he could still hear the music and see the dancers. Reluctant to leave, he walked in quick steps to the master of ceremonies and asked, "Master, why were six rows of dancers employed for the ceremony?"

The master of ceremonies was an elegant, well-built man in his fifties, with fair skin and a black beard combed into three tufts. Taking a look at Kong Qiu, he replied slowly, "The eight-row dance is used exclusively for the king, while the six-row dance is adopted for the lords of the vassal states. As the ruler of Lu, the Duke of Zhou is naturally entitled to the six-row dance."

Kong Qiu asked, "The Duke of Zhou helped King Wu and King Cheng in the establishment and consolidation of the dynasty. He is surely comparable to King Wu in terms of achievement. Why is he not entitled to the eight-row dance?"

The master of ceremonies replied, "Though the Duke of Zhou achieved the greatest merits under heaven, he never ruled from the throne for a single day, and is therefore by no means entitled to the eight-row dance. Considering his special contributions to the dynasty, King Cheng had actually issued an edict granting him permission to use the eight-row dance. However, he vigorously declined, for he was unwilling to go against the established rites. Therefore the Duke of Zhou's refusal to use the eight-row dance is in conformity with the rites he advocated."

Kong Qiu went on to ask some more questions about the sacrifice, to which the official replied with great patience. Then Kong Qiu bowed deeply and said, "Thank you very much, master, for taking so much trouble." Taking leave of the official, he turned away and left the temple.

Impressed by this great eagerness to learn, the master of ceremonies gazed after Kong Qiu until he passed out of sight at the turning of the street.

Leaving the temple, Kong Qiu felt excited and did not want to return home at once. He walked down the east-west street until he arrived at an intersection. Looking to the north, he saw an earthen platform to the west of the road not far away. Surrounded by pines and junipers, the platform looked quiet and still in contrast to the bustling streets nearby. Approaching it, he remembered that the platform had been built by Boqin, the Duke of Zhou's son and the first ruler of Lu. Kong Qiu walked around the platform and found it overgrown with weeds and overrun with wormwood, as if no one had used it for a long time. The sight plunged Kong Qiu into deep thought. He thought of how Boqin had built the platform on which to look west to the Zhou capital and long for his father. The ruler of Lu today, though a descendent of the Duke of Zhou, had nevertheless completely forgotten about his ancestor. What a shame! Wasn't it lamentable that the most essential rites were forsaken because of decline of the ruling house!

Back home, Kong Qiu continued to put all his energies into studying rites, music, writing, and mathematics and practicing archery and chariot driving. Dissatisfied with what he had already achieved, he made a firm resolution to be more conversant with the six arts.

To his surprise, people began to talk about him after his visit to the temple of the Duke of Zhou. Formerly, people had often praised him for his rich knowledge, but now they talked about his ignorance, saying that he knew practically nothing.

One day Kong Qiu was practicing archery with some youths when one of them came up and whispered to him , "Kong Qiu, people have been talking about you."

His eyes wide with surprise, Kong Qiu asked, "What did they say about me?"

"They said you asked all kinds of questions in the temple because you knew nothing about the sacrificial rites."

"What else did they say?"

"They said you were totally ignorant."

Kong Qiu retorted, "They do not understand me in the least. I am alert and eager to learn, and I am not ashamed to learn from others, even those below me in rank. In my opinion, there are many people of learning in the world. When I walk in the company of other men, there must be one from whom I can learn something. According to the teaching of the ancients, when you know something, acknowledge that you know it, and when you do not know something, acknowledge that you do not know it—that is true knowledge. What can you get by pretending to know something that you actually know nothing about? I know a little more than others just because I study hard and often ask questions. No one is born with knowledge, which must be gained through diligent study. Though some people are more clever than others, still they should keep learning in order to advance themselves. There is no limit to knowledge!"

Finding these words interesting and reasonable, the young man nodded his agreement. More youths gathered around to listen to Kong Qiu.

Kong Qiu ran his eyes over the crowd and raised his voice. "I took an interest in learning in early childhood. At the age of fifteen I decided to devote myself to it."

The youths were greatly affected by what he said. After finishing the archery practice, they continued to talk about Kong Qiu's ideas. Those who had considered Kong Qiu ignorant changed their mind and came to admire and respect him. Some even began to regard him as a sage.

A year passed and Kong Qiu was nineteen now. His fame spread quickly, until even the court of Lu heard about his learning.

After the morning audience one day, Duke Zhao of Lu sent for Jisun Yiru, Shusun Chengzi and Mengsun Xizi and asked them, "I have heard that Kong Qiu, the son of the late Minister of Zou, Shuliang He, is a very learned man. Is that true?"

Jisun was a fat and short man. He liked to stare at others through narrowed eyes. Shusun was of medium height with a thin face. He seldom expressed his opinion. The two of them looked at each other and made no reply to the duke's question.

Duke Zhao looked at the three ministers one by one, eagerly waiting for an answer.

Mengsun said, "I have also heard about it, but it has not been confirmed. I dare not make a definite reply."

Duke Zhao said, "In that case, bring him in for an audience. If he is indeed a learned man, I will appoint him to an important position."

Jisun was displeased to hear that. Shusun acted as if he had heard nothing and did not give his opinion.

Mengsun said, "As Your Lordship wishes, I will send for him immediately." He dispatched someone to invite Kong Qiu to enter the palace.

Kong Qiu was then reciting *The Book of Poetry* at home. He was very fond of the folk songs for their sincere emotions and elegant style.

Hearing a knock at the gate, Lady Qiguan hurried to open it. She started at the sight of the duke's messenger.

Adjusting his dress and hat, Kong Qiu walked out into the courtyard and bowed in salute, saying, "Forgive me for coming out late to welcome you!"

Without taking the time to exchange formalities, the messenger said briefly, "His Lordship has issued an edict inviting you to enter the palace for consultation without delay."

The news came as a pleasant surprise to Kong Qiu, who left with the messenger at once, without saying good-bye to his mother and wife.

The palace of Lu was of a grand scale and graceful style, its buildings all well-appointed. Entering the palace for the first time, Kong Qiu could not help feeling nervous even though he knew that nothing untoward would happen to him. Following the messenger, he arrived at the rear palace and fell on his knees in salute. All smiles, Duke Zhao invited him to sit down. He thanked the duke and, lifting the front of his dress, took a seat to the right.

Duke Zhao said, "Kong Qiu, I hear you are conversant with the classics and have mastered many skills. Today I would like to hear your opinions about how to govern the state."

Kong Qiu left his seat and knelt, saying, "As a humble commoner,

Qiu dare not talk nonsense."

"Straighten yourself!"

"Thank you, Your Lordship." Kong Qiu stood up and returned to his seat.

Duke Zhao asked, "What was the governing principle adopted by the ancient sage kings?"

Kong Qiu replied unequivocally, "The ruler should serve the people."

"What was the Duke of Zhou's major achievement?"

"He established the rites and composed music."

"The present situation is characterized by the fact that the state of Qi is strong while Lu is weak. In order to make Lu more powerful than Qi, what measures should I adopt?"

Lowering his head, Kong Qiu thought for a while, then said, "In my opinion, If Lu is to become powerful, the first step is to restore the ancient rites of Zhou, establish a benign government, and show true concern for the common people, guiding them by morals and governing them by rites. Those in office should suit their action to their words and be exemplary in their behavior. Only thus will orders be carried out and prohibitions be observed. To achieve all this, it is paramount that we appoint people who are both virtuous and capable to fill offices, and promote people of integrity who have long been forgotten. If people, high and low, are united as one and pull their full weight, Your Lordship can rest assured that Lu will surpass the state of Qi."

Filled with joy, Duke Zhao said, "You are a sage. Would you like to stay in the court to be my consultant?"

This would be the perfect opportunity for Kong Qiu to give full play to his talents and realize his aspirations. However, it came so suddenly that he was struck dumb, not knowing how to reply.

Jisun was a man who disliked capable people out of jealousy. He was greatly upset when he realized that Kong Qiu was indeed conversant with statecraft and that Duke Zhao was going to appoint him an official. Glancing at Duke Zhao, he interposed, "Your Lordship, Master Kong Qiu is indeed commendable, considering his youth and talent. However, an appointment to office is an important decision that should be taken only after careful consideration, so that the person appointed will fulfill his duties competently."

Duke Zhao knew all too well that Jisun was jealous of talented people, but as the chief minister his words carried weight. The duke did not want to argue with him in front of Shusun and Mengsun. Furthermore, the duke did not know Kong Qiu very well and feared that the ministers would not be convinced of his wisdom if Kong Qiu received an appointment on his words alone. Therefore he said, "The chief minister's words are reasonable. We'll give the matter further thought and discuss it later."

Kong Qiu had heard about the "three Huans" long before. Jisun was arrogant and domineering, making decisions in the court without authorization. Shusun was hesitant and indecisive, frequently changing his stand in the power struggle among the three houses. Mengsun was a simple-minded and honest man, but he was ignorant and incompetent and had little control of the overall situation. Kong Qiu looked at them with disdain, regret and indignation. Disdain because these ministers were fully occupied in the power struggle, neglecting state affairs; regret because Lu, controlled by such people, would surely decline; and indignation because the court was manipulated by such men. He wished he could stand up and rebuke Jisun for all his despicable actions. However, he checked himself, for he was after all a well-educated and cultured man. Instead he said with a false smile, "Kong Qiu lacks talent and learning. He sincerely asks the instruction and benefaction of Your Lordship and the ministers!"

Well pleased with the eloquence and graceful manners of the youth before him, Duke Zhao stood up and took a step forward, saying, "You are the descendent of the great sage king Cheng Tang. I hope you can make further progress, just like a boat sailing upstream, so that one day you will become a real sage of our nation and our age."

Rearranging his garment, Kong Qiu fell on his knees and said, "I will always remember Your Lordship's invaluable advice. And I will study hard and not fall short of Your Lordship's expectations." With that he stood up and, in a calm and resolute air, left the rear palace. Once beyond the gate, he was greatly relieved and walked in the quiet backyard of the palace in sprightly steps, feeling like a bird spreading its wings. He rejoiced at his meeting with the Duke of Lu; this was an exciting day in his life, a day to be remembered. He believed that someday the duke would accept his advice on governing the state and make Lu strong. There were many obstacles, such as Jisun, who looked like an insurmountable wall. Nevertheless, he was convinced that a journey began with the first step. Now that the first step had been taken, the second and the third step whould follow, and sooner or later his dream would come true. He hoped it would not be too far away. He was full of confidence about his predictions. In fact he had already gained greatly by his visit to the court, during which both Duke Zhao of Lu and Jisun addressed him as Fuzi, or the Grand Master. Thereafter he was generally called Kong Fuzi.* No sooner had he arrived home than he heard a baby crying. Smiling with joy, he hurried into the room and saw his newborn son, a white and plump baby. After saluting his mother, he took the baby in his arms and looked at it closely. Zhengzai felt a surge of emotions, a mixture of both grief and joy. After all these years she and her son had at last made it to this day. Quietly she whispered to her deceased husband, "Your spirit in heaven may at last rest in peace."

Lady Qiguan asked her husband tentatively, "Let's choose a name for the baby."

Putting the baby in her arms, Confucius walked around the room, unable to think of anything. He went to the courtyard and looked around, but no idea came up. He came back into the room and sat there thinking hard, but again failed to find an ideal name.

That night Confucius found it hard to go to sleep. He had just been doubly blessed by the audience with Duke Zhao and the birth of his son. He thought how he would improve the situation in the state of Lu, and educate his son so that he would take up the same cause as his father when he grew up. When he finally dozed off, it was almost daybreak. Half asleep, he found himself in a carriage, arriving at Hao, the capital of Zhou. The city had wide streets and numerous richly ornamented buildings. Men and women walked in separate paths, the young showed great respect for the old, and the merchants did not cheat in their dealings. While he was lost in thought, the carriage drove straight into the palace. He was about to dismount and kneel in obeisance when an old man came up smiling and said, "No formalities, please. You must be Kong Qiu from the state of Lu?" Surprised, Confucius bowed with clasped hands and replied, "I am Kong Qiu. How do you recognize me?" The old man said, "I am the Duke of Zhou you've been thinking about. Knowing you will come today, I have been waiting for you." Looking closely, Confucius found the Duke of Zhou to be a strong man with white hair and beard and kind, benevolent-

---

*This name, Kong Fuzi, or Kong the Grand Master, was Latinized into Confucius by Western Catholic missionaries in China during the early 17th century.

looking eyes. He said hastily, "I do not deserve the welcome of a superior man like you." The Duke of Zhou said, "I am doing this not just to welcome you but to help Lu. I heard that you are a promising young man with great learning. The future of Lu will depend on you." Confucius said, "I really wished I could assist the Duke of Lu in this respect. But I felt alone and weak, not knowing what to do." Putting on a stern expression, the Duke of Zhou said, "With enough resolution and perseverance, you will surely succeed." Before he could ask the Duke of Zhou questions on governing the state, Confucius was awakened by the baby's crying.

The courtyard was bathing in sunlight. The old scholar tree looked especially beautiful in the golden sunlight.

Having swept the courtyard, Confucius was reflecting on his dream the night before and trying to find a name for his son, when he heard someone knocking at the gate.

Chapter Four

Confucius Becomes Keeper of Granaries and Visits the Peasants; Reappointed to Keeper of Livestock, He Punishes a Crooked Subordinate

Opening the gate Confucius was surprised to see the duke's messenger carrying two live carp in his hand.

Hurriedly Confucius invited the messenger into the room.

The messenger said, "Having learned of your newborn son, His Lordship has sent me to bring you these two carp in congratulation."

Greatly moved, Confucius said, "I have never done anything for Lu and really do not deserve His Lordship's gift!"

The messenger replied, "Master, it would be better if you accept the gift and return His Lordship's favor in the future."

Confucius accepted the carp in both hands. Then the messenger took his leave and returned to the palace. Gazing after the messenger until he was out of sight, Confucius took the carp into the room, when suddenly he got an idea. "Right, I'll name my son Li* and his styled name will be Boyu**." Then he explained to his mother and wife, "We had our son only yesterday, and today the lord sent his gift. This is something to be remembered, something to be proud of. Therefore I want to name the baby Li. As Bo refers to the eldest, Boyu would be a most suitable styled name.

Finding his thoughts acceptable, both Zhengzai and Lady Qiguan expressed their agreement.

The birth of Kong Li brought laughter and happiness to the family and also a burden for Confucius. He had to devise a plan to support this family of four. By that time Mengpi had already moved out and set up his own family with his mother and wife.

In that year a few changes took place in the life of Confucius. He was appointed a minor official. In the city of Cheng under the jurisdiction of Mengsun Xizi there was an official in charge of granaries

---

* "Li" meaning carp
** "Yu" meaning fish

and collection of land tax who was discovered to have practiced graft. Mengsun had not been able to replace him for lack of a suitable candidate. The first time when he met Confucius in the court, he considered him very talented. It was near harvest time, and Mengsun decided to appoint Confucius an official in the city of Cheng, not only to fill the vacancy but also to see if he really had the capability to work in the government. Having reached the decision, he sent for Confucius.

The messenger arrived at Confucius' house and explained why he had come. Confucius promptly left with him, and on his way he thought to himself, "Though Mengsun Xizi is not a learned man himself, it is commendable that he should treat learned people with respect. If I should get his recommendation, I will surely make remarkable achievements in order to lay the foundation for realizing my great aspirations in the future." Soon he arrived before the gate of Mengsun's residence. It was a big house with an extensive courtyard: not so imposing as at Jisun Yiru's house, the gate tower was nevertheless constructed in grand style.

The messenger said, "Master, please come in!" Confucius was jostled out of his deep thought.

Following the messenger along the winding paths in the quiet courtyard, Confucius walked through three gates before he arrived at Mengsun's chamber. Confucius realized that, by receiving him at the back room, the host was treating him as an honored guest.

It soon became clear that he had guessed correctly. At the messenger's announcement, Mengsun emerged from the inner room to greet Confucius. When Confucius bowed in obeisance, Mengsun bowed in return and invited him into the inner room.

After they had taken their seats as host and guest, Mengsun said, "Ever since I heard your speech at court, I have held you in great respect and admiration. Today I have prepared a humble meal and some wine to express my admiration for you. I hope you will honor me with your acceptance."

Bowing slightly, Confucius replied, "I have not contributed to the state and therefore do not really deserve your high commendation."

By this time the servants had laid out the table, and Mengsun invited Confucius to take his seat. After declining as modesty demanded, Confucius took his seat as guest.

After three rounds of wine, Mengsun began to ask Confucius if he would like to take up an official position. Confucius replied that he would be willing to try.

Mengsun said, "Considering your virtue and talent, you are fully qualified to be a minister. However, time is not yet ripe. At present there is a vacancy in the city of Cheng under my jurisdiction for a keeper of granaries. The position is indeed insignificant. I wonder if you would deign to take it?"

Confucius replied, "Since you bestow such great favor on me, how could I decline your offer!"

Greatly pleased, Mengsun raised his cup and drank with Confucius. Then he told Confucius about the wrongdoings of the discharged official and the measures that should be taken when he took office.

Bidding Mengsun good-bye, Confucius returned home and told his mother and wife about his appointment. Then he began preparations to make his journey to the city of Cheng to assume office.

The former official and his subordinates had committed fraudulent practices, putting the better part of the taxes received into their own pockets. After taking office, Confucius studied the account books carefully, finding them full of errors, inconsistencies and alterations. He sent for the runners and said to them in a very kindly manner, "I have been appointed by Minister Mengsun to take up this post. Due to my predecessor's incompetence, the accounts he left are confusing and need to be carefully audited. I will continue to use the services of the staff members of this office, and I hope you will fulfill your duty and work together to meet the tax collection quota this year."

The runners showed contempt for the young official before them and one of them replied, "We will try our best to carry out your order, officer." He uttered the word officer with disrespect.

Confucius ignored it. He divided the city into five sections and assigned each runner to one area to make tax collection.

After the runners had left, Confucius changed into commoner's clothes and went out to mingle with the locals. Walking along small paths around the fields, he was pleased to see the rice that had just been harvested had plump ears and big grains. Arriving at a threshing ground, he heard some women singing,

In the ninth month the ground is pressed;
In the tenth month the rice is harvested.
When the food crops arrive at the ground,

All the family become busy.

The song was clear and joyful. People seem to be drunk with happiness at the bumper harvest. But suddenly the song changed its tune, turning sad and rueful:

Ai—
We the peasants!
We have harvested the food crops
And turned them in at the government office.
We busy ourselves from dawn till night,
Weaving straw ropes.
No sooner have we finished mending the thatched houses,
Than it's time to sow the crops again.

Listening to the song, Confucius was at first elated, then became a little startled. He knew the song, which was from *The Book of Songs*, almost by heart, but he had never understood its real message until this moment. He said to himself, "Indeed, a few words have said it all, about the joys and sorrows of the peasants in a year of their life. Harvests are not produced easily!"

He approached the threshing ground. Seeing him, the women stopped singing and began to work attentively with lowered heads. Some children playing among the hay stacks came up and looked at him curiously. One of them asked, "Where do you come from, and who are you looking for?"

Before Confucius could find a suitable reply, the other children began to ask questions. "Why do you come here?" "Are you lost?" "Are you hungry?" "Are you thirsty?" Looking at their innocent faces and listening to their simple and kindly words, Confucius was much moved. He said with a smile, "Many thanks to you! I am neither hungry nor thirsty."

He walked over to some peasants who were taking a break, sat down and began to chat with them. The hearts of peasants were pleasant like the cool, clear weather in autumn. In a few minutes they were all chatting like old friends. The children stood around watching and laughed along with the adults as if they too were part of the conversation.

Confucius asked, "It looks like you have a good harvest this year."

"Yes, a very good harvest." the peasants replied.

"Do you have any difficulty paying the land tax?"

At the mention of tax, the smiles vanished from the faces of the peasants, and they fell silent.

Confucius watched their expressions carefully and waited patiently for their reply.

After a long pause, one peasant scrutinized Confucius carefully and deciding that from his broad forehead, dark eyebrows, big eyes, and graceful manners there was no ulterior motive in his asking, said, "Actually, considering this year's harvest, most households will have no difficulty paying all the taxes. However," and he paused to look around him before he continued, "the tax collectors are such corrupt people. In collaboration with their superiors, they cheat the common folks whilst the minister is kept in the dark. The utensil they use to collect the grains are larger than the standard size, so they can gain a lot at the expense of us peasants. Given that, why should we be willing to pay the tax?"

Another peasant said, "I heard a new official has been appointed this year. I wonder if this one will be different from the last."

"There have always been more corrupt officials than upright ones. This one will surely be no exception!"

"He might be even worse than the last one!"

"Maybe we will be fortunate enough to have an honest official this time."

"If that is so, we will be blessed. Let's pray that heaven may be kind to us!"

Excusing himself from the warmhearted and honest people, Confucius made his way to other villages. He heard the same story in each one and decided that he had learned all he wanted to know.

The following day when the peasants came to pay land tax Confucius observed the proceedings and discovered that the utensils the collectors used did indeed appear unusual. He asked the runners to bring more, but they were all found to be of the same size. Confucius then asked some of the peasants living nearby to bring some of their own utensils which turned out to be much smaller than the ones used by the runners.

Returning to the office, Confucius sent for all the runners and demanded, "Have you always collected land tax in this way?"

The runners replied in trepidation, "We plead guilty! We plead guilty!"

Confucius said sternly, "Vicious people like you must be severely punished; otherwise you would not understand the authority of the king's law." With this he meted out punishments according to the severity of their offenses. A few were expelled and the two most hated runners were sent to Confucius' superiors to receive their just deserts.

Having done that, Confucius then had the peasants elect the most trusted members of their community to help him collect tax. He ordered that those who paid tax ahead of schedule would enjoy a ten percent reduction and those who paid tax on time a five percent reduction. Those who did not observe the deadline would have to pay ten percent more and those who refused to pay tax would have their land confiscated and reallocated to others. If anyone was not able to pay tax due to crop failure, then they would be eligible to apply for tax exemption.

Thus the peasants found out to their joy that the new official was just and honest and meted out rewards and punishments in due accord. In addition, they trusted the tax collectors as they had been elected by themselves, therefore they came willingly to pay their tax. Confucius was always on hand to supervise the procedure for fear that someone would try to cheat the people again. One day a peasant carrying some grain on a shoulder pole arrived to pay his tax. He looked pale and was dressed in ragged clothes. Confucius approached him and asked, "Is your family in difficulty? Why are you dressed in so ragged a fashion?"

The peasant looked to be in his late thirties, strong and well-built. He gazed at Confucius for a moment and asked, "You are our new official, aren't you?"

"Yes," replied Confucius.

The peasant put down his load, shook the dust from his clothes and bowed, saying, "Our family has had a good harvest this year. We have more than enough to eat and wear. Paying tax is no problem."

Confucius looked at him inquisitively.

The peasant asked, "But, you find it strange that I am dressed in these poor clothes, don't you?"

Confucius nodded.

The peasant was on the verge of tears when he replied, "My wife died three years ago, leaving me with my teenaged son. Though we are not very poor, our life is hard. Look at me: My clothes are worn out even though I have good cloth."

Confucius said, "In that case, why don't you find another wife?"

The peasant replied, "A bright moon cannot compare with the lamp, and a good stepmother cannot compare with the real mother. I have not married for fear that my new wife may maltreat my son."

"There are more good people than bad in the world. The new wife you choose may not necessarily be partial."

"You are perhaps right, but I feel I cannot take the risk."

Confucius smiled sadly and turned to look at another poorly dressed man. He was thin and lame in the right leg, and carried his heavy load with some difficulty. Confucius approached him and asked, "Why are you dressed so poorly too?"

The man replied, "I was handicapped as a child, and my life has always been hard. According to the law I can enjoy tax exemption. But in all these years I have paid tax in full. Sometimes when there was a crop failure I pleaded with the official for a reduction or exemption, but received only a scolding or a sneer. I am afraid ..."

Confucius understood what he meant. He said, "You are afraid my order may not be truthfully carried out?"

The peasant lowered his head and did not reply.

Confucius said, "You are exempt from tax. Take this load of grain back home!"

The grateful peasant bowed repeatedly, not knowing what to say.

The onlookers heard and saw what had happened, and all of them praised Confucius for his benevolence and justice.

When the story spread, the peasants became more willing to pay tax and that was how it happened that tax collection was completed ahead of schedule.

Confucius brought the taxed grain to Mengsun Xizi in person, explaining the methods he had used to encourage tax payment. When Mengsun discovered that the year's tax income was twenty percent more than that of the past few years, he realized what deception had been practiced. He said with a deep sigh, "So many officials and their subordinates seek private gains at public expense!" Confucius then told him the wrongdoings of the tax collectors and their punishment. Mengsun said, "You have proved yourself to be honest and capable. It is highly commendable that you could see through the fraudulent runners at your very first official position."

Taking leave of Mengsun, Confucius returned home. He read books, practiced the rites, and sometimes went out to visit friends and consult their opinions.

When the time came to collect tax the following year, Confucius, with the experience of the first year and familiarity with the procedure still clear in his mind, was not expecting any trouble. At the appointed date he arrived at the city of Cheng, sent for the peasants who had helped him collect tax the previous year, and told them to inform all the households to pay tax on time. To his puzzlement, only a few small households paid their tax in the next five days. All the larger households refused to pay.

Confucius sent the peasants loyal to him to find out the reason behind it. However, people who refused to pay tax would not offer any explanation. When urged to pay tax, they promised that they would, then went back on their word. Left without a choice, Confucius went in person to investigate.

In the Spring and Autumn Period, a minister usually divided his manor into several cities and appointed a steward to be the magistrate of each city. The magistrate of Cheng was Gong Ke, one of Mengsun Xizi's stewards. He was a deceitful man with a lozenge-shaped face and triangular eyes. Appointed to such an important position, he considered Mengsun gullible and, instead of repaying his kindness, tried to cheat him in every way possible. The keeper of granaries was a subordinate of the city magistrate. Gong Ke had been highly displeased when Mengsun appointed Confucius to the position without consulting him. The former officer was his trusted follower and had sent him part of the embezzled tax income each year. Confucius, however, did not send him anything; instead he totally ignored him. Enraged, Gong Ke sent men to find the two expelled runners and together they visited the households in secret and ordered the people to pay tax directly to the magistrate, not to the keeper of granaries.

Dressed in plain clothes, Confucius went to visit the peasants, who treated him with trust and told him all that he needed to know. When Mengsun sent someone to report on the progress of tax collection, Confucius informed him of what Gong Ke had done. A few days later Mengsun sent men to announce to the larger households that they must pay tax in accordance with the regulations issued by Confucius, that all matters concerning tax collection was to be dealt with by Confucius alone and the magistrate not allowed to interfere in any way. Within seven days, the tax collection task was fulfilled.

One day Mengsun sent for Confucius and said to him kindly, "The vegetable garden and animal farm are ill managed and deteriorating rapidly. You are young, capable and experienced. I want to change your position and appoint you as keepr of livestock. What do you think?"

A keeper of livestock was a junior official in charge of the vegetable garden and animal farm. When Confucius considered the offer and did not reply promptly, Mengsun added, "It is of course both dirty and tiring to deal with cattle, sheep, mules and horses all day long. The job would put you to some inconvenience."

"I would not mind that," replied Confucius. "I am only worried that I might not be able to do the work well."

Mengsun broke into a big smile and said, "You have displayed your abilities already and need not be so modest."

"Since you place so great a trust in me," said Confucius, "I will do my best to manage the garden and farm well."

"When will you be able to take office?"

"It depends on your arrangement."

"How about tomorrow?"

Confucius nodded his consent.

The next morning Confucius went to his new office. Entering the courtyard, he found it overgrown with weeds and strewn with rubble. He made his way slowly into the office, which was covered by a copious layer of cobwebs. Involuntarily he sighed, and turning to look at the courtyard he saw an old man hobble into the house. Confucius hurriedly went to meet him.

The old man asked, "You are the new officer, aren't you?"

Confucius replied, "Yes, I am."

The old man said, "I heard about it only this morning. The other runners still don't know. Otherwise they would have come to receive your orders."

Confucius asked with a straight face, "Where have they gone?"

The old man sighed, "After the dismissal of your predecessor two months ago, they have done nothing but receive their pay. They fool around in the garden all day and slaughter pigs and sheep to feed themselves."

No sooner had he finished his words when two strong men came hurriedly into the courtyard and asked the old man, "Where is the new officer?"

The old man glared at them, then pointed to Confucius, saying, "This is our new officer."

The two men laughed, covering their mouths with their hands. "You must be joking! If he were the officer, we could be the magistrate."

Anxious, the old man pulled them by the clothes and said, "How can an old man like me tell lies! He is really our new officer."

The expressions of the two men became thick with fear as they said, "We had eyes but did not see, so we committed a great offense. Please forgive us!"

Confucius asked coldly, "Where are the other runners?"

The two men looked at each other but did not know how to reply.

Confucius studied them. They were red-faced, big-eyed, looking simple and honest. He kept his fierce stare trained upon them until they lowered their heads in shame, then asked, "What are your names?"

The old man replied for them, "One is named He Zhong and the other Ping Cheng. They are upright in character but have bad tempers."

Confucius smiled lightly and said, "I can see that." Then he ordered, "You two, go and find the other runners!"

"Yes, Officer!" They left in a hurry. Soon they returned with all the other runners.

Standing on the terrace in front of the hall of his office, Confucius addressed them in a stern voice, "You are all runners paid by the government for your work. Why were you not in the office doing what you are paid to do?"

The twenty or so runners stood in the courtyard, listening. They reacted with different expressions to Confucius' words.

Confucius added, "Open your eyes wide and take a look: What has become of this office!"

The runners remained silent.

Confucius said, "Come with me to have a look at the cattle, sheep, mules and horses in the farm!"

Arriving at the farm, Confucius frowned more deeply. The farm was surrounded by a dilapidated hedge made of wooden piles and bamboo poles. The farm was really filthy and smelled terrible, steeped in urine and excrement of animals, with flies and maggots everywhere. Confucius walked around the cattle pen and examined those pens that kept the sheep, mules and horses. Most of the animals there were only skin and bone. Unable to contain his anger anymore, he asked loudly,

"Who is the supervisor here?"

A short man replied in a low voice, "I am the supervisor here, Officer."

Confucius looked at this man. He had a pointed chin, sunken cheeks and small eyes. Confucius asked him, "What's your name?"

The supervisor replied, "My family name is Gu and my given name is Hua."

"Gu Hua!"

"Here!"

Confucius said in a stern and determined voice, "I'll allow you five days in which to mend all the hedges in this farm and clean away all this unsighting mess. From now on you must have the entire place cleaned regularly!" He went up to a stable and saw that the manger contained grass but no feed. He asked, "How is it that these horses eat only grass but no feed?"

Gu Hua could find no reply.

Sweeping his eyes over the runners, Confucius shouted, "He Zhong, Ping Cheng!"

He Zhong and Ping Cheng stepped out and answered, "Here."

Confucius ordered, "Starting from today, you will help Gu Hua manage the farm. You have a short time to do a good job!"

The two men replied confidently, "Yes!"

After Confucius had left, Gu Hua blinked his small eyes, trying to look modest and sincere, and said, "Brothers He Zhong and Ping Cheng, I have turned the farm into a mess because of my lack of ability. Today Officer Kong has appointed you overseers, so you must assume responsibility for the farm. I suggest ..." He watched the two men for their reaction and went on, "I suggest that the two of you take charge of the farm, and I can work as your assistant to find grass and feed and deliver pigs and sheep."

He Zhong waved his hand and said, "This won't do! This won't do! Brother Gu Hua, I think it would be better if you take charge, and Ping Cheng and I will assist you."

Ping Cheng also smiled fatuously, "Right, Brother Gu. We will be your assistants."

Gu Hua smiled cunningly, saying, "Please don't decline my offer. If you regard me as your elder, just accept this arrangement."

Left without a choice, the two men acquiesced.

After careful investigation and deliberation in a relatively short span of time, Confucius worked out a set of regulations for meting out rewards and punishments according to performance. In less than a year the entire office and the farm became well-governed. Well fed, the cattle, sheep, mules and horses were plump and sturdy.

One day Mengsun Xizi came for a visit, and Confucius took him around the place. Immensely pleased, he said in appreciation, "Master, you have exceptional talent!" Suddenly the smile vanished from his face, and he asked in puzzlement, "Now that there are so many plump pigs and sheep, why do you send me only ten every month?"

Confucius was dumbfounded at the question. He said, "I have always stuck to the number you set for me: ten pigs and ten sheep every month."

Shaking his head, Mengsun said, "What I have received from you is but five pigs and five sheep."

Confucius realized that someone must have been cheating him. Feeling downcast, he said to Mengsun, "Minister, something is wrong. I will report to you at your residence after getting to the bottom of it."

Mengsun also felt angry that he had been deceived and returned to his residence in low spirits.

Returning promptly to the office, Confucius called Gu Hua, He Zhong and Ping Cheng to the front of the hall and demanded in a loud voice, "Which of you sends pigs and sheep to Minister Mengsun's residence?"

Gu Hua replied in trepidation, "I send them at the appointed time."

Confucius asked, "How many do you take each month?"

Blinking his eyes, Gu Hua replied, "Ten each month."

Confucius asked, "Is it ten pigs and ten sheep, or ten pigs and sheep?"

Gu Hua hummed and hawed and finally said, "Ten pigs and ten sheep."

"Then why did Minister Mengsun receive only five pigs and five sheep?"

"Well, ..."

Confucius said sternly, "Tell the truth!"

Gu Hua fell on his knees and, trembling with fear, replied, "I sold half of the pigs and sheep in secret."

"And where is the money?"

"I spent it."

Confucius paused for a minute, then announced, "A petty man like you is by no means qualified to work for the government!" He deprived Gu Hua of his post and ordered him to return all the money he had obtained by illicit means.

After this incident Confucius became keenly aware of the unpredictability and pitfalls in official circles. He had not expected to encounter power abuse, such as committed by Gu Hua, in such an insignificant office. Torn by mixed feelings of regret and indignation, he made a decision.

Chapter Five

Confucius Has His Mother Buried by
His Father's Side;
He Travels a Long Distance to Study Music
After a Famous Master

Confucius came to see Mengsun Xizi with the decision in his mind. Having recounted Gu Hua's misconduct, he said, "You have treated me with great favor, making me keepr of granaries and then keeper of livestock. I will remember this with gratitude always. However, after much thought, I have decided not to accept an official position again."

Surprised, Mengsun asked, "You have dealt with Gu Hua's case properly and should be commended for it. Why do you want to resign?"

Confucius said, "I took positions in the government with the aim of serving the nation. As keeper of granaries, I tried my best to collect tax and keep the accounts clear. As keepr of livestock, I tried my best to have the animals well fed. If the runners were lazy I exhorted them with patience. If the runners did wrong I punished them according to law. I think I have fulfilled my duties. However, when I look at the world, I see nothing but the decline of the ruling houses, the breakdown and the degeneration of social and moral conduct, and the disintegration of music and rites. Even if I can make the accounts clear, the cattle and sheep plump, my subordinates honest and the runners diligent, I can contribute precious little toward upholding the way of Zhou and strengthening the ruling house of Lu. I might as well try to put out a burning cart-load of firewood with a cup of water."

Mengsun asked, "In your opinion, what should be done about it?"

Confucius said, "If we implement the benevolent rule as exemplified by King Wen and King Wu of Zhou and eliminate profiteering and other malpractices among the ministers and officials, the state of Lu will grow steadily stronger, and the people will become more and more wealthy. When that day comes, virtuous people from neighboring states, having heard what has happened, will be drawn here."

They were talking intimately when a steward entered to announce

a visitor. A young, anxious-looking man came into the room. He was of medium height, well-built and with a ruddy complexion. Confucius recognized him as Yan Lu. Yan Lu, whose styled name was Wu You, was a childhood friend of Confucius'. He was born in the twenty-seventh year of Duke Xiang of Lu (546 B.C.) into a poor family and herded cows as a boy. Seeing that he was perspiring, Confucius asked anxiously, "Brother, what has happened? What has brought you here in such a hurry?"

Yan Lu said, "Elder Brother, I just called at your house, where I found your mother seriously ill. You'd better return immediately!"

Startled, Confucius took leave of Mengsun and returned home with all haste.

Zhengzai was lying in bed. Her face was pale and her eyes closed.

A flustered Lady Qiguan was waiting at the bedside.

Kong Li, then four years old, did not know what was wrong, but walked around shaking the bed and moving the chair. Confucius had also a daughter, named Wuwei, who was just learning to talk.

Confucius threw himself in front of the bed. "Mother! What's wrong? Why did it happen so suddenly?"

Slowly opening her eyes, Zhengzai coughed lightly and said in a weak voice, her eyes brimming with tears, "I feel tight in my chest and short of breath. I am afraid I won't get well again."

Confucius said, "No, you are not yet forty, please don't think that way! I will go and find the doctor at once. You will surely get well again."

Confucius stood up, intending to fetch the doctor.

Zhengzai caught his hand with some difficulty and said, "Qiu, you have not let down your father and grandfather; you are modest and eager to learn, and have succeeded in your study. Today you are an officer; it is an official post even though it is low in rank. You must be honest and fair and handle matters impartially. Do not associate with evil persons and snobs. If turning the tide is beyond your power, you can at least preserve your own integrity. Make a good name to be handed down in history, as your grandfather wished!"

Confucius said, "Your son will always remember this."

Zhengzai continued, "Always keep in mind your grandfather's last words; let them urge you to exert yourself and constantly review your deeds and speech."

Confucius said, "I understand."

Thinking for a while with her eyes closed, Zhengzai then said, "Your brother is handicapped; you should help him if he is in difficulty."

Confucius was about to reply when Mengpi arrived. Hearing Zhengzai's words, he said in tears, "Mother, don't leave us!"

Taking him by the hand, Zhengzai said, "I am dying. The Kong family has contributed greatly to the state of Lu. The two of you must follow the example of your ancestors!"

It was then nightfall, and it grew dark in the room. Lady Qiguan lit a small oil-lamp. Zhengzai's face turned from pale to yellow. All members of the family stood around her bed.

Confucius said to Yan Lu, "I cannot go away right now. Brother, please go and find a doctor!"

Yan Lu left in great haste. A short while later he returned with the doctor. After feeling the patient's pulse, the doctor took Confucius aside and said to him, "Her pulse is very weak, and her breath is dwindling. Prepare for the burial!" With this he left.

All the family members kept watch by Zhengzai's bed, hoping she would open her eyes and say something. To listen to her, they all held their breath. Time passed by at an agonizingly slow pace. They waited until dawn, when she finally opened her eyes. The last moment of darkness had gone, and light was coming in through the window. Zhengzai attempted to speak. Confucius realized this was what was commonly known as the last radiance of the setting sun. He stood with his hands by his sides, waiting for his mother's exhortation. Zhengzai finally opened her mouth and said haltingly, "Practice benevolence and serve the nation well. There's something I have kept from you. Your father is buried at ..."

"Where is my father buried?" Confucius asked anxiously.

"He is buried at ..." She used up her last breath but failed to say anything, then closed her eyes forever. This was the spring of the fourteenth year of Duke Zhao of Lu's reign (528 B.C.). She was thirty-nine years old.

The family wailed in grief before gathering themselves together to prepare for her funeral. Yan Lu remained in the house to help.

Having placed her in the coffin, it was Confucius' wish that she be buried with his father. But where was his father's grave? When Shuliang He died, Zhengzai kept his place of burial from Mengpi and Kong Qiu because she did not want them to go there offering sacrifices

to the neglect of their studies. She tried to tell them the place before
her death but failed. The family had moved back to Qufu after
Shuliang He's death; therefore none of the neighbors knew Shuliang
He's burial place. Confucius and Mengpi discussed the problem and
carried Zhengzai's coffin to a street corner called Wufu, hoping to find
someone who might tell them what they wanted to know. They waited
from morning to noon. A lot of people came to watch, but none of
them knew the burial place of Shuliang He. The two brothers were
waiting anxiously when a woman in her fifties approached them. She
was grey-haired above her wrinkled face, dressed in a robe of coarse
cloth. She walked to the coffin, paid her respects to the dead, and
turned to ask Confucius and Mengpi, "Why have you placed your
mother's coffin here?"

Confucius said, "I want to have my mother buried together with
my father, but I don't know where my father is buried. Therefore we
have put our mother's coffin here in the hope that someone may help
us."

The woman said, "I am Wan Fuman's mother, and your mother's
good friend. I know where your father is buried."

Confucius and Mengpi prostrated before her and touched the
ground with their heads in obeisance: "Please tell us!"

When the woman told them Shuliang He's burial place the two
brothers thanked her repeatedly and following her instructions, carried
their mother's coffin to Fang Mountain.

Fang Mountain sloped down from east to west. The funeral
procession climbed the mountain until they reached a ridge, where
they had a complete view of Fang Mountain winding ahead like a giant
dragon. A few thick cypress and Chinese juniper trees grew on a piece
of level ground. Looking at the map drawn by Wan Fuman's mother,
Confucius recognized it to be his father's grave. They quickened their
pace.

Arriving before Shuliang He's grave, Confucius and Mengpi fell
on their knees in obeisance and prayed. They buried their mother to
their father's right, facing south, and returned home in tears.

Confucius passed the next three days in a daze. After rising on
the fourth day, he felt his mind had cleared a little, and his tired body
was more relaxed than before. After breakfast he began to study. He
valued time as if it were gold and did not want to waste it. He fumbled
through the bamboo slips on the wooden board, looking for *The Book*

of Changes.

Yan Lu came running and said eagerly, "When I was walking down the street just now I heard people talking about Nan Kuai, Chief Minister Jisun's retainer, who just raised a rebellion in the city of Fei."

Confucius looked at Yan Lu in astonishment.

Yan Lu continued, "The people of Fei rose up and attacked Nan Kuai. He was defeated and fled to the state of Qi."

Confucius heaved a sigh of relief.

Having brought the news, Yan Lu returned to herd his cows and sheep.

After seeing Yan Lu out, Confucius picked out *The Book of Changes.* He tried to read but could not concentrate. He thought about what Yan Lu had told him, and remembered what Jisun Yiru had done. A few years before, Jisun went to pay homage to Mount Tai, totally ignoring the rites of Zhou, which stipulated that only the king of Zhou and the rulers of the states were entitled to conduct such a ceremony.

Confucius thought a lot. He was worried that someday Jisun might raise a revolt, just as his steward had revolted against him. Such power struggle among the ruling class would victimize the common people of Lu and propel the state of Lu into further decline. Confucius knew that given his position and status, he could only think about the problem but could not hope to solve it. However, he was anxiously waiting for a chance to become a court official.

According to the custom of that time, the son should observe a three-year mourning after the death of his parent. During that period he could neither play the *qin* guitar nor sing songs. Conversant with the rites, Confucius went by the ancient custom, for three years staying home all day to read or practice rituals. Only Yan Lu came often to ask him questions and bring him news. Though Yan Lu made a living as a herdsman, he was greatly concerned about affairs of the state. He often pricked up his ears when people talked about current affairs and political situations.

In the spring of the seventeenth year of Duke Zhao of Lu's reign (525 B.C.) Tan Zi, ruler of the state of Tan, made a visit to Duke Zhao. A dependency of Lu, the state of Tan held birds in high regard. Birds appeared in their totems and were even used to name their official positions. Confucius had learned about this custom long before but did not know the reason behind it. Therefore he wanted to inquire about it from the people of Tan. When Yan Lu learned of Tan Zi's visit to Lu, he hurried to inform Confucius.

Having just completed three years' mourning for his mother, Confucius did not want to miss this good chance, and followed Yan Lu to the Lu court. On the way he met Mengsun Xizi. Confucius saluted and asked, "Minister Mengsun, I have heard that Tan Zi has come to pay respect to our lord. Is that true?"

Mengsun replied, "Yes, he came three days ago."

Confucius then told Mengsun what he intended to do.

Mengsun said with regret, "Unfortunately, he left Lu for Tan more than two hours ago."

Confucius was thoroughly disappointed to hear this.

In autumn that year Tan Zi came again to visit Duke Zhao, at which time Mengsun sent someone to inform Confucius.

Dressed in formal clothes, Confucius went and waited in front of the guesthouse where Tan Zi stayed.

Tan Zi paid his respects to Duke Zhao, who invited him to a banquet that evening. After the banquet Tan Zi returned to the guesthouse.

Confucius came up and bowed in obeisance, saying, "I have heard that in your state flying birds are highly revered, and even official positions are named after them. Can you tell me why it is so?"

It was said that the ruler of Tan was a descendent of Shao Hao, so Tan Zi started by saying, "The ancestor of the state of Tan is Shao Hao." Looking at Confucius proudly, he continued, "When our ancestor established the state, two pheonixes happened to alight on a parasol tree. He interpreted it as an auspicious sign. Since then phoenix has been regarded as an auspicious bird. Later more birds came to be included in the pantheon. The custom of using the names of birds in officialdom started with Shao Hao." He went on to explain the official system of Tan in detail, and Confucius listened attentively. Tan Zi then described other aspects of Tan. When he learned that the person before him was Confucius, whom he had always admired, he became more modest in his attitude and said, "I have heard your name long before. Please accept my apologies for not recognizing you!"

Confucius thanked him over and over and then bade him good-bye.

In the eighteenth year of Duke Zhao of Lu's reign (524 B.C.) the states of Song, Wei, Chen and Zheng suffered successively from fires.

Some people in Zheng suggested that they offer sacrifice to heaven, saying, "If we don't remove the calamity by offering sacrifice to heaven, fire will break out again in the state of Zheng." The ruling minister of Zheng, Zi Chan, said, "Heaven's rule is illusive, whereas man's rule is practical. Since we cannot go up to heaven, how can we understand it?"

Confucius had always respected Zi Chan. Zi Chan, named Gongsun Qiao, was Duke Mu of Zheng's grandson and a virtuous chief minister of Zheng. Confucius knew a lot of stories about him. The state of Zheng was sandwiched between Jin and Chu. Both Jin and Chu were big and powerful, while Zheng was small and weak. Zi Chan became governor of the state in the thirtieth year of the reign of Duke Xiang of Lu (543 B.C.). He advocated frugality and military consolidation. The people did not understand him at first and wrote a song to curse him:

> Thrift, thrift,
> He praises thrift all day,
> And good clothes are not allowed to be worn.
> Army, army,
> He wants to build the army strong.
> What to do about the land lying waste?
> If someone offers to kill Zi Chan,
> We will follow him wholeheartedly!

A learned and talented man himself, Zi Chan promoted people of virtue and ability to high positions. When an important decision was to be made about state affairs, he consulted Gongsun Hui, who was conversant with situations in the various states, went out to the suburbs to have a talk with Bi Shen, a man who thought deeply and planned carefully. At the same time he sought advice from the common people. Then he consulted the wisdom of Feng Jianzi to make a decision and finally sent You Ji, who was good at diplomacy, on diplomatic missions to carry out the decision. After such detailed and careful procedures, Zi Chan never made a single mistake. Governed by him for three years, the state of Zheng attained social stability and achieved a succession of diplomatic victories. Thereupon the common people of Zheng composed another song:

> Our children are taught by Zi Chan;
> Our land is developed by Zi Chan.

Zi Chan must not die;
Who is to succeed him if he dies?

Confucius was much influenced by Zi Chan in his emphasis on people instead of heaven, his circumspection and cautiousness, and his concern for the welfare of the nation. Whenever he heard people praising Zi Chan for his achievements, Confucius' admiration for him grew and he wished he could take Zi Chan as his teacher and learn the methods of running the nation well and bringing peace and security to the people.

Confucius became more and more learned after diligent study and persistent investigation. One day, after teaching a few characters to his son, Kong Li, and his daughter, Wuwei, he played the *qin* and sang songs. The sound of the *qin* seemed to him high-pitched and crisp, lacking melody and depth. He stopped to contemplate for a moment, then started playing again, but was still not pleased with the sound. He stood up facing the wall and considered the problem for a long time. Suddenly he realized what was wrong. "I have upgraded myself in the other branches of knowledge, but have not been taught well with regard to music." So he decided to find a famous master to teach him.

He had long heard that the master musician of Jin, Shi Xiangzi, had made great achievements in mastering the *qin*, and wanted very much to learn from him. In the spring of the nineteenth year of the reign of Duke Zhao of Lu (523 B.C.) Confucius said good-bye to his family and friends and set out for Jin.

He traveled for more than ten days, encountering all kinds of hardships until he finally arrived at the foot of Taihang Mountain. The mountain stretched as far as the eye could see, with high peaks in the clouds and numerous gullies and valleys. There were green and luxuriant pines and cypresses, with kites and vultures flying in the sky and deer and cranes roaming about on the ground. The sun was setting in the valley, with half the sky turning red in the evening glow. At the sight Confucius knew it was going to be fine again tomorrow. The crow of chickens and the barking of dogs could be heard, and cooking smoke arose slowly from the thatched houses, making a lovely, poetic scene in the last glow of the setting sun.

As it was getting dark, Confucius put up at an inn by the road at the foot of the mountain. Exhausted by the day's journey, he slept soundly in the barely furnished room.

After breakfast the next morning, he started to climb the mountain, following other travelers. The narrow lane was lined with thistles and thorns and gigantic ancient trees. He lost count of how many streams he had crossed or how many ridges he had passed over. The scene before him was constantly changing, now a wide valley, now a precipice. He could not see far ahead and had to watch his steps carefully. It was not until twilight that Confucius climbed over the Taihang, and the boundless loess plateau stretched before him with its network of gullies and rivers washed by rain year after year. Cooking smoke was again rising from the villages. It reminded him of what he had gone through the whole day, the rugged paths and precipitous hills. Feeling dizzy and sore all over his body, he was nevertheless glad and proud that he had left the mountain behind him. It occurred to him that the road ahead might be more rugged and present even greater difficulties. "No matter what happens, I will travel down the road until I reach my goal," he said to himself and, dragging his tired legs, kept on walking.

Spring was a windy season on the loess plateau. Gusts of strong wind carrying loess blew against him, making him unable to open his eyes or move forward easily. To evade the attack of the flying loess, he often had to stop and cover his eyes with his hands until the wind abated, then moved on.

Finally he arrived at the capital of Jin. This was also an ancient city with wide bustling streets and fine buildings. Eager to find the master musician, he began to ask around for the residence of Shi Xiangzi, not pausing to enjoy the sights.

Confucius found Shi Xiangzi's house on a quiet alley, its black-painted gate ajar. On the wall facing the gate was written a giant character, *fu*, meaning good fortune.

Confucius patted the dust off his clothes and knocked at the gate.

It opened slowly and Confucius found himself facing a gray-haired old man with a square face, looking kind and benevolent. Confucius took one step forward and said with a bow, "You are Shi Xiangzi, I presume?"

The old man returned the salute and said, "Yes, I am. Where do you come from, and what do you have to teach me, having arrived at my humble abode?"

Confucius said, "I am Kong Qiu from the state of Lu. I have come specially to learn from your skills at the *qin*."

Shi Xiangzi said with a smile, "I have heard you are a sage with great learning and exceptional talent, and I have longed to meet you. It is my good fortune that you have come to visit me so unexpectedly."

Confucius said, "Your fame has spread far and wide in the world. I have come here specially to learn from you."

Shi said, "I am not really worthy of the fame. Since you have traveled a long distance to visit me, please come in and let's talk." He took Confucius by the hand and led him into the house.

After they had taken a seat, Shi said, "You have displayed your sincerity by enduring the hardships of a long journey. I will teach you all I know about the art of playing the *qin*."

Half rising from his seat in a salute, Confucius said, "I owe you many thanks!"

Shi said, "I can play the *qin* because I am a minor official responsible for playing chime stones. Now let me show you how to play the *qin*." He stood up, walked to a table and pulled back a black cloth to reveal an ancient *qin* painted jet-black. Having adjusted the chords, he began to play with rapt attention. The music was deep, melodious, thrilling and uplifting.

Well taught by his grandfather in childhood, Confucius was highly conversant with music. Intoxicated in the sound of the *qin*, he felt so comfortable he forgot all about his hunger, thirst and fatigue.

After completing each piece of music, Shi stopped to explain its meaning. Confucius listened earnestly and remembered what he heard very clearly. Pleased with his sincerity, Shi soon revealed everything he had learned about music in dozens of years, and Confucius was filled with gratitude. They talked heartily together like old friends and that evening Shi invited Confucius to have dinner and to stay in his house. In the days that followed, they kept each other company from morning till night practicing and discussing music together.

Under Shi's instruction, Confucius made rapid progress in his musical understanding and skills. Shi also gained much knowledge while listening to Confucius speaking on subjects both ancient and modern. About ten days later Confucius attained great facility at fingering. Now when he played the *qin*, the music sounded moving and pleasant, just like words spoken from one's heart.

One day Confucius kept playing the same piece of music time after time. Smiling with satisfaction, Shi said, "You have grasped the essentials and become quite skilled at it. You may practice a new tune."

Confucius said modestly, "I have learned to play the tune but do not yet understand its principle." So he kept on practicing.

After a while Shi said, "Judging from what I have heard, you have already understood the principle of playing the *qin*. You can change to a new tune."

Confucius said, "I do not yet understand its meaning."

After a while Shi said, "You have already understood its meaning. Now you can start practicing another tune."

Confucius said, "I have yet to find out who composed the piece, his character and aspirations."

Some moments later Confucius assumed a serene and serious expression as if he were standing on a hill gazing into the distance. Taking a deep sigh, he said, "At last! Now I understand it! A broad mind, high aspirations, great integrity and lofty sentiments; who could have written a tune like this except King Wen of Zhou? He had such a broad view that the whole world was in his sight."

"Master, you are incredible! When my teacher taught me the tune, he told me that it was called 'King Wen's Composition'! You have got a real understanding of its meaning, and your skills are superb! How amazing!"

Confucius and Shi Xiangzi became close friends and a month passed like this, when Confucius said, "Thanks to your instruction, I have somewhat improved my skill at playing the *qin*. I have stayed here for over a month now. It's time for me to return home."

"It is hard to tell when we will ever meet again," Shi replied. "Why not stay for a few more days?"

Repeatedly urged by Shi, Confucius agreed to stay.

Three days later Shi invited Confucius to a farewell banquet. After three rounds of wine Shi asked, "You are well versed in matters about heaven and earth, ancient and modern, and have the reputation of a sage all across the dukedom. Why don't you render service to the state by taking an official position in the court of the Duke of Lu?"

Confucius said, "It is in Lu that I was born and grew up; of course I want to devote myself to its welfare. But right now the ruling house is feeble while wicked ministers take control of the court. Under such circumstances, it is not suitable for me to serve in an official position. I have to devote myself to learning and wait for a change of the tide."

Shi sighed, "It is easy to recognize a gentleman but difficult to recognize a petty man. However, petty men often enjoy high positions whereas gentlemen are left out in the cold, all because the ruler has shut his eyes and stopped up his ears. As a popular saying goes, good medicine tastes bitter to the mouth, and honest advice sounds unpleasant to the ears. Few people like bitter medicine or good advice!"

Confucius said, "If only heaven would open his eyes and bring the sage kings Yao, Shun, Yu and Wen back to life!"

Drinking wine to alleviate their distress, the two of them had a rambling chat about everything under the sun and did not retire to bed until late into the night.

The following morning after breakfast, Confucius made ready to depart. Shi accompanied him until they were outside the city. "We will have to part in the end even if I travel with you for a thousand *li*, so let's say good-bye here," Shi said.

Confucius said, "I am extremely fortunate to gain your misplaced appreciation. I will never forget what you have done for me and hopefully will return the favor in the future. Take care of yourself! I must leave."

Shi replied, "We will meet again sometime. Let's take good care of ourselves."

Traveling across mountains and streams, Confucius returned to Lu by the way he had come.

As soon as Confucius entered the gate, Lady Qiguan, Kong Li and Wuwei came up to welcome him. Lady Qiguan relieved him of his luggage, while Kong Li and Wuwei patted him to get the dust off.

Confucius had just taken his seat when Yan Lu arrived in high spirits. As soon as he saw Confucius, he began to ask a lot of questions: Is the capital of Jin big and pretty? Was the journey difficult? What kind of a person was Shi Xiangzi? Confucius did not know which of these questions to answer first.

Yan Lu said, "Now that you are well versed in all the six arts, you can take me as your disciple."

Confucius said, "Up till now schools have always been run by the government. There is no precedent of a private school. You must realize that education is no trivial matter; if ill managed, it would harm the young people by leading them astray."

Yan Lu said, "With your great learning and sincerity in dealing with the others, your school will attract too many students for you to handle. And the students will only worry that there is too much for them to learn. How can that come to any harm?"

Confucius said, "Your words are reasonable, but I have to consider such a matter carefully before I can make a decision."

No sooner had he finished his words than the ground shook violently. The house shuddered and the trees rocked. The sickles and pickaxes in the room bumped against one another, creating a great clattering.

Rushing out of the house, they looked back and saw that a crack had appeared in the wall and much cogongrass had slipped down from the roof. Looking around, they saw nothing but fallen walls and collapsed houses, with a dust cloud arising over everything.

Yan Lu's family was poor and lived in a dilapidated house. Worried about their safety, he said, "I will go home to have a look!" With this he made off at once.

Telling Lady Qiguan, Kong Li and Wuwei to stay outside the house, Confucius quickly followed Yan Lu into the street.

Chapter Six

Confucius Starts to Take on Disciples;
Duke Jing of Qi Seeks to Enlist Real
Talents into His Service

Walking along the street with Yan Lu, Confucius saw only desolation all around. The houses, which had been standing just a moment before, were now either tilted or had crumbled to the ground. Not yet recovered from the shock, people stood before the gates of their houses praying to heaven.

The lane on which Yan Lu lived was narrow and ragged, with small run-down thatched houses sparsely distributed on both sides. Curiously, few of these small and low thatched houses had collapsed. Upon entering into Yan Lu's house, they found his wife standing at a loss in the courtyard. At the sight of her husband and Confucius, she gradually calmed down and, pointing to the house, said, "Look, the back wall has crumbled."

Yan Lu and Confucius went to the back of the house and found a big hole in the back wall. They repaired it with mud and stones, finishing the job in less than two hours.

All people in the city were busily mending and strengthening their houses against the danger of further collapse.

Having fortified his own house, Confucius returned to his studies.

In the twentieth year of Duke Zhao of Lu's reign (522 B.C.) Confucius was twenty-nine years old, or thirty by the nominal age. After many years of study and investigation, he had acquired much knowledge with respect to both self-cultivation and statecraft. He cherished great aspirations but still felt uncertain how to establish himself in society.

Yan Lu visited him every day, asking a lot of questions and requesting to be accepted as a disciple. Asked to start a private school and take on students, Confucius said, "It is easy and convenient when the two of us get together and exchange our viewpoints on learning, but it would be entirely another matter if I start a school."

Yan Lu said, "The teacher is only responsible for guiding in the right direction; the rest depends on the students themselves. You can

teach the way you want, and the students will learn in their own ways."

Confucius put on a stern expression and said, "If I start a school, I will hold myself responsible for all the students. People differ greatly in their natural abilities, their likes and dislikes, their disposition and their skills. To teach them well, one must apply the method suited to their individual characteristics."

"Master, your words are most sensible!" Yan Lu fell on his knees and touched the ground with his forehead, saying, "Your disciple pays respect to the master."

Confucius hastily helped him up with both hands, saying, "Why are you being so obsequious?"

"It is proper that a disciple shows his respect to the master in such a way."

"In that case, I have no choice but to take you as my disciple, do I?"

"Actually, I have been your disciple for a long time already."

After that the courtyard of Confucius' house became a classroom, as he took on several students. Luckily there was an old scholar tree that provided a cool shade.

One day Confucius was teaching his students when someone knocked at the gate. Kong Li had sharp ears and was therefore the first to hear it. He ran swiftly to open the gate.

It was a stranger in his twenties. He was of average stature, and had large eyes and thick eyebrows.

Kong Li stared at him for a moment, then asked, "Who are you looking for?"

The visitor asked politely, "Excuse me, is this Confucius' residence?"

"Yes, it is. Please come in."

Hearing the exchange, Confucius and Yan Lu came out of the room to meet the visitor in the courtyard.

The visitor introduced himself by saying, "I am Zeng Dian from the city of Nanwu. Your name has long resounded in my ears. I have come especially to learn from you." Without waiting for a reply, he put down the bundle from his shoulder, adjusted his dress, and prostrated himself before Confucius. "Disciple Zeng Dian pays respects to the master!"

Zeng Dian, whose styled name was Zi Xi, was born in the twenty-seventh year of the reign of Duke Xiang of Lu (546 B.C.) in the city of Nanwu in the state of Lu.

Looking at the ardent and ingenuous youth before him, Confucius was filled with a sense of mission. It was then that he made his decision to start a private school. He helped Zeng Dian on his feet and said, "Please come in and talk with me."

Inside the room, Confucius introduced Yan Lu, Kong Li, Lady Qiguan, and Kong Wuwei to Zeng Dian.

After saluting Lady Qiguan, Zeng Dian opened his bundle, took out ten pieces of dried meat, and said, "As I live in a poor area, I can prepare no better gift to the master than these ten pieces of meat. Please accept my humble offering."

Taking the meat, Confucius said with sincerity, "I attach little importance to gifts but great importance to teaching. Now that I start to teach, I will eliminate the outmoded conventions in government schools. I will treat without partiality all those who want to study with me, regardless of their social status. Even so, since the giving of an initial gift to the master is such a common practice, I will accept as my disciple anyone who wants to study with me and brings ten pieces of dried meat as a gift."

At that time government schools were so costly that only officials and wealthy people could afford to send their children there. By accepting only ten pieces of dried meat as school fee, Confucius provided the children of poor families with the chance of receiving an education. Furthermore, he was well-known and his fame as a sage had spread to the neighboring states. Thus in a very short time he gathered a lot of students.

In teaching, Confucius adjusted his method to individual differences and proved skillful at giving systematic guidance. Sometimes he lectured in the courtyard under the old scholar tree, talking about *The Book of Poetry*, *The Book of History*, *The Book of Rites*, *The Book of Changes*, and *The Book of Music*. Sometimes he sat in his room and answered questions from his disciples. Sometimes he took his students out to the suburbs, balancing their temperament in play and sightseeing.

One day Confucius was teaching his students in the courtyard when a man burst in. He was tall and sturdy, with a square face and a high forehead. Wearing a warrior's hat decorated with chicken feathers, a long silk gown, a pair of heavy boots, and a sword hanging from his waist, he looked neither like a warrior nor like a scholar. He approached Confucius in giant steps and said in a hoarse voice,

"Disciple Zhong You pays respect to the master!"

Zhong You, styled name Zi Lu, was also known as Ji Lu. He was born in Bian in the state of Lu in the thirty-first year of Duke Xiang of Lu's reign (542 B.C.).

Confucius looked at him doubtfully, and then scolded him, "You dress in showy clothes and stalk in as if there were no one else present: You don't look like a scholar in the least. The water of great rivers comes from high mountains, but at the source it is so shallow a wine cup cannot float on it. Things become entirely different at the middle and lower reaches; you cannot cross it without boarding a big ship and braving violent winds. Now you dress in magnificent clothes and assume an overweening air, who would dare point out your mistakes?"

Zi Lu lowered his head and went out without replying. A moment later he came back dressed like a warrior and, drawing his sword, began practicing swordplay in the court. He swirled like a sparrow hawk spreading its wings and leapt like a dragon leaping out of the water, creating flashes of white light and whistling sounds with his sword. The spectators were enthralled by his performance when he suddenly took a giant stride, stopped abruptly, and put away his sword. He said to Confucius, "In ancient times every gentleman carried a sword with him for self-defense. I heard that your father was a brave commander, who still enjoys great fame among the people of Biyang. Master, since you are strong, you should also practice the sword and other martial arts as a heritage from your ancestors."

Confucius said, "In ancient times a gentleman established himself on loyalty and benevolence. Faced with people who were not charitable, he tried to educate them by loyalty and truthfulness; faced with people who were domineering, he tried to influence them by benevolence and righteousness. By doing so he would achieve good results. Why was there any need for him to defend himself with a sword?"

Zi Lu inclined his head and listened attentively.

Confucius continued, "I heard that Cheng Tang did not draw his sword in self-defense when he led an punitive expedition against King Jie of Xia; nor did King Wu draw his sword when he headed the expedition against King Zhou of Yin. Yet they both achieved victories. This is called subduing others by virtue. In my opinion, you can only truly subdue someone by virtue. This has been proved by numerous events. On the other hand, people subdued by force seldom accept the situation wholeheartedly."

Filled with veneration, Zi Lu said in a low, muffled voice, "After hearing your instruction today, I feel like someone who, having lived in a dark room for a long time, suddenly sees a bright light and feels enlightened in his heart. Please wait a moment. I will come back after I have changed my clothes."

Confucius was pleased by his simplicity and straightforwardness despite his impudent manners.

When he came in for the third time, Zi Lu was dressed like a scholar. He walked in small, quick steps and looked straight ahead, bearing no trace of the warrior.

Confucius said seriously, "Zi Lu, please listen to me. In my opinion, if someone likes to boast about his bravery and excellence, he must be a vain and arrogant person without substance. If someone makes a point of being smarter than others and is full of pretenses, he must be a petty man. On the other hand, a gentleman is bighearted and never makes pretenses. If he knows something, he acknowledges that he knows it; if he does not know something, he acknowledges that he does not know it. If he can do something, he acknowledges that he can do it; if he can not do something, he acknowledges that he can not do it. This is the true mark of a upright gentleman!"

Zi Lu said, "I understand!"

Confucius took a great liking to this frank and honest disciple. He asked with a smile, "Zi Lu, what's your greatest talent?"

"As you have just seen, I am very good at swordplay."

"I am asking about your literary instead of martial talents. I can see that you are fairly well endowed. What do you want to learn?"

"I don't really understand how one's eagerness to learn may benefit him. Please explain this to me!"

Pausing to think for a while, Confucius replied slowly, "Without several loyal ministers to offer him advice, the ruler will surely commit mistakes and bring calamities to the state. Without several good friends to offer him advice, the scholar will not make rapid progress in his studies for lack of criticism. You can not ride a fine horse without using the rein or make wood straight without using the rope. A person who has learning will be sharp-eyed and clear-minded, and able to deal with affairs efficiently. A person who is averse to learning and does not cultivate himself will degenerate, make mistakes and eventually be punished by law. Therefore a gentleman must devote himself to learning."

Still unconvinced, Zi Lu argued, "Many things in the world are created with an innate strength. Take the bamboo on Nan Mountain, for instance. It grows straight even though no one trims it. Arrows made of the bamboo can pierce the hide of a rhinoceros. Is not bamboo created with this inner strength? What does this have to do with learning?"

"Yes, I see your point. However, if we attach sharp copper heads to the bamboo arrows, won't they pierce the hide of rhinoceroses more easily?"

Zi Lu thought this reasonable and nodded.

Confucius added, "If a person with good natural endowments studies diligently, he will make even greater achievements, just like the bamboo arrows with copper heads."

Zi Lu asked, "If there is someone dressed in ragged clothes but hiding a precious jade in his bosom, what should he do?"

Confucius replied without hesitation, "If the state is being ruled by a fatuous and self-indulgent sovereign, he should take his jade and hide himself in the mountains; if the state is being ruled by a virtuous and sensible sovereign, he should put on a magnificent dress and display the jade."

"I will follow your advice, master, displaying myself in front of gentlemen and concealing myself in front of petty men," Zi Lu said.

Thus Confucius and Zi Lu talked on while the other disciples sat around and listened. At this moment someone came with the news that Yan Lu's wife had just given birth to a baby boy. Confucius told Lady Qiguan to take six pieces of dried meat and gave it to Yan Lu by way of congratulation. Yan Lu accepted the gift with gratitude and, making a deep bow, returned home.

As it was still early, Confucius looked into the bundles of bamboo slips and picked out the one he wanted from *The Book of Poetry*:

Let's pick Cheqian,*
Pick it quickly.

Let's pick Cheqian,
Pick it up quickly.

Let's pick Cheqian,

---

*Asiatic plantain.

Take it up quickly.

Let's pick Cheqian,
Strip it off quickly.

Let's pick Cheqian,
Wrap it in the gown quickly.

Let's pick Cheqian,
Wrap it up in the gown quickly.

Confucius chanted the poem, and the disciples chanted after him.

Just then someone came with the news that Zi Chan, the virtuous chief minister of Zheng, had died.

Zi Chan was never far from Confucius' thought. Confucius had always wanted to find an opportunity to meet Zi Chan, and the news came as a heavy blow. He regretted that he had not visited him before and blamed heaven for not allowing such a good man to live a few more years. He stood there quietly and broke into tears.

Zi Lu was a frank and outspoken person. Puzzled with Confucius' grief, he asked, "Master, Zi Chan was the chief minister of Zheng, so his death does not incur loss to Lu. What's more, you don't know him personally. So why are you weeping for him?"

Confucius said, "Zi Chan was a truly superior man. In twenty years or more he turned Zheng from a weak and poor state into a strong and wealthy one mainly because of four reasons: First, he was upright and well-behaved, conducting himself with caution and sticking to the rites of Zhou. Second, he served his lord earnestly, treated people of inferior ranks with respect, and consulted people from all circles so that he could avoid making mistakes. Third, he advocated frugality, opposed extravagance, and loved the people as if they were his own children. The people were able to live in peace and happiness because of his good management of the state. Fourth, he executed a benevolent rule, employed people and resources with care and did not make the people do anything against righteousness. Since he had such fine virtue and merits, how can I help admiring him? I had long wished to visit and learn from him, but my wish was not to be fulfilled. How can I help feeling regret? Now that he is dead, I will never have a chance to meet him. How can I help feeling grief?"

Zi Lu realized that he neither understood Zi Chan nor Confucius, so he did not venture to speak again.

Confucius remained in low spirits for several days. One day a rainbow spanned the clear sky right after a storm. Confucius was overjoyed: "There are so many beautiful miracles in nature!" He wanted to go out in the fine weather after the storm and take a trip to the suburbs.

His mother had told him several times that he had been born under Mount Niqiu. Why not take a trip there?

By that time Confucius had accepted quite a few disciples who later became well-known, including Min Shun, Qin Shang, Ran Geng, and Qidiao Kai. Min Shun, styled name Zi Qian, was born in Lu in the sixth year of Duke Xiang of Lu's reign (536 B.C.). Qin Shang, styled name Pi Ci, was born in Lu in the twenty-sixth year of Duke Xiang of Lu's reign (547 B.C.). Ran Geng, styled name Bo Niu, was born in Lu in the twenty-eighth year of Duke Xiang of Lu's reign (545 B.C.). Qidiao Kai, styled name Zi Kai, who was also known as Zi Ruo, was born in the state of Cai in the second year of Duke Zhao of Lu's reign (540 B.C.).

Confucius relayed his plan to his disciples, who agreed to it with enthusiasm. Since he was very fond of books, he selected some bamboo slips from his collection to take with him. Then they set out.

In summer, Mount Niqiu was covered in ancient trees and luxuriant grass in which locusts leapt and grasshoppers chirped. Confucius and his disciples climbed halfway up the mount and sat down in front of the mountain-god temple. After catching his breath, Confucius spread the bundle of bamboo slips in his hand. His disciples gathered around him and found it to be *The Book of Poetry*.

Zi Lu asked in surprise, "Master, why are you so fond of *The Book of Poetry*?"

Confucius replied in an animated voice, "The theme of the three hundred poems in *The Book of Poetry* can be summed up in one phrase: Sincerity of feeling and purity of the mind. Why don't you all study *The Book of Poetry*? By studying it you can enliven your imagination, sharpen your sight, improve your ability to understand and cooperate with others, and learn the technique of employing parables in your speech. The book can teach you the right ways to serve the ruler as well as your parents, and also acquaint you with many birds, animals, and plants. *The Book of Poetry* brings me both solace and inspiration.

That's why I often study it." Gazing at the flowing river at the foot of the mountain, he was lost in thought.

Most of the time the Yishui River was a gentle flow crystal clear. Right after the storm, however, it had become muddy and torrential. Looking at the rushing river, Confucius sighed, "Time flows on just like this, not ceasing day or night! Life is short; in the time for a galloping horse to pass a crack, it will be gone. You should cherish time and study diligently in order to learn as much knowledge as you can."

The disciples replied in unison, "Yes, we understand."

Looking in the spirited faces of his disciples, Confucius began to consider their character and disposition one by one. Yan Lu was faithful and steady; Zi Lu, impetuous and straightforward; Bo Niu, stable and experienced; Qidiao Kai, smart and keen; Zi Qian, kind and filial. He considered how he could teach them according to their individual dispositions and have them employed according to their talents when the opportunity came. He placed his hopes for the future on his disciples.

Confucius was very gratified by the behavior of his disciples. Zi Qian lost his mother when he was a child, and his father remarried. His stepmother, though not fond of him, treated him tolerably well at first. Later she gave birth to two sons, whom she treated much better than him. In winter one year she made three cotton-padded coats. Two thin ones were for Zi Qian's younger brothers, who felt warm wearing them and even sweated while working. Zi Qian was given the thick one, but he shuddered with cold. Seeing this, his father thought he was putting a show on purpose to scandalize against his mother and struck him with a whip. The coat was torn, and some reed catkins drifted out. Filled with rage, the father grasped the whip and shouted, "Come here, you despicable woman!" Knowing that she was in the wrong, the stepmother came out from the inner room and fell on her knees before her husband, trembling with fear and begging for mercy. At this Zi Qian also fell on his knees and begged on his stepmother's behalf, "Father, please calm your anger. Stepmother has always been good to me; the cotton-padded coat was just an accidental mistake. Please forgive her!" Not fully appeased, his father threw away the whip and said, "I'll send her back to her parents!" Zi Qian said, "Father, you can not do that. Even if stepmother does not treat me well, I am the only one who suffers. If you divorce her, both my two brothers and I will suffer from hunger and cold." On hearing this, the stepmother felt ashamed for what she had done and wept with remorse. Thereafter she treated Zi Qian with great affection, and Zi Qian's fame as a filial son spread all over the states.

Confucius was fond of praising others for their merits but refrained from discussing their shortcomings. He considered it a rule to be observed by all gentlemen; only petty men liked to rake up other people's faults but said nothing of their merits. Looking at his disciples and thinking of their virtues, he felt a great satisfaction in his heart.

They enjoyed the scenery in the mountain with its flowers, grass, birds and rocks, and returned home in high spirits.

Confucius continued to teach his students every day in the courtyard. His fame grew by each passing day and spread far and wide.

One day after the morning audience Jisun Yiru returned to his residence. At the sight of his steward Yang Hu, he suddenly felt a sense of aversion. Recently he had heard many rumors about Yang Hu building up his personal influence. He thought there must be some truth in these rumors, for there could be no smoke without fire. Therefore he intended to appoint some new stewards to check and weaken Yang Hu's influence. After careful deliberation he focused his attention on Confucius' disciples. So he invited Confucius to his house and, assuming an unusually modest appearance, said with a smile, "According to what I heard, since you started teaching, many people of outstanding talents have come from various states to be your disciples. I wonder if you could recommend a few of them to take up official positions."

Confucius thought for a while and, bowing slightly, replied, "Though I have many disciples, few of them are qualified to be officials in terms of talent and virtue. At present only Zi Lu is suitable to serve in the government."

Jisun asked anxiously, "How about appointing him to the position of city magistrate?"

Confucius said, "Zi Lu is honest, straightforward, and resolute, and will be just and achieve merits in his position. However, his rashness and impetuousness makes him unsuitable for an appointment right now."

"Perhaps you would keep this in mind and recommend a few suitable candidates for official positions in the future?"

Confucius smiled, "It is to benefit the state that I am teaching my disciples. Once there are suitable candidates, I will surely recommend them to you."

Taking leave of Jisun, Confucius felt exhilarated. The sky looked unusually blue and the street unusually wide. He seemed to realize the significance of his cause for the first time.

At home, he was pleased to find some of his favorite disciples, including Zi Lu, Yan Lu, Qin Shang, Ran Geng, Min Shun and Qidiao Kai, absorbed in their studies in the courtyard.

At the sight of Confucius, Zi Lu stood up and asked, "Master, what did the chief minister want to talk with you about?"

"It was about official positions."

"Did the chief minister invite you to be an official?"

"No. He wanted to appoint some of you."

"The master is not yet an official, how can we be officials? Master, did you comply with his request?"

"No, I didn't."

The disciples sighed with relief and went back to their studies.

After a while, Min Shun asked, "Master, what kind of people are suitable to be officials?"

Confucius replied without hesitation, "Those who have distinguished themselves in their studies are suitable candidates for official positions."

"What should an official pay attention to?"

"An official serves both the King of Zhou, his lord, and the common people. He should be loyal to the king, respect his lord, show concern for the people, and solicitation for children and elderly people. He should have a concrete plan and a strong confidence, without which nothing will be achieved. Furthermore, he should seek opinion and advice from various people, ..."

The discussion was interrupted by the arrival of a messenger from the state of Qi. Adjusting his dress, Confucius hastened to meet him at the gate.

The messenger bowed deeply and said, "The Duke of Qi and Chief Minister Yan has come to Lu and are staying at the guest-house. They need to seek advice from the master and invite you to come."

Yan Ying, styled name Ping Zhong, became a senior minister after his father's death in the twenty-sixth year of the reign of Duke Ling of Qi (556 B.C.). He retained the position during Duke Zhuang of Qi's reign. When Duke Jing became sovereign in 547 B.C., Yan Ying was appointed chief minister. He played a major role in formulating the domestic and foreign policies of Qi and his achievements were great. He was therefore one of the people Confucius admired. Confucius had heard a lot of stories about him: how he bluntly advised against the sovereign's decision and corrected his mistakes, how he advocated frugality and set an example by not eating meat or wearing silk clothes, and how he had an astute mind, was an eloquent speaker, and did not submit to humiliation when he went to Chu as an envoy.

Confucius was overjoyed at the news of Yan Ying's visit, for he had long hoped to learn from this venerable man. So he followed the Qi messenger excitedly and arrived at the guest-house. After an exchange of greetings, Duke Jing of Qi said, "I have heard of your name for a long time. It is my great fortune to meet you today."

Confucius said, "I have a fame that I do not deserve."

Duke Jing asked bluntly, "Please tell me, why was Duke Mu of Qin able to gain supremacy over all the other states?"

Confucius gave a start and thought to himself, "So you also want to be the overlord of all the states?" He examined Duke Jing's appearance again. He was in his forties and had a slender figure, a lean face, a pair of eyes shining with arrogance, and three tufts of sparse but well-combed beard. Duke Jing's expression testified to Confucius' impression, and he shuddered inwardly with fear. After thinking for a moment, he said, "Duke Mu of Qin was able to dominate all the states mainly because he was good at employing the right people."

"Both Duke Jian and Duke Ding of Zheng employed Zi Chan, so they can be considered to be good at employing capable people. However, neither of them was able to win supremacy over the other states. Why was that so?"

"The state of Zheng has the powerful Jin to its north and the powerful Chu to its south. It was very weak and its people dispirited until Zi Chan helped the Duke of Zheng to govern the state. Now it has grown much stronger, its people live happy and peaceful lives, and all the other states regard it with a new sense of respect. What has been achieved is indeed remarkable. If the Duke of Zheng had not employed Zi Chan, the state of Zheng would undoubtedly have declined further."

Yan Ying, a short man in his fifties, listened quietly to the conversation. When Confucius finished speaking, he raised himself from the chair and said, "According to what I have heard and seen, you are indeed conversant with affairs both ancient and modern. If you have aspirations, courage and ideas, why don't you apply to the Duke of Lu for a position and thus employ your talents for the benefit of your nation?"

Confucius said, "I have learned nothing but what has been passed down from the ancients, which is different from what is needed for governing a state. What's more, in today's turbulent world upright people are placed at a disadvantage. I think I'd better be teaching."

Yan Ying said, "Are you really resigned to living like a hermit all your life?"

Confucius smiled and did not make any reply. Yan Ying looked puzzled.

Chapter Seven

Confucius Visits Lao Zi in the Royal Capital;
He Studies Music from Chang Hong
While Staying with Lao Zi

After a while, Confucius broke up the silence. "When time is ripe for me to join the government, I think I might have a try."

Duke Jing of Qi and Yan Ying asked Confucius a few more questions about ancient and modern affairs in the various states, to which he replied by quoting copiously from various sources. Duke Jing nodded his head repeatedly and expressed his admiration. Yan Ying, however, shuddered with apprehension. "If the Duke of Lu should appoint him to an important position, Lu would probably be the supreme power among the states," he said to himself.

As it was getting dark, Confucius took his leave. The other two stood up and saw him out.

Confucius continued to study diligently and teach untiringly. Time passed quickly. At the end of the year the students took their leave one after another and returned home to spend the New Year with their families. Confucius felt lonely and was lost in contemplation. In the third month that year Prince Ping of Chu had Senior Minister Wu She and Wu She's son Wu Shang executed. Wu She's other son, Wu Yuan, fled to the state of Wu. In the tenth month Hua Hai, Xiang Ning and Hua Ding in the state of Song plotted together against their sovereign. When their plot was uncovered, Hua Hai and Xiang Ning fled to the state of Chen, and Hua Ding fled to Wu. In the eleventh month Dong Guo, the grandson of the late Marquis Ling of Cai, killed Marquis Ping of Cai and set himself up as Marquis Dao. Thinking over all of these events, Confucius sighed, "What a year of turbulence!" Again he thought of Zi Chan, whose death he considered to be the greatest loss of the year. A man of strong character, Confucius could not help feeling grieved whenever he thought of Zi Chan. He hoped someone like Zi Chan would emerge again to restore the rites of Zhou and bring order to the chaotic world.

In the twenty-first year of Duke Zhao of Lu's reign (521 B.C.) Confucius was thirty years old. He continued to teach his disciples at

home. In the third month King Jing of Zhou ordered the Wushe Bell to be cast in bronze. In summer Hua Hai, Xiang Ning and Hua Ding returned to the state of Song, captured the city of Nanli and sought help from the state of Wu. Wu sent troops and inflicted a crushing defeat on Song. In the eleventh month three states, Jin, Qi and Wei, sent troops to rescue Song, routing Hua Hai, Xiang Ning and Hua Ding.

In the spring of the twenty-second year of Duke Zhao of Lu's reign (520 B.C.) the state of Qi sent troops to attack the state of Ju. Hua Hai, Xiang Ning and Hua Ding fled Nanli to the state of Chu. In the fourth month King Jing of Zhou died, and King Dao succeeded to the throne. Prince Ji Chao killed King Dao and proclaimed himself king. Duke Qin of Jin sent a punitive expedition and set up Prince Ji Gai as King Jing of Zhou.

In the sixth month of the twenty-third year of Duke Zhao of Lu (519 B.C.) Ji Chao sent troops to attack the royal capital. King Jing of Zhou fled to the city of Liu and took refuge at Diquan. Marquis Dao of Cai died and was succeeded by his younger brother, who became Marquis Zhao of Cai. In the seventh month Wu sent troops to attack Zhoulai. With the assistance of Chen and Cai, Chu attacked Wu. A great battle was fought at Jifu in which Chu suffered a grave defeat.

Whenever Confucius learned of such events, he was filled with worry. In their scrambling for power and profit, the vassal lords wrought great calamities on the lives of the common people. He saw the decline of government by rites and the rise of government by law. Early in the third month of the sixth year of Duke Zhao of Lu (536 B.C.) the state of Zheng had its penal codes cast on a bronze tripod. This made Confucius realize how difficult it would be to restore government by rites.

In the twenty-fourth year of the reign of Duke Zhao of Lu (518 B.C.) Mengsun Xizi fell ill. Lying in bed, he was filled with a deep remorse. He hated himself for his ignorance and incompetence. His unfamiliarity with diplomatic formalities had brought him shame when he accompanied Duke Zhao on a visit to Zheng. He often lost his arguments with Jisun Yiru and Shusun Chengzi because of his inability to quote the classics to illustrate his points. "I won't let my sons go on living like this!" He struggled to sit up and sent for his two sons, Mengsun Heji and Nangong Jingshu, and said to them, "It seems that I won't be long for this world. After my death, both of you should go and take Confucius as your master. I know Confucius pretty well. He is conversant with the six arts and and has a wide knowledge. He has been teaching disciples for several years. If you study with him modestly, you will surely become men of great ability."

Both sons promised to do exactly as their father would have them do.

After Mengsun Xizi's death, the two brothers went to visit Confucius according to their father's instruction. It was a warm spring day. Confucius was explaining *The Book of Rites* to his students when Mengsun Heji and Nangong Jingshu called. They fell on their knees in obeisance to Confucius.

Confucius hurriedly helped them up and said, "Why do the two of you salute me in this way?"

Mengsun Heji said, "We have come to study with you."

In the Spring and Autumn Period senior ministers were hereditary. At the death of Mengsun Xizi, Mengsun Heji, as the eldest son and therefore the legitimate successor, became a senior minister himself. Confucius despised people who put on airs but who had neither learning nor ability. Looking at the two aristocratic youths prostrating in front of him, Confucius was greatly pleased, feeling as if the world had changed and the state of Lu would have a bright future. So he accepted them as his disciples without the least hesitation.

As Mengsun Heji was then in mourning for his father, he asked Confucius, "Master, how can one be called filial?"

"When his father is alive, he observes his aspirations. When his father is dead, he observes his behavior. If he sticks to the ways of his father for a long time, he can be called filial."

"In that case, how can he strive to be filial?"

"One can be filial by not going against the rites."

"I will do as you have instructed," Mengsun said.

After receiving these two disciples, Confucius felt more confident of his cause. In order to teach well, he continued to study untiringly. One day he expressed his intention to visit Lao Zi and ask questions about the rites. Nangong Jingshu informed Duke Zhao of Lu of this, who gave his approval readily. He permitted Nangong Jingshu to accompany Confucius on the trip and, in addition, made them the present of a chariot with two horses and a driver.

Confucius was very happy with the duke's gift. Having properly arranged the affairs at home, he set out with Nangong Jingshu for the royal capital.

Nangong Jingshu was formerly named Mengsun Wen. As he lived at a place called Nangong, he adopted it as his surname. He was a tall and handsome youth with a round face, ruddy complexion and graceful manners. Intelligent yet modest, he was diligent in his studies and constantly asked Confucius a multitude of questions. Very much pleased with him, Confucius wanted to teach him everything he knew and answered all his questions fully.

The three of them had a pleasant journey, enjoying the scenery as they traveled. At twilight one day they arrived before a high mountain, where they saw several people using a net to catch birds. Confucius bade the driver stop the chariot and dismounted with Nangong to take a look. Confucius was puzzled to find that the only birds they had caught were young ones; there was not even one adult bird in the net. He saluted the catchers and asked, "Why have you caught only young birds, but no adult ones?"

The bird catchers were pleased with Confucius' politeness. An old man replied, "The adult birds are cautious and difficult to catch. The young birds are greedy after food and therefore easy to catch. That is why we have come to catch the fledglings. If the young sparrows follow the adult ones closely, then it would be difficult to catch them. If the adult sparrows were like the young ones, seeking after food in disregard of the danger to their lives, they, too, would be easy to catch."

Confucius was deeply impressed. He said to Nangong, "The cautious birds can stay away from calamities, while the greedy birds will lose their lives. They decide their own fate, be it fortune or misfortune. The same is true with people. One should not seek small gains yet forget the principle of righteousness. He who stays near vermillion gets stained red, and he who stays near ink gets stained black. Therefore a cultured man should select people of virtue as his masters and learn from them. If instead he stays away from superior men and keeps the company of petty men, seeks profit and neglects righteousness, he will bring misfortune upon himself just like the greedy young sparrows."

Nangong listened attentively and found the master's words very enlightening.

Confucius added with a sigh, "If a man does not plan for the future, he will surely find himself in trouble soon. You must keep this in mind!"

Nangong said, "I will."

They mounted the chariot and drove on. A few days later they approached Luo, the royal capital, so named because of its location to the north of the Luoshui River.

The Zhou Dynasty was established in 1122 B.C. with its capital at the city of Hao. In the early Eastern Zhou the capital was relocated in the city of Luo. Lying to the east of Hao, Luo was sometimes referred to as the eastern capital.

When the capital came into sight in the distance, Confucius and his two companions felt glad and cheerful, wishing they could reach the city in a single step. In the evening glow they could not see the city clearly, so they used their hands as eye-shade and looked ahead. The ancient capital, where the king of Zhou lived, was indeed magnificent. As if sensing their eagerness, the horses quickened their pace without being urged.

At the news of Confucius' arrival, Lao Zi came out of the city in a chariot to meet him. He ordered the servants to wipe the path clean for the occasion. Confucius was overjoyed when he learned Lao Zi had come to meet him. He dismounted from the chariot, adjusted his gown and with both hands offered Lao Zi a wild goose, a customary gift at the time. Lao Zi, whose family name was Li and given name Er, was also called Lao Dan. Born in the state of Chu, he was appointed by the king of Zhou to be an official historian in charge of the royal library. He was a very erudite person of noble character and high prestige. At that time he was already a grey-haired man over seventy years old. After an exchange of greetings, they mounted their chariots and entered the city together.

Upon entering the city Confucius was amazed by its magnificence. He had never seen prosperity on this scale before. The street was bustling with activity. There were people leading camels and walking in a leisurely pace. People hurried by carrying heavy loads. Teams of soldiers marched, carrying spears on their shoulders. There were colorfully decorated chariots drawn by big horses. There were people putting on monkey shows, practicing club-play, selling flowers, or displaying singing birds. Shops of various heights and sizes lined both sides of the street, with all kinds of goods for sale.

Lao Zi accompanied them to the inn where his guests were to put up. The next morning Confucius rode in his chariot to visit Lao Zi at his house.

Arriving in front of the house, Confucius descended from the chariot and knocked on the gate.

The gate-keeper announced their arrival to a delighted Lao Zi. Accompanied by Nangong, Confucius entered the room and took his seat. He said to Lao Zi, "I admire your great knowledge and understanding of the rites, music and morals, and have come with my disciple to learn from you. Please teach me!"

Lao Zi said, "Since you have traveled such a long distance to meet me, I will tell you everything I know. However, my knowledge extends only to morals and the rites; as for music, I have never studied it carefully. I will introduce the two of you to my old friend Chang Hong. Just like his grandfather and his father, he is the grand musician for the king and is highly accomplished in the art of music. He will be able to teach you."

Confucius said, "That would be excellent. Now I have a question for you. People say the rites today can not compare with those in ancient times. Would you please tell us about the ancient rites?"

Lao Zi said, "The decline of the rites was caused by the enfeeblement of the royal house of Zhou and the power struggle among the vassal lords. The ancient rites were formulated by the Duke of Zhou when he served in the court under King Wu and then King Cheng. At the height of its power and splendor, the Zhou Dynasty had a complete set of rites to which everyone, from the highest class to the lowest, conformed. After the founding of Eastern Zhou, however, the royal house gradually declined and the struggle for supremacy among the vassal lords became more and more aggravated, so much so that the ancient rites were all but extinct. Fortunately, some of them have survived in places such as the suburban shrines, the royal palace, and the ancestral temple of the royal house. It is said that in order to understand something you have to see it with your own eyes. I will take the two of you to some of these places to have a look." With this he rose and led Confucius and Nangong to visit Mingtang, the Hall of Brightness.

Mingtang was the place where the King of Zhou presided over important ceremonies. Neatly arranged and elegantly colored, it looked simple yet serene. Standing in the hall, they felt as if they were witnessing a scene hundreds, even thousands, of years old. Confucius looked around and found the wall painted with many figures. On the wall at the front were painted a succession of kings, including, from right to left, Fu Xi and Nü Wa, Zhu Rong, Shen Nong, Huang Di, Zhuan Xu, Di Ku, Tang Yao, Yu Shun and Xia Yu. Painted in colour, the figures were carrying compasses, carpenter's square, shovels or halberds. They had various expressions and looked very vivid and lifelike. All the kings took the form of human figures except Fu Xi and Nü Wa, who had human heads and torsos but dragon-like tails.

Nangong, pointing to the pictures of Fu Xi and Nü Wa, asked, "Master, why do Fu Xi and Nü Wa have dragon-tails?"

Confucius looked at Lao Zi, who gave a slight nod, beckoning him to reply to the question. So he said, "It is said that in the beginning there were no people in China. Later Fu Xi and Nü Wa were sent from heaven. As deities they appeared strange, with human heads and bodies and dragon tails. They got married and gave birth to humans; therefore we regard them as our ancestors and call ourselves descendants of the dragons. Fu Xi is also known by some other names, such as Mi Xi, Bao Xi, Pao Sheng, Fu Xi, Xi Huang and Huang Xi. He taught the people to make nets, fish, hunt and herd animals, and also invented the eight trigrams. According to another legend, Nü Wa made clay figurines which became the first humans. Later heaven collapsed, and great floods and fierce beasts brought calamity to the world. Nü Wa smelted some stones of five colors with which she mended heaven. Then she took the legs of a giant turtle and used them to support the four corners of heaven. Thus heaven stopped leaking and had no danger of further collapse. She also subdued the floods and killed the beasts, thus enabling people to live in peace and contentment."

Fascinated by the legend, Nangong listened with rapt attention.

On the south wall were pictures of two ugly figures. Confucius walked up and learned from the caption that the one to the east was King Jie of the Xia Dynasty and the one to the west was King Zhou of the Yin Dynasty. Each of them had a woman under him, looking ferocious and hideous. Nangong snorted with disgust and went on to look at other pictures.

On the east wall was painted a picture of the Duke of Zhou serving office under King Cheng. Big and tall and assuming a kindly appearance, the Duke of Zhou was saluting reverently to King Cheng. The young King Cheng sat in the royal seat and listened quietly to the Duke of Zhou's report. Confucius saw at last the person he had always admired, and felt a resurgence of his great affinity for this man even though it was no more than a picture. Curiously, the Duke of Zhou as depicted in the picture looked similar to the image he had seen in his dreams. He felt joyful and greatly satisfied, absorbed before the picture until Lao Zi urged him to move on when he looked down and saw some two to three hundred bronze wares of superb workmanship on display.

After looking at these, Confucius left the Mingtang and moved on to the royal ancestral temple, which had been established in honor of Hou Ji, the sire of the Zhou rulers. Hou Ji's mother was said to be Jiang Yuan, the daughter of Youtai Shi. One day she saw a giant footprint in the field and stepped on it playfully, thereby falling pregnant. She considered the baby a scourge and decided she had to dispose of it. She left it in a back alley, but the passing cattle and horses delicately stepped around it. She then left it to the mercy of the deep forest, but there being a lot of people there the child was recovered. Then she put it on a frozen pool, but the birds gathered around and protected it from the cold with their wings. Astonished, Jiang Yuan decided to take the baby back and bring it up. The boy had high ambitions even when he was small. He liked to cultivate hemp and beans, which grew well under his care. After he grew up, he devoted himself to growing crops and had bumper harvests year after year. Hearing of him, Emperor Yao appointed him a teacher of agriculture, and all the people learned to grow crops using methods he devised. Thus he brought benefit to the whole nation and achieved much of great merit. Emperor Shun appreciated him deeply and commented that people had often suffered from famines until they began to grow crops in accordance with the seasons and Qi's instruction. Qi, meaning "desertion," was adopted as the name of Hou Ji, because of his mother's initial intention to desert him. Later Emperor Shun gave him a manor at Tai, where he changed his name to Hou Ji.

Confucius knelt in a salute, before reluctantly leaving the hall. He turned and saw a bronze statue in front of the terrace on the right. The mouth of the statue was covered by three pieces of white silk. He walked up to the statue and read the small, finely written characters on its back.

It is an ancient rule that man should be cautious in his speech. Please stick to the rule. Do not talk too much for it often brings defeat. Do not take unessential action for it often causes trouble. Guard against indulgence in pleasure and do not do anything that may cause you remorse. Do not say it causes no harm, for it may bring protracted misfortune. Do not say it does not harm, for it may bring great catastrophe. Do not say it inflicts no injury, for the calamity may spread like prairie fire. Do not think your speech and actions go unknown, for both Heaven and evil spirits are watching you closely. A small fire, if not put out in time, will turn into a blaze. A small stream, if not stopped in time, will turn into a big river. Tiny silk threads, if left unbroken, will turn into a net. A young sapling, if not felled in time, will grow into a big tree that can not be cut down unless with an axe. Beware of the root of all troubles, and grasp the key to good fortune. An overbearing man will come to a sorry end, and a proud man will one day meet his rival. The robbers blame the robbed for being too wealthy, and the common people are all afraid of being rich. A superior man understands he can not transcend the world, so he places himself in a lowly position, thereby winning admiration. Others may strive to be strong, but I assume a humble attitude, so no one will contend with me. Others may marvel at my behavior, but I persevere. Others may become doubtful, but I remain firm and steadfast. I conceal my talents from the world and do not compete with others. Even though I achieve honor, no one can bring me any harm. The rivers are superior to the valleys because they assume a lowly position. Heaven is partial to no man, but men of benevolence will be blessed. Bear this in mind! Bear this in mind!

Having finished reading, Confucius remarked to Nangong, "I have learned from this article that a man should not speak or act rashly; otherwise he will meet defeat and trouble. *The Book of Poetry* rightly says: I move cautiously, as if facing a deep gulf or walking on thin ice. We must bear the words of the ancients in mind that all troubles come from a loose tongue. Therefore we must speak and conduct ourselves with the utmost care."

By that time the sun was setting. Lao Zi began to feel hungry and invited Confucius and his disciple to accompany him home for lunch.

After the meal Confucius said, "My knowledge of the various systems of rites is incomplete, and I have not yet grasped their essential meaning. Please explain this to me."

Lao Zi said, "The rites in their highest sense can determine the fate of a nation. King Yu of Xia, Cheng Tang of Yin, kings Wen, Wu, and Cheng of Zhou and the Duke of Zhou were able to win people's support and maintain peace in the country just because they adhered to the principles of proper behavior. In contrast, King Jie of Xia and King Zhou of Yin acted against the rites and brought turbulence to the country. The people, living in poverty, rose in revolt and put an end to their rule. Therefore all the sage kings in ancient times acted in accordance with heaven and acted in the interests of the country and the people."

"What is the original meaning of *jiaoshe*, the grand sacrifice?" asked Confucius.

"*Jiao* means sacrifice to heaven, which is offered in winter, and *she* means sacrifice to earth, which is offered in summer."

"What is the procedure for sacrifice to heaven offered by the king?" Confucius asked next.

"The first step is a pray offered in the ancestral temple to select the date for the ceremony. Divination is carried out by using tortoise shells and grass leaves. On the day of the divination the king stands in Ze Palace to receive the diviner's sacrificial oath to heaven. At the conclusion of the divination ritual, the oath is pasted to the outermost gate of the royal palace, informing all officials to prepare for the ceremony by fasting and bathing. On the day of the grand sacrifice, the road is cleared and posted with guards, and even people who have just lost one of their parents are not allowed to weep. The king, dressed in fur and riding in a plain-colored chariot preceded by twelve banners painted with designs of dragon, tiger, the sun and the moon, dismounts the chariot before the altar and changes into a garment decorated with a dragon design especially made for offering sacrifice to heaven, and a crown with twelve strings of jade. Then comes the offering of wine, the burning of incense and firewood, and the reading of the oath."

"I have heard Tan Zi say that if proper manners are observed in the family, the relationship between the junior and senior members will be kept in good order; if the women observe proper manners, the household will enjoy harmony; if the king observes proper manners, all the court officials will show their respect; if all the officials observe proper manners, victories on the battlefield will be achieved. But what will happen if proper manners are not observed on these occasions?"

"If on these occasions proper manners are disregarded, society would be like a blind man riding a blind horse, not knowing that he is on the verge of a cliff. The result would be a lack of order between the junior and senior members, disharmony in the household, lack of virtue on the part of the king, lack of respect on the part of the officials, and self-defeat of the army. This would lead to endless troubles."

Just then Chang Hong called. Lao Zi introduced him to Confucius and Nangong Jingshu, and explained that Confucius wanted to study music from him.

Chang Hong was in his forties, with a square face, big eyes, and graceful manners. He smiled modestly, "It is said that a guest does not visit two hosts at the same time. Why should an ignorant person like myself be forced to display his ignorance? How embarrassed I would be if I should fail to answer the questions."

Confucius stepped forward and bowed in obeisance. "Please do not refuse my request. The music of King Wu has deep meanings which I do not quite understand. There is a phrase that goes like this: 'Wu has been in wariness for a long time.' What does it mean?"

Chang Hong said, "King Wu of Zhou was worried that he might lose the respect of his subjects so he composed the song in order to admonish the people."

"What's the meaning of 'Stretch the limbs and stamp the ground early'?"

"That one should take action at the right time so as to obtain good results."

Confucius thought for a while, then asked, "What's the meaning of 'Slowly and repeatedly, stand waiting for a long time'?"

Chang Hong said, "The music of King Wu was meant to praise King Wu's exploits in attacking King Zhou of Yin and establishing the Zhou Dynasty. 'Slowly and repeatedly' describes the many difficulties that King Wu endured before subduing King Zhou; 'Stand waiting for a long time' describes King Wu waiting for the vassal lords to come and pay homage to him."

Having said this, Chang Hong took the qin from the table and played the music 'Great Wu' from beginning to end. The music had a wide range and rose and fell like waves. Sometimes it flowed unhurried like a small stream. Sometimes it floated like a dancing butterfly. Sometimes it rose like thousands of horsemen galloping on the battleground, then fell like the flood passing through high mountains. Absorbed in the music, Confucius saw in his mind's eye vivid scenes such as King Wu leading the troops, and the vassal lords paying homage to him.

The music culminated in a melodious tune. As if awakened from a dream, Confucius started and gasped with admiration.

Chang Hong said, "The music is divided into six parts: In part one, the troops set out amidst the beat of drums. In part two, the Yin Dynasty is destroyed by the expedition. In part three, the troops return on a southward expedition. In part four, the southern frontier is fortified. In part five, the kingdom is divided into fiefs. In part six, the great exploits of the king are praised."

Confucius felt that Chang Hong's words sprang from an accurate insight and thus enabled him to understand the essence of "Great Wu." As a master musician, Chang Hong was also very excited to have at last met someone who really understood music. They talked of the subject congenially, Confucius bringing the subject around by asking Chang Hong to compare the merits and demerits of the music of Wu and the music of Shao.

Chang Hong explained, "Shao music belongs to Shun, while Wu music belongs to King Wu. Shun governed the country by inheriting the virtue of Yao, and King Wu saved the people by deposing King Zhou of Yin. They are about the same in terms of merits. But speaking specifically of the music, Shao music, in my opinion, sounds harmonious and pleasing to the ear, beautiful in both sound and words, thus it is the acme of perfection. Wu music, on the other hand, is beautiful in sound but somewhat obscure in meaning. Thus, while it can be called good, it still falls a little short of perfection."

Confucius went on to inquire about the relation between sound and meaning. Chang Hong answered all his questions with patience, giving concise and thorough explanations. As it was getting dark, Chang Hong took his leave. Confucius and Nangong, too, bade goodnight to Lao Zi and returned to the inn.

The following day Confucius and Nangong rode in their chariot to enjoy the sights of the city of Luo. They also went to the Luoshui River, where poplar and willow trees grew along both banks. The sound of the fishermen's songs came from the boats sailing up and down the river. On their way back to the inn, they saw many wanderers and beggars. Confucius was sorely distressed and said to himself, "The royal house has become so powerless that these people do not have enough to eat and wear. How sad and lamentable!"

In the next few days Confucius continued to probe Lao Zi on a wide range of subjects who was so learned that he was able to give detailed replies to all these questions. As the time came for Confucius to leave, Lao Zi went to see him off and said to him, "According to what I have heard, the ancients usually gave two types of farewell gifts. Wealthy people offer money, while people of virtue and learning offer advice. I have no money and will offer you a few words of advice. First, in my opinion, most of what you are studying right now has been handed down from ancient times. You must not regard it as infallible. Second, it is true that people of a certain status should ride a chariot when going out, but if a chariot is not available they can still go out. There is no need to stick fast to the ancient rites in all cases. Third, people of virtue and learning are usually calm and inconspicuous. It is the same in doing business. A good merchant does not display his best wares."

With these words Lao Zi suggested the weak points in Confucius. Confucius considered the advice sound and of good reason, and said in gratitude, "I have benefited greatly from your instruction on this visit to the capital. I will always remember your exhortation and advice." Then he mounted the chariot and set off.

Upon his return to Lu, Confucius went to the court to report to Duke Zhao of Lu, who wanted to know all about Confucius' visit to the royal capital. Confucius gave a vivid and succinct description of the trip. Immensely pleased, Duke Zhao said, "After a long and arduous journey, you have come back with fruitful results. You have brought good fortune to me and the state of Lu!"

Confucius expressed his thanks and returned to meet his family and disciples.

Ran Geng asked, "Master, what kind of person is Lao Zi?"

Confucius said, "It is hard to describe him clearly. To my knowledge, the bird on the wing can dart into the clouds, yet it can be shot down by arrows. The fish, swimming in water, can plunge to the bottom of the river, yet it can be caught by the fishermen's net. A beast can run very fast, yet it can be caught by the hunter. Only the dragon is beyond the reach of men. It can swim in the four seas or ride on clouds and fogs, going freely wherever it wants. I can not say what kind of person Lao Zi really is, but perhaps he can be compared to the dragon."

In the next few days Confucius expounded the rites to his disciples and told them what he had learned from Lao Zi, making explanations in terms of situations in the state of Lu. He thought that the rites of Zhou were complex and difficult to master, but they are meticulous and deliberate and by strictly following them one could win people's support and govern the state well. In his mind he was drawing up his blueprint, waiting for a chance to persuade Duke Zhao of Lu to put the rites of Zhou into practice.

One morning Confucius was just about to start teaching when Zi Lu arrived. "You have come just in time," said Confucius. "I am talking about the rites of Zhou. Come and listen!"

Zi Lu said, "Master, nowadays the rites and the music have already fallen into disuse. Who will ever want to practice the rites of Zhou?"

Confucius felt that Zi Lu was being impudent, so he said sternly, "As a grown man, you must not draw a conclusion so rashly!"

Zi Lu said, "Master, please listen to me. Chief Minister Jisun is using eight rows of dancers in ceremonial offerings to his ancestors. You have told us that only the King of Zhou is entitled to the eight-row dance. A vassal lord can use the six-row dance, and Chief Minister Jisun can only use the four-row dance. Is he not openly defying the rites of Zhou by using the eight-row dance for himself?"

Confucius was so indignant his face turned pale, and his hair stood on end.

Zi Lu continued, "He is also constructing a ceremonial gate."

Confucius broke into a rage. "This is really outrageous! If this can be tolerated, what can not?"

At the unprecedented outburst of their master, the disciples were all stupefied.

Chapter Eight

Helped by Virtuous Ministers, Duke Zhao of Lu Escapes from the Jaws of Death; Receiving Timely Reinforcements, Jisun Yiru Turns Defeat into Victory

It was all too natural that Confucius should fly into such a rage. At that time the residence of a minister was usually built along a central axis with five or three gates. When all the gates were opened, a person standing in front of the main gate could see the back garden. On the other hand, the palace of the sovereign had nine gates. The courtyard was divided into the front and rear parts by a partition gate built separately behind the second gate. As the gate was kept shut unless an important ceremony was being held in the palace, it was also called the ceremonial gate. Both the eight-row dance and the ceremonial gate belonged to the privilege of the King of Zhou alone. Jisun Yiru, however, had appropriated both practices for himself. Thus Confucius hastened in great rage to the court to report the matter to Duke Zhao of Lu.

Duke Zhao had already learned something about Jisun's behavior. After hearing Confucius out, he too was filled with indignation. "Chief Minister Jisun has usurped sovereign power and behaved in the most unscrupulous manner. He has become a thorn in my side. I want to be rid of this scourge, yet he controls half of the state and has three thousand troops under his command. How can I cope with him? In your opinion, master, what shall we do about it?"

Confucius calmed down and felt he had to speak his mind. He looked around and finding no one else in sight, whispered, "Lack of forbearance in small matters will confound great plans. Considering the overall situation, you had better be patient and take no action until the opportunity arises."

Looking sad and worried, Duke Zhao sighed deeply. "As Chief Minister Jisun has appropriated the state authority to himself, and yet instead of attending to state affairs, he indulges himself in wine and pleasure. The ministers are at odds, and this year's disastrous drought

has resulted in a poor harvest, threatening people with hunger and cold. If the state keeps on deteriorating like this, people will become increasingly dispirited. What can we expect if things go on like this!"

Confucius said, "It takes more than a single day for a river to freeze over, and it takes a long time for an illness to become really serious. The present situation has to be dealt with by careful consideration and with a long-term plan." They talked on for a while, then Confucius took his leave.

By his great learning and good manners, Confucius won the appreciation of Duke Zhao, who often invited him to come to the palace for intimate discussions.

As Confucius became increasingly well-known, the number of his disciples also grew steadily. Greatly concerned with state affairs, he hoped that Duke Zhao, having recognized his learning and talent, would appoint him to an important position. However, Duke Zhao listened to his views but did not offer him any office. Confucius had no choice but to continue his studies. By way of self-consolation, he said to his disciples, "Is it not a pleasure to review from time to time what one has learnt before?" At that time people of virtue and learning placed great emphasis on learning from one another. Having learnt the art of qin from Shi Xiangzi, rituals from Lao Zi and music from Chang Hong, Confucius had a deeper understanding of the importance of such exchange. He said, "Is it not a delight to have friends come from afar!" Though feeling sad and worried that he was not understood by others, he said to the students, "Worry not about having no position, worry more about lack of learning. Don't worry about not being understood; if you have true learning and talent, you will surely be understood." He was convinced that one day he would be appointed to an important office by his sovereign.

In the autumn of the twenty-sixth year of Duke Zhao of Lu's reign (516 B.C.) a minister of Lu, Hou Zhaobo, selected three strong game fowls for a cockfight with Jisun. Cockfighting was one of their favorite hobbies. Jisun had won most of the contests, which puzzled Hou Zhaobo. He thought to himself, "He is a powerful minister, but why are his fowls also so powerful?" He racked his brains and suddenly a thought occured to him. He decided to investigate the matter personally to see if his suspicion was well founded.

The fight was to take place on the fifteenth of the ninth month. They chose to fight on one of the Lu army's drilling grounds. The well-to-do were all fond of watching such scenes of excitement and fun, so in the early morning that day the ground was crowded with people, among them was Minister Shusun. The people strained their necks, waiting anxiously for the fight to begin.

Hou was the first to arrive. He was tall but stooped a little. He glanced at the spectators and sat down in his seat, looking full of confidence. He was followed by a large retinue of stewards and guards carrying caged fowls and fully armed with swords and broadswords.

Soon after, Jisun also arrived. He was potbellied and walked with a swagger. He sat down in his seat, took a look at the spectators, and glanced sideways at Hou. He was also surrounded by a team of haughty-looking stewards and guards. Jisun said sarcastically, "You are early, Minister Hou. You must be sure of your success."

Hou replied, "Minister Jisun, you are very good at raising game fowls and have won every fight up to now. I fear I am not your equal."

The procedure of the contest had been agreed on. There would be three games fought between three fowls from each side. The loser of a game would pay the winner five taels of silver. Yang Hu explained the rules to the spectators, then announced the start of the fight.

A cage was opened on each side, and two fowls rushed out toward each other, flapping their wings to intimidate the other. They stopped at a distance of three feet, stuck up their tails, lowered their heads, and stared at each other, the feathers along their neck standing up. It happened that Jisun had three red fowls, while Hou's three fowls were all multicolored. The two fowls stood their ground and did not start fighting at once. The onlookers waited patiently. The red fowl, like its master, was eager to win and attacked first. It leapt toward the spotted fowl and attacked with both beak and claws. Unafraid, the spotted fowl ran forward a few steps and passed safely beneath the claws of the red fowl. Having missed a shot, the red fowl turned and scurried toward the spotted fowl, this time keeping itself close to the ground. The spotted fowl leapt and flew over the head of the red fowl. After a few turns like this, the red fowl, feeling discouraged, stopped attacking. Taking the chance, the spotted fowl leapt forward, bit the red fowl on its comb, and attacked its stomach with the claws. Crowing in pain, the red fowl became weak on its legs and hit the spotted fowl's head with the wings. Surprisingly, the spotted fowl also let out a cry of pain, released its bite and flopped to the ground. Struggling to its feet, shuddering with pain, it flapped its wings and wiped its eyes with its claws, obviously losing its sense of direction. The red fowl seized the opportunity, leapt over and attacked with both beak and claws. Hiding its head under the wings, the spotted fowl was completely defeated. The people were all puzzled by what had just happened. They found it difficult to understand why the red fowl could turn defeat into victory, and why the spotted fowl lost the fight when it had already gained the advantage.

Greatly pleased, Jisun threw a triumphant glance at Hou.

Feeling despondent, Hou ordered a steward to take five taels of silver to Jisun.

Taking the silver on his master's behalf, Yang Hu announced in a loud voice: "The second game!"

The two sides released another two fowls from the cages. Once out of the cage the two fowls started fighting. This time the spotted fowl attacked first, and the red fowl beat back vigorously. A fierce fight ensued between the two fowls, each trying to subdue the other. After about a dozen turns, the red fowl began to show signs of fatigue; it could only parry the other's blows without being able to hit back. After another five turns, the red fowl squatted on the ground and hid its head, enduring the scratch and snip of the spotted fowl.

Hou burst out laughing. "Chief Minister, you have to admit defeat this time!" He ordered a steward to get the silver from the other side.

Jisun remained calm and unperturbed. "Minister Hou, the fight is not yet over. How can you tell I have lost?"

As if encouraged by the remark, the red fowl suddenly flapped its wings violently, and a cloud of dust rose up. The spotted fowl cried painfully and wiped its eyes with the claws. The red fowl stood watching for a moment, then moved up sideways to the spotted fowl and revenged itself by scratching and snipping. The spotted fowl lost the fight again.

The spectators realized what had happened and started to comment among themselves. "Something is wrong about the red fowl's wings." "You are right. The spotted fowl could no longer see though it was not hurt in the eyes." "This is strange, very strange!"

Hou also realized what had happened. He calmly took out five taels of silver and handed it to a steward.

Taking the silver, Yang Hu asked, "We have already won two games out of three. Shall we proceed to the third game?"

Hou said, "Since we have agreed on three games, of course the third game will be played."

Yang Hu said, "It seems that Minister Hou would not give up until the last minute."

Hou did not want to argue with him. He took the cage handed to him by a steward, let out the third spotted fowl and combed its feathers with his hands. Then he handed the fowl to the steward, who carried it in his arms and put it onto the ground the moment Yang Hu released from the cage the third red fowl.

The red fowl very much resembled its owner in disposition: impatient and eager to win. It rushed forward fiercely and pecked at the comb of the spotted fowl. Cautiously the spotted fowl turned and intercepted the red fowl's head with its tail. Taking the spotted fowl's dodge as a sign of weakness, the red fowl leapt after it trying to reach for its comb. But the spotted fowl was very patient. Whenever the red fowl leapt up, it lowered its head and stuck up its tail to ward off the attack. Gaining no advantage after a dozen leaps, the red fowl felt discouraged and stood watching its opponent. The spotted fowl turned and suddenly dashed toward the red fowl. Fierce in attack but inadequate in defense, the red fowl met its opponent hastily and was bit on the comb. The spotted fowl raised its beak and scratched the red fowl's stomach with the claws. The red fowl was dripping with blood on its comb, and its stomach suffered several cuts. Unable to cope anymore, it turned to flee, leaping over the heads of the spectators with all its might. The spotted fowl also leapt over and pursued its opponent relentlessly.

The spectators thronged over to watch. Faced with a high stone wall that it could not leap over, the red fowl hid its head in a fissure in the wall and endured the pecking and clawing of the spotted fowl. The spotted fowl's claws were so powerful that with every scratch it plucked a few feathers off the red fowl. The onlookers gasped.

Yang Hu came running. Forgetting all about manners, Jingsun and Hou also came running. Hou said, panting, "Chief Minister, this time you have definitely lost."

Red-faced and out of breath, Jisun could find no word in retort. He looked at the defeated fowl in bewilderment.

The spotted fowl was relentless. It had almost plucked all the feathers from the red fowl, but it continued to scratch and peck.

Yang Hu ran over and caught the spotted fowl. Looking closely, he found two sharp copper hooks attached to the fowl's claws.

At sight of this Jisun demanded indignantly, "Minister Hou, so this is the kind of fowls you use for cockfights?"

Hou knew he was in the wrong, but he was not intimidated. He ordered a steward to bring the badly injured red fowl, whose remaining feathers still smelled of mustard. He also demanded in a loud voice, "Chief Minister, why is there mustard powder in your fowl's feathers?"

As far as Jisun could remember, no one had ever challenged him openly as Hou did just now. Enraged at the humiliation, he snatched the spotted fowl from Yang Hu's hand and hurled it onto the ground with all his might. The spotted fowl moved its wings a couple of times, then became motionless. Yang Hu drew his sword and cut the dead fowl in two.

Undaunted, Hou also killed the red fowl in his hand by forcefully hurling it onto the ground.

The guards on both sides drew their swords, ready for a fight. There was a tense pause.

At this Shusun came up and squeezed himself between Jisun and Hou. He gestured the guards to put away their weapons and said with a smile, "Take it easy! Why should the two of you dispute over such a trivial matter? Cockfighting is just a form of amusement and is not worth getting so upset about. Why don't the two of you return home, rest and calm down?"

Intending to gain the upper hand, Hou said indignantly, "I lost the first two rounds of the cockfight today, and I have offered the chief minister ten taels of silver. But I won the third round. Would the chief minister please give five taels of silver to me?"

Jisun glanced at Hou and simply snorted.

Hou countered with the same snort of contempt.

To be held in defiance by Hou was something Jisun had not expected, for he was used to having everyone, including Duke Zhao of Lu, submit to his authority. Such humiliation was too much for him to bear. He beat his chest madly and screamed, "Who do you think you are! How dare you speak to me like this?"

Yang Hu drew his sword and took a step toward Hou.

Hou looked around and was relieved to find his stewards and guards stand in readiness for combat. So he did not step back.

Shusun shook his hands. "Ministers, please check yourselves and order your guards to step back!"

Under the circumstances, to step back first would signify weakness and a loss of face. Therefore neither of the two opposing sides was willing to do so. It became a deadlock.

Shusun finally realized the crux of the matter. He shouted, "Stewards and guards, take away your weapons and step back!"

Neither Jisun nor Hou contradicted the order. So their stewards and guards put away their weapons.

Shusun said to Jisun, "Chief Minister, please return to your residence!"

With a sweep of his wide sleeves, Jisun went away, still fuming with rage. He stuck out his stomach and raised his eyes to the sky, trying to look proud and dignified.

Shusun then said to Hou, "Minister Hou, please return to your residence!"

Hou had mixed feelings about this. He did not know whether to thank Shusun or rebuke him.

Jisun was well-known for his ruthlessness. On his return, Hou was filled with anxiety. That night he summoned a few trusted stewards to make a plan in case of emergency. Under the oil-lamps the stewards appeared tired and nervous. Hou regretted having offended Jisun. It was no good hitting the rock with an egg, he told himself. But what had been done could not be undone. Looking anxiously at his stewards, he hoped they would come up with some good ideas. But they remained silent.

Hou realized that a catastrophe was imminent. He snapped at his distressed-looking stewards, "It is said that one maintains an army for a thousand days so that he can use it for an hour. Now that hour has come. On ordinary days you talk so eloquently, but most of what you talk about is useless. Now I need you to come up with some useful ideas, and you say nothing. Are you all wine skins and rice bags?" After this outburst, he again felt regret, fearing that his words might be heard by Jisun's men. He walked out to the courtyard and looked up into the sky. A bright, round moon was hanging in the sky, now and then concealed behind some white clouds. On a night like this he would usually sit down and watch the moon in the company of his family, but this very night he felt no inclination to do so. Instead, the moon and the stars peeping behind the clouds seemed to be mocking him. He cocked his ears and listened, but the night was quiet. He sensed that behind such silence, something ominous was brewing. He was caught in panic. At this moment dogs' barking rose in the distance.

Unable to stay calm, he went back to his room with the determination to cast the die. He ordered the stewards, "Assemble the guards immediately and follow me to attack his house!"

One steward advised him against this, saying, "Minister, it is not that we are afraid to fight to our death, but that Jisun is so much stronger. We have little hope of gaining victory in a head-on fight with him. We should practice restraint and bide our time."

Hou thought this reasonable and lowered his head to reconsider.

Another steward added, "To succeed against Jisun, we would have to join forces with a few other houses."

Hou said, "You are right. Leave and rest!"

That night passed without untoward incidents. The next morning a guard hurried in to report, "Minister, Yang Hu has led troops and captured some of our land."

Hou almost fainted. Stamping his feet, he said, "I am done for! He has beaten me at last." With this he slumped into his seat.

After a few moments Hou regained his composure and dressed in his official garment, went to see Duke Zhao of Lu.

Duke Zhao had long wanted to be rid of Jisun, whom he regarded as his worst enemy. After hearing Hou's report, he ordered Hou to lead troops to attack Jisun.

Hou returned home and laid out a plan with his few trusted followers. They decided to launch an attack after dusk.

It was a moonless night, the sky covered with dark clouds, when Hou and a large band of his troops set out for the chief minister's residence. Having thrown a tight cordon around the house, Hou gave the order to attack. All of a sudden the torches were lit and battle-cries pierced the sky.

Above the chief minister's residence, the sky was ablaze and deafening battle-cries could be heard. Jisun was awaked before the guards came to report the attack. It was not unusual that a domineering person like him should be ill-informed; his use of the eight-row dance in ancestral worship had been widely criticized both by court officials and the common people, but he had heard nothing of it. When he built the ceremonial gate in his residence, even a magnanimous person like Confucius denounced him to Duke Zhao. Listening to the battle-cries and looking at the light of burning torches, Jisun could not quite believe his own eyes and ears. When he came to his senses, Hou had broken into the first courtyard and was advancing to the rear courtyard. At his manor, the city of Fei, Jisun had three thousand crack troops trained by Yang Hu, but here in his residence there were only a few dozen armed guards. Outnumbered by the attackers, they were quickly disposed of.

Jisun ordered Yang Hu to seek help from the Mengsun and Shusun houses with all haste. No sooner had Yang Hu left through the back gate than Hou, sword in hand, entered Jisun's bed-chamber. Jisun only had half a dozen guards by his side. Hou said to him, "Chief Minister, if you are sober enough, tell your guards to withdraw, so that they would not die unnecessarily for you."

Jisun stuttered, "Minister Hou, What ... what do you want to do?"

Hou shouted, "Tell your guards to step back. Otherwise..."

Two guards at Jisun's side tried to fight back and were instantly cut down. Jisun realized that to fight back would only mean death for him. Thus he bowed deeply and said, "Minister Hou, both of us serve in the court under our sovereign. Please take pity on me and pardon me for the sake of our sovereign!"

"Chief Minister, it is by the order of our sovereign that I have come to subjugate your house!"

Greatly frightened, Jisun fell on his knees and beat his head on the ground repeatedly. "Minister Hou, please let me go!"

"You can't go now!" It was Duke Zhao's voice.

Jisun looked up and saw Duke Zhao arriving with another band of troops. He crawled toward Duke Zhao and pleaded, "Your Lordship, I am guilty and deserve to die ten thousand deaths! But you and I have the same ancestors. Please spare my life for the sake of our ancestors!"

Duke Zhao asked, "Do you still want to stay in Lu?"

"No, no, I will leave for another state." Jisun touched the ground with his head and four limbs like a huge frog.

In the meanwhile Yang Hu was trying to persuade Shusun to go to Jisun's rescue. "Minister, the three houses of Jisun, Shusun and Mengsun are like melons growing on the same vine. Hou Zhaobo is now besieging Chief Minister Jisun. If he should capture the residence and kill the chief minister, the houses of Shusun and Mengsun would be in danger. In my opinion, you'd better send guards immediately to rescue the chief minister. In this way Hou's rebellion will be subdued, the state of Lu will be preserved, and the common people will be protected from calamities. Otherwise you could come to the same end as Chief Minister Jisun. The common people would suffer, and the power of the state of Lu might even fall into the hands of Hou Zhaobo."

Shusun said hesitantly, "But Hou is acting by Duke Zhao's order. I've received report that our lord has also led a band of troops to attack Jisun."

Yang Hu said slyly, "Our sovereign is only temporarily deceived by Hou, who intends to sow discord among the three houses and take advantage of it."

Shusun was mulling over his words when Yang Hu added, "Hou is a narrow-minded man who is not easy to get along with. Just think about his dispute with Chief Minister Jisun over something so trivial as a cockfight. If he should come to power in Lu, would life be easy for you and the house of Mengsun?"

Shusun had witnessed the cockfight himself. Though Jisun was overbearing in manners, Hou was no less assertive. They were equally matched in their ruthlessness. He finally agreed to send troops to rescue Jisun.

In the same manner Yang Hu succeeded in bringing Mengsun round to his views. Then he returned to the chief minister's residence, leading the joint forces from the Shusun and Mengsun houses.

Jisun knew that he must play for time. So he remained on his knees kowtowing and pleading.

Growing impatient, Hou urged Duke Zhao, "Your Lordship, Jisun is guilty of flouting the law and numerous other crimes. Why should we delay his execution?" With this he raised his sword, ready to bring it down on Jisun's head as soon as Duke Zhao issued the order.

Frightened out of his wits, Jisun whined, "Your Lordship, please spare me!"

Hou looked at Duke Zhao. Time crawled slowly. The atmosphere was tense in the room.

After some deliberation, Duke Zhao finally said, "Kill!"

Hou was about to bring down his sword when there came from outside a burst of battle-cries. A guard by Jisun's side hurled his broadsword and cut off Hou's hand that held the sword. The sword clanged to the ground in front of Jisun Pingzi. Taking a glance at Hou's broken arm, Jisun suddenly felt strong again. He sprang to his feet and retreated toward a corner of the room.

Hou was screaming in pain. His face pale with terror, Duke Zhao fled through the rear gate accompanied by his guards, leaving Hou

Zhaobo behind.

The situation had changed dramatically. Yang Hu appeared before his master and struck Hou at his waist, chopping him in two. He saluted Jisun saying, "Forgive my delay."

Jisun said, "You have come just in time. A moment later and I would be a ghost under Hou's sword."

Yang Hu asked, "Where has that befuddled sovereign gone?"

Jisun said, "He has fled through the rear gate."

Without another word, Yang Hu led his men in pursuit.

Hearing the sound of pursuers behind him, Duke Zhao told his guards to throw away the torches and move on in the dark.

Yang Hu went on a hot pursuit. Duke Zhao's men fought their way ahead, leaving many corpses behind them. When Duke Zhao was only a short distance ahead, Yang Hu shouted, "Fatuous lord, stop fleeing and meet your death!"

The cries of the pursuing troops echoed in the capital of Lu and reverberated in the field.

Duke Zhao dashed forward along the bumpy road, not knowing what kind of fate awaited him.

Powerfully built and well versed in martial arts, Yang Hu killed the fleeing guards as easily as if he were cutting radish. Duke Zhao began to despair when he found the guards by his side dwindling fast. He tripped and fell into a ditch.

Yang Hu ran up to him and burst out laughing. "Fatuous lord, you could not escape even if you had wings. Meet your death now!" With this he threw his sword into the ditch.

Duke Zhao took up the sword with shaking hands.

Yang Hu said, "Cut your own throat, quick! Otherwise I'll order my men to cut you into pieces!" His voice was so blaring that Duke Zhao's ears buzzed.

At this moment a band of men suddenly arrived on the scene. Yang Hu took a long halberd from a soldier's hand and made ready to fight. He found the men were led by Zi Lu riding on a horse. Yang Hu asked, "Why do you come here?"

Zi Lu said, "To kill traitors like you and rescue our lord!"

A battle ensued, but neither side could gain the advantage. Zi Lu had come by Confucius' order to rescue Duke Zhou, so he did not intend to fight a prolonged battle. He helped Duke Zhao out of the ditch and put him onto a horse, then fought his way eastward.

Yang Hu led his men in a pursuit. Unable to catch up, he returned to report to Jisun at his residence.

Leaving Yang Hu and his men behind, Zi Lu accompanied Duke Zhao and headed toward the road leading to the state of Qi. At a crossroad they encountered another group of men. Terrified, Duke Zhao let out a cry, "Heaven wants the end of me! I am doomed!"

Chapter Nine

Gao Zhaozi Treats a Man of Inferior
Rank with Respect;
Yan Ying Is Jealous of Confucius
for His Talent

Zi Lu said, "Don't be afraid, Your Lordship. The band of troops in front of us is led by my master, who has come to see you off."

Duke Zhao was greatly relieved. Now he came to realize that Confucius was a man of rare abilities and regretted that he had not made him a high official. Torn by feelings of shame, regret, and indignation, he did not know what to say. He was lucky to have escaped alive. As an old saying goes, "As long as the green mountains are there, one need not worry about firewood." Thinking in this way, he rode his horse toward Confucius.

The dark clouds grew thinner, now and then penetrated by the moonlight. Confucius paid respects to Duke Zhao, saying, "Your Lordship has suffered great alarm. I have waited here for a long time. Please dismount and leave in the chariot."

Yan Lu helped Duke Zhao off the horse. With bitter remorse Duke Zhao said to Confucius, "I deeply regret not having appointed you to high office, and my mistake resulted in this catastrophe. Now my officials and I must leave our homeland."

Confucius said, "You may drive to the state of Qi and take refuge there until the trouble in Lu is over."

Duke Zhao said, "You have known both the Duke of Qi and Chief Minister Yan for a long time. Why not come to Qi with me?"

Confucius thought for a moment and said, "As there is no grudge between Jisun and myself, I don't think he will persecute me. The Duke of Qi and Chief Minister Yan have been your friends for many years. If you go to them in difficulty, they will surely give you the help you need. Please leave here at once in case something untoward happens again!"

Duke Zhao mounted the chariot, the driver raised the whip, and they set out for the state of Qi. Terribly upset and disconcerted, Duke

Zhao looked ahead listlessly, not knowing what the future had in store for him. The road from Lu to Qi passed through high mountains and over downs. The bumpy journey on the winding road seemed to signify to the duke that he would spend the rest of his life in hardships and misfortunes. When Duke Zhao arrived at the capital of Qi, Duke Jing of Qi arranged for him to stay at Qianhou.

After the chariot of Duke Zhao passed out of sight in the undulating downs, Confucius returned home with his disciples, his heart heavy.

After Duke Zhao of Lu's exile to Qi, Jisun grew even more powerful in the court while the households of Shusun and Mengsun became further weakened.

In the eleventh month of that year Duke Yuan of Song died. His son, Tou Man, succeeded to the dukedom. He was known as Duke Jing of Song.

During the next few months Confucius felt gloomy. Living in the state of Lu without a ruling lord, he felt the pain of the lack of opportunity for such person of high aspirations as he to reach his goal. When he heard that Duke Jing of Qi was broad-minded, showed respect to talented people, and had courteously allowed Duke Zhao of Lu to stay in Qi, he decided to go there with his disciples in search of a chance to give play to his talents.

After committing his family to the care of Kong Li and Nangong Jingshu, he set out in his chariot with several dozen disciples. They traveled north, braving the cold wind of early spring. Aware of their master's downcast mood, the disciples seldom spoke. On the afternoon of the second day they arrived at the foot of Mount Tai. Looking up, Confucius saw the highest peak of Mount Tai surrounded by white clouds. He was too heavy-hearted to enjoy the sight. Instead, he felt that he could be compared to the clouds drifting along aimlessly.

While they were walking, they heard someone crying in utter bitterness and grief. Confucius saw that it was a middle-aged woman standing in the field by the road. He said, "Zi Lu, that woman must have suffered a heavy blow to be weeping like this. Go and ask her why she comes here weeping all by herself in the field." Zi Lu went up to the woman, saluted and asked, "Excuse me, why are you weeping here by yourself?"

Wiping off her tears, the woman looked Zi Lu up and down, then replied, sobbing, "First my father-in-law and husband were eaten by tigers. Now my son was also eaten by a tiger. Three generations of my family have all died in this way. I have no one to complain to, so I come here to recount the injustice to heaven."

Zi Lu was a staunch, upright and kind-hearted person, and felt deep sympathy for the woman. Restraining his grief, he asked in puzzlement, "If this place is overrun by fierce tigers, why haven't you moved to another place?"

The woman said, "Because here I don't have to pay taxes and levies."

Zi Lu felt sad and distracted. Saying a few comforting words, he returned to tell the story to Confucius.

After hearing Zi Lu out, Confucius looked up to the sky and sighed deeply, "Tyranny is fiercer than tigers!"

Later this same day they arrived at Qingshi Pass. Confucius told Zi Lu to stop the chariot, and they got out to take a look. Qingshi Pass, built with stone slabs on the ridge of Mount Lu, served as the borderline between the states of Lu and Qi. Gazing at the characters "Qingshi Pass" written in broad, forceful style, Confucius called to his mind the wars, negotiations, and intermarriages between Qi and Lu. He said to himself, "The borderline between Qi and Lu is so clear-cut, yet there have been so many territorial conflicts between the two states. This shows how greedy man's heart can be." He turned to gaze at the land of Lu, where all things were coming alive in a light, warm breeze. Green buds appeared on willows, and grass was beginning to sprout from the ground. But the season of spring did not bring joy to his heart. In his mind's eye he again saw the overbearing face of Jisun Yiru. Mounting the chariot again, he left his homeland and headed for the land of another state. All sorts of emotions welled up in his heart. He wondered what kind of faces and eyes he would meet in the strange land as the chariot drove on along the steep, winding mountain path.

They came to a big river when they heard someone wailing. Confucius listened attentively, then said to his disciples, "It does not sound as if the man is lamenting the loss of a dear one." As the chariot approached the man, Confucius took a good look at him. His face was dirty, his hair dishevelled, and he was holding a sickle and a rope in his hands. He was wailing without shedding any tear of grief. Dismounting the chariot, Confucius walked up to him and asked, "Who are you?"

The man replied, "I am Qiu Wuzi."

Confucius asked again, "This is not a place of burial, so why do you come here to weep?"

Qiu Wuzi said, "In my life I committed three mistakes, which I was unaware of at the time. Now it is too late for me to repent. That's why I am weeping with remorse."

Confucius said, "Could you tell me honestly what your three mistakes are?"

Qiu Wuzi took stock of Confucius, then said slowly, "I was eager to learn as a child, so I traveled from place to place for the advancement of my learning. I returned home in old age to find that both my parents had passed away. For all the knowledge I have mastered and all the rules of propriety I have practiced, I failed to fulfill my filial duties. This is my first mistake. For a long time I served the lord of Qi and was devoted to my work. He indulged himself in pleasure and luxury, but I failed to stop him. This is my second mistake. I was fond of making friends and treated all of them with sincerity. However, they requited my kindness with enmity and broke away from me. This is my third mistake. It is not until now that I come to realize that things did not change the way I hoped, just as the tree can not keep still if the wind goes unabated. I wanted to fulfill my duties to my parents, but they passed away before I had a chance to do so. I wanted to advise the lord against his errors, but he would not listen to me. I wanted to make friends, but my friends abandoned me. Tell me, what's the point for a person like myself to go on living?" Having said this, the man threw himself into the waves.

Hurriedly, Confucius called his disciples to rescue the man. But the river was deep and flowed very fast. Qiu Wuzi was instantly swallowed up and carried away.

The suicide that took place right before their eyes made all of them feel sad. They looked at one another, not knowing what to say.

Confucius said, "There is some truth in what Qiu Wuzi said. The son should always keep his parents' age in mind, feeling both happy and anxious as they grow older. When his parents are alive, he should not go on a long journey, unless there is a definite direction in which he goes." He looked at his disciples one by one. "You have to think about this carefully. Those with no one to take care of at home may accompany me to Qi, the others should go back to Lu. It's hard to tell when the disorder in Lu will come to an end, and the pursuit of learning can not be completed in a single day. In a situation like this, one's duties to the parents take precedence."

At Confucius' words some disciples became hesitant about proceeding. Thirteen of them took leave of their master and returned home.

Qi was a big and powerful state in the east. During the rule of Duke Huan of Qi (685 to 643 B.C.) the capable and virtuous chief minister, Guan Zhong, carried out reforms which greatly strengthened it. Duke Huan had assisted the state of Yan to defeat invaders from the north, rescued the states of Xing and Wei, joined forces with other states of the Central Plain to attack Cai and Chu, signed a treaty with Chu at Zhaoling, pacified the internal strife in the royal house of Eastern Zhou, and hosted several meetings with other vassal lords. He became the first overlord in the Spring and Autumn Period. By the time Chu Jiu, Duke Jing of Qi, came to power, the state of Qi had been somewhat weakened, but it remained a formidable power. Duke Jing of Qi was now eager to flex his muscles and restore Qi to its former glory. Acting in the way becoming the sovereign of a big power, he provided a sanctuary for Duke Zhao of Lu, captured the city of Yun from the state of Lu and relocated him there.

Confucius and his disciples traveled by day and rested by night. One day they saw in the distance Linzi, the capital of Qi. The city wall was high and long, and the city gate looked strong and magnificent. Confucius thought to himself that, with its fertile land and vast population, it was no wonder that Qi had been a leader of the states. Thus thinking, he arrived before the city gate. A group of people were already waiting there, headed by a middle-aged man of tall stature and graceful manners. At the sight of Confucius' chariot he came up a few steps and bowed with hands clasped. "Is it Confucius that rides in this chariot?"

Confucius replied, "Yes. Who are you? How did you recognize me?"

The middle-aged man said, "My name is Gao Ting, and I come from the same clan as Minister Gao Zhaozi. On hearing of your visit, Minister Gao asked me to come and welcome you outside the city. I've been waiting here for some time."

Confucius had heard of Gao Zhaozi, a famous minister of Qi, though he had not met him before. He was pleased to learn that Gao Zhaozi had sent men to welcome him. Hurriedly he dismounted the chariot, adjusted his garment, and returned the salute. After an

exchange of greetings, they remounted their chariots and rode to Gao
Zhaozi's residence.

The capital of Qi was a prosperous city with wide streets, a large
population, and booming markets. Gao Zhaozi, informally dressed, was
standing in front of a high gate tower waiting for Confucius. A man
in his fifties, he had a wide forehead, deep-set eyes, and three tufts of
beard, looking elegant, alert, experienced, honest and frank.

The chariot stopped at the gate. Gao Zhaozi came up smiling.
"Master, your arrival has lit up my humble abode. It is my greatest
honor!"

Confucius dismounted and returned the salute, saying, "Lu is
suffering from a calamity and my disciples and I have come to Qi. I
hope you can afford us some help."

Gao said, "It is my duty to help you when you are in difficulty.
Please come in and let us talk!"

The two of them walked in through the gate hand in hand.
Confucius found himself in a large, quiet courtyard. There was an
exquisite rockery by a pool, with lilacs growing in the east and green
bamboos in the west.

They entered the upper room at the front and took seats as host
and guests. After inquiring Confucius on his trip, Gao ordered a feast
to be prepared to welcome Confucius and his disciples.

When the evening feast ended, Gao had some guest rooms
cleaned and invited Confucius to stay. Confucius declined politely, but
when Gao insisted with full sincerity, he said, "The guest should listen
to the host. I agree to your arrangements."

The two of them felt like old friends though they met for the first
time. That night they talked by candlelight until midnight. In their
conversation Gao became more and more aware of Confucius' outstanding talent and persuaded him to stay on to serve in the court of
Qi under Duke Jing. Gao said, "It is fitting that you served the Duke
of Lu in your homeland. But the duke has now fled Lu, and the
calamity of Lu has not come to an end. The court is under the control
of Chief Minister Jisun, who is engaged in a power struggle with the
houses of Shusun and Mengsun. Under the circumstances, how is it
possible for you to give rein to your talents and fulfill your aspirations
there? After careful consideration, I think Qi is the most suitable place
for you to succeed in your aims. Since the time of Duke Huan and
Chief Minister Guan Zhong, Qi has been the leader of the states,

protecting them against invading barbarians. It enjoys great prosperity, and its population is still growing. Our present ruler, Duke Jing, cherishes a great ambition. With a talented person like you to assist him, he would be like a winged tiger and become the leader of the vassal lords."

Confucius said, "Guan Zhong was a benevolent man. Without resorting to military means, he assisted Duke Huan to become the leader of the lords. This testified to his exceptional talent and wisdom. However, if Guan Zhong had not met Bao Shu, he would not have had the chance to put his ability to good use, the way a piece of jade will not be appreciated if it remains buried underground. Therefore one has to rely on a lot of factors in order to achieve great things. A fine horse that can cover a thousand li in a single day is indeed precious, but the man who can recognize such a horse is even more precious, for it is up to him that the horse will give full play to its strength. Otherwise, the horse would die in distress. So I regard Guan Zhong as a benevolent man, but Bao Shu deserves the name even more."

Gao listened attentively and thought Confucius' words carried an underlying message. He decided to find a chance to recommend Confucius to Duke Jing.

It was already past midnight by the sounding of the night watches. The two of them began to feel tired and retired for the night.

Confucius lay in bed, staring through the window into the courtyard. The moon, at the last quarter, hung in the sky like a sickle, looking cool and chilly.

The next day Confucius sent Min Shun to the city of Yun to call on Duke Zhao of Lu, and sent Zi Lu to inform Yan Ying of his coming visit. Yan Ying was a very short man, but he had outstanding ability. He once succeeded in getting rid of three chief generals by using two peaches. Gongsun Jie, Tian Kaijiang and Gu Yezi were three generals of exceptional courage, who had achieved great merits for Qi. However, they treated Yan Ying with arrogance and contempt, so he went to Duke Jing and accused them of lacking loyalty and devotion to the sovereign, treating their superiors with disrespect, and failing to protect the people against either internal oppression or invasion from outside. People like them, he said, would surely bring calamity to the nation someday. Duke Jing consented to his plan of eliminating the three generals. When they were called to the court, the duke had two peaches brought out while Yan Ying explained to them, "In recognition of your great contributions to Qi, His Lordship has given the three of you two fresh peaches. You may divide them among you according to your merits." As soon as he finished speaking Gongsun Jie said, "So the one who gets no peach must be lacking in courage and merits?" He stood up and took a peach. At this Tian Kaijiang stood up hurriedly and took the other one. Gu Yezi sighed, "Judging by my merits, I also deserve a peach. Unfortunately there are only two, so I will have none." He stood up and drew his sword. The atmosphere became tense. Gongsun Jie and Tian Kaijiang suddenly realized their mistake and said loudly, "We are not as brave as General Gu in battles, and our merits can not compare with his. It is greedy of us to take the peaches before him." They put down the peaches, drew their swords and cut their own throats. Faced with this tragic scene, Gu Yezi said, "Both General Gongsun and General Tian have died, yet I remain alive: this is against the principle of benevolence. For me to give people something to laugh at yet feel no sense of shame: This is against the principle of righteousness. To repent for my action but refuse to die: this is lack of courage. Now that the two of them have died because of the peaches, how can I stay alive to enjoy the peaches by myself?" He also drew his sword and killed himself.

Riding in his chariot along the street, Confucius called to his mind the many things Yan Ying had done. He admired Yan Ying for his ability but blamed him for being narrow-minded and intolerant of people superior to him in one way or another. He felt sorry for Gongsun Jie, Tian Kaijiang and Gu Yezi, who were so simple-minded and gullible that they died without knowing why. Thinking thus, Confucius shuddered inwardly. "Shall I return? No, I mustn't." He was acquainted with Yan Ying. According to custom, it was his duty to call on Yan Ying; otherwise it would be a breach of etiquette. Pulling himself together, he bade the charioteer to drive on. The image of Yan Ying again emerged before his eyes: his astute mind, changing expressions, and great eloquence. He remembered the story of Yan Ying's visit to Chu as an envoy. To humiliate Yan Ying and the state of Qi, the Prince of Chu had a small gate built beside the main gate. When asked to enter by the small gate, Yan Ying said, "When I visit a state of dogs, I will enter through the dog-gate. Today I am an envoy to Chu, so I can not go through this gate." At this the prince had no choice but to allow him to enter by the main gate. When Yan Ying came before him, the prince said with contempt, "Are there no other people than you in Qi who can be sent here as an envoy?" Yan Ying responded with a description of the vast population of Qi. The prince said depreciatingly, "In that case, why has a person like you been chosen as the envoy to Chu?" Yan Ying replied, "There is a rule in Qi stipulating that an envoy must be well matched to the ruler of the state he is being sent to. If the ruler is virtuous, a virtuous person will be chosen as the envoy; if the ruler is fatuous, a fatuous person will be chosen. That is why I, as the most fatuous person in Qi, has been sent here." The prince was struck dumb, not knowing what to say. Unwilling to admit defeat, he thought of another trick, and invited Yan Ying to a banquet in the palace. As they raised their wine cups to drink, the guards brought in a man with hands bound behind him. The prince asked, "Who is he?" One of the guards replied, "He is a native of Qi." The prince asked again, "What has he done?" The guard replied, "He is a thief." The prince turned to Yan Ying, "So the people of Qi are very good at stealing, aren't they?" Yan Ying replied, "I hear that the tangerine fruits that grow south of the Huai River taste nice, but those growing north of the river are inedible. Why is it so? Because of differences in the nature of land and climate. That man did not steal in Qi, but after coming to Chu he has become a thief. Might it be possible that the land and climate in Chu have the peculiar effect of turning people into thieves?"

The vivid scenes moved quickly before Confucius' eyes.

Zi Lu reined in the horses, and the chariot came to a stop. Confucius saw Yan Ying standing at the gate and got down from the chariot. After an exchange of greetings he followed Yan Ying into the drawing room. Yan Ying was well known for his frugality. The room only had a few pieces of old furniture with barely any decoration.

Looking at Confucius' disciples, Yan Ying said with a sigh, "It is only a few years since we last met, yet you have gathered so many talented disciples."

Confucius said, "I teach disciples only because it gives me the comfort to do so. I do not really deserve my fame."

Yan Ying said, "A few years from now and you will probably have all the talented people as your disciples. Maybe an old man like myself would have to address you as my master."

Confucius knew only too well that Yan Ying was a jealous person. He wondered whether Yan Ying was offering a compliment or being jealous. He said with a forced smile, "Chief Minister, your fame has spread far and wide. I am only afraid I would not deserve to be your disciple."

Yan Ying asked, "Are you planning a short sojourn or a long stay in Qi?"

Confucius said, "I have come here to call on the Duke of Lu and visit some old friends."

At their last meeting Yan Ying had found Confucius superior to him in ability. He feared that, if Confucius decided to stay in Qi, Duke Jing might appoint him to a high office. If that happened, his authority as chief minister would be threatened. On learning that Confucius did not plan to stay long, he felt greatly relieved and began to talk more easily with a smile playing around the corners of his mouth. "Qi and Lu are good neighbors, and there have been several marriages between our ruling houses. In the past we enjoyed a harmonious relationship and shared prosperity and glory. But Jisun has now usurped the power in Lu, and as a result the Duke of Lu has suffered some hardships. Fortunately Duke Jing has gladly received the Duke of Lu and captured the city of Yun for him, enabling him to live on Lu territory again."

Confucius had only come to pay a courtesy call. On hearing these words he said, "Someday the ruler and people of Lu will repay Duke Jing's kindness." After saying a few more words of gratitude, he took his leave.

He returned to Gao Zhaozi's house to find Gao Ting there, who said to him, "I can neither grow crops nor go fishing nor hunting. I only want to wear a straw-cape, offer sacrifice to heaven, and live a leisurely life away from the turbulence of the world. Master, could you please tell me what makes a superior man?"

Confucius said, "Being aware of what you say and do, and preserving your purity. Practice benevolence. Only a wise man can prevent his speech and conduct from bringing him distress and trouble. Therefore you should avoid trouble by being careful and avoid calamity by being respectful and frugal. You should respect and become close to virtuous and cultured people, even if they are a thousand li away. You should rebuke and shun evil and petty people, even they happen to be your next-door neighbors."

Just then Gao Zhaozi returned from the court and said to Confucius with excitement, "When Duke Jing heard of your visit to Qi at the morning audience, he was eager to meet you. Please come with me to the court at once!"

Highly pleased, Confucius followed Gao to the Qi palace which consisted of many imposing houses with a very big courtyard. The ground was laid with square stones and the wall built of stone slabs. The palace buildings were richly ornamented with carvings and colorful paintings. In front of the palace there was a tall wide terrace encircled with granite banisters. Confucius was surprised to find there was not a single tree in the palace grounds, and asked Minister Gao why this was so.

Gao replied in a low voice, "Trees in the courtyard could be used as hiding places. The lord prohibits the planting of trees in the court for the sake of his personal safety."

Confucius wondered why the Qi sovereign should go in constant fear of his safety.

After Confucius saluted him in the rear palace, Duke Jing offered him a seat. When Confucius had sat down, the duke asked, "What should human relationships be like?"

"Rulers, subjects, fathers and sons must fulfill their respective duties," Confucius replied.

Duke Jing smiled, "Right! If the ruler does not act like a ruler, the subject does not act like a subject, the father does not act like a father, and the son does not act like a son, even if there is plenty of grain, I would not have any to eat!"

After a moment of silence Duke Jing asked again, "I have ruled the state for many years. I have shown loving care for the common people and selected capable people to fill offices. I have won the support of my officials and my people and received praise from all sides. But I have failed to restore Qi to its former glory under Duke Huan. Why is it so?"

"In order to make the state strong and the people wealthy, a key point is to denounce extravagance and practice frugality."

Duke Jing was very glad to hear this. "Chief Minister Yan has mentioned this to me repeatedly. Now you also stress this point. Great minds indeed think alike! So I realize extravagance must be avoided if I want to make Qi strong and powerful."

They went on talking in this way about matters of governing the state. After that, Duke Jing often sent for Confucius to talk with him. He even offered to give the land of Nixi to Confucius as his manor.

However, Confucius declined. "The ancients said that one should not accept what he does not deserve. I have made no contribution to Qi and therefore do not deserve a manor."

"You have broad and profound knowledge. I often consult you about affairs of the state, and you have given me good advice. You deserve to be given a manor like Nixi."

When he saw Confucius was adamant in his refusal, Duke Jing did not compel him further.

Confucius and his disciples stayed on in Gao Zhaozi's house, reading books and practicing rituals. One day Min Shun returned from the city of Yun and reported to Confucius, "Our lord is good in health but does not look in high spirits." Confucius was relieved to hear that things were normal with the Duke of Lu. He then took his disciples out on an excursion in the capital city. The city was divided into two parts: the Greater City and the Lesser City. The Greater City was nine li long from south to north and seven li wide from east to west. It was the dwelling place of officials, the common people and merchants. The Lesser City was four li long from south to north and three li wide from east to west. It consisted of the palace complex of the Qi ruler. Compared with the capital of Lu, the Qi capital had about the same area, and there were also eleven gates in its city walls. The streets and lanes in the city were clean and tidy. There were ten big streets twenty to sixty feet in width. Four main streets crisscrossed in the city center. This was also the most prosperous area in the city, with throngs of people and chariots. Under the city wall were water outlets built with stone slabs. There were three layers, each consisting of five square openings. Inside the opening the stones were interlocked to allow water to flow out but prevent people from entering the city through it. Ditches and canals intercrossed in the city to discharge the water accumulation. All of these were well designed and carefully constructed. Confucius looked for a long time and sighed with admiration. It was twilight when they returned to Gao's house. Confucius felt the air was damp and stuffy. He also found drops of water on the surface of the water tank, and sparrows were jumping and chirping in agitation on the roof, unwilling to return to their nests. He realized that there was going to be a heavy rain, so he said to Gao, "Judging from the various signs, it is going to rain heavily. We should tell the officials and the people to dredge the ditches and make other preparations against flood."

Gao admired Confucius greatly and believed he must be right.

That evening, when he took up the matter with Duke Jing, Duke Jing summoned the court officials to the palace and told them to organize the people to prepare against the coming flood.

Yan Ying advised against it, saying, "Kong Qiu is just a pedant who swallows ancient learning without digesting it. He knows little about what actually takes place between heaven and earth. How can there be a heavy rain in the wheat harvest season?"

Duke Jing hesitated and did not know what to do. So he told the officials to return home.

Soon afterward thunders rumbled across the sky, then a heavy rain followed. Hurriedly Duke Jing summoned the court officials to an emergency meeting to discuss what measures should be taken.

Aware of his error, Yan Ying stood with his head bent and did not venture to say anything. The other officials looked at one another and failed to come up with any useful suggestion. Gao Zhaozi, standing in the rank of civil officials, was the only one who remained calm.

Chapter Ten

Listening to Shao Music, Confucius Forgets the Taste of Meat; Nangong Shi Comprehends His Master's Message by Reciting a Peom

Gao Zhaozi remained well at ease because he had sent mounted envoys to the various cities to notify the magistrates to organize the people in preparation against flood. Accordingly, he reported to the duke what measures he had taken beforehand.

Duke Jing of Qi felt greatly relieved. All smiles, he said, "It's indeed fortunate that you have taken the necessary precautions. Otherwise the people of Qi would suffer a calamity." Then he told the court officials, "Kong Qiu is really incredible! Usually we don't have heavy rains like this until the end of the sixth month, but it's only the beginning of the fifth month now! It's amazing that he could have made such an accurate prediction!"

The court officials, deeply impressed, murmured their admiration. The only one who remained sullen was Yan Ying, who grew more and more worried over Confucius' superior talents.

The heavy rain lasted a whole day and night. All the surrounding states suffered crop failures due to waterlogging caused by the volume of water, but Qi, having taken timely precautions, was able to minimize its losses. After this incident Duke Jing treated Confucius with increased respect and began to address him as master. He often invited Confucius to discuss affairs of the state.

One day, when the two of them were talking about music, Duke Jing summoned the court musician. This was a man in his fifties dressed in scholar's robes. He had bright eyes and a grey beard stretching to his chest, and his manners were composed and graceful. At the sight of him Confucius was delighted.

Duke Jing bade the musician play a piece of ancient Shao music in praise of the sage King Shun. The musician displayed his great expertise in the performance by achieving a total unity of the content and form. The music sometimes sounded like a breeze in spring brushing against

one's cheeks, sometimes like great waves surging on the shore. It was joyful like pearls falling into a jade saucer and as bright and clear as the unclouded moon.

Confucius was totally absorbed in the music. As soon as the musician finished playing, he sprang to his feet and exclaimed, "Excellent! It's no wonder that Chang Hong, the King of Zhou's musician, holds the Shao in the highest esteem. It's a perfect integration of sound and meaning. In comparing Wu and Shao, Chang Hong said that Wu, though pleasing to the ears, is obscure in its message. Now I realize how correct he is." With this he sat down at the qin and started learning to play the Shao, the best music he had ever heard. He went on practicing and asking questions for a long time without showing any sign of fatigue.

Watching Confucius in such a state of enchantment, Duke Jing said, "There is plenty of time ahead of us. Why are you so anxious?"

Confucius stopped playing, took leave of Duke Jing and the musician, and returned to Gao's house. He was delighted to have heard such beautiful music but regretted that he could not learn to play it well sooner. He began to practice day in and day out. Food no longer appealed to him, and he could not even tell the taste of meat when he ate it. He sighed, "I never thought music could be so powerful and intoxicating!"

One day in autumn Duke Jing invited Confucius to join him on a hunting excursion to the suburbs. They found themselves in a golden field with green mountains in the distance and white clouds in the sky. Drawing in a deep breath of the fresh air, Confucius felt relaxed and joyous. He feasted his eyes on the beautiful scenery around him.

When the horses and chariots arrived at a mountain foot, Duke Jing signaled with his bow to the subaltern in charge of the place. The subaltern, not knowing he was being called for, did not respond. Enraged by the disrespectful behavior of the subaltern, Duke Jing had him brought before him and demanded, "I have come here to hunt. When I signaled to you just now with my bow, why did you pay no attention?"

Calm and collected, the subaltern replied, "According to the hunting rules set by our late sovereign, a red banner with a bent pole is used to summon ministers, a bow is used to summon officers, and a leather hat is used to summon subalterns. When I saw the bow but no leather hat, I thought some officers were being called for, not myself. So I did not move. I beg Your Lordship to pardon me!"

Duke Jing glanced at his followers and said, "The late sovereign's rules must not be changed lightly." He turned to the subaltern, "You are not guilty!"

The subaltern, having expressed his gratitude, retreated.

Confucius watched the subaltern walk into the distance, then said with a sigh, "That subaltern abides strictly by the rules set by the late sovereign. He surely is familiar with the rites!"

Duke Jing nodded his agreement. Looking at the beasts and birds around them, he ordered, "Open the nets, and put arrows to your bows!"

After a frenzy of shooting and chasing, they returned with a good catch.

At the morning audience the next day Duke Jing spoke highly of Confucius' knowledge and virtue to his officials and expressed his intention to appoint him to an office. "I have always been fond of people of talents," he said, "and talents such as Kong Qiu's are very rare indeed. My honored officials, what position do you think I should give him?"

With a sweep of his wide sleeves, Yan Ying bowed and said, "Your Lordship, the so-called scholars like him are flashy and without substance. They have a high opinion of themselves and do not submit to anyone. They oppose frugality and advocate extravagance, spending a fortune on funerals and burials. What would happen if this should become common practice among our people? These people make a living by canvassing. How can we rely on them to govern the state? In the early years of Zhou, the rules of rites and music laid down by the Duke of Zhou were practicable, but today they have been almost forgotten. It is these rules that Confucius is now stressing the most, the rules about how to receive guests, how to walk properly, how to wear one's clothes and hat, and even how to adjust one's expression and styles of speech to the different class of people one is dealing with. Such rules are very complicated, hard to grasp, and they serve no practical purpose. If we should carry them out in Qi, our state would regress six hundred years to the early days of the dynasty!"

Another minister named Li Chu chimed in, "These so-called scholars are capable of nothing but empty talk. Their high-sounding words are totally useless. We must not fall into their trap!"

Duke Jing was a bit startled. "A trap?" He looked at Li Chu inquisitively.

Li Chu was short and fat, and he had a gourd-shaped face with small, rolling eyes. He said with an ingratiating smile, "If Kong Qiu were really talented, why didn't he make use of his talents in Lu? Why did he allow the Duke of Lu to flee his homeland and take refuge in Qi?"

While Yan Ying's words revealed a weak spot in Confucius' theory, Li Chu's remark also sounded somewhat reasonable. Thus Duke Jing said nothing further of giving Confucius an office.

After that, Duke Jing changed his attitude toward Confucius and began to keep him at a distance. At first he showed Confucius due respect out of courtesy, but then became more and more indifferent. One day Duke Jing said to Confucius, "I can not treat you as a higher minister the way the Duke of Lu treats Jisun, nor can I bring myself to treat you as a lower minister. Your place is therefore somewhere in between."

Hearing this, Confucius realized at once that Duke Jing was cold-shouldering him. He knew to his disappointment that his opportunity to achieve his political aspirations in Qi had gone. On his return to his friend's abode he told Gao Zhaozi that he intended to leave for Lu and it was only on Gao's insistence that he reluctantly agreed to stay on in Qi.

One day Duke Jing said bluntly to Confucius, "I can not appoint you to carry out the reforms."

Though this was not unexpected, Confucius could not help feeling sad and despondent. Back at Gao's house, he bade his disciples prepare for their departure.

At the end of the year Confucius, as usual, reviewed the situations in the various states. In the ninth month Prince Ping of Chu died and was succeeded by his son Zhen, who became known as Prince Zhao. In the eleventh month the state of Jin attacked and captured the city of Gong from the royal domain of Zhou. Princes Zhao and Zhaobo fled to Chu, carrying the documents and files of Zhou with them. King Jing of Zhou sent an expedition against Chengzhou. "When will the wars come to an end and the world regain its peace?" Confucius sighed.

In spring of the twenty-seventh year of the reign of Duke Zhao of Lu (515 B.C.) the state of Wu sent troops to attack Chu. Confucius sighed deeply on hearing the news. He had discovered that he could not carry out his plan of regulating the world by rules of proper conduct in the state of Qi, anymore than in his home. He decided to return to Lu. One day, after Gao Zhaozi had left home to attend the morning audience, Confucius and his disciples set out for Lu.

Confucius was in a confused state of mind, feeling as bewildered as when he first came to Qi. It was hard to find someone who really understood him.

One day they encountered a chariot in which sat a middle-aged man of an average height, who was dressed like a scholar. He looked very handsome and had graceful manners. Confucius said to Zi Lu, "I think the person sitting in the coming chariot must be a man of virtue and culture. Go and inquire as to his name."

Zi Lu approached the chariot and bowed with clasped hands. "Excuse me, could you tell us where you are from and what your name is?"

The man raised himself in his seat and replied, "I am Ji Zha from the state of Wu."

"Ji Zha?" Confucius repeated the name to himself and almost exclaimed with excitement. Ji Zha was not only very learned but also a superior man of widespread renown. He was the fourth son of Shou Meng, the late Prince of Wu. When Shou Meng wanted to pass the throne to him, Ji Zha declined obstinately, so that Shou Meng's eldest son was chosen as the successor. Later the eldest son offered the throne to Ji Zha, who declined a second time, so that the second son was chosen instead. Later the throne was passed on to the third son. When the third son died, Ji Zha managed to excuse himself again, unwilling to take the throne for himself. Thus the third son's son, Liao, became the new ruler of Wu.

Confucius had heard many stories about Ji Zha. On his way to visit the northern states as a state envoy, Ji Zha passed Xu and called on its ruler. The ruler of Xu took a fancy to Ji Zha's sword but could not bring himself to ask for it as a gift. Ji Zha wanted to give the sword to him, but as an envoy he must wear his sword in accordance with the rites. Having completed his missions in the northern states, Ji Zha again passed Xu on his return journey with the intention to offer his sword to its ruler. He regretted to learn, however, that the ruler of Xu had died of illness. Ji Zha went to visit the latter's grave and, after offering a sacrifice, hung his sword on a tree beside the grave. Someone asked him, "Now that the ruler is dead, what's the point of hanging your sword on a tree?" To this Ji Zha replied, "I have promised to myself to give my sword to him as a present, and I must keep my promise even though he is dead." Later, the people of Xu composed a song in Ji Zha's praise:

Ji Zha from Yanling
Is a man of his word!
He hung a sword worth a thousand pieces of gold
By the side of his deceased friend's grave.

The stories about Ji Zha flashed in Confucius' mind. Having always wanted to meet Ji Zha, the unexpected encounter came as a gift from heaven. Dismounting the chariot, he walked forward in quick steps and bowed deeply. "Kong Qiu from Lu has admired your fame for so long and is greatly honored by this unexpected meeting!"

Ji Zha got down in a hurry and returned the salute. "The honor is entirely mine, master. I only regret that we did not meet earlier." Pointing to a handsome youth standing behind him, he continued, "This is my eldest son, Yi, who has accompanied me on this journey to look for a teacher. How lucky I am to meet you here! I would like him to study with you. Please accept him as your student."

A smart and quick-witted youth, Ji Yi knelt down before Confucius said anything. "Disciple Ji Yi pays respects to his teacher!"

Confucius said to Ji Zha with a smile, "My only fear is that I am not as good as my name, and may lead your son astray."

"You are being too modest. Some of your disciples have already attained great fame, not to say yourself," replied Ji Zha.

Confucius helped Ji Yi on his feet. Ji Zha took Confucius by the hand and together they sat down by the road to have a hearty talk.

To have learned the Shao was the best thing that happened to Confucius during his stay in Qi. He asked, "The Shao was written before the Wu, yet the former is easy to understand and the latter obscure. Why is it so?"

Ji Zha replied, "Maybe it's because of the difference in situation faced by Shun and King Wu of Zhou. For Shun, life was smooth and easy. Yao married his two daughters to him and later passed on the throne to him. No one ever criticized him. Therefore he had plenty of leisure to invent the five-string qin and compose "The Song of the South Wind," in which he wrote, "Gentle south wind, you have enhanced the wealth of my subjects." What a joyous mood he was in! As for King Wu of Zhou, life was an arduous journey. He led troops personally to attack King Zhou and ward off the tribesmen, suffering numerous hardships. Because of this the Wu contains some messages that are difficult to decipher."

Confucius went on to ask questions concerning rites and customs in the state of Wu, to which Ji Zha replied fully. Then they parted.

Ji Zha continued on his way to Qi with his son, having agreed with Confucius to leave Ji Yi with him on their visit to Lu.

Confucius and his disciples continued their journey. Three days later they were about forty li to the capital of Lu, when a mounted soldier of Wu approached. The soldier dismounted and said, "Master,

Minister Ji ordered me to inform you of his eldest son's death of a sudden illness at Yingbo."

Deeply grieved, Confucius bade the disciples return to Lu and arranged for Zi Lu, Min Shun and a few others to accompany him to Yingbo for Ji Yi's funeral.

The funeral ceremony was very simple. Baring his left arm, Ji Zha felt the earth covering the grave with his hands and said in a hoarse voice, "My son was always very strong, but then he died a sudden death and had to be buried in a strange land. Is this destined to happen to him?" After the funeral Ji Zha offered his thanks to Confucius and his followers, then took his leave.

Confucius traveled on toward the capital of Lu. Back home, he learned to his great distress that his elder brother, Mengpi, had died in his father-in-law's house in Wei. He was about to blame Lady Qiguan for failing to inform him, when Nangong Jingshu explained, "When your elder brother died, a messenger was sent to Qi, only to learn that you had left for Lu. Then he headed for Lu in haste, but found you had gone back to Qi. The messenger did not meet you on the way as he had taken a different path. That's why you did not get the news in time."

Confucius was deeply grieved to have lost his only brother. He bade his son Kong Li fetch his cousins, Kong Zhong and Kong Wujia, who could assuage their grief by a change in surroundings.

Having sent Kong Li off, Confucius began to teach lessons to his students. He talked about *The Book of Poetry*, saying, "The book contains three hundred poems, which can be divided into three parts, the Feng, the Ya, and the Song. The Feng refers to the ballads in Zhounan, Zhaonan, Bei, Yong, Wei, Wang, Zheng, Qi, Wei, Tang, Qin, Chen, Gui, Cao and Bin."

Qidiao Kai asked, "Why are the ballads called the Feng?"

Confucius nodded, "That's a good question! I'll explain to you clearly. There are two main reasons that the ancients referred to ballads as the Feng. First, the poems in this part reveal in both form and content the customs of the various places, and the word *feng* can mean 'local customs.' Second, the word *feng* can also refer to the wind, which has great variety in size, volume, strength, and tone quality. The same is true of the poems in this part, which therefore resemble the wind in nature. That's why they are called the Feng."

The students listened attentively and suddenly the scales fell from their eyes.

Confucius continued, "I've made a rough count and discovered that the Feng take up more than half the volume of the book. Most of the poems are good, except a few ballads from Zheng and Wei, which are licentious. I'll take them out when I edit the book."

Zi Lu asked, "What about the other two parts, the Ya and the Song?"

Confucius said, "You are really impatient! I am just coming to it." He said after a pause, "The Ya consists of two sections, the Greater Ya and the Lesser Ya. There are more than a hundred hymns, mostly written by literati of the royal capital of Zhou. The Song has three sections, the Song of Zhou, the Song of Lu and the Song of Shang. There are about forty poems in praise of the exploits of the deceased rulers, such as Kings of Zhou, Dukes of Lu, and Dukes of Song."

After explaining the arrangement of *The Book of Poetry*, Confucius began to talk about the poem "Yi" in the Greater Ya. When they came to the lines, "A stain in a white jade tablet can be removed, but it's impossible to remove a stain contained in speech," Confucius said, "What a wise remark! Of course a flawless jade is lovely, but even if there is a flaw, it can be removed by grinding. It is different with one's speech and conduct. Once a mistake is committed, it can not be removed. That's why the Duke of Zhou exhorted people to beware of their speech, for too much speech brings defeat; and to beware of their conduct, for unnecessary conduct causes trouble. You must all bear this in mind: Be cautious in both your speech and conduct!"

The students said in unison, "We will bear this firmly in mind!"

After that the students began to take a strong interest in *The Book of Poetry* and studied it quite often. Nangong Shi was so fond of the book that he was never without it.

Nangong Shi, with Zi Rong as his styled name, was also called Nan Rong. As a favorite disciple of Confucius, he displayed a thorough understanding of his master's teaching. On one occasion he asked Confucius, "Yi was very good at archery, and Ao at fighting in the river. But neither of them came to a good end. On the other hand, Yu and Ji tilled the field with the common people and did not excel in military exploits. Yet both of them had the world under their control. Why is it so?" Confucius did not reply. When Nangong Shi had left, Confucius said, "He is a real superior man! How he admires virtue!" As Confucius seldom described any of his disciples as a superior man, his remark testified to the rare rapport between the master and the disciple.

One day Confucius was talking about the Wu and the Shao music when Kong Li entered, followed by Kong Zhong and Kong Wujia. Zhong, with Zi Mie as his styled name, had grown into a handsome lad. Wujia was a pretty girl with a sweet temper. They bowed to Confucius in salute and went in to meet Lady Qiguan. Confucius let Kong Zhong stay in the house and study with him. Wujia was made to live with Confucius' daughter and studied womanly virtues and skills with Lady Qiguan.

One early morning Confucius found Nangong Shi reading the poem "Yi," lingering over the lines, "Speak with caution, conduct yourself with reverence, and maintain graceful manners. A stain in a white jade tablet can be removed, but it's impossible to remove a stain contained in speech." Greatly pleased, Confucius went to Lady Qiguan and said, "Nangong Shi is cautious in his speech and conduct and strives to preserve his purity. If the ruler is wise and the state prosperous, he would serve in an office and not waste his talents. If the ruler is fatuous and the state in turbulence, he would not mingle with the evil-doers and get himself into trouble. I want to marry my niece to him. What do you think?"

Lady Qiguan said, "Nangong is your disciple, someone you know extremely well. It's most suitable to marry Wujia to him."

Confucius continued, "Gongye Chang is wise and well-cultivated. He can endure great hardships and humiliation. I want to give Wuwei to him. What do you think of that?"

After a pause Lady Qiguan said, "Since you think them well-matched, you can take the decision."

Having discussed the matter with his wife, Confucius went to talk with Nangong and Gongye, who readily accepted the proposal.

Confucius felt very glad to have successfully arranged the marriages of his daughter and niece. He went out into the courtyard to enjoy the spring breeze under the starlit sky.

Just then Yan Lu arrived to report, "Master, I have just heard in the street that Prince Guang of Wu has sent Zhuan Zhu to assassinate Liao, King of Wu, then set himself up as the new king."

Confucius sighed deeply. "Minister Ji is such a modest man, whereas the royal descendants of Wu are so greedy and unscrupulous that they fight fiercely among themselves. There is no crime they would not stoop to! Minister Ji is right now on a mission to Qi. He might be still kept in the dark."

Yan Lu said, "He will hear of it soon."

Confucius fell into deep thought.

After Liao succeeded to the throne, Guang, the son of the eldest son of the late king of Wu (Shou Meng), bore an intense hatred against him. At his order Zhuan Zhu, the assassin, pretended to be a cook and got his way into the kitchen in the royal palace. At a banquet Zhuan Zhu hid a dagger in a cooked fish and, while serving the dish, brought out the dagger and stabbed Liao to death. Thus Guang became the new king. He was generally known by the name of He Lu.

About five days later Ji Zha suddenly arrived in Lu. He went to see Confucius and said to him, "I have come here specially to visit you. My nephew Liao has been murdered by another of my nephews, Guang, who has taken the throne for himself. I am going to Wu to offer my condolences to the deceased king. After that I have nothing to do except living like a hermit in my manor, Yanling."

Confucius said, "Isn't it a terrible waste for a talented person like you to live like a hermit and not work for your state?"

Looking up into the sky, Ji Zha sighed sadly. "Guang has obtained the throne by unrighteous means. Who knows how many people will come to harm because of him? If I return to serve an office under him, I would be helping a tyrant to do evil." With this he took leave of Confucius and mounted his chariot.

Confucius said in a choking voice, "Take care, Minister Ji!"

Ji Zha returned the salute. "Take care, master!"

After offering his condolences to Liao, Ji Zha retired to his manor, Yanling, where he lived like a hermit, unmoved by Guang's repeated invitations to serve in the court, until his death.

When Confucius returned to his homeland in Lu Jisun Yiru was still in control of the court, bringing turbulences to the state and causing great sufferings to the people. Bracing himself, he called on Jisun in an attempt to persuade him to fetch Duke Zhao back from the city of Yun. But Jisun flatly refused, to the great disappointment of Confucius.

One day he and his disciples walked sixty li to the south, arriving at Zhu, Lu's vassal state. The capital of Zhu was small but well located. It was like a small basin, with its city walls built in connection with the surrounding mountains. To its north was Mount Yi. Admiring the view, they entered the city.

Hearing that Confucius was coming, Duke Zhuang of Zhu sent men to welcome him.

Confucius explained, "My students and I have come only to climb Mount Yi and dare not disturb your sovereign."

The envoys returned to report to Duke Zhuang, who sent a guide to accompany Confucius and his students to Mount Yi.

Arriving before the mountain, Confucius dismounted the chariot and looked up. He saw that the entire Mount Yi consisted of huge rocks just like an artificial rockery.

Treaded by numerous climbers, three paths had formed leading to the top. The eastern path wound along the mountain foot and reached the top of the eastern peak before it turned and headed for the main peak. It twisted among ancient trees and huge rocks. The western path led upward along the ridge of the mountain, with stone steps chiseled out of granite. It was very steep, looking like a ladder hanging from the sky. The middle path passed through a depression and went up directly to the main peak. It consisted of stone steps half hidden among the forest.

Studying the paths carefully, Confucius decided to take the eastern path. They enjoyed the views while climbing. There were rocks of diverse shapes resembling tortoise, crane, tiger or leopard. There were also fountains, sounding like the jingle of bells, the beating of drums, or the clattering of horses' hoofs.

Halfway up the mountain Confucius pointed to a room-sized cave and said jokingly, "This stone cave could be made into a classroom." Later, people spoke of the cave as "the place where Confucius taught his disciples."

The guide said, "There are innumerable caves in the mountain; the biggest of them can hold several hundred people."

Encouraged by this remark, Confucius continued climbing with nimble steps.

Stopping in front of a heap of black stones, Confucius asked in puzzlement, "Where do these black stones come from?"

"No one has yet come up with a plausible explanation," the guide replied.

Examining the stones, Confucius saw that each of them was separate from the others. He muttered to himself, "Where could all these stones have come from?"

The guide remarked, as if answering Confucius' question, "It is said that after the goddess Nü Wa had finished mending heaven with stones of five colors, a few stones were left. They rolled in the wind and brought havoc to the people on earth. The Queen Mother of the Western Heaven then sent a celestial force to collect the stones and put them together to form Mount Yi."

Confucius listened enrapt to the beautiful legend, his lips curved in a shadow of a smile from time to time.

Pointing to a stone shaped like a wooden pole, the guide said, "Look, master, this is the Queen Mother's jade hairpin."

Confucius laughed heartily.

Wild flowers were blooming in a profusion of colors. Reaching the top of the eastern peak, they looked down the slope to the back and saw luxuriant pines, from which emanated a peculiar fragrance. Looking north, they saw the Lu capital amid the curls of cooking smoke. Taking several breaths of the fresh air, Confucius said, "It is well said by the ancients that one can broaden one's views by climbing high. From the eastern peak, even the entire state of Lu appears small!"

An eagle soared in the sky, now flapping its wings forcefully, now gliding slowly with its wings spread wide. Suddenly it dived steeply climbing again with a hare in its grasp. At the sight of this Confucius commented, "In nature the strong are always devouring the weak!" He thought of the connection between nature and society, animals and people. He firmly believed that the nature of man can be improved by means of education. Again he vowed to himself that he would train his disciples into men of virtue and courage and persuade people to behave according to the rites.

Gazing at the peaks of Mount Yi, he was lost in thought. The sight of the high mountains broadened his mind and made him think more freely. Then he hit upon an idea.

Chapter Eleven

Confucius and His Disciples Climb
Mount Tai to Broaden Their Vision;
Tracing the Source of the Sishui River
They Compare the Past with the Present

Confucius discovered that mountain climbing could broaden one's view, build up one's confidence, and enrich one's imagination. Therefore he decided to lead his disciples to climb Mount Tai. After his return to Lu from Mount Yi, he made his preparations and set out.

Mount Tai in spring was full of life, with its luxuriant grass and trees, birds and animals. Encircled in the rising mist, it looked like a noble lady wearing a thin veil standing behind a door curtain made of pearls. At the foot of the mountain Confucius and his disciples dismounted the chariot and began to climb up. They found to their delight that there were too many things for the eyes to take in: rocks of exquisite shapes, strange-looking trees, fragrant grass and colorful butterflies.

Halfway up the mountain their brows were beaded with sweat. Stopping to regain his breath, Confucius listened to the soughing of the wind in the pines and looked at the waterfalls. What a scene of beauty and harmony, he thought to himself. If only the rules of propriety formulated by the King of Zhou could touch everything like a spring breeze, causing the flowers to bloom and the trees to grow; if only his ideas could rush down unobstructed like the waterfall, nourishing the land and everything on it! He knew that these were merely fantasies, and that reality was entirely different. One could not hope to achieve anything in society unless one was prepared to endure hardships. This was just like climbing the mountain; it took a little effort to make each step upward.

Zi Lu and Yan Lu walked on either side of Confucius and sometimes supported him with their hands.

Confucius said, "You don't have to do that. Everyone should climb the mountain relying on his own strength."

They looked up and found the peak was not very far away.

However, the path became more and more steep and, as few people had ever reached the top, the narrow, winding path had become blocked by thistles and thorns. This made the climbing more difficult. Zi Lu went up to the front and cleaved through the thistles, clearing a way for those who followed behind.

On top of the mountain, Confucius gazed at the floating clouds below and felt as if he had approached heaven, as if he could touch the blue sky with his hand. He span around lightly for a few times on a stone slab, feeling light-hearted and pleased. Suddenly he sighed, "When I reached the top of Mount Yi I found the state of Lu small. Now that I have reached the top of Mount Tai, I find the entire world small. The higher one stands, the broader one's view grows."

Standing on the mountain-top, Confucius and his disciples feasted their eyes on the sights all around them. When the sun began to descend in the west, they retraced their path down the mountain and then set off home in their chariot.

On their way back they met a grey-haired old man. Dressed in a light fur coat with a black belt, he was playing a *qin* and singing joyfully in a loud voice, as if he had not a single care in the world.

Perplexed, Confucius got off the chariot and asked, "Where are you from? And why are you singing so joyfully?"

The man replied, "I am Rong Qiqi. Of the many things in life that please me, three are my favorites: The heaven has given birth to ten thousand things, of which human beings are the most precious. I happen to be a human being. This is the first of my three favorite things. For human beings, a difference is made between men and women: Men are superior to women. I happen to be a man. This is the second of my three favorite things. People cannot decide how long they are going to live. There are those who died without seeing the sun and moon, and those who died in their swaddling clothes. At ninety-five, I am still alive, and can play the *qin* and sing songs. This is the third of my three favorite things. Poverty is common among the people, and death is waiting for everyone. I can live and die just like anyone else. What worry should I have?" Having said this, he started to play the *qin* and sing in a loud voice, looking joyful and complacent.

Confucius said to his disciples, "Excellent! This is a man who knows how to bring joy to himself!"

Back home, Confucius considered Rong Qiqi's words carefully and suddenly realized that they were intended as a warning to him.

"He is exhorting me to be content with my lot and stop my persistent pursuit," he said to himself, clenching his fists. "This won't do. I must aim to achieve my goal!"

The goal that Confucius envisaged was the establishment of an ideal social order in which all the vassal lords paid homage to the King of Zhou. It resembled a pagoda which, having no steps, was out of reach. He was determined to build the steps, and the task was indeed too formidable for him to undertake single-handedly. Fortunately he had many disciples of outstanding talents, who would undoubtedly help him build the steps. He decided to expand his teaching practice. To admit more students, he had several large thatched houses built to the west of his residence and used them as classrooms.

Thereafter Confucius taught his students there tirelessly. He used the elicitation method of teaching, encouraging the students to ask questions and then answer the questions themselves.

One day Confucius was standing in the courtyard deep in thought when Kong Li walked by in quick steps. Confucius stopped him and asked, "Have you studied *The Book of Poetry?*"

Kong Li replied, "No, not yet."

Confucius said, "Unless you study *The Book of Poetry*, you will not know how to speak properly."

So Kong Li began to study *The Book of Poetry* assiduously. He grew more and more interested and could recite many poems from the book as well as understand their meanings.

The next time when Kong Li walked past Confucius in the courtyard, Confucius asked, "Have you studied *The Book of Rites?*"

Kong Li replied, "No, not yet."

Confucius said, "Unless you study *The Book of Rites*, you will not know how to conduct yourself properly in society."

So Kong Li began to study *The Book of Rites* assiduously. He made fast progress, learning a lot about the rules of proper conduct.

Confucius was delighted by his son's progress.

In the twenty-eighth year of the reign of Duke Zhao of Lu (514 B.C.) Wei Shu, after coming to power in the state of Jin, wiped out two domineering ministers, Qi Shi and Yangshe Shi. Then he divided Qi Shi's land into seven counties and Yangshe Shi's land into three counties, and appointed people of virtue and talent to govern them.

Hearing the news, Confucius said with delight, "What Wei Shu has done conforms with righteousness and therefore has the support of the people far and near!"

He had always regarded as his comrades people who practiced benevolence and rules of propriety in their office. Therefore, when he heard of Wei Shu's righteous action, he was very excited and praised him generously to many people.

One day when Confucius was teaching *The Book of Rites* to the students, he again spoke of Wei Shu with appreciation.

Zi Lu asked in puzzlement, "Master, you have been praising Wei Shu for the past few days. How great is his achievement?"

Confucius smiled, "Qi Shi and Yangshe Shi acted against benevolence and righteousness. By eliminating them Wei Shu was carrying out the will of Heaven. He has now divided their land into ten counties and appointed people of virtue and talent, including his own son, to magistrates. This shows that he knows his subordinates well enough to assign them suitable positions. How can I help feeling glad when there are virtuous people like Wei Shu in our time?"

Zi Lu asked tentatively, "In that case, Jin has a bright prospect, does it not?"

Confucius said, "There are many virtuous people in the state of Jin. If Bo Hua were still alive, the world would already have been put into order."

Zi Lu asked in perplexity, "Who is Bo Hua? Could you tell me more about this man?"

Confucius said, "Bo Hua was from the city of Tongdi in the state of Jin; therefore he was called Bo Hua of Tongdi. As a child he was intelligent and eager to learn; as a grown-up he was brave and unyielding; in old age he was benevolent and treated with courtesy those inferior to him in rank. In possession of the above three virtues, one can govern the world without difficulty!"

Zi Lu said, "Eager to learn as a child and brave as an adult—these things are easy to achieve. But how is it possible for a man of virtue to show respect for people inferior to him?"

Confucius said slowly, "According to what I have heard, one is sure to gain victory by attacking a small army with a large one. And one is sure to obtain all people of virtue in the world by treating reverently those who rank below him. Formerly, when the Duke of Zhou served in the court of King Cheng, he was the highest official with the entire world under his control. Despite his honors and position, he held virtuous and talented people of low origins in high regard. On one occasion he received and talked with a hundred and seventy people in a single day. Why did he behave that way? Because he wanted to select suitable people to fill important offices. In fact, every virtuous man should be able to treat those below him with courtesy."

Confucius had scarcely finished his words when Yan Lu came in. He saluted and said, "Master, I just heard that Duke Zhao has moved from the city of Yun to Qianhou in Jin."

Confucius sighed deeply. "The ancients said that a country cannot last a single day without a ruler. At present our sovereign has left his homeland, the court is dominated by Jisun, and the people are living in misery. When will this come to an end!"

Squaring his shoulders and rubbing his hands, Zi Lu said, "Master, let me raid the Chief Minister's residence and kill Jisun. Then we can fetch back our lord, and Lu will be freed from its troubles."

Confucius flared up. "Stop talking nonsense! Haven't you heard of the saying that a fierce tiger is no match for a pack of wolves? Even if you had three heads and six arms, you would still be no match for thousands of crack troops. What's more, a wily hare has three burrows. Jisun has set up many defense lines in his manor. How would you be able to cope with all that! Once a battle takes place, it is the innocent soldiers and the common people who will suffer the most."

Choked with resentment, Zi Lu said in a muffled voice, "Do you mean we just have to sit here and let him do whatever he wants?"

Confucius said quietly, "I will go to the chief minister's residence and persuade him to send an envoy and fetch back our lord."

"What if he refuses to listen to you?" asked Zi Lu.

Confucius said, "Man is different from metal, stone, grass and trees because he has feelings. If I talk to him explicitly about the consequences of his action, how can he remain unmoved and persist in his way?"

Seeing that Confucius had made up his mind, Zi Lu harnessed the chariot and drove it for Confucius.

The chariot pulled up in front of the gate of the chief minister's residence. Hearing the report of the gate-keeper, Jisun Yiru came personally to welcome Confucius. He had a pointed head, short legs, and a big stomach. To the puzzlement of Confucius, instead of putting on airs as usual, he smiled cordially, "Pardon me for not coming earlier to welcome your arrival!"

Confucius said, "I have come uninvited to trouble you. Please do not blame me for it!"

Jisun smiled again. "You are being too polite, master. Please come into the room where we can talk!"

Entering the room, they took their respective seats as host and guest. Narrowing his eyes, Jisun asked, "What do you have to teach me, master?"

Confucius went straight to the point. "Our lord has left the state for many years. If the situation remains unchanged, Lu will steadily weaken. If there should be an invasion against us, the result would be unthinkable."

Jisun's smile froze. He said with a straight face, "So you want me to fetch back Duke Zhao, don't you?"

Confucius half rose from his seat. "That is indeed what I have in mind."

Jisun's face turned livid. "For no reason at all, Duke Zhao led troops to attack me and was defeated and exiled. He has got what he deserved!"

Confucius said quietly, "It is better to resolve past grudges than bear them always in mind. I hope you will change your mind for the sake of our state and the common people."

Jisun retorted, "Having fled, Duke Zhao is no longer the ruler of Lu. I am planning to set up his younger brother Song as our new sovereign."

Confucius' face changed color, and he said hastily, "Chief Minister, that would be most inappropriate. The ancients exhorted people not to take action which is not fully justified. To set up Song as the sovereign when Duke Zhao is still alive is exactly such an unjustified action. Please think twice."

Jisun saw reason in Confucius' words. He stroked his beard and was silent for a long time.

"In my opinion, the best option would be to receive Duke Zhao back to Lu."

Confucius waited hopefully for Jisun to give an unequivocal answer, but Jisun remained silent. It was suffocatingly quiet in the room. There was no sound except their breathing. After a spell of embarrassing silence, Jisun shook his head slightly.

Disappointed, Confucius sadly took his leave. Jisun politely saw him to the gate.

Caught in a gust of cold wind, Confucius shuddered. He felt sorely disheartened, realizing that there was no hope of Duke Zhao's return as long as Jisun remained in power in Lu. What else was there to do? Back home, he felt lonely, confused and downcast. After careful consideration, he concluded that the only thing he could do was to devote himself totally to the teaching of his students. He would impart to them his ideal, which would grow like a seed and bear fruit someday. This would be part of the steps he planned to build that would lead him to the pagoda of his dream. He had always believed that by perseverance one would realize one's dream. He was convinced that the day would come when he climbed to the top of the shining pagoda. Needless to say, he would have to endure numerous hardships.

In autumn that year the state of Lu enjoyed a favorable climate, with the crops growing very well. At twilight one evening, after explaining a passage in *The Book of Changes*, Confucius said to his disciples, "I was born and raised in Lu. I have always drunk water from the Sishui River. Yet I don't know where the source of the river is."

Zi Lu said eagerly, "The Sishui River originates at the western foot of Peiwei Mountain, to the east of my hometown. There are four gushing springs, which converge into a stream to make up the river."

Confucius said, "Well, let's go and have a close look at the source of the river tomorrow, shall we?"

The disciples unanimously agreed.

Zi Lu then gave a vivid description of the scenery around Peiwei Mountain after which the disciples returned home to prepare for the trip.

Early next morning Confucius took a look at the cloudless sky and said to his disciples, "It's going to rain today. Take your raincoats with you."

Looking up at the clear sky, the disciples were puzzled. Though they did not quite believe it was going to rain, they took their straw rain capes with them as Confucius had told them.

Following the chariot of Confucius, they set out in high spirits, going out the capital city's east gate to head for Peiwei Mountain along the ridge of Fang Mountain. Fang Mountain stretched in an unbroken chain of undulating hills. The Sishui River was winding and turbulent. The ground rose steadily from the capital of Lu to Peiwei Mountain. The Sishui River, originating at Peiwei Mountain, flowed westward along the northern side of Fang Mountain. It was girded by two green ribbons of willow trees. Cranes danced lightly on the sandy beach, and flocks of gulls leisurely strolled on the surface of the river.

A violent wind arose, and a dark cloud floated from the northeast. In an instant big clusters of dark cloud filled the sky, blocking the sun. As soon as the wind stopped it began to rain heavily.

Confucius told the disciples to put on their rain capes and go and find a shelter nearby.

After they had settled down in an inn, Min Shun asked Confucius, "Master, the sky was so clear when we set out this morning. How did you know it was going to rain?"

Confucius said, "It is written in *The Book of Poetry* that the approaching of the moon to the Bi star signifies heavy rain. Yesterday evening I looked up at the sky and found the moon very close to the Bi star. Though the sky was clear this morning, the air felt rather moist, which was unusual in autumn. Therefore I concluded it was going to rain heavily today."

The landlord had prepared a simple meal and invited them to have supper.

Zi Lu knew Confucius liked to eat ginger raw, so when he found no ginger in the plate, he asked the inn-keeper to bring some, which he washed and put into the plate.

After the meal they went to bed. The next day they continued their journey.

It was an overstatement to call Peiwei a mountain, for it was only a few dozens of feet high and less than one li in circumference. From a great distance Zi Lu pointed and said, "Look at Peiwei Mountain!"

Confucius looked ahead but did not see what he was looking for, as he did not regard the small mound as a mountain.

When the chariot arrived before Peiwei Mountain, the two horses neighed and stopped. Confucius looked ahead and indeed saw four fountains gushing high into the sky. He got down from the chariot and walked quickly to the fountains. The disciples also forgot their fatigue after a long journey and gathered around the fountains to enjoy the marvelous sight.

The four springs were gushing out constantly, with pearl-like bubbles and the sweetness of honey, murmuring all along into the Sishui River, which flowed on to nourish the land and irrigate the cultivated fields.

The disciples cupped the spring water in their hands and drank heartily.

Confucius also scooped up some water and drank a mouthful, relishing its sweetness and freshness. He remarked, "Wonderful! I did not know there is such a fairyland in the world!"

Zi Lu was very excited and danced joyfully. "Master, come here and have a look!"

Following him, Confucius looked ahead and saw a lot of fountains. One of them was creating pearl-like bubbles, and another was spurting so forcefully that it carried along with it thin, grain-like sand.

Zi Lu pointed at the fountain with yellow sand and said, "This is called washing-rice fountain." Pointing to two small fountains side by side, he said, "This is the double-eye fountain." Leaping and crying like a boy, he told the names of the fountains aligned alongside each other: "Gold-string fountain, silver-string fountain, pearl fountain, reclining-ox fountain, ..."

"How many fountains are there altogether?" Confucius asked.

Zi Lu answered, "It is said there are seventy-two in all, but the actual number far exceeds that. Look, there are fountains all over the place."

Confucius looked in that direction. A small lake was formed to the southeast of Peiwei Mountain. Numerous streams of spring water were gushing out around the lake, like a group of dragons spitting pearls and pieces of jade.

They feasted their eyes on the sight with delight. Some disciples began to name the fountains according to their shapes. Intoxicated in their play, they forgot about all their worries.

At this moment several people gathered around to watch. They were sallow of face and as thin as skeletons, regarding Confucius and his disciples curiously. Confucius' heart sank, and he shivered. If there were still people suffering from hunger and cold in a year of bumper harvests, it was not hard to imagine what a year of natural disaster would mean to the common people. He thought of Bo Qin, who eliminated undesirable customs, practiced the rules of proper conduct, and pacified the border lands. Under his rule the people grew wealthy, and Lu became powerful. Since then the situation in Lu had deteriorated to such an extent that its sovereign had now been driven into exile. He wished he could break into the chief minister's residence and persuade Jisun Yiru to make up with Duke Zhao and receive him back to Lu. Then he remembered Jisun's haughty appearance, and he lost heart. What was the point of making another futile attempt?

At dusk, when Confucius arrived home from Peiwei Mountain, Wuwei carried the supper prepared by Lady Qiguan to her father. Wujia was a very bright child. Finding her uncle in a bad mood, she patted his clothes to clean the dust and asked him a lot of questions until Confucius finally smiled.

That evening Confucius remained awake in bed until almost daybreak. Suddenly he found himself in Hao, the royal capital. In the centre of the city stood a high and magnificent palace. Hundreds of civil and military officials, formally dressed, lined up to enter the palace. Their shout of salute was deafening. Curiously, Confucius walked up in quick steps and, hiding himself behind a pillar, peeped into the palace. In the hall sat a boy of about eleven, and at his side stood the Duke of Zhou, looking kindly and graceful. The boy must be King Cheng, thought Confucius. At this moment King Cheng said, "My honored ministers, please present your memorials one by one!" At once the Duke of Zhou, with a sweep of his broad sleeves, bowed deeply and said in a clear, unhurried voice, "I have heard that the ruler of Lu has lived in exile at Qianhou in the state of Jin for many years since he was driven away by his chief minister, Jisun Yiru. It is highly inappropriate for the ruler of a state to take refuge in another state. If such a situation is allowed to continue, the relationship between the old and the young, the superiors and their subordinates would be disrupted, and the rituals and music would cease to exist. I beseech Your Majesty to send a thousand war chariots on an eastward expedition against Lu to wipe out Jisun and receive the Duke of Lu back to his home state. This will demonstrate the authority of the king, reestablish the proper order of superiors and inferiors, and propagate the rites and music. I hope Your Majesty will issue an edict." King Cheng of Zhou looked at the court officials with a dazed expression and did not say anything for a long time. The court officials said in unison, "Jisun Yiru has wrought havoc on Lu. We appeal to Your Majesty to issue the edict!" King Cheng turned abruptly to the Duke of Zhou, "I approve of what you said. Select a thousand war chariots at once for an expedition against Lu, eliminate Jisun and rescue the Duke of Lu!" The Duke of Zhou cried loudly, "Thank you, Your Majesty!" At this Confucius struck the pillar with his fist and almost shouted with joy. Hearing the noise, two guards carrying long halberds hastened toward him and demanded angrily, "Who are you? Why do you hide here and listen to secret discussion of government affairs?" Confucius bowed with his hands clasped and said, "I am Kong Qiu from the state of Lu. Because our ruler has been forced into exile for several years, I have come to the royal capital to ask His Majesty to send troops to rescue Lu. On hearing of His Majesty's consent to send troops, I was overcome with joy. Please do not be angry with me." Just then the Duke of Zhou, beaming with satisfaction, came up and said to Confucius, "Kong Qiu, you should return to Lu in haste to assist the Duke of Lu to govern the state!" Confucius bowed deeply and said, "I will do as you have told me!" He was about to turn away when his foot hit the wall, which made him cry out in pain. He was awakened and realized he had been dreaming.

The wonderful dream contrasted sharply with reality, which made Confucius very sad. As it was near dawn, Confucius dressed up and walked out the door. A few puffs of cloud hung in the sky, and the stars appeared unusually bright. A group of wild geese flew south in a regular formation, crowing. The rueful crow made him think of Duke Zhao of Lu. He could imagine how the duke longed for his homeland and his eyes dimmed with tears.

He felt disconsolate and uncertain, like a man standing at a crossroad, not knowing which path to take.

He could only find solace in teaching his disciples and collecting and collating ancient texts. He vowed to himself that he would edit *The Book of Poetry*, *The Book of History*, *The Book of Rites*, *The Book of Changes*, and *The Book of Music*, eliminating the false and retaining the true, so that future generations would be able to read the classics in their best form. He also planned to write down in detail the history of the state of Lu, which would serve as a mirror for future generations.

He was thinking about his plan for the future when Kong Li appeared and saluted respectfully. Confucius said to him, "I have heard that the only thing that can keep a man busy all day is the pursuit of learning. Exceptional beauty in appearance is nothing worth noticing, great strength is nothing to be feared, and a famous family name is nothing to brag about. Even great fame can not compare with the craving for learning. People of virtue and culture must study with diligence. Only in this way can they understand things past and present. This can be compared to a pool into which many streams of water flow and which is surrounded by grass and reeds. No matter how people guess and explore, they would not know where all the water is coming from."

Kong Li said, "I understand. I promise to study diligently."

In the winter of the twenty-ninth year of the reign of Duke Zhao of Lu (513 B.C.) the state of Jin had a giant tripod cast and the penal code carved on it. At the news Confucius sighed deeply and said to his disciples, "Such practice will disrupt the proper order among the people. Jin is going to perish!"

The shining pagoda that Confucius dreamed of had many levels. At the top was the King of Zhou, below him the vassal lords, then the ministers, then the scholars, and at the bottom were commoners and slaves. To have the penal code carved on the tripod was a threat to this pagoda. Confucius felt distressed and anxious; he could find no way to protect the dignity and entirety of the pagoda. He could only think hard in perplexity.

In the thirty-first year of Duke Zhao of Lu's reign (511 B.C.) the Jin ruler sent an envoy to Lu. At the news, Confucius hurried to the guesthouse to visit him.

Chapter Twelve

Jisun Yiru Exhorts His Son for the Sake of the Family;
Confucius Explains the Meaning of the Slanting Vessel to His Disciples in the Temple

When Confucius called on the Jin envoy at the guesthouse, the envoy told him, "The Duke of Lu has lived for a long time at Qianhou in Jin. Though he has been treated kindly, this cannot compare to living in his own state. Therefore our lord intends to send him back to Lu so that he can reach a reconciliation with his ministers."

Highly pleased at the news, Confucius took leave of the Jin envoy at once and went to see Jisun Yiru.

Having already met with the Jin envoy, Jisun was considering the Duke of Jin's proposal, but had been unable to reach a decision. Confucius' visit provided him with a chance to extricate himself from this awkward position. After Confucius explained the message delivered by the Jin envoy, Jisun said, "I've been thinking about it since you took the matter up with me last time. You are right about it: It goes against the rules of propriety for a state to have no ruler. I have just made up my mind to go to Jin in person to fetch back our sovereign."

Confucius said, "It is highly commendable of you, Chief Minister, to let the state and people take precedence over personal grudges."

Jisun acted quickly. He bade Yang Hu select two hundred crack troops to accompany him on his journey to Jin.

The following day Confucius led a dozen of his disciples to see Jisun off at his residence, after which they returned home in high spirits. He selected auspicious dates for the weddings of his son, daughter and niece. After that he again devoted himself to teaching, while waiting anxiously for Duke Zhao's return.

Jisun, at the head of fifty chariots, travelled day and night and soon reached Qianhou in the state of Jin. He bade Yang Hu call on

Duke Zhao to inform him of their intention to fetch him back.

Duke Zhao heard Yang Hu out, walked up and down for a while, then returned to his seat, wondering whether Jisun was sincere in his mission or merely playing a trick. As a sovereign in exile, Duke Zhao longed to return home and to extinguish the bitter memories of living in a strange land. When the day finally came for him to return, he grew apprehensive. He was afraid that Jisun might be hatching a plot against him. With dazed eyes he stared hard at Yang Hu.

Yang Hu's insolence was well known in Lu. He returned Duke Zhao's gaze with a withering look. Duke Zhao shuddered inwardly and felt gooseflesh rise over his entire body.

Just then Jisun himself approached Duke Zhao, his fat body staggering somewhat as he walked. He fell on his knees, saying, "A guilty minister kowtows to Your Lordship!"

It was the first time Duke Zhao had ever heard Jisun admit his guilt, and he could not help suspecting it to be a trick. He felt dizzy and confused, torn by conflicting emotions. After a long pause he said in a distorted voice, "You may stand up, my honored minister!"

With his porcupine-shaped body, Jisun found it much easier to kneel down than to get up. He thanked the duke and tried to stand up, but when he propped up one leg, he lost his balance and nearly fell onto his back. Yang Hu caught his right arm and dragged him upward, but Jisun's left foot tripped on the wide brim of his robe. Luckily Yang Hu was strong enough to pull him to his feet. When he finally stood firm, he was already gasping for breath.

When Duke Zhao politely asked him to take a seat Jisun bowed with clasped hands: "Thank you, Your Lordship." He had barely sat down when he rose again. "Your Lordship," he said, "the unhappy episode in Lu has become a thing of the past. I want to forget old grudges and hereby beg you to return to Lu for the sake of the state and the common people."

From his experience Duke Zhao had ample reasons to regard Jisun with deep-rooted mistrust. Looking at him closely, Duke Zhao suspected that something sinister was hidden behind the false smile on his face, and his words sounded full of deceitful wiles. After a long pause, the duke finally said with a soft sigh, "I have not presided over the court for such a long time, and now I am like a candle flickering in the wind. It would be useless for me to return to Lu. It would be better if my last days were spent here."

Jisun said, "A headless man cannot walk, and a headless bird cannot fly. How can Lu go on without a ruler? Please consider this matter carefully!"

Duke Zhao found his words reasonable, but shuddered at the expression on his face. After a few more moments of hesitation, he had made up his mind to stay in Jin. He said to Jisun, "I am grateful that you have put away old grudges and travelled such a great distance to fetch me. However, being old and decrepit, I have no hope of achieving anything great on my return to Lu, so I'd better stay here."

Jisun felt humiliated by what he regarded as Duke Zhao's insensitivity and lack of understanding. His first impulse was to burst into a fury and rebuke Duke Zhao. But he was no longer the quick-tempered youth of many years ago. Restraining his anger, he managed to adopt a sincere expression and said, "In that case, I would not force you to return. Take care of yourself. I shall take my leave."

Duke Zhao sprang up, his lips trembling, and half wanted to say, "Wait a minute, I'll go back with you!" But fear got the better of him, so that he ended up muttering, "Take care of yourself, honored minister."

Jisun walked out of the room, indignant and disgruntled. He left Jin for Lu without even saying good-bye to the Duke of Jin.

They made the journey home in a listless mood. After many days of arduous travel they arrived north of the Lu capital at twilight. Looking south, Yang Hu saw in the distance a chariot surrounded by several dozen people outside the city's north gate. He reported this to Jisun.

Jisun sighed, "This must be Confucius and his disciples. They must have come here several times in these days to wait for our sovereign's return. Loyalty like this is indeed rare!"

They approached the group and saw that it was indeed Confucius and his disciples.

Craning his neck, Confucius looked at the oncoming chariots one by one. Failing to find Duke Zhao in any of them, he suddenly turned pale, and his heart sank.

Jisun appeared and recounted how Duke Zhao had insisted on remaining in Jin. Raising his head, Confucius gazed into the sky in the northwest, tears welling up in his eyes. His dream of restoring Lu to its former glory had been dashed to pieces.

In winter of the thirty-second year of his reign (510 B.C.) Duke Zhao died of illness at Qianhou in the state of Jin. At the news Jisun immediately set up Duke Zhao's younger brother, Song, as the new ruler. He became known as Duke Ding of Lu.

Born and brought up in the inner quarters of the palace, Duke Ding had grown used to indulgence in wine and pleasures. After his ascension he paid little attention to affairs of the state but instead whiled away his hours in the company of his wife and concubines enjoying dance and songs. Half a year passed in this way.

In summer of the first year of Duke Ding of Lu's reign (509 B.C.) Shusun Chengzi brought back the remains of Duke Zhao of Lu from Qianhou. On hearing that Duke Ding intended to have some slaves buried alive with the deceased duke, Confucius hurried to the palace. "Since ancient times benevolent rulers are distinguished by their love of people, who make up the foundation of a nation," he said to the duke. "You have to rely on people to make the state strong and powerful. It has been rightly said that a state with people's support will prosper, whereas a state without people's support will perish. Formerly, Duke Mu of Qin loved people and showed great skill at selecting talented people to fill offices. As a result, Qin was turned from a remote and backward state into a strong and powerful one. However, when Duke Mu died some people were buried alive with him, which caused fright and anger all across the state. As a common saying goes, the overturned cart ahead may serve as a warning to the carts behind. If you want to make Lu prosper and the people support you whole-heartedly, you'd better give up the practice of immolation."

Duke Ding was in his fifties, looking thin and weak. His face turned sullen on hearing Confucius' words. He wanted to express his displeasure, but he knew that Confucius' words were not unreasonable. So he said quietly, "You are absolutely right, master. I will listen to your advice and will not immolate people for the late duke's burial."

Confucius knelt and said, "Your wisdom is a true blessing to the state and the people!"

Duke Ding combed his beard with his fingers and said with a smile, "You may stand up, master."

Confucius rose and took his leave.

Soon after, Duke Zhao of Lu was buried to the east of the capital. A high grave was built of earth, and dozens of junipers and cypresses were planted around it.

The climate was highly irregular for autumn that year. It snowed heavily by the end of the ninth month, and many crops were destroyed by frosts.

In the fifth month of the second year of the reign of Duke Ding of Lu (508 B.C.) a city gate and two temples caught fire and was burnt to the ground.

Misfortunes befell Lu in rapid succession. Deeply worried, Confucius decided to offer advice to assist Duke Ding in managing the state. With this in mind he entered the palace to see Duke Ding.

Stepping inside the palace gate, Confucius heard music from the rear palace, by which he speculated that Duke Ding must be enjoying dance and music again. Arriving at the rear palace, he found Duke Ding lying on his back in a divan, with his eyes fixed on the dancing girls, his hands patting his legs.

A palace attendant approached him and reported in a low voice, "Your Lordship, Kong Qiu has come to call on you."

Duke Ding turned to glare at the attendant, then continued to watch the dance.

Standing outside the gate, Confucius saw clearly what had happened. He was on the brink of losing his temper, and wanted to step forward and demand in a stern voice, "As the sovereign you indulge yourself all day in wine and songs to the neglect of state affairs. You have betrayed your ancestors above and the common people below. How can you hope to govern the state well in such a manner?" He felt his face flush and cautioned himself, "By all means remain calm and tranquil. You should advise the sovereign in kind words and persuade him to consider the interests of the state and people."

The music stopped. The attendant waiting by Duke Ding's side stepped forward and reported timidly, "Your Lordship, Kong Qiu has come to call on you. He has been waiting outside the gate for a long time."

As if awakened from a dream, Duke Ding straightened himself in the divan and said with a broad smile, "Bring him forth at once!"

The attendant cried, "Let Confucius enter the palace!"

Holding his breath, Confucius walked up to Duke Ding and knelt. "Kong Qiu pays homage to Your Lordship!"

Duke Ding waved his sleeve lightly. "You may stand up, master."

"Thank you, Your Lordship!"

Duke Ding told Confucius to take a seat. After the latter had sat down, he asked, "What important matter do you wish to take up with me?"

"Your Lordship," Confucius replied, "in the past few years Lu has been afflicted with various calamities. Our state will grow steadily weaker unless we take timely measures to restore the rites and consolidate the government. If we allow the situation to continue, the future does not bear thinking about!"

Duke Ding was dumbfounded by Confucius' blunt remark. After a long pause, he said, "This has been on my mind also. What good ideas do you have to offer?"

Clearing his throat, Confucius said with great seriousness and sincerity, "It is said that the river does not freeze over in a single day. For many years Lu has suffered both domestic troubles and incursions from beyond its walls, resulting in poverty and lack of faith among the people. In my opinion, in order to govern the state well, as the first step we must set the people's mind at ease. When people are calm and contented, the state will prosper; when people are worried and disgruntled, the state becomes weak. If we want to set the people's mind at ease, the most important thing to do is to enable them to have enough to eat and to wear. At present we have starving people everywhere; many have left Lu for other places in search of a better life. We should open the official granaries to feed the famished refugees, so that they would love their lord better than their own parents. Second, punishment should be pronounced against the corrupt officials, who seek private gain by unscrupulous means at the expense of the people's livelihood and state security. Those guilty of minor misconducts should be fined money and grain and deprived of their official posts; those who have committed serious crimes should be thrown into prison and have their property confiscated. Third, if we select people of virtue and talents to fill offices, virtuous people will come to us from afar without being invited. If, on the contrary, we reject superior men and employ petty men, virtuous people would leave for faraway places. Fourth, the peasants should be encouraged to till the land and craftsmen rewarded for their contribution to the state. Fifth, we should set up more schools and promote education, so that people can obtain good education regardless of their class origin."

As soon as Confucius finished speaking, Duke Ding exclaimed, "Good, very good! Your talents and wisdom are as good as your fame. I am already planning ..."

Just then a palace attendant approached with the report that the chief minister had arrived.

Duke Ding said, "Call him in!"

After the attendant had left Duke Ding said to Confucius, "I am planning to appoint you to an office. What do you think?"

After a long pause, Confucius said, "It is the duty of every subject to serve the state. I am ready to receive your appointment!"

At this moment Jisun Yiru entered the palace, his fat body hobbling from side to side. He kowtowed and took a seat to the left of the duke.

Confucius saluted to Jisun, then took his leave.

Duke Ding turned to ask Jisun, "My honored minister, what has brought you here?"

When Jisun heard of Confucius' visit to the palace, he wondered whether the latter had been summoned by the duke or had gone on his own initiative to offer some advice. This was the reason why he had hastened to the palace. No sooner had he taken his seat than Confucius rose to leave, which seemed strange to him. Duke Ding's question took him by surprise, so he murmured, "Well, I have just come to keep Your Lordship's company to watch the song and dance performance."

Annoyed at his awkward expression and mumbled words, Duke Ding said with a straight face, "Honored minister, Confucius is a man with rare talent and insight. I want to make him an official. What do you think?"

Jisun was intensely jealous of Confucius for his talent and wisdom. He felt apprehensive about what might happen if Confucius was given an important post. The incident of his forcing Duke Zhao into exile would be written down in history records to be denounced by future generations. The people would blame him for causing internal strife in the Lu court and bringing about Lu's steady decline. And Confucius would replace him as the dominant figure in the court. He regretted that he had not received Confucius as his steward and thus made him a submissive follower. Clasping his fists, he wished he could have all those who were superior to him in talent strangled and ground to pieces. He wanted to shout, "No! No! As long as I am alive, Confucius must not be made an official!" But he checked himself. He was old enough to face reality. At that instant it suddenly occurred to him that a more important move would be to prevent Duke Ding from employing Confucius and cultivate his son, Jisun Si, to take up the chief minister's chair. Having spent the better part of his life in the court, he was able to regain his composure quickly and said in a calm voice, "Your Lordship, Confucius is indeed world-renowned for his wisdom. He understands things in heaven and on earth, ancient and modern. He is the person I admire the most. However, he is after all a scholar. A scholar can be compared to the moon's reflection on the water surface, or flowers in the mirror: good to look at but without substance. He may serve well as a teacher. If appointed to an important post, he might cause great harm."

On hearing this, Duke Ding felt hesitant. He stood up and thought for a while, then said, "I'll have to give the matter some consideration. Let's discuss it later!"

Jisun was greatly relieved to hear this. Returning home, he called his son Jisun Si to him and said, "I am near the end, with one foot in the grave. To retain the chief minister's position for the family, you must learn some practical skills, especially the way to deal with people. For hundreds of years the chief minister's office has been coveted by many people, including the families of Shusun and Mengsun. Now Confucius is also a contender on the scene. By no means should he be taken lightly. He is prudent and experienced, and has won the lord's favor. Whenever I think of him I felt jealousy and fear. He seems to be a threat to myself and to you. You must find ways to check and dispel him, preventing him from becoming a high official."

Jisun Si took after Jisun Yiru in visage, but contrasted him in stature. While Jisun Yiru was short and dangerously fat, Jisun Si was tall, a little stooped and piteously thin. Looking at his son closely, Jisun Yiru felt he had so much to say. He wanted to teach his son in a single breath all about how to be a chief minister.

Having grown up in the chief minister's house, Jisun Si was quite familiar with his father's official manner of speech and conduct. He considered himself fully qualified to succeed to his father's office and hoped for the day to come soon. So he paid but slight attention to Jisun Yiru's exhortations. He was thinking instead how he would enjoy himself when he became chief minister.

Annoyed at his son's inattentiveness, Jisun Yiru raised his voice in rebuke. "Have you heard everything I said? Why are you always so absent-minded? If you don't pay attention you will bring disgrace to our ancestors. The glory of the Jisun family must not be ruined like this!" Feeling numb and dizzy, he gripped his head with his hands and sighed again and again. "I am nearly seventy and weak from illnesses. You must not turn a deaf ear to my words like this!"

Reluctantly, Jisun Si moved close to his father.

Burning with anxiety, Jisun Yiru said, "Yang Hu is also a problem. He has served as a steward in our household for many years and achieved great merits, but he is very deceitful and not to be trusted. He is not only skilled at martial arts, but he can also lead troops in battle. At present he has several thousand soldiers under his command, and according to my sources of information he is in frequent contact with the stewards from the Shusun and Mengsun families. If they should raise a revolt, the outcome would be unthinkable." Filled with fear and apprehension and dogged by illness, he felt his days were numbered. He said with a sigh of grief, "It seems that I am not long for this world. You will have a very heavy burden on your shoulders."

Jisun Si knew nothing about the dangers involved in his forthcoming official career. In his imagination, a chief minister was simply someone who enjoyed an extremely high status and almost unlimited power, who could indulge himself in all kinds of pleasures and get away with just about everything. He was envisaging his future: Escorted by stewards and guards when he went out, welcomed by his wife and concubines when he returned home, held in awe and respect by all officials and the common people, and obeyed unquestionably by his own family. He could hardly contain his joy at the thought that this was not a dream but something that would come true in the near future. Thus he paid no attention to what his father was saying. His lips trembling with anger, Jisun Yiru demanded, "Have you heard clearly what I told you?"

"Oh?" Jisun Si was jostled out of his daydream. "Yes, I ... I have heard it clearly."

"And what did I tell you?" Jisun Yiru asked, pointing his son's nose with his finger.

Jisun Si stared blankly.

Jisun Yiru said in exasperation, "It is the misfortune of our family and ancestors to have an unworthy descendant like you!" His voice grew muffled and weak.

Taking a close look, Jisun Si discovered his father lying limp in his seat, his eyes staring obliquely, his mouth twisted and foaming.

Jisun Si called in the servants and had him carried to bed. From that time on Jisun Yiru was afflicted by paralysis that confined him to bed, reliant on his servants for all his daily needs. Without his father to exhort and keep an eye on him, Jisun Si felt as if some invisible fetters had been removed and began to devote all his time to wine and women.

Confucius felt very glad after his visit to Duke Ding, who promised to appoint him an official. Considering it a good opportunity to realize his political ambitions, he drew up a plan for assisting the duke to govern the state and waited for the time to come to put the plan into effect. However, because of Jisun Yiru's objection, Duke Ding abandoned the idea of appointing Confucius to office and did not take up the matter again. In vain Confucius waited for a summons from the duke. Feeling more than a little frustrated, he continued to devote himself to teaching.

One day, after expounding some passages from *The Book of Rites*, Confucius was taking a rest in the courtyard when Zi Lu burst in and reported, "Master, I have just heard that Duke Zhang of Zhu had died, and five people were buried alive with him."

Hearing this, Confucius said with great annoyance, "In his life Duke Zhuang of Zhu failed to bring prosperity to the state or peace and comfort to its people, whereas at his death he brought them the shadow of death. The decision was taken by Duke Yin, who has apparently thrown benevolence to the winds! It seems that the people of Zhu will have a hard time under his rule."

In autumn of the fourth year of the reign of Duke Ding of Lu (506 B.C.) Confucius visited the temple of Duke Huan of Lu with his son, Kong Li, his nephew, Kong Zhong, and his disciples. In the courtyard inside the temple there were red-leafed pistache trees, wild chrysanthemums, and green cypresses and junipers, a glorious interplay of colors in the morning light.

Having saluted the statue, Confucius and his disciples looked at the bronze vessels in front of the statue. These vessels, round or square in shape, showed fine workmanship. Confucius stopped before a strange-looking vessel and examined it with great interest. Hanging on a wooden frame with two axles, the vessel had a rectangular opening at the top and a round bottom. Confucius asked of the curator, "What kind of vessel is this?"

"This is called the slanting vessel," replied the man.

Confucius said to his disciples, "According to what I have heard, the slanting vessel has a great moral to teach about the doctrine of the mean. When empty, it slants; when filled with a proper amount of water, it stays upright; when filled to the brim, it overturns. Why don't we bring some water and have a demonstration?"

Strong and nimble, Zi Lu picked up a pail and returned immediately with it filled with water.

Confucius said, "Watch carefully, all of you! Zi Lu, pour water into the vessel!"

Zi Lu lifted the pail and emptied half the water into the vessel, which swayed and then became still.

Confucius said in a loud voice, "A bit slower!"

Zi Lu stopped pouring and held the pail over the vessel.

Confucius said, "I want all of you to see for yourselves the moral behind this. Now pour water into the vessel slowly."

As water kept flowing into the vessel, it changed from a slanting position to become upright.

Confucius said, "If more water is poured into it, the vessel will turn over."

Zi Lu asked, "Shall I?"

Confucius said, "Yes, go ahead."

Before the pail was empty, the vessel began to tilt. When Zi Lu emptied the pail of water into the vessel, it toppled, splashing its contents all over the ground.

"Do you understand now? Since fullness leads inevitably to downfall, one must always guard against self-satisfaction. A person of outstanding intelligence should always look out for possible weaknesses in his intelligence. A person of exceptional merits should always think about his possible failings. A person of great courage should bear in mind his possible cowardice in some aspects of life. A person of immense wealth should prepare himself for hard days to come. Only thus can one give full play to one's advantages, and avoid turning them into disadvantages and obstacles. Is this clear to you?"

The disciples, comprehending the words from their own perspectives, nodded their appreciation.

Confucius smiled with satisfaction.

After lingering to enjoy the sights for some time, the disciples returned home with Confucius.

In the sixth month of the fifth year of Duke Ding of Lu's reign (505 B.C.) Jisun Yiru died, and the position of chief minister was succeeded to by his son, Jisun Si, who historically became known as Ji Huanzi.

Before Jisun Si could consolidate his position, Yang Hu, colluding with his cousin Yang Yue, and Gongshan Buniu, another steward in the Jisun household and magistrate of the city of Fei, spread a dragnet for him.

Chapter Thirteen

Two Cousins Set a Trap by
Giving a Banquet at Pu Garden;
The Lu Sovereign Sends an Expedition
Against the City of Huan

Having inherited the position of chief minister, Jisun Si was feeling extremely pleased with himself. After breakfast he donned his official garment and hat, and walked briskly out of his room to the front courtyard. To his surprise, he found the courtyard planted with armed guards each a few steps apart. He drew a deep breath, realizing that something was terribly wrong. Plucking up his courage, he called out, "Servants! Send for Head Steward Yang Hu!" With his high position and status, he was wont to having a dozen people answering his call at once, but this time no one paid any attention to him. Flying into a rage, he roared at the guards as he walked toward the gate, "What are you doing here? What has happened?" The guards at the gate, however, refused to let him leave. Sweeping his broad sleeves, he said, "This is absurd!" The courtyard was silent except for the chirping of cicadas, which irritated him. In his confusion, the words of his father suddenly came to his mind: "Beware of Yang Hu." He wondered, "Is he behind all this?" Unable to restrain his anger, he blurted out, "What a treacherous jackal!" He looked at the guards with his angry eyes but recognized none of them. It was too late, he thought to himself. I have become his prisoner, a bird in his cage.

He guessed correctly. It was indeed Yang Hu who had sent guards to surround his residence and put him under house arrest. Yang Hu was very pleased with what he had done. He threw out his chest and spoke arrogantly. He wanted to replace Jisun Si and take control of the Lu court. From many years' experience of serving in the court, he knew that in order to achieve great things military strength was not enough. He must also rely on scholars. After careful consideration, he decided to invite Confucius to be his advisor.

One day he had a steamed suckling pig prepared and rode in his chariot to call on Confucius.

Confucius had once been humiliated by Yang Hu. Though he did

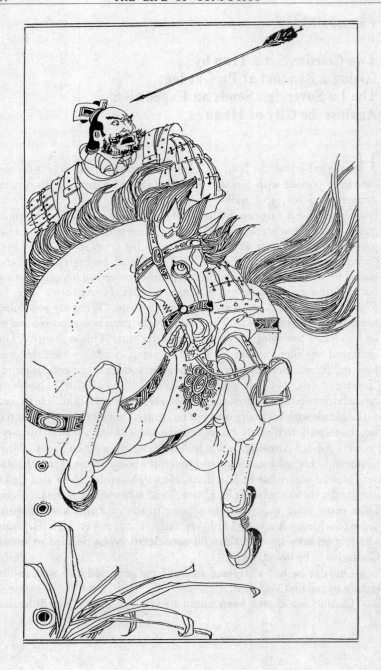

not hold the old grudge against him, he hated such people who went against the rules of propriety. On hearing that Yang Hu was coming to pay him a visit, he decided to avoid him. Dressed in formal clothes, he was about to leave the house when Yang Hu arrived in front of the gate.

Confucius had no choice but to retire to the inner room and told Kong Li to receive Yang Hu.

Yang Hu entered the courtyard radiant with smiles and greeted Kong Li with clasped hands. "I have come today to visit your father, whose fame I have known for a long time."

Kong Li, returning the salute, said, "My father left home this morning and has not yet returned."

Surprised, Yang Hu rolled his eyes and decided that Confucius was deliberately avoiding him. Suppressing his anger, he said calmly, "I have prepared a simple gift for the master. Please accept it." He beckoned a servant to bring the suckling pig into the courtyard.

Kong Li insisted on declining the gift, but Yang Hu would not listen. "Sorry to have troubled you," he said, and took his leave.

According to customs, when offered a gift one must pay a return visit to give his thanks. Confucius found himself in a dilemma. He had always held ancient rules of propriety in high esteem. If he did not pay a return visit, he would violate the rules and be mocked. But, if he called on Yang Hu to thank him, he would be blamed for associating with an evil person and betraying the Duke of Lu. After some thought he came up with an idea. He sent his disciple Qidiao Kai to keep tabs on Yang Hu's house, so that he could pay a visit to Yang Hu when he was not at home. In this way he would avoid meeting Yang Hu without violating the rules. On the third day Yang Hu was seen to have left home in his chariot, and Qidiao Kai hurried back to report to Confucius.

Confucius promptly mounted his chariot and headed for Yang Hu's house with Zi Lu. At the gate he exchanged a few words with the guards, telling them to report his visit when Yang Hu returned. Then he rode home with a light heart. At a street corner, however, a chariot headed toward them, and in it sat Yang Hu. Confucius was surprised and confused, not knowing quite what to say.

Yang Hu leapt out of his chariot, took two steps forward and bowed with clasped hands. "Master, you engage in discussions about the classics and state affairs all day. Why don't you join the government?"

Reluctantly Confucius climbed down from the chariot and returned the salute. "I have been eager to learn since my childhood and have read some books since. Thus I have acquired some knowledge. As for affairs of the state, I know very little about them."

Dissatisfied with this reply, Yang Hu asked with a straight face, "Are you a gourd hanging under the eaves of the house, good to look at but of no practical use? Wouldn't the gourd become useful if it is cut in two halves to make ladles?"

Confucius was struck with the remark. He had longed to serve in the government and help governing the state. He said, "Am I a gourd? No, I am not. I am prepared to enter office." The moment he uttered these words he regretted it. He wanted to be an official, but not under Yang Hu. He fell into awkward silence.

With his wily eyes Yang Hu watched Confucius closely and found he was not speaking sincerely. He said, "A great man understands his times. I hope you will reflect upon the situation and come to your decision soon!"

Their talk was growing disagreeable, so they took leave of each other after exchanging a few more words.

When Confucius got home, Zi Lu asked coldly, "Master, are you really going to be an official?"

Confucius sighed, "Those who do not share the same viewpoints will not lay plans together. How is it possible for me to work for Yang Hu?"

Zi Lu broke into a smile. "Master, so you only exchanged a few polite words with him out of courtesy!"

Confucius said, "Everyone is after wealth and honors. However, wealth and honors obtained by unrighteous means are like floating clouds to me. I have no use for them at all."

Zi Lu nodded with a smile.

Yan Lu approached Confucius followed by a youth. He said, "Master, this is my son, Yan Hui. He is sixteen. I have not brought him here earlier because I did not have ten pieces of preserved meat to offer. I have already taught him some basic knowledge. Please accept him!"

Yan Hui's styled name was Zi Yuan. He was also called Yan Yuan. Born in the twentieth year of Duke Zhao of Lu's reign (522 B.C.), he was short, thin, and sallow. After his father finished speaking, he fell on his knees and said, "Disciple Yan Hui pays respects to his master!"

Confucius smiled, "I did say that anyone who offers a gift of ten pieces of meat will be accepted as my disciple regardless of his origin. But I did not say only those who offer such gifts will be accepted. Yan Hui, please get up!"

Thus Yan hui became a disciple of Confucius' just like his father. Confucius was to accept a few more disciples, including Ran Yong, Ran Qiu, Shang Qu, and Liang Zhan. Ran Yong's styled name was Zhong Gong. Ran Qiu's styled name was Zi You; he was also called Ran You. Shang Qu's styled name was Zi Mu. The three of them were all natives of Lu. Liang Zhan, whose styled name was Shu Yu, came from the state of Qi. All of them were of the same age, born in the twentieth year of Duke Zhao of Lu.

Again Confucius abandoned hope of entering office and devoted himself to teaching. In the meantime, having completed editing *The Book of Poetry*, he embarked upon *The Book of History*, *The Book of Rites* and *The Book of Music*.

After putting Jisun Si under house arrest, Yang Hu began to throw his weight about in the court. The court officials bore an intense hatred against him but dared not oppose him openly. They worked in secret to find a way to deal with him.

Yang Hu became worried over the hostility of the court officials. He knew that it was unwise to incur public wrath. Cudgeling his brains, he decided upon the strategy of drawing the majority of the officials in and isolating the rest. He withdrew the guards keeping watch on Jisun Si and then made preparations for a covenant with Duke Ding of Lu and some other officials. He selected the Zhou Altar as the site for making the covenant. The altar was named after the Duke of Zhou, the first ruler of the state of Lu.

In the sixth year of the reign of Duke Ding of Lu (504 B.C.) Yang Hu coerced Duke Ding, Jisun Si, Mengsun Heji and Shusun Chengzi into making a covenant at the Zhou Altar. They then swore an oath to the people at the Yin Altar and offered sacrifice to the gods at Wufu Street. Yang Hu planned to destroy anyone who went against the covenant.

Yang Hu's plans were optimistic. He planned to replace Jisun Si and become the chief minister himself.

In the second month of the seventh year of Duke Ding of Lu's reign (503 B.C.) Qi returned two cities, Yun and Yangguan, to Lu. Yang Hu took the two cities under his control. As none of the court officials challenged him openly, Yang Hu thought the time had come to eliminate the three Huans. By that time Shusun Chengzi had died and was succeeded by his son, Shusun Zhouchou. So the heads of the three powerful households included Jisun Si, Mengsun Heji and Shusun Zhouchou.

On a quiet winter night in the eighth year of Duke Ding of Lu's reign (502 B.C.) the sky was covered by dark clouds, and snowflakes were falling thick and fast. In the inner room of Yang Hu's house, Yang Hu, Yang Yue and Gongshan Buniu sat before a square violet table under a dim light, their faces wearing a murderous look.

Shaking his broad shoulders, Yang Hu picked up a large piece of beef and put it into his mouth, chewed hastily and swallowed it. Suddenly he slammed the table and stood up. "As stewards we have lived like grass under a stone slab, unable to straighten up and raise our heads. Now the ruler is fatuous and incompetent, and the three households inert. Why don't we join forces with the stewards from the houses of Mengsun and Shusun, and have Jisun Si, Mengsun Heji and Shusun Zhouchou ..." he drew his right hand to his chest and closed it into a tight fist.

Yang Yue shot him a look with his frog-like eyes and hushed him. Looking around stealthily, he put his thick lips to Yang Hu's ear. "At present we are not strong enough and have to give the matter careful consideration."

Gongshan Buniu had a pointed chin, sunken cheeks and small, rat-like eyes. He combed his beard with his hand and said through clenched teeth, "We must take advantage of the present situation and make a surprise attack."

"What is your plan?" Yang Hu asked eagerly.

Gongshan Buniu smiled cunningly and explained his plan. Yang Hu and Yang Yue smacked their lips in appreciation.

Early the next morning the clouds dispersed to reveal a clear sky. Dressed in casual clothes and shoes, Jisun Si moved from his inner room to the courtyard and stopped at the piece of ground where snow had been cleared by the servants. He tightened his belt, tied up his sleeves and began to practice shadow boxing.

After completing several sets of exercise, he felt entirely relaxed. Wiping the sweat from his forehead, he was about to begin another set when he heard a horse neighing outside the gate. Straightening himself, Jisun Si saw a young soldier standing in front of the gate.

Jisun Si looked on with puzzlement as the young soldier walked in. "Who are you?" Jisun Si asked, a little confused.

The young man brought out an invitation card from his inner pocket, stepped forward and bowed. "My master is giving a banquet at Pu Garden tomorrow. He invites the chief minister to attend."

When Jisun Si took the card, two big characters, "Yang Hu," caught his attention. His heart sank, and his frown became even more knotted. He was afraid that Yang Hu was setting a trap for him. He shuddered at the thought of the days when he was under house arrest at Yang Hu's order. He did not really dare to attend the banquet. But it would be rude to decline the invitation, which might be a sincere one. He hesitated, unable to make up his mind. After a long moment of silence he finally came to his decision. Lightly tapping the invitation card with his fingers, he said, "Please inform your master that I will attend the banquet at the appointed time."

The young soldier made another deep bow. "Thank you, Chief Minister. I shall take my leave."

After the soldier had left, Jisun Si was deeply disturbed. That night he kept turning in bed, unable to sleep. He rose early at dawn, only to be annoyed by the ominous cawing of crows. He practiced a set of shadow-boxing absent-mindedly. Feeling the wind cutting to his bones, he rubbed his hands and returned to his room.

Immediately after breakfast Yang Hu and Yang Yue arrived at the gate in their chariots. After an exchange of courtesies they set out in their chariots for Pu Garden. Yang Hu sat in the first chariot, looking calm and well at ease. Jisun Si sat in the second one, uneasy and fidgety. In the third chariot sat Yang Yue, as alert as a hunting dog who had just found the game. The snow-covered road was slippery, and the strong horses pulling the chariots sweated profusely.

They left the smooth main road behind them and came up to a downy area. Jisun Si's anxiety increased. The driver appeared to be signaling to him with his eyes. Just then a gust of wind lifted up a swirl of snow, which settled over him. While brushing off the snow, he glanced behind him to see a group of Yang Hu's men following him closely, swords in hand. In the chariot behind, Yang Yue also had a sword in his hand. He watched Yang Hu attentively as if watching for some signal.

Jisun Si was terrified. Forcing himself to stay calm, he whispered to the driver, "This does not look at all good. Turn right at the next crossroad and head for Minister Mengsun's residence at full speed. Otherwise we are done for!"

These words were spoken in sadness and despair. The driver nodded and reined in the horses slightly. The chariot slowed down and increased its distance behind Yang Hu's chariot.

At the next crossroad the driver relaxed the rein and whipped the horses twice. The chariot turned onto a side road and sped on toward

Mengsun Heji's residence.

Seeing this, Yang Yue pressed forward in pursuit. Taking an abrupt turn, the chariot lurched, with one of its wheels caught in the gully. Leaping out of the chariot, Yang Yue ordered the soldiers to push the chariot while he took the whip from the driver's hand and lashed the horses fiercely.

By the time they got the chariot back unto the road, Jisun Si had already moved a long distance ahead.

When Yang Hu realized what had happened he turned his chariot back to pursue Jisun Si. He shouted, "Fast! Fast! Don't let him escape!"

Like a wolf at feeding time, Yang Yue stood in his chariot with bloodshot eyes and releasing a barrage of arrows.

When Yang Hu and Yang Yue reached the house of Mengsun Heji, they saw an empty chariot parked in front of the gate. Jisun Si had been received into the house and protected by Mengsun Heji's guards.

Yang Hu and Yang Yue were furious. Standing in the chariot, Yang Hu shouted, "Minister Mengsun, please turn Jisun Si over to us!"

No sooner had he finished shouting than Mengsun Heji walked out the gate. Yang Hu did not dismount but bowed with clasped hands. "Minister Mengsun, please turn Jisun Si over!"

With his guards behind him, Mengsun Heji was not to be intimidated. His eyes wide with anger, he severely rebuked, "Humph! How dare a treacherous steward like you challenge me! Today I will teach you a lesson. Warriors!"

The guards answered in unison, "Here!"

Mengsun Heji swept his hand and shouted, "Shoot!"

Arrows flew like rain from behind the wall and the gate tower. Mengsun Heji then gave a loud shout, "Warriors, kill!" At his order the guards swarmed out of the gate.

In the entangled fight that ensued, Yang Yue was shot by several arrows and fell from his chariot.

Finding things had taken an ugly turn, Yang Hu retreated, leaving Yang Yue's body behind. Several of his followers that lagged behind were killed by arrows.

Mengsun Heji led his men in a pursuit, then returned to his house.

When Mengsun Heji entered the hall, Jisun Si knelt and kowtowed his gratitude. "I would not have escaped death but for your help. I will never forget what you've done for me!"

Helping him up with both hands, Mengsun Heji said, "I am

unworthy of such courtesy, Chief Minister."

Jisun Si said, "Of course you deserve my salute, for you are comparable to my parents, having saved the life which they gave me."

Mengsun Heji said, "Since we share the same ancestors and serve in the same court, it is only proper that we should help each other out in difficulty." He bade the servants prepare a feast to help Jisun Si get over the shock.

Just then Shusun Zhouchou arrived, having heard of the incident. Mengsun Heji invited him to join them at the banquet.

The three of them took their positions as host and guests and offered one another toasts. After three rounds of drinks Shusun Zhouchou said, "The stewards have been working in collusion to get rid of us. Yang Hu will not take his defeat lying down. We must take ample precautions."

A guard ran in to report, "Yang Hu has taken our lord under duress and is now leaving the palace with troops to attack us."

Mengsun Heji brought his fist down on the table and shouted, "That traitor is being too intolerable!" He then told the guards to take their positions and the archers to lie in an ambush.

Mengsun Heji clasped his hands in a salute and said, "I am not strong enough and will need reinforcements from both of you."

Jisun Si said, "I am to blame for causing this trouble and will spare no efforts to deal with it!"

Filled with indignation, Shusun Zhouchou said, "I will not live under the same sky with these traitors! Minister Mengsun, please get two horses ready for Minister Jisun and me."

Mengsun Heji walked to the door and shouted, "Get two fine horses ready, quick!"

A short while later a guard came leading two big and strong horses. Jisun Si and Shusun Zhouchou took leave of Mengsun Heji, mounted their horses and disappeared into the darkness.

Carrying his sword, Mengsun Heji climbed up the gate tower to look into the distance, where the street was lit up by torches lining up like a dragon.

Yang Hu headed in his chariot for Mengsun Heji's house, having coerced Duke Ding of Lu to come with him.

Concealing himself in the gate tower, Mengsun Heji watched the approaching enemy and waited for the moment to attack.

Yang Hu saw Mengsun Heji's house was wrapped in darkness, with only one lantern hanging on the gate tower. He combed his beard and laughed out aloud. "Minister Mengsun, you are done for! Warriors, attack! Whoever kills Mengsun Heji will receive a great reward!"

The soldiers, holding spears, swords and halberds, dashed at Mengsun Heji's house, shouting battle-cries.

At Mengsun Heji's order a hail of arrows was let off, killing and wounding Yang Hu's men by the dozen. The battle-cries intermingled with the clanging of weapons and the moaning of wounded soldiers.

Seeing Mengsun Heji had been well prepared for the attack, Yang Hu turned to flee, but from the distance came two bands of troops holding torches, with cries piercing the sky. Yang Hu's men scattered in all directions, trying to flee the ambush. To his alarm, Yang Hu found himself encircled by the troops from the houses of Jisun, Mengsun and Shusun, and the encirclement kept tightening. He had to abandon Duke Ding of Lu, and managed to break away with his chariot.

At the morning audience the next day Duke Ding sat in his chair, not fully recovered from the shock. The court officials kowtowed in obeisance and arranged themselves in two ranks according to their positions.

Placing his hands on the table, Duke Ding asked, "My honored ministers, do you have anything to report this morning?"

Instantly Jisun Si raised his jade tablet and cried in a loud voice, "I have something to report to Your Lordship."

In a slightly agitated voice he announced, "In defiance of the law, Yang Hu has raised a revolt against his superiors and caused great confusion to the court and the common people. I beseech Your Lordship to dispatch a punitive expedition!"

His voice trembling with indignation, Duke Ding said, "It was abominable of Yang Hu, who dared hold me under duress! Who is willing to lead the expedition?"

Two generals stepped forward at the same time to answer the call. They were Shen Juxu and Yue Qi, both in their thirties, hefty and full of vitality.

Greatly pleased, Duke Ding said, "I order you to lead a hundred war chariots each to pursue and attack Yang Hu."

The two generals knelt to receive the order and retreated. At the head of two hundred chariots, they took the road by which Yang Hu had fled.

Leading the remainder of his troops, Yang Hu had fled in the night to the city of Huan. He was filled with despondence and rage. Unwilling to admit defeat, he ordered the soldiers to close the gate and strengthen the city wall and sent a mounted messenger to seek help from Gongshan Buniu in the city of Fei. He was preparing for a last-ditch fight.

At twilight Shen Juxu and Yue Qi arrived at Huan with their troops.

Hearing the news, Yang Hu cautiously approached the gate tower with a few followers. He was a little afraid at the sight of the enemy. Both Shen Juxu and Yue Qi were generals well-known for their bravery, and the troops they led were strong and well-trained. Faced with such a superior force, Yang Hu grew as restless as ants on a hot pan.

Standing under a banner embroidered with an enormous character, "Shen," Shen Juxu demanded sternly, "Yang Hu, you were born and raised in Lu, and enjoyed the favor of our lord. Instead of repaying his kindness, you became a traitor. Why?"

Yue Qi, standing under a banner embroidered with an enormous "Yue," also exhorted Yang Hu to surrender to save innocent soldiers from dying because of him.

Yang Hu bit his teeth and let out an insidious laughter. "How dare you brag like this, you petty scoundrels! Soldiers, shoot!"

From behind the city wall arrows flew out like a swarm of grasshoppers, but were all knocked down by Shen Juxu and Yue Qi's soldiers, who kept a long distance from the city wall.

Yang Hu shouted madly, "Draw your bows strongly! Strongly!"

His men kept shooting without striking anything. A little frustrated, he stamped his foot and, grabbing a bow from a soldier's hand, drew it with all his might and shot an arrow toward Shen Juxu's head.

Shen Juxu dodged nimbly to the left and caught the arrow in his right hand.

The soldiers gave a loud shout of approval. Yang Hu was so enraged that the veins on his neck bulged. He put another arrow to his bow and shot toward Yue Qi's chest.

Yang Hu was a good shot. The arrow flew squarely at Yue Qi's chest. Yue Qi, however, stayed motionless, as if nothing had happened. Many soldiers were breathless with anxiety, and some even screamed. When the arrow almost reached his chest, Yue Qi put his sword to his chest so that when the arrow hit the sword it bounced back and fell onto the ground.

After an initial pause of astonishment, the soldiers let out a loud cry of appreciation.

Yang Hu felt discouraged. He was physically exhausted. He staggered and propped himself up against a wooden pillar. He was almost in despair, gazing listlessly to the southeast. Huan was located to the north of the Lu capital, while Fei was to the east. Yang Hu was placing his hope in Gongshan Buniu.

It was nightfall. The cold north wind made the melted snow freeze again. Yang Hu shuddered from cold and hunger, and his mouth felt dry. Beneath the city gate he saw torches being lit up, and battle-cries could be heard every now and then. He looked to the southeast but saw nothing except darkness. He began to blame Gongshan Buniu for failing his promise to provide help when help was most needed. Then he realized that it would take at least one day and one night for the messenger to return from Fei with reinforcements, if there was any. He knew to his terror that the city of Huan could not hold out for so long. Furthermore, Gongshan Buniu might be unwilling to help.

Yang Hu guessed rightly. Gongshan Buniu had promised to assist in eliminating Jisun Si, Mengsun Heji and Shusun Zhouchou and had planned the banquet at Pu Garden himself. But his real intention was to sit on top of the mountain to watch the tigers fight and come down to reap the spoils when either or both sides were wounded. So when Yang Hu's messenger arrived at Fei, Gongshan Buniu had him killed in secret.

Standing on the gate tower, Yang Hu watched the enemy troops down below and waited in vain for reinforcements.

Shen Juxu and Yue Qi ordered their men to use scaling ladders to mount the city wall.

Having ordered his soldiers to shoot arrows in defense, Yang Hu fled the city in the company of a few trusted followers.

Shen Juxu and Yue Qi captured the city, inflicting great casualties on the enemy, but after a thorough search they failed to find Yang Hu. They held a brief discussion and then Shen Juxu went on with the search in the city while Yue Qi left the city with twenty war chariots to pursue Yang Hu.

Yue Qi looked closely at the crossing and found hoof prints on the road to Yangguan. So he gave the order to travel down the road in pursuit.

At dawn when they reached Yangguan, they found Yang Hu standing on the wall atop the city gate.

Like a cornered beast, Yang Hu made ready for a last-ditch struggle. Finding Yue Qi had only a few troops who had traveled all night on icy roads, Yang Hu decided to go out the city to give battle. Followed by a few trusted followers, he rode out and braced himself for a good fight.

An intrepid fighter, Yue Qi drove his chariot forward. The two of them stopped, facing each other at a shot's distance. The banner on Yue Qi's chariot was fluttering in the northwest wind. Drawing his sword, Yue Qi pointed at Yang Hu and said, "Traitor! Dismount and surrender! If you resist, you will die with no burial ground!"

Yang Hu said, "Don't brag like that. You are tired out from a night's traveling. I have been waiting to catch this tired hare you are."

Annoyed, Yue Qi swept his hand and shouted, "Soldiers, attack!" The twenty chariots drove forward like arrows shot from the bow. Waving his sword, Yang Hu threw himself into battle. Many horses were wounded, and their riders toppled. After about thirty rounds, Yang Hu felt numb in his arms and limp in his legs. He could only parry the enemy's blows without being able to strike back. Looking around, he found to his fright that only three of his followers were left. While fighting, he tried to find a path of retreat. Yue Qi kept up a close chase until he cut down the last three of Yang Hu's men. Unable to hold out any longer, Yang Hu sped his horse and fled to the east.

Yue Qi drove his chariot in pursuit, but the rugged mountain path made the chariot slow down and lag far behind Yang Hu's horse. Yue Qi got down from the chariot, jumped onto a fine horse, and galloped down the road.

Yang Hu had just heaved a sigh of relief when he heard hoof beats behind him. Turning to look, he found Yue Qi on horseback approaching him. Prodding the horse, he galloped to a nearby hill. The horse stopped before a granite precipice, and he had to dismount and climb up the hill on foot. When Yue Qi came up to the precipice and looked around, Yang Hu shot his last arrow. The arrow whizzed toward Yue Qi's forehead. With a loud cry he dropped from the horse.

Chapter Fourteen

Yang Hu Has a Narrow Escape from Lu to Qi; Duke Jing of Qi Fails to Satisfy the Demand of Duke Ding of Lu

Yang Hu saw that Yue Qi was shot down from his horse. Standing on the precipice over thirty feet high, he let out a roar of laughter. Then, gathering his strength, he leapt down from the precipice. Sword in hand, he dashed toward Yue and brought the sword down on his chest. To his astonishment, Yue sprang up and dodged nimbly.

A moment before, when Yang concealed himself behind the trees and rocks, Yue was unable to see him. So when the arrow came, he acted as if he were wounded in order to induce Yang to come out. Frightened by this unexpected turn of events, Yang fell back a few steps before he collected himself.

Pointing at Yang with his sword, Yue said, "Traitor, come here and prepare to die!"

Yang faltered. He had not realized Yue was so accomplished in martial arts. While preparing to fight, he tried to think of a way of escape, saying, "Don't brag like that. Who knows which of us will be cut down?"

With nothing more to say, Yue struck down with his sword, and Yang raised his sword to ward it off. The two swords clashed, producing sparkles. They fought fiercely, sometimes shielding themselves behind rocks or tree trunks, sometimes leaping onto a tree branch, where they continued their fight.

Knowing that Yue's men might arrive any minute, Yang wanted to fight a quick battle. Giving out an angry roar, he threw himself at Yue who, standing by a big tree, did not fight back but dodged to the left. Yang's sword was caught in the tree trunk, which sent him into a fit. At this Yue came forward to attack, and Yang, having no place to cover himself, leapt onto a tree branch. Eager to gain the final victory, Yue also leapt up, but unfortunately landed on a dead branch, which crashed. He fell to the ground.

Congratulating himself on his good luck, Yang looked up to see his steed grazing under the precipice. He ran over, mounted the horse,

and galloped toward the Qi-Lu border.

Yue had sprained his lower back in his fall. By the time he struggled to his feet, Yang had already passed out of sight.

At this time the soldiers arrived on foot. They helped Yue Qi onto his horse, and he proceeded to the city of Huan, where he joined forces with Shen Juxu. Together they returned to the capital and reported the outcome of the battle to Duke Ding of Lu.

Thereupon Duke Ding had an official letter sent to Duke Jing of Qi asking his assistance in capturing Yang Hu.

Just as the troops of Shen Juxu and Yue Qi were recovering from the battle with Yang Hu, another steward of the Jisun family, Gong-shan Buniu, raised a revolt in the city of Fei. This again plunged the state of Lu into chaos.

In Mengsun Heji's house, Nangong Jingshu was trying to persuade his elder brother to recommend Confucius to Duke Ding for a high official position. He said, "Confucius is widely known for his outstanding virtue, great learning, and faithful devotion to the state and the sovereign. Failure to employ him in the government would only result in ridicule from the common people, disappointment on the part of talented men, and damage to the state, which would then be liable to internal strife and incursions from the outside. At present Yang Hu has fled to Qi, but he might not be reconciled to his defeat and want to effect a comeback, just like dying embers that may glow again. Yesterday Gongshan Buniu revolted in Fei, so we have one trouble following another. This may lead to great catastrophe unless we arrest it as quickly as possible. I hope you will go to the sovereign in the interest of the state and people and, risking his displeasure, insist that he appoint Confucius to an important position. It would be a great blessing for Lu if you should succeed!"

Mengsun sighed, "I know the master well. However, our lord spends all day enjoying wine and dance, and Jisun also indulges himself in merrymaking to the neglect of state affairs. This has enabled traitors like Yang Hu and Gongshan Buniu to exploit the situation to their advantage. If ruler and ministers had worked together with one heart to govern the state, Lu would not have suffered one calamity after another!"

Nangong said in an agitated voice, "Do you mean there is nothing we can do when our state is on the verge of downfall?"

Lowering his head, Mengsun said, "Well, I feel really helpless, with nothing to contribute to our state's welfare and safety!"

"It's precisely because of this that you should recommend people of virtue and talent to high positions," Nangong said.

Mengsun said, "A person who loves money will only become more greedy when he obtains it. Once a person who loves power obtains it, he will never pass it on to someone else!"

Looking perplexed, Nangong said, "Our master's appointment would not necessarily reduce the chief minister's power."

"Jealousy is common to all people, and a narrow-minded person like Jisun is more jealous than others. If the master should take office and achieve great distinction, Jisun would undoubtedly try to play down the master's achievements or even persecute the master ruthlessly."

With his hands behind him and looking up into the sky, Nangong Jingshu sighed deeply. "How difficult it is! There must be nothing more difficult than to really get to know someone." After a pause he added, "So there's nothing we can do but let our master remain like a piece of fine jade buried in the ground?"

"Well..." Mengsun paused for a while then continued, "I will get him appointed magistrate first. If he does well at the post, the sovereign will probably promote him to high office. But it also depends on our master's luck."

Nangong smiled understandably.

Their discussion of the matter concluded, Mengsun set out for the palace to see Duke Ding.

Duke Ding stood facing his court officials, looking haggard and deeply worried.

Mounted scouts brought in reports one after another. "Your Lordship, Gongshan Buniu is heading for the capital with his troops." "Your Lordship, Gongshan Buniu claimed he would capture the capital in ten days."

Glaring in anger, Shen Juxu rubbed his fists, eager to have a fight.

Filled with indignation, Yue Qi was on tenterhooks, ready to leave for battle at any moment.

Duke Ding stood up to speak when Shen said, "Your Lordship, last time the expedition against Yang Hu was not fully successful, so that he was able to escape to Qi. I offer to lead troops to attack Gongshan Buniu, so that I can make amends for my faults."

Yue chimed in, "I am the one to blame for Yang Hu's escape. I ask to be given the chance to atone for my crime by leading troops to attack Gongshan Buniu."

Duke Ding said, "The two of you have led many expeditions and achieved outstanding merits for the state. What fault is there for you to atone for! At present Gongshan Buniu has raised a revolt in Fei, a city of difficult access. If he should achieve victory on the battlefield he would march on to capture the capital. If he suffers defeat, he would probably flee to a neighboring state. Hereby I appoint Shen chief field commander and Yue his deputy. Each with two hundred war chariots under your command, the two of you will set out to attack Gongshan Buniu and recapture Fei. I would be very glad if you catch him alive or have him beheaded. Failing that, you may also consider your task accomplished if you drive him out of Lu."

Shen and Yue knelt' to accept the order. Walking out of the palace, they immediately summoned the troops and set out toward Fei.

There were nothing but hills and downs between the capital and the city of Fei. At the head of the troops, Shen and Yue traveled for a whole day and reached a mountain ridge at twilight. The north wind was fiercely blowing, with a coldness that cut into the bones. They could now see in the distance on the opposite mountain ridge a general's banner embroidered with "Gongshan" in large characters. This was flanked by banners featuring figures of dragon, tiger, snake and bird. Enraged by the sight, Shen swore to himself, "Traitor, I will fight you to the death!"

Eager to give battle, Yue said with a bow, "General, let me attack with a hundred chariots."

"Take it easy, Minister Yue. We have complicated terrain before us, and our men and horses are tired after a long journey. Tonight we'll camp here, and tomorrow morning we can decide our next move after studying the surroundings."

"What if Gongshan Buniu makes a surprise attack?"

"Since we have just arrived, it is unlikely that Gongshan Buniu will take action before he finds out about our strength. We only have to post a lot of sentries and keep a good watch."

Thereupon they made camp on the spot. At dusk the wind grew stronger. Shen hit upon an idea and hurried to Yue's tent.

"General!" Yue sprang to his feet and asked eagerly, "What's on your mind?"

Shen came close to him and whispered, "It is very dark, and the wind is very strong. A perfect time to make a surprise attack."

"But our men are indeed tired, and we have yet to familiarize ourselves with the terrain. To sally forth now would..."

Shen interrupted him, "Don't you worry about it, Minister Yue. To fight at night one must rely on strategy instead of strength. What I have in mind is an attack by fire."

"Oh well, but wouldn't we be killing too many innocent soldiers?"

"There is never too much deception in war, as the ancients taught us. Why are you being so kind-hearted? Gongshan Buniu is a rebel and traitor, and those who obey his command are helping a villain to do evil. If they are burnt to death, they get what they deserve. Moreover, more people would get killed if we engage in battle with them."

"When shall we set out?"

"In the dead of the night, of course."

They selected a hundred crack troops and had plenty of firewood and pine resin collected.

At the third watch of the night Shen called the one hundred soldiers to him and said to them with great determination, "The rebels consider themselves safe behind the barrier of the mountain. You must be brave and resolute. Move to windward of the enemy, light the firewood and resin, then return immediately."

The soldiers replied in a rumbling voice, "Yes!"

Having seen the soldiers off, Shen and Yue stood watching outside the tent. After about an hour, they were greatly relieved to see fire breaking out in many places to the windward of the enemy.

Abetted by the strong wind, the little spots of fire spread rapidly and set the whole place ablaze. The soldiers and horses caught in the fire cried and wailed, many burned to death. The rebels were defeated without a fight, and those who survived the fire fled overnight to the city of Fei.

At daybreak Shen and Yue led their high-spirited troops and set out toward Fei. Having suffered a defeat, Gongshan Buniu had the city gate closed and would not venture out to give battle.

Standing before the city gate, Shen shouted to the rebel soldiers, "Listen, officers and soldiers on the city wall! You are the subjects of our lord, yet instead of rendering your service to the state, you join a rebellion. How do you account for your action?"

Yue drove forth in his chariot and cried, "Think of your parents, wives and children. Why do you obey a traitor like Gongshan Buniu?

If you have him bound up and brought to us, you will remain the subjects of Lu and may choose either to serve under General Shen or return to fulfill your duties to your parents and tend on your wives and children. With the troops here we can capture the city with little effort, by which time all of you will lose your lives. To die or to live —it is up to you quickly to decide!"

A man emerged on the gate tower. He was very thin and shifty-eyed. Taking a close look, Yue found the man to be none other than Gongshan. He bit his teeth and rebuked, "Traitor, surrender! If you fall into my hands I'll tear you to ten thousand pieces!"

Gongshan shaded his eyes with his hand and looked into the distance, paying no attention to Yue's words.

The besiegers and the besieged reached a stalemate.

Mengsun Heji entered the palace when Duke Ding was disposing troops for battle, so he had to wait. After Duke Ding had finished the deployment, Mengsun Heji said, "Your Lordship, Confucius is a very learned person well versed in both the letters and martial arts. Considering our need of talented people in the government, why not employ him?"

Duke Ding looked at the court officials and asked, "My honored ministers, what's your opinion?"

The officials began to think what position could be given to Confucius when Jisun Si interposed, "Your Lordship, as a scholar Confucius is very good at talking about poetry and history and producing elegant pieces of writing. As for serving in the government, he is an amateur."

Mengsun persisted, "Chief Minister, at his youth Confucius proved himself well when he was keeper of granaries and then keeper of livestock."

Jisun retorted, "But that is not exactly the same as serving in the government."

Mengsun realized that Jisun was doing his utmost to prevent Confucius from obtaining an office. It would be futile to argue with him. So he fell silent.

"Let's talk about the matter later. End of the audience!" said the duke.

On his return from the palace, Mengsun described to Nangong what had happened in the court. "There is nothing more I can do. An arm is no match for a leg in strength."

Having told Confucius of the news, Nangong said in consolation, "Master, don't lose heart. Someday our lord will surely give you an important position!"

Confucius forced a smile to his face. "It isn't that easy! People with courage and intelligence being appointed to high positions—such cases have been precious few since the dawn of history. For me there is plenty of work to be done, teaching my students and collating ancient documents. What else do I wish for!"

"The world is being unfair to you, master!" Nangong said with agitation.

"There is no need to blame heaven or other people for one's misfortune. As I said I have work to do."

A man burst into the room. He was in his forties, with a scholar's cap on his head and a whip in one hand, looking neither like a scholar nor a soldier. As Confucius and his disciples looked on, the man saluted with clasped hands, "Minister Gongshan has sent me to call at the master's house. He wants to pay his respects and invite the master to come to Fei to lay plans with him."

Returning the salute, Confucius hesitated for a few moments, then said, "This is something very important. Allow me some time to think it over before I give a reply to Minister Gongshan."

"Very good. I will stay in the inn and await your favorable message." The visitor bowed deeply and left.

Zi Lu grew so angry his eyes were bloodshot. As soon as the visitor walked out the gate, he said to Confucius in a loud voice, "Master, you talk to us about benevolence and righteousness all day. But now you want to serve under an evil man like Gongshan Buniu just because you can not enter the government for the time being. Aren't you afraid of being ridiculed and denounced by the people?"

Confucius was struck speechless and blushed to the roots of his hair. Feeling deep regret, he said to himself, "It is said by the ancients that a dragon only enters clear water, and a phoenix only alights on the parasol tree. How can I waver because of a little frustration?" He turned to Zi Lu and said earnestly, "I was not wrong in regarding you as a good disciple. You are probably the only one who can criticize me so bluntly!"

Zi Lu said, "Don't be offended, master. I made those caustic remarks because I was so disturbed."

By this time Confucius had regained his composure. He said with a smile, "I should consider myself fortunate if other people often point out my errors and mistakes. Why should I take offense?"

Nangong said, "Master, Zi Lu is a careless speaker. Please do not take his words to heart."

Confucius said, "Nangong, even you don't understand me, do you? Though Zi Lu is unpolished, he understands me. Knowing that I would not be offended, he reproved me bluntly. I am fond of him for his frankness, honesty, and purity of mind. Since he became my disciple no one has dared to humiliate me."

Nangong realized then that his anxiety had been unnecessary. He thought for a while and asked tentatively, "Master, let me go to the inn and tell the messenger to return to Gongshan Buniu immediately."

At this Zi Lu said, "Master, let me go to the inn and kill that messenger. That would save us a lot of trouble!"

Confucius put on a stern expression and said, "Don't be so hotheaded! It has been a time-honored rule that one never executes the envoy from an enemy state. That man has come simply to pass on a message from Gongshan; how can you kill him?"

Finding the master's words wholly reasonable, Zi Lu lowered his head and spoke no more.

Confucius then asked Nangong to go to the inn at once and inform the messenger that he would not accept his offer.

When the messenger returned to Fei, it was under siege by Shen Juxu and Yue Qi's troops. He looked on from the distance but failed to find a way to enter the city. So he wrote down the message of Confucius' declination on the shaft of an arrow and, when it got dark, climbed up a mound and shot the arrow onto the city wall.

The arrow was picked up by a sentry and submitted to Gongshan Buniu.

After reading the message on the arrow shaft, Gongshan clenched his teeth and reached a decision. He called all his officers to him and said in a hoarse voice, "We are under siege by Shen Juxu and Yue Qi. If we fight them head-on we would meet certain defeat. Nor can we hold out long if we stay to defend the city. I think the best choice is to break out of the encirclement."

The officers said without much faith, "We will act by your order, Minister Gongshan."

Gongshan briefed his officers on the battle plan, and they left to carry out his order.

In the third watch of the night, the besieging troops launched their attack under a star-lit sky, trying to climb up the city wall by scaling ladders.

All of a sudden the south gate was opened, the suspension bridge lowered, and a band of troops rushed out with loud battle-cries.

Shen and Yue directed the troops to intercept the oncoming enemy, meanwhile sending orders to block all the other city gates lest Gongshan tried to flee through one of them.

A fierce battle ensued. Like cornered beasts, the troops of Fei put up a desperate fight, but they met with strong resistance from the besieging troops. Before long, corpses piled high and blood flowed in streams.

At this moment many of the besieging troops hastened to the east gate, with loud cries of "Give chase!" Gongshan Buniu, who was a great fighter, had just broke out of the east gate single-handedly.

In the darkness Gongshan was fleeing at full speed, pursued by Shen Juxu and Yue Qi. The three horses sped on in the direction of Qi. Knowing that he was no match for the two, Gongshan Buniu turned down a small path. Shen and Yue followed him closely.

Coming to a deep ravine, Gongshan's horse lurched to the right abruptly, and began pacing in circles. Shen and Yue took the chance to approach him and were about to get at him when he galloped downhill. They turned and followed him.

They climbed over downs and hills and crossed some streams, until they came to a valley near the Qi-Lu border. Riding on a frozen river, Gongshan began to feel tired and was gasping for breath. Suddenly the horse tripped and fell, dumping him onto the ice. He slipped for more than thirty feet. He tried several times to get up on his feet, only to fall down again over the slippery ice. Then he saw to his fright that Shen and Yue had reached the river bank. Gathering up all his strength, he finally shuffled his way to the northern bank of the river. He jumped up, drew his sword, and made ready for another fight.

At this moment both Shen and Yue also fell on the surface of the river. Gongshan picked up some fist-sized stones from the ground and threw them at the two men, who rolled on the ice and dodged the shots successfully, to Gongshan's disappointment. He realized that he had better flee, but his horse, having struggled to its feet, was still pausing on the ice. He stamped his feet and called to his horse at the top of his voice. Hearing the familiar voice of its master, the horse raised its head, cocked its ears, and with sudden vigor struggled its way to the northern bank. Gongshan took the rein, mounted the horse, and fled at full speed.

With great difficulty Shen and Yue made their way to the northern bank of the river, and soon were joined by their horses. They mounted the horses and continued their pursuit. However, unlike Gongshan, they were not familiar with the terrain. After making a few turns, Gongshan vanished out of sight. Not knowing which path to take, Shen and Yue stopped to watch. Suddenly they heard the neighing of a horse on Qingshi Pass and saw a mounted figure there. By the time they reached the pass, Gongshan was nowhere to be seen.

Shen was filled with regret. He struck a nearby pine tree with his sword, cutting the thick trunk in two.

Yue beat his chest and sighed, "Well, he has fled to Qi!"

The two of them returned in a mood of great despondence to the city of Fei, where they checked the captives and spoils, then led the troops back to the capital.

Having been informed of the outcome of the battle, Duke Ding of Lu came out to receive them outside the palace.

At the sight of Duke Ding, Shen and Yue hastily dismounted their chariots, walked up in quick steps and knelt before the duke, saying, "Your guilty subjects pay respects to Your Lordship!"

Looking immensely pleased, Duke Ding said with a broad smile, "You have brought peace to the people by wiping out Yang Hu and subduing Gongshan Buniu. I am ready to congratulate your officers and men on their outstanding merits. Why do you talk about being guilty? Please raise yourself and come into the palace so we can talk."

The two of them followed Duke Ding into the palace and gave a brief report on the battle with Gongshan Buniu. Thereupon Duke Ding had an official letter written for an envoy to take to Qi. After that, he ordered Shen and Yue to reward the troops with bounties.

When the Lu envoy reached the Qi court, a palace guard demanded, "Where are you from and what has brought you here?"

The envoy brushed his clothes and said with a bow, "I am a envoy from Lu and I request a meeting with the ruler of your honorable state."

The guard examined him again and asked, "Do you carry a letter with you?"

The envoy said, "Please report to your lord that I have a letter which I must hand to him directly."

The guard returned the salute and told him to wait, then went into the palace to report. The guard was gorgeously dressed and richly ornamented, wearing a sword adorned with a jade piece dangling from the hilt, creating a jingling sound.

In the magnificent palace Duke Jing of Qi sat in his chair, with civil and military officials aligned before him in two ranks.

The palace guard entered and knelt to report, "Your Lordship, an envoy from Lu requests to meet you."

Duke Jing asked with surprise, "Has he brought an official letter?"

The guard said, "He says he would offer it directly to Your Lordship."

Duke Jing frowned and hesitated for a moment, then said in a low voice, "Send him in!"

The guard retreated at once.

Outside the palace the Lu envoy, hearing the summons, adjusted his clothes and entered with a determined step. He passed between lines of armed guards and arrived before Duke Jing. "A humble servant pays respects to Your Lordship," he saluted on his knees.

Duke Jing eyed the well-mannered envoy and asked, "Are you an envoy from Lu?"

"Yes, I am."

"Have you brought a letter from your lord?"

"Yes, I have."

"Pass it to me."

The envoy produced a piece of white silk from inside his sleeve and with both hands raised it high over his head.

Duke Jing took it, spread it out and glanced at it. He said to himself, "Last time the Duke of Lu sent us a letter saying Yang Hu had fled to Qi. Now according to this letter, Gongshan Buniu has also fled to Qi." Turning to look at his officials, he asked, "My honored ministers, have you heard anything of this?"

The officials looked at one another, but none of them said anything.

After a few moments Chief Minister Yan Ying shuffled his way out of the rank and said to the duke, "Your Lordship! It is easy for a man or two to go into hiding in a large state like Qi. In my opinion, we should send men out on a hunt, then inform the Duke of Lu of the result."

Duke Jing's knitted brows became smooth again, and he said hastily, "Yes, that will do." He told the Lu envoy to return to the guesthouse and in the meantime sent some men to investigate the matter. It was then discovered that Yang Hu had already left Qi for Jin; as for Gongshan Buniu, no one seemed to know his whereabouts. Duke Jing had a letter written and gave it to the Lu envoy to take it back to the Duke of Lu.

When he read the letter, Duke Ding of Lu was very displeased. "What? Yang Hu has fled to Jin? So a powerful state like Qi was incapable of capturing a fugitive!"

The court officials, in no position to comment on this, remained silent.

After the audience, Mengsun Heji went to Confucius' house and told him about Yang Hu's flight to Jin.

Confucius gazed into the sky and heaved a deep sigh. "Years ago a man named Qing Fu emerged in Lu and brought numerous troubles. The people of Lu said that Lu would not be free of troubles until Qing Fu's death. Today we have Yang Hu, who has brought calamity to the state and the people. By fleeing to Jin he has taken misfortunes with him. If Zhao Jianzi drives him away, there would be peace. If Zhao lets him stay and appoints him to high office, that would be like welcoming a robber or leading a wolf into the house; there would be no end of troubles in the future."

Mengsun said, "Zhao Jianzi is a man of wisdom and insight. I think he knows what kind of person Yang Hu is and will have no use for him."

Confucius said, "A wolf waving its claws and showing its teeth is indeed fearful, but people will try to kill it or drive it away, knowing it for what it is. But a wolf dressed up like a man is much more dangerous because of its disguise. We may regard Yang Hu as such a wolf!"

Mengsun said, "I can enter the palace and ask the lord to send a letter to Jin requesting its assistance in eliminating this scourge."

Confucius said, "There are different opinions regarding the same person. When I consider someone bad, you may not necessarily agree with me, and vice versa. Yang Hu is a deceitful man endowed with a glib tongue; he can tell lies with great eloquence. It was exactly urged by him that you helped Jisun drive the Duke of Lu to Qi, wasn't it?"

His face flushing with shame, Mengsun said, "I was deceived and took his evil words for truth. Looking back on it, I feel ashamed and hardly dare face my ancestors, the late duke and the people. It will be the regret of a lifetime!"

"All men make mistakes," Confucius comforted him.

"Yes I know, but the consequences of my mistake are grave indeed."

"Let bygones be bygones. The important thing is to focus our attention on the future."

At this juncture Nangong Jingshu appeared and announced with great excitement, "Master, His Lordship invites you to enter the palace as he has a matter to discuss with you."

"Do you know what it concerns?" Confucius asked.

"His Lordship is probably considering an appointment for you."

Confucius' eyes flashed, and he smiled with great pleasure. He went at once to change clothes and left for the palace accompanied by Nangong.

Chapter Fifteen

**Confucius Governs Zhongdu Well by Punishing
Profiteers and Eliminating Outdated Customs;
The People Build Water Conservancy Projects
and Subsequently Enjoy a Bumper Harvest**

Jisun Si had suffered continuous setbacks since he became chief
minister. Repeatedly urged by Mengsun Heji, he finally agreed to make
Confucius his household steward and prepared to recommend him as
magistrate of the city of Zhongdu. Duke Ding of Lu consented readily
and bade Nangong Jingshu invite Confucius to the palace. Always
eager to serve in the government, Confucius was overjoyed as he set
out for the palace.

Duke Ding stood up to receive him as Confucius entered the rear
palace.

Confucius saluted to Duke Ding and, after the duke had sat down,
knelt and kowtowed in obeisance, then took his seat.

Duke Ding looked thin and languid. He said in a listless voice,
"Master, you are a sage known far and wide for your great learning. I
intend to appoint you magistrate of Zhongdu. What do you think of
it?"

Confucius got up and kowtowed again. "Thank you, Your Lordship, for this great favor!"

Duke Ding said, "You may raise yourself." When Confucius had
returned to his seat, he continued, "Zhongdu is a piece of flat, very
fertile land. However, it has been suffering from disorder because of
ill-government by its former magistrates. When you take office, you
must manage it to the best of your ability. If you achieve distinction,
I will give you a more important position."

Confucius said, "I was born and raised in Lu. It is my duty to
render my service to our state. I will never forget your favor and your
instruction."

As if a great burden had been lifted off him, Duke Ding felt a
deep relief and asked in a spirited voice, "How do you plan to manage
Zhongdu?"

With great assurance Confucius replied, "I will educate the people in the ways of the ancient kings, so that they treat their parents with filial piety, their elder brothers with proper respect, and their friends with honesty and faithfulness. There will be proper sequence among juniors and superiors, the men and women will fulfill their respective duties of tilling the field and weaving cloth, the merchants will be fair and honest in their dealings, ..."

"Well, well," interrupted Duke Ding with excitement. "My honored subject, you are indeed a man of great learning, talking with such eloquence! You may choose an auspicious day on which to take office."

It was spring, when tender sprouts began to appear in willows and poplar trees in the breeze. One day in the ninth year of Duke Ding of Lu's reign (501 B.C.) Confucius, having bade farewell to his wife and children, mounted his chariot and set out for Zhongdu in the company of a few disciples.

Zhongdu was ninety li from the capital of Lu. In his excitement Confucius traveled fifty li and entered the jurisdiction of Zhongdu without feeling the slightest fatigue.

Zi Lu, dressed in an old sheepskin overcoat, was driving the chariot. His forehead streaming with perspiration, he threw open the overcoat and slowed his pace. Yan Hui, who was small and thin, was also sweating under his cotton-padded coat and gradually fell behind the chariot. The others, including Min Shun, Ran Geng, Qin Shang, Zeng Dian and Qidiao Kai, had all taken off their cotton-padded coats and flung them over their shoulders. Sitting in the chariot, Confucius gazed ahead, many thoughts flashing across his mind. In a high, upright poplar tree two magpies were leaping about and chirping merrily, as if offering their congratulations to Confucius and his disciples. Though he did not believe in good or ill omens,* Confucius was nevertheless pleased at the sight of the magpies and listening to their joyful twittering. He looked up and saw an eagle flying around high in the sky among the clouds. He was filled with all kinds of emotions. He reviewed his life in his mind, his humble origin, the frustrations he had encountered, the decline of Lu, and the internal struggle in the court. He thought of the fatuousness of Duke Ding, the incompetence of the chief minister, the power struggle among officials,

---

*The chirping of a magpie was taken for a good omen by Chinese in the old days.

and the sufferings of the common people. He could hardly remember how much ridicule and rebuke as well as praise and recommendation he had received. He forced himself to snap out of his reminiscences and concentrate on the present and look into the future. The present situation was just like the road under his feet, bumpy and tortuous. As for the future, he had already worked out several blueprints for governing Zhongdu, appropriate for the need of a small change, a big change, or an overall change in the city. He opted for the most radical plan, intending to experiment with his political ideals in Zhongdu.

When they came to a fork in the road with several restaurants and wineshops Confucius said to Zi Lu, "How about having lunch here?"

"I've been feeling hungry for some time already. Wait till I find a good place for us." Zi Lu went and arranged a meal for the company.

They were about to set out again after lunch when a magnificent chariot came from the west. When it approached the restaurants, the driver stopped the two horses, and a handsome youth dismounted. He was medium in stature and well-built, with an elliptical face, dark eyebrows and big eyes. Dressed in a light lambskin coat and silk boots, he looked extremely elegant. Confucius and his disciples marveled at the sight of him. Looking disdainful, Zi Lu cocked his head and sneered, "Humph! A dandy from a wealthy family out to swindle and bluff!"

Confucius reprimanded him in a low voice, "Don't judge people by appearance only!"

Instead of entering one of the restaurants, the youth came up to Confucius, bowed politely, and asked in a soft voice, "May I venture to ask if the elder before me is Confucius?"

Surprised, Confucius looked at the man closely but did not recognize him. "I am Kong Qiu from Lu," he said. "And you ..."

The young man dropped on his knees and said, "I am from the state of Wei. My family name is Duanmu, my given name Ci, and my styled name Zi Gong. Having learned of your great fame, I was going to the Lu capital to study with you. It is my good fortune to meet you here unexpectedly."

Addressing Duanmu Ci by his given name, Confucius said, "Raise yourself, then we can talk."

Zi Gong got up and, without taking the time to brush off the dust from his dress, exchanged greetings with Zi Lu, Min Shun, Yan Hui and the rest of the company. He then asked in a low voice, "Where are you heading for with the master?"

Zi Lu, who had changed his attitude to Zi Gong because of the latter's gracious manners, said, "The Lu ruler has appointed the master as the magistrate of Zhongdu. We are on the way to his office."

Zi Gong said with another bow, "Congratulations, master!"

Confucius said, "Duanmu Ci, since you have become my disciple, you may accompany me to my office."

Zi Gong said "Yes" and, not delaying to have lunch, invited his fellow disciples to mount his chariot and set out after Confucius.

Arriving at the magistrate's office at Zhongdu, Confucius immediately put his plans into effect. Officials who were honest and law-abiding were promoted, those who lacked ability were deprived of their posts, and those who had made private gains by taking advantage of their positions were thrown into prison.

After this the office took on a new look. Confucius then appointed some of his disciples to serve under him. The local gentry began to treat him with increased respect.

Confucius was anxious to learn something of the customs and social conditions at Zhongdu. One day, after sending his disciples out to gather information, he changed into plain clothes and left his office. Walking along a small lane, he was saddened by the sight of broken walls and dilapidated houses everywhere. Just then he heard someone cursing in a hoarse voice. He went up and saw over a half crumbling earthen wall a middle-aged man standing in the courtyard, knife in hand, cursing loudly at a skinned goat on a chopping board. Finding it strange, Confucius coughed slightly and, pushing open the low wooden door, walked into the courtyard. After greeting the man he asked, "Why are you shouting angrily at a dead goat?"

The man looked strong and well-built. With a thump he planted the knife on the board and, after making a casual gesture of greeting, replied, "You don't understand. People used to be honest in Zhongdu, making fair deals and not taking advantage of children or the elderly. But in recent years the morals have got worse and worse. Take my trade, for instance. Since Shenyou Shi started selling goats, numerous people have been cheated by him."

"Who is Shenyou Shi? And how dare he act so unscrupulously?"

The man examined Confucius again, then said, "You did not look like a native of this place."

Confucius smiled and nodded.

"Shenyou Shi came from an ordinary family in Zhongdu. Three years ago he began trading in live goats. He purchased goats at a low price and fed them with salted fodder for a couple of days. The goats got very thirsty eating this kind of fodder and began to drink plenty of water. Then he drove them to the market. The buyers, not knowing what he had done, liked his goats for being so plump and competed with each other to buy them. I never went and bought goats from him. But yesterday, when I happened to be out, my family bought this goat from him. Look!" He pointed to the goat on the chopping board. "Water is dripping from the mutton."

Confucius went up for a closer look, then asked, "If Shenyou Shi is such a wicked person, why hasn't anyone come up to accuse him and have him punished?"

The man looked around and lowered his voice. "At present Shenyou Shi can really give himself airs! With his ill-gotten wealth he has ingratiated himself with some officials and thus become a local tyrant. There is no one in Zhongdu who dares to challenge him!"

Confucius nodded understandingly, then asked, "Which official does he have connection with?"

The man looked around again and whispered, "It is Cheng Bi, a runner of the former magistrate. He backed Shenyou Shi up, and in return for that Shenyou Shi bribed him heavily. The two of them work hand in glove and ride roughshod in the city." He paused for a moment, then continued. "I heard a new magistrate has been appointed. His name is Kong Qiu. Now this is a remarkable man! As soon as he took office, he dealt all those corrupt runners a head-on blow. Even Cheng Bi was said to have been thrown into prison. Fantastic, don't you think? However, Shenyou Shi has become so used to his dishonest trade that he continues to cheat and exploit others even after he lost his backer. Well, it is rightly said by the ancients that money can gain one access to the gods. Maybe Magistrate Kong has already been bribed by Shenyou Shi. People always show respect for the rich, and even dogs only bite the poor." He noticed that Confucius had turned yellow in the face, so he pointed to a stump and said, "I have talked for so long without asking you to take a seat. Please do not be offended."

"You are being too kind. Thanks so much for treating an uninvited visitor with such sincerity. I must take my leave now."

After Confucius had returned to his magistrate's office, his disciples also came back one after another to report what they had found out. Zi Lu said, "Master, I paid a visit to a gentleman called Liang Cai. According to him, there are three things that are most abominable in Zhongdu. First, Shenyou Shi sells live goats fed with salted fodder; it's the same as filling mutton with water. Second, Gongshen Shi, the son from a scholar's family, has married a beautiful and wanton woman named Qi, who has an affair with someone. Third, a wealthy man named Shenkui Shi has violated the rites by celebrating his family weddings with music in the hall and dance in the courtyard, a privilege only a crown prince is entitled to."

Zi Gong said, "I heard many people talk about Shenyou Shi's behavior in the market. As for the other two things, I have heard nothing about them."

Confucius asked the other disciples, who gave the same reply as Zi Gong.

The following day happened to be a big market day in Zhongdu. Confucius went to the pork and mutton market accompanied by Zi Lu and Zi Gong. Looking around, they saw a man displaying a group of goats. He was short, stout, with a bald head and a creamy face covered with whiskers. Walking to and fro, he shouted, "Look at my goats! Every one of them is plump and fat. Mutton is a good thing indeed. If you eat mutton and drink mutton soup in winter, you will feel warm in your heart. If you eat mutton and drink mutton soup in summer, you will feel cool. If you eat mutton and drink mutton soup in spring and autumn, you will feel more comfortable than ever."

Zi Gong, born into a merchant's family in the twenty-second year of Duke Zhao of Lu (520 B.C.), was then only nineteen years old. His upbringing had imparted good business acumen to him and made him an eloquent talker. Standing among the prospective buyers, he suddenly asked, "Sir, could you tell us what else is so special about your goats?"

Shenyou Shi gave a little start. He glanced at Zi Gong and said with irritation, "Don't you have eyes? Can't you see for yourself what is special about my goats?"

Being quick-tempered, Zi Lu got angry at the caustic remark. Taking a step forward, he said in a loud voice, "All we can see is the skin of these goats. Who knows what it's like inside the skin?"

Touched on the raw, Shenyou retorted angrily, "Are you saying I have instilled water into the live goats?"

Zi Gong said, "Whether you have done it or not depends on your conscience."

Zi Lu added, "No one knows better than you whether you have done something wrong."

His trick exposed, Shenyou put on a ferocious expression and roared, "If you want to buy my goats, come and buy them. If you don't want to buy, go away at once! I have no time to waste with you!"

Walking up to him, Confucius said in a quiet tone, "Have you never heard of the saying, 'Polite manners lead to wealth'? As a merchant, why do you have to get so angry over such a trivial matter?"

Under the calm gaze of Confucius, Shenyou felt a little daunted, knowing that the man before him was not to be taken lightly. He said in a less agitated voice, "Sir, didn't you hear how they abused me?"

"If you have not instilled water to the goats, why should you be so touchy about it?"

"So you also suspect me?"

"Since you are offended by other people's suspicion, why not prove on the spot that your goats have not been filled with water? Come on, I'll buy a goat and have it butchered as a test!"

Shenyou felt himself cornered. He curled himself up and squatted on the ground, not saying anything.

Confucius bade Zi Lu take out a silver ingot and put it before Shenyou. He said to the onlookers, "I heard that Shenyou has fed these goats with salted fodder, so they must have drunk a lot of water, from five or six to over a dozen catties each. Now I want to have a test on the spot. If any of you would do me a favor by selecting a goat and slaughtering it, I will pay for the goat."

Plucking up his courage, Shenyou sprang to his feet, shouting, "Sir, we have no grudge against one another. You cannot treat me like this!"

Confucius said, "But I must have a test."

Shenyou extended his arms and showed his fists, as if ready for a hand-fight.

Ignoring him, Confucius turned to the onlookers and asked, "Who wants to help?"

Zi Lu, growing impatient, repeated the question, "Who wants to help?"

A sturdy man in his forties came up and said in a loud voice, "Let me be the butcher!"

On closer look, Confucius recognized him as the man he met

yesterday. The man borrowed a knife from a meat counter nearby, took one of the goats, and slaughtered it with great dexterity. After weighing the butchered goat, he placed it on the chopping board. At once water began to drip from the cuts. After about an hour he weighed it again and found it had lost six catties. Ripples of murmured comments ran through the crowd, and Shenyou Shi became the target of common denunciation. "You are dead to all sense of shame!" "You will come to no good end, cheating people like this!"

Confucius, taking a quick decision, addressed the people, "Shenyou Shi has traded in live goats for many years. If he did his business honestly, he would deserve encouragement. However, he fed the goats with salted fodder and made them drink a lot of water. If a goat purchased from him is not slaughtered in five days, it will die. He must be severely punished for cheating people, otherwise there would be no hope of ridding the market of profiteers like him. Furthermore he has aligned himself with corrupt officials to bully and suppress the people. Thus I, the new magistrate, decides to fine him five hundred taels of silver, to be submitted in ten days. One day's delay will be punished by an increase of ten taels to the total sum. Shenyou Shi, do you have any objection to this?"

Shenyou was dumbfounded. Bending forward, he walked up to Confucius, fell on his knees and kowtowed repeatedly. "I had eyes but failed to see Mount Tai. Please forgive me for offending you! Your charges against me are all sound. I plead guilty."

By this time a large crowd had gathered around them, listening attentively when Confucius continued to speak. "If you want to trade in live goats in the future, you must do honest business and treat the people fairly. You must not attempt again to bribe the officials in order to suppress the people. If you should be found guilty of such actions, there would be severe punishment for you! Now go back and prepare to pay the fine!"

Then, amid murmurs of appreciation among the crowd, Confucius left for his office accompanied by his two disciples.

Back in the magistrate's office, Confucius bade Yan Hui write an announcement recounting how Shenyou Shi had fed goats with salted fodder, for which he was fined five hundred taels of silver, and exhorting merchants to do business honestly and deal with all customers fairly. The announcement was copied on pieces of white silk and put up on the four gates of the city. After that Confucius went on to deal with the other two affairs mentioned by Liang Cai.

He could find no easy solutions for the two affairs. Qi, the unchaste woman, had offended public decency. Shenkui, relying on his wealth, had usurped princely rituals at wedding ceremonies in his household. Both of them had violated the rules of proper behavior, but neither had broken the law, so that the authorities actually did not have the power to intervene. He thought for a long time but failed to find a good solution, so he called his disciples to him and asked their opinions.

Zi Lu suggested, "Nothing can be easier. I'll go and tell Gongshen to write a certificate of divorce and send Qi home. As for Shenkui's violation of the rites, it just shows he has more money than he can spend properly. Won't it be nice if we fine him a large sum and use it for defence expenses?"

"But since Gongshen has not come to our office to place a complaint, it is not suitable for us to deal with the matter directly."

"But we can't let her go on in this way!"

"We have to think about it. Gongshen has been kept in the dark about his wife's affair. Even if he learns about it, he may not want to make it public. As for Shenkui's violation of the rites, if we impose a forfeit without justification, he is sure to feel unconvinced."

"We can wait till another wedding takes place in Shenkui's household, then intervene," proposed Zi Gong.

"This is a good solution, but it would take a long time to carry it out. We cannot afford to wait so long if we want to fight extravagance."

Yan Hui said, "Master, since Shenkui's family is very wealthy, we can order him to pay a large sum to subsidize the government's military expenses. In this way we can both contribute to the state treasury and check extravagance."

Confucius nodded his appreciation, then asked, "And what do you propose to do about Qi?"

"We may have a children's rhyme composed about Qi's misconduct. In three days Gongshen will hear about it, and then he will surely divorce her."

"Can you write the rhyme?"

Gazing up at the ceiling for a while, Yan Hui chanted, "In the city of Zhongdu something bad has happened. In Gongshen's family, the wife has lost her chastity. The husband will have to send her home quickly, if he wants to wipe off the shame."

Quite satisfied, Confucius let Yan Hui write down the rhyme on a piece of silk and had it taught to children in the street. Then he bade Zi Gong write a letter and had it sent to Shenkui's house.

A few days later Shenyou paid in the forfeit of five hundred taels. Gongshen, sure enough, divorced his wife, Qi. The Shenkui family handed in three thousand taels of silver as military expenses.

One day Confucius went out with his disciples to observe the peasants till their field. He climbed to a small hill in the south of the city and looked around. The ground had cracked because of dryness, and dust was flying everywhere. He went on to visit some more places and saw similar sights. Having gathered enough information, he returned to his office.

Confucius ordered the runners to invite five highly regarded peasants to his office and treated them as honored guests. He asked in a respectful voice, "Could you tell me how to prevent the field from cracking?"

The peasants replied in unison, "By using water."

Confucius smiled and asked, "But where can we find water, and how can we lead it to irrigate the field?"

One peasant said, "Zhongdu consists mostly of flat land, so it is not difficult to dig wells here. By digging plenty of wells, we will no longer worry about the lack of water in the field."

Confucius asked again, "If it is not difficult to dig wells, why haven't people already done it?"

Another peasant replied, "Due to military conscription there aren't enough able-bodied laborers left in the villages. In addition, the heavy tax makes us peasants live in poverty, without enough food or clothing. We all long to go to another place, and are reluctant to make the efforts to dig wells to water the fields. It is only our attachment to our humble home that has kept us here."

Confucius suddenly saw the light. "Are there any big rivers or hills in Zhongdu?" he asked.

One peasant replied, "Thirty li to the north there is a big river called Wenshui. It originates from Mount Tai, and its sweet and clear water is most suitable for irrigating the fields. There are a lot of low hills about twenty li to the north."

Confucius was not unfamiliar with the Wenshui River, but he had not realized its vicinity to Zhongdu. He said excitedly, "I intend to appoint the five of you to head a project to dig wells and ditches, which can be used for irrigation when we have a drought and for drainage in case of flood. What do you think?"

The peasants replied in unison, "Honorable sir, who does not want a better life? But with our stomach barely half filled, we don't really have the strength for the project."

Confucius said, "I'll ask permission from His Lordship to open the state granaries to feed all famished peasants."

Prostrating themselves, the peasants said, "You have given us a second life! Thanks Heaven, Zhongdu will be saved!"

The following day Confucius and his disciples went to the Wenshui River. Even in the dry season the river had strong currents. Willows grew on both banks of the river. Beside the river there ere many densely populated villages, which showed signs of prosperity with the crowing of chickens, the barking of dogs, the neighing of horses, and the braying of donkeys. Confucius said to himself, "Water! Water is the source of cultivated fields, crops and prosperity!"

From a forest by the river came the cries of turtledoves which, intermingled with the babbling of the river, sounded exceptionally pleasing and harmonious. Confucius remarked, "Turtledoves! Their cries signify the time for sowing the five crops."*

On his way back to the office, Confucius saw many tracts of field that had been tilled but that they were too dry for planting. Those that had not been tilled had cracked. He decided to ask permission from Duke Ding to open the granaries to relieve the starving peasants. Then he would use the forfeits paid by Shenyou and Shenkui to subsidize poor peasants so that they could buy farm tools and irrigation equipment. He would also organize the peasants to dig wells and ditches and lead the Wenshui River to irrigate the dry fields.

Back in his office, he described his plan to his disciples, who all expressed their admiration. He wrote a memorial and had it sent to the capital. To his great joy Duke Ding granted his request. He carried out his plan step by step. The peasants, having received relief food and bought farm tools with subsidies, set to work vigorously digging wells and ditches. In spring that year Lu suffered a severe drought, and people in many places found it impossible to grow any crops. In Zhongdu, however, seeds were sown on time, and before long the fields were a delightful green.

---

* Rice, two kinds of millet, wheat and beans.

Confucius went on next to rectify social order. In three months the general mood of society took on a remarkable change. In the market one could find high-quality goods at reasonable prices, and even children and the elderly were in no danger of being cheated by the merchants. People conducted themselves according to the rites and had a strong sense of honor, treating their elders with respect and their juniors with loving kindness. Pleased with what he had achieved, Confucius wrote an announcement giving detailed instructions on people's daily lives. The announcement said, "Elders and juniors must eat separately, and the strong and the weak be given different tasks. Men and women must walk in separate paths and not touch in giving or receiving. Do not pick up things others lost, or adorn daily utensils with carvings. The inner coffin should be four inches thick, and the outer coffin five. Build graves by the hills, and do not erect memorial tablets for the dead. All residents of Zhongdu must abide by the above rules." After the announcement was put up, it achieved the desired effect. Half a year later there was such an improvement in society that people no longer had to lock their gates at night.

In summer that year, when heavy rains resulted in a flood, Confucius ordered his disciples and the runners to supervise the peasants to drain off the flood and prevent waterlogging. When autumn came they had a bumper harvest of the five crops, and all the granaries were filled to the brim. The peasants held Confucius in great awe and admiration, regarding him as a living god. Whenever he made an announcement or issued an order, they carried it out without the least hesitation.

In order to provide for the vagrants Confucius bade wealthy families invest in handicraft mills, which employed men to make pottery and melt bronze and women to weave cotton and silk. The wares and cloth they produced were sold to various states, including Qi, Wei, Jin, Zheng, Wu, and Chu. Zhongdu became a prosperous business site, with merchants coming from far and near.

Confucius was very pleased with the situation. One day he and his disciples were discussing plans for further improvement of Zhongdu, when a runner came in to announce some visitors.

Confucius said, "Invite them to come in!" He stood up and went to the door to receive the guests.

The runner returned with three young men. They wore cotton-padded clothes and carried parcels on their backs. Reaching the steps before the door, they put down their parcels and knelt. "Disciples pay respect to the master!" They chorused.

"Where are you from, and what are your names?" asked Confucius.

A tall and handsome young man replied, "My family name is Bi, my given name Buqi, and my styled name Zi Jian. I am a native of Lu."

Another young man, who was of medium height and had bright, shining eyes, said, "My family name is Wuma, my given name Shi, and my styled name Zi Qi. I come from the state of Chen."

The third youth, who was very short and looked homely with his small face, small nose, and small eyes, said in a surprisingly sonorous voice, "My family name is Gao, my given name Cai, and my styled name Zi Gao. I am from Qi. I met these two brothers on the way, and have come with them to study from the master."

Confucius said, "Raise yourselves and let us talk."

They entered the room and took seats. Confucius introduced them to Zi Lu and the other disciples, then asked their ages. The three of them happened to be born in the same year and were all twenty years old.

Confucius could not help feeling satisfied, having done well both in his official post and teaching career. Just then a runner came in and cried, "An edict from the lord!" Not knowing whether it was good or bad news, Confucius hurried out to receive the edict.

Chapter Sixteen

Confucius Becomes Minister of Justice and
Resolves a Dispute Between Father and Son;
He Recommends Two Disciples to Be Stewards
at the Chief Minister's House

With both hands Confucius took a piece of yellow silk from the messenger, opened it, and read the following: "Honored Subject Kong: I have learned of your outstanding achievements in Zhongdu in the past year and intend to promote you to an important office. Return immediately to the capital."

Holding the piece of silk in his hands, Confucius was overcome with exhilaration. In his mind's eye the yellow silk resembled a golden bridge leading to the capital and to his political dream. He muttered to himself, "The rites of Zhou will be restored and the Duke of Zhou will smile in heaven!" Restraining his excitement, he said to his disciples, "His Lordship has ordered me to return to the capital. Dispose of the affairs at hand, then bundle up your baggage and prepare to leave with me!"

Confucius bade Zi Gong take the messenger to the guest-house and keep him company, and returned to his room to prepare for departure. In his room there were stacks upon stacks of bamboo slips and silk. In the past year he lived apart from his family and had only his disciples and these books for company. He began packing the books and in the meanwhile looked back to the year's experience of running the city of Zhongdu. What he had achieved so far, he decided, relied largely on knowledge gained from these books, and for this reason he treasured them even more than before.

That night he turned and tossed in bed, unable to sleep, for he had so many things to think about. Zhongdu had changed a lot, but that was only the beginning. He wished he could stay on to govern it for several more years until his political ideal was completely realized here. However, Duke Ding's promise of an important office in the government appealed to him even more. What he wanted to do was the complete restoration of the rites of Zhou in the whole world, and

he was not to let such a good opportunity slip by. Looking into the future, he envisaged three steps for his career. First he would help Duke Ding govern the state of Lu well. Second, he would persuade the other vassal states to follow suit. Third, he would help the King of Zhou implement the rites of Zhou all over the country, thereby setting up an ideal social order.

When the roosters had crowed three times he got up and walked to the door. When he saw his disciples putting baggage onto the chariot, he felt at once sad and joyous.

In early dawn a big crowd gathered before the gate of the magistrate's office. There were members of the local gentry, merchants and common people coming to see him off, bringing presents of chicken eggs, dried meat, dates, silk, and bronze wares. They did not speak, but their eyes were brimming with tears of gratitude and regret.

At the sight of this Confucius felt a pain in his chest, and tears welled up in his eyes.

As soon as they saw him, people thronged forth to offer their presents. At the head of them was a grey-haired old man, who raised a basket of eggs high above his head, saying, "Honored sir, this is a token of thanks from your humble subject. By all means accept it!" The others also insisted on offering their presents while uttering words of deep gratitude.

"Elder!" Confucius choked on his words. "Please, I really appreciate your kindness, but cannot accept your present."

"But these are tokens of our highest regard!" shouted the crowd. Standing on the terrace, Confucius did not know what to say. Just then Zi Lu arrived with the chariot. Confucius hastily mounted the chariot and with clasped hands bade the people good-bye. The street was lined up with people, who had come to see him off with their smiles and tears. He sometimes waved his hands, and sometimes bowed with clasped hands, offering his thanks to the people for their kindness. When the chariot finally rumbled out the south gate, he found to his surprise that another crowd of people had gathered there to bid him farewell. He dismounted from the chariot and addressed them in a loud voice, "I have done very little and do not really deserve your kindness. Please return to the city!" With this he bowed several times and got up his chariot, turning to wave good-bye to the people.

On his return to the capital, Confucius went directly to the palace to see the duke and thank him for his great favor.

Duke Ding was in the best of moods. "You really have exceptional abilities to have governed Zhongdu so well in less than a year. Can you tell me how you achieved such remarkable results?"

"Relying on the authority of the King of Zhou and Your Lordship, I implemented the rites set up by the Duke of Zhou and made simple changes beneficial to the common people."

Duke Ding asked tentatively, "Can Lu be governed well by the same practice?"

Confucius replied with great assurance, "The important thing is to implement the rites and rules established by the Duke of Zhou, educate the people in ways of proper conduct, and act in the best interests of the people. In this way not only Lu but the entire world can be governed well."

"Excellent!" exclaimed Duke Ding. "I intend to appoint you as Minister of Construction. What do you think of it?"

"The Minister of Construction has the vital task of supervising on the one hand the planning, design and construction of temples, palace buildings and the capital, and on the other hand the construction and maintenance of roads and bridges. What he does is all for the benefit of the state and the people. I will do my best to fulfill my duties in return for your favor!"

"At the audience tomorrow morning I shall inform the court officials of my decision."

Confucius kowtowed his thanks and returned home.

It was the beginning of the tenth year of Duke Ding of Lu's reign (500 B.C.). Confucius met and exchanged greetings with Lady Qiguan, Kong Li, Wuwei and the disciples who had stayed in the capital. He went to bed early that night. The following day Confucius took office as the Minister of Construction. Apart from fulfilling his official duties, he continued to teach his disciples.

Among his many disciples, Confucius found Yan Hui and Zi Gong to be very exceptional. Being quiet in disposition, Yan Hui never made casual remarks. Zi Gong, on the other hand, was an eloquent speaker. One day, after Confucius explained the poem "Big Rats" from *The Book of Poetry*, the disciples asked many questions. Yan Hui, however, was lost in thought and did not venture to speak. Confucius had noticed that Yan Hui had studied tirelessly all day but had seldom made any inquiry about what he learned. When asked a question, however, he could always come up with a very good answer.

On one occasion Confucius said to Zi Gong, "Yan Hui never disagrees with me even when we talk for a whole day. He seems to be slow. But when he studies on his own, he not only understands fully but is also quite creative. He is not slow at all."

"What kind of person am I then?" Zi Gong asked.

Confucius thought for a while, then replied, "You can be compared to a vessel."

"What vessel?"

"A vessel for holding grains on grand ceremonies."

Quite pleased, Zi Gong turned to leave, but was stopped by Confucius, who said to him, "You must realize that a superior man should not be like a vessel, which can be used only for a single purpose."

"Master, how can one become a superior man?"

"Do more and talk less. Before you talk about something you advocate, do it first. In this way you can become a superior man."

Knowing that Confucius was referring to his verbosity and impulsiveness, Zi Gong said with a blush, "I understand."

Confucius was very pleased with the progress his disciples were making. He devoted much of his attention to his official duties and soon achieved great distinction. Duke Ding then appointed him to Minister of Justice.

In his new position Confucius was responsible for exterminating rebels and bandits, arbitrating quarrels among the people, and meting out punishments for criminals. On the third day after he took office Confucius was leafing through the documents when two people ran into the hall, crying and screaming, the gatemen having failed to stop them.

Confucius looked up with surprise and saw two men grappling their way to his desk. One was about forty and the other some fifteen or sixteen. Their hair disheveled, and with mud all over their bodies, they each knelt before him and cried, "Your Excellency, please uphold justice on my behalf!"

"Who are you?" asked Confucius, looking them up and down. "Why are you quarreling like that?"

The older man said, "Your Excellency, this is my son, who was spoiled by his mother in his childhood. He does neither farm work nor housework. Since his mother's death I have become busier than ever, yet he continues to idle about and does no decent work. This morning

I tried to persuade him to go work in the field. Instead of doing what I said, he hit me. That's why I have seized him and brought him here. Please back me up!"

The boy said, "My father is very unreasonable. All he has done is rebuke me or beat me. Look!" He tore open his shirt and exposed many bruises. "This is what he did to me!"

Confucius asked, "What are your names?"

The father said, "My name is Hu Jue, and he is Hu Qian. We live to the northeast of the capital. Our family has tilled the field for generations."

Pointing to the bruises on Hu Qian's chest, Confucius asked, "Did you cause these bruises?"

Hu Jue patted his swollen cheeks and said, "Your Excellency, just look what he did to me!"

Confucius asked in a stern voice, "Hu Qian, why do you idle about and not help your father with the farmwork?"

His head drooping, Hu Qian said nothing.

Confucius asked again, "Hu Jue, why did you not reason with your son but beat him so often?"

Hu Jue lowered his head with nothing to say.

It was very quiet in the hall. Confucius racked his brains but failed to come up with a good solution. When he happened to look out and saw some swallows flying about catching insects, it suddenly occurred to him that there was a swallows' nest under the eaves of the prison. He put on a stern expression and said severely, "The father does not act like a father, and the son does not act like a son. This is really outrageous! Runners!"

Four runners came up to the hall and said, "Here!"

Confucius said, "Put the ill-bred father and son into prison!"

Hu Jue and Hu Qian stared with disbelief, then shouted that they were wronged.

Ignoring them, Confucius swept his hand, and the four runners grabbed Hu Jue and Hu Qian and shoveled them into prison.

Confucius sent for the prison warden and told him in a low voice, "Take good care of them and give them enough to eat and drink. If possible, draw their attention to the swallow-nest under the eaves."

The warden received the order in great puzzlement.

Confucius, feeling confident, went on to read the documents.

Hu Jue and Hu Qian, hoping for a just settlement of their dispute, did not expect to be thrown into prison. Filled with anxiety and indignation, they squatted in separate corners of the prison cell and sulked. They found it hard to comprehend why the Minister of Justice, who was universally praised for his ability and benevolence, could have dealt with their case in such a way.

At lunch time the warden brought them the meal and placed it outside the door, calling Hu Jue and Hu Qian to come out to eat. They sat on the ground and, opening the rice basket and broth pot, saw to their surprise very good cooked rice and meat broth. They became even more puzzled than before.

Just then swallows twittered in the nest under the eaves. Hu Jue and Hu Qian looked up to see a swallow standing on the brim of the nest feeding its young. Five fledglings, with their mouth wide open, received food from the big swallow. Running out of food, the big swallow flew away, and another big swallow, which had been waiting nearby, flew to the nest and started feeding. By the time it finished, the first swallow came back with more food. Thus the two swallows took turns feeding their young, not resting for a moment.

At the sight of this Hu Jue recalled with a pang the hardships he had gone through bringing up his son. The scene of the two swallows feeding their young also made Hu Qian realize how much his parents had done for him. He began to feel guilty and to blame himself. Breaking into tears, he cried, "Father, I am worse than a beast!" He fell on his knees before Hu Jue. "Punish me! Beat me! Rebuke me!"

At this Hu Jue also started sobbing.

Hu Qian shuffled toward the warden and begged, "My father has done nothing wrong; I am the one to blame. Please let my father go! Only I deserve to be imprisoned!"

The prison warden came to realize what Confucius had intended to achieve. He ran up the hall and reported, "Your Excellency, Hu Qian has admitted he was in the wrong. He is weeping in remorse. What shall we do?"

Pleased by the news, Confucius said, "I'll go and take a look."

He followed the warden to the prison, where Hu Jue and Hu Qian were weeping loudly, cupping their heads with their hands. Confucius asked, "Hu Qian, have you realized your mistake?"

"Yes, I have."

"What is it?"

"I was ungrateful and would not repay the kindness of my

parents."

"What do you propose to do in the future?"

"I'll mend my ways and turn over a new leaf in my life."

Confucius then asked Hu Jue, "Hu Jue, do you realize your mistake?"

"Yes, I do."

"What is it?"

"I failed to teach my son properly."

Confucius said, "If the son is ill-bred, the father is to blame. Well, you may get up!"

Then he continued, "In observance of the rites, the old should treat the young with loving kindness, and the young should treat the old with respect. What a shame when the old do not love the young and the young do not respect the old, the way you used to be!" After a pause, he said, "Now that you have both realized your mistakes, I'll let you return home. Do not make the same mistakes ever again!"

With tears of gratitude Hu Jue and Hu Qian kowtowed repeatedly to Confucius, then returned home together.

The incident caused a sensation in the state of Lu, and people all admired Confucius for his outstanding wisdom. When Confucius entered the palace the following day to attend the morning audience, Jisun Si accosted him at the gate and asked bluntly, "Minister of Justice, you once mentioned that to govern a state well, filial piety must be advocated. Having violated the rule of filial piety by suing against each other, Hu Jue and Hu Qian deserve the most severe punishment. However, instead of punishing them for their crime, you set them free. How do you account for it?"

"Chief Minister," Confucius replied, "nowadays the various states in their contention for supremacy place military strength before the rites. If our state does not advocate filial piety, how can we justify ourselves for punishing the common people for being unfilial? If we fail to educate people in the rules of proper conduct, and then execute them for committing mistakes, we would be committing the mistake of executing the innocent. *The Book of History* says, 'Cultivate virtuous behavior and exercise punishment with caution, do not hold prejudice against widows and widowers, employ those who deserve trust, respect those who deserve respect, punish those who deserve punishment, and make the people understand the reasons behind all these. Only by observing the above rules in exercising punishment will the people be convinced and devote their efforts to work instead of going against the law.' The book also says, 'Punish those who deserve punishment, and execute those who deserve execution. Do not follow your personal inclinations when making a decision.' All the sayings above are quoted from 'Exhortations to Kang,' written by the Duke of Zhou to exhort his younger brother, Kang Shufeng. The central theme lies in the line 'cultivate virtuous behavior and exercise punishment with caution.' Nowadays moral education has been weakened, and punishment by law strengthened. When people break the law, they do not know why. That's why as punishment has increased in severity, robbers have increased in numbers. I could not bring myself to have the son of the Hu family executed just because he failed to get an education in correct conduct. Therefore I had father and son locked up in prison to make them realize their respective mistakes and reach a reconciliation. The happiness of the family was thus ensured with the father showing loving care for his son and the son showing filial piety toward his father. I have done all this according to the Duke of Zhou's instruction!"

Combing his grey beard with his fingers, Jisun heard Confucius out attentively, then said with a smile, "Minister of Justice, you have such a clear picture of the current world in your mind! I can rely on your talents to assist our lord to govern Lu."

By then all court officials had entered the palace. Confucius said, "Chief Minister, we should also ..."

Jisun gave a little start, "Oh, it's time for the audience. Let's go in at once!"

After the morning audience Jisun asked Confucius, "Minister of Justice, you have many talented disciples. May I have several to be my household stewards?"

Thinking of the hardships he had gone through in his official career, Confucius paused to give Jisun a closer look, then said, "Though I have many disciples, few of them are fit to be officials. At present only Zi Lu and Ran Qiu are suitable."

"In that case, may I have the two of them as my stewards?"

"Zi Lu is honest but impulsive and plain-speaking. It is better for him to delay entering office. Let Ran Qiu alone join your household staff."

"I hope you will take up the matter with Ran Qiu and tell him to come to be the head steward of my house as soon as possible."

Confucius consented and left the palace. He told Ran Qiu about it at once.

Ran Qiu had studied with Confucius for many years and displayed his talents for office. He had yearned for a chance to enter office for a long time. Thus he received the news with great pleasure. The next day he went to Jisun Si's house to accept his position.

Since he became Minister of Justice, Confucius had been kept very busy. One day when a local archery festival was going to be held, Confucius said to his disciples, "I have not used the bow for a long time. Let's go to take part in the archery festival, shall we?"

The disciples agreed and began to change into warrior's dress and take out their arrows and bows.

Zi Lu, who had received his education in martial arts before he came to study with Confucius, was especially delighted. Confucius and his disciples arrived at Juexiang Garden, where a huge crowd of archers and spectators had already gathered. According to the rites of the Zhou Dynasty, two ministers of the court were appointed to supervise the practice of archery, a required training for all able-bodied men. Those who excelled in the art could either serve in the army or perform rituals at banquets or sacrificial ceremonies. On the day of the local archery festival, Juexiang Garden always attracted many archers and spectators.

Confucius made his way to the shooting ground accompanied by his disciples. There were three leather targets, each with a red spot in the center surrounded by black circles. Confucius frowned and said, "The range is a little too short."

The disciples looked back to see many young and middle-aged archers, bow and arrows in hand, eager to start practicing.

Intending to test Zi Lu on his leadership ability, Confucius said, "You will be the chief supervisor for today's shooting practice. You may organize the people to start practicing now."

Feeling greatly flattered, Zi Lu turned to the crowd, bow and arrows in hand, and addressed them in a loud voice, "The archery festival is a joyful occasion. Officers and men from defeated troops are requested to stand in the back and not try to be the first to practice."

As soon as he finished these words a few people stepped back from the crowd.

Zi Lu continued, pointing to the space in front of him, "Those who have achieved merits for the state, who treat their parents with filial piety and their friends with brotherly love, and who have outstanding virtues are invited to stand here."

At his words some more people drew back of their own accord. Now the shooting ground became much less crowded than before.

Zi Lu bade Zi Gong, Yan Hui and Ran Yong shoot first. Standing abreast, the three of them put one foot forward, drew their bows fully, and discharged the arrows, which whizzed toward the targets, hitting squarely on the bull's-eyes. A drum was beaten to announce the good results, and there came a loud shout of appreciation from the onlookers. Then the three of them hit the bull's-eyes with the second and third arrows, causing the crowd to applaud them for a long time.

Zi Lu then let the rest of his fellow students shoot, and the results were uneven. After most of them had practiced, he said to Confucius, "Master, it's your turn now."

Confucius said, "I have come today as an onlooker. It's your turn."

Zi Lu was glad to hear this, for he had longed to have a go himself. He drew his bow and shot three arrows in a row, hitting the bull's-eye with each arrow. The crowd let out a great roar of appreciation.

Smiling with satisfaction, Confucius said to his disciples, "I have greatly enjoyed your performance today. Some of you are very skilled at archery. It's late now. Let's go home."

On their return they were still in high spirits, talking about the day's practice. Confucius was very pleased with the skills of his disciples and especially with the leadership talents displayed by Zi Lu and said to him, "During today's practice I came to realize your great abilities in leadership. The chief minister happens to be looking for stewards. Shall I recommend you to him?"

"I'd rather drive the chariot for you, master, than take office."

"It is for the purpose of serving the state that we study the classics and practice the rites. How can you waste your talents by driving the chariot for me for the rest of your life? A dragon can only show its power by entering water. It's time for you to take a swim in the sea."

"I'll do as you tell me, master. When shall I start?"

"The chief minister seems to be very eager. You can call on him today and act on his instruction."

"Master, I have never served an office before and need your help and guidance."

"Just relax and do what you consider your duty. I'll keep an eye on you for sure."

Zi Lu smiled ingenuously and said, "I can not go straight to the chief minister's residence without being invited; otherwise people would laugh at me and think of me as a title-crazy man. I will need someone to introduce me."

"I'll pay a visit to the chief minister myself and explain it to him. He is sure to appoint you to an important position."

"Thank you so much, master."

Confucius considered for a moment, then said, "Actually, you can accompany me to the chief minister's house, so that he will have a chance to test your ability."

Zi Lu nodded his agreement. They went together to the chief minister's house. When Zi Lu answered fluently all the questions put to him about state affairs, Jisun Si was immensely pleased and appointed him to head steward. Subsequently Zi Lu carried out his duties with great resolution and efficiency, and Jisun was very satisfied.

It was then spring in the third month. In his capacity as Minister of Justice, Confucius was able to effect a marked improvement in the general mood of society in Lu. He was more convinced than ever that the restoration of the rites of Zhou was no longer a dream, but an attainable goal. He again saw in his mind's eye the shining pagoda, the symbol of an ideal social order, towering like a great mountain and radiant as the sun.

One day, on his way home from the morning audience, Confucius felt the spring in the air and said to his disciples when he arrived home, "Spring is already with us now, and there are flowers everywhere. How about an excursion to the Sihe River?"

The disciples readily agreed and set out with Confucius. As soon as they were out of the city by the north gate, they saw a row of willows standing by the river like a green curtain. Arriving at the dike, they relished the sight of the rushing stream, the sound of birds singing, the bright sunlight, and the fresh air. Wild flowers growing by the river gave off an intoxicating fragrance, and clouds formed into various shapes in the sky. They all enjoyed the sight and made merry. Confucius stood by the river and gazed at the rushing stream for a long time.

Zi Gong asked, "Master, whenever we come to a great river, you stop to gaze at it. Why?"

Confucius paused at the question, then replied, "Water has a variety of features. When rising, it will gradually submerge the small islets in the river. The process is natural and effortless, yet irresistible, just like the power possessed by people of culture and virtue. It always flows downward in an orderly way, as if exhorting people to proceed in an orderly sequence. It keeps rushing on without drying up, as if it were the source of all things under heaven. While flowing it produces a variety of sounds, as if playing a piece of music. Originating in high mountains, it runs down thousands of valleys and ravines with great intrepidity, resembling a man of courage. Whether in a lake, a pool or a container, it has a level surface, reminding us of the unbiasedness of the law. It can fill a container but never rises above it, showing the quality of uprightness and sense of proportion. It comes from the distance and disappears into the distance without losing its serenity and purity, just like a man who retains his innocence wherever he goes. Though there are twists and turns in its course, it always heads for the east, like a man determined to reach his goal in spite of difficulties. Therefore, when coming to a great river, people of culture and virtue always stop to contemplate it."

Zi Gong sighed with fascination, "I never thought there could be so much meaning in the movement of water!"

Watching the flowing water, the disciples fell into a lively discussion about its numerous marvels. Only Min Shun and Yan Hui contemplated the river in silence.

Confucius recalled the great waterfalls in Mount Tai and thought of his political ambitions. He comforted himself, "Though there is a long distance to go for the complete restoration of the rites of Zhou, I have at least taken a big step forward. If only I can keep proceeding in this way, ..." Feeling as if he had no time to lose, he called his disciples to him, and they started the journey home.

On their way home the disciples talked and laughed. Suddenly Confucius saw something nearby and said something they dared not even think about. All the disciples were dumbfounded.

Chapter Seventeen

Li Chu Seeks a Chance to Humiliate the Lord of Lu; Confucius Trains the Army in Case of Emergency

"The land around here is excellent," Confucius said to his disciples, pointing to a small mound by the road. "When I die, this would make an ideal burial ground for me."

The disciples, who held Confucius in the highest esteem and wished him a long life, had never given thought to his death. Moreover, he was then only fifty-one years old. Thus they were all struck dumb by his remark.

At the sight of their stunned looks, Confucius smiled. "Why should you be so startled by the mere mention of my death? Who can expect to live forever? Yet I am not ready to die now, for I have much work to do. I was talking about the future."

"Master," asked Zi Gong, "the ancients often selected a place near a river or a mountain for their burial ground. But there is no river or hill nearby; what's so good about this site?"

Pointing to the mound again, Confucius said, "When I am buried here after death, I will have the Sihe River to the north and the Lu capital to the south. Listening to the sound of the currents in the river, I will be able to tell the season and the climate, and by gazing into the clouds in the sky I will know if Lu is enjoying peace and prosperity."

Now the disciples realized what Confucius meant when he mentioned his death, and they stopped worrying. There was again laughter and heated discussion among them.

Listening to his disciples' animated talk and thinking of the great changes that had taken place in Lu, Confucius was filled with joy. His mind drifted to the Duke of Zhou and the rites of Zhou, and he began to consider how he could restore the rites and put an end to the great turbulence in the world.

After Duke Ding of Lu made Confucius a high official, the city of Zhongdu and then the entire state of Lu showed remarkable

improvements, so that the neighboring states regarded Lu with increasing respect. Duke Jing of Qi, who had always wanted to be a leader of the various vassal states of Zhou, became worried over the situation. He feared that Lu would threaten Qi's supremacy someday if it continued to grow stronger. He also regretted that he had not listened to Minister Gao and enlisted the service of Confucius.

It was springtime. In the rear palace of Qi, flowers were in full bloom, and butterflies danced here and there in the garden. A winding path led to quiet corners in the rockery, where box trees and wistaria grew and flourished. Two grey magpies frolicked among the grass and rocks, chirping merrily. Lotus leaves spread over the surface of the pool, and weeds shaped like pines grew underwater. Dragonflies skimmed the surface and fish swam leisurely in the bottom of the pool. A frog crouching on a lotus leaf was waiting patiently for an edible insect. Beside the pool stood a small pavilion with a thatched roof, long upturned eaves, and a placard bearing the inscription, "Pavilion for Refreshing the Mind." Inside the pavilion there was a square stone table surrounded by four drum-shaped stone stools, and on one of these stools sat Duke Jing of Qi. He had a haggard and anxious look on his face that contrasted sharply with the liveliness of the garden.

The two grey magpies continued to hop and chirp. If in a better mood, Duke Jing would listen and watch the birds delightedly, just as if he were enjoying a song and dance performance. On this particular day, however, he found the birds irritating, and bent down to pick up a stone.

Just then a short, fat man entered the garden by the round entrance. The muscles on his face were twitching, his small eyes rolled, and even his grey beard quivered. He looked grotesque in an oversized official robe. Walking on tiptoe, he approached Duke Jing.

Duke Jing, angry at the two magpies, threw the stone. Startled, the birds flew away. Duke Jing turned and caught sight of Li Chu.

Li Chu hurriedly bowed and asked, "Is something troubling you, Your Lordship, sitting all alone here in the pavilion?"

Duke Jing replied with a deep sigh, "Since the lord of Lu employed Confucius, Lu has become well governed in a short time. According to what I have heard, Zhongdu was run by Confucius for only one year, and now people in that city do not pick up and pocket what are lost on the road, and do not have to lock their doors at night. The other states are following his practice. In this way Lu will surely grow so strong in a few years that all the states will have to treat it with awe and respect. The outcome is unthinkable!"

Moving a little closer, Li Chu said in a low voice, "In that case, why don't you find a way to stop this?"

Duke Jing spread his hands in a hopeless gesture. "What is there to be done?"

Blinking his small eyes, Li Chu said, "We can write a letter inviting the lord of Lu to meet with us in Jiagu. At the meeting we can resolve old grudges with Lu on the one hand, and at the same time teach Confucius a lesson, so that he will not dare take any action against us in the future."

"Speaking of old grudges," said Duke Jing, "Qi and Lu have plenty between them. Only recently Yang Hu and Gongshan Buniu fled to Qi one after the other. When the lord of Lu sent letters requesting us to capture them, we did not take it seriously and failed to secure either one. How can I face the lord of Lu when he might ask me about it?"

"But Yang Hu stayed in Qi for only a short time before he left for Jin," said Li Chu. "As for Gongshan Buniu, he is currently staying on the Qi-Lu border with some rebel troops from Lu. If Lu is unable to eliminate its traitor, why should we go out of our way to do the job for it?"

"Your argument is reasonable, but I still don't like to be blamed for providing sanctuary for a pack of rebels."

"If Qi and Lu conclude a meeting in Jiagu successfully," said Li Chu, "they can join forces in an attack against Gongshan Buniu. Wouldn't that be the best solution?"

"Very well said!" exclaimed Duke Jing with great pleasure, springing to his feet. He was about to tell Li Chu to begin planning for the meeting when he checked himself. "The meeting is a very important matter," he said. "We must discuss it with the chief minister."

"Yes," Li Chu nodded. "I'll go straight away and ask his opinions."

Duke Jing made his way to the rear palace, turning the plan over in his mind, while Li Chu went to the chief minister's residence to see Yan Ying.

Yan Ying had also been worrying over the changes in Lu. He was afraid that Confucius' influence would spread from Lu to Qi and to the entire world. He was green with envy. Standing in the courtyard, he gazed around restlessly, at the same time racking his brains to find a way to stop Confucius. At the sight of Li Chu he hurriedly ushered him into the parlor.

Looking at Yan Ying's downcast expression, Li Chu asked, "Chief Minister, you do not look well. Are you feeling all right?"

Yan Ying sighed deeply, "Well, I feel sick at heart."

"I see," said Li Chu, rolling his eyes. "Your heart must be under attack from external fire."

"Minister Li, haven't you heard that Lu is growing strong day by day? In the world today the strong will live, and the weak will perish. How can I help worrying when we have a neighboring state like this?"

Hearing this, Li Chu was very glad. "Chief Minister," he said earnestly, "that is exactly why I have come here. If we don't want Lu to surpass Qi, we must find a way to stop its growth."

Yan Ying's knitted brows became smooth. "So we share the same view," he said. "But how do you propose to check Lu's growth?"

When Li Chu recounted in detail his plan for a Qi-Lu meeting in Jiagu, Yan Ying smiled approvingly. "At the audience tomorrow morning we can take up the matter with His Lordship. Then we will send an official letter to the lord of Lu."

The next morning Duke Jing described the plan to his court officials, who all agreed to it. He then ordered Li Chu to write a letter proposing a meeting with Lu in Jiagu on the 15th of the sixth month that year.

On receiving the letter from Duke Jing of Qi, Duke Ding of Lu arranged for the Qi envoy to stay in the guesthouse, then summoned the court officials to a meeting to discuss the matter. All officials arrived except Confucius, who was then touring the Sihe River. Duke Ding sent a guard posthaste to find him.

Returning from his trip, Confucius and his disciples had no sooner entered the north gate than a mounted guard approached them, dismounted and saluted. "Minister of Justice," he said, "His Lordship wants to see you at once to discuss something urgent."

Confucius was startled. In those chaotic years the law of the jungle prevailed, and a weak state like Lu was never free from the danger of being invaded, ransacked or even destroyed. He dared not think what the news might be. Bidding the disciples to go on home, he followed the guard to the palace.

The atmosphere was tense in the court. Duke Ding sat in his chair, sullenness written large on his face. Jisun Si, Shusun Zhouchou, Mengsun Heji, Shen Juxu, Yue Qi and other court officials stood in two ranks. Dead silence reigned in the hall.

Confucius kowtowed to Duke Ding, then got up and took his position in the rank of civil officials.

Duke Ding said, "My honored ministers, the lord of Qi has sent us a letter suggesting a meeting with me in Jiagu on the 15th of the sixth month. At present Qi is apparently superior to Lu in strength. It is strange that Duke Jing of Qi should go out of his way to show his respect for a weak neighbor. Therefore I dare not agree to his proposal rashly, but have summoned you to discuss it."

The officials responded differently on hearing the news. Some were startled and very much afraid, some were stupefied with a blank look on their faces, while some stayed calm and confident.

Jisun Si was the first to speak. "The lord of Qi is a very wily man, who have a handful of crafty and fawning officials like Li Chu in his employ. There is no way that we could tell what trick he is up to. Your Lordship must not risk himself by attending the meeting."

Shusun Zhouchou agreed. "Your Lordship," he said, "this is an important matter that needs careful deliberation."

Mengsun Heji said, "Qi has invaded our land several times in the past. Now it suddenly changes its policy, offering to make an alliance instead of coercing us by its military strength. I think there is something fishy about it. We can not be too careful."

"I venture to disagree," said Shen Juxu. "Qi did invade us on several occasions, but that happened years ago. Now that they have come to offer their friendship, it would not be civil for us to refuse!"

"Minister Shen is right," said Confucius. "We must respond to a courteous gesture with courtesy."

Duke Ding thought for a moment, then said with apprehension, "Minister Kong, though you have a good point there, there is no telling what will happen at the meeting. If I go, I will need an official in charge of the ceremonies, a capable man versed in both the letters and martial arts. Now who can recommend such a man to me?"

There was no response.

"Who will be the master of ceremonies for Qi?" Confucius asked.

Duke Ding said, "Yan Ying, the chief minister of Qi."

"Great attention must be paid to rules of propriety in interstate relationships," remarked Confucius. "Since Qi has put its chief minister in charge of the ceremonies, Lu should also choose Minister Jisun for that position."

Hearing this, Jisun Si turned pale with fright. After a long pause, he muttered, "To preside over such ceremonies is an important matter. Without much talent or learning, I am really not fit to do this. Your Lordship must forgive me. Ministers, please recommend someone else, so that he will bring honor to His Lordship and our state."

Confucius said, "Chief Minister, when dealing with another state we have to do everything on an equal footing. If Qi has chosen its chief minister as the master of ceremonies, Lu will have to choose you. If someone else should be appointed to the position, we would become a laughing-stock among the states for going against the rites. This is a matter of the utmost significance. You really must not decline any further."

The other officials agreed. "Chief Minister, the minister of justice is right." "For this meeting, we must have the chief minister to preside over the ceremonies." "You should not decline, Chief Minister. Just go ahead and accompany His Lordship to the meeting."

When Duke Ding glanced at Jisun Si tentatively, he saw the pleading look in the latter's eyes and refrained from speaking.

The officials continued arguing over the matter. Clearing his throat, Confucius said in a loud voice, "Your Lordship, we can not justify our action unless we abide by the rites. For the meeting in Jiagu, we must have the chief minister in charge of the ceremonies."

Duke Ding asked, "Minister Jisun, what do you say?"

Jisun Si knitted his brows and said in a low voice, "Your Lordship, we can not predict what will happen at the meeting in Jiagu. It may proceed smoothly or lead to an armed conflict. I am really not suitable to shoulder such an important task and beg Your Lordship to select someone else."

"Who do you think is such a suitable person?" asked the duke.

"The minister of justice is wise, courageous, and well versed in both the letters and martial arts. Besides, he is a very eloquent speaker. I think he is the most suitable person to serve as the master of the ceremonies for the Jiagu meeting."

"Well," Duke Ding said hesitatingly. "That would go against the rites."

"Not at all," said Jisun Si. "You can appoint the minister of justice to acting chief minister for the occasion."

The court officials murmured their appreciation of the idea. Duke Ding muttered, "Well—"

"Your Lordship," said Confucius. "I do not deserve such an honor."

"Minister of Justice," said Jisun Si. "With your outstanding ability, you will surely fulfill your duties as the master of ceremonies perfectly. Do not decline any further!"

Confucius was about to speak again when Duke Ding interposed. "Minister Kong, since the chief minister has recommended you with such sincerity, and the other ministers have expressed their approval, you don't have to decline anymore. There is no reason why you can not be the acting chief minister!" He looked around and asked, "My honored ministers, what do you think of this arrangement?"

The officials replied in unison, "Your Lordship has made a wise decision!"

Duke Ding said, "Minister Kong, please don't let us down. Please accept the appointment."

Confucius saluted solemnly to Duke Ding and the court officials and said, "Many thanks to Your Lordship and the ministers for thinking so highly of me!" He paused for a little while, then continued, "People who uphold the rites can not afford to neglect armed force either. A state intending to make peace with a neighbor must have military strength to back it up. Formerly, Duke Xiang of Song was humiliated during his visit to Chu just because he did not take the troops with him. The overturned cart ahead is a warning to the carts behind. We must take ample precautions against emergencies."

"You are absolutely right!" cried the duke. "What do you think should be done?"

Passing his fingers through his beard, Confucius said, "Your Lordship should get General Shen and General Yue to accompany you as ministers of defence during the meeting."

Duke Ding sighed with relief. "You may make arrangements as you consider necessary."

Confucius turned to ask Shen Juxu and Yue Qi, "What do you think?"

"We are willing to receive your order, Minister of Justice!"

"The two of you will please start drilling the troops tomorrow. It is your duty to keep the soldiers strong and the horses sturdy."

"Yes, we understand!" Shen and Yue responded.

Early the next morning several hundred war chariots were assembled on the drill ground. Carrying banners embroidered with designs of dragon, tiger, bird and snake, the chariots were arranged in several formations suited to fighting in different types of terrain such as mountains, forests, rivers, and plains.

On the general's platform were planted two big banners carrying the characters "Shen" and "Yue." Shen Juxu and Yue Qi directed the chariots from the platform. After three bursts of drum beats, a band of chariots carrying dragon banners drove to the center of the drill ground in an orderly formation. Each chariot was drawn by four horses, two on each side of the shaft. They began rehearsing an attack through the river, turning now to the left and now to the right in a variety of battle arrays. Having completed the practice, they left the drill ground in good order. This was followed successively by the other three bands of chariots rehearsing for battles in mountains, on plains and in forests. After that, a mock fight between two armies ensued. Amid the deafening sound of drum beats, battle-cries and gongs, the two armies became engaged in a tangled fight. When this was over, some soldiers began practicing hand-to-hand combat, each displaying his skill at using the sword, broadsword, spear, or club. Finally came the practice of archery. As war chariots made up the main force for most battles, it was paramount for an army to have skilled archers. Shen and Yue had always attached particular importance to training their men in archery. Now the archers came forth in groups of ten, took aim at the targets and, at Shen's order, each discharged three arrows. Very few of them missed their shots, to Shen's great satisfaction. He then ordered all other troops to join in the archery practice. It was not until noon that Shen called an end to the drill and allowed the troops to take a rest. After that, Shen and Yue took turns drilling the troops.

When Duke Jing of Qi received Duke Ding of Lu's reply to his letter, he summoned Yan Ying and Li Chu to the rear palace and discussed with them the preparations for the meeting in Jiagu.

Li Chu said, "Your Lordship, the meeting will be conducted in Lu territory, but Qi should take precedence over Lu."

Duke Jing gave him a puzzled look.

Li Chu explained, "There are three reasons for this. First, the meeting is proposed by Qi, so Qi will naturally be the leader. Second, since Jiagu is Lu territory, Lu will be the host and Qi the guest. Out of courtesy the host should allow the guest to take precedence. Third, Qi is superior to Lu in strength. It has been common practice since ancient times for the weak to submit to the strong."

Yan Ying disagreed. "Minister Li, you are mistaken. When two states come together for a meeting, they should deal with each other on an equal footing. It would be inappropriate for us to try to gain advantage over trivial matters."

Li Chu said, "But how will we be able to check Lu in this way?"

"We have to work out a long-term plan about this," said Yan Ying. "What we need to do now is to establish a friendly relationship with Lu."

Duke Jing of Qi concurred. "Minister Li, the chief minister is quite right. Since the meeting is not far away, the two of you must make preparations for the meeting in strict accordance with the rites. Do not cause unnecessary complications which might give people reason to laugh at us!"

Yan Ying and Li Chu replied in unison, "We'll comply with your order!" They left the palace and returned to their residences.

Yan Ying felt intensely jealous whenever he thought of Confucius. Though he had advised Duke Jing to adhere to the rites at the meeting, he wished he could somehow destroy Confucius once and for all. Returning home, he was so restless he could not sit squarely in his seat. He recalled with pride his political achievements: killing three unruly generals with two peaches, bringing glory to Qi on his visit to Chu, and strengthening Qi by the advocation of frugality. However, he could not suppress his despondence when he looked at the present situation. He had thought himself capable of helping Duke Jing become a leader of all lords; this had always been the ultimate aim of his political career. After dozens of years, however, Qi failed to grow strong but instead had begun to decline steadily. Then there came Confucius, who seemed to be superior to him in every aspect. Someday, he thought, Lu would surpass Qi and even become the leader of all the vassal states. Looking in the bronze mirror, he saw a grey-haired man with barely a trace left of his former vigor and vitality. He would like to begin all over again, but he felt old and weak, unequal to the task he wanted to undertake. He spent a sleepless night, racking his brains over the predicament, trying in vain to find a way to prevent Confucius from turning Lu into a powerful state.

At the same time Li Chu was thinking of something quite different. It was with the aim of humiliating Duke Ding of Lu and Confucius that he had proposed the Qi-Lu meeting in the first place.

He hoped thus to boost Qi's morale and bring shame to Lu. Though many of his previous plans had run foul, Li Chu was convinced that it would work out this time. He knew that it would be out of the question for Duke Jing to bring crack troops with which to overpower Duke Ding of Lu at the meeting. That would result in universal condemnation against Qi. He had to find a more subtle way to subdue Lu.

Li Chu had someone write the music for a poem from *The Book of Poetry*, "Riding in the Chariot," which recounted the illicit love affair between Wen Jiang and Duke Xiang of Qi. Then he had the song taught to some attractive dancing girls, who would perform at the Jiagu meeting to humiliate Duke Ding of Lu.

Confucius was also busy preparing for the meeting. He ordered Shen Juxu and Yue Qi to keep drilling the troops selected to accompany Duke Ding to the meeting. He drew a picture of the platform to be constructed for the meeting in accordance with ancient customs. He read through historical documents from which he copied descriptions of interstate meetings, studied them carefully, then devised the procedure for the Jiagu meeting, paying attention to every detail.

Soon it was the end of the fifth month. As the date of the meeting was drawing near, Confucius went to find out how Shen Juxu and Yue Qi had been doing with the training of the troops. Arriving at the drill ground, he mounted the general's platform to take a look. At the sight of him the officers and men put more effort into their exercise. The banners featuring dragon, tiger, bird and snake fluttered in the strong southeast wind. The war chariots first practiced various battle formations for fighting in the river, on the plain, in the forest and in the mountain, then arrayed themselves for a mock battle of attack and defense. Confucius was pleased with what he saw.

After about two hours both officers and men were sweating all over. Taking a look at Shen Juxu, Confucius found him beaming with vigor while directing the troops with his commanding flags. When he looked at Yue Qi, however, Confucius was startled to find him sallow in the face. Beads of perspiration were streaming down his forehead, his hand holding the flag trembled, and he bit his lower lip so hard that blood trickled down to his chin. Confucius ran up to him and said, "General Yue, you are ill. Return to your residence at once and send for a doctor!"

Yue Qi said, choking with gratitude, "Minister of Justice, you have come personally to supervise the training of the troops. How can I put down my commanding flag and leave?"

Confucius said, "It is only half a month to the meeting. How will you fulfill your mission if you go on like this? Go home at once and find a doctor!"

With a sweep of his flag, Shen Juxu ordered the troops to stop practicing, then ran over to Yue Qi. "General Yue," he said with disapproval, "why didn't you tell me about your illness? How are you feeling?" He gave a start when he felt Yue Qi on the forehead. "You are having a high fever," he said, and wiped off the blood from Yue Qi's chin.

Confucius said, "Go home at once! I'll go and find the court physician for you."

Some officers came over and carried Yue Qi into a chariot, which drove him home.

Hearing Confucius' report, Duke Ding was startled. "The meeting is very near," he said. "If General Yue is severely ill, how will he be able to lead the troops?"

"There is no need to be anxious, Your Lordship. General Yue must be suffering from a wind-cold illness due to over-fatigue. He will surely recover in three days if well treated by the court physician."

"In that case, send the court physician to his house at once!"

Thereupon Confucius accompanied the court physician to Yue Qi's residence. After feeling the patient's pulse, the physician diagnosed wind-cold illness and prescribed some medicine accordingly. After taking the medicine for one day Yue Qi felt his illness much alleviated. Three days later he was back in good health. Greatly pleased, Confucius ordered Shen Juxu and Yue Qi, "The meeting is about ten days away. The two of you have done well training the troops. To keep the officers and men in good shape, you should stop training for a few days and allow them to take a rest."

"We'll carry out your order!"

"However, you must have the chariots and banners examined, so that repairs can be made if necessary. All the chariots must be in good condition and all the banners intact."

"We'll carry out this order!"

"Then you should select a crack force for the meeting, excluding anyone who is weak or ill."

"We'll carry out this order!"

Having made these arrangements, Confucius felt a little tired and went for an outing with Min Shun and Zi Gong. When they walked out of the south gate, the sight before them reminded Confucius of his childhood. Gazing at the altar by the Yishui River, Confucius remembered the time when he had come here to watch the grand sacrifice. He was then living with his mother and brother.

Zi Gong asked, "Master, what is that earthen platform? What do people use it for?"

As if awakened from a dream, Confucius gave a little start, then replied, "That is the altar for the grand sacrifice."

Pointing to another earthen platform to the east, Zi Gong asked, "What about that one?"

"That is the platform where sacrifice is offered to Heaven to ask for rain."

Zi Gong asked again, "Why can't the same platform be used for the two sacrifices, since they are both offered to Heaven instead of Earth?"

"The ancients attached great significance to sacrificial rituals and put stress on the correctness of every detail. The grand ceremony is offered annually, whereas the sacrifice for rain is held only at the time of drought. They are different in function and must be conducted differently."

Zi Gong asked hesitantly, "Master, are there really gods in heaven?"

Confucius gazed up into the sky, pausing for a moment. "There are the sun, the moon and the stars in the sky. Apart from that, I suppose the sky must be empty."

"In that case, why do people offer sacrifice to Heaven so devoutly?"

"People need something to hope for. They regard a drought as Heaven's punishment of their misdeeds, so they offer sacrifice to Heaven by way of appeasement. But it does not always lead to rain. As I can remember, there have been many instances when sacrifices were offered without producing a single drop of rain, so that all the crops dried up in the end."

"When a man dies, will his soul live on?"

"A dead man can be compared to a lamp that has used up its oil. Nothing is left of him except the body."

"If there is no soul living after death, why do you offer sacrifices to the ancestors?"

"I regard ancestral worship as an occasion to eulogize the virtue and merits of our forefathers. When offering the sacrifice, I feel as if my forefathers were standing in front of me and giving me instructions on how to conduct myself properly. Therefore I never ask anyone else to offer the sacrifice on my behalf."

"Minister of Justice!"

Hearing the sudden shout, Confucius looked up to see a soldier running toward him. He was still gasping for breath when he came before Confucius to report, "Minister of Justice, something serious has happened! General Shen has ordered me to ask you to return to the city immediately!"

Chapter Eighteen

Lu Gains a Diplomatic Victory
at the Jiagu Meeting;
The Entire State of Qi Mourns
Yan Ying's Death

Confucius gave a start and asked hastily, "What's the matter?"

"Many soldiers are suffering from coughs, headaches and fever."

Confucius said, "I'll go and have a look!"

Arriving at the camp, Confucius heard the sound of coughing everywhere. He visited some sick soldiers and found they showed the same symptoms as Yue Qi. It seemed strange that they should suffer from wind-cold illness in summer, but on second thought he realized what had happened. Exhausted by the rigorous training under Shen Juxu and Yue Qi in the past few days, the soldiers had become susceptible to the attack of wind and cold. He sent for a doctor and had him prescribe some medicine for the sick soldiers. Then he sent men to buy a lot of ginger, had them cut into slices and boiled into soup. He ordered every soldier to drink the ginger soup three times a day, one large bowl each time. Confucius had always been fond of ginger, which had the function of enhancing appetite and warding off dampness and cold. As the day of the meeting was drawing near, he felt anxious over the ill health of so many soldiers and went to inspect them several times a day. To his great relief, all the sick officers and men recovered fully in a few days due to timely treatment. He invited Shen Juxu and Yue Qi to his office and briefed them on the procedures for the meeting.

On the 13th of the sixth month of the tenth year of Duke Ding of Lu's reign (500 B.C.) Duke Ding set out for Jiagu accompanied by Shen Juxu and Yue Qi, each leading five hundred war chariots. They proceeded at a leisurely pace and arrived at Mount Tai at dusk. Confucius dismounted and approached Duke Ding. "Your Lordship," he reported, "we have arrived at Mount Tai."

With Confucius to supervise the rites at the meeting as his acting chief minister and numerous war chariots to protect him,

231

Duke Ding felt happy and lighthearted. He said, "Help me out and let me take a look at Mount Tai."

Two soldiers hurried forward and helped Duke Ding dismount the chariot.

Duke Ding looked around him. At the sight of an endless line of war chariots, he felt a surge of courage and reassurance. When he turned to look at Mount Tai, he was overcome with awe and respect. Making a deep bow he said, "Mount Tai, if you have divine power, please bless me with a peaceful journey. If my wishes are fulfilled, I will send men to offer sacrifice to you each year."

Confucius was not pleased to hear this. He said hastily, "Your Lordship, it is getting late. Shall I order the troops to make camp here tonight?"

"Please do," replied the duke, and Confucius had the order passed on to the troops.

They broke camp early the next morning. The sky was suffused in a rosy light as the sun emerged from behind the mountain. Wisps of cooking smoke rose continuously from the villages nearby. The undulating hills were shrouded in mist.

Duke Ding set out in his chariot after offering another prayer to Mount Tai. In the afternoon they reached Jiagu. Sitting in the chariot, Confucius looked ahead and gasped in admiration. A small piece of flat land formed between two mountain ridges, slanting from northwest to southeast. It resembled an armchair, with the two ridges as its armrests. Under each of the mountain ridge there was a big rushing river, and between the two rivers there was a low hill. The rivers converged at the narrow end of the hill, sending great waves into the sky. This low hill had been chosen as the site for the Qi-Lu meeting. The soldiers built a platform according to the plan drawn by Confucius. Three stone steps led to the earthen platform, which faced a relatively large piece of smooth ground. Confucius watched with satisfaction. Just then the men of Qi, carrying colorful banners, arrived at the opposite mountain ridge. Confucius ordered the troops to make camp in a battle formation.

At nightfall the moon, almost full, emerged from behind the clouds to shine on the camp-sites of the Qi and Lu armies. Suddenly a violent wind rose, and dark clouds floated across the sky, concealing the moon. It became pitch-dark, as if the ground had been covered by a giant earthen pot. Soon torches appeared on both camp-sites.

Inside the tent Confucius said to Shen Juxu and Yue Qi, "Send patrols at once! We can not be too careful."

"Yes!" replied the two generals.

Confucius added, "When our lord meets the duke of Qi tomorrow, the two of you must take your cue from me."

"Yes!"

Having seen Shen and Yue off, Confucius sat down in his tent and considered what might happen at the meeting the following day. Waving his broad sleeves to chase off the buzzing mosquitoes, he tried to guess what Duke Jing of Qi, Yan Ying and Li Chu planned to do.

In the camp-site of the Qi army, Li Chu sneaked out of his tent and rushed into the tent of Duke Jing.

Startled, Duke Jing looked closely under the dim lamplight and recognized Li Chu. He stared at him and asked, "Why are you still up? Is there something urgent?"

Glancing around to make certain that Duke Jing was alone, Li Chu said in a low voice, "When Your Lordship meets the Duke of Lu tomorrow, I plan to ..." He moved closer to Duke Jing and whispered.

After hearing him out, Duke Jing said with a frown, "The matter deserves careful consideration. We have to talk it over with the chief minister."

Li Chu waved his hand, saying, "The chief minister is a long-time friend of Confucius. Furthermore, he has grown timid in his old age. He would definitely object to this if we tell him. Please believe me. I guarantee the plan will be carried out successfully."

Duke Jing looked at Li Chu doubtfully for quite a long time, then nodded slightly.

In the morning a gentle breeze blew through the trees and flowers in the mountain.

The two parties stood on the mountain ridges facing each other. A banner leader, holding a yellow banner, swept three times to the left, three times to the right, then held it in front of him. Next the drum leader beat the bronze gong twenty-one times, its sound resounding in the valley. After that, the sovereign lord from either side walked slowly toward the platform, headed by a band of banner men. Having crossed the stone bridges over the big rivers, Duke Jing of Qi and Duke Ding of Lu dismounted to exchange greetings, then walked up the slope, pausing to rest for a while on the level ground in front of the platform. Confucius and Yan Ying bade the musicians play a tune for receiving the guest, then led Duke Ding and Duke Jing toward the steps, with Confucius on the left and Yan Ying on the right. They turned and gestured for Duke Ding and Duke Jing to ascend the platform. Duke Ding and Duke Jing lifted the left foot at the same time onto the first step, then placed the right foot beside the left. After a slight pause, they climbed the second step. On reaching the platform, the two dukes took their respective seats facing south. As Jiagu was Lu territory, Duke Jing of Qi took the seat of the guest on the left. Apart from the two dukes, there were only a few soldiers on the platform carrying banners or holding canopies for their lords. Confucius and Yan Ying stood under the platform along with the musicians, dancing girls, and the rest of the soldiers.

When the music stopped, Duke Ding and Duke Jing stood up together, lit three joss sticks each, and knelt to pray to Heaven: "We meet here in Jiagu today to establish everlasting peace and friendship between Qi and Lu. From now on we shall regard each other as brother. When Qi is in trouble, Lu will come to help. When Lu is in trouble, Qi will come to help. With Heaven and Earth as our witnesses, we shall never go back on our covenant." They kowtowed to Heaven, received wine cups from the guards, and offered sacrifices to Heaven and Earth. Then they offered each other a toast by way of congratulation and returned to their seats.

The musicians began to play again. Listening to the melodious tune, Duke Ding was filled with satisfaction, as if he no longer had a single care in the world.

Duke Jing said, "It is a happy occasion for Qi and Lu to meet here today. I have some exotic song and dance performances prepared. Let's enjoy them together."

Li Chu, who had been waiting anxiously, waved his arm. Instantly a group of savage-looking men carrying spears, swords and shields scrambled up to the platform amid the sound of drum beats. Dressed in animal skins and their chests bare, they jumped around making funny gestures.

Duke Jing said proudly, "This is the dance of the Laiyi people, whose state was destroyed by Qi many years ago."

Duke Ding became so frightened his face turned pale.

Lifting the front of his garment, Confucius hurried up the steps, went up to Duke Jing and demanded loudly, "Your Lordship, we have come here for peace. Why should the war dance of savages be performed?"

Uninformed of Li Chu's plan, Yan Ying also ran up the platform and said to Duke Jing, "Your Lordship, how can we use such a dance at a grand ceremony like this?"

Unable to justify himself, Duke Jing blushed and waved his arm. "Dismiss the dancers!" he shouted.

This greatly disappointed Li Chu, who had hoped to use the savage dance to intimidate Duke Ding. He quietly approached a group of dancing girls and spoke a few words to them, then turned to climb up the platform and said to Duke Ding and Duke Jing with a deep bow, "Since Your Lordships do not like the song and dance of savages, how about a performance by our palace dancers?"

Duke Ding, not fully recovered from the alarm, said nothing.

Duke Jing nodded his consent.

At Li Chu's beckoning, twenty-four colorfully dressed dancing girls mounted the platform and began to perform a palace dance. They gently twisted their slender waists and spread their long sleeves in a series of graceful movements, and their singing was both sonorous and melodious. When they finished performing the Shao music, Confucius finally broke into a smile.

Then the tune changed abruptly, and the dancing girls began to sing "Riding in the Chariot" from *The Book of Poetry*:

> *The chariot rolls on,*
> *With embroidered side-doors and a red fur canopy.*
> *Along the road flat and smooth,*
> *Wen Jiang is leaving Qi for Lu at daybreak.*

Hearing this, Confucius gave a little start.

The dancing girls continued:

> *Four black horses look handsome and strong,*
> *With soft reins dangling to the ground.*
> *Along the road flat and smooth,*
> *Wen Jiang is leaving Qi for Lu at daybreak.*

Confucius shot a glance at Duke Jing of Qi, who seemed to be enjoying himself. Yan Ying looked calm and expressionless.

> *The Wenshui River has greatly swollen.*
> *People are bustling about in the streets.*
> *Along the road flat and smooth,*
> *Wen Jiang is enjoying the sights.*

> *The Wenshui River has drastically swollen.*
> *People are hurrying in the streets.*
> *Along the road flat and smooth,*
> *Wen Jiang is relishing the sights.*

Confucius became flushed with shame. This was a poem satirizing the illicit affair between Wen Jiang and Duke Xiang of Qi. After marrying Duke Huan of Lu, Wen Jiang found an opportunity to return to Qi and have a rendezvous with her brother. It was a disgrace for both Lu and Qi. Confucius wondered why Li Chu should have arranged for the dancing girls to sing such a song.

The dancing girls continued, the words growing more explicit:

> *His wife loves her brother;*
> *What can he do about it?*

Confucius could not take it any longer. Springing to his feet, he placed his hand on his sword, stared Duke Jing in the eyes, and demanded in a stern, sonorous voice, "These people deserve a thousand deaths for humiliating Their Lordships on such a solemn occasion! Please order your generals to execute them on the spot!"

By now Duke Ding of Lu had also realized the implication of the song. He turned livid with rage, gasping for breath.

Before Duke Jing was able to respond, the dancing girls had sung the subsequent lines:

> *The son, being filial, has no other choice*
> *But to build a trysting nest at the border.*

The men of Qi roared with laughter. Li Chu laughed more heartily than the others.

Confucius was so enraged that his hair stood on end. He shouted, "At this meeting Lu and Qi have made peace and become brothers. How dare these dancing girls humiliate Their Lordships with their song? Ministers of Defense of Qi, please have them beheaded on the spot!"

The two Qi ministers stood under the platform, not knowing what to say.

Confucius shouted angrily, "Ministers of Defense of Qi, please come up to the platform immediately!"

The two ministers looked at Duke Jing, who acted as if he had not heard anything.

Unable to contain his anger, Confucius said to Duke Jing, "Since Lu and Qi have become brothers, the defense ministers of Lu may act on behalf of the defense ministers of Qi." He beckoned toward the ground below the platform, saying, "General Shen and General Yue, please come up to the platform!"

Shen Juxu and Yue Qi ascended the platform at once and beheaded the two leading dancers. The other dancers were terrified, some paralyzed with fright while others scurrying down the platform.

Duke Jing of Qi trembled with fear, unable to say a word.

Li Chu hid himself behind Duke Jing and held his breath.

Only then did Yan Ying realize Li Chu's real intention in sponsoring the Qi-Lu meeting. He felt both regret and shame. Being an experienced diplomat, he quickly regained his composure. "There is no need to worry," he said to Duke Jing. "Confucius is a man who attaches great significance to the rules of propriety. He won't do anything that goes against the rites." He turned to Duke Ding. "What has happened just now is our fault. We failed to make proper arrangements, so that the dancing girls sang a licentious song by mistake. Please forgive us!" Then he bowed to Confucius, saying, "Minister of Justice, please calm your anger! I really did not know it beforehand. I apologize for what has happened."

Returning the salute, Confucius said with lingering anger, "Chief Minister, I have a question for you. Qi is a great state. Instead of adhering to the rites of Zhou and upholding the glory of our common ancestors, you played the music of barbarians, danced the dance of barbarians and sang licentious songs. Even I blushed with shame on your behalf. How do you feel about this, Chief Minister?"

As Confucius' rebuke was severe but well justified, Yan Ying lost his habitual eloquence and could not come up with a reply.

That evening Duke Jing sat in his tent in a despondent mood with Yan Ying and Li Chu.

Duke Jing slowly raised his head and said with displeasure and regret, "Minister Li, I do not want to blame you, but it is my impression that Confucius guides his ruler with ancient rules of propriety and righteousness, whereas you guide me with crude customs of savage people. Why?"

Li Chu remained silent, his mind churning. He had hoped to humiliate the duke of Lu, ruin Confucius' reputation, and check Lu's growth. However, against all his expectations, Confucius struck back and sent the duke of Qi and his ministers into a fix. He had made a fool of himself trying to be clever.

As the atmosphere grew tense in the tent, Yan Ying spoke up. "Your Lordship," he said, "this meeting place can be compared to a battleground. Though we lost the first round, that does not mean we have been defeated. When the treaty is signed tomorrow, we can find a way to gain the upper hand."

Li Chu slapped his leg and stood up. "The chief minister is absolutely right!" he said. "In my opinion, ..." The three of them began discussing what to do in the following day.

The next day, when all the articles had been agreed upon and the treaty was going to be signed, Li Chu suddenly proposed an additional article stipulating that whenever Qi launched an expedition against an external enemy, Lu must join the expedition with three hundred war chariots; otherwise it would be guilty of violating the treaty.

Duke Ding was astounded. That article would make Lu a dependency of Qi. He turned to look at Confucius.

Confucius called another minister of Lu named Zi Wu to him, and the two of them discussed the matter in a low voice. Then Zi Wu went back and said to Li Chu, "Since Qi and Lu have become two brotherly states, it is only natural for one side to help the other if there is an expedition. However, Lu also proposes an additional article: Qi must return the occupied territories of Huanyang, Yun and Guiyin to Lu; otherwise it would be guilty of violating the treaty."

Duke Jing and his two ministers were struck dumb. As the demand was entirely justified, they had no reason to refuse. Reluctantly he agreed to return Huanyang, Yun and Guiyin to Lu and had it written in the treaty.

Duke Ding was overjoyed and admired Confucius greatly for his courage and resourcefulness.

With the treaty signed, Qi and Lu concluded their meeting in Jiagu.

The men of Lu returned to the capital in high spirits. As for the men of Qi, it was an entirely different matter. Duke Jing sat sulking in his chariot. Yan Ying was lost in thought. Li Chu was filled with regret for fear that Duke Jing might blame him for this situation. Back in the capital, Yan Ying looked unusually haggard with his lean face and sunken eyes. He shuffled his way to Duke Jing and said in a soft voice, "Your Lordship, we did not get what we wanted at the meeting. However, Qi has conducted itself according to the rites by making some necessary concessions to Lu, apologizing for our mistake and returning some occupied territories. A great man knows when to yield. We don't have to worry over such a temporary setback."

Duke Jing smiled sadly.

Though he advised Duke Jing to take it lightly, Yan Ying was heavy-hearted himself. On his return to his residence, he felt so exhausted he could hardly move his legs. Struggling to the bed, he slumped down and felt sore all over his body. The ceiling seemed to be whirling and the bed shaking. He closed his eyes, feeling as if the world were turning around very fast.

For three days he was mostly lost in a coma and neither ate nor drank. Whenever he woke up he muttered the name of Confucius repeatedly.

He had always been intensely jealous of Confucius. There was a time when he considered himself a great hero capable of holding up the sky in spite of his short stature. However, he could not help feeling a sense of inferiority by the side of Confucius, who was conversant with all the six arts and displayed remarkable ability in both civil and military affairs. The day Duke Ding of Lu appointed Confucius to high office, Yan Ying's worst nightmare came true. Whenever he thought of this, he was filled with a sense of helpless rage, and his head ached so much that he felt he was going to die. But he did not want to die, for his ambition remained unfulfilled, the ambition of turning Qi into the most powerful of all the states.

The court physician visited him three times a day, but none of the medicines prescribed by him produced any effect. His condition continued to deteriorate.

One day when Duke Jing came personally to see him he said

in a weak voice, "Your Lordship, Qi will be the leader of the states someday! But there is Confucius in the state of Lu ..." He paused, two large teardrops rolling from his eyes.

Duke Jing felt greatly distressed, and his eyes also dimmed with tears. He said in a hoarse voice, "Honored minister, you'd better ..."

"Your Lordship," said Yan Ying. "It is better to strengthen oneself than to thwart the growth of one's opponent. We must attain power and prosperity for Qi!" There was a sudden surge of vigor in his voice, and his eyes brightened when he remembered the many things he had achieved. Given the opportunity, he would follow Lu's example and help Duke Jing restore the rites of Zhou in Qi. He would govern the state with benevolence and achieve a harmonious relationship with the common people. By winning people's support he would be able to make the state strong. Lost in thought, he almost forgot about his illness. Then his heart sank as he brought himself to face the dismal reality. He closed his eyes. He wanted to die happy with all his aspirations fulfilled instead of dying with a heavy heart because of Qi's steady decline. What could he do now? He opened his eyes again and said in a barely audible voice, "Your Lordship, after I die, my funeral should be conducted in the most simple manner."

Duke Jing nodded and was about to speak when Yan Ying's hand dropped abruptly.

Duke Jing called Yan Ying by his name but failed to get any response. He had died with his eyes still open.

As the chief minister Yan Ying was widely admired for his advocation of frugality in affairs of both the family and the state. The story of his successful mission to Chu, where he won honor for his state by his eloquence and wisdom, was known to every household. At the news of his death the entire state of Qi went into mourning. On the day of his burial many people joined in the funeral procession of their own accord, dressed in heavy mourning garments. Many people wept with grief.

Yan Ying was buried outside the inner city of the Qi capital. A high mound was constructed above his grave.

For several days people traveled to his grave to show their respect by burning incense and offering sacrifices.

After Yan Ying's burial, Duke Jing appointed Li Chu chief minister, which caused heated discussion both in and outside the court. Some ministers headed by Gao Zhaozi blamed Li Chu for bringing shame to Qi at the Jiagu meeting. Even Yan Ying's death, they argued, was partly the result of what Li Chu had done, so he shouldn't be appointed to such an important position. Other officials headed by General Tian Chang regarded Li Chu as a resourceful and loyal minister who had worked with heart and soul for Qi's good and therefore fully deserved the appointment. As for Duke Jing, he had his own considerations. He could not very well punish Li Chu for the fiasco at the Jiagu meeting, for Li Chu was acting with his permission. Once he had made Li Chu chief minister, he could not diminish his own authority by changing his mind even though many court officials objected to the appointment.

On his return to Lu, Confucius gained resounding fame by the diplomatic victory at the Jiagu meeting, and Duke Ding treated him with increased respect and favor. One day he walked out into the street dressed in a homely garment and light shoes, followed closely by two runners.

In the downtown area of the Lu capital the merchants were shouting their wares.

Confucius stopped in front of a butcher's shop.

The shop owner handed a piece of pork to an old man and said with a smile, "Five catties of pork. Take care!"

The old man was about to take the pork when Confucius stopped him. "Wait!" he said to the shop owner. "Please weigh it again. Let's see if it is indeed five catties."

The shop owner forced a smile. "Honored sir, please come in and have a seat."

Confucius said with a straight face, "I am asking you to weigh this piece of meat again!"

The shop owner muttered, "But I weighed it just now!"

"Was it full measure?"

The shop owner did not dare reply.

Confucius picked up the steelyard and weighed the meat himself. Pointing to the beam of the steelyard, he said, "Look, it is four and a half catties. Why did you sell it as five?"

The shop owner said hastily, "It was careless of me to make such a mistake. I'll let him pay the price of four and a half catties."

Confucius gave him a stern look. "No! You tried to cheat an old man and should be punished for it. You must give the meat to him for free!"

"That would not be fair!" cried the shop owner.

"Does this old man often come here to buy meat from you?" asked Confucius.

"Yes," said the old man. "I am a regular customer."

Confucius asked the shop owner, "Is he telling the truth?"

The shop owner replied in a low voice, "Yes."

Confucius said sternly, "When he came to buy five catties of meat, you gave him only four and a half. Since he often buys meat from you, who knows how much you have overcharged him? I am letting you off lightly by a fine of merely four and a half catties!"

The man became tongue-tied and lowered his head.

Just then they heard someone crying for help.

Chapter Nineteen

On Shimen Mountain the Disciples
Express Their Aspirations;
Among Apricot Trees the Master Sings
to the Accompaniment of the Zither

When Confucius looked up he saw a local bully taking liberties with a girl. He handed the pork to the old man and told him, "You may take it away!"

The old man said with a bow, "Many thanks, sir!"

Returning the salute, Confucius headed for the bully and demanded sternly, "Where are you from, you scoundrel, and how dare you humiliate a girl in broad daylight!"

The bully glared with his triangular eyes and dashed toward Confucius. "Ha! Ha! Who do you think you are, pretending to be a hero!" He raised his hand to strike Confucius.

Confucius dodged to the side, and the bully ran into the two runners walking behind Confucius.

"Arrest him!" cried Confucius.

The runners grabbed the bully tightly.

Confucius said, "A villain like him must be severely punished. Take him to prison!"

The runners left escorting the villain. The girl thanked Confucius and left. By this time some people had recognized Confucius. "The minister of justice has upheld the law by punishing the wicked and protecting the innocent. He deserves our respect and admiration!" One of them commented.

Confucius smiled at them, then walked away in giant strides. He went straight to the palace and, informed by an attendant that Duke Ding was enjoying the flowers in the garden, went there to find him.

Roses were in full bloom in the palace garden. Duke Ding was taking a stroll, enjoying the beautiful sights as if he hadn't a single care in the world.

Confucius approached him, bowed and said, "Your Lordship, at present there is neither internal trouble nor incursion from the

outside, and ..."

Duke Ding interrupted him, saying with satisfaction, "Right, the state is prosperous, the people are enjoying a peaceful life, we have good weather for the crops, and even the flowers look unusually attractive this year. Let's enjoy the good fortune heaven has bestowed on us!"

Confucius said after a pause, "But things are not exactly as what you said."

Surprised, Duke Ding asked, "Well?"

Confucius bowed again. "Your Lordship, though Lu has neither internal disturbance nor foreign invasion, there are some defects."

Duke Ding asked in astonishment, "What defects?"

"There are, for instance, merchants who dominate the market, charging exorbitant prices and giving short measure, and local villains who defy the law, bullying the weak and doing all kinds of evils."

Duke Ding relaxed his brows and smiled. "Well, I'll let you formulate regulations and mete out severe punishments to such people!"

"Your decree will be carried out!" With that Confucius left the garden and returned to his office at once to begin work on the regulations. He called his disciples to him and said, "At present Lu has established an alliance with Qi, so that the two states are like two brothers. Qi has returned to us the three places of Huanyang, Yun, and Guiyin, which it took from us by force many years ago. With no internal or external troubles to worry about, our lord begins to indulge himself in wine and pleasure, neglecting affairs of the state. Actually we are threatened by many crises. The social order is breaking down, with evil people throwing their weight around. The three houses have become more powerful than ever; their private forces grow steadily stronger, and their city walls keep getting higher. Gongshan Buniu, though defeated and driven to Qi, has been enlisting men in the border area preparing for a comeback. Without the elimination of these scourges our state will not be able to enjoy peace. I intend to promulgate a few regulations and have them implemented by force in order to ensure peace and stability in the state. Do you have any good suggestions to make about this?"

No sooner had Confucius finished his words than Zi Lu sprang to his feet. "Master, nothing can be easier than this! We can issue announcements and orders to stop the confusion in Lu the way we did in Zhongdu. Since the three houses have violated the rites by building the walls of their manors too high, we can send troops to tear down the walls by force. As for Gongshan Buniu, who hides himself in the mountain area near the border, just give me five hundred war chariots and I'll wipe him out in a single battle!"

"There is some truth in what you just said, but you have oversimplified the whole matter. Social disorder as we have today has resulted from many years of ill-management. It takes more than a day for a river to freeze over or for a tree to grow very tall. We can not expect to eradicate deep-rooted social evils overnight. The three houses have become so powerful that Lu's prosperity or downfall depends on them. How can you match them in strength? And how can you speak and act rashly against them, when you are the head steward in the chief minister's house? As for Gongshan Buniu, he is good at deceptive plots as well as martial arts. How can you possibly cope with him when even Generals Shen and Yue failed to capture him?"

Zi Lu wondered if Confucius was expressing doubt over his ability or trying to goad him into action. He sat down and listened to what his fellow disciples had to say.

Fair-skinned and soft-spoken, Ran Qiu looked much more like a scholar than Zi Lu. Facing his master, he stood up, brought his feet together and said, "Master, since Lu and Qi have just made an alliance, we can ask our lord to send a letter to Qi requesting that they send troops to drive Gongshan Buniu out of Qi territory. At the same time we'll also send troops to intercept him. Thus the joint forces of Lu and Qi will be able to wipe out Gongshan Buniu and his rebel army. Only by eliminating this mortal malady can we clear the path for governing Lu according to the rites."

With his big eyes and dark eyebrows, Mi Buqi looked quite astute. He bowed to Confucius with clasped hands. "Master and my fellow students," he said, "let me say a few unwise words. If a state is to be prosperous, its people must be at peace. Though there is no apparent turbulence in Lu, we can not tell when a calamity will befall us considering the situation in the world, with the strong always ready to devour the weak. Furthermore, we have the three powerful families in Lu that are not only engaged in a struggle among themselves but also attempt to usurp the authority of the ruling court. There are, in addition, local despots and villains who act outrageously at the expense of the common people. If we allow this situation to continue, how will

Lu be able to achieve stability? If there is no stability, how can it ever grow strong and prosperous? Therefore we must issue orders and promulgate regulations to punish the local tyrants, subdue the rascals, encourage men to till the land and women to weave cloth, protect fair dealings by merchants, carry out water conservancy projects, set up handicraft mills and business centers, and promote education. When people become wealthy, the state will be powerful. When the state is powerful, it can free itself of both external and internal troubles. If the ruling house can assert its authority, the three families will naturally decline."

Listening to him, Confucius looked pleased.

Yan Hui said, "Master, you were able to make a complete change in Zhongdu in only one year by implementing some regulations. Now we only have to revise these regulations and apply them to the entire state of Lu. People will obey the law just as grass will bend in a strong wind. In a year's time Lu will also undergo a complete change."

"Will you take up the task of revising those regulations?" asked Confucius.

"Yes, I will do it to the best of my ability."

While Confucius was talking with the disciples, a boy some twelve to thirteen years old called at the gate. The gate-keeper asked, "Where are you from, young boy, and why do you come to the office of the minister of justice?"

The boy had large eyes and hair long to his shoulders. He looked at the gate-keeper and said, "I come from Hu Village. My father told me to come and learn from the master."

Hu Village was a backward place notorious for the immoral conduct of its people. Hearing the boy's reply, the gate-keeper sneered, "How can a hopeless person like you bring yourself to see the master? Go back where you came from at once!"

The boy protested, "You are being unreasonable! Though Hu Village has a bad name, surely not everyone from there is a bad person. How can you turn me away like this?"

Growing impatient, the gate-keeper brushed the boy off with his hand, saying, "I don't have time to waste on you. Go away!"

The boy left in a huff.

When Confucius and his disciples walked out of the office, the gate-keeper reported the incident to him, confident that he had done the right thing. To his surprise, Confucius said with a frown, "Why didn't you report to me at once? The young boy came to learn from me by his father's order, so he must be a filial son. Though living in Hu Village, he has come to seek learning, so he must be intelligent. I would be only too pleased to have a filial and intelligent person as my disciple. How can we shut the door on him?"

Realizing his mistake, the gate-keeper lowered his head and fell silent.

Confucius said, "In the future you must be more careful and guard against rash action. When did he leave?"

"Only a moment ago."

"Go and invite him back!"

The gate-keeper ran off at once and soon returned with the boy.

The boy came up to Confucius and knelt to kowtow. "Master, you are famous for your virtue and learning. My father told me to study the rites with you."

"Get up, and we can have a talk."

The boy got on his feet and stood by the side of Confucius.

"What's your name?"

"My name is Xiang Xin, and my styled name is Zi Qiu," replied the boy.

Confucius went on to ask a few questions about basic knowledge, to which the boy replied fluently. Highly pleased, Confucius talked with him for about two hours before Xiang Xin took his leave and went home.

Gazing after him, Confucius remarked, "It is said that people in Hu Village are coarse and ill-mannered. But isn't Xiang Xin well-behaved?"

Puzzled, Zi Lu asked, "Master, Hu Village is a place where evil people are assembled. Other people would avoid dealing with anyone from that place, but you treated the boy with great kindness. Why?"

"Since that boy wants to get away from what is evil and approach what is good, it is our duty to help him. Have you never heard the saying, 'A superior man is always ready to help others attain a worthy goal'?"

"Yes, I have," replied Zi Lu.

"All of you should attempt to acquire the virtue displayed by the clear water in the river: It not only maintains its own purity but also washes away unwholesome elements from others."

The disciples took their leave, still thinking about their master's remark.

That evening Yan Hui finished revising the regulations. Early the next morning he submitted the revised version to Confucius, who made a few changes and bade his disciples make several copies of it on pieces of white silk. Then he had them posted on the gates of the capital and sent to magistrates of other cities to be carried out all over Lu. Half a year later there was a marked improvement in the general mood of the society.

Spring arrived again after winter, bringing life back to earth. Confucius rejoiced at the progress Lu was making toward prosperity. One day he left the city for an outing accompanied by Zi Lu, Yan Hui and Zi Gong. After walking about thirty li they arrived before a big river. Confucius looked up to see two high, steep peaks facing each other. They stretched to the east, with the river in between. In the dry season there were no torrential waves in the river. However, many streams flowed down from the mountain, creating a lot of waterfalls. Beautiful pebbles could be seen through the crystal-clear river water, some as large as bowls while others as small as apricots. Some were as white as jade and some shining like pearls. Confucius dismounted from the chariot to have a closer look. He sighed to himself, "I didn't expect to see such a beauty spot here. It would make an ideal dwelling place for the immortals!"

Zi Lu unharnessed the chariot, tied the horses to a tree, and walked over to a stream. He cupped some water with his hands and drank two mouthfuls. "How sweet it is!" he exclaimed, and, kneeling by the stream, he lowered his head and drank directly from it. Having drunk his fill, he was about to get up when he saw some small fish and shrimps in the water. "There are fish and shrimps here!" he cried with excitement. Just then a small crab crawled out from a fissure in the rock. When he tried to snatch it, the crab swiftly fled back inside the fissure.

"Don't drink the stream dry!" Zi Gong joked. "Elder brother, are you looking at yourself in the water or studying the rock?"

Zi Lu took Zi Gong by the hand and said, "Come over and take a look! There are fish, shrimps and crabs here!"

Zi Gong looked into the stream, intrigued by what he saw, but he said nonchalantly, "That's nothing to get excited about! Where there is water, there are bound to be fish, turtles, shrimps and crabs. Nothing can be more natural."

Confucius called to the two of them, "Let's climb up the mountain!"

Zi Lu and Zi Gong agreed and helped Confucius climb up. In spring everything in the mountain was full of vitality. The masson pines were giving off their peculiar fragrance. The gutweed was in full bloom. The birds were singing and building their nests. The lively scene filled Confucius with delight.

On reaching the summit, they looked around and found themselves surrounded by green hills. Confucius looked down at the river winding like a white ribbon between two mountain ridges. The two precipices underfoot looked like a pair of screen doors. If the doors could be shut, locking the entire valley, the river would form a lake. Confucius tried to think what such a lake would look like. He asked his disciples, "Do you know what the mountain is called?"

Zi Lu said, "There are many mountains in the world that don't have a name. Maybe this is one of them."

"Such a great mountain deserves a name," said Confucius. "I would call it the Stone Gate Mountain."

The three disciples clapped their hands, thinking it an appropriate name.

Confucius sat down on a stone slab and said, "Whenever I climb up a mountain I feel exhilarated. With a big mountain stretching below, a man can broaden his view, uplift his mind and contemplate the future. Faced with this beautiful sight, why don't you all say something about your aspirations?"

Zi Lu was the first to speak. "I want to lead a band of forces carrying banners of dragon, tiger, bird and snake and shouting deafening battle-cries. At the head of such an army, I will rout the enemy and capture their cities, winning a hundred victories in a hundred battles. Only I am endowed with such talents. As for Yan Hui and Zi Gong, they can do no more than serve as minor officers in my army to carry out my orders."

Confucius remarked, "You are indeed a brave warrior!"

Zi Gong spoke up with great confidence. "If Qi and Chu should fight in the field," he said, "and neither of them would back up though both have suffered great casualties, I will put on a splendid garment and visit the commanding generals of both sides, exhorting them to put an end to the battle by making them realize their mistakes. Only I am capable of accomplishing such a task, though I could take Zi Lu and Yan Hui along as my followers."

Still keeping his countenance, Confucius remarked, "A good speaker like yourself is indeed fit for a diplomatic career."

Yan Hui smiled but did not say anything.

"Yan Hui, why don't you say something? Don't you cherish any ambitions?" Confucius asked.

"Zi Gong is skilled at diplomacy, and Zi Lu is skilled at commanding troops. What else is left for me to do?"

"I just want all of you to talk about what you most like to do. Why don't you just say a few words?"

Straightening his short and thin body, Yan Hui said with assurance, "According to what I have heard, lavender and the stinking grass can not be kept in the same vessel; nor can the sage king Yao and the despot Jie rule in the same country. That's because they are opposite in essence. What I really want is to serve under a sage ruler. I will teach the people in the five essential virtues to make the father righteous, the mother benevolent, the elder brother friendly, the younger brother respectful, and the son filial. Then I will educate the people in rites and music, so that they will conduct themselves properly and treat one another with courtesy. Even without city walls, people will no longer attack one another. The day will come when the weapons are destroyed to make farm tools, when one can herd cattle, sheep, mules and horses in the field with no danger of being disturbed, when no one is separated from their loved ones, when there is no longer any war. When that day comes, who will need Zi Lu's bravery and Zi Gong's eloquence?"

Impressed, Confucius said, "Yan Hui, you have made virtue your ultimate aim. That's wonderful!"

Zi Lu asked with a bow, "Master, which of our aspirations do you opt for?"

"To waste no property, bring no harm to the people, and put an end to war and dispute—that's what Yan Hui wants. Naturally I agree with him."

Zi Lu retorted, "There has not been a single instance where the ancients subdued a revolt or established a new state without resorting to force. Both civil administration and military strength make up the foundations of a state. What's wrong about leading troops to battle?"

"Force should be employed, only after reason has failed to achieve the aim. When a person can be persuaded to mend his ways, we should not use force against him; when a person can be influenced by virtue and benevolence, we should not exhort him in blunt words. The best method of education is to influence people by subtle persuasion."

"Well," said Zi Lu, "there are so much for us to learn!" He thought for a while, then asked, "Master, what's your greatest aspiration?"

"I wish for the old to live in peace and comfort, my friends to trust me, and my descendants to cherish my memory."

"What's the relationship between learning and virtue?"

Confucius thought for a moment, then asked, "Do you realize that the six virtues can lead to six evils?"

"No, I don't," replied Zi Lu.

Confucius pointed to a rock by his side. "Sit down, and let me describe to you in detail these six evils and six virtues. If a man is benevolent but does not love learning, he will be easy to fool. If a man is clever but does not love learning, he will be licentious. If a man is honest but does not love learning, he will be easy to deceive. If a man is straightforward but does not love learning, he will be a caustic speaker. If a man is brave but does not love learning, he will be apt to provoke trouble. If a man is staunch but does not love learning, he will act recklessly."

Yan Hui asked, "Master, what is benevolence?"

"Restrain oneself and return to the rites of Zhou—this is called benevolence."

"But how can one attain benevolence?"

"If you speak and act in accordance with the rites of Zhou, you may be called benevolent. Once you achieve this, everyone in the world will look up to you as a benevolent man. You only have to rely on yourself to attain benevolence, without anyone else's help."

Yan Hui did not fully understand, so he asked again, "Can you tell us the key to the attainment of benevolence?"

Confucius stood up and said seriously, "Do not look at anything that is contrary to the rites, do not listen to anything that is contrary to the rites, do not speak anything that is contrary to the rites, and do not do anything that is contrary to the rites."

Overjoyed as if he had just been given a precious treasure, Yan Hui said, "Though I am stupid, I will follow your instructions, master."

"Master," asked Zi Lu. "You have a wide range of knowledge. Were you born with it, or have you acquired it through study?"

Confucius smiled. "Of course I have acquired it through study."

"What man may be called eager to learn?" asked Zi Lu.

"One may be called a superior man eager to learn if he does not satiate himself when eating, attaches little importance to daily comforts, fulfills his duties with diligence, speaks cautiously and modestly, and constantly attempts to rectify himself by calling on people of culture and virtue."

The four of them walked downhill along the same path by which they had come. They began to feel very hungry. Confucius said, "There are no restaurants around. Where can we have our meal?"

Zi Lu pointed to a peasants' house not far away. "Cooking smoke is rising from that house. Let's go there and ask for a meal."

Zi Gong objected. "In such a wild place, we can expect nothing but a very coarse meal. How will our master be able to eat that?"

Confucius said, "Let's go and take a look."

When they arrived at the small, dilapidated house, Zi Lu went up to knock at the wooden door. An old man came out, took a good look at them, and asked, "Is there something you want?"

Zi Lu made a deep bow and said, "Grandpa, we are travellers. I wonder if you could give us a meal. We will pay for it. Please help us!"

The old man said, "There is no need for you to pay. However, our meal is so coarse you probably won't be able to swallow it."

"Just prepare us a simple, everyday meal," said Zi Lu. "Don't take too much trouble about it."

The old man took out some wooden stools, invited them to sit down and wait for a moment, and returned into the room to cook the meal. After some time he brought out four crocks on a cracked plate. The crocks, blackened by smoke, looked coarse and dirty. Placing the plate on a stone slab under the eaves, he handed the crocks to Confucius and his three disciples. When Zi Gong opened the crock, he found it filled with coarse rice covered with a thick layer of chaff. Its peculiar odor made his stomach turn. Hurriedly he covered the crock, not knowing what to do. Zi Lu forced himself to eat a few mouthfuls, then gave up. As for Yan Hui, he ate up his share at one go, wiping his lips with satisfaction. Confucius also ate up his crock of cooked rice, showing no sign of reluctance, then he said to Zi Lu, "Pay the old man and thank him for the meal. We'll have to return."

Zi Lu brought out a few pieces of silver and handed them to the old man, saying, "Grandpa, thank you for the meal. Please accept this."

The old man said, "Even people who live in wilderness stress the importance of righteousness. Why should you thank me for such a coarse meal?"

Confucius said, "We have come uninvited to trouble you and must thank you for your kindness. Please accept it!"

Zi Lu placed the pieces of silver in the old man's hand, and they bade him good-bye.

When they were out of the thatched house, Zi Lu asked, "Master, you once said that rice can not be refined too much, nor can meat be minced too much. Just then that old man used coarse crocks for cooking, and the meal tasted terrible. How were you able to eat that?"

"It is true," said Confucius, "that the crocks were crude and the meal did not taste good at all. But the old man was treating us with sincerity and kindness. How could I hurt his feelings?"

Zi Lu felt instant regret, wishing he had eaten up the entire crock of rice. Zi Gong, however, pretended that he had not heard the master's words and walked behind them without saying anything.

Reaching the chariot, Confucius turned to take another look at Stone Gate Mountain. Reluctant to leave, he took out his zither and walked over to a group of apricot trees, where he pulled up the hem of his garment and sat down. Having adjusted the chords, he began to play and sing.

The poplar is large and tall.
Do not cut it down, do not chop it,
For Zhao Bo once slept under it.

He paused, as if lost in reminiscences about Zhao Bo, then went on singing.

The poplar is large and tall.
Do not cut it down, do not break it,
For Zhao Bo once rested under it.

The poplar is large and tall.
Do not cut it down, do not pull it up,
For Zhao Bo once reposed under it.

Zhao Bo, whose family name was Shi, founded the state of Yan in the early Zhou Dynasty. He assisted King Wu of Zhou to destroy the Shang Dynasty and was subsequently enfeoffed at Yan. He was a sage ruler whom Confucius held in high esteem. Listening to the

melodious music and the song, the disciples felt as if they could see
Zhao Bo wandering under the poplar. Sitting rigidly upright, Confucius rested for a while, then continued.

> It is so merry by the stream;
> The good man is feeling well at ease.
> He sleeps alone, wakes alone and speaks alone;
> A joy like this is unforgettable.

He shifted his gaze from the stream to the valley.

> It is so merry in the mountain;
> The good man is feeling so cozy.
> He sleeps alone, wakes alone and sings alone;
> A joy like this is hard to forget.

Then he turned to gaze at the hill.

> It is so merry on the plateau;
> The good man is strolling with a light heart.
> He sleeps alone, wakes alone and lies in bed alone;
> A joy like this can not be conveyed.

Zi Lu, Yan Hui and Zi Gong listened for a moment, then took
out a piece of white silk, spread it to reveal some poems from *The Book
of Poetry*, and began to sing along with their master.

> You have given me a papaya,
> And I return you a piece of jade.
> It is not meant for gratitude,
> But a token of our everlasting love.

The sound of the zither became crisp and clear, and the tune
joyful. While singing, they saw in their mind's eye a couple of youth
exchanging their love tokens.

> You give me a peach,
> And I return you a piece of jade.
> It is not meant for gratitude,
> But a token of our everlasting love.

> You give me a plum,
> And I return you a piece of jade.
> It is not meant for gratitude,
> But a token of our everlasting love.

Confucius put down the zither and began to stroll among the blossoming apricot trees. Bees flew among the trees to gather pollen from the flowers. He marveled at their agility, joy and industry. "Come here and have a look!" he called out to his disciples. Zi Lu, Yan Hui and Zi Gong tucked away the white silk and came over. "Look at the bees. They are brave, industrious, and friendly to one another. They come together in large numbers to gather honey without causing any trouble. In this respect the bees are much superior to man. The confusion in our time is really dismal. Just think about some of the things that happened in recent years. In spring of the fifth year of Duke Ding' reign, the men of Zhou killed Prince Chao in Chu. That summer Yue invaded Wu. In the first month of the sixth year of the reign of Duke Ding, the state of Zheng destroyed the state of Xu. When will we be able to restore the rites of Zhou if people keep on fighting among them in this way?"

Zi Lu asked, "Master, Lu has achieved unprecedented progress toward peace and prosperity since you became minister of justice. Why are you given to sadness instead of feeling glad?"

Confucius smiled. "It is true that we have made some progress in Lu, but many things have yet to be done. For one thing, Lu will not be free of danger until Gongshan Buniu is eliminated. Furthermore, the city walls of the three houses are a violation of the rites. Unless they are reduced in height, we will have no hope of restoring the rites of Zhou."

On their return to the city they met Duke Ding outside the city gate watching kites. At the sight of Confucius Duke Ding said, "My honored minister, it is such a beautiful day in spring. Come over and enjoy these kites with me!"

Confucius hurriedly dismounted and knelt in obeisance. "Kong Qiu pays homage to Your Lordship!"

Without moving his gaze from the kites, Duke Ding said nonchalantly, "You may rise, honored minister."

Confucius looked at Duke Ding's face caught in the last rays of the sun and felt much displeased. After the meeting in Jiagu the duke paid little attention to state affairs but had begun to indulge himself in pleasure, and Confucius had long wanted to advise him against it. He stood by Duke Ding's side and said in a low voice, "Your Lordship, I was not informed that you were going to watch the kites here today."

"Oh," said the duke carelessly. "I just decided to come here on impulse."

Confucius frowned and said bluntly, "But your every remark or move may influence the prosperity or downfall of the state!"

"Really? A single remark can make a state prosperous? Can you give me an example?"

"It is not that simple. However, people say that it is not easy for the ruler or the subjects to fulfill their respective duties. If the ruler realizes the difficulty involved in his duty but tries his best to fulfill it, can't we then say that the state will become prosperous because of a single remark?"

Duke Ding no longer watched the kites but turned to look at Confucius attentively. "Well, can you give me an instance where a single remark brings about the downfall of a state?"

"It is not that simple. However, on one occasion a ruler remarked that he enjoyed nothing better than to have no one disobey him. If a ruler makes a wrong remark but no one dares disobey, can't we say that the state will deteriorate because of a single remark?"

Duke Ding considered Confucius' words carefully and finally said, "You are indeed a sage, honored minister!"

Just then a palace guard came running in and reported, "Your Lordship, Gongshan Buniu has returned to Lu and recaptured the city of Fei."

Duke Ding was enraged by the news and was rendered speechless.

Chapter Twenty

The Lu Army Gains a Victory by Luring
the Enemy Away from His Base;
Fighting Against Overwhelming Odds,
the Rebel Troops Suffer a Crushing Defeat

"Your Lordship, please return to the palace and summon the court officials to a meeting," suggested Confucius.

Duke Ding turned to the guards, "Let's return to the palace!"

The guards hurriedly helped Duke Ding onto the chariot and escorted him back to the rear palace.

It was growing dark. Duke Ding sighed deeply, looking downcast and gloomy, then asked Confucius, "Honored minister, Gongshan Buniu must have evil intentions that do not bode well for us. I want to send troops to wipe him out immediately. What do you suggest?"

"The city of Fei is a manor of the chief minister. After Gongshan Buniu's escape to Qi, the chief minister appointed Shusun Zhe magistrate of Fei. Shusun Zhe, however, has always worked hand in glove with Gongshan Buniu. I suspect that Gongshan Buniu was able to capture Fei this time partly because of Shusun Zhe's coordination. Therefore we must not take rash action, but must make careful preparations to ensure our success."

"After Gongshan Buniu fled to the mountains," said the duke, "I thought he would no longer cause any trouble and did not expect him to return to Fei so quickly. You must be right in saying that he had Shusun Zhe's cooperation. But what do you think we should do?"

Confucius was about to speak when a palace guard rushed in and saluted to Duke Ding, saying, "Your Lordship, Hou Fan, one of Minister Shusun's stewards, has raised a revolt in the city of Hou."

Stupefied, Duke Ding flopped down into the chair.

The guards swarmed up to him, stroking his chest and patting him on the back. After a while Duke Ding regained his composure. He looked at Confucius pleadingly. "Honored minister, one disaster has followed another. What shall we do?"

Confucius glanced at the palace guards and attendants. Taking

the cue, Duke Ding swept his arm. "Retreat, all of you!"

The palace maids and the guards withdrew at once.

"Your Lordship," Confucius began, "the chief minister, Minister Shusun and Minister Mengsun, relying on the power of their household stewards, have kept increasing the height of their city walls and expanding their private troops. This not only goes against the rites of Zhou but also threatens the safety of the ruling court."

"I have long hoped to eliminate these menaces. What do you think we should do?"

"We must reduce the city walls of these three houses to make them conform to the rites."

"What if Jisun, Shusun and Mengsun refuse?"

"At the audience tomorrow I will speak to the court officials, explaining that the city walls of the three houses exceed the limit according to the rites of Zhou. The chief minister, Minister Shusun and Minister Mengsun may feel displeased, but being well acquainted with the rites, they are not likely to argue irrationally. With their acquiescence, we will be able to destroy the city walls of their manors."

"What if they refuse to do so?"

"If they should disobey, we can dismantle the city walls by force. Now Hou Fan has revolted in Hou, while Gongshan Buniu and Shusun Zhe has captured Fei. It provides a good opportunity for us to take military action."

"The Lu army is not very strong and may not be equal to the task of destroying the city walls of the three houses."

Confucius reassured the duke, saying, "Your Lordship need not worry. In their attempt to build up their strength the three houses have accumulated many grievances against one another. We will be able to make use of this." He then explained his plan in detail.

Duke Ding nodded his head and finally broke into a smile. "You may proceed with your plan," he said. "Set to your tasks immediately!"

"I'll obey your order!"

"Honored minister, this matter is of utmost importance. Please be very cautious!"

"Please set your mind at ease. I will deal with it to the best of my ability."

After seeing Confucius off, Duke Ding remained worried and returned to his bed-chamber without eating supper. For the first time he began to realize his mistake. Since he became ruler of Lu, he had spent all his time in sensual pleasures, enjoying songs and dance, allowing himself to become accustomed to the flattery of sycophants. "Why wasn't I aware of the threats?" he asked himself, gazing at the swaying bamboos outside the window. "Well, I never thought about them." Again his mind drifted to the palace maids, their beautiful songs and voluptuous dance movements. Hastily he checked himself and tried to concentrate on the present crisis. He imagined the heated argument at the morning audience the next day: Jisun Si would fly into a fury, Mengsun Heji would pretend compliance, and Shusun Zhouchou would not give an unequivocal reply. He was grateful to Confucius, who destroyed Li Chu's plan to insult him in front of Duke Jing of Qi, enabled Lu to grow strong steadily by implementing appropriate measures, and worked out a plan to weaken the three houses. The duke felt too agitated to sleep.

In the meantime Confucius was thinking how to deploy the troops to wipe out the rebels.

Duke Ding felt guilty when he held the morning audience the following day, the 10th of the third month of the twelfth year of his reign (498 B.C.), something he had not done for a long time. After the court officials had saluted him, he said in a loud voice, "My honored ministers, do you have any questions to debate?"

All the officials had learned about Hou Fan's revolt and Gongshan Buniu's return to the city of Fei. Failing to come up with any solution, they looked at one another and said nothing. It was so quiet in the hall one could have heard a pin drop.

Confucius emerged from the rank of civil officials holding a jade tablet in both hands. He came up to Duke Ding and bowed deeply, saying, "Your Lordship, Hou Fan has raised a revolt in the city of Hou, and Shusun Zhe has also revolted in Fei. Gongshan Buniu has returned and joined forces with Shusun Zhe."

Duke Ding asked eagerly, "I have learned all this. The question is, how shall we subdue the rebels?"

Quoting from ancient documents, Confucius replied, "The rites of Zhou stipulate that there should be no weapons in any household and no large city walls should be built in any manor. The situation in Lu, however, goes against the rites. There are private troops in some households, and the walls of some manors are so high that they are comparable to the royal capital. I beseech the chief minister, Minister Shusun and Minister Mengsun to set up a good example by destroying the city walls in their manors and placing their private troops under the command of the state. In this way the rites will be upheld, and the ruling house strengthened. When the rites are upheld, the people will give their support. When the ruling house is strengthened, the state will grow powerful, and the people wealthy."

Stunned, Mengsun Heji stole a glance at Jisun and Shusun, who to his surprise appeared calm and well at ease.

All the officials were waiting for the three of them to respond.

With two of his household stewards turning against the state, Jisun was unable to cope with the situation all by himself. On hearing Confucius' words, he was very pleased, for he wanted to use the authority of the state to defeat the rebel troops under Gongshan Buniu and Shusun Zhe. "It is my stewards," he said to Confucius, "who violated the rites by building high city walls. I support the Minister of Justice's suggestion." He stepped forward and saluted to Duke Ding. "Your Lordship, I think we can proceed as the minister of justice has proposed. Let's first destroy the city walls, then gather the private troops together."

Shusun, who was in the same predicament as Jisun, said earnestly, "Your Lordship, let's carry out the plan proposed by the minister of justice!"

Mengsun did not expect the two of them to assume such an attitude and wondered whether the opinions they were expressing were the ones they really held.

Growing impatient, Duke Ding raised his voice and asked, "Minister Mengsun, what is your opinion?"

Mengsun composed himself and said hesitatingly, "Well, I think ... we can proceed as the minister of justice has proposed."

Duke Ding was overjoyed that the matter could have been settled so smoothly and quickly. He sprang to his feet, intending to ask who would be willing to lead troops to fight Hou Fan and Shusun Zhe. Then he checked himself when he remembered what Confucius had said to him earlier. So he announced, "The audience is over!"

Returning from the palace, Confucius invited Shen Juxu and Yue Qi to his office and told them about his plan. "If either of you have any suggestions," he said, "please do not hesitate to tell me."

"Minister of Justice," Shen said, "your plan is really foolproof. I'm sure we will achieve total victory by following it strictly."

Yue said, "Minister Mengsun's manor, Cheng, is very near to the capital. I heard that even now Gonglian Chufu, one of Mengsun's stewards and the magistrate of Cheng, is strengthening its walls. Is it not possible that he would take advantage of our weakness to attack after our troops have set out for Hou and Fei?"

Confucius smiled. "It is commendable of you, General Yue, to pay attention to such details. In my opinion, Gonglian Chufu is building the city walls for defense purposes. He does not have the strength to take drastic military action."

Still worried, Yue said, "Minister of Justice, you'd better be careful!"

"I will," replied Confucius.

Shen and Yue returned to deploy the troops according to Confucius' order, and Confucius went in person to call on Mengsun Heji.

At the news Mengsun Heji came out to receive Confucius. As he had formerly acknowledged Confucius as his master, he fell on his knees to kowtow, but Confucius stopped him. "Don't stand on ceremony, Minister Mengsun. I have come to ask you a favor."

"Master, please come into the parlor where we can talk."

They went to the parlor and took the seats of host and guest. "Master, tell me what I can do for you, and it will be done," said Mengsun.

Confucius said, "At present Hou Fan has revolted in Hou, and Shusun Zhe has revolted in Fei in collusion with Gongshan Buniu. Since the state of Lu is facing such difficulties, I hope you will go and persuade Gonglian Chufu to stay calm and reduce the city walls to the scale sanctified by the rites. In this way you can avoid using force and win the praise of both the court officials and the common people."

Of the three houses, the Mengsun was the weakest. Mengsun Heji heard Confucius out glumly, thought for a moment, then said, "The present crisis can be attributed to the chief minister and Minister Shusun, who have been building up their private forces for quite a long time."

"I have come here today," said Confucius, "to remind you that further crisis can be avoided if you persuade Gonglian Chufu to conform to the rites."

"These treacherous stewards are indeed hateful. I will follow your advice, master, and go to persuade Gonglian myself."

"That is excellent. I will take my leave then."

The following day a band of troops set out for Hou carrying two banners embroidered with names of the commanders, "Shen" and "Yue." Shen Juxu and Yue Qi sat in their chariots at the head of the army. They stopped and made camp in front of Hou. The soldiers approached the city gates to challenge the enemy every day, but they did not seem eager to launch an attack.

Hou Fan dared not come out the city to give battle, for he knew both Shen Juxu and Yue Qi were formidable opponents. He stayed in the city for three days, watching the enemy from the gate tower. As his troops and the residents in the city began to grow restless, Hou Fan dispatched two messengers, who slipped out of the city in the dead of night and went to Cheng and Fei to ask for reinforcements. The besieging troops paid no attention to them and let them get away.

In the city of Fei, Gongshan Buniu and Shusun Zhe were busy recruiting soldiers to expand their troops. They sent out men to gather wood for making war chariots, and many families in the surrounding areas were robbed of planks they had reserved for making coffins or even those already made. The rebels caused such confusion in the city that even the dogs and fowls had no peace. Complaints could be heard everywhere.

With their skills in martial arts and a hundred war chariots under their command, Gongshan Buniu and Shusun Zhe had been fondly hoping to capture the Lu capital, kill Duke Ding and his officials, and set up a new ruling court, in which Gongshan Buniu would be the sovereign and Shusun Zhe the chief minister. To turn their dream into reality at the earliest chance, they intensified the training of the troops. Loud battle-cries reverberated over the drill ground, and war chariots patrolled the streets all day.

One day a scout arrived to report, "Honored sir, Shen Juxu and Yue Qi have led troops to attack Hou."

"What?" Gongshan Buniu leapt out of his chariot and caught the scout by his hand. "Is the information reliable?"

"I saw it with my own eyes. The troops carried the generals' banners emblazoned with the huge characters 'Shen' and 'Yue'."

Filled with excitement, Shusun Zhe said, "Big brother, let's set out at once!"

Gongshan Buniu leaned back and broke out laughing. "Thank Heaven for giving me such a good opportunity! Guards, pass on my order to the troops: Stop drilling and make ready to set out!" Suddenly his face fell. He paced around a couple of times and batted his eyes, muttering to himself, "That stupid duke has learned of my revolt in Fei. How could he have ordered both Shen Juxu and Yue Qi to attack Hou? Could this be a trap?"

Shusun said, "Big brother, you are worrying too much! That fatuous duke is only interested in wine and women. What does he know about strategy?"

Gongshan pulled a long face. "You are mistaken! Of course the duke is stupid and ignorant, but Confucius is a wise and prudent man. How could he have been so careless? We must not be deceived by their cunning moves and take rash action!"

Just then another scout arrived. "Honored sir, Shen Juxu and Yue Qi have left the capital to attack Hou."

Gongshan asked loudly, "Are you sure?"

"Yes, I saw it with my own eyes."

"Did you see Shen Juxu and Yue Qi?"

"Yes, I did. According to your order, I dressed myself like a pedlar and stood watching by the road. Shen Juxu and Yue Qi passed right before my eyes in their chariots. They looked truly grand!"

"What?" Gongshan's eyes bulged.

Frightened, the scout dared not speak again.

Gongshan swept his hand and said, "Away with you!"

The scout ran away as fast as he could.

Shusun bowed with clasped hands, saying, "Big brother, the two scouts have brought the same news. Let's set out at once! If we let the opportunity slip, it may be lost forever!"

Gongshan stamped his foot and decided to cast the die. He told Shusun to summon all the officers to a meeting in the magistrate's office.

"Brothers," Gongshan began, "we have endured great sufferings hiding in the mountains and sleeping in sheds. Why? Because we want to rise head and shoulders above the others! We are all of us men of great strength and courage. There is no reason why we should remain servants forever!"

Shusun said, "Big brother, all of us are willing to follow your order to fight the fatuous duke. Once we succeed, you will be the ruler of Lu, and the rest of us will become court officials. At present the entire Lu army has set out to attack Hou. We should take advantage of this to capture the poorly defended capital."

"Brothers, what do you think of this?" Gongshan asked the other officers.

The officers were all desperados who clamored, "We are willing to follow your order!"

After the babble subsided, Gongshan stood up. "Good! We are only one hundred li from the Lu capital. We will set out this afternoon and arrive there at dawn tomorrow. Once our expedition is successfully carried out, I'll reward all of you according to your merits. I hope you will charge forth bravely and not stop fighting until that incompetent ruler is killed."

"What shall we do with the officials we capture?" asked Shusun.

Gongshan bit his teeth forcefully. "Kill them all! Only thus can we make a complete change in Lu." Suddenly he thought of Confucius and added hastily, "Confucius alone should be kept alive."

"Big brother, why will you treat with consideration a man like Confucius who once humiliated you?" Shusun asked.

"It is true that among all the court officials of Lu, Confucius alone humiliated me on one occasion. However, he is a man of great knowledge and exceptional wisdom. If I could persuade him to assist me, not only the state of Lu but the entire kingdom of Zhou would be within my reach. Why should I be in a hurry to kill a man so useful to me? Furthermore, because he humiliated me, I will deliberately treat him with magnanimity so as to leave a good name in history."

"When shall we start out?" asked Shusun.

"To move swiftly is the best tactic in war," declared Gongshan. "Let's summon the troops and set out at once. All of you, tend to your respective duties!"

The officers swarmed out of the magistrate's office and, gathering the troops under their command, headed for the Lu capital.

In order to surprise the enemy, Gongshan ordered the bells on the horses taken off so that the troops could proceed quietly.

At dawn they arrived at Fangshan Mountain only about ten li from the capital. Bidding his men to stop, Gongshan climbed up a mound and gazed into the distance, but he could see nothing due to a thick fog. There was a deadly silence except for the rising and falling of cocks' crowing. Caught in a gust of cold wind, Gongshan shuddered. He regained his composure and muttered to himself, "This is the chance of a lifetime. I must stick to my decision!"

"Big brother, we're only an hour from the capital. Why did you order the troops to stop?" Shusun asked.

"We do not know the strength of the troops defending the capital. We must prepare ourselves against emergencies!"

"Since Shen Juxu and Yue Qi have gone off to attack Hou, there will be few troops left in the capital. We can capture it at one go. Why do you worry so much?"

"Confucius is too clever to leave the capital undefended. I suspect that ..."

Shusun interrupted, "Even a wise man can make a mistake. Moreover, how could he know we are coming to capture the capital?"

Just then a mounted soldier arrived and reported, "Honored sirs, a messenger from the magistrate of Hou arrived in Fei with the news that Hou has been under siege from a superior force led by Shen Juxu and Yue Qi. The magistrate dared not venture out to fight the enemy and requested you to send reinforcements."

Gongshan was at last relieved of his apprehension. Believing that he would soon enter the capital, he could no longer contain his excitement and let out a shout of laughter. "Foolish duke, your end is come!" He drew his sword and said to Shusun, "Order the troops to advance. Whoever kills the weak-minded ruler will be amply rewarded!"

Shusun mounted his chariot and announced in a loud voice, "Officers and soldiers! Minister Gongshan has given the order to attack the city before daybreak. Whoever enters the city first and kills the witless ruler will receive the greatest reward!" He drew his sword and shouted, "Charge!"

At once the capital was shaken by the sound of rolling chariots, galloping horses and soldiers' battle-cries.

The ground in Fangshan Mountain slanted downward from east to west. Gathering speed, the war chariots charged forth with great momentum.

Eager to gain victory, Gongshan and Shusun no longer bothered to keep the troops in formation but charged ahead in their chariots. They soon arrived at the foot of the mountain.

All of a sudden there arose the deafening sound of bronze gongs as many war chariots emerged from the forest. They arrayed themselves like a pincer and began to close in on Gongshan Buniu and Shusun Zhe.

The two of them were flabbergasted. Under the first rays of the morning sun they saw many more chariots riding out of the forest. The generals' banners were embroidered with the big characters of "Shen" and "Yue" respectively.

The rebel troops were thrown into consternation. They could not understand how Shen Juxu and Yue Qi could have returned so swiftly from Hou.

All this had actually been arranged by Confucius according to the strategy of "luring the tiger out of the mountain." He selected two soldiers who looked like Shen Juxu and Yue Qi respectively, dressed them in generals' robes and seated them in generals' chariots. Then he ordered a general named Zi Wu to lead a band of forces, apparently under the command of the two substitutes, to besiege Hou. Shen Juxu and Yue Qi stayed in the capital and dispatched scouts to observe the movements of the enemy. Informed of the coming of Gongshan Buniu and Shusun Zhe, they hastily summoned the troops and lay ambush in the forest.

Realizing that they had fallen into a trap, Gongshan and Shusun turned their chariots and tried to flee. By this time the road was crowded with chariots and horses going in all directions as the rebel troops were thrown into total confusion.

Shen Juxu and Yue Qi pursued the enemy and kept shooting arrows.

Gongshan and Shusun fled as fast as they could. Many of their men were shot dead. Some soldiers, injured by arrows, fell from the chariots and were trampled to death.

Gongshan turned into a small lane, with Shusun close at his heels. Rebel soldiers were flying in all directions, some toward Fei while others into the forest.

Shen said, "General Yue, I'll pursue the enemy here, and you can lead fifty chariots and reach Fei by a roundabout route. By capturing it you can cut off the escape of the rebels. We'll join forces in Fei after gaining victory."

Whereupon, Yue Qi left for Fei with fifty war chariots.

The road was strewn with broken chariots and corpses. By the time Gongshan reached Gumie, he found himself left with only about twenty chariots following him. He wanted to rest, but Shen Juxu's banner appeared in the distance. Knowing it would be difficult for him to escape, he decided to put up a desperate fight. "There are two choices for us to make," he announced to his followers, "either to be captured and executed, or to turn and fight the pursuing enemy with all our might. What do you think?"

"We are willing to follow your order!" the soldiers chorused.

With a ferocious look on his face, Gongshan shouted in a hoarse voice, "Officers and soldiers! Turn your chariots and charge at the enemy!"

The soldiers turned their chariots to fight their pursuers.

This was a small piece of flat ground surrounded by farmlands planted with wheat just turning green. The two opposing forces began to fight fiercely. After about a dozen rounds, Gongshan lost another five chariots.

Gongshan grew more and more anxious. Just then Shusun was injured by an arrow and fell out of his chariot with a scream. Shen Juxu's men swarmed up, and a short moment later Shusun had arrows all over his body. At the sight of this Gongshan Buniu was greatly startled.

Shen Juxu shouted, "Gongshan Buniu, step down the chariot and give yourself up! Otherwise you will come to the same end as Shusun Zhe!"

Gongshan whispered to the driver, "Unharness a horse, quick!" At the same time he stood up in the chariot and gazed into the distance as if he had found something. Sure enough, Shen Juxu's men also turned to stare in the same direction.

Gongshan leapt from the chariot onto the unharnessed horse, struck it with the handle of his sword and galloped away.

"Shoot him!" cried Shen Juxu.

It was too late. The arrows fell to the ground before they reached Gongshan.

Furious, Shen said to his soldiers, "Kill all the rebels!"

The soldiers surrounded what was left of Gongshan Buniu's troops and killed everyone who dared resist.

Shen drove his chariot to pursue Gongshan, who vanished into a dense forest by the Sihe River. Filled with anger and shame, Shen muttered to himself, "What a sort of general am I, who can not catch and kill such a traitor!" When he reached the forest, which the chariot could not enter, he unharnessed a horse, swung onto it and sped on. He crossed the Sihe River and climbed over a hill, where he found Gongshan on another hill in the distance. Knowing he could not catch Gongshan this time, Shen returned. He began to place his hopes on Yue Qi.

In the meanwhile Yue Qi led another band of forces to the poorly defended Fei and captured it with little fighting. He ordered the soldiers to close the city gates and hide the war chariots inside the city, making ready to venture out as soon as Gongshan Buniu returned. When Gongshan did not appear, Yue Qi felt a little puzzled and said to himself, "Have the rebels all been wiped out by General Shen? Or has Gongshan Buniu had a narrow escape?" He stood watching on the gate tower and saw a mounted soldier galloping toward the city gate.

Chapter Twenty-one

Confucius Advises the Duke of Lu to
Restore the Rites of Zhou;
Qi Uses Beautiful Maidens to Disrupt the Lu Court

Arriving before the city gate, the soldier dismounted, bowed with clasped hands and said, "General Yue, Shusun Zhe was shot dead at Gumie, and the rebel troops were completely wiped out. Gongshan Buniu alone had fled to Qi."

"Where is General Shen?" Yue Qi asked.

"He is gathering forces at Gumie and preparing to set out for Hou."

Yue Qi had the city gate opened to let the soldier in. He ordered his men to stay in Fei to dismantle the city wall and set out in a chariot by himself, heading for Hou by a shortcut.

On the road to Hou he caught up with Shen Juxu and rode along with him. To confuse the enemy, they had their banners concealed.

At the sight of many war chariots approaching the city, Hou Fan, the magistrate of the city of Hou, was overjoyed, taking it for reinforcements from Gongshan Buniu and Shusun Zhe. He ordered his men to make ready to leave the city and prepare for battle. To his bitter disappointment, the newly arrived troops joined the ranks of the besiegers.

Shen and Yue met Zi Wu, and together they rode around the city to observe the terrain, then returned to the camp-site.

Hou Fan stood on the gate tower, his knees knocking together with fear. He regretted having overestimated his own strength. He racked his brains for a way out. To fight the enemy head-on would mean certain defeat. If he capitulated, he would doubtlessly spend the rest of his life in prison. The best choice was to abandon the city and flee, but how could he break out of the encirclement in face of such overpowering forces?

The sun was setting. He narrowed his eyes in the sunlight, his lean face looking more dismal than ever. Then he recalled how he had sent messengers one after another to sneak out of the city at night and go to Cheng and Fei to ask for help, to the ignorance of the besieging

forces. This was his last hope, like a piece of wood caught by a drowning man in a swift river. He turned to gaze down at the city of Hou and felt a return of confidence. He had hoped to use Hou as a power base from which he could recruit followers until he became strong enough to capture cities and overthrow the rule of Duke Ding. He would then preside over the court and rule the entire state. As if encouraged by his daydream, he placed his hand on his sword and watched down the city gate with shining eyes.

Having finished deploying the troops, Shen went up to the city gate in his chariot. He pointed at Hou Fan with his sword and shouted, "Traitor, come down and surrender!"

Hou Fan let out a fit of hideous laughter. "Minister Shen, you are supposed to be a very capable general. So, why have you not done anything since you besieged the city many days ago?"

Shen laughed, "Traitor, you have fallen into my trap. The Shen Juxu you saw was a fake." He swept his hand, and Yue Qi came up in his chariot accompanied by the soldier who looked like Shen Juxu. "Take a close look. Can you tell which of us is genuine?"

Hou widened his eyes in surprise but could not tell them apart. Filled with shame and regret, he shouted, "Shen Juxu and Yue Qi, I won't stop fighting until I kill both of you! You are both generals of Lu, yet you have played such a dirty trick. Neither of you deserves to be called a gentleman!"

Shen laughed. "Isn't it ridiculous for a traitor to talk about being a gentleman? Are you ignorant of the principle that there can not be too much deception in war? An idiot like you trying to raise a revolt is just like an insect trying to shake a mighty tree, don't you think?"

Overcome with shame, Hou shouted hoarsely, "Men, hand me a bow and arrows!"

A soldier standing by his side hastily handed him a bow and some arrows.

He took three steps forward, placed an arrow onto the bow and shot it at Shen.

Shen dodged, caught the arrow in his hand, and threw it onto the ground with a sneer.

Hou shot two more arrows, which were both caught by Shen. He screamed angrily.

Yue shot three arrows in return. Hou hid himself behind a pillar, on which the three arrows landed.

Stroking his slightly bruised cheek, Hou realized he was no match for the enemy forces. He retreated into the gate tower and, though Shen Juxu, Yue Qi and Zi Wu kept shouting curses, did not venture out again.

After dark Shen Juxu ordered drums to be beaten as a signal for attack. The troops moved toward the city, keeping out of the shooting range of arrows, and shouted battle-cries loudly.

Hou panicked and ordered his archers to shoot arrows.

Arrows fell like rain from the city wall but failed to injure a single person. After several rounds Hou realized he had been fooled and shouted to the archers, "Stop shooting! Don't shoot again without my order!"

Having achieved the desired effect, Shen ordered the drummers to keep beating the drums, then sent a crack force to mount the city wall with scaling ladders. A few of them got on the city wall and embarked on close combat with the defending troops. Though some ladders were cut down by the defenders, with the climbers falling down the city wall, reinforcements were sent in by Shen. After heavy fighting the defending troops began to waver. Knowing the battle was lost, Hou exchanged clothes with a soldier and ran toward the east gate along a small lane, hoping to find a chance to get away.

The attackers broke through the south gate, shouting victoriously, and replaced the banners on the city wall with their own.

Shen Juxu ordered torches to be lit. The city wall and surrounding areas were bathed in light as bright as day.

To prevent Hou Fan's escape, Shen had ordered Yue Qi and Zi Wu to lay siege to the east and north gates respectively. Just as the torches were lit up, Yue Qi saw a soldier gliding down the city wall along a rope. He aimed an arrow at the soldier and hit him squarely on the back. With a scream the soldier dropped to the ground.

The east gate was also captured by the attackers. Many rebel soldiers surrendered. Upon entering the city, Shen, Yue and Zi headed straight to the magistrate's office, where even after a thorough search they failed to find Hou Fan. Among the dead bodies inside the south gate they found one dressed in Hou Fan's clothes, but it was not Hou. So they continued their search.

It suddenly occurred to Yue that he had shot down a soldier at the east gate. He said, "General Shen, I shot someone dressed like a soldier trying to escape by the east gate. It might be Hou Fan in disguise."

"Let's go and take a look!"

They went to the east gate and found the body. Under the torchlight, they recognized to their great relief that the man was indeed Hou Fan. Then they began to clean up the battlefield.

Early the next morning Shen ordered the troops to reduce the height of the Hou city wall according to Confucius' instruction. He feasted the officers and men for the victory and gave them three days off. Then they set out for the city of Cheng.

On hearing the news, Gonglian Chufu climbed up the city gate to watch the oncoming troops. He had no intention to resist by force, for that would mean certain defeat. Instead, he planned to gain a victory with his tongue. When Shen Juxu, Yue Qi and Zi Wu arrived before the city, Gonglian Chufu had the city gate opened and the suspension bridge lowered, and came out of the city all by himself. Gonglian Chufu was in his fifties, handsome, fair-skinned, with a beard that reached to his chest. Walking in steady steps and smiling all over his face, he approached the three generals, bowed politely, and said in a stentorian voice, "I did not know the three generals were coming to our city and have failed to welcome you properly. Please forgive me!"

Shen and his companions returned the salute, dismounted the chariot, and said, "We are uninvited guests and did not expect you to welcome us."

Taking a look at the contingent of troops, Gonglian asked deliberately, "May I ask why you have come with so many troops? Is it a drill or an expedition?"

Treated with courtesy by Gonglian, Shen did not know how to reply. "Well," he turned to look at Yue and Zi, who were also looking at him uncertainly. In fact, none of the three knew how to deal with people like Gonglian with his refined, gentlemanly manners, sagacious and brave as they were in face of ferocious adversaries like Gongshan Buniu, Shusun Zhe and Hou Fan.

Gonglian asked, "Are you keeping something from me? You are not come here to attack me, are you?"

The three generals remained silent.

"Please enter the city and let's have a talk!"

Taking a look at the high city wall of Cheng, Yue Qi muttered, "To speak the truth, His Lordship has ordered us to—to—"

"The three of you are the pillars of our state," said Gonglian Chufu. "You are famous all over the kingdom for your courage and bravery. You find it easy to defeat a superior enemy force, so why is it so difficult for you to say a few words?"

Yue threw out his chest. "Because the city wall of Cheng is too high, which goes against the rites of Zhou, His Lordship has ordered us to reduce it."

Gonglian Chufu said with a smile, "You are mistaken, General Yue. The rites of Zhou are largely out-of-date. The scale of a city, for instance, should be determined according to its location and strategic significance. Cheng can be compared to a gate guarding Lu against Qi. If Cheng is safe, Lu is safe; if Cheng is in danger, Lu will be in danger. At present Qi is much stronger than Lu. If we undermine the defence in Cheng by reducing the height of its city wall, an invading army from Qi would be able to ride straight into Lu without meeting much resistance. If we consolidate the city wall in Cheng, invasion from Qi can be effectively warded off. I beseech you to consider this carefully before taking any action."

Shen said, "Though your argument is somewhat reasonable, we have come by the order of His Lordship. How could we return without fulfilling our task?"

"It's quite easy. I will accompany you to the capital and explain the matter to His Lordship myself."

Finding no response from the three men, Gonglian continued, "Generals, please lead your troops inside the city to take a rest. I will go to the capital by myself and report to His Lordship. I will assume full responsibility for my action. What do you think?"

The three generals were moved by the great courage displayed by the magistrate of Cheng, and they decided to lead the troops back to the capital and report to the duke of Lu at once.

When Confucius learned the news from a scout, he was both glad and annoyed. Glad because Shusun Zhe and Hou Fan had been eliminated and Gongshan Buniu, who had fled to Qi, would definitely not dare return to Lu in his remaining years. Annoyed because Shen Juxu should have been persuaded by Gonglian Chufu not to reduce the city wall of Cheng. He was still angry over the matter when the three generals arrived to ask punishment from him.

"You have achieved great merits by killing Shusun Zhe and Hou Fan, driving away Gongshan Buniu and cutting down the city walls of

Fei and Hou. What did you do that calls for punishment?"

Shen Juxu described how Gonglian Chufu had refused to have the city wall of Cheng reduced.

Hearing him out, Confucius found Gonglian Chufu's argument could not be faulted. Formerly he had sent Mengsun Heji to advise Gonglian Chufu not to take any military action. Only thus were they able to cut down the city walls in Fei and Hou successfully. When Confucius thought about all this, his displeasure subsided, so he said with a smile, "I must congratulate you on your great exploits! You may return to your residences to relax yourself."

Thus ended a dramatic episode in the history of Lu, the destruction of the three great cities.

Mengsun Heji was grateful to Confucius who, in his opinion, must have spared the city of Cheng out of partiality toward his disciple. Jisun Si was glad that Shusun Zhe had been killed and Gongshan Buniu driven away, but he was angry with Confucius for destroying the city wall of Fei. Shusun Zhouchou, bearing a similar grudge, began to keep aloof from Confucius. Though he was aware of their change of attitude toward him, Confucius did not pay much attention. He was too much preoccupied with his task of making Lu strong.

Duke Ding of Lu was very grateful to Confucius and often invited him to the rear court to talk about politics, government, and the rites. One day Duke Ding asked, "Honored minister, the ancients said that when the Great Way prevails, the whole world will live as one. I want to understand the meaning of this remark. Could you explain it to me?"

The ancient adage was one of Confucius' favorites, and he had always wanted the opportunity to explain it to the duke. However, he said by way of modesty, "I know only a little about this."

"Don't be so modest. Please tell me what you know."

"The ancient sage rulers selected men of virtue and ability to fill offices. They kept their word and maintained peace and security. Thus a person not only treated his own parents with respect but also treated other people's parents in the same manner. He not only treated his own children with loving care but also treated other people's children in the same manner. Therefore the old lived out their lives in security, the strong gave full play to their ability, and the widows, widowers, orphans, and elderly people without children could all make a living. A valuable item, if left in the street, would not be taken away.

Everyone worried that he could not contribute to the others. There were no wicked men in powerful positions, no robbers and bandits. No one picked up lost articles in the street, and one need not lock the door at night. This is called the Great Harmony. Such were the times of the sage rulers Yao and Shun."

Pleased, Duke Ding asked, "I want to attain the Great Way. How shall I proceed?"

"When Yu, Cheng Tang, King Wen, King Wu, King Cheng and the Duke of Zhou ruled the kingdom, they all abided by the rites. The rites were the foundation of the authority of the king as well as the vassal lords. By sticking to the rites, the ruler can implement regulations, advocate benevolence and righteousness, propagate moral education, and harmonize the relationship between ruler and subjects. The government rules by the principle of justice. Without justice, the position of the ruler will be in peril, and the officials will seek personal gains at the expense of public welfare. So the saying goes, 'If the upper beam is not straight, the lower one will go aslant.' All the ancient sage rulers upheld justice in governing the world. Heaven begets the seasons and earth begets riches, while people multiply and become members of the society after receiving instruction from the teachers. The above four processes can run smoothly only when the ruler upholds justice. A sage ruler regards the entire kingdom as one community and treats his subjects without partiality, listening to their speech, observing their conduct, understanding their emotions, watching their fulfillment of duties, and striving for a harmonious relationship with all of them."

"What are the people's emotions?"

Confucius replied, "It refers to the seven innate emotions which are joy, anger, sorrow, fear, love, hate and desire."

Duke Ding of Lu asked again, "What are the human duties?"

"The ten human duties comprise loving care on the part of the father, filiality on the part of the son, kindness on the part of the brother, respect on the part of the younger brother, righteousness on the part of the husband, virtue on the part of the wife, charity on the part of the old, obedience on the part of the young, benevolence on the part of the ruler and loyalty on the part of the subject."

"What is the human harmony?"

"Harmony in human relationship is achieved when the ruler keeps his word and strives to maintain peace."

The duke narrowed his eyes, pondering over Confucius' words, when the latter added, "The ancient sage rulers regulated the seven human emotions, nurtured the ten human duties, won people's trust, maintained peace and security, advocated compromise and avoided conflicts—all these are manifestations of the observance of the rites. People can not live without cloth, silk, beans, and grain, and the relationship between man and woman is also needed by everyone. On the other hand, people want to escape from poverty, hunger, illness and death. A ruler must try his best to obtain for his subjects what they need and protect them from what they abhor."

Duke Ding smiled. "Honored minister, you are indeed a sage!" He paused for a moment, then changed the subject. "Honored minister, when we passed Mount Tai on our way to Jiagu last year, I promised the mountain god an annual sacrifice on the 13th of the sixth month if the meeting was a success. As the date is near, who do you think can be appointed to arrange for the sacrifice?"

Not much interested in the matter, Confucius answered, "You may choose a court official who is attentive and responsible."

Duke Ding decided to put Nangong Jingshu in charge of the matter.

Much improvement was made in the state of Lu as a result of Confucius' efforts in persuading Duke Ding to rule according to the rites of Zhou. In his spare time Confucius continued to teach his disciples.

Lu's steady growth in strength greatly disturbed Duke Jing of Qi, who intended to become the overlord of all the states.

Sensing the duke's anxiety, Li Chu suggested, "Your Lordship, since you are worried over Confucius' assistance to the duke of Lu, why don't we try to sow discord between them?"

Duke Jing spread his hands in a helpless gesture. "That is easier said than done!" he said. "Since Confucius took office in the Lu court, he has achieved many things in a surprisingly short time, which have pleased the duke of Lu greatly. How will we be able to sow discord between the two of them?"

Li Chu replied with a wily smile, "There is something you do not realize, Your Lordship. Confucius is a man who cherishes high aspirations, while the duke of Lu is a fatuous ruler with a weakness for wine and women. If we select some dancing girls and offer them to the duke of Lu as a gift, he will surely be glad to accept it. After that he will become too absorbed in watching the performance of the dancing girls to attend to state affairs. When Confucius discovers that his ambition can not be fulfilled in Lu, he will not hesitate to leave for another state. Then we will no longer have any need to worry about Lu."

Duke Jing was overjoyed. "What a wonderful idea!" he exclaimed. "Honored minister, you may go and see to it in person!"

"I'll carry out your order!" said Li Chu. He left the court and sent men all over the state to select beautiful maidens. Eighty young girls, both pretty and bright, were collected in a month. Li Chu had them trained in singing and dancing.

In the third month of the thirteenth year of Duke Ding of Lu's reign (497 B.C.) Duke Jing of Qi wrote an official letter to Lu. He gave the letter to Gongsun Yunyan, a court official, who set out for Lu with a hundred and twenty fine horses and eighty dancing girls. After traveling for six days, they arrived at the south gate of the Lu capital. Gongsun Yunyan bade the dancing girls rest while he entered the city alone.

Duke Ding was watching a song and dance performance in the palace, when a guard hurriedly came up and reported, "Your Lordship, an envoy from the duke of Qi has brought a gift of eighty dancing girls and a hundred and twenty fine horses."

Duke Ding was immensely pleased. He waved the performers away and asked anxiously, "Where is the Qi envoy?"

"He is waiting outside the gate."

"Bring him here at once!"

Called by the guard, Gongsun Yunyan straightened his garment and walked into the palace. After kowtowing to Duke Ding, he took the letter from his sleeve and respectfully held it overhead with both hands. "This is the letter from our sovereign," he said. "Please read it."

A palace attendant took the letter and handed it to Duke Ding.

Duke Ding opened the letter and read it quickly, apparently pleased with its content. "Take the Qi envoy to the guest-house where he can rest!" he ordered.

Gongsun Yunyan bowed and thanked the duke.

After Gongsun Yunyan had gone, Duke Ding ordered, "Open the gate and let in the dancing girls!"

"I'll pass on your order!" cried the attendant.

"Wait!" The duke said, suddenly realizing his rashness. "I have to discuss the matter with the chief minister and the minister of justice."

Sitting at the dinner table that evening, Duke Ding had no

appetite, for his mind kept drifting to the dancing girls outside the south gate. He looked up and shouted, "Guard!"

A guard ran up and knelt before him.

"Tell the chief minister to enter the palace at once to discuss something important!"

After the guard had left with the order, Duke Ding drifted into a daydream, trying to imagine how the dancing girls looked.

"Your Lordship, the chief minister has come," announced a guard.

Duke Ding collected himself. "Let him enter!"

After saluting the duke, Jisun Si said excitedly, "Your Lordship, the Qi envoy has pitched a tent outside the south gate, where he is organizing the dancing girls for a rehearsal. The news of their arrival is spreading so quickly that a huge crowd has gathered to watch. All the dancers are very young and extremely pretty. They have such sweet voices, and they move with such grace and charm that you would mistake them for fairies descending from the sky!"

Duke Ding was fascinated.

At the sight of the duke's expression, Jisun Si asked, "Your Lordship, why don't we open the city gate and let them in?"

Duke Ding took up the letter from the desk and handed it to Jisun Si. "I have to consult the minister of justice before reaching a decision."

Jisun Si smiled. "Your Lordship, the duke of Qi is making a friendly gesture. In my opinion, we have to accept the gift, or the duke of Qi would be offended. We can accept the gift now and offer something in return in the future."

"So you think we can accept it?"

"Yes!" Jisun replied with assurance.

The two of them laughed happily together.

"Where are the dancing girls? Honored minister, take me there to have a look!"

"They are performing outside the south gate. We'd better change into plainclothes. Otherwise we may be recognized by some officials and give rise to undesirable comments."

The two of them changed their clothes, left the palace by the rear gate in two small chariots, and headed for the south gate of the city. As they drew near, they could hear the melodious music. "Faster!" Duke Ding urged the driver.

The drivers cracked their whips, and the chariots sped to the south gate. Duke Ding and Jisun leapt out and climbed briskly up the gate tower.

The dancing girls murmured among themselves, "The duke of Lu has come to watch us!"

All the girls came out of the tent and began to sing and dance in the most alluring manner.

Fascinated by the music, singing and dance, Duke Ding and Jisun were beside themselves with excitement and forgot all about their dignity. They ran down the gate tower, ordered the soldiers to open the city gate and lower the suspension bridge, and went out the city to mingle with the crowd of spectators.

After a while Jisun pulled Duke Ding out of the crowd and whispered, "Your Lordship, there are a hundred and twenty fine horses in the shed to the east!"

His eyes widening with greedy delight, Duke Ding said, "Quick, take me there!"

They approached the shed and saw by the moonlight many big and sinewy horses. Startled by the sight of strangers one of the horses suddenly neighed. Duke Ding started and drew back a few steps. The horses calmed down and resumed eating. Duke Ding cried, "Wonderful!"

Jisun beckoned him to keep quiet.

Just then the dancing girls began to sing.

The peach tree is so luxuriant,
Its blossoms so bright and lovely.
The young maiden is going to marry
And start a happy family.

Duke Ding was so enchanted by the singing that he moved back to the watching crowd around the dancing girls without realizing what he was doing. Just then a few clouds drifted over and hid the moon from view. It became suddenly dark on the ground. Duke Ding looked up at the clouds with irritation. The dancing girls continued their singing.

My sweetheart is nowhere to be seen,
And I am filled with anxiety.
Only when I see him
And draw close to him,
Will my heart rest at ease.

Duke Ding could no longer contain his excitement. He shouted, "Open the gate and let them enter the city!"

Scarcely had he finished these words when they heard someone shouting an order in the distance, "Draw the suspension bridge and close the gate!" Duke Ding and Jisun felt as if cold water had been poured on them.

Chapter Twenty-two

Wallowing in Pleasure, Duke Ding of Lu Neglects State Affairs; Disappointed with the Fatuous Sovereign, Confucius Leaves His Homeland

By the familiar sound of the voice the duke and his chief minister knew it must be Confucius. Early that day Confucius had left the city by the west gate for an outing in the company of some disciples. When they came to the eastern dike of the Sihe River, he sat down and began to sing to the accompaniment of his zither:

> When in the tenth month the Yinshi Star rises to mid-heaven,
> They are building a new palace at Chuqiu.
> Judging direction by the shadows of the sun,
> They are building new houses at Chuqiu.
> They plant hazel and chestnut trees,
> As well as maple, idesia, catalpa and phoenix trees,
> Whose wood can be made into musical instruments.

The tune was vigorous and his voice deep and melodious. He saw in his mind's eye the prosperity of the state of Wei under the rule of Duke Wen. Then he changed to another tune, which was more joyful and lighthearted:

> Standing on the relics,
> He gazes at Chuqiu.
> Gazing at Chuqiu and Tangyi,
> He measures the mountains and the hills.
> He walks down to observe the field
> And consults the oracle, which is auspicious.
> The word is indeed very suitable.

He looked up into the distance as if he were gazing at Chuqiu and Tangyi himself: the mulberry trees, the green field of crops, the singing birds and running deer, the men plowing in the field and the women gathering mulberry leaves. How he wished he could see such a prosperous scene in Lu!

The rhythm of the music grew faster. As he became totally absorbed in the poem, his singing mingled harmoniously with the music:

The timely rain has fallen,
Tell the driver it is going to be a fine day.
Tell him to get up early to drive the cart,
To the mulberry field over there.
That honest man
Has a careful and far-reaching thought,
He breeds three thousand strong horses.

Having finished the song, he lingered on with the picture in his mind. He felt as if he was nearer than ever to realizing his political ideal.

The disciples had often accompanied Confucius on such excursions. When he started to play the zither and sing, they either joined in the singing or took out the books and read.

Confucius put down the zither, got on his feet, and looked at the vast wheat field. "My students," he said, "Lu has rid itself of internal strife and external threats. The government is instituting a benign rule and the people have begun to enjoy a better life. You may give full play to your talents to serve the state!"

Before the disciples could make any comment, Confucius suddenly turned to look into the distance. They stood up and looked in the same direction and saw someone riding a horse toward them. When he stopped before them and jumped off the horse, they found him to be Zi Lu.

When Confucius saw Zi Lu arrive in such haste, he realized that something important must have happened and urged Zi Lu to tell him.

Panting for breath, Zi Lu said, "Master, I found you at last!"

"What has happened?"

"An envoy from the duke of Qi, Gongsun Yunyan, has brought our lord a gift of eighty dancing girls and a hundred and twenty fine horses."

"Has His Lordship accepted the gift?"

"I don't know."

Hearing this, Confucius turned to his disciples. "We must return to the city at once!"

Back in the capital, Confucius went straight to see Shen Juxu and told him, "General Shen, the duke of Qi has sent our lord a gift of eighty beautiful maidens and a hundred and twenty fine horses. He clearly hopes thereby to weaken and destroy Lu. You must order the soldiers to guard the city gates closely to prevent the men of Qi from entering the capital."

"I will go at once to carry out your order."

Confucius felt a little better. He went to the chief minister's residence to see Jisun Si, hoping to take him along to the palace to advise Duke Ding against accepting the gift from Qi. To his surprise, the guard informed him that Jisun Si had left for the palace. Wondering what Jisun Si had in his mind, he set his face toward the palace, but by the time he got there he was told that Duke Ding was out.

"Could it be ..." Confucius asked himself. "Could they have gone to watch the song and dance performance?" Burning with anxiety, he hastened to the south gate, where somewhat to his relief he saw only two small, plain-looking chariots. However, he was furious when he found the gate wide open and the suspension bridge lowered. He shouted to the soldiers guarding the city gate, "Draw the bridge and close the gate!"

The soldiers obeyed his order without delay.

Just then Shen Juxu arrived. Confucius asked him in a deprecating tone, "General Shen, why was the city gate wide open?"

Puzzled, Shen did not know how to reply.

An officer came up to them and explained, "Minister of Justice, His Lordship and the chief minister arrived a moment ago, and the gate was opened to allow them to go out and watch the song and dance performance."

Confucius was flabbergasted. The news shattered his hopes. He stood there in a daze for a long time. The melodious singing of the dancing girls pierced him like a dagger. He felt pained and dizzy, as if he were falling from the top of a mountain into a bottomless pit.

When the city gate closed on them, Duke Ding and Jisun were mortified. They no longer had any appetite for the performance but began to worry how they could enter the city in a decent way. They racked their brains but failed to come up with an idea.

After recovering from the shock, Confucius said to Shen, "Tell the soldiers to open the city gate and let His Lordship and the chief minister enter!"

Duke Ding and Jisun were greatly relieved when the city gate was opened and the bridge lowered. They hurriedly entered the city, keeping their eyes on the chariots and avoiding Confucius' gaze.

Confucius said with a bow, "Your Lordship, Chief Minister, please mount the chariots and return to the palace!" His tone was mild but not without a touch of indignation.

Duke Ding muttered, "Honored minister, please accompany me to the palace."

Back in the palace, Duke Ding fidgeted in his chair with an awkward look on his face. Jisun, who seated himself to the duke's left, showed no sign of embarrassment as if he had nothing to feel ashamed of.

Confucius was convinced that Duke Ding and Jisun's behavior had brought shame not only upon themselves but also upon the state of Lu. He would not look squarely at them for fear that they would grow more ashamed.

The atmosphere was tense. The three of them sat there awkwardly, no one venturing to speak first.

Duke Ding calmed down gradually. He coughed slightly and said, striving to sound nonchalant, "Minister of Justice, the duke of Qi has sent us a gift of eighty dancing girls and a hundred and twenty fine horses. What shall we do about it?"

Confucius replied bluntly, "Your Lordship, at present Qi is powerful and Lu weak, so it is obvious that Qi harbors some hostile design against us by offering the gift in such an obsequious way. We must by no means accept it!"

Jisun disagreed. "Minister of Justice, since the meeting at Jiagu, the duke of Qi has treated Lu with sincerity. He returned Yun, Huanyang and Guiyin to Lu unconditionally. Why should he be harboring evil intention by offering us a gift at this time?"

Confucius answerd, "The two situations are different. During the Jiagu meeting, the duke of Qi adopted Li Chu's wicked plan and tried to humiliate our lord, first by the savage dance and then by a licentious song. When the trick did not work, he did not give up but demanded an additional article to the treaty, requesting Lu to send three hundred chariots to join any of Qi's expeditions. They agreed to return us the three places only after we demanded it formally, declaring that otherwise they would be violating the treaty. Now we must consider our position carefully. It is common knowledge that one appears humble when he wants a favor. Since Qi wants nothing from us, why should it be so humble? Furthermore, we have done Qi no big favor, neither do we have any ill intention against it. So why should Qi send us such a generous gift? Therefore I think there must be some ulterior motive behind this. I beseech you to consider this!"

"Honored minister," said the duke, "an exchange of goodwill between two states has been common practice since ancient times."

Confucius said, "The ancient rites are of course held in high esteem in Lu, the manor of none other than the Duke of Zhou. But Qi's gift of beautiful maidens is quite another matter. It is difficult to deal with women and petty men. When you treat them with favor, they will become disrespectful. When you keep aloof from them, they will become resentful. We can easily imagine what the duke of Qi has in mind by sending the gift of eighty beautiful women."

Duke Ding smiled. "Honored minister, you are making the whole thing more complicated than it really is. Are you implying that those fragile-looking girls are more dangerous than flood and wild beasts?"

Confucius replied, "It is easier to subdue the flood or wild beasts than to check women and petty men. I am worried that the duke of Qi wants to use these women to—" he did not finish his words.

Duke Ding blushed, knowing what Confucius wanted to say. He tried to look innocuous. "Honored minister, you may express your opinion."

Confucius hesitated, then said, "Your Lordship, in my opinion, we may accept the fine horses and prepare an ample gift in return. As for the eighty dancing girls, we'd better return them to the duke of Qi. That would save us a lot of trouble and enable them to be reunited with their families. They must be suffering great sorrow having been forced to leave their homeland at such a young age! A benevolent ruler loves the people. I hope Your Lordship will have pity on them."

These words filled Duke Ding with shame and anger. "So you are saying I would not be benevolent if I let the dancing girls stay," he said to himself. He tried hard not to let anger get the better of him.

Jisun stroked his beard and said slowly, "Minister of Justice, you are quite mistaken. The dancing girls were recruited by the order of the duke of Qi, who should therefore be held responsible for their sorrow, if there is any. Moreover, if His Lordship accepts the girls, they will stay to sing and dance in the palace. They will have no more worries in the world but can enjoy themselves all their life."

"But I am worried that—"

"That will be all!" Duke Ding snapped, extending his right hand.

Confucius stood up and bowed. "Your Lordship, Lu has gone through many hardships and is just beginning to see some improvements, and ..."

Duke Ding interrupted him impatiently. "I've made up my mind. You may take your leave now!" With this he swept his sleeves and retreated into the inner room.

Jisun looked quite pleased with what had happened while Confucius returned home with a heavy heart.

The next morning Duke Ding sent Jisun to receive Gongsun Yunyan into the palace and treated him as an honored guest. He accepted the fine horses and dancing girls and offered in return a gift of two thousand taels of gold. He also had Gongsun Yunyan amply rewarded.

Having fulfilled his mission, Gongsun Yunyan went back to Qi.

Duke Ding could hardly contain his cravings for the eighty dancing girls who had now become part of his harem. However, he was sensible enough, after some consideration, to allocate twenty of them to Jisun Si. The rest he kept in the palace, spending days and nights in their company. He was so wrapped up in his sensual pleasures that for many days he failed to hold a single audience.

Confucius was filled with rage and despair. He knew it would be futile to advise Duke Ding against his wrong behavior. He stayed home in a gloomy mood, feeling at a loss what to do.

His disciples had a heated talk over what Duke Ding and Jisun Si had done.

Zi Lu said, "Master, the duke and the chief minister are enchanted by the dancing girls. There is no longer any hope for Lu to grow strong. Let's leave for another state."

Confucius stared at him blankly. "We must be patient. Maybe they will change their mind. The grand sacrifice will be held tomorrow. If His Lordship sends us the sacrificial items, there is a chance that we will still be useful. Otherwise we will have to leave, as His Lordship will have no use for us."

The grand sacrifice to Heaven was held each year in Lu in accordance with the rites of Zhou. A high earthen platform was constructed for the purpose on the northern bank of the Yishui River south of the capital. After the ceremony, the sacrificial items would be distributed to the court officials as a token of the sovereign's care for his subjects and of Heaven's blessings for the people.

Confucius longed to stay in Lu, his homeland, and devote all his efforts to its prosperity. He waited anxiously for a messenger to come from Duke Ding after the sacrifice. For three days he waited in vain. Finally he gave up and decided to leave Lu.

In the evening Confucius sat under the dim light of an oil-lamp, his face pale and tired. He picked up the zither and began to sing:

> *I gather licorice on top of Shouyang Mountain,*
> *Men's false words should not be believed.*
> *Listen instead to honest words and advice,*
> *And not take false words for true!*

As he sang, his eyes brimmed with tears. Lady Qiguan, who sat by his side, also rubbed her eyes. For many years she had shared woes with him. While he worried over the fate of the nation, she worried over his health.

Confucius put down the zither and said to Lady Qiguan, "His Lordship has accepted the gift from the duke of Qi and has not attended audience for several days. I have decided to leave Lu for another state."

Lady Qiguan was already an old woman, grey-haired and wrinkled. She said in a hoarse voice, "You have already traveled from place to place without attaining the chance to realize your dream. I am afraid that you will only be disappointed again."

Her words made Confucius feel more depressed. With the world suffering from turbulence and the vassal lords preferring force to benevolence, it would be going against the tide to advocate the rites of Zhou. However, Confucius thought he had no choice. "No matter how difficult and frustrating it will be," he said to Lady Qiguan, "I have to live my life according to the rites of Zhou."

Lady Qiguan knew him too well to contradict him. She went about helping him pack up for the journey. Confucius selected a few books in bamboo slips and pieces of silk to take with him. He was about to take a rest when some disciples arrived.

Zi Lu said as soon as he came into the room, "Master, have you made up your mind? When shall we leave?"

Ran Geng picked the snuff of the lamp with a grass stick. Looking at Confucius, he asked, "Master, the world is large but disordered. Where will we be able to find a suitable place?"

"The rites and music formulated by the Duke of Zhou are universally sound and will remain so. Their current disuse has been caused by militarist attitudes of the vassal lords. I don't think that, among the rulers of the various states, there is not even a single one who agrees with me."

Min Shun said, "Master, good intentions are seldom understood. This time we must make sure that the ruler we serve is indeed someone who wants to establish a benevolent government."

"I feel a bit confused at this moment," admitted Confucius. "I want to leave Lu, but I don't know where exactly I should go."

Yan Lu said, "Master, my family is poor, I have to stay home to support them. Though Yan Hui is not very clever, he enjoys studying with you. Please take him with you so that he won't lag behind in his studies."

"Who else will accompany me on a long journey?" asked Confucius.

Zi Lu responded at once, "I will!"

Other disciples also expressed their willingness to go.

Much moved, Confucius said, "We'll start off tomorrow. Now you go home and say good-bye to your family and prepare for the trip!"

The disciples bowed and took their leave.

"Zi Lu and Ran Qiu," said Confucius, "as the chief minister's stewards, you don't have to go with me."

Zi Lu said hastily, "Master, you once said that people who have different attitudes do not lay plans together. I find myself at odds with the chief minister in both speech and conduct. I want to take this chance to resign my office in his house."

Confucius nodded. Though rude and rash sometimes, Zi Lu was one of his favorite disciples. Kind, honest and straightforward, Zi Lu was also very solicitous in looking after Confucius' daily needs. With Zi Lu by his side Confucius felt warm and secure.

Ran Qiu said, "Master, the chief minister pays little attention to state affairs but spends all his time enjoying himself. I also want to leave him and go with you."

Confucius nodded again.

Having seen them off, Confucius still did not feel sleepy. He had many things to think about. He went out of the house and walked to the Temple of the Duke of Zhou. In the darkness he could make out the profile of the temple against the sky, serene and majestic. The cypresses and junipers stood like guards protecting the temple, the statue of the Duke of Zhou, and the rites he had established for the kingdom. The gate to the temple was tightly closed. Though he wanted to enter the temple and look at the statue, Confucius was reluctant to trouble the keeper. So he stood before the temple trying to envision the Duke of Zhou's appearance.

Suddenly there arose a racket among the birds settling in the trees as a crow alighted on a twig already occupied. Confucius shuddered. It seemed that the world was never free of conflicts, even in the dead of a silent night.

Then he saw a lantern approaching. When the man came near, Confucius recognized the old keeper. He was nearly seventy and had grey hair and beard. "Master," he said, "still up so late? Is there anything wrong?"

"I couldn't sleep at home, so I came here to pay respects to the Duke of Zhou. I thought you must have gone to bed already."

The old man said, "The older one grows, the more useless one becomes. The oil for the lamps was used up yesterday, but I forgot all about it until this evening, so I went to my daughter's to get some. My daughter is really good to me; she let me stay for dinner there."

"You enjoy a good life in old age and have a filial child. You can be called a happy man."

"A man is always happy if he is contented!"

Confucius thought of his son, Kong Li, who was still childless after many years of marriage. Brushing the unhappy thought from his mind, he said with a smile, "Since you are in a good mood this evening, shall we go together and pay respects to the Duke of Zhou?"

The old man was surprised. "Master, I have been keeper of the temple for dozens of years, and no one has ever come to visit it at night. Are you leaving soon?"

Confucius replied with a sad smile.

"Follow me!" said the old man.

The two of them came to the main hall. Standing before the statue of the Duke of Zhou, Confucius was torn between conflicting emotions. He was glad and exalted, yet also regretful and ashamed. From the statutes left by the Duke of Zhou, he had learned how to be a man and how to govern a state according to the rites. Yet he found it impossible to put what he had learned into practice. Confucius knelt and kowtowed to the statue, his eyes filled with tears.

The old man stood watching silently by the side.

Confucius stood up and went out the temple. He turned to look back, as if he were bidding a final farewell to some good friend. He thanked the old man and went out into the street. The moon had risen high, bathing the ground in silvery light. Then he heard to his surprise some voluptuous music. He looked around and found himself near the palace. He frowned with distaste and walked briskly home.

Lady Qiguan sat waiting for him by the lamplight, with some clothes piled up in front of her. She gave him an inquiring look, not knowing what to say to comfort him. When he lay down in his clothes, she asked, "So you are definitely leaving?"

"On my way back from the temple just now, I heard music still in the palace. When a man follows a path of unrighteousness, it is unlikely for him to pull himself away. It seems that Lu will be ruined by those dancing girls from Qi. I have to leave Lu if only to regain my peace of mind."

The next morning Confucius' house was filled with disciples who came to see their master off. Confucius said to them, "I will be gone for at least three to five years. You must not neglect your studies during this time." He turned and said to Kong Li and Kong Zhong, "After I leave, you must take good care of your mother."

Kong Li and Kong Zhong said, "We will, father. You may trust us!"

Sparrows chirping in the old locust tree added confusion to the scene. Confucius checked up the luggage on the chariot and said to the disciples, "I must leave now."

"Where are we going, master?" asked Zi Lu.

"The goal of my life is to restore the rules of propriety in the world," said Confucius. "I will go wherever there is a chance to put my ideals into practice."

The disciples all looked blank.

Zi Lu said, "I have a brother-in-law who serves in the court of the duke of Wei. Let's make his house our first stop, shall we?"

Confucius thought for a while, then said, "Wei is not far from Lu. We might as well go there." There were other reasons that he agreed to go to Wei. First, Wei had enjoyed thirty-eight years of peace and security under the rule of Duke Ling. In addition, with Shi Yu dead and Qu Boyu old, Wei was in short of talented officials, so that he had a chance of obtaining a high position in the Wei court.

"Let me drive the chariot on this long journey," Zi Lu said.

"Among the six arts, I am best at driving the chariot. Let me drive for the master instead!" Ran Qiu took the whip from Zi Lu and mounted the chariot.

Zi Lu helped Confucius onto the chariot, and the disciples bade their master farewell. Some of them were sobbing.

The chariot left the city by the west gate and headed for Wei. Again and again Confucius turned to look at the capital. He felt sorry for the misfortune that had befallen his homeland and regret for his inability to save the situation.

Apart from Zi Lu and Ran Qiu, there were about thirty disciples who accompanied Confucius on this journey. These included Min Shun, Ran Geng, Ran Yong, Yan Hui, Zi Gong, Zai Yu and Bi Buqi. While Confucius rode in his chariot, some disciples sat in Zi Gong's chariot and some walked.

As their journey got underway, someone came running from behind. They looked back and recognized the court musician, Shi Ji.

Coming up to Confucius, Shi Ji bowed and said tearfully, "Minister of Justice! You must not go! You should stay in your homeland and make it prosper!"

Confucius replied helplessly, "His Lordship has totally neglected state affairs after he received the gift from Qi. Lu will surely decline. Of course I want to stay in my homeland, but I am compelled to leave!"

"Yes," agreed Shi Ji. "It is not your fault. I was only thinking for our state. Wherever you go, please do not forget about your homeland." He broke into tears.

Restraining his own tears, Confucius said, "Take care, sir! I have to leave now."

They got on with their journey and traveled for several days until they arrived before a mountain.

Zi Lu said, "Master, we are at the border."

"Stop the chariot!" said Confucius. He got down and, gazing into the distant hills, remembered the many mountains he had climbed, the sense of freedom he had experienced on Mount Yi, and the great aspirations inspired by Mount Tai. A few pheasants, crackling and pursuing one another, alighted on the stone slab, then vanished again into the forest. For a flitting moment Confucius almost felt a deep longing for a peaceful, carefree life. He looked back to the east, but the Lu capital was already blocked by some hills. He said to Zi Lu,

"Bring me my zither. I'll sing a song to cheer us up."

Zi Lu took the zither and put it in front of him.

Confucius sat down and began to play. He sang:

I am forced to leave
By the gossip of those women.
Falling into a trap set by seductive women,
The sovereign will cause harm to the state.
Why should I shed tears of sadness?
Let me enjoy the rest of my life in leisure!

Listening to the song, the disciples were all brought to the verge of tears.

When Confucius stopped playing, he stood up and made a deep bow toward the east. Then he got on the chariot to continue the journey.

When the company arrived at a small town of Wei, Confucius suddenly cheered up.

Chapter Twenty-three

Confucius and His Disciples Arrive
in the State of Wei;
The Duke of Wei and His Consort Have
an Argument in the Garden

When they arrived at the town where the streets were crowded with people, Confucius sighed with pleasure. "I didn't realize the state of Wei was so prosperous. So many people in such a small town!"

It was the first time during their journey that Confucius smiled. The disciples also felt glad.

"Master, when the population has grown, what should be done next?" Ran Qiu asked.

"Make the people rich," replied Confucius promptly.

"When the people have become rich, what should be done next?"

"Set up schools and give the people a good education."

Wei was one of the smaller states. When Duke Wen of Wei came to power in 659 B.C., Duke Huan of Qi led a joint force of various states to help him build the Wei palace. This was eulogized in the *Book of Poetry*. Though Duke Wen of Wei ruled the state well, Wei remained small and weak compared with the greater powers contending for supremacy. Thus Confucius was surprised to find so many people in a small town. He began talking to his disciples on various subjects. In his opinion, Ran Qiu was intelligent, cautious and suited to a career in the government, but he did not study hard enough. So he said, "Qiu, I was not born with knowledge. I have acquired what I know by learning."

Ran Qiu realized at once the underlying message of Confucius' remark. He tried to find excuses for himself, saying, "Master, it isn't that I don't like what you teach. I am simply not clever enough to grasp it."

"One who lacks strength will stop halfway on his journey," said Confucius. "As for you, I think you have barely set out!"

Ran Qiu was struck speechless, unable to retort. After a while he asked, "Master, do you feel any resentment being forced to leave Lu

like this?"

Looking up into the sky, Confucius said, "It was my own decision to leave my homeland. I blame neither fate nor people for my misfortune. Otherwise I would be constantly filled with resentment. No, I don't blame anyone for what has happened." Even as he said this, he felt an unspeakable sorrow in his heart.

Zi Lu leapt out of his chariot and came up to Confucius. "Master," he said, "let's rest for a while!"

Confucius nodded his consent.

Zi Gong helped Confucius dismount and asked, "Master, what do you plan to do after leaving Lu?"

Confucius said, "When the government is wise and honest, the superior man should take office and help govern the state. When the government is corrupt, the superior man should leave for another place. As long as one lives, one must have something to aspire to and not drift along aimlessly. My greatest ambition is to rid the government of corrupt officials, eliminate evil and deception, put an end to war, restore the rites stipulated by the Duke of Zhou, and achieve Great Harmony in the whole world. It is to find a way to realize my ambition that I am leaving my homeland."

Ran Geng, who was a man of few words, now also joined in the conversation. "What's the difference between a superior man and a petty man?" he asked.

"A superior man is strict with himself and tolerant of others. A petty man does the contrary."

Min Shun asked, "Master, how does a superior man deal with his cause?"

"A superior man must be in keeping with the times when he works for his cause. He talks about it with modesty, treats it with sincerity and carries it out according to the rites."

"Does a superior man also bear grudges?" asked Zi Lu.

"A superior man only worries about his lack of ability and does not blame others for not understanding him."

Zi Lu looked surprised and unconvinced.

Confucius added, "If a superior man holds a grudge, it could only be caused by his failure to achieve anything and win the people's praise."

They mounted the chariots and continued their journey. Soon after, they arrived at Diqiu, the capital of Wei.

Ran Qiu came up to Confucius and reported, "Master, a small boy is standing in the way for no apparent reason."

Confucius looked up to see a boy of some eleven to twelve years old. Dressed in clothes made of coarse cloth, he had hair to his shoulders, a round, darkish face covered in dust, and a pair of large, bright eyes. Looking a little angry, the boy gestured for them to make a detour. Surprised, Confucius bade Ran Qiu stop the chariot, and dismounted and went up to the boy. "Child, why do you stand in our way?"

"You talk and behave like a gentleman, but you can't tell between right and wrong!"

Confucius was so surprised he did not know how to reply.

"Sir," continued the boy, "where do you come from, where are you going, and what's your name?"

Confucius found the boy's behavior quite amusing. He said, "I am Kong Qiu from the state of Lu."

The boy looked Confucius up and down and said doubtfully, "Kong Qiu is said to be a sage who knows everything under the sun. But why are you being so unreasonable?"

"You—" said Zi Lu, growing impatient and irritated.

Confucius stopped him. "Do not be so hasty!" He turned again to the boy and said, "May I ask why I am being unreasonable?"

The boy pointed to the road, "Look, I have constructed a city there. Now tell me, is it proper for the chariot to take another route or for the city to be destroyed to make way for the chariot?"

Confucius looked down and saw a miniature city built out of mud. It had a tower over each of the four gates and a palace building at the center of the city. He turned to the boy, who looked as proud as a peacock. Confucius muttered to himself, "Well, there is indeed a small city. Of course the chariot should take a roundabout way." He bade Ran Qiu turn the chariot to the side.

At this the boy said, "Well, you are really a sage who knows the rules of proper behavior!" He knelt before Confucius, saying, "A child pays respects to the master!" he cried.

Confucius helped him up with both hands and asked, "What's your name?"

"My family name is Xiang and my given name Tuo."

"Are you a native of Wei?"

Xiang Tuo replied, "Yes." Then he asked, "Master, are you

traveling through Wei or are you going to stay here for some time?"

Having not yet made up his mind, Confucius could not answer the question and just shook his head.

Xiang Tuo soon lost interest and went back to his mud city.

Led by Zi Lu, Confucius arrived at Yan Zhuozou's house. It had a very big courtyard surrounded with stone walls.

Hearing of their arrival, Yan hurried out to welcome them. He was a man in his fifties, tall, square-faced, dressed in a faded official garment. He said with a broad smile, "Forgive me for not coming to receive you earlier!"

Confucius bowed with clasped hands. "My disciples and I have come to trouble you. Please do not take offense!"

"Your arrival has brought glory to my humble abode. Let's skip formalities and enter the room to talk!"

Confucius and his disciples entered the room and took their seats. "Master, are you just passing by or..."

Zi Lu put in, "The duke of Lu acted against the rites and accepted a gift from the duke of Qi. The master was compelled to leave."

Yan frowned with puzzlement. "It is common practice for neighboring states to exchange gifts. Why should the master be so offended?"

Zi Lu replied, "It would not have mattered much if the duke of Qi had sent gold, silver or other treasures. What he sent was beautiful women!"

Yan Zhuozou seemed to have understood the situation at once. "Oh well, no wonder." He lowered his head and thought for a while, then said to Confucius with a smile, "Though my house is simple and humble, there are many rooms in it. You and your disciples might as well stay here, so that I can learn from you whenever I have a question."

Confucius bowed slightly in his seat. "I am away from my homeland and know no one else here in this strange land. I am very grateful to you for letting us stay!"

"Your name has spread far and wide in the world," said Yan. "At the audience tomorrow morning I will request His Lordship to give you an important position!"

As this was exactly what he wanted, Confucius smiled his assent.

Yan told his housekeeper to prepare a banquet in honor of Confucius and his disciples.

The next morning Yan informed Duke Ling of Wei of Confucius' stay in his house.

Greatly pleased, Duke Ling said, "Heaven is doing me a great favor by sending a great sage here! He is suffering from a misfortune. If I employ him now, he will surely try his best to work for the benefit of Wei. My honored ministers, what do you think of this?"

Not knowing why Confucius had come to Wei, the officials could not offer their advice, so they remained silent.

Duke Ling realized he was being too hasty, so he said, "Well, there is no need to give him an official position right away. Since he has left Lu for Wei, I should treat him with proper respect. I will give him the same salary as he received in Lu as the minister of justice."

Three days later Duke Ling had the salary sent to Confucius, who went at once to the palace to offer his thanks.

Duke Ling, who considered himself a sage ruler, came out of the rear palace to welcome Confucius. Duke Ling was a thin man of nearly seventy.

Moved by such courteous reception, Confucius bowed deeply and said, "Kong Qiu feels quite ashamed to receive the salary he does not deserve!"

"Master, you achieved great merits assisting the duke of Lu, and your fame as a sage has spread all over the country. Your arrival at our state is indeed a great honor." He took Confucius by the hand and led him into the palace.

After they had taken their seats, Duke Ling said, "Master, as minister of justice in Lu you enjoyed high honor and great power. What do you plan to do now that you have resigned your post?"

Confucius replied seriously, "In my opinion, one should worry about his inability to fulfill his duties instead of his inability to obtain official position. What I seek is truth. If I learn the truth in the morning, I would die in the evening without regret."

"Wei enjoyed great prosperity under the rule of my ancestor Duke Wen," said Duke Ling. "Since then there have been six rulers, Duke Cheng, Duke Mu, Duke Ding, Duke Xian, Duke Yang and Duke Xiang, but none of them succeeded in restoring Wei to its former power and glory. Though I am advanced in years I still want to do my best for Wei. Is there any way to make the state strong?"

Duke Ling's words sounded ambitious but lacking in confidence, so Confucius said noncommittally, "A superior man follows no set rules in dealing with the affairs of the world. There is nothing that he must do or must not do. He simply does what he thinks suitable and proper."

The duke did not quite understand and forced a smile.

As the conversation was going nowhere, Confucius took his leave. On his return to Yan Zhuozou's house, he met a middle-aged peasant who had come in a hurry. Gasping for breath, the man asked, "Are you Confucius, the sage who knows everything under the sun?"

Surprised, Confucius asked, "What's the matter?"

"My bull has been fighting with a neighbor's bull for two hours outside the city. We tried every way to separate them, but in vain. If the fight continues like this, both bulls will be injured. I have therefore come to seek your advice."

"I'll go and take a look," said Confucius.

Zi Lu hurriedly harnessed the horses to the chariot, and they set off at once. Going out the south gate, they saw a crowd stand there watching. Two bulls, their horns interlocked and their feet sunk in the ground, had reached a stalemate. Neither wanted to back down.

Confucius dismounted, walked up to the two bulls and watched them for a while. "Bring me a basin of cold water!" he shouted.

Someone ran to a farmhouse nearby and returned with a pot of cold water.

Confucius took the pot, went up to the bulls, and poured the cold water squarely on their heads. Both bulls gave a start and fell back.

The owners of the bulls thanked Confucius, and the onlookers marveled at his ingenuity. The incident soon became the talk of the city.

After that, people often came to call on Confucius and asked his advice on various subjects. As Confucius had nothing to do in Yan's house except teaching his disciples, he received the visitors warmly and tried his best to help them.

One day he was teaching his disciples when two small boys, quarreling with each other, came to him. Confucius looked up and recognized one of the boys, Xiang Tuo. He was about to ask why they had come when Xiang Tuo fell on his knees. "Xiang Tuo pays respects to the master!"

The other boy paused, then also knelt and kowtowed. "Wen Jing pays respects to the master!"

Looking them closely and trying to guess why they had come, Confucius said, "Get up and speak!"

The two boys stood up and looked at each other defiantly. Wen Jing put out his tongue and made a face at Xiang Tuo.

Confucius could not help smiling. He asked, "What were you quarreling about?"

Xiang Tuo said, "I told him the sun is nearer to us in the morning because it looks bigger. But he said the sun is nearer to us at noon. So we have come to you to make a judgement for us."

Wen Jing said, "The sun is of course nearer to us at noon, because it is so much hotter. Suppose there is a fire. Do you feel warmer when you are close or far away?"

Xiang Tuo retorted, "When you look at the same object, does it appear bigger when it is close or far away?"

The two went on arguing, pursing their lips contemptuously.

Confucius faltered at the question, for he had never thought about it before. He stood there thinking for quite a long time, then broke into a smile. He said with assurance, "The sun is the same distance from us in the morning and at noon."

Both Xiang Tuo and Wen Jing asked, "But why—"

Holding out his hand to stop them, Confucius explained, "When it comes out in the morning, the sun is shrouded by the fog over the earth, which reduces its light. Therefore we can gaze at it directly, and it appears big and close to us. By noon the fog has dispersed, and the sun gives out its full radiance so that we dare not look at it directly. Thus it appears small and distant."

Fully convinced, Xiang Tuo and Wen Jing smiled and left with dancing steps.

The disciples were all pleased by Confucius' reply to the question, which had appeared to them difficult to answer.

Confucius had studied the six arts tirelessly in order to serve his sovereign and help make Lu a powerful and prosperous state, so that the other states would follow suit and the rites would be restored in the entire kingdom of Zhou. However, he had been forced to leave his homeland and try his fortune in another state. He was deeply mortified, hoping that Duke Ding of Lu and Jisun Si would change their mind someday and invite him to return to Lu. He waited for two months without receiving any news from Lu.

Duke Ding of Lu was having conflicting feelings. Immediately after Confucius left Lu, he summoned Jisun Si to the rear palace and said to him, "Honored minister, the minister of justice has left because

I offended him by accepting the dancing girls sent by Qi. What shall we do now?"

With twenty dancing girls allotted to him, Jisun was having a good time and did not think much about the welfare of the state and the people. He replied absent-mindedly, "The minister of justice was born and raised in Lu. He has great learning and is well versed in the rites. I am sure he will return to serve his native state someday."

"I intend to send an envoy to invite him back. What do you think?"

"Your Lordship, the minister of justice is a very obstinate man. If we send an envoy to call him back, he will definitely refuse. It is better to let him suffer a few frustrations in the various states, then he will return without being invited."

"He showed great wisdom and courage at the Jiagu meeting, and the policy he formulated has been very effective in governing the state. I am afraid of being ridiculed by my offspring for driving such a capable man away!"

Jisun lowered his head and thought for a while. "Your Lordship," he said, "the minister of justice left Lu because of the dancing girls. It is said that a malady can only be cured by removing its cause. If you really want him back, you'll have to return the dancing girls to Qi." He looked at Duke Ding, whose face twitched uncontrollably, and added with emphasis, "The decision is yours to make!"

Duke Ding had wallowed in wine, music and women for so long and become so infatuated with the dancing girls from Qi that he could not bear even the thought of parting with them. He sighed deeply and said languidly, "Well, let's wait for him to return of his own accord!"

Jisun felt greatly relieved, as if a heavy stone had been removed from his chest.

Thus Confucius became less and less on their minds, until he was totally forgotten.

Having recognized Confucius' great talent, Duke Ling of Wei began to consider using his service. After the audience one morning, he went to enjoy the flowers accompanied by his wife, Nan Zi. It was a very big garden with a pool in the center. Behind the pool rose a rockery made of rocks of various shapes, around which all kinds of flowers grew. A small path wound its way around the rockery. Nan Zi, in her late thirties, was wearing a red silk gown and a jade pin in her hair. She had a slender figure, an oval face, and appealing eyes. She plucked a red rose and handed it to Duke Ling.

Thinking about Confucius, Duke Ling was not paying much attention to Nan Zi. He took the flower absent-mindedly and just held it in his hand.

Nan Zi pursed her lips in displeasure. She took Duke Ling by the arm and shook him, saying, "My Lord, put it in my hair!"

When Duke Ling turned and gazed at her dazedly Nan Zi broke into a smile.

Duke Ling put the flower to his nose, took a sniff, and said with intoxication, "My lady! Let me put it in your hair."

Nan Zi leaned herself close to Duke Ling.

Looking at his half-witted appearance, Nan Zi felt revolted. With her good looks, she thought, she deserved a handsome man as her lover, not a doddering old man like Duke Ling. She was not satisfied with her marriage even though it had given her great wealth and comfort. She felt as if her heart had drifted away, leaving only an empty shell in Duke Ling's arms.

By now Duke Ling had fully regained his senses. Holding her in both arms, he rocked her gently and asked, "My lady! Are you all right? Why do you have such a strange look?"

Nan Zi gazed at him, and in her narrowed eyes he seemed to have undergone metamorphosis, turning into the man of her dream. He was tall, had thick eyebrows and large eyes, and he was very good to her, attentive to her every need. Their every meeting brought her raptures. Imagining Duke Ling to be her lover, Nan Zi pushed herself firmly against him and let him shower her with kisses.

Just then two palace maids entered the garden to pick flowers. At the sight of Duke Ling and Nan Zi they retreated quietly.

But Duke Ling had seen them. He pushed Nan Zi away and continued to walk down the small path by himself, looking at flowers.

Forced out of her daydream, Nan Zi was filled with both shame and rage.

The two of them walked on, feeling bored. Duke Ling said, "My lady, have you heard of the sage who arrived in our state recently?"

"Are you talking of Confucius from Lu?"

"Yes. He is indeed a sage who knows everything under the sun!"

Nan Zi took a close look at him. "Do you plan to appoint him to high office?"

Duke Ling replied with great self-satisfaction, "In fact I do."

Nan Zi plucked a leaf, tore it into pieces and threw them away spitefully. She said with contempt, "So the poor pedant has come to Wei to try his fortune! What does he know except a few lines from ancient books? If he were really capable, why didn't he remain in Lu to assist the duke govern his home state?"

Duke Ling was dumbfounded. Though the wife of a sovereign was not supposed to interfere in state affairs, he was so infatuated with Nan Zi that to please her he often acted on her opinions. When he saw that Nan Zi was close to an angry outburst, he hastily explained, "I have heard that Confucius is conversant with the six arts, and he is also the descendant of the sage king Cheng Tang. As acting chief minister, he achieved a stunning diplomatic victory for Lu at the Jiagu meeting. As magistrate of Zhongdu he ran the city so well that robbers and thieves were virtually eliminated. As minister of justice he..."

Looking contemptuous, Nan Zi interrupted, "My Lord, according to what you have just said Confucius must be a living god!"

Aware of her irritation, Duke Ling said by way of compromise, "Well, it was just a thought."

Nan Zi said, gritting her teeth, "In my opinion, he might have come here with an ulterior motive. Maybe he wants to do us harm."

Duke Ling was startled on hearing her words. He remembered how his ancestor Duke Yi was murdered by tribesmen who invaded Wei, captured the capital, and destroyed the palace. The people of Wei made Duke Dai their ruler, who died of illness only a year later, and was succeeded by Duke Wen. Duke Wen moved the capital to Chuqiu and then to Diqiu. Thanks to the assistance of the joint forces led by Duke Huan of Qi, Duke Wen was able to build the new capital and the palace and promote agriculture. After that, Wei had a respite from turmoil until Duke Ling became ruler. He shuddered at the thought that Confucius might be plotting against him. Then he saw in his mind's eye how Confucius looked: courageous but not impetuous, kind, polite, and graceful. It was hard to believe that such a man could harbor any evil intentions.

As if having read his thoughts, Nan Zi said in an overbearing tone, "If Confucius were not plotting something, why has he brought so many people with him?"

Duke Ling could not answer her question. He looked at her timidly, as if begging for her forgiveness. Nan Zi looked back at him compellingly. Her eyes could be sharp and piercing as well as alluring and seductive.

Under her gaze, Duke Ling was at a loss and did not know what to say.

Nan Zi went on relentlessly, "Which ruler does not want his state to be strong and prosperous? If Confucius were really capable, he should have stayed in Lu as minister of justice to give full play to his talents. Why should he leave his homeland and seek his fortune in a strange land?"

Duke Ling thought her words reasonable and did not argue with her.

Pleased with herself, Nan Zi demanded, "A superior man should return the kindness he has received. The duke of Lu treated Confucius with great favor, but instead of repaying such kindness he found an excuse to run away. Isn't this the conduct of a petty man?"

Duke Ling was silent. After a long pause he asked tentatively, "My lady, what do you think we should do about Confucius?"

Batting her eyes, Nan Zi said, "We only have to make a test to find out if something is genuine gold or not."

Chapter Twenty-four

The Wanton Consort Has an Affair
with a Courtier;
A Brave General of Wei Subdues a Rebellion

"Why not," Nan Zi suggested, lowering her voice to a whisper, "send a man outwardly to assist Confucius in daily affairs but actually to spy on him? In this way we will find out his real intention without incurring any embarrassment."

Accustomed to yielding to Nan Zi's caprices, Duke Ling agreed to her plan. He praised her for her cleverness and asked, "My lady, which man shall we choose?"

"I have already found a brave and cautious man for the task. Can you guess who it is?"

Duke Ling gave her a vacant look.

Nan Zi said in a sweet tone, "It is none other than your favored minister Gongsun Yujia."

Duke Ling was displeased and pulled a long face.

Gongsun Yujia was tall, handsome and well-mannered. Much appreciated by Duke Ling, he was appointed to junior minister in the court. However, Duke Ling later found out about his traits of craftiness and deceit and began to keep him at a distance. Duke Ling's apprehension was not entirely unjustifiable. Five years before Nan Zi and Gongsun Yujia, both in their mid-thirties, had started a clandestine affair.

It all began on a lovely day in spring. Relying on Duke Ling's favor, Gongsun could enter and leave the palace as he pleased. One day when he strolled into the palace garden he saw a palace maid plucking flowers for Nan Zi and became instantly seized by her exceptional beauty. She had a slender figure dressed in a red blouse and a green skirt, her hair elaborately woven like a conch. Her eyes were large and lovely, her eyebrows curved like the crescent moon, and she moved among the flowers with great dexterity and charm.

Unable to constrain himself, Gongsun sneaked up to her and suddenly took her in his arms. The palace maid was scared out of her wits. She dared not scream and was too weak to fight him. Gongsun

kissed her frantically, while his hands moved all over her. The maid
collapsed to the ground, staring blankly into the sky.

Gongsun lifted her by both hands and looked around, when he
heard someone cough slightly behind him. He turned and to his horror
saw Nan Zi standing there. He put down the palace maid and fell on
his knees. "Your humble servant deserves death! Please have mercy on
me!"

Nan Zi sneered at him and said loudly, "Well, a court official
taking liberties with a palace attendant on palace grounds. Do you
confess your guilt?"

Gongsun said repeatedly, "Your humble servant is guilty, very
guilty!"

"What punishment do you deserve?"

"Your humble servant deserves ten thousand deaths!"

"Good!" said Nan Zi with a drawl. "I'll go to His Lordship at once
and ask him to order you to be torn apart by five horses!"

Gongsun broke down completely. He beat his head on the ground
and pleaded, "Have mercy! Have mercy!"

Nan Zi frowned and said in a milder tone, "You will receive mercy
on three conditions."

Gongsun kowtowed. "If Your Ladyship can forgive me, I will agree
to a hundred, even a thousand conditions, not only three."

"Good!" Nan Zi said in a measured tone. "Listen carefully. First,
you will refrain from contact with any palace maid; second, when you
attend court audiences, you must always speak in favor of my opinion;
third, you must do whatever I want you to do."

"I promise to do all these things."

"Swear to Heaven!" demanded Nan Zi.

Gongsun Yujia said immediately, "With great sincerity I swear to
Heaven: I will follow the three rules laid down by Her Ladyship,
otherwise I would be exterminated by Heaven and Earth!"

Nan Zi smiled. "Minister Gongsun, you may get up now."

Gongsun got on his feet, his face flushed and his forehead covered
in sweat.

"Minister Gongsun, raise your head!"

"Your humble servant is guilty and dares not raise his head."

"Your guilt is forgiven!"

Gongsun slowly looked up.

The two of them were instantly dazed. Gongsun had entered the palace many times and on some occasions accompanied Duke Ling and Nan Zi to watch song and dance performances. But never before had he had a chance to take such a close look at Nan Zi, whose flawless beauty surpassed every woman he had ever seen. As for Nan Zi, Gongsun Yujia also appeared to her like a perfect specimen of a man. His body was strong and well-built, and his eyes sparkled with intelligence. Compared with him, Duke Ling was just a rawboned ugly old man. She told herself that this was the ideal lover she had been looking for.

They stared at each other for quite a few moments. Straining to calm herself, Nan Zi ordered, "Follow me!"

Gongsun followed her steps obediently, not daring to breathe aloud.

Coming to a round gate in the garden, Nan Zi said in a mild but determined voice, "I've been told you are very accomplished in the martial arts and can walk on walls and rooftops. His Lordship happens to be sick today. This is a chance bestowed by Heaven. You must come to see me in the rear palace in the dead of night!"

Trembling with fear, Gongsun stammered, "Your Ladyship, this ... this would be an unpardonable crime. Your humble servant dare ... dare not risk his life..."

Nan Zi smiled lightly. "Hmph! Are you the man you appear to be?"

"But that would be an unpardonable crime! I beg you..."

Her eyes widening in anger, Nan Zi said, "Well? Do you remember the oath you swore to Heaven just now?"

Gongsun fell silent.

Nan Zi said sternly, "Remember: come in the dead of night! Otherwise I would inform His Lordship of your behavior today. Then you would find it too late to repent!" With this she walked briskly back to the palace.

On her return to the palace she sent for Qiu Lian, the palace maid who had plucked flowers in the garden for her that day.

Qiu Lian fell on her knees and pleaded with trepidation, "Your slave has done wrong! Please spare me!"

Nan Zi laughed softly. "You've done nothing wrong; that rascal is to blame for assailing you. Now get up!"

Qiu Lian expressed her gratitude and rose to her feet.

"From now on you will attend on me day and night." When Nan

Zi went on to give her a detailed instruction, Qiu Lian was scared speechless. Nan Zi pulled a long face and said, "Do you want to stay alive or not?"

Qiu Lian could do nothing but nod her assent.

Back at home, Gongsun paced restlessly up and down in his room, unable to decide what to do. If he missed the appointment, Nan Zi would report the matter to the duke. But if he went to see her, he might fall into her trap. After much consideration he decided to go. If he disobeyed Nan Zi, he would definitely be put to death. If Nan Zi had really taken a fancy to him, he would not only escape death but also satisfy his lust.

Toward the third watch of the night he arrived outside the palace in a black, close-fitting dress and a pair of soft-soled shoes. At the third watch he looked around to make sure that no one was in sight, then leapt onto the palace wall. He bent down, tightened his abdomen and landed into the courtyard soundlessly. Even Qiu Lian, who had been waiting by the gate to the rear palace, did not hear any noise. He ran briskly along the wall and, finding the gate ajar, slipped inside. His sudden appearance took Qiu Lian quite by surprise.

By the dim light from the room, he saw the shadow before him and mistook it for Nan Zi. So he picked her up and said softly, "My lady, I've kept you waiting for too long." As he was walking into the room with Qian Lian in his arms, he ran into Nan Zi. Taking it for a trap, he put down Qiu Lian and knelt. "Your humble servant has come at your order!" he said. "Please spare me!"

Nan Zi's anger gradually dissipated. When she spoke her voice was gentle. "Get up at once!"

Gongsun scrambled to his feet, and his eyes fell on Nan Zi's alluring figure. When their eyes met, he became spellbound. After some dithering, he suddenly took Nan Zi in his arms and placed her onto the bed, not bothering to extinguish the light.

After a long night of pleasure Nan Zi took Gongsun by both hands and said in a sweet voice, "A good time can not last forever! It's almost daybreak, so you must hurry back."

Gongsun kissed her. "I wish I could lie by your side until we are both in the same coffin."

Displeased, Nan Zi covered his mouth with her hand and said disapprovingly, "What an inauspicious remark!"

Gongsun hastily corrected himself, saying, "I want to keep you company all my life!"

Light began to appear in the window. Gongsun put on his clothes in great haste and made for the door.

Nan Zi cried out angrily, "Come back!"

He stopped and asked timidly after a long pause, "Does Your Ladyship have any more instructions for me?"

"I allowed you to take liberties with me all night, and you want to leave without a word of thanks?"

Gongsun said with a smile, "Well, it is getting late..."

Nan Zi had to go straight to the point. "When will you come again?"

"I am at your beck and call!" With this he bowed deeply. "Your humble servant must take his leave!"

On his way out he saw Qiu Lian nodding at the door.

Gongsun stopped to stroke her breasts and shower her with kisses, then left quietly.

After that, Nan Zi had Gongsun eat out of her hand. They continued to have their rendezvous in the rear palace, and Nan Zi grew even more aversive to Duke Ling of Wei. Whenever a grand banquet was given in the palace with song and dance performances, Nan Zi and Gongsun would exchange amorous glances.

Gossip traveled fast among the court officials. Duke Ling also suspected that Nan Zi might be unfaithful to him, but to retain his dignity he suppressed his suspicion and acted as if nothing had gone wrong.

When Nan Zi recommended Gongsun Yujia to keep tabs on Confucius, Duke Ling was suddenly reminded of his longtime suspicion, and he felt too confused to say anything.

Nan Zi had no choice but to summon all her womanly charms to subdue the duke. She pressed herself against him and smiled her sweet smiles until Duke Ling finally succumbed. "Well, your suggestion is accepted. Tomorrow morning I will inform Gongsun Yujia of his mission."

Just then they were startled by someone bursting into the garden. They looked closely and recognized the duke's son, Kuai Kui, then some forty-seven to forty-eight years old. He ran up to Duke Ling and said in short gasps, "Gongsun Shu has raised a revolt in his manor, Kuang. His men are marching toward the capital!"

Accustomed to living in peace and luxury, Duke Ling was struck speechless for a few minutes by the news of a revolt by his minister. Finally he muttered, "My son, who can lead troops to resist and destroy the rebels?"

"Father, Wangsun Jia is very good at martial arts and military strategy. Why not send him to lead an expedition against Gongsun Shu?"

Duke Ling called out, "Guards! Send for Wangsun Jia at once!"

The guards standing outside the garden left immediately to find Wangsun Jia.

Duke Ling and Kuai Kui returned to the rear palace and waited anxiously for Wangsun Jia's arrival.

When the guards returned with Wangsun Jia, not waiting for him to salute, Duke Ling said anxiously, "Honored minister, I've always known you to be good at leading the army. Gongsun Shu has just raised a revolt and is marching toward the capital. I intend to put you in command of a band of troops to subdue the rebels. What do you think?"

Wangsun, in his forties, was tall, well-built and had large eyes with thick eyebrows. He said with great confidence, "It is for an emergency like this that the troops are kept. I promise to defend the state with my life!"

Duke Ling began to breathe with more ease and regained his normal complexion. Raising his voice, he said, "Excellent! You may set out with the troops at once!"

Wangsun stood there without moving.

Realizing his mistake, Duke Ling asked, "Eh, how many troops do you need, honored minister?"

"Three hundred war chariots would be enough."

"You may gather the troops by my order and set out at once!"

"I'll carry out Your Lordship's order!"

Wangsun first sent out a few scouts, then summoned the troops and left for Kuang.

They had traveled barely thirty li when a mounted scout returned to report, "Gongsun Shu and his men are only ten li away."

Wangsun ordered the troops to stop and shift into a battle formation, ready to intercept the oncoming rebel army.

About an hour later, dust arose in the distance. Wangsun mounted his chariot and shouted to his men, "Officers and men! The rebel army is coming. To protect the peace of our state and the happiness of our people, everyone should fight the enemy bravely!"

They could hear the horses' neighing and battle-cries uttered by Gongsun Shu's men. War chariots and foot soldiers carrying motley banners appeared. The biggest banner was embroidered with two large golden characters, "Gongsun."

Gongsun Shu was a very hefty man. Riding in his chariot, he stopped at an arrow's distance from Wangsun and said with a false smile, "Minister Wangsun, the duke of Wei is incompetent and Nan Zi is faithless. Do you expect to come to a good end by serving such a ruler? It would be wise for you to join forces with me. Together we will march to the capital and get rid of this witless ruler. Then together we can rule the state of Wei."

"Traitor, how dare you talk to me like this! His Lordship has bestowed much favor on you, but instead of returning his kindness, you betray him. If you put down your arms, dismount the chariot and let yourself be tied up, maybe our lord will spare your life. Otherwise you will find it too late to repent!"

Still unperturbed, Gongsun Shu said, "Minister Wangsun! It is said that a truly wise man moves with the tide. Nowadays wars are breaking out everywhere, and the strong always subdue the weak. If you are a man, why don't you lead a band of forces and fight on your own? Someday you may become a lord yourself. Aren't you after wealth and honor, just like everyone else? Now come with me to attack the capital!"

Enraged, Wangsun Jia picked up his bow and shot two arrows, hitting and breaking the pole of Gongsun Shu's banner, which fell to the ground in front of Gongsun Shu.

This sent Gongsun Shu into a fury. He drew his sword and shouted, "Soldiers, charge! Whoever kills Wangsun Jia will be amply rewarded!"

Wangsun called out, "Wait!"

Gongsun staggered at the thunderous roar.

Wangsun continued, "It is you who starts this rebellion, so why should your soldiers die because of your guilt? If you are brave enough, come forward by yourself. Let's fight it out man to man."

Gongsun Shu liked the idea, for he was extremely proud of his skill in martial arts. "Agreed!" he cried. "We will fight between the two of us. If you defeat me, I will led my men back to Kuang. But if I happen to beat you?"

Wangsun Jia replied with full confidence, "If you defeat me, I will withdraw my troops!"

"Do you mean what you say?" asked Gongsun Shu.

"A worthy man is as good as his word!"

Gongsun was convinced that Wangsun was no match for him. He was eager to win the fight so he could go on to attack the capital. He leapt out of his chariot and walked up, sword in hand.

Wangsun placed his sword into the hilt and stepped forward.

The two of them stopped at a distance of twenty steps. Wangsun said, "Minister Gongsun! As the saying goes, a single mistake may result in repentance of a lifetime. You have already committed a heinous crime by starting a revolt. If you repent now, follow me to the court and plead guilty to His Lordship. There is a chance that you will be forgiven. If you persist in your dangerous course, you will not only come to a miserable end but you will also be condemned as a traitor through the ages."

"Minister Wangsun, though you have outstanding abilities, you can find no way to use them. A real man can only serve a hero but not a fatuous ruler!"

"So you are going to fight to the bitter end?"

"I will not feel satisfied until I have stormed the palace and killed the impotent duke."

"Let me tell you something. Your dream does not have the slightest chance of coming true."

"Let's stop wasting time. How shall we start fighting?"

"In the courteous way, of course."

Gongsun untied his sword and threw it to the ground. He tightened his belt and sleeves and made ready to attack.

Wangsun also placed his sword onto the ground, straightened his garment and prepared to fight.

Gongsun was about to attack when Wangsun waved his hand. "Minister Gongsun, the result of our fight will affect the fate of Wei and also the lives of our men. Tell your men not to move without order if you are a brave man."

Gongsun turned and shouted, "Soldiers, no one shall move without my order!" Then he turned to Wangsun, "Minister Wangsun, you should also make this clear to your own troops."

Wangsun shouted to his men, "When I fight with Gongsun Shu, you shall only look on without saying anything, let alone making any move. Whoever disobeys shall be executed!"

Gongsun Shu was relieved. He still did not consider Wangsun a formidable opponent. Bowing slightly with clasped hands, he said, "Minister Wangsun, please begin!"

Wangsun said, "Please begin!" He stood there without making any move.

Gathering his strength, Gongsun stepped forcefully toward Wangsun, his hands moving swiftly like a snake just coming out of its hole.

When he came near, Wangsun suddenly leapt over his head.

Gongsun was surprised that Wangsun Jia could have jumped so high. He turned and threw himself at Wangsun, extending both arms and drawing back his legs like an eagle heading for its prey.

Wangsun dodged by falling back swiftly.

Failing to harm his opponent by two of his favorite combat moves, Gongsun began to grow impatient. He headed toward Wangsun, striking with his fists and feet.

Wangsun did not show any sign of weakness but fought him head-on. They exchanged about fifty moves, kicking up a great dust around them. Gongsun began to feel a little weak in the arms and short of breath. He suddenly bent down and extended his feet, hitting Wangsun's shin and sending him sprawling. He leapt into the air, intending to stamp his opponent with his feet. Supporting himself on his hands, Wangsun withdrew his legs and hit Gongsun's feet with his own, sending the latter away for a long distance. Unprepared, Gongsun fell to the ground.

The soldiers on both sides were now cheering and encouraging their commanders.

Gongsun got to his feet, wiped the sweat and mud off his face, and tried to collect his senses. He looked up and saw Wangsun gazing him mockingly. Shamed into anger, he picked up his sword and dashed toward Wangsun with a roar.

Wangsun evaded several thrusts bare-handedly, falling back step by step until his own sword was within reach. He kicked it up with the left foot and caught it in his hand.

The two started fighting with their swords. After about thirty moves Gongsun felt weak in his legs and numb in his hands. Realizing that he was inferior in strength, he decided to employ one of his tricks. He thrust out his sword and, when Wangsun stepped back in evasion, turned and ran. He stopped beside a willow tree and, just as

Wangsun came up, attacked suddenly with his sword.

Crying out in surprise, Wangsun dodged just in time, so that the sword only tore a hole in his sleeve.

Gongsun emerged from behind the tree and moved toward Wangsun, who turned and ran for dear life.

Gongsun pursued him swiftly, intending to finish him off.

Wangsun stopped abruptly, turned and stabbed Gongsun's right arm with his sword. Gongsun staggered, dropping his sword onto the ground. He cried out painfully. Wangsun lifted his right feet and kicked Gongsun on the lower abdomen, then drew the sword to strike. Gongsun, however, leapt backward and scurried away.

Having lost his esprit, Gongsun jumped into his chariot and drove off at once. Wangsun led the troops in a pursuit, routing Gongsun's army. Climbing up a mound, Wangsun ordered his men to shoot down numerous men and horses of the fleeing enemy. Gongsun was able to lead the remnants of his troops back to Kuang.

Having cleared up the battleground, Wangsun returned to the capital with his triumphant troops and the captured soldiers and horses.

Duke Ling of Wei and all the court officials went out the city to welcome the return of the expeditionary force. The city residents also poured out into the street to cheer their heroes.

Duke Ling was overjoyed that Wangsun could have defeated the rebel army in such a short time. That evening he gave a sumptuous feast in the palace to celebrate the victory. He was soon captivated by the song and dance performance and felt as if he no longer had a single care in the world.

Nan Zi said to him seriously, "Your Lordship, could there be a special cause for Gongsun Shu's revolt? For many years Wei has enjoyed peace and comfort. Why did such an incident take place barely a year after Confucius' arrival? Is this merely a coincidence?"

Hearing this, Duke Ling sent for Gongsun Yujia and gave him some instruction.

Gongsun Yujia nodded his head repeatedly.

Chapter Twenty-five

Confucius Is Kept Under Surveillance in Wei; He and His Disciples Are Surrounded at Kuang

As Duke Ling of Wei grew suspicious of Confucius he finally agreed to send Gongsun Yujia to keep watch on him. When Gongsun Yujia came to Yan's house, Confucius was discussing rites with his disciples in the courtyard. He went up and made a deep bow. "Gongsun Yujia has come at His Lordship's order to tend daily affairs for the master. If you need my help in anything, just tell me."

Confucius was surprised, wondering why Duke Ling had done this. He returned the salute and said, "I am grateful to His Lordship for his kind treatment. I don't know how I can repay his favor by sending you here to take care of my disciples and me."

"I am a rough fellow. If there should be any negligence or mistake on my part, I hope you will forgive me!"

"Minister Gongsun, you are being too modest. How can I take up your valuable time?"

"I am merely carrying out His Lordship's order. What's more, you are widely known for your virtue and talent. Staying close to you, I will have a chance to learn something about civil and military affairs so that I can serve my state better in the future."

"In that case I have no objection to your staying," said Confucius.

Zi Gong was not at all pleased. As a native of Wei he knew Gongsun Yujia's reputation only too well. In his opinion, it was a shame to allow such a person to stay at Confucius' side.

After this, Gongsun Yujia followed Confucius closely all day. He came on the pretext of tending daily affairs for Confucius, but he did practically nothing useful. After about a month Confucius began to tire of him.

One day Duke Ling of Wei summoned Confucius into the palace and said to him politely, "Master, you have stayed in our humble state for over six months. If there is anything we failed to do, please do not

be offended!"

Confucius said with a smile, "Having received what I do not deserve, I am wondering how I can ever repay your kindness."

Duke Ling said, "I've been worrying a lot since Gongsun Shu's revolt, which took me by complete surprise. You are well versed in both civil and military affairs. If a higher minister should raise a revolt, how shall we deploy the troops to subdue him?"

Confucius assumed a serious expression. "I am a scholar who knows something about the rites but nothing about military affairs."

Duke Ling was quite displeased. He had heard of Confucius' exploits in leading the troops to subdue the three major cities in Lu. In his opinion, Confucius was obviously unwilling to talk about the topic, for he was after all not a subject of Wei. Thinking about this, Duke Ling began to regret having treated Confucius with so much generosity.

At the sight of Duke Ling's unhappy look, Confucius felt uneasy and rose to take his leave.

Back in Yan's house, Confucius recalled what had taken place in the past six months, feeling very depressed. Apart from teaching his disciples and solving some problems for the local residents, he had achieved virtually nothing. He lamented the time he had wasted. Concluding that Duke Ling was not the kind of wise ruler he had been looking for, Confucius decided to leave Wei. He told the disciples of his intention, and they unanimously agreed to leave.

During his stay in Wei Confucius had called on various civil and military officials. He became good friends with an old court official named Qu Boyu. Since he was leaving Wei, he went to pay Qu Boyu a last visit, accompanied by Yan Hui, Zi Lu and Zi Gong. At the news of their arrival Qu Boyu came out the gate to receive them.

Twenty years Confucius' senior, Qu Boyu was grey-haired but still hale and hearty. Pleased to see Confucius, he bowed with clasped hands. "Master, you spent all day teaching your disciples and have not been to visit me. Did I offend you by my negligence last time?"

Returning the salute, Confucius said, "As a man without an occupation, I dare not trouble you too much."

"You are being too modest, master! A traveler has no one but his friends to rely on. Away from your homeland, you are bound to feel unhappy sometimes, so you should often go out and try to forget your worries. Now please come to the upper room where we can have a talk!"

The two of them walked into the room side by side, and the three disciples followed behind.

Qu was a man of high aspirations. He liked others to point out his mistakes and was quick at correcting them. Therefore he was deeply respected by Confucius. Formerly, a minister named Shi Qiu (styled name Zi Yu) kept sending memorials to Duke Ling of Wei advising him to get rid of a crooked court official and replace him with Qu Boyu. However, Duke Ling did not take his advice. Before he died, Zi Yu said to his son, "Qu Boyu is capable enough to be the chief minister, but I have failed to persuade His Lordship to employ him. After I die, do not conduct a mourning for me in the main room. This will be my posthumous advice. If His Lordship gets the message, he will perhaps appoint Qu Boyu to high office." Moved by Zi Yu's insistence, Duke Ling finally appointed Qu Boyu a court official. Later, Qu Boyu resigned from his post due to Duke Ling's ineptitude and bigotry. On hearing this Confucius remarked, "What a superior man Qu Boyu is! When the ruler was sagacious, he came out to assume office and made use of his talents. When the ruler acted fatuously, he went away and concealed his abilities."

About three years before Qu Boyu had sent a household steward to the state of Lu to visit Confucius, who received him in his office. Confucius asked the envoy, "Minister Qu has resigned because of his old age. What is he doing at home?" The steward replied, "Minister Qu is striving to reduce and avoid mistakes. However, he grows worried that he has not achieved this." Confucius was greatly pleased with the reply. After the envoy had left, he remarked, "What an envoy! What an envoy!" The incident left a deep impression on him.

Looking at the venerable old man before him, Confucius felt a surge of conflicting emotions. He did not want to leave, but he had to. Having so much to say, he did not know how to begin.

Qu Boyu looked closely at Yan Hui, Zi Lu and Zi Gong and said to Confucius with deep emotion, "Master, by teaching poetry and the rites to your talented disciples, you will earn a lasting reputation in history. Could you tell me what ultimate goal do you set for your disciples?"

Pleased with the question, Confucius replied, "What you just asked is of the utmost importance! In my opinion, a man must have a goal in life; only thus can his life be both colorful and worthwhile.

According to *The Book of Rites*, when the Great Way prevails the whole world will become one community. Since the origin of man in China when Fu Xi and Nü Wa married, many sage rulers have emerged. We have Zu Rong, Shen Nong, Huang Di, Zhuan Xu, Di Ku, Yao, Shun, Yu, Cheng Tang, King Wen and King Wu. All of them strived to attain the Great Way, working hard all their lives to make the country strong and the people wealthy. Unfortunately, there were also some despots such as King Jie and King Zhou, who did not rule the country well. Instead, they only sought to satisfy their evil desires and brought havoc to the common people. As my lifelong ambition, I want to persuade the ruler of a state to follow the example of the ancient sage kings and guard against the evils of the ancient despots, establishing a benevolent government and eliminating warfare. The Great Way can be achieved in one state first and then spread to the whole world. It is my hope that my disciples would also make this their lifelong cause."

"It is indeed commendable that you take it upon yourself to propagate the rites! Judging by what I have experienced, however, you failed to achieve your aim in Lu and will probably fail again in Wei."

"Whatever happens, a man should never lose his courage and perseverance. I will not change my mind in the face of difficulties."

"I'm afraid you may run into trouble by advocating something that goes against the tide."

Confucius said with determination, "A benevolent man sometimes has to risk his life for the sake of benevolence but never tries to save his own life at the expense of benevolence. We would have no use for music and the rites if we do not stick to the rules of benevolence and righteousness."

Qu smiled sadly. "In today's world people attach much greater importance to military strength than to the rites. Your ideas are fine, but you will find few people agree with you."

Confucius fell silent. After a while he said, "What you said is right, Minister Qu. The ancient rites have been forgotten by many people. I can describe the rites of Xia, but it is not being practiced by Xia's offspring, the ruler of the state of Qi. I can also describe the rites of Shang, but it is not being practiced by Yin's offspring, the ruler of the state of Song. This is due to the lack of adequate historical documents on the one hand and people of virtue on the other. If there had been ample documents and numerous virtuous people, the situation would have been totally different. Therefore I spend most of my time teaching the rites to my disciples. Someday the government of rites will be accepted by the vassal lords and the king of Zhou, because it is so wished by the common people."

"Master, among the rites of Xia, Shang and Zhou, which do you prefer?"

"The rites of Zhou have been formulated on the basis of the rites of Xia and Shang. They are therefore the richest and most refined. Therefore I favor the rites of Zhou."

"What do you think of Ning Wuzi?" asked Qu.

Confucius was quite familiar with Ning Wuzi, a minister serving under Duke Wen and Duke Cheng of Wei, so he replied definitely, "He is an intelligent man."

"How can you tell?"

"When the state was in peace and the ruler wise and benign, he displayed his talent by offering useful advice to the lord. When the state was in turmoil and the ruler foolish and rash, he feigned stupidity and ignorance. Other people may equal him in terms of talent but not in terms of stupidity and ignorance."

Qu laughed heartily. "You are perceptive, master! You have such a deep insight into the affairs of the world!" He paused a little, then said jokingly, "Master, are you not more intelligent than he?"

"How can I compare with him!"

"My fatal weakness," said Qu, "is that I am too frank and outspoken. I often inspire enmity in others just because I say what I think without much deliberation."

Confucius said, "In my youth I went to learn from Lao Zi in the Zhou capital, where I saw an article written on a bronze figure. It said, 'It is an ancient rule that man should be cautious in his speech. Please stick to the rule. Do not talk too much, which often brings defeat. Do not take unessential action, which often causes trouble.' The truth of these words has been proved by my experience since then. Shi Xiangzi, the court musician of Jin, once told me that good advice sounds unpleasant to the ears just as good medicine tastes bitter to the mouth. However, few people are wise enough to listen to unpleasant advice!"

They talked for a long time. Confucius did not take his leave until sunset.

Learning that Confucius and his disciples were about to leave, Yan Zhuozou hastily had a farewell banquet prepared for them. He tried to persuade Confucius to stay, but Confucius had made up his mind. Yan Zhuozou made him the gift of a little silver for traveling expenses.

Early the next morning Confucius and his disciples left the Wei capital by the south gate and headed for the state of Chen. In late autumn, it was hot at noon but very chilly in the morning. As they traveled along the dusty road, the cropped fields, the undulating downs and the woeful cry of wild geese flying overhead all added to their desolate mood. Confucius thought of his wife, Lady Qiguan, and his children. He also thought of the disciples in Lu, wondering if they had given up their studies. Suddenly a large stretch of red leaves in the hill ahead of them caught his attention. His face lit up with pleasure. "Look at the hill ahead of us!" he called out to his disciples. "What a lovely sight!"

His disciples had been trudging along behind the chariot, their faces covered with a thick layer of dust. Hearing the master's call, they ran up to his chariot and looked ahead. What they saw delighted them.

"What a wonderful place! It would be nice to stay there for a few days," said Zi Lu.

"What our master wants is to make the whole world into such a beautiful place," commented Ran Geng.

Confucius was pleased that his disciples understood him so well.

A chariot sped toward them. Confucius looked up to see a youth in his twenties, dressed in a scholar's robe and sitting in the chariot. The youth lifted the hem of his robe, leapt off the chariot and came up to Confucius. He bowed with clasped hands and asked, "Venerable sir, are you coming from the capital of Wei? Have you met Confucius?"

Zi Lu said hastily, "You have asked the right person!"

Zi Gong stepped forward and stopped Zi Lu. "Why are you looking for our master?" he asked.

The youth took a look at them and replied, "I am a native of Chen. My family name is Gongliang, my given name Ru and my styled name Zi Zheng. I have heard of Confucius' reputation for a long time and want to study with him as his disciple. A month ago I went to Lu, where I learned that the master had left for Wei. I am on my way to Wei to look for him."

Zi Gong's heart warmed toward the youth with his graceful manners and elegant dress, who reminded him of the time when he sought the tutorship of Confucius many years ago. "This is the master himself," he said.

Overjoyed, Gongliang Ru wiped off the dust from his clothes, adjusted his hat, and knelt before Confucius' chariot. "Your disciple Gongliang Ru pays respects to the master!"

Confucius was very glad to have such a handsome, well-mannered youth to be his disciple. "Gongliang Ru, please get up and let's talk."

Gongliang got on his feet and stood by the chariot, waiting anxiously for Confucius to speak.

Confucius said, "We are now heading to the state of Chen. It is hard to tell how many roads I will travel and how many obstacles I will encounter. Judging from your fine clothes, you must come from a wealthy family. Will you be able to bear the difficulty and distress of a wandering life?"

Gongliang Ru said, "Though I come from a wealthy family, my father has been very strict in teaching me. I have not only learned a little about poetry and rites but I have also practiced martial arts. With a strong physique, I can endure whatever hardships I may come across."

Confucius nodded with satisfaction. "Get on the chariot and follow me to Chen then!"

Gongliang said, "Master, traveling long distances on foot would be too much for my fellow disciples. There are many horses and chariots in my house. Let me return home and bring back a few chariots for my fellow disciples. Further down the road you'll enter a mountain area with very beautiful scenery. You may stay in a hostel for a few days and enjoy the local sights until I return with the chariots."

Confucius hesitated.

Zi Gong said, "Master, this sounds like a good idea. Let him return to bring the chariots, and we can find a hostel to stay in. We will have time to enjoy the views and practice the rites there."

"We might as well," agreed Confucius. "Gongliang Ru, come back and join us quickly!"

"I understand." With a deep bow Gongliang mounted his chariot and set off for Chen.

Confucius and his disciples put up in a hostel before the mountain slope, where chrysanthemums were in full bloom and persimmons had turned yellow in maturity amid the gentle autumn breeze. They continued their study of poetry and rites there, and sometimes climbed up the hill to enjoy the sights.

At twilight one day, Confucius stood on the terrace before the hostel and looked south, for he expected it was time for Gongliang Ru to return. In the distance five small dots were moving. As they drew nearer they turned out to be five chariots.

The disciples also came out and stood by their master's sides. In a short while five brand-new chariots came before them. The horses were big and strong. All the disciples were filled with joy.

When Confucius and his disciples set out the following day, they made a very impressive convoy with their seven chariots.

The sun was blotted out by dark clouds, and it became unusually hot and stuffy. Confucius said, "As a common saying goes, coldness in spring or heat in autumn signifies rain. We have to make haste to find a hostel, or we will be traveling in rain along muddy roads."

At this the disciples all whipped the horses to a swift trot, soon arriving at the Kuang area. Yan Ke, who was driving the chariot for Confucius, remarked, "Master, it was here that Yang Hu broke into the city when he fled from Qi to Jin." A local resident who happened to be passing by heard the remark.

Yan Ke, whose styled name was Zi Jiao, was a native of Lu. When Yang Hu fled from Qi to Jin, he stopped in Kuang to enlarge his forces, causing much harm to the local people, who bore an intense hatred against him. Hearing Yan Ke's casual remark, the local mistook Confucius for Yang Hu and went hastily to report to Gongsun Shu.

After his defeat by Wangsun Jia, Gongsun Shu had spent over a month nursing his wound. Then he stayed in Kuang, not daring to venture out. When he heard Yang Hu had come to the city, he immediately summoned his troops and set out.

Confucius and his disciples, all riding in chariots for the first time, reached a mountain ridge with red-leafed trees and yellow grass. As they were enjoying the view, a light rain started. They went down the mountain ridge into a pass when, at the signal of a whistle, Gongsun Shu and his men suddenly emerged and surrounded them.

Taken by surprise, Confucius could only stare at them blankly. A hefty man standing on a war chariot and holding a sword in his hand was staring at Confucius fiercely. Pointing to Confucius with his sword, he shouted, "Yang Hu, you owe us a debt in blood. I was wondering where to find you, and here you are to seek your own doom! Think on this, this day next year will be the first anniversary of your death!" He finished his words with a sweep of his sword, and his men tightened the encirclement.

Zi Lu leapt from the chariot and walked up to him. He bowed deeply and asked, "My I learn your honorable name?"

Throwing out his chest, the man replied, "I am Gongsun Shu!"

"Just now I heard you call the name Yang Hu. Who do you take for Yang Hu?"

Gongsun Shu pointed at Confucius with his sword. "That's him!"

Zi Lu broke out laughing.

"Who are you?" demanded Gongsun Shu. "And why do you laugh?"

"My family name is Zhong, my given name You, and my styled name Zi Lu. I laughed because you mistook my master for Yang Hu."

Gongsun Shu gave Confucius another look and shook his head. "I don't believe you. Yang Hu is said to be very tall, just like him."

Zi Lu said, "The two of them may look alike, but they are totally different in nature. Yang Hu is a traitor who has left Lu for Jin. As for my master, Confucius, he is universally respected for his virtue. How can you compare one with the other?"

"You are telling me this is Kong Qiu?" Gongsun asked doubtfully.

"Yes," replied Zi Lu.

Gongsun ordered his man to fall back for an arrow's distance. Still suspicious, he kept the encirclement around Confucius and his disciples and decided not to leave until he discovered their true identity.

Confucius told his disciples not to take any rash move for fear of causing more trouble.

The rain did not stop at nightfall. They felt hungry, thirsty, and extremely tired. The air was chilly in the autumn breeze. As it grew dark, the cry of birds and animals in the mountains sounded sad and fearsome.

At dawn the rain stopped, and a round moon emerged from the dispersing clouds. At the sight of the bright moon, Confucius felt better. He drifted into a dream, finding himself riding at full speed toward the royal capital. Meeting him in front of the palace, the Duke of Zhou demanded sternly, "Kong Qiu, why do you come to the capital instead of helping the duke of Lu govern the state?" Confucius replied, "Following your order, I served His Lordship with all my heart. I adopted a benevolent policy and propagated the rites, and was able to make some improvements in Lu. However, after His Lordship accepted eighty dancing girls and a hundred and twenty fine horses from Qi, he indulged himself in pleasure-making for three whole days without attending to state affairs. Unable to take it any longer, I left Lu in search of a sage ruler elsewhere. I arrived in Wei, but its ruler turned out to be weak and incompetent. Now I am heading for Chen, but the men of Kuang surround us and do not allow us to leave." The Duke of Zhou said, "Perhaps all this is decreed by fate." "But I do not want to succumb to adverse fate," said Confucius. "My only wish is to govern the state by rites and music and work for a world of peace and harmony." "Good!" said the Duke of Zhou. "I have found someone to carry on my cause!" Just then Confucius was awakened by the neighing of horses. It was already daybreak. Red leaves laid scattered on the ground around them. Gongsun Shu's men were still holding the encirclement a short distance away. Some were practicing spear play and others brandishing the clubs.

Confucius got up and found himself covered by Zi Lu's padded jacket. He got out of the chariot and handed the jacket to Zi Lu, whose lips had turned crimson with cold. "Put it on!" Confucius said to Zi Lu with pity.

"I am strong enough to withstand the cold," said Zi Lu.

Confucius looked at the other disciples, who all appeared haggard and afraid, so he decided to cheer them up. "Since the time of King Wen," he said, "the world's culture has been inherited by us. Qi is stronger than Lu but inferior in terms of culture, institutions and rites. By making great efforts to propagate the rites, Qi might be able to catch up with Lu. If the culture and rites of Lu spread elsewhere, harmony will be achieved in the whole world. If Heaven wants to destroy this culture, we won't be able to learn it. If Heaven does not want this culture destroyed, how can the people of Kuang harm us?" He spoke with great confidence, and his disciples felt reassured.

Unable to ascertain the identity of Confucius and his disciples, Gongsun Shu would not allow them to leave. He kept them there for five days. Running out of food, they had to dig for wild vegetables. They grew listless with hunger and their mouths were parched with thirst.

Gongliang Ru said, "Master, it is said that a man would rather die on his feet than live on his knees. We should fight bravely instead of lying here without doing anything! I would rather die than putting up with such humiliation."

Confucius turned to Zi Gong, "You are a very good speaker. Go and talk to Gongsun Shu. He may be persuaded to let us go."

Zi Gong said, "I can only persuade people amenable to reason. As for someone like Gongsun Shu, who is incapable of being brought to reason, I would be totally helpless."

"Why not give it a try?" said Confucius.

"I'll do as you say!" Zi Gong straightened his clothes and walked toward Gongsun Shu.

Gongsun was sitting in his chariot eating mutton, his cheeks smeared with fat. When Zi Gong approached, he stared askance at him and said, "Well? Dizzy on an empty stomach? Move forward on your knees and I will give you a piece of bone for you to chew." He threw a rib to the ground.

Constraining his anger, Zi Gong said in a mild tone, "Respected sir, we are merely a group of scholars traveling through here. There has never been any bad blood between us. Why don't you allow us to leave?"

Gongsun swallowed the mutton in his mouth and mumbled, "Someone recognized him as Yang Hu, but he said he is Kong Qiu. Who can attest to it?"

"I can," said Zi Gong.

"You belong to his group, of course you will speak in his favor."

"In that case, I'll go back to the Wei capital to find someone."

Gongsun rolled his eyes and threw his chin up. "I don't believe anyone from the Wei capital!" he shouted.

Zi Gong knew it would be a waste of time to reason with him any further. He returned and reported to Confucius what had happened.

"Well," said Confucius. "If Heaven does not want us to perish, we'll find a way out of here."

Gongliang Ru suggested, "Master, we have no choice but to fight our way out of here. Otherwise we will all starve to death."

Zi Lu agreed. "Master, there is no other choice. Let's do it tonight."

Confucius finally nodded his agreement.

At the third watch they uttered a loud cry and charged out with Zi Lu and Gongliang Ru in their chariots at the front, followed by Yan Ke, who drove the chariot for Confucius. The men of Kuang pursued them for a while, then gave up. The seven chariots sped on for over thirty li. At dawn they stopped, only to find Yan Hui missing. Confucius was so upset that he beat his chest and stamped his feet.

Chapter Twenty-six

Confucius and His Disciples Return to Wei; Lady Nan Zi Meets with Confucius

While breaking out of the encirclement, the chariots rode at full speed on the bumpy road. Yan Hui, who was weak and thin, and limp with hunger, fell from the chariot into the grass by the road. His first impulse was to call for help, but he checked himself for fear of impeding the others' escape. He got on his feet and ran after the chariots. At daybreak he finally caught up with Confucius and the other disciples.

Confucius was so happy to see him that his eyes brimmed with tears. "I thought you had been killed by the men of Kuang," he said. "I did not expect to see you again."

Panting heavily, Yan Hui replied earnestly, "Master, when you are still alive, how dare I die!"

Confucius was much moved by this remark. "Get on the chariot," he said, "and let's continue the journey."

By this time the sun had risen. Yellow and red fallen leaves swirled in the autumn wind. A group of wild geese, uttering doleful cries, flew south in an orderly formation. Confucius thought of his homeland. He had been hoping for Duke Ding of Lu to change his mind and send men to fetch him back, but this had not happened. His efforts to restore the rites of Zhou in the world proved futile time and again. Forcing himself to calm down, he looked up at the white clouds drifting in the blue sky. Suddenly a few wisps of cloud appeared to him like war chariots arrayed for battle. "Is that a sign of war?" he asked himself, but he quickly brushed the idea away. Feeling both tired and hungry, he said to his driver, Yan Ke, "Let's stop to eat somewhere."

Soon they arrived at a small town with several restaurants in the street. "Master, let's eat here, shall we?" Yan Ke asked.

Confucius licked his parched lips and nodded his consent.

After they entered a restaurant and took their seats, the waiter began to describe the menu of the day. Zi Lu interrupted him. "Don't bother. One big bowl of noodles with fried bean sauce for each of us."

The waiter announced loudly to the cooks, "A big bowl of noodles with fried bean sauce for each!"

Zi Lu added, "Get a piece of ginger and cut it into thin slices."

The waiter again conveyed the message to the cooks.

Confucius and his disciples waited for the meal, their stomach churning. After what seemed like hours the waiter emerged with the bowls of noodles on a wooden tray. They bolted down their noodles, then continued their journey, traveling over sixty li until, at dusk, they arrived at a place called Pu.

Confucius said, "It is getting late. Let's find a clean place where we can stay the night."

They stopped when they came to a big river with two hostels along its bank.

Behind the hostels there was an orchard where the red leaves of pear trees were falling to the ground. A sudden gust of wind carried the leaves into the air, then blew them away into the distance.

The disciples stood and watched the sight.

Confucius gazed after the leaves and was suddenly seized by an intense feeling of sadness. The beautiful red leaves that he so admired were being ruthlessly swept away by the autumn wind, and he could do nothing about it. He looked down into the river, where a few red leaves were being carried away by the current.

The disciples stood around him talking. Zi Lu approached him and said, "Master, shall we stay the night here?"

Confucius gazed at the leaves in the river without saying anything.

Zi Lu went into the hostel on the right and returned. "Master," he said, "the rooms in that hostel are not big but very clean. Let's stay here, shall we?"

Confucius readily agreed.

They dismounted the chariots and unsaddled the horses. After supper they went to their respective rooms to rest. All of them slept soundly, having had a most tiring day.

Getting up early the next morning, they heard a racket outside, whereupon, Confucius told Ran Qiu to go and see what had happened.

Ran Qiu opened the gate and was startled to see a crowd of men carrying all kinds of weapons. The leader was a hefty middle-aged man with big rolling eyes, heavy eyebrows and thick whiskers. Placing his left hand on the sword hanging from his belt and pinching his right temple with his right hand, he said with a sneer, "Are you a follower of Kong Qiu?"

"Yes," replied Ran Qiu.

"What's your name?"

"My family name is Ran and my given name Qiu."

"Are you a native of Lu?"

"Yes," replied Ran Qiu. He bowed with clasped hands and asked, "May I have your name please?"

Without returning the salute, the man replied in a husky voice, "I am Gongshu Shi."

Ran Qiu bowed again, "May I ask why you have come with so many people?"

Gongshu Shi replied insolently, "To capture Kong Qiu!"

"My master has never offended you, so why do you want to capture him?"

"The duke of Wei is an evil man, and I have gathered troops ready to storm into the palace and cut off his head. Just at this moment you suddenly show up here. Are you not sent here to spy for him?"

Ran Qiu found the situation both funny and annoying. He said in a mild tone, "Gongshu, even if the duke of Wei has made mistakes, he has also worked for the benefit of the people. How can you treat him like that?"

Gongshu Shi cocked his head and swept his hand. "Stop talking nonsense! Tell Kong Qiu to come out! I have something to say!"

Reluctantly Ran Qiu returned and reported the matter to Confucius.

Smoothing his clothes, Confucius went to the gate. Before he could say anything, Gongshu demanded in a peremptory voice, "Are you Kong Qiu from Lu?"

Confucius stepped up and clasped his hands in a salute. "I am Kong Qiu from Lu. May I ask why you have come with your followers?"

Gongshu Shi answered nonchalantly, "Well, the duke of Wei is a wicked man, and he has thrown the entire state into total chaos. I am leading my troops to attack Diqiu and kill him."

For a short while Confucius felt dizzy. As more and more people resorted to force and violence, his dream of restoring the rites of Zhou appeared more and more ephemeral.

"Kong Qiu, Are you a spy sent by the duke of Wei?" Gongsun demanded.

The accusation was so ridiculous that Confucius felt it beneath his dignity to reply.

Gongshu Shi drew his sword and, brandishing it, asked in a menacing voice, "Tell me, are you sent by the duke of Wei?"

Confucius paced up and down the terrace for a while, muttering to himself, "Am I a spy?" Aware that this was not the time to speak honestly, he said, "Gongshu, my disciples and I are heading for Chen and only happen to pass here. I have no interest in what happens between the Wei palace and Pu."

Gongshu rolled his eyes. "I don't believe you! I heard people say that the duke pays you a very handsome salary. Now it has been a rule since ancient times that a man should not accept something he does not deserve. As a scholar you must have known that!"

"Well, it is exactly because I did nothing to deserve His Lordship's favor that I decided to leave Wei for Chen with my disciples."

"In that case, will you swear not to inform the Wei ruler of my gathering troops here?"

"I am heading for Chen."

"But what if you happen to go to Diqiu?"

"I will not mention what happened here."

Gongshu strode up to Confucius and extended his hairy hand.

Confucius, who always held treacherous people in contempt, did not respond.

"You are making fun of me!" roared Gongshu furiously, drawing his sword.

Confucius smiled, "Why do you have to be so impatient?"

Replacing the sword into the sheath, Gongshu asked, "So you are willing to swear by striking palms?"

Confucius nodded and extended his right hand, which Gongshu hastily struck with his.

Confucius did not feel very happy at being forced to smack palms with a rebel leader. "Gongshu, now my disciples and I can get on with our journey, can't we?" he asked coldly.

Gongshu Shi hesitated for a while, then turned and shouted, "Men, let's get out of here!"

When the rebels had left, Confucius bade the disciples get on the chariots. They rode for a dozen li before coming to a fork in the road. Suddenly Confucius said to Yan Ke, "Let's return to Diqiu by a roundabout route!"

"Master, I thought we were going to Chen," said Yan Ke in

surprise.

"I have just changed my mind," declared Confucius.

Yan Ke turned the chariot and struck onto a side road to the right.

After a while Gongliang Ru caught up to Confucius and said, "Master, we are taking the wrong road."

"I know," said Confucius. "I don't want to go to Chen right now."

"Where are we going then?" asked Gongliang Ru.

"To Diqiu."

Zi Gong also gained upon them. "Master, why are we going to Diqiu?" he asked.

"Because I want to inform the duke of Wei of what is happening in Kuang and Pu."

Zi Gong was surprised. "Master, you always stress the need to keep faith . Why do you want to break a promise you made only a moment ago?"

Confucius replied, "There is no need to go by a promise made under duress. Even if Heaven learns about this, it will not blame me. If I do not tell the duke of Wei about the rebels and let him send troops to exterminate them, how will I ever have a chance to restore the rites of Zhou?"

Knowing it would be in vain to argue with Confucius, Zi Gong mounted his chariot without more ado.

Arriving at Diqiu, Confucius led his disciples straight to Qu Boyu's house.

Pleasantly surprised by their arrival, Qu hurriedly smoothed his clothes and came out to welcome them.

Qu Boyu and Confucius entered the room hand in hand and took their seats as host and guest. "Do you plan to stay long in Wei this time?" Qu asked.

Confucius sighed. "I wanted to lead my disciples to Chen, but unfortunately we met some wicked people on the way. First we were besieged at Kuang by Gongsun Shu, who mistook me for Yang Hu. It was not until five days later that we managed to get away. Then we arrived at Pu, where Gongshu Shi is planning a revolt against the duke of Wei. He took me for a spy and would not allow us to leave until I promised not to tell anyone of his plot."

Qu said, "It is well said that eminent people suffer more hardships than obscure people. You left Diqiu for only half a month, yet you met with so many humiliations. What has the world come to!" He paused for a moment, then asked, "What do you plan to do now?"

Confucius thought for a while, then replied, "I want to inform the duke of Wei of the situation in Kuang and Pu, and I also want to stay here for a while and try to learn more about situations in other states."

Qu smiled broadly. "In that case," he said, "you and your disciples can stay under my roof. Though it is not much of a house, there are ample rooms for the guests."

"Well—" Confucius hesitated.

Qu said, "Please do stay here. Then I can also benefit from your instructions." He bade the house servants clean the guest rooms and prepare a feast to welcome Confucius and his disciples.

That evening Confucius and Qu had a long talk, discussing current affairs as well as events in the previous dynasties. They did not go to bed until late at night.

For a long time Confucius could not sleep. The hardships he had suffered in Wei showed him the great difficulty he would have to overcome in order to restore peace and prosperity in the present world. However, he thought he could make a new start in Wei by helping the duke of Wei subdue the rebels.

The next morning Confucius left immediately after breakfast for the palace to see Duke Ling of Wei, who received him very politely. "Master," said Duke Ling, "it is most fortunate that you have returned! I hope you will stay on in our humble state and help me govern it!"

Confucius knitted his brows and said in a low voice, "I have returned to Diqiu because of something that is most important to the security of Wei."

Duke Ling's interest was aroused and he listened attentively as Confucius continued, "I left Diqiu for Chen, but was first besieged by Gongsun Shu at Kuang, then encountered Gongshu Shi raising a revolt in Pu. So I changed my mind and returned to report to you. It is necessary to summon the two ministers of defense to lay plans for the extermination of the rebels."

Duke Ling remained silent for a long time. In his opinion, Gongsun Shu had suffered a grave defeat and could not cause much trouble. As for Gongshu Shi in Pu, for all his bragging about attacking Diqiu, he would not be a threat to the Wei capital either, for Pu was a long distance from Diqiu but very near to the states of Jin and Chu and could serve as a buffer area against incursions from the two neighboring states.

Confucius waited and waited. Finally Duke Ling said coolly, "I'll consider the matter carefully and discuss it with you later.'"

Confucius was perplexed by Duke Ling's response. He wondered how a ruler of a state could remain so unperturbed at the news of revolts in his very own territory. He could not understand what Duke Ling had in mind. He took his leave and returned to Qu Boyu's house with a heavy heart.

At the sight of Confucius' worried look Qu at once knew what had happened. To make him feel better, he talked with him on various subjects. Confucius greatly enjoyed their conversation and only regretted that there were few people who understood him so well.

That winter Confucius stayed in Qu's house, where he continued to teach his disciples, describing to them in great length the exploits of the ancient sage rulers.

In spring of the fourteenth year of Duke Ding of Lu's reign (496 B.C.), Confucius was teaching his disciples when an envoy of Nan Zi called at the house. Recognizing the envoy to be Gongsun Yujia, Confucius recoiled inwardly. With great reluctance he asked, "Minister Gongsun, what business has brought you here?"

Gongsun Yujia said with a bow, "Her Ladyship has learned of your great fame and wants to listen to your instruction in person!"

Hearing this, Confucius was all in a fluster, not knowing how to reply.

"Master," urged Gongsun Yujia, "please mount the chariot and go to the palace instead of keeping Her Ladyship waiting!"

This was a hard decision for Confucius to take. If he refused to go, he would be blamed for discourtesy; if he accepted the invitation, he would be in danger of jeopardizing his own reputation by dealing with an infamous woman. He lowered his head and thought hard. Repeatedly urged by Gongsun, he could not come up with a good excuse for not going and reluctantly agreed to go. He called Zi Lu to drive him to the palace.

A colorful pebbled road, lined by a variety of flowers in full bloom, led to the exquisitely decorated palace building where Nan Zi lived.

Gongsun Yujia entered the chamber and reported on his knees, "Your Ladyship, Confucius has arrived."

"Let him come in at once!" said Nan Zi in an affectedly sweet voice.

Gongsun Yujia announced loudly to the guards, "Let Confucius enter the palace!"

At that moment many thoughts swirled in Confucius' mind. He was aware of Nan Zi's influence on Duke Ling of Wei; with her words she could either persuade him to take the right path or lead him astray. Therefore the influence of such a woman on the ruler could well determine the fate of a state. Getting good advice from her, the ruler would gather honest and talented people around him, reduce taxation and levy, and restore the rites of Zhou. Infatuated with her charms, he might grow fatuous and dissipated, turning a deaf ear to honest advice and causing the state to deteriorate. Confucius told himself that this might be a chance for him to persuade Nan Zi to exert a positive influence on Duke Ling. Hearing the summons, he walked briskly into the palace, holding his breath and lowering his head. Falling on his knees, he said, "Kong Qiu from Lu pays respects to Your Ladyship!"

Looking through the door curtain made of strings of pearls from her inner room, Nan Zi had a clear view of Confucius. She took a close look at him and muttered to herself that Confucius was not only wise and learned but also had very graceful manners. She slowly left her seat and made a bow. "I heard of your fame a long time ago, master. I have fulfilled a great wish by seeing you today. Please rise!"

Confucius could only hear the tingling sound made by the jade jewelry Nan Zi was wearing. He stood up but kept his eyes fixed on the ground. "Kong Qiu is too stupid to deserve your praise. What does Your Ladyship have to teach me?"

"According to what I have heard, you were able to make great improvements in the city of Zhongdu after governing it for only one year. When you were minister of justice in Lu, you educated the people so well that it became unnecessary to lock the gates at night. What special methods did you employ to achieve all this?"

"Thanks to the kindness and wisdom of the duke of Lu, the people were obedient. As for me, I only tried to implement the rites of Zhou."

"Could you help Wei to achieve prosperity in the same manner?" asked Nan Zi.

His eyes glittering, Confucius replied, "Every land under heaven belongs to the king. Since Wei is also within the domain of the king of Zhou, how can I refuse to do my best for it?"

"I intend to recommend you to His Lordship someday," said Nan Zi. "What do you think?"

Confucius said, "After I left Lu, I want to offer my advice to the lords of the various states in order to restore the rites of Zhou. If the duke of Wei can be the first to adopt my advice and uphold the rites of Zhou, it won't be long before Wei will become free of internal turmoil and external threats. When the people enjoy a peaceful life, they will carry out their respective duties faithfully, and prosperity will be achieved in the entire state of Wei. When that time comes, all the other states will vie with each other to follow Wei's example!"

"It is admirable that you cherish such great aspirations!" said Nan Zi. Then an idea occurred to her. Though Confucius had done nothing suspicious in Wei, he was after all a native of Lu. How could she be sure of his loyalty to Wei? If he worked hard to make Wei strong, would he have a mind to usurp the duke's authority? Furthermore, what if he should learn about her clandestine relationship with Gongsun Yujia? At this very thought, her heart began thumping violently. Forcing herself to calm down, she muttered in a low voice, "Master, you may leave now. Wait till I report to His Lordship and ask him to give you a proper position."

Confucius bowed deeply. "I will take my leave then."

Nan Zi got up and returned the bow, accompanied by the jingling sound from her jade pieces.

Coming out of the rear palace, Confucius sighed with great relief and walked lightly to his chariot. Throughout their journey back to Qu Boyu's house, Zi Lu was in the sulks silently driving the chariot.

When they got back, he said with exasperation, "Master, you are someone widely admired and respected! And Nan Zi is someone widely despised! How could you humiliate yourself by kneeling before her?"

Confucius knew that Zi Lu had misunderstood him. He said calmly, "Among my many disciples, you are the one who knows me the best. Do you still have doubts about my integrity?"

Zi Lu rubbed his neck and lowered his head, not saying anything.

Confucius added, "I am very well acquainted with Nan Zi's behavior. I went to visit her because in the first place, she is the duke's wife, so it would be discourteous to decline her invitation. Secondly, she enjoys the duke's favor. If she recommends me to the duke, he will surely listen to her. Thirdly, by meeting her I will have a chance to persuade her to mend her ways."

Zi Lu interrupted him, "I am afraid that your action may not be well understood by others. You have put your reputation in jeopardy by going to see her."

"Real gold fears no fire—a superior man is not afraid of rumors against him."

"But I still think it a very demeaning thing for you to call on her," insisted Zi Lu.

When he failed to convince Zi Lu, Confucius grew anxious. "I really did not want to see her, but I had to accept her invitation! If I were not telling the truth, let Heaven punish me! Let Heaven punish me!"

Zi Lu was finally convinced by Confucius' words.

Confucius went on teaching his disciples. He often thought of Nan Zi's promise to recommend him to Duke Ling. To realize his dream of restoring the rites of Zhou in the entire kingdom, he had to begin with the lord of a vassal state. He waited for over ten days without receiving any message from Duke Ling.

One day he was teaching his disciples *The Book of Music* when an envoy from the duke arrived. His eyes flashed with hope.

Chapter Twenty-seven

Confucius Accompanies the Duke of Wei
on an Excursion;
The Duke's Son Attempts to Assassinate
His Mother

Confucius thought Duke Ling of Wei was going to employ him. His face radiant with smiles he went out to receive the envoy.

The envoy bowed deeply. "His Lordship is going on an excursion in the suburbs tomorrow and invites you to go with him. Will you accept the invitation?"

Greatly pleased, Confucius bowed in return. "I am more than glad to accept His Lordship's invitation. I will go to the palace early tomorrow morning."

"Very good! I will take my leave then."

Having seen the envoy off, Confucius was in a very agitated mood. He regarded the invitation as a signal that Duke Ling would soon appoint him to high office.

Returning to his disciples, he finished the piece of music he had been teaching and sent them away. Then he speculated as to why Duke Ling invited him to join the trip.

Early the following morning Confucius arrived in his chariot outside the palace gate. Under the colorful banners there was a magnificent chariot surrounded by many elegantly dressed palace guards. The chariot was much bigger than normal size. It had a wooden parasol draped with yellow silk, and its doors and windows, embedded with gold and silver, were carved into pictures of the eight trigrams, a chariot team, and animals including dragon, tiger, snake and bird. Confucius could not help marveling at the superb workmanship, yet in the meanwhile he felt ashamed of Duke Ling's extravagance.

Just then a loud cry came from the palace. "His Lordship approaches! Prepare the chariot!"

The driver cracked the whip in his hand and the well-trained horses stepped backward, pushing the chariot into the palace gate.

In a short while the chariot came out with Duke Ling and Nan

Zi on board. Duke Ling gestured to Confucius with his hand. "Master, please join us!"

Confucius looked in the direction and found an ordinary-looking chariot behind. His heart sank. On receiving the invitation, he had expected to make the trip with Duke Ling alone. If Nan Zi were to accompany them, she would stay in the chariot behind while he and Duke Ling rode in the same chariot. Now he found himself in a most awkward position.

The guards opened the door of his chariot and placed a three-rung stepping stone underneath. "Please mount the chariot!" they urged.

Confucius could hardly bear the humiliation. He felt as if people all around were staring at him with mockery and contempt in their eyes. His limbs felt so numb he could hardly move them. The guards virtually had to carry him into the chariot.

Sitting in the chariot, Confucius felt as if he could hear Duke Ling and Nan Zi chatting intimately, and he was filled with both shame and indignation. Fortunately the doors and windows of the chariot were draped with silk curtains, so that people in the street could not see who was riding in it. He lifted the window curtain a little and peeped into the street. Instantly he met the curious stare of the spectators and hastily tucked it into place. After what seemed an eternity the chariot finally stopped, and Confucius heard Duke Ling's loud voice, talking and laughing. The door of the chariot was opened and he found himself before a river bank lined with willows, poplars and elms.

Confucius wished he could be transported out of this place at once, like a bird longing to escape from a cage. However, he waited quietly and stepped out of his chariot only after Duke Ling and Nan Zi had dismounted theirs. As spring was the low-water season in Wei, the river had dwindled into a small, narrow stream, where cranes, gulls and other aquatic birds were meandering about in search of food. He looked up to the trees lining the river banks and drew in a deep breath of the fresh morning air.

At the sight of the birds Duke Ling shouted excitedly to the dozen guards close at his heels carrying bows and arrows, "Shoot arrows, quick!"

The guards at once put arrows onto their bows.

"Please wait!" Confucius blurted out.

Both the guards and Duke Ling were astonished. "Master, what do you mean?" asked the duke.

Confucius said, "Your Lordship! It is common practice not to shoot birds in spring. Right now all kinds of birds are breeding and tending for their young. If a big bird is shot down, a whole nest of small birds will starve to death. Please take pity on the small birds and do not shoot their parents!"

Duke Ling looked at Confucius as if he were a total stranger. "I am really impressed by your kindheartedness to the birds!" he said flatly. He turned and gestured to the guards. "You may leave now, all of you!"

Nan Zi knitted her brows, looking not at all happy.

Confucius looked at Duke Ling's followers and was very glad to find Zi Lu among them.

Zi Lu caught Confucius' eyes and walked up to him in quick steps.

"Have you brought my chariot?" asked Confucius.

"Yes, it's over there!" Zi Lu pointed to the team of chariots behind them.

Confucius said in a low voice, "When we return, I will ride in my chariot and go back straight to Master Qu's house."

Zi Lu was surprised but could not very well ask any question in front of Duke Ling and his guards, so he nodded his agreement.

Duke Ling had expected to have a good time watching his guards shooting the birds by the river. Compelled by Confucius to give up the plan, he soon lost interest before the beautiful scenery. He stretched himself with a yawn. "Master," he said, "let's return to watch the dance in the palace!"

Confucius said, "Your Lordship, I have to go back to Master Qu's house to teach my disciples. Forgive my not accompanying you."

"Well, suit yourself," said Duke Ling indifferently.

Relieved, Confucius turned and whispered to Zi Lu, "Go and drive the chariot to the small path. We'll return to the city by a roundabout route."

By this time Nan Zi had grown impatient and began pestering Duke Ling to go back.

Duke Ling gave the order: "Return to the city!"

Gazing after Duke Ling's entourage, Confucius wondered how he could expect such a ruler to restore the rites of Zhou and bring peace and prosperity to the state of Wei. Listlessly he got on his chariot. He regretted having accepted the duke's invitation and thus brought disgrace on himself. He sighed and groaned in deep agony and frustration.

"Master," asked Zi Lu, "why are you feeling so despondent? Isn't it an honor to accompany His Lordship on a trip?"

Confucius said indignantly, "I have met many people who are fond of women, but to abandon virtue because of a woman is really going too far!" He paused a little, then added, "Well, I have never met a man who loves virtue more than he loves women."

Upon their return, Qu Boyu came out the gate to receive them. All smiles, he was about to offer his congratulations when he saw the sad and hurt look on Confucius' face. Taken completely by surprise, he could not find the right words to say in consolation. "You must be tired, master!" he muttered. "It is fortunate for you to accompany His Lordship on the trip today! I have not yet had such an honor."

Confucius smiled sadly. "The duke is getting old and does not attend to state affairs wholeheartedly. I won't stay long in Wei."

Hearing this, Qu felt so grieved that his eyes brimmed with tears, for he knew Confucius was telling the truth. "All this has resulted from the decline of the royal court," he said sadly.

"Minister Qu," said Confucius, "we must not lose hope. Even though the vassal lords often fight among themselves, the king of Zhou still rules in the royal capital. If the rites of Zhou can be implemented, peace and harmony will surely be achieved in the entire world."

"If you receive an important office from the ruler of a state, what will you be able to do?" Qu asked.

Confucius said confidently, "If I am asked to help govern a state, there will be marked improvements in the first year and great prosperity in three years."

"How will you be able to achieve that?"

"The key to governing a state is righteousness. If I am appointed to govern a state, I will try my best to be just and honest. If I can keep myself just and honest, why should there be any difficulty in governing the state? If I can not keep myself just and honest, how will I be able to instruct others?"

Qu thought for a while, then said, "Master, I don't want to boast, but when I was a minister in the court, I maintained my integrity and refused to be contaminated by evil influences. And yet I achieved precious little in my office. Why?"

"Your virtue and honesty will be duly recognized by the people," said Confucius. "However, you failed to lead the duke to the right path. A ruler had control over the fate of the state; he might cause it to prosper or decline by a single word of his. A state can be made prosperous only if its ruler can be made virtuous."

Qu smiled. "Master, you have opened my mind with your words!" He combed his beard with his fingers and pondered. "It is easier to sift gold from the sand than to spot a truly remarkable man! Where can you find a virtuous ruler?"

"It was because of this that I left Lu for Wei. Since I can not achieve my purpose here, I will leave Wei for some other state."

Qu Boyu fell silent.

That evening Confucius was too agitated to fall asleep. Looking up through the window, he felt as if his lifetime goal was just like the bright moon, splendid but always out of reach. He recalled what he had been through in the past decades, the hardships and frustrations he had endured. He thought of his mother's tender care and his grandfather's deathbed wish. He remembered the internecine strife in the Lu court, Yang Hu's arrogance, Duke Jing of Qi's capriciousness, Lao Zi's great learning, Duke Ling of Wei's powerlessness and stupidity. Some of his memories were joyful, some sad and irksome. How he wished he could dispel evil forces and bring peace and order to the whole world! He sat up and felt very giddy. He sat quietly for a while, draped a piece of clothing over his shoulders and walked into the courtyard. In the spring the night wind was sometimes warm, sometimes chilly. Looking up at the starlit sky, he saw the Milky Way giving off a bluish light. He gazed at the Big Dipper that guided those who had lost their way in the night. He muttered to himself, "A state governed by virtue and benevolence will be like the Big Dipper, pointing out the directions for all the other states." He wanted to bring the entire world into harmony, just as the heavenly bodies moved year after year in an orderly sequence. The king of Zhou would then enjoy the same position as the Big Dipper, surrounded and supported by all his subordinates in the various states. Lost in contemplation, Confucius bowed deeply to the Big Dipper.

The first cock's crow awakened Confucius from his reverie. He shuddered with cold and went back to his room.

For several days Confucius remained in low spirits. Affected by his mood, the disciples also grew quiet and seldom laughed and talked aloud.

One day at noon one of the disciples, Zai Yu, felt sore all over his body and dizzy in his head, so he went to sleep in his room. Confucius was so angry that he stamped his feet. "Decayed wood can not be carved, and crumbling walls can not be painted! A man only lives for a few dozen years. Why should he waste his time sleeping in the daytime, instead of working to improve himself!"

Min Shun pleaded on Zai Yu's behalf, saying, "Master, perhaps he is not feeling well today."

"Well, perhaps," said Confucius. "But a man must be strong-willed and not let himself be brought down by a minor ailment. Of course people are different in temperament. Some are diligent, some are lazy. What else do I have to say about Zai Yu?"

In the meanwhile something ominous was taking place in the Wei court. Duke Ling had a son named Kuai Kui, who was nearly fifty. Having learned of the affair between Nan Zi and Gongsun Yujia, he decided to find a chance to punish them. However, he had to wait patiently for an opportunity, for he was no match for Gongsun Yujia in combat.

One evening, when Duke Ling gave a banquet for his courtiers, Kuai Kui could not help noticing, along with other officials, the frequent exchange of amorous glances between Nan Zi and Gongsun Yujia. He walked up to Duke Ling and whispered, "Father, I have drunk too much and am not feeling well. I want to return to my chamber and rest."

Duke Ling was too absorbed in drinking to pay much attention. "Do as you wish, my son!" He turned and raised his wine glass. "Honored ministers, our state is enjoying peace, security and favorable climate. Why not celebrate our good fortune with songs and dance? Let's drink three cups to ... to..."

Nan Zi took him by the hand and said sweetly, "Your Lordship, too much wine harms the mind. Let's stop drinking and call out the dancers."

Duke Ling shook off Nan Zi's hands and stumbled to his feet. Raising his cup he said, "Let me drink three cups first. Honored ministers, bottoms up!"

After he had emptied three cups in a row, Nan Zi called out, "Let the dancers appear!"

Instantly the dancers came up to the center of the hall and began to perform to the accompaniment of soft and melodious music.

Meanwhile, Kuai Kui was fuming in his chamber. He said to himself, "I address Nan Zi as mother, but I am ashamed of her conduct! What's more, my father seems to be totally ignorant of her transgressions!" He stared fixedly at the candle flame in front of him and felt as if he could see Nan Zi's face, full of alluring charms. "A demon!" he shouted, sweeping the candlestick onto the floor. The room became totally dark, but Nan Zi's bewitching smiles still lingered in his mind's eye. "If I don't get rid of her, there would be no peace in Wei!" He thought of informing his father of the matter, then gave up the idea. Suddenly he took the sword hanging on the wall, drew it from the sheath and made a few thrusts.

Dressed in close-fitting clothes, he headed, sword in hand, for the site of the banquet where the music was still playing. Then he stopped abruptly. "Ridiculous!" he said to himself. "How would I be able to kill her in front of so many guards and officials?" Just then the singing and the music stopped, and Duke Ling was escorted by attendants into his bed chamber.

Kuai Kui turned and ran into the court where Nan Zi lived, and hid himself behind the gate, intending to attack Nan Zi on her return.

The palace maid Qiu Lian had been dozing off in a seat by the gate. Hearing some noise, she cried out in surprise. "Who is that?"

Kuai Kui whispered, "It's me, Kuai Kui."

Qiu Lian relaxed a little. "Why do you come here so late at night?" she asked.

Kuai Kui panicked. He walked up to her and placed his sword on her neck. "Little bitch!" he said sternly. "Did you help Nan Zi and Gongsun Yujia get together?"

Qiu Lian was so scared that her whole body shook uncontrollably. "I dare not! Please spare me!" she pleaded, tears rolling down her cheeks.

"Do you know anything about their illicit affair?"

Qiu Lian did not reply.

"Did you pass messages for them?"

Qiu Lian found herself in a quandary as to what to say to his questioning.

With a twist of his wrist, Kuai Kui cut off Qiu Lian's head with the sword. He kicked her body, which slumped before Nan Zi's bed, splattering blood all over the place.

At this moment a woman outside the room said in a severe voice,

"Qiu Lian, it's so dark in the room. Why haven't you lit the lamps?"

Recognizing Nan Zi's voice, Kuai Kui concealed himself and made ready to attack.

Nan Zi had not lived in the palace for many years without learning the dangers lurking even in the most heavily guarded ground. At first she thought Qiu Lian had fallen asleep, but when she called again without receiving an answer, she realized that something was wrong. She turned abruptly and walked away from the room, trembling. Surprised, the guards and attendants did not know what to do. At this moment Kuai Kui leapt out of the room into the courtyard and shouted sternly, "Where are you going, you bitch? Come and meet your death!"

Nan Zi was scared out of her wits when she turned around and saw the murderous-looking Kuai Kui.

Sword in hand, Kuai Kui threw himself toward Nan Zi. He moved so fast that his sword was near Nan Zi before the guards could do anything to stop him.

Nan Zi cried out in fear and dropped to the ground on her back. Kuai Kui raised his sword and was about to strike down when another sword intercepted his. He looked up and saw Gongsun Yujia. Foaming with rage, he said, "It is most unlucky for Wei to have a traitor like you! Throw down your weapon and meet your death!"

Gongsun sneered, "Don't brag like that! When I tie you up and bring you to His Lordship, I will be amply rewarded, and you will be punished with death. Don't you realize you are trying to assassinate his favored wife?"

By now Nan Zi had already got on her feet and was walking away escorted by the guards. Kuai Kui rushed toward her, but he was beaten back by Gongsun Yujia. As their swords clanged together, Kuai Kui felt numb in his arm, and his hand was damp with blood from the crack in his hand. He shouted, "Guards! Kill that bitch!"

Paying no attention to him, the guards escorted Nan Zi away from the scene.

"Well, are you going to kill yourself, or do you need me to do it for you?" Gongsun asked.

Kuai Kui knew that he was no match for Gongsun Yujia. "A petty man like you has no right to talk to me like that!" he said. "If you have the least sense of shame, you should cut your own throat with your sword!"

At this moment there rose loud cries all over the palace ground. "Catch the assassin!" "Close the gates!" "Don't let him escape!" Torches and lanterns were lit up everywhere.

Gongsun Yujia was a very wily person. He had grown suspicious when Kuai Kui showed signs of drunkenness after drinking very little wine. He could think of two possibilities. As Kuai Kui was nearly fifty, he might be plotting a coup to replace his father. On the other hand, he might have learned something about Nan Zi's illicit affair and was therefore plotting against her. After the banquet, Gongsun Yujia had trailed Nan Zi and her attendants into the palace. Thanks to the darkness of the night and his familiarity with the place, he had not been discovered by anyone. When Nan Zi called Qiu Lian without getting any answer, he knew his suspicion was well-founded. He drew his sword and made ready to rescue Nan Zi. However, he had to deal with the situation for his benefit. To save Nan Zi's life would be undoubtedly an exceptional merit, but his affair with Nan Zi would make things complicated. What would the court officials and the people in the street think of him? In addition, it would not be difficult for him to capture or kill Kuai Kui, but he did not think it wise to do so, for Kuai Kui was, after all, Duke Ling's son. He decided to let Kuai Kui escape.

Hearing the loud cries all around, Kuai Kui panicked and wanted to flee. He made a feint by thrusting his sword forward, then ran away.

Gongsun told the guards who had just arrived to pursue in the opposite direction while he followed Kuai Kui himself.

Coming to the high palace wall, Kuai Kui had nowhere to go. He turned and prepared to put up a desperate fight.

Gongsun thrusted his sword forcefully, jamming it into a fissure on the wall.

At this Kuai Kui came forward to attack, and Gongsun dodged by stepping back. The cries of the guards were coming nearer and nearer. Kuai Kui suddenly hit upon an idea. He leapt onto the sword planted in the wall, then leapt again to the top of the wall, vanishing into the darkness.

Duke Ling was furious. "Shut all the city gates! Search the entire city! Don't let the treacherous son escape!"

Hearing the duke's order from outside the palace wall, Kuai Kui realized he could no longer stay in Wei. He ran with all his might to the west gate. As he heard the clatter of a horse's hoofs behind him, he stepped aside and concealed himself. When the horse came before him, he dashed to it, killed the rider with the sword, and leapt onto the horse. The mounted guard he had just killed happened to be heading for the west gate to pass on Duke Ling's order. When Kuai Kui arrived at the west gate, the guards there were surprised.

"I am on a very important mission," said Kuai Kui. "Open the gate immediately!"

The guards tried to delay by asking some irrelevant questions. "What's so urgent that you have to leave the city at such an hour?" "Why are you going all by yourself?" "For the sake of your safety, we can not allow you to leave the city without His Lordship's order."

Growing impatient, Kuai Kui cut down a soldier with his sword and said sternly, "Open the gate! Otherwise all of you will suffer the same fate as this!"

Flabbergasted, the guards opened the city gate and lowered the suspension bridge.

Stabbing the horse's rump with the hilt of his sword, Kuai Kui galloped out as swiftly as a flying arrow.

Having gone about five li, Kuai Kui turned to take a look. A band of soldiers carrying torches were coming in his direction. Not daring to delay, he sped on toward the state of Jin.

Duke Ling of Wei found it difficult to get over the shock of the incident. He could not help wondering why Kuai Kui wanted to assassinate Nan Zi, and why Gongsun Yujia should have failed to capture Kuai Kui. He remembered that the history of the state of Wei was never free of internecine strife in the ruling house. It suddenly occurred to him that it had been too much of a coincidence for Gongsun Yujia to be on the spot at the right moment to save Nan Zi's life. "How did he get into the forbidden ground of the inner palace?" he wondered. Seized with indignation, he rose and walked out of the room intending to question Nan Zi on the matter. But on second thought he stopped himself. "She would not admit to it for sure," he told himself. "Without any evidence I would achieve nothing and only create a scandal." He returned to his bed-chamber, bitter and confused, for a restless night.

The next day he ordered Nan Zi's residence to be heavily guarded on the pretext of ensuring her safety, but his real intention was to give Gongsun Yujia no chance to approach her. Furthermore, he went to her place every day to keep her company. However, the more frequently he came to visit her, the more aversive she grew toward him. Gradually his zest for her also subsided.

One day Duke Ling was sitting in the palace, worrying over the security of his days to come, and wondering if some other court official would turn against him someday. It suddenly occurred to him that Confucius might have some advice to offer, so he decided to send for him at once.

Chapter Twenty-eight

Master and Disciples Discuss State Affairs by the Yellow River; Courtiers of Jin Compete for Control of Its Army

Upon Confucius' arrival in the palace the duke of Wei came right to the point. "My unfilial son has failed in his evil plot and fled to Jin. Could you tell me, master, how I should deal with the matter?" he asked.

Seeing Duke Ling's careworn visage, Confucius hesitated for a long time. Nan Zi deserved severe punishment, for her licentiousness had brought disgrace to the ruling house of Wei. However, considering his position as the son of the duke of Wei and as a court official, Kuai Kui should have tried to hush up the scandal instead of attempting to assassinate Nan Zi himself. Because Nan Zi was Duke Ling's wife and Kuai Kui Duke Ling's son, the incident could be said to have taken place within the family circle. Confucius moved his lips a little but failed to come up with any words.

Duke Ling looked at Confucius hopefully, like a patient waiting for the doctor's prescription. But the doctor failed to prescribe anything.

After a long pause Confucius finally said, "No matter what you do, you can not disregard either the relationship between father and son, or that between husband and wife. Now your son has fled to Jin and will probably never come back to harm your wife. So why not let your wife and son live on separately in this manner?"

Duke Ling of Wei was not at all satisfied with the noncommittal reply. Then it occurred to him that as an outsider Confucius was not really in a position to comment on what had taken place in the ruling house of Wei. He said with a smile, "Your words are reasonable, master. Let's see what this unfilial son of mine will do next!"

In the fifth month of 495 B.C. Duke Ding of Lu died, and his son succeeded to the dukedom as Duke Ai of Lu. When Confucius heard the news, he felt a glimmer of hope. The new sovereign might

send an envoy to invite him back someday.

One day, when Confucius led his disciples on an outing, he climbed up an earthen hill and looked east to Lu, wondering when he would return home, and when his homeland would be strong and prosperous. His efforts had been mostly futile and the future looked uncertain, but he would not allow himself to give up hope. Just then two turtledoves flew overhead. At the sight of the birds Confucius thought of a song from *The Book of Poetry* and began to sing:

> The cuckoos build their nests in mulberry trees;
> The little birds dart among date trees.
> Behold the man of virtue!
> His attitude is so serene.
> His attitude is so serene,
> An example to be followed by states of all sides.

As he sang, Confucius saw before him the man of virtue eulogized in the poem. The day would come when he finally found such a virtuous ruler, tall, benevolent, serene and dignified.

> The cuckoos build their nests in mulberry trees,
> The little birds dart among hazelnut trees.
> Behold the man of virtue!
> A model for the whole nation.
> A model for the whole nation,
> Let's wish him an everlasting life.

As Confucius sang, his disciples joined in.

Just then a band of horses and chariots carrying numerous banners came along the main road, creating quite a racket. Confucius knew it must be Duke Ling of Wei and his attendants. He said to his disciples, "The duke is come. Follow me down the hill and line up to welcome him." He lifted the front of his robe and walked down slowly to the side of the road, followed by his disciples in an orderly formation.

When Duke Ling's chariot drew up, Confucius walked up briskly and said with a deep bow, "Your Lordship, where are you heading?"

Duke Ling smiled blandly, "I am not feeling well these days. Today I just come out for some relaxation."

"It is indeed fortunate for you to be in such a fine mood!" said Confucius, by way of carrying on the conversation. Duke Ling, however, neither dismounted from his chariot nor deigned to pick up the thread of the conversation. He simply cocked up his head and gazed after a lone wild goose flying to the north.

Thus slighted, Confucius felt a pang of shame and indignation. After Duke Ling's chariot passed before him, he immediately returned with his disciples to Qu Boyu's house, where they packed up their luggage and took leave of their host.

The brightness of the clear spring day contrasted sharply with Confucius' gloomy and dejected mood. Traveling along the dusty road, the disciples wondered where they were going.

Zi Lu finally broke up the silence by asking, "Master, we left in such a hurry today. Where are we going now?"

Confucius gazed up into the sky. "The fish can swim anywhere it likes in the wide sea, and the bird can fly anywhere it likes in the vast sky. According to what I have heard, the state of Jin has been well governed in recent years. Let's go there!"

The disciples felt their mind at ease again and began to chat and laugh among themselves as they journeyed along.

A few days later they reached the bank of the Yellow River. At the sight of the torrential Yellow River they uttered cries of wonder. Confucius dismounted and stood on a mound by the road to look into the distance. The Yellow River truly merited its name, for the water, the river bed and the banks were all yellow. It resembled a giant yellow dragon rushing to the east. Confucius stood gazing at the yellow current and reviewed his previous comment on the quality of water. Descending the mound, he walked down the river bank and went up to the rushing stream. He felt awed by the power of the water carrying the yellow earth all the way to the sea. He looked toward the east, feeling as if the yellow earth under his feet were moving gradually toward the sea. He wondered if the day would come when the sea might become filled with yellow earth.

"Master," called Zi Lu behind him, "The ferry is here. Shall we cross the river?"

Confucius looked up at the wooden ferry-boat filled with people, horses and chariots. "Yes, let's cross the river!" he said. Lifting the hem of his garment, he walked briskly toward the boat.

The boat, specially designed for ferrying across the Yellow River, was very wide, flat, clumsy and stable. It had four chariots, a few horses and some thirty to forty passengers on board. Apparently the passengers came from all walks of life, some wearing splendid clothes while others plainly dressed or even in rags.

Standing on the stone terrace, Confucius gazed attentively at the passengers descending the boat. Suddenly a middle-aged man in a scholar's robe caught his eye. Though not very tall, the man appeared well-built and stood upright. He had a ruddy complexion and seemed to be in his late forties. As he stood on the bow and looked toward the shore, his eyes met with those of Confucius. The two of them felt an instant rapport, as if they had known each other for a long time.

Leaping off the boat, the man walked up to Confucius, stopped at a few steps' distance, and bowed with clasped hands. "Do I have the honor of meeting Confucius from Lu?" he asked.

Confucius saluted him in return. "I am Kong Qiu from Lu. How did you recognize me?"

The man glanced at the disciples standing behind Confucius and laughed heartily. "If you were not Confucius," he said, "how could you have so many brilliant followers!"

Confucius took a step forward and bowed again. "May I have your honorable name," he said, "and could you tell me where you come from?"

The man waved his hand lightly. "I feel quite ashamed of my unworthiness. My name is Yang Jin, and I used to be a local magistrate in Jin. Though my ability was limited, I managed to govern the place well. I wanted to try harder and really achieve something when Zhao Jianzi killed two virtuous ministers, Dou Mingdu and Shun Hua. He is still in a murderous mood, and many people's lives are still in danger. I am thus compelled to resign and leave my homeland."

Confucius was flabbergasted by the news. He did not know Dou Mingdu and Shun Hua personally, but from what he had heard he knew them to be both men of virtue. Without their assistance, Zhao Jianzi would not have achieved his present position, yet now he had both of them executed. Speechless Confucius gazed to the northwest as if mourning for the death of the two virtuous ministers.

Though he had never met Zhao Jianzi, Confucius had a good understanding of his character. Zhao Jianzi, also named Zhao Yang, was a powerful minister of Jin. When Yang Hu fled from Qi to Jin, Confucius had remarked that he would bring trouble to Jin.

Zi Lu came up to Confucius. "Master, your prediction has proved correct."

Confucius sighed. "An evil man will never mend his ways. A man like Yang Hu brings calamity wherever he goes." When he turned to gaze at Yang Jin, he could not help feeling deep sympathy for him, for both of them had suffered the same misfortune. He wanted to describe his experience and vent his frustrations, but it would only aggravate their gloomy mood. Restraining his feelings, he said, "So where are you going now?"

"A fine bird chooses a good tree to nestle in, and a superior man chooses a sage ruler to serve. I want to find a sage ruler under whose rule I can realize the goal of my life."

"What's the goal of your life then?" Confucius asked.

"I will begin by assisting a sage ruler to restore the rites and establish a benevolent government, until finally Great Harmony is achieved in the whole world."

Confucius was so excited that he walked up to Yang Jin and took him by both hands. "Your goal is the same as mine. It is because of this that I have left my homeland with my disciples. It has been well said that virtue can find its company. Since we are fortunate enough to meet today, why don't we travel together?"

Yang Jin bowed deeply before he replied, "Master, your fame has spread far and wide. How could I travel with you as equal?"

"The hardest thing to find in the world is a person who really understands you. We cherish the same ideal, so let's work together for the restoration of the rites!"

Yang Jin still declined the offer, saying, "First I want to find a quiet place where I can get over my mood of dejection. After that I will decide where I want to go next."

Disappointed, Confucius let go of Yang Jin's hands. "Since you have your own plan, I will not insist."

Yang Jin said with a salute, "Take care, Master! I hope we will meet again!"

Returning the salute, Confucius said, "Take care!"

Yang Jin mounted his chariot and drove on to the east.

Gazing after the chariot, Confucius and his disciples uttered sighs of admiration and regret.

As the sun went down to the west, a thick layer of dark cloud spread across the sky. Confucius stared at the river rushing east, its waves and swirls appearing to symbolize the numerous hardships and retrogressions of history. He stood there watching and wondered if the water of the Yellow River would ever become clear.

At this moment the ferry-boat left the ford for the other shore.

"Master, shall we get on our way?" Zi Lu asked.

Confucius sighed deeply. "When I was young," he said, "I went to Jin and studied the zither under Shi Xiangzi. I meant to learn something more on this trip to Jin, but Zhao Jianzi has discarded the rites and music and killed innocent people. As the saying goes, 'Do not drain the pond for fish, otherwise the dragon will not go and take up its abode there.' It seems unsuitable for us to go to Jin right now."

"Where shall we go then?" Zi Lu asked again.

"Let's return to Wei!" said Confucius after a long pause.

The disciples had different expressions on their faces, but none of them said a word. The only sound they heard was the Yellow River rushing by.

After Zhao Jianzi killed Dou Mingdu and Shun Hua, he went on to build his personal forces with an eye to eliminating all his opponents and taking control of the Jin court.

The other two powerful ministers of Jin, Fan Shi and Zhongxing Shi, were unwilling to submit. Instead, they both began to train their private troops, making ready to contend for power with Zhao Jianzi.

In autumn of the nineteenth year of Duke Ding of Jin's reign (493 B.C.) Fan Shi and Zhongxing Shi joined forces. They gained support from the state of Zheng, which agreed to send them a great deal of provisions.

When he heard the news, Zhao Jianzi immediately summoned all his officers to discuss the situation. Late in the evening, about a dozen people gathered in Zhao's parlor. Zhao combed his beard with his fingers and said with great assurance, "I have just seen a report that Fan Shi and Zhongxing Shi will receive provisions and reinforcements from the state of Zheng. It is a good chance for us to defeat them separately. Each of you must try his best to fulfill the task assigned to him!"

The officers responded with a bow, "We are willing to receive your order!"

"Good!" Zhao stood up and walked back and forth in the room. "First I will have a band of troops to attack the provision carts from Zheng. If their provisions are destroyed, the enemy will fall into confusion!"

The officers, eager to win merits, all expressed their willingness to go.

Zhao looked around and said loudly, "Listen carefully! If the battle is won, I will report to His Lordship for ample rewards. A meritorious high-ranking minister will be endowed with a county, a low-ranking minister will get a prefecture, and a gentleman will receive a hundred thousand mu of land."

The officers responded in unison, "You are wise and virtuous, minister!"

Stepping forward, Zhao said, gesturing with his hand, "Fan Cai, listen!"

"Here!" Fan Cai stepped out.

"You will lead a hundred chariots and lie in ambush in the pine forest to the left of Heifengkou. When the provision carts entered the valley, close in on them from behind!"

"Understood!" said Fan Cai.

Zhao shouted again, "Chen Zhuang, listen!"

Chen Zhuang stood up. "Here!"

"You will also lead a hundred chariots and lie in ambush in the forest to the right of Heifengkou. When the provision carts enter the valley, join Fan Cai and close in on them from behind."

"Yes!" Chen Zhuang replied sonorously.

Zhao seemed to gain more confidence from the attitude of his officers. "Sima Long, listen!"

Sima Long responded in a muffled voice, "Here!"

"You will lead three hundred chariots and lie in ambush to the north of Heifengkou. After the provision carts have all entered the valley, attack them head-on!"

"Yes!"

"The three of you must coordinate well, eliminate the Zheng forces and capture all the provisions!"

The three officers replied, "Yes!"

"All the other officers will follow me. We will lie in ambush twenty li north of Heifengkou to intercept the reinforcements from Fan Shi and Zhongxing Shi."

"Yes!" replied all the officers.

"We will set out at midnight. Now you may leave and prepare!"

It was a starless night, the sky covered in dark clouds. Fan Cai, Chen Zhuang and Sima Long led their troops toward Heifengkou, where they concealed themselves before dawn. This was a danger zone of high hills and dense forests. The valley wound between two mountain ridges, sometimes so narrow as to allow only one chariot to pass at one time, and sometimes so wide that hundreds of chariots might converge to give battle. Crystal-clear river water flowed over pebbles of different sizes.

Heifengkou was an opening in the mountain ridge to the south. The small rugged path leading to it was the only way by which the Zheng army would arrive. Densely grown pine trees blocked out the sunlight, and a fierce wind was always whistling.

The dark clouds grew even thicker. At daybreak a dull thunder rolled across the sky, followed by a heavy rain. Floodwater rushed down the mountains and flowed out of the valley. Only a moment later the sun came out, painting the mountains and trees in a rosy hue.

"A rainbow!" cried a soldier.

"Silence!" snapped Fan Cai. His darkish face appeared a little sallow due to nervous tension. He looked up into the sky and, at the sight of the rainbow, regarded it as a good omen. He bowed to heaven devoutly and prayed, "May Heaven bless us with a total victory!"

The soldiers were all delighted to see the rainbow in the blue sky. The tension before a major battle was somewhat relieved as they enjoyed the sight. A short while later the rainbow began to evaporate and soon vanished out of sight.

Fan Cai looked south through the pine forest. Along the road leading to Heifengkou some people were traveling by twos and threes, but not a single chariot was to be seen.

They waited anxiously for a long time until the sun began going down and they all felt very hungry. Just then they saw in the distance a few dark spots, which gradually turned into a long procession of carts. Excited, Fan Cai ordered the soldiers to take cover. He looked ahead and found to his satisfaction that all the footsteps and ruts on the road had been washed away by the rain. "Heaven bless our commanding general!" he said to himself.

The provision carts halted abruptly at the mountain slope. Three mounted soldiers came galloping to Heifengkou, where they peered in all directions. Finding nothing suspicious, they galloped back.

About an hour later, the three mounted soldiers returned to Heifengkou and again looked around carefully. Satisfied with what they had seen, they galloped down the slope again.

After a short while the carts began moving up the slope toward

Heifengkou, their wheels creaking over the rugged, stone-strewn road. Fan Cai and his men made a careful count of the carts that emerged from Heifengkou one after another. When the two hundredth cart had entered the valley, Fan Cai and Chen Zhuang made a whistling signal simultaneously and the troops charged out amid loud drum beats and battle-cries.

As it was difficult for the chariots to travel along the mountain ridge, both Fan Cai and Chen Zhuang left their chariots in the pine forest and dashed down the mountain slopes at the head of the troops, closing in on the men of Zheng from both sides of Heifengkou.

Totally taken by surprise, the men of Zheng fell into confusion as they attempted to withstand the attack. It was not long before over half of them were cut down. Some horses were injured, some broke loose and ran wildly, and some rolled down the valley, dragging the carts with them.

The Zheng soldiers in the valley, instead of turning to aid those in the rear, fled for all they were worth. Some even threw the sacks of grain off the carts to hasten their escape.

Just then Sima Long, who had lain in ambush at the other end of the valley, shouted, "Charge! Anyone who achieves merits in the battle will be amply rewarded!"

The soldiers rode forth in their chariots and shot arrows at the men of Zheng, who were too confused to put up an effective fight. Many were wounded or killed and the others, except for a lucky few, became prisoners.

Sima Long, Chen Zhuang and Fan Cai led their soldiers to clean up the battle ground. To their great joy, their own casualty turned out to be negligible. Moreover, except for a few that had fallen into the valley, most carts remained intact with the sacks of grain. Sima Long ordered the troops to escort the prisoners and the provision carts out of the valley and march back to camp. After traveling for a short while, they saw a thick cloud of dust arising in front of them and heard drum beats and battle-cries.

Sima Long said, "General Chen and General Fan, it must be our commanding general fighting against Fan Shi and Zhongxing Shi, who have come to meet the men from Zheng. Let's leave some men behind to escort the carts and lead the troops to attck the enemy and help the commanding general."

"Your idea sounds great," Chen Zhuang agreed.

"Let's do it now!" said Fan Cai.

The three of them charged forward at the head of their troops and a fierce battle took place on a piece of flat ground. Among the numerous banners embroidered with the patterns of dragon, tiger, snake and bird, three general's banners stood out bearing the characters "Fan," "Zhongxing" and "Zhao" respectively.

It was near dusk. Fan Shi kept shooting arrows at Zhao Jianzi desperately. Zhongxing Shi was so fuming with rage that his eyes almost popped out of their sockets.

Sitting squarely in his chariot, Zhao Jianzi directed the movement of his troops with a small flag in his left hand and a sword in his right hand. At the sight of Sima Long, Chen Zhuang and Fan Cai, he knew at once that the attack against the provision carts from Zheng had succeeded. "General Fan," he ordered, "lead some men and close in on the enemy from the right! General Chen, you will close in on the enemy from the left! General Sima, lead your troops and move to the rear of the enemy to block his way of escape!"

The three generals left to carry out the orders.

In the meanwhile Fan Shi and Zhongxing Shi also came to realize the provisions from Zheng had been captured by the enemy. They decided to fight to the bitter end. Fan Shi suggested, "Minister Zhongxing, I'll stay here while you go and attack the enemy from the rear."

"Zhao Jianzi is a very wily person," cautioned Zhongxing. "Be careful, Minister Fan!"

"You should also beware of his subordinates!" said Fan Shi.

"I understand!" Zhongxing Shi then left for the north with his troops.

When Zhao Jianzi saw this from his chariot, he knew at once the enemy's intention. "After you divide your troops in two," he thought to himself, "I will wipe you out separately!" Thus he rearranged his armor and said to his men, "Fan Shi and Zhongxing Shi have become a sure catch! Whoever kills Fan Shi will be generously rewarded!"

Soldiers can always be made brave by a high reward. No sooner had Zhao Jianzi finished his words than a chariot dashed toward Fan Shi.

Fan Shi gave a start at the oncoming chariot. Then he calmed down and quickly drew his bow and shot an arrow, hitting the driver on the head. Out of control, the chariot charged into Fan Shi's formation, where the three soldiers on board were instantly cut down and chopped into pieces.

When another chariot was about to charge forth, Zhao Jianzi stopped it. "Wait! Do not fight the enemy one by one. Let's fight them together. Follow me!"

At his order, numerous chariots rumbled forward. Fan Shi grew fearful and turned his chariot to flee, at the same time ordering his men to shoot arrows. Both sides suffered losses in the tangled fighting that ensued. As the road became blocked with the damaged chariots, Zhao Jianzi had to take a roundabout route to chase the enemy. After traveling a while, his chariot stopped before a small river.

The soldiers who had crossed the river called out, "Commander, leave the chariot and come over!"

He was still hesitating when an enemy chariot rushed at him at full speed. Zhongxing Shi put an arrow to the bow and shot at Zhao Jianzi's chest.

With a loud cry, Zhao fell out of his chariot.

Chapter Twenty-nine

Father and Son Fight for the Dukedom of Wei;
Confucius and His Disciples Encounter Some Bandits

When Zhao Jianzi saw the arrow coming toward him, he dropped off the chariot and the arrow landed on the chest of the soldier behind him.

Zhao got to his feet, climbed back into his chariot and, with a wave of his sword, ordered his men to shoot arrows.

By this time four bands of forces had formed a tight encirclement around Fan Shi and Zhongxing Shi. At Zhao Jianzi's order, arrows flew thick and fast, cutting down numerous enemy soldiers.

At nightfall Fan Shi and Zhongxing Shi had only a dozen chariots left. Recognizing defeat, they fought their way out of the encirclement. Zhao Jianzi pursued them for a while, then had the gongs beaten to recall the troops.

After this victory Zhao Jianzi was able to strengthen his position and eventually to establish a new state called Zhao.

Confucius and his disciples strolled along the Yellow River for a few days before embarking on their journey back to Wei. One evening it was too hot and stuffy in the hostel room to sleep, so they went out to enjoy the cool air in the courtyard, where they saw two men, one young and the other elderly, in the shadows talking about Zhao Jianzi.

"What a stormy age this is!" said the older man. "Zhao Jianzi is indeed a wicked man. First he murdered Dou Mingdu and Shun Hua, and now he is all puffed up after defeating Fan Shi and Zhongxing Shi. Unlucky for him, Fo Bi just rose up against him in Zhongmou."

The youth said, "In times of turbulence the world is dominated by a handful of powerful men. Who can tell if the state of Jin will be ruled by Zhao or Fo in a few years' time?"

"Ordinary people like us have no use for honor and fame. We only want to live in peace, but even that is too much to expect nowadays."

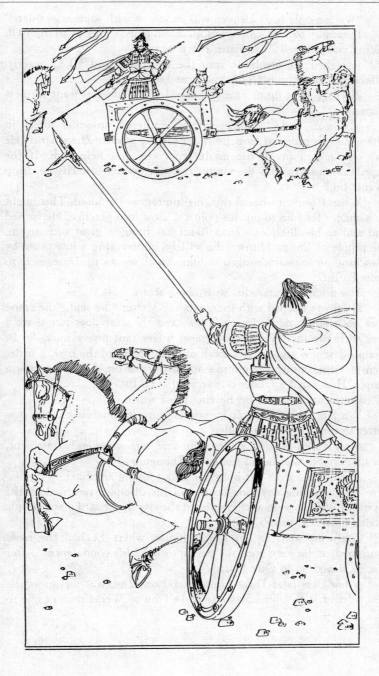

"We can only hope Heaven will endow us with some sage rulers!"

Listening to the conversation, Confucius thought to himself, "What evil plot will Zhao Jianzi hatch next?"

Just then a man burst into the courtyard and asked eagerly, "Please tell me, who is Confucius from Lu?"

Zi Gong went up to him and asked, "Why do you want to meet Confucius?"

The man said, "Minister Fo has gathered up some forces in Zhongmou in order to launch an expedition against Zhao Jianzi. He has sent me to invite the master to come and help him. If the expedition is successful, the master can stay on to assist His Lordship to rule Jin."

When Confucius heard this, his interest was aroused. This might be a chance for him to put his political ideas into practice. He turned and said to his disciples, "Zhao Jianzi has brought great suffering to the people of Jin, so Minister Fo will be undertaking a just cause by launching an expedition against him. Shall we go to Zhongmou to assist Fo Bi?"

The disciples responded with blank stares.

Zi Lu was flushed with indignation. "Master," he said, "the crane does not share a nest with the crow, and the deer does not share a cave with the fox. While Zhao Jianzi wages sanguinary wars, Fo Bi recruits deserters and traitors. Both of them disregard the rites, murder men of virtue, usurp their lord's authority and oppress the common people. How can we render our service to Fo Bi?"

Confucius hesitated on hearing these words.

Yan Hui said, "What Zi Lu said is quite reasonable, master. It is better to think it over carefully."

After a spell of silence Confucius said with some embarrassment, "Zi Lu is right. We should not go to Zhongmou."

At this the envoy left quietly without saying anything.

The following day Confucius and his disciples returned to the capital of Wei. As soon as they entered the city they heard many people talking about the duke's death.

Confucius went to Qu Boyu's house, where he had the news confirmed, so he went into the palace to offer his condolences. After that he stayed on in Qu's house.

A few days later Duke Ling's grandson, Zhe, was set up as the new ruler of Wei, later known as Duke Chu of Wei. Envoys came to offer congratulations from all neighboring states except Jin, which previously had sent Zhe's father, Kuai Kui, to a place called Qidi and helped him take control of this fertile area and build up his forces there.

Qidi, which faced Jin across the Yellow River, was a strategic place linking with Jin, Zheng, Wu and Chu. On hearing of his father's death, Kuai Kui sent an envoy to Zhe with a letter expressing his intention to return to Wei to succeed to his father's position. However, before his death Duke Ling of Wei had said to Zhe, "Kuai Kui betrayed me and attempted to murder his father's wife. He has now fled to Qidi, where he plans to usurp the dukedom with the help of Jin. How can I have such a traitor for my successor! When I die, you shall become the sovereign of the state. You must try your best to make our state prosperous. Build a strong army so that you will be able to subdue revolts and ward off invasions from outside. If Kuai Kui returns with his forces, you must lead the army in person to defeat and kill him. Failing that, you should at least drive him away and keep him out for as long as he lives!"

Thus when Duke Chu of Wei received Kuai Kui's letter, he threw it to the ground with great annoyance. "Since he has turned against my grandfather," he said to the envoy, "I no longer have anything to do with him. My grandfather has passed the dukedom to me. Return and tell him that he must leave Wei in a few days. Otherwise he will die a graveless death!"

Trembling in fear, the envoy stumbled his way out of the palace and returned to Qidi to report to Kuai Kui.

Kuai Kui turned crimson with anger. "I swear I won't rest," he said between clenched teeth, "until I have killed this treacherous son and become the ruler of Wei!" His first impulse was to lead his men to attack Diqiu, capture his son and tear him into pieces. Then he calmed down a little, aware that to attack the Wei capital with his army of merely a hundred chariots would be like throwing an egg against a stone. He decided to cross the Yellow River to ask Zhao Jianzi for help.

After capturing the provision carts of Zheng and driving Fan Shi and Zhongxing Shi out of Jin, Zhao Jianzi continued to build up his forces. One day he was sitting in his house thinking over his plan for further expansion when a guard entered to announce the arrival of Kuai Kui.

"Invite him to come in!" Zhao Jianzi said, quite pleased.

The guard showed Kuai Kui into the parlor, where Zhao stood up to receive him.

They took their seats as host and guest and exchanged greetings. "Is there something you want to see me about?" Zhao asked.

Kuai bowed slightly and said in a disconsolate tone, "Let me be candid, Minister Zhao. My father just passed away and has been succeeded by my unfilial son, Zhe. I sent him an envoy with a letter asking him to resign in my favor, but he refused in the most spiteful words. How can I swallow such an insult! If he can be so vile and heartless, why should I deal with him with courtesy!"

Zhao rolled his eyes. "You are not saying you and your son will draw swords on each other, are you?"

Fuming with rage, Kuai said, "I want to lead an army to attack the capital and kill this sinful son of mine. Otherwise I will be too ashamed to go on living in this world!"

Looking doubtful, Zhao asked, "How many war chariots you have?"

Kuai Kui replied with a sigh, "Only a hundred."

Zhao felt a surge of ambition. If he helped Kuai overtake the Wei capital and replace Zhe as the ruler of Wei, he would obtain a very loyal ally. To goad Kuai into action, he said, "To fight Zhe with a hundred chariots would be like throwing an egg against a stone. I advise you to hold back your anger and let the matter rest. After all, Zhe is your own son."

Kuai Kui pulled a long face at the words. "You have it wrong," he said with great agitation. "By refusing to abdicate in my favor Zhe has proved to be an unfilial son. How can someone who is unfilial to his father be a good ruler of a state?"

Zhao said with a broad smile, "In that case, you have already made up your mind?"

Kuai clenched his fists and said savagely, "I swear I will get rid of this wicked son of mine!"

"All right, I will send Fan Cai to Qidi with two hundred war chariots and put them under your command. What do you think?"

Kuai hastily bowed. "Many thanks, Minister Zhao!"

Zhao sent for Fan Cai and said to him, "At present our friend here is having some difficulty. You must lead two hundred chariots to Qidi, where you will join forces with him to attack the Wei capital."

Fan replied with a bow, "I'll carry out your order!" He turned and saluted Kuai, "Fan Cai will be at your service!"

Immensely delighted, Kuai smiled gratefully. "I am incredibly fortunate to have Minister Zhao's sincere friendship and General Fan's help. I will repay your kindness after I succeed!"

Zhao waved his hand. "Don't mention it!"

Eager to take action, Kuai asked, "When shall we set out, Minister Zhao?"

"The decision is yours!"

"If General Fan can gather the troops this evening, we shall start off tomorrow morning. How about that?"

"That will be fine."

That evening Zhao Jianzi gave a banquet both to welcome Kuai Kui and to bid Fan Cai farewell.

Early the following morning Fan and Kuai set out with two hundred war chariots. The day was hot and stuffy without the slightest wind, and the ground was as hot as a food steamer. Soaked in sweat, the men and horses trudged on toward the Yellow River.

At twilight a few days later they arrived at the river bank, where they found only four ferry-boats. As they were preparing to cross the river, a violent wind arose, and big clusters of dark clouds emerged from the south. A torrential rain followed shortly afterward and did not stop until an hour later, when night fell and stars appeared in the sky. The water in the Yellow River was greatly swollen, rushing downstream in a thunderous roar. Looking back to the west, they found the ground which had been parched a moment before flooded by the river.

The soldiers were all drenched like drowned rats. Fan Cai walked to the ferry crossing and shouted to the boatmen, "Get your boats ready to ferry my chariots across!"

A boatman hurriedly came over and pleaded with him.
"General," he said, "We have strong wind causing big waves now. It would be dangerous to cross the river at night. Let's wait till tomorrow morning!"

"What?" Fan Cai gave them a fierce look. "You think I won't pay you?"

Another boatman hastily bowed and replied in trepidation, "That's not on our mind, general. It is our duty to help you!"

Fan Cai took a look at the river. "The rain has stopped, the wind has abated, and the stars have come out. Cross the river this evening, and you won't even have to sweat in such cool weather."

The boatmen were about to plead further when Fan swept his arm and said sternly, "Save your breath and row the boats over here!"

The boatmen had no choice but to row the boats to the ford carefully and set off for the other shore with Fan Cai's war chariots. Fortunately the wind had calmed down. The four boats hurried to and fro between the two shores. Next morning all two hundred war chariots had crossed the river.

As soon as he stepped on Wei territory, Kuai Kui felt high-spirited and full of confidence. Looking at the war chariots behind him, he felt as if the Wei capital were already within his grasp. He returned to Qidi and put his one hundred war chariots under Fan Cai's command. "General Fan," he asked tentatively, "when shall we set out to attack the Wei capital?"

"We should stay here for a few days to rest our men and horses. In the meantime we need to work out a detailed plan to ensure the success of our action."

Kuai Kui, however, was eager to storm into the capital and set himself up as the ruler of Wei. "General, your troops have come here without concealing their movement. If we do not take action quickly and surprise the enemy, my unfilial son will have time to prepare against us."

"Of course undue delay may cause trouble, but at least we must find out about the terrain surrounding the capital before we launch our attack."

"There is no need to worry!" said Kuai. "The Wei capital is surrounded by open country with only a few streams. There is no dangerous terrain!"

Fan Cai frowned, "The last thing we need is a piece of flat land when we launch a surprise attack. How will we be able to conceal our movement?"

"We can attack at night," suggested Kuai.

"There doesn't seem to be a better alternative," Fan said reluctantly.

That evening the sky was covered in dark clouds, and the air seemed to have stopped flowing. Amid the cries of crickets and humming of mosquitoes, the creaking noise produced by the war chariots sounded alarmingly loud. Fan looked up into the starless sky and hoped that a wind would rise to hush up the noise of his marching troops.

They came before a river when a strong wind came. Small waves rose in the river, and the reeds fluttered with a rustling sound. Kuai started and had gooseflesh all over.

Fan got up in his chariot and looked warily into the reeds, for the rustling sound made him feel nervous. He said to Kuai, "It is not difficult to hide several hundred chariots over there among the reeds. Let's send a few scouts to take a look before deciding on our next move."

"General Fan," said Kuai Kui, trying to boost his courage. "It is over forty li from the capital city. We have come here unknown to god or ghost; how could there be an ambush?"

"One can never be too careful when directing the troops," said Fan. He turned and shouted, "Stop!"

No sooner had he said this than a whole legion of war chariots emerged from the reeds accompanied by loud drum-beats and battle-cries.

Kuai was so startled that he beat the horses violently, making them go around in circles.

Fan quickly deployed his forces to meet the attack. He shouted at the enemy general, "Announce your name!"

"I am Wangsun Jia," replied the Wei general, who stood in his chariot, sword in hand. "Who are you?"

Fan Cai answered haughtily, "I am Fan Cai, a general of Jin!"

"Fan Cai! As a Jin general you should be assisting your lord to guard Jin against foreign invasion. Yet you have come with a large force to attack Wei. Why?"

"Because the state of Wei is suffering from gross depravity and wickedness. Think carefully, General Wangsun! At the death of the late duke of Wei, he should be succeeded by his son, who is still alive. However, the grandson has usurped what rightly belongs to his father in defiance of his filial duties. Does he not deserve to be punished by an expedition?"

"This is Wei's internal affairs and none of Jin's business. Furthermore, Kuai Kui must blame himself for all this," retorted Wangsun Jia. "What can he expect after he turned against his father and attempted to murder his father's wife? Why should you risk your life for an unworthy man like him? You'd better return to Jin with your forces!"

Kuai Kui shouted from his chariot, "Wangsun Jia, if you have the slightest knowledge of the rites, you will withdraw your troops at once. Don't you know who I am?"

Wangsun Jia sneered. "A short time ago you were famous and highly respected in Wei, but unfortunately you ruined your own fame by going against His Lordship. Now a new ruler has been set up in Wei. You have not a place to put your feet on in Wei. If you are clever enough, run away and make your living in another state!"

Kuai roared furiously. At his order the soldiers released a hail of arrows, shooting down quite a few people in the ranks of the Wei army.

Enraged, Wangsun said, "I have already made a concession to you. If you take my generosity for weakness, you will suffer for it!"

Kuai intended to charge across the river with the war chariots, but Fan stopped him. "Don't be so hasty. The enemy hides in the dark while our troops are in the open. It would be difficult for us to fight under such circumstances. We must lure the enemy out of the reeds." He ordered, "Retreat quickly!"

Just then a gust of wind swept across the reeds while the sky was lit up in a flash, revealing a multitude of war chariots lined up across the river. Fan Cai gasped with astonishment.

As if sensing the workings of his mind, Wangsun shouted, "General Fan, a wise man knows when to give in. If you return to Jin with your troops, I promise you won't lose a single man or horse. If you should decide to resist, you would only meet death! Please be wise to the situation and make your choice now!"

Dissatisfied with Fan Cai's order for retreat, Kuai Kui could no longer contain his anger. "Don't retreat! Charge forth! Whoever kills Wangsun Jia will get the biggest reward!"

Under conflicting orders, some chariots dashed forth while others fell back, resulting in a great confusion.

After some rumbling thunder it started to rain heavily. Wangsun shouted, "Officers and men, kill!"

Loud drum-beats mingled with the sound of falling rain. The war chariots from the two sides became embroiled in a tangled fight. Many soldiers were stabbed, trampled or crushed to death. As Wangsun Jia embarked on a hot pursuit after Fan Cai, Kuai Kui fled the battle-ground for Qidi with a few dozen chariots.

Fan Cai kept turning back to shoot arrows while retreating. He hit one of the horses drawing Wangsun Jia's chariot, which ground to a stop. Taking the opportunity, Fan Cai got away and returned to Qidi.

Kuai Kui and Fan Cai lost over a hundred war chariots, while Wangsun Jia lost only about fifty. After this battle, Kuai Kui grew cautious and no longer dared take any rash action. He stayed in Qidi drilling his troops and biding his time. His presence in Qidi became a headache for Duke Chu of Wei, who had to be constantly on the alert against emergency.

Living in Qu Boyu's house, Confucius learned to his distress what had happened. One day he said to his disciples, "The fight between the sovereign and his father has sent the people of Wei into confusion. It is unsuitable for us to stay here any longer."

"Where shall we go then?" Zi Lu asked.

Confucius seemed to have considered the matter long before. He replied promptly, "Song is the place where my ancestors once lived. Let's go to Song."

The disciples said in unison, "We'll follow you wherever you go, master!" Already accustomed to a wandering life, they packed up without delay and set out promptly. It was a cool morning, the air fresh and clear right after a light rain, when they came to an open country in Song a few days later. Willows lined up along the river bank, and various trees grew in the field. Swallows flit over the trees while eagles soared high in the sky. Confucius heaved a sigh of relief at the peaceful scene.

At noon they felt hungry, but saw no inn nearby. Confucius looked at his disciples and found them all soaked in perspiration. When the chariots came to an old camphor tree with a large canopy, he suggested, "It is too hot. Let's rest here for a while."

The disciples were only too glad to concur. They stopped the chariots by the tree and sat down to rest in the shade. Two magpies leapt and twittered beside their nest built on a twig, as if teaching their young to sing and fly. The grains in the field were just putting forth ears. Confucius was pleased at the prospect of a bumper year for the people of Song. Many swallows and dragonflies were wheeling in the air catching insects. His interest aroused, he said to his disciples, "The scenery here is as beautiful as a painting. Let's practice the rites under this camphor tree!"

The disciples shouted their agreement.

Confucius first explained in detail some rules given in *The Book of Rites*. When they were about to start practicing, they heard a big noise. A band of people rushed toward them from the south, headed by a hefty man with an ugly face and tangled whiskers. At his command some fifty to sixty men formed an encirclement around Confucius and his party.

Surprised, Confucius went up and asked, "May I know who you are? Why do you surround us?"

The man replied in a hoarse voice, "I am Sima Huantui of Song."

The name was not totally unknown to Confucius. A man of humble origin, Sima Huantui had built up his personal influence during the internecine fights in the Song court. He was powerful enough to act as he pleased in the court and even defy the authority of Duke Jing of Song. He had no patience with time-honored rules and practices and did not hesitate to act against them. On one occasion he ordered a stone coffin carved out for himself; the project took three years at a preposterous cost.

Faced with the malicious-looking man, instead of cowering in fear like many of their fellow disciples, Zi Lu, Gongliang Ru and Ran Qiu stood firmly by Confucius' sides, sword in hand, ready to fight with all their might.

"Master, let us attack and kill these ruffians," Zi Lu said.

Confucius hastily stopped him. "Don't be so hotheaded. This man would not harm us without cause. Put away your swords and let's ask him some questions." He walked up to Sima Huantui and introduced himself.

Sima Huantui straightened his neck, squinted at Confucius, and asked haughtily, "I know you are Kong Qiu. Where are you going?"

Confucius replied, "My students and I are heading for Song."

"What tricks were you playing under this tree?" asked Sima Huantui with a sneer.

"I was teaching my students to practice the rites," replied Confucius calmly.

"Those teachings of yours are old and stale and should have been buried in a coffin long ago! But you take them as something precious and brag about them everywhere. Who knows how many rulers and men of virtue you have harmed?"

Confucius was struck speechless by this fierce abuse. Realizing the futility of arguing with him, he paid no more attention to him, but went on with his explanation of the rites to his disciples.

For a while Sima Huantui stood there uncertainly, then he swept his arm and shouted, "Cut down this tree!"

His men swarmed toward the camphor tree, brandishing their swords and axes, in a short while the tree fell to the ground. The magpie-nest was smashed and the fledglings were killed. The two big magpies flew around over the men's heads, crying. They charged at Sima as if determined to take revenge.

Sima flourished his sword to strike at the magpies, which fought him desperately, dodging his sword and trying to claw his head. Unable to hit the birds with his sword, Sima shouted to his men, "Shoot! Shoot them!"

Instantly arrows flew at the birds, killing two on the spot.

Still gasping with anger, Sima went up to the dead birds and stabbed them with his sword. Then he ordered his men to surround Confucius and his disciples again.

Yan Hui came up to Confucius and said, "Master, it is impossible to reason with such people. Let's be on our way!"

"Don't be afraid!" said Confucius with composure. "Heaven has bestowed me with virtue. What can Sima do to me?"

It was getting dark, but Sima and his men refused to go away.

Confucius and his disciples had been kept there since noon. They were hungry and thirsty.

"Master, let's fight our way out!" Zi Lu suggested.

Gongliang Ru agreed. "Yes, let's fight our way out, master! Zi Lu and I will lead the way, and you and the others will follow us."

Confucius only sighed but would not say yes or no to their suggestion.

Chapter Thirty

Zi Gong Calls on a Village Woman to Learn a Secret Method; Confucius Tells Duke Min of Chen the Origin of a Strange Arrow

With repeated pleadings on the part of Zi Lu, Ran Qiu and Yan Ke, Confucius finally agreed to fight their way out of Sima Huantui's encirclement.

For fear that Confucius would come to harm if captured by Sima Huantui, Zi Lu whispered to him, "Master, these people seemed to be very cruel and heartless. Let us exchange our clothes to confuse them."

Confucius hesitated, but Zi Lu took off his robe and helped Confucius off with his. The disciples let out a loud shout and dashed forward together.

Sima had come in order to drive Confucius out of Song. When Confucius and his disciples charged at them, he told his men to make way. However, after Confucius and his disciples had broken out, Sima and his men pursued them for a while just to intimidate them further.

Confucius and his disciples fled for dear life, arriving in the capital of Zheng one after another. Confucius stopped at the east gate, where he dismounted the chariot and gazed back. The disciples were even more worried when they could not find their master. Zi Gong arrived at the west gate, where he met an old man in his sixties looking like a recluse. He was of medium height and had greying temples and a beard to his chest. He had a ruddy complexion and large, piercing eyes. Zi Gong went up to him, bowed, and asked, "May I ask if you have seen my master?"

"Who is your master?"

"Kong Qiu from Lu."

The old man broke into a fit of laughter. "There is a man at the east gate," he said, "who has a very graceful appearance. He resembles the sage ruler Yao in his cheeks, and his neck looks like that of Gao Tao, Yao's minister of justice. His shoulders reminds one of Zi Chan of Zheng, and below his waist he looks pretty much like Yu the Great,

who led the people to tame the flood. However, for all his elegant appearance, he cuts a sorry figure just now. I would compare him to a homeless dog."

Hearing these words, Zi Gong did not know whether to thank the man or to rebuke him.

The old man laughed again and left.

Zi Gong hurried to the east gate, where he found Confucius gazing to the east, his head held up.

Zi Gong felt so sad and bitter that tears swelled up in his eyes. "Master!" he cried in a choked voice.

"It's you!" Confucius exclaimed with joy, rubbing his eyes. "Where did you go? I was so worried about you."

"After we fought our way out last night, I lost my way. At daybreak I reached the west gate, where an old man told me to find you here. Have all the others arrived?"

"Yes, they have," Confucius replied.

Zi Gong then recounted the words of the old man.

Confucius smiled bitterly. "He said I look like ancient sage kings —such compliments I do not really deserve. As for comparing me to a homeless dog, that's not far from the truth. Look!" He spread his arms and shook the dust off Zi Lu's long gown that he was wearing. "Am I not in a sorry state?"

The disciples were all down in the mouth. None of them ventured to say anything.

Finally Min Shun, somewhat encouraged by the sight of the streams of people coming and going through the east gate, said to Confucius with a bow, "Master, since we have arrived in Zheng, let's call on its ruler and stay here for a few days, while we decide where to go next."

As a small and weak state, Zheng was not the ideal place in which Confucius could build up a benevolent government and transform the entire world with the restoration of rites. He stared at his disciples and sighed deeply. "We have no other choice now. Zi Gong, since you are a good speaker, go and inform the Duke of Zheng of our arrival!"

Zi Gong agreed and, beating the dust off his clothes and adjusting his hat, rode into the city.

Confucius and the other disciples also entered the city. They ate at an eating-house and went out on to the street, where they stood waiting for Zi Gong's return.

Duke Sheng of Zheng had ruled the dukedom for eight years. An ambitious man in his twenties, he often dreamed of making Zheng one of the most powerful states in the kingdom. At this particular moment he was again day-dreaming: Zheng enjoyed a most strategic location, with Qi and Lu to the east, Qin and Jin to the north, Chu and Wu to the south and the royal capital to the west. If he could use every possible means to bring the surrounding states under submission, he would be able to order them around in the name of the king. When that day came even the king of Zhou would have to bow to his wishes. Extremely pleased with this prospect, he ordered music and dance to be performed.

The guards passed on the order. A short while later sixteen dancing girls walked in to the accompaniment of music and began to dance, twisting their waists and swinging their long sleeves. Duke Sheng beamed with delight and satisfaction.

Just then a guard entered and reported, "Your Lordship, Zi Gong, a disciple of Kong Qiu from Lu, begs for an audience."

"What?" Duke Sheng stood up, but immediately sat down and leaned back in his chair. He closed his eyes and thought for a while. The teaching of Confucius, in his opinion, was completely outdated. The only way to make Zheng strong was building up its military power. If allowed to stay, Confucius might obstruct his cause by advocating the rites. "Pass on my words," he said finally. "I have no time to meet him. Tell them to leave Zheng as soon as possible!"

Zi Gong was getting impatient waiting outside the palace gate. When the guard finally came out with the duke's order, Zi Gong was filled with indignation. He swept his arm and left without a word.

When Confucius and his disciples saw Zi Gong, their hearts sank, and when Zi Gong told them what had happened they were all sorely disappointed.

Confucius said, "Well, there are both big and small states, and there are both virtuous and ignorant people. What can we do with an unreasonable man like him! If we can not stay here, we will simply go and find another place. Since it's still early, let's get on our way to Chen!"

Gongliang Ru was greatly pleased. "Master," he said, "Chen is my homeland. Last time we failed to go there because of Gongshu Shi's revolt. This time let me drive the chariot for you and lead the way."

They got on their chariots and started off at once. A few days later they reached Chen. They were driving along the road when they heard someone singing in a forest of mulberry trees:

The world is full of strange things
Too difficult for one to understand.
If you can not string the nine-twist pearls,
Come ask me at Xie Village.

It was the voice of a woman, clear and melodious. Confucius gazed into the forest and saw a middle-aged woman singing the song while picking mulberry leaves. Though he did not know what the song was about, Confucius memorized the words.

On their arrival at the capital of Chen, Gongliang Ru located a clean inn where they settled down for the night. Early the next morning a messenger arrived. Confucius hastily went out to meet him.

The messenger was in his forties. He bowed to Confucius and said politely, "I am Gongye Ming, a messenger of His Lordship the duke of Chen. He invites the master to enter the palace!"

This invitation was a welcoming change after what they had experienced of late with Sima Huantui and Duke Sheng of Zheng. All smiles, Confucius said to the messenger, "Please allow a few minutes for me to have my disciples prepare the chariot. We will leave as soon as possible."

Gongye Ming agreed and waited.

Confucius called Zi Lu to him and said in a low voice, "The duke of Chen wants to see me, and you will come with me. We have suffered a lot since we left Wei. It is lucky for us to have the duke's invitation. You must act cautiously and not brag and boast in the palace."

Zi Lu nodded his head. "I understand, master."

Confucius mounted the chariot and followed Gongye Ming to the palace. Duke Min of Chen met him at the palace gate. "You are a great sage of our time," the duke said. "It is a great honor for me and my people to have you come such a long distance to visit us!"

Confucius bowed deeply. "Please forgive me for troubling you!"

Duke Min was then in his fifties. He was a tall man with a long face and deep wrinkles on his forehead. He gestured for Confucius to enter the palace. "This way, please!"

Confucius stood at attention and also gestured with his hand, "After you, Your Lordship."

Bothering no more about formalities, the duke took Confucius by the arm, and the two of them walked into the palace together.

After they had sat down and exchanged greetings Duke Min asked a lot of questions, to which Confucius replied carefully and convincingly. All the court officials present marveled at his great knowledge.

Duke Min exclaimed with admiration, "No wonder people everywhere regard you as a sage!" Suddenly he assumed a serious expression, looking Confucius in the face. "Our late sovereign has left me with a string of nine-twist pearls, but the string has broken. No one can string the pearls together again, for the opening in each pearl has nine twists. Since you are recognized as a great sage, you must be able to solve this problem. I hope you will help me."

Confucius bowed slightly in his chair. "I have acquired my knowledge," he said, "by studying diligently. The nine-twist pearls you just mentioned is something I have never seen or heard of. May I have a look at them?"

"Bring the pearls here!"

At the duke's order, two palace attendants brought in a square purple box, knelt before the duke and opened the box.

Confucius was deeply impressed by the sight. In the box lay twenty-one pearls the size of dates with all the colors of the rainbow. He took one into his hand and examined it carefully. The opening for the string to pass through had indeed nine twists. "What a priceless treasure!" he said with wonder. Then he felt a little embarrassed. How could he string the pearls together?

Duke Min and the court officials looked at him with anticipation, as if waiting for a doctor to prescribe for a fatally ill patient.

Just then Confucius remembered the song of the woman collecting mulberry leaves. He stood up and bowed with clasped hands. "Your Lordship, the pearls are too intricately made for me to string them in a short time. If you entrust them to me, I will try to find a solution."

Duke Min looked inquisitively at his officials, who all appeared apprehensive. He stood up slowly and said, "Of course you are trusted, master. No one in the world would ever doubt your integrity! Though the nine-twist pearls are a treasure of our state, I am sure I can entrust them to you."

"In that case, I will take them with me."

Duke Min still felt somewhat at a loss.

"You can expect good news," Confucius added confidently. "The pearls will be strung together in three days." With this he took his leave.

After Confucius and Zi Lu had left, the court officials all looked disconsolate. Gongye Ming said, "Your Lordship, what shall we do if something should go wrong?"

After pondering for a while Duke Min said, "Confucius has always practiced benevolence and righteousness. The pearls are absolutely safe with him. However, we have to worry about thieves and robbers."

"Yes," agreed Gongye Ming.

"The matter is not so serious, really," said the duke. "I'll just send some guards to protect the pearls in secret."

The officials agreed that it was a good idea.

When Confucius left the palace with the pearls, Zi Lu said disapprovingly, "Master, didn't you tell me to act cautiously and not brag and boast? But it was you who boasted. It is possible that no one had ever strung these pearls together. The duke might be playing a trick to humiliate you. If you fail to solve the problem, people will laugh at you. What's more, the world is overrun with thieves and robbers. If the pearls are stolen, how will you be able to prove your innocence? Your fame will be ruined!"

Confucius said with a smile, "What you said is right."

Zi Lu looked at Confucius in surprise, waiting for an explanation.

"On our way to the Chen capital the other day," said Confucius, "I heard a woman who was gathering mulberry leaves say that she knew how to string the pearls."

Zi Lu said with puzzlement, "I accompanied you all the way to Chen and did not remember someone teaching you how to string pearls!"

"Did you remember the song sung by the woman in the mulberry trees?" asked Confucius.

Zi Lu shook his head.

"Well," Confucius changed the subject. "As you said, it is important that we guard against thieves and robbers. You, Ran Qiu and Gongliang Ru are both smart and brave. Back in the inn, the three of you will be responsible for the safety of the pearls."

Zi Lu was pleased with the task entrusted to him.

Back in the inn, Confucius called his disciples to him and said earnestly, "We have just arrived in Chen, and the duke treats us politely. He has twenty-one nine-twist pearls for which the string has broken. Unable to string them together again, he has asked us for help.

The pearls are a treasure handed down from ancient times. The ancients said that a superior man is always ready to help others. However, the opening in each pearl has nine twists, so that it is extremely difficult to pull a string through it. Does any of you know a method of doing it?"

Zi Lu brought in the pearls and passed them round among fellow disciples, who only marveled but could not come up with a way to string the pearls together.

Confucius asked, "Zi Gong, did you hear someone sing a song in the mulberry trees on our way here the day before yesterday?"

Zi Gong said, "Yes, I did. The song goes, 'The world is full of strange things too difficult for one to understand. If you can not string the nine-twist pearls, come ask me at Xie Village.' She must know the secret method to string the pearls."

Confucius smiled gladly. "Zi Gong!" he said. "You are attentive and have a good memory. Tomorrow morning you will go and find the woman at that village and return with the secret of the pearls!"

"I will do my best to accomplish the task," promised Zi Gong.

"Ran Qiu and Gongliang Ru," Confucius said, "the two of you will help Zi Lu to ensure the safety of the pearls!"

Ran Qiu and Gongliang Ru replied in unison, "We understand!"

Early the next morning Zi Gong took leave of Confucius and drove to Xie Village, arriving there before noon. He stopped the chariot outside the village and looked around. Many mulberry trees were growing around a few dozen thatched cottages, but no one was in sight. Just then he heard someone singing in the mulberry trees:

The world is full of strange things
Too difficult for one to understand.

Delighted, Zi Gong left the chariot and ran quickly in the direction where the song was coming from. When he got there, he found himself facing a village woman. Her darkish face had a ruddy complexion and her body was well-built. She wore an apron round her waist and a square kerchief on her head, and she had large, sparkling eyes. Zi Gong saluted with joined hands. "May I ask if this is Xie Village?"

"Yes, it is," replied the woman after returning the salute. "Are you a disciple of Kong Qiu from Lu?"

Surprised, Zi Gong replied, "Yes, my name is Duanmu Ci, and I am a disciple of Confucius."

The woman asked, "Haven't you come to ask my help about some problem?"

"Yes." Zi Gong bowed again. "When we arrived in Chen, the duke asked us to help him string some pearls together. We don't know how to do it because the opening in each pearl is long, thin and twisted. When we passed here the other day we heard your song, so I have come today to ask for help."

The woman heaved a deep sigh. "It is hard to say how many talents are stifled and wasted nowadays. The ruler can only spot the few people under his nose and has no idea that people of great talents and bravery can be found everywhere."

"Do you mean to say—"

"Let's not talk about that," interrupted the woman. "I'll tell you how to string the nine-twist pearls right now."

"That would be wonderful!" Zi Gong exclaimed. "Many thanks!"

"Fill the opening with honey, stick a piece of raw silk to the tail of an ant and place the ant in the same box with the pearls. In a single night the ant will string all the pearls together with the silk."

The scales fell from Zi Gong's eyes and he thanked the woman again and again. He gazed after her till she returned to her house and entered the wooden door, then drove back to the capital.

Confucius and his disciples immediately tried the method. When they opened the box the next morning, they found to their great joy that all the twenty-one pearls had been strung together on the silk. Confucius told the disciples to attach a silk string to the piece of raw silk and pull the string through the pearls. Soon all the pearls were strung on the silk string.

Greatly pleased, Confucius said, "There is much truth in the words of that village woman. She must be the wife of a recluse. If a village woman has such great wisdom, there must be numerous things that we don't know or understand. There is indeed no end to learning!"

After breakfast, Confucius and Zi Lu went to the palace to return the pearls.

Duke Min of Chen was immensely pleased. "Master," he said, "you have accomplished a great task for me. This has removed a great weight from my mind. You will be duly rewarded!"

"I am just happy to help," Confucius said. "As for reward—"

Duke Min interrupted him, saying, "It is inconvenient for you and your disciples to stay in a hostel. May I give you a house as a gift?"

Confucius declined. "The ancients said that one should not receive a reward which one does not deserve. I appreciate your kindness but can not accept your offer."

The duke urged again, but Confucius would not accept the gift. Finally Duke Min said, "Well, I won't force you to accept my gift. You and your disciples may stay on in the hostel."

After that Duke Min often invited Confucius to the palace and talked with him. He was deeply impressed by Confucius' discourse on world affairs and admired him greatly for his knowledge and wisdom.

After the morning audience one day, Duke Min retreated to the rear palace, intending to enjoy some music and dance. Just then a guard entered carrying in his hand a dead eagle with an arrow still planted in its body. "You idiot!" rebuked the duke angrily. "Why do you come to me with a dead eagle? What's wrong with you?"

The guard fell on his knees and replied in a trembling voice, "Your Lordship, I was passing the front court when I saw this eagle fall from the sky with the arrow on it. I do not know whether it's a good or ill omen, so I decided to present it to you."

Widening his eyes, Duke Min gestured with his hand. "Bring it here!"

The guard presented the eagle on both hands.

Duke Min stood up to examine the eagle. He pulled out the arrow and looked at it carefully. The arrow was made of stone and bamboo, which was quite peculiar, for at that time most arrows were made of iron or copper. Duke Min thought for a while and sent someone to invite Confucius.

Confucius was not surprised when the messenger arrived, for Duke Min often invited him into the palace whenever he had any difficult question. He did not set out for the palace until he finished teaching his disciples. Zi Lu again drove the chariot for him.

Duke Min was eager to know the origin of the stone arrow. As soon as Confucius arrived, he asked, "Master, nowadays people use copper or iron to make arrowheads. However, this eagle was shot dead by a stone arrow. Can you tell me where this arrow comes from? What people make such arrows?"

Confucius took the arrow in his hand and examined it. "Well," he said, "this arrow has a long history."

"Tell me about it!" urged Duke Min.

"It originated in the ancient state of Sushen in the north."

"Where is this Sushen?"

"Sushen is also known as Xishen and Jishen. In the Shang Dynasty people of Sushen lived in an area north of Buxian Mountain, stretching from the middle and lower reaches of the Heilong River to the west and the sea to the east. They were good at making arrows, for they made their living by hunting and fishing. When King Wu of Zhou destroyed Shang, all the barbarian tribes had to pay tribute to him. The tribute from Sushen was stone arrows just like this one. King Wu distributed the arrows among his children, one of whom, a daughter, was enfeoffed in Chen, and also among officials to remind them of their duty to guard Zhou territory."

Duke Min listened with rapt attention as Confucius recounted the history of the stone arrow. He did not know whether to believe the story.

Aware of the duke's doubts, Confucius said, "If you want to verify the story, you may send someone to check the storehouse of ancient relics."

Duke Min followed this advice and, sure enough, stone arrows were found in the storehouse which looked exactly the same as the stone arrow taken from the dead eagle. "Master," the duke exclaimed with admiration, "you are acquainted with everything under the sun. You are really my good teacher!"

At this Confucius got up from his seat and saluted, saying, "I do not deserve such praise!"

"The able man will serve as teacher," said the duke, smiling. "Did not the ancients say so?"

Confucius felt very uneasy receiving such excessive praise and took his leave.

Back in the hostel, Zi Lu described what had happened to his fellow disciples.

Zi Gong remarked, "If we compare learning to a wall, our walls are all very low. With the wall between us, we can still see each other and find out about each other's learning. It's not the same with our master. The wall of his learning is several times higher than ours."

"You are indeed a good speaker, brother," said Zi Lu with a smile. "The comparison you make is vivid and accurate."

The disciples fell into a heated discussion. Some agreed with Zi

Gong while others disagreed. Yan Hui, however, did not say anything.

Zi Lu went up to him and slapped him on the shoulder. "Yan Hui," he said, "when you make a remark, it often wins the master's approval. How would you describe our master's learning?"

Yan Hui smiled, but did not speak.

Zi Lu urged, "Let everyone air his own views! There is no need to keep your opinion from us."

"We can express our views freely among ourselves," said Yan Hui, "but it is a different matter as regards our master. He is not only rich in knowledge but widely respected for his virtue. I dare not comment on him."

"Our master treats us as his own children," said Zi Gong. Why can't you talk about him? Tell us your opinion!"

Urged repeatedly by the other disciples, Yan Hui finally said, "The more I look up at our master's teaching, the higher it soars; the more I delve into it, the deeper it becomes. One moment it spreads in front of me like a road, but suddenly it is behind. In spite of this, our master is good at leading me forward step by step. He has broadened my mind with ancient culture and regulated me with the rites, so that I could not stop learning even if I wanted to. I exhaust myself in study until I feel I can carry on by myself. However, when I want to take a step forward, I still do not know which way to go."

"It is you," said Zi Gong in admiration, "who has the best understanding of our master's teaching!"

Just then Qidiao Kai bursted into the room. "Where is our master?" he asked anxiously.

The other disciples were stunned.

Chapter Thirty-one

Confucius Describes the Attributes of a Benevolent Man; On His Deathbed Jisun Si Thinks of Confucius

Zi Lu asked, "Brother, what's the matter? Why are you in such a fluster?"

Qidiao Kai sighed. "People in the street say that Chang Hong, the king's musician, has been executed."

They all felt sad at the news. Min Shun said, "Chang Hong was one of the few people our master admires. When the master went to the royal capital to study rites from Lao Zi, he also learned music from Chang Hong. The master will surely be grieved to learn of his death."

"This is just hearsay," said Yan Hui. "Maybe it is not true. Let's not tell the master for the time being."

"I agree," said Ran Qiu.

Just then Confucius walked into the room. The disciples fell silent, not knowing what to do.

Sensing the unusual atmosphere, Confucius asked, "What has happened? Why do you look like this?"

Zi Lu stepped forward and said, "Chang Hong was killed by the people of Zhou."

As if getting a heavy blow in the head, Confucius felt numb and dizzy. His face turned pale, his lips trembled, but no word came out of his mouth.

Zi Lu and Min Shun hastily supported him with their hands.

After a long time Confucius recovered from the shock. "The ways of the world have changed," he sighed. "People who advocated the rites have been killed one after another. How can we restore the rites of Zhou in such a world?"

Following this incident Confucius remained in a despondent mood for many days, sighing and groaning all the time.

One clear day Confucius, feeling a little better, stood in the courtyard and gazed to the east. The disciples knew he was again thinking of his homeland and family members, so they gathered around to chat with him in order to relieve his sorrow.

Zi Lu said, "Master, you once told Yan Hui that benevolence means regulating oneself with the rules of propriety. But the king of Zhou executed Chang Hong, a talented and benevolent man, and Zhao Jianzi killed Dou Mingdu and Shun Hua. If such things continue to happen—"

Ran Qiu winked at Zi Lu, beckoning him to stop.

Zi Gong chimed in, hoping to divert Confucius' attention from the death of Chang Hong. "Master, how can one attain benevolence?"

Though Confucius attached great importance to benevolence, he did not talk about it very often, so he was pleased by Zi Gong's question. "Well," he said, "let me say something about benevolence." He took his seat and the disciples gathered around him.

"One can only attain benevolence by persistent cultivation and learning," said Confucius. "He should have a good foundation and gradually build on it, just like a workman who must first sharpen his tools if he wants to do his work well. If we want to cultivate benevolence here in Chen, we must treat the virtuous officials with respect and make friends with people of culture."

Gao Cai stepped out from behind Zi Lu. Compared with Zi Lu, he looked very short and thin. He lowered his usually stentorian voice and asked, "Master, what's the difference between a benevolent man and a wise man?"

"The benevolent man has a tranquil disposition, takes pleasure in mountains, and therefore enjoys a long life. The wise man has an active disposition, takes pleasure in streams, and therefore enjoys a happy life."

"If we tell a benevolent man that another benevolent man has fallen into a well, will he jump into the well?" Zai Wo asked.

"Why should you do that?" said Confucius, shaking his head. "You can tell a benevolent man to go away and not return, but you must not cheat him or trap him. Even if you can cheat him sometimes, you should never fool him."

"I understand," said Zai Wo.

Zi Lu suddenly asked, "When Duke Huan of Qi killed his elder brother, Jiu, Zhao Hu, Jiu's tutor, committed suicide because of shame and despair. However, Guan Zhong, who was also Jiu's tutor, was shameless enough to live on." He paused, looking at Confucius in the face. "Can Guan Zhong be regarded as a benevolent man?"

"After Duke Huan of Qi killed his elder brother, Jiu, he appointed

Bao Shuya, who had accompanied him during his exile, his chief minister. Bao Shuya was very good at discovering people of ability and placing them at suitable posts. As he knew Guan Zhong was more capable than himself, he recommended him to Duke Huan. Following Bao Shuya's advice, Duke Huan appointed Guan Zhong to a high post and let him carry out reforms all over the state. Guan Zhong consolidated government administration of the capital and its surrounding districts, instituting a military establishment in the better part of the capital. A scholar, after passing three tests, would be made an assistant to a senior official. Different tax rates were determined according to the quality of land, plundering of livestock was prohibited, and the burden of levy relieved. The government promoted the development of salt and iron industries, regulated the manufacturing and control of currency, and adjusted market prices, thus greatly augmenting the strength of the state. Furthermore, calling on the other vassal lords to 'support the king and dispel barbarians,' Duke Huan became the first overlord in the Spring and Autumn Period."

Recalling the exploits of Duke Huan, Confucius felt a deep admiration for Guan Zhong and Bao Shuya. "It was with Guan Zhong's help," he said, "that Duke Huan hosted several peace-making meetings of the lords, thereby preventing war among the states and promoting production. Because of this, people were able to live in peace and enjoy the fruits of their labor. This was Guan Zhong's benevolence!" He paused for a while, then repeated, "This was Guan Zhong's benevolence!"

Unconvinced, Zi Gong remarked, "Guan Zhong can not be regarded as a benevolent man! Duke Huan killed his brother, Jiu, who was Guan Zhong's lord. But Guan Zhong went to serve Duke Huan instead of sacrificing his life for his lord as Zhao Hu did."

Confucius said seriously, "Guan Zhong assisted Duke Huan in gaining dominance over the other lords and bringing order to the whole world. Today we still enjoy the benefits he brought us. Without Guan Zhong, we would have been reduced to barbarians wearing ragged robes and with our hair down. Why should you judge Guan Zhong in this way? Why should you attach more importance to minor errors instead of the great cause of restoring rites to the world?"

Zi Gong lowered his head for a few minutes, then asked, "Master, if someone can bring bountiful benefits to the common people and help them achieve a better life, will you call him benevolent?"

"Far more than benevolent!" replied Confucius with a smile. "He would be a sage for whom even Yao and Shun would be no match. What is benevolence? A benevolent man is one who helps others establish what he wants to establish himself, and helps others to achieve something he wants to achieve himself. To treat others as one wants to be treated oneself is the way to be benevolent."

"If one governs a state by benevolence, what will happen?" asked Zi Gong.

"He will be in the same position as the Big Dipper," replied Confucius, gesturing with his hands. "He remains still in the center, while the other stars move around him."

"If a sage ruler appears," asked Zi Gong, "how long will it take to establish a benevolent government?"

"Even if there is a sage ruler," replied Confucius, "it will take at least thirty years to establish a benevolent rule."

The disciples were all astonished.

"To govern a state well," explained Confucius, "there must be a complete system of regulations, a strong army and virtuous ministers. Only thus can we guard the state against internal revolts and invasions from outside. When the state is peaceful, people will be in harmony. When the people are in harmony, the government will be efficient. When the government is efficient, the people will become wealthy. When the people are wealthy, the state will grow strong. To stray from this would be attending to trivialities and neglecting the fundamentals."

The disciples murmured their appreciation.

Zi Gong asked, "How can we obtain people's trust and govern the state well?"

"You have asked a very good question, Zi Gong!" said Confucius approvingly. "The ancient kings governed the world by benevolence. If the king obtained people's trust by his cleverness but failed to educate them in benevolence, he would lose their trust gradually. If the king obtained people's trust by his cleverness and educated them in benevolence, but failed to treat them seriously, people would not live in harmony. The king must obtain people's support by his wisdom, instruct them in benevolence, treat them seriously, and mobilize and employ their labor reasonably. Only in this way could he retain people's support forever. People's support is the key to prosperity and strength."

"I would like to attain benevolence," said Zi Gong, "but it is beyond me at this stage. May I have a single sentence to guide my action for life?"

Confucius thought hard, his brows drawn together. "Well," he said slowly, "I would say loyalty and forgiveness."

Zi Gong looked at him inquisitively.

"Do not impose on others what you do not want for yourself," explained Confucius.

"Yes," Zi Gong said. "I do not want to be bullied, nor do I want to bully others."

"Very good!" said Confucius. "Unfortunately you have not yet achieved this."

Zi Gong blushed.

Confucius regretted having spoken so bluntly. "Zi Gong," he said, trying to ease the awkward atmosphere. "How do you compare yourself with Yan Hui?"

Zi Gong thought for a while and replied respectfully, "How can I compare myself with Yan Hui? When he is told one thing, he understands ten. When I am told one thing, I understand only two. I am no match for him."

Confucius combed his beard. "I agree. You are no match for Yan Hui."

"Master," said Zai Yu with a bow, "people all praise the greatness of Yao and Shun, but I do not fully understand their merits. Could you tell us about them?"

Confucius looked up into the sky. "Zai Yu," he said, "what you just asked is of the utmost importance. During his rule Yao appointed officials to establish the calendar and teach the people to grow crops according to the seasons. He exercised a benevolent rule and brought benefits to the whole world. When he was old, he did not pass on the throne to his son; instead, he traveled all over China in search of virtuous people until he found Shun. After testing Shun for three years, he allowed Shun to administer the government in his place. At his death he was succeeded by Shun. How great Yao was! Nothing is higher or larger than Heaven, and Yao was the only man who learned from Heaven. His benefits were so bountiful that people did not know how to praise him. His merits were so great that no one can compare with him to date. The rites he established were so fine that it is impossible to find any fault in them."

The disciples listened attentively.

"When Shun came to the throne," continued Confucius, "he removed the four evil officials Gun, Gong Gong, Huan Dou and San Miao from their posts and became a sage ruler. Like Yao he traveled all over China selecting virtuous people to serve in the government, and finally chose Yu as his successor."

Zai Yu saluted again and asked, "Master, would you tell us about Yu the Great's exploits?"

"Yes, tell us about Yu," the other disciples chimed in.

"All right," agreed Confucius with pleasure. "He was said to be Gun's son. Appointed by Shun to harness the floods, he divided China into nine prefectures and led the people to dredge the rivers and construct ditches and canals. In the thirteen years of his fight against the floods, he passed by his home three times and did not enter it. Because of his success in harnessing the floods, he was chosen by Shun to be his successor. Upon Shun's death, Yu became king. I regard him with deep reverence and find no reason to blame him. He ate meagerly, but had magnificent robes made for sacrificial rites; he lived in a squalid house, but devoted all his efforts to flood-fighting projects. Yao, Shun and Yu were indeed great! They ruled the entire world, but they did not indulge themselves in comforts or pleasure. On the contrary, they spent all time working for the benefit of the people. How great they were!"

Thus Confucius stayed on in the state of Chen, teaching his disciples and discussing various subjects with them. One day in autumn Duke Min of Chen invited Confucius to join him on an excursion to the suburbs. Riding in the same chariot, they arrived at an open field painted red and yellow by sorghum and millet, their heavy ears undulating slightly in the breeze. "What a good harvest Chen will enjoy this year!" said Confucius.

Duke Min of Chen beamed.

Confucius, however, fell into a sad mood, for the beautiful view before him contrasted with the plight faced by the state of Lu. In the fourth month that year Lu had suffered a great earthquake, resulting in heavy losses. This was followed by a drought in many places, where people's lives became endangered by famine. He could think of only two incidents to comfort himself. His son, Kong Li, had a boy by his wife. The boy was called Kong Ji and had Zi Si as his styled name. Confucius was very happy to have a grandson to carry on the family line. The other incident was the burning down of the temples of Duke Huan and Duke Xi of Lu, which had been built against the rites of Zhou. "Heaven has punished those who defy the rites!" Confucius had said to himself on hearing the news.

An eagle soared high in the sky, flying to the east. Confucius felt an intense longing for his homeland.

In the meantime Jisun Si had become bedridden because of heart failure. Listening to his uneven heartbeats, staring at the beams and pillars in his house, he lamented the many calamities Lu was suffering, the earthquake, the droughts, and the fires. "I am responsible for all this!" he sighed. Looking at his bony hands, he realized with a shudder that his days were numbered. He could not suppress the sense of shame and regret when going over his life in his mind. Those innumerable days of merry-making now appeared to him not only wasteful and useless but also extremely dull. He saw clearly the ineptitude of Duke Ding and the wisdom of Confucius, but the situation was beyond redemption. Duke Ding was buried in his grave, and Confucius was wandering in another state. "What about myself?" Jisun Si held his head in both hands and groaned. "What will people say about me after my death?" He could hardly thought of anything worthwhile that he had accomplished in his lifetime.

For all the doctor had done for him, Jisun Si's health deteriorated day by day. He decided to make an excursion to the countryside and take a last look at the land of Lu.

As the chariot rode out of the south gate, tracts of unevenly grown sorghum and millet came into sight. Many withered stalks could be seen among the ripe crops. Jisun Si felt ashamed for having failed to run the state well and give the people a good life. "Drive the chariot around the city," he told his son Jisun Fei, who was sitting by his side. "I want to take a good look at it."

The chariot drove on slowly. Jisun Si found the creaking of the wheels was getting on his nerves. The high city wall reminded him of Yang Hu's revolt and Gongshan Buniu's attack. "Lu was almost ruined in their hands!" he thought with a shudder, but he did not want to blame himself too much for the setbacks suffered by Lu. Duke Ding's ineptitude, in his opinion, was chiefly responsible for the steady decline of the state.

Just then a grey magpie flew overhead, crying mournfully, and alighted on a willow tree by the city moat. It wobbled a little, tightening its grasp to prevent itself from falling. It went on crying mournfully, with its head cocked and its wings sagging. At the sight of the bird Jisun Si remembered the ancient saying, "When a bird is dying, its cry is pitiful; when a man is dying, his words are kind." He heaved a deep sigh for the dying magpie and for himself as tears came to his eyes.

Gazing at the city wall and gate towers as the chariot rumbled along, Jisun Si remembered how Confucius had successfully dismantled the walls of the three cities. If he and the late Duke Ding had listened to Confucius' advice and declined the gift of Qi, and worked hard for the prosperity of the state, Lu might have grown into a great power among the states. The more he thought of this the more remorseful he became. His eyes blurred and his head swam. Covering his eyes with his hand, he forced himself to calm down. "Lu was the manor of the Duke of Zhou," he said to Jisun Fei. "The Duke of Zhou is the common ancestor of our sovereign and the Mengsun, Shusun and Jisun houses. Many outstanding men have emerged in Lu, and today we have Confucius, a man of great knowledge and ability. He is so exceptional that many people are jealous of him. Despite my position as chief minister, I also felt jealous of him. Now I am sorry for what I have done. If he had been given a high official post, Lu might have become strong and prosperous. The ancients said that past experience is a guide for the future. After my death, you must try to invite Confucius back. By asking his advice, you will be able to assist His Lordship to make Lu strong!" His tone was firm, but his voice dwindled to a whisper.

Jisun Fei nodded and urged the driver to return immediately.

Back in his house, Jisun Si was already in his last breath. Jisun Fei had the servants move him onto the bed. His eyes half open, Jisun Si said in a hardly audible voice, "Remember to invite Confucius back to assist His Lordship."

Jisun Fei bent down and held his father's head in both hands. "Father, is there anything else you want to tell your son? Please speak!"

Jisun Si's lips trembled, but he stopped breathing before he could say another word.

Jisun Fei wailed for a long time, then proceeded to arrange for his father's funeral. After that he succeeded his father as chief minister.

At the morning audience one day Duke Ai of Lu had a look of despair on his face. "Honored ministers," he said, "this year our state has suffered drought and earthquake. The losses caused by such disasters are very serious, and people are left without enough to eat or wear. What shall we do about this?"

The court officials knit their brows in distress and lowered their heads.

This was the first time Jisun Fei attended an audience, so he felt a little timid. Looking around him, he stepped forward and said, "Your Lordship, the people have neither grain nor cloth. To save their lives we have to open the state granaries to relieve the hungry."

"Well," Duke Ai hesitated. "The grain storage may not be enough to feed so many people."

"There is no better alternative," said Jisun Fei.

"Your request is granted," said Duke Ai reluctantly. "The state granaries will be opened to relieve the hungry."

The court officials chanted in unison, "May His Lordship be praised for his wisdom!"

"Your Lordship," Jisun Fei said again, "before my father passed away, he spoke highly of Confucius. He bade me ask Your Lordship to invite Confucius back to Lu."

"Confucius once served as minister of justice," the duke said, resting his chin on his hand. "He left Lu because our late duke accepted the gift from Qi. Since then he has traveled to many states but failed to utilize his talents. If we call him back, he will surely agree. What do you think, honored ministers?"

A tall man with broad shoulders emerged from the rank of civil officials. His name was Gongzhi Yu. "Your Lordship," he said in a loud voice, "Confucius has left Lu for many years; it is hard to say what is on his mind just now. In my opinion, we'd better begin by inviting his disciple Ran Qiu. This is a man of exceptional ability!"

"Minister Jisun, what do you think?"

"We can invite Ran Qiu back first," replied Jisun Fei. "Then we can ask Ran Qiu to invite Confucius back."

"Who is willing to be the envoy to Chen?" asked the duke.

"Your humble official is willing to go," said Gongzhi Yu.

"That would be fine," Duke Ai said with a smile. "Get prepared and set out immediately!"

Gongzhi Yu received the order and left the palace. A dozen days later he arrived at the Chen capital.

The arrival of an envoy from Lu filled Confucius with joy. He hastily straightened his robe and went out to meet him.

Gongzhi Yu bowed with joined hands. "Master," he said, "you left Lu a few years ago and have traveled from state to state ever since. How have you been in all these years?"

"You must have something very important to tell me," said Confucius, "if you have troubled yourself to travel such a long distance."

"His Lordship has sent me to invite your disciple Ran Qiu to return to Lu," said Gongzhi Yu.

At this Confucius' face became flushed with joy.

Chapter Thirty-two

**Duke Min of Chen Hunts Auspicious Animals
Despite Confucius' Objection;
A Wu General Is Persuaded by Confucius
to Withdraw His Invading Troops**

Confucius said with a smile, "It is my duty to contribute to the welfare of Lu, my homeland. His Lordship's invitation has given Ran Qiu a chance to serve his state. I will go and tell Ran Qiu at once."

Confucius returned to his room and called Ran Qiu to him. "Ran Qiu," he said, "His Lordship and the chief minister want you to return to Lu. They will probably appoint you to a high post. I have faith in your talents for administrative affairs. I hope you will make use of this opportunity and work diligently for the benefit of Lu." He stood up and gazed to the east, then sat down again. "Though it is small and weak, Lu originated as the manor of the Duke of Zhou; it has a complete system of rites and music. Under a benign government, it won't take long for Lu to attain peace and prosperity. The other states will follow its example, and harmony will be restored to the whole world."

Ran Qiu had a blank look on his face. He knew little about the situation in Lu and therefore did not share Confucius' confidence. "If the chief minister gives me an important position," he asked, "what shall I do first?"

Wearing a worried look, Confucius replied, "Due to the serious drought this year the people of Lu are suffering for lack of food. When people do not have enough to eat, the state will not enjoy peace and stability. When you return, you should try your best to assist the chief minister and ensure that the people obtain enough food and clothing."

Ran Qiu hesitated, feeling the heavy burden on his shoulders. "I will do as you say, master," he said at last.

Moved to an intense longing for his homeland, Confucius said in a hoarse voice, "If you become a high official, do not forget to fetch me back!"

"Trust me, master!" said Ran Qiu, his eyes dimmed with tears. "I

will persuade His Lordship and the chief minister to invite you back as soon as possible."

After Ran Qiu had left, Confucius again fell into a gloomy mood. When night fell and the moon rose in the east he stood at the door, looking west to the royal capital, then east to Lu, thinking of his homeland and the king of Zhou.

When he got up the next morning, he found the courtyard strewn with leaves fallen from the ginkgo tree. He strolled back and forth, saddened by the coming of autumn. He had fallen into the habit of standing in the courtyard and watching the tall ginkgo tree after he finished teaching his disciples. He lowered his head and was startled to see that his beard had turned totally grey. "Sorrow hastens the coming of old age!" he sighed bitterly. Suddenly he threw out his chest, thinking he would go and recommend himself to Duke Min with the promise to make Chen strong and prosperous in three years. However, he was too proud to do so.

Duke Min of Chen treated Confucius with great favor, providing him with food and clothing all year round and often asked his advice on all kinds of problems. When he went out the city for an excursion, he sometimes invited Confucius to accompany him.

It snowed several times that winter. One day Duke Min asked Confucius to accompany him to the suburbs and watch his men hunting in the snow. Riding in the same chariot, they left the city by the north gate. The ground and the trees were all covered in snow.

Duke Min asked, "Master, it is very cold today. Are you all right?"

"Thanks to your warm solicitude," replied Confucius, "I have more than enough clothing and bedding for all the seasons." He lifted the hem of his robe, revealing the white lambskin underneath. "How can I feel cold wearing such fine lambskin as you have bestowed on me?"

A look of satisfaction showed in Duke Min's face as Confucius continued, "This year Chen has enjoyed good weather for the crops. The people are fortunate enough to have ample food and clothing."

Duke Min was disappointed, for Confucius did not praise him but only talked about the weather and the people. Sensing the duke's displeasure, Confucius changed the topic. He pointed to a group of running deer. "The deer is an auspicious animal. It is a good omen for Your Lordship to encounter this animal first on your excursion. Surely Chen will enjoy another bumper harvest next year."

Duke Min's face lit up with pleasure. "Listen!" he called out to the guards. "Tell the hunters to catch those deer!"

"Please don't!" cried Confucius. "The deer eat grass and cause no harm to men, so they have always been regarded as an auspicious animal. It would not be right to catch them."

The smile vanished from Duke Min's face.

Aware of the duke's displeasure, Confucius refrained from speaking again.

At Duke Min's order, the hunters spread their nets and drew their bows, closing in on the deer, which tried in vain to break out of the encirclement. The hunters shot their arrows from all directions, and the deer fell to the ground one after another. At the sight of this Confucius began to feel an aversion to Duke Min. How could such an ignorant ruler run the state well?

"Wonderful!" exclaimed Duke Min, looking at the dead deer on the ground. "Wonderful!" He no longer paid any attention to Confucius.

Confucius could not bear it any longer. He sighed heavily and closed his eyes, not saying a single word.

Duke Min finally regained his composure. Taking a glance at Confucius, he folded his arms and stopped shouting. When the hunters had gathered all the deer, he ordered, "Return to the palace!"

The snow had begun to melt. Drawn by four strong horses, the chariot drove slowly along the muddy road. On their return to the capital, they found icicles of various shapes hanging from the eaves of many houses. Reflecting the sun, the icicles appeared beautiful.

Confucius was not in the mood to enjoy the view. Once they entered the city, he took leave of Duke Min and returned to the hostel. After that, although Duke Min continued to treat him as an honored guest, he no longer felt the same toward the duke. Confucius and his disciples stayed in Chen for three years, during which time the state of Jin grew steadily strong and often fought with Chu, the big southern state. Caught between the two powers, Chen suffered many disturbances.

One day in spring of the sixth year of Duke Ai of Lu's reign (489 B.C.) Confucius gazed at the tender leaves in the ginkgo tree and sighed with sorrow. He was already sixty-two. At that time a man seldom lived to be seventy years old. "I don't have many years to live," he mumbled to himself. He did not want to stay on in Chen, but where could he go? Wei was excluded because Duke Chu of Wei had no qualms of conscience even though his father, Kuai Kui, was still in exile. He could not be regarded as a legitimate ruler. The state of Jin was strong, but the court was presided over by Zhao Jianzi, who adopted a warlike policy, discarded the rites, and eliminated those who disagreed with him. The state of Song was small and weak, and it had barbarous men like Huan Tui at the helm. As for Qi, Duke Jing of Qi had died and was succeeded by his son Yan Ruzi, about whom Confucius knew very little. Finally he thought about Chu in the south. Prince Zhao of Chu had ruled for twenty-seven years. Though he was advanced in years, he still had high ambitions. Under his rule Chu was strong enough to challenge Jin openly. Confucius finally decided to try his fortune with Prince Zhao of Chu, who he hoped would share his political views.

The disciples were all glad when Confucius told them his decision, and together they began packing.

The next morning they called on Duke Min to say good-bye and started out toward Chu.

Three days later they reached the Chen-Cai border. Coming to a junction of three roads, they were about to head for Chu by way of Cai when a contingent of troops emerged in the southeast, carrying a banner embroidered with the character "Wu." Confucius gave a gasp of astonishment, for he knew this must be an invading army.

The army was indeed sent by the prince of Wu, Fu Chai, to invade Chen. In their conflicts Chu and Jin often used Chen as a springboard. Fu Chai wanted to check the expansion of Chu and Jin by subduing Chen and turning it into a protectorate.

The chariot carrying the general's banner stopped in front of Confucius. A hefty man stood up in the chariot and pointed at Confucius with his sword. "Hey," he shouted in a gruff voice. "Who are you? Why have you come here with these chariots? Are you sent by Chen to stop me?"

Confucius walked up to the man slowly and asked, "Where are you coming from, general? And where are you going?"

The man pointed to the general's banner above his head. "I am sent by the prince of Wu," he said haughtily, "to lead an expedition against Chen."

"At present Wu is strong and Chen weak," said Confucius. "And it is the duty for the strong to help the weak. If Wu uses its strength to bully the weak, is it not going against benevolence and righteousness? How can you justify Wu's action?"

The Wu general did not know what to say.

"The ancient men of virtue did not oppose all wars," continued Confucius, "for a war may be either just or unjust. When it aims to help the kind and punish the wicked, to save the weak against the strong, people will support it. If its aims are to help the wicked and bully the weak, people will curse it. Since you have come to attack Chen without a just cause, the people of Chen will put up a desperate fight, and the neighboring states will undoubtedly help Chen and regard Wu as their common enemy. You will be widely denounced even if you gain a victory, for you have chosen evil over righteousness. If you lose the battle, you will bring great losses to Wu as well as Chen. In either case you will be committing an unpardonable crime!"

The Wu general was struck speechless by Confucius' argument. He looked back at the large contingent of troops and muttered, "Well, I don't know...."

Confucius said, "In my opinion, you should lower your banners and muffle your drums, and lead the troops back to Wu. By doing this you will save both Chen and your men from a grave calamity." He pointed to the ranks of the Wu army. "You are standing at the junction of the roads. If you chose the right path, you will achieve your goal. If you choose the wrong path, you will not only fail to reach your goal but ruin your reputation forever. Which course will you follow? This is a question you must decide for yourself!"

"May I have your honorable name?" asked the Wu general.

"This is—" Zi Lu said hastily.

Beckoning Zi Lu to stop, Confucius bowed with joined hands. "I am Kong Qiu from Lu."

The Wu general rubbed his eyes and stared at Confucius, then leapt out of the chariot and knelt. "Wuma Cheng had eyes but failed to see. Please forgive me, master!"

Confucius walked up to him and helped him up with both hands. "You overwhelm me with a salute I do not deserve, general."

"You are a sage of our time," said Wuma Cheng excitedly, getting on his feet. "It is a blessing from Heaven for me to meet you!"

Confucius was more concerned over the fate of the Chen people. "General Wuma," he asked anxiously, "what do you think of what I just said?"

"All your words are like jewels. I will write to the prince advising him against attacking Chen. I will go back with the troops as soon as I receive his edict."

Confucius smiled joyfully. "I admire you deeply for your adherence to righteousness!"

"Make camp on the spot!" Wuma Cheng ordered his officers. "Anyone who harasses the local inhabitants will be executed!" He turned and said to Confucius, "Master, you are one of the people I admire most. Let me be your host for a few days!"

Confucius gladly accepted the invitation. He introduced his disciples and followed Wuma Cheng to the roadside.

By this time the soldiers had set up the general's tent. Wuma Cheng took Confucius' left arm in both hands and led him into the tent. After they were seated as host and guest, Confucius began explaining his views on benevolence, righteousness, rites, wisdom and honesty. Wuma Cheng was filled with admiration.

That night Wuma Cheng wrote a letter and sent it to the prince of Wu by a mounted messenger.

In the meanwhile Duke Min of Chen was filled with trepidation at the news of the oncoming Wu army. He had ruled Chen peacefully for thirteen years and had no idea how to fight wars. He summoned all the court officials to discuss the situation and prepare for resistance, at the same time sending an envoy to Chu to ask for help.

When he received the news, Prince Zhao of Chu also held an audience to discuss the matter. They decided to send some troops to rescue Chen. In addition, an envoy was dispatched to the Chen-Cai border to invite Confucius to come to Chu.

Wuma Cheng's letter sent Fu Chai into a rage. "How can a general be stopped from attack by a few words!" he roared to his officials, who expressed different opinions over the incident. After a while Fu Chai calmed down. However, considering it again, he said, "There is some truth in what Confucius said. An expedition should be launched for a good cause. Chen is a small state that does not pose any threat to us. By attacking it I would give people a good reason to criticize me." After much consideration he decided to cancel the expedition and call Wuma Cheng back.

One day Wuma Cheng was talking with Confucius in the tent when a messenger arrived with the prince of Wu's letter. Wuma Cheng hurriedly got up from his seat to receive it. Spreading the yellow silk he read the following: "Honored minister, you benefited from the words of Confucius, and I have benefited from yours. A calamity has been avoided, and benevolence and righteousness retained. You are ordered to gather the troops and return immediately." After he finished reading, tears welled up in his eyes. With both hands he handed the silk to Confucius.

Confucius was also greatly moved. "General Wuma," he said, smiling, "please get ready to go. After seeing you off I will head for Chu by way of Cai."

Wuma Cheng ordered pigs and sheep to be slaughtered to feast the troops and invited Confucius and his disciples to join in the celebration of the averting of an imminent war. "Master," he said to Confucius with full sincerity, "I have benefited a great deal even though we met only a few days ago. I admire you for your noble character and broad vision and will make your instruction my lifelong motto."

"I am not worthy of such praise," said Confucius uneasily.

Wuma Cheng leapt onto his chariot and turned back, bowing with joined hands. "Take care, master! We'll meet again!"

"Take care, general!" said Confucius, returning the salute. "We'll meet again!"

Gazing after the retreating Wu troops, Confucius was filled with delight, for what had just happened seemed to testify to the power of the rule by rites. If the ruler was virtuous, benevolence and justice would prevail. He gazed until the Wu troops had gone out of sight, then called on his disciples to resume their journey.

They made their way to the southwest in high spirits. The field was green with trees and grass. Confucius felt so lighthearted that he wanted to sing. Suddenly he heard a child's voice singing a children's rhyme:

> When crossing the river
> The prince of Chu got a fruit of duckweed.
> It was as big as a dou measure,
> As red as the sun.
> When cut open and tasted,
> It was as sweet as honey.

Confucius looked into the distance and saw a small boy sitting on a buffalo. He held a short flute in his left hand and a piece of willow in his right hand. As he sang, he lightly touched the buffalo on its head and its thick and crooked horns. When he finished the song, he placed the willow under his leg and began to play the flute. The tune came out loud and clear; first it was "The Seventh Month," then "Big Mice," both songs being from *The Book of Poetry*. Confucius and his disciples were astonished by the expertise with which the small boy played these tunes. The music reminded Confucius of the days when he served as keeper of granaries in Lu.

Climbing up a slope, they found themselves facing a land of downs. Confucius' thoughts drifted to the downs in his hometown, the scenery by the Sishui River, the land and people of Lu. He was stabbed by an intense longing.

When they came to a big river, Confucius got down from the chariot and gazed at the stream flowing gently. Green reeds grew on the dike, and flocks of gulls strolled in the river. An angler sat motionless in a small boat floating downstream.

Confucius looked around but did not see the ferry crossing. He turned to Zi Lu and said, "Zi Lu, go and inquire where the ferry crossing is. We have to cross the river."

Zi Lu climbed over the dike and saw two old men, one tall and the other short, driving a buffalo to plough the field. He went up and bowed with his hands joined in front of his chest. "Could you tell me where I can find the ferry across the river?"

The taller man asked, "May I know who you are?"

"I am a native of Lu," replied Zi Lu. "My family name is Zhong, my given name You, and my styled name Zi Lu. My I have your honorable name?"

The short one said, "I am called Chang Ju, and he is called Jie Ni. Who is the man gazing at the stream over there?"

Zi Lu said proudly, "He is my master."

"Who is your master?" asked Chang Ju.

"Kong Qiu," replied Zi Lu.

"Which Kong Qiu?"

"Kong Qiu from Lu."

Chang Ju smiled contemptuously. "Is he not a sage who knows everything under the sun?"

Zi Lu was astonished by this response.

"In that case," continued Chang Ju, "he already knows where the ferry crossing is."

Zi Lu frowned with displeasure.

Jie Ni said in a deprecating tone, "At present there are more evil people than good in the world. You have been following your master to escape the evil in search of the good. Where can you find them? Why do you not, like us, withdraw to a remote place and live a carefree life?" With this he went on ploughing the field, paying no more attention to Zi Lu.

Zi Lu returned to the riverside despondently and recounted the words of Chang Ju and Jie Ni to Confucius.

Confucius was disappointed to hear Zi Lu's story. "Since we are unable to live in remote mountains with birds and beasts," he said, "what do we live for if we stop dealing with people? If people were living in peace and harmony, I would not have to leave my homeland and wander from place to place. Some men in power adopt a warlike policy and try to bully others into submission, thus bringing great suffering to the people. That is why I strive for a benevolent government that rules according to the rites. If everyone should follow the example of Chang Ju and Jie Ni, who would work on behalf of benevolence and virtue?"

By this time the small boat carrying the angler had drifted near them. Zi Lu went up and learned the location of the ferry crossing from the angler. They proceeded there and crossed the river.

Sulking over the words of the two old men, Zi Lu gradually lagged behind the others. As he hurried on the way, he met an old man carrying a hoe on his walking stick. Zi Lu saluted him and asked, "Did you see my master?"

"Who is your master?" asked the old man.

"Confucius from the state of Lu," replied Zi Lu.

"How can he be called a master," said the old man, "if he does not toil with his four limbs and can not tell the five grains apart?"

"May I have your honorable name?" asked Zi Lu.

"A humble man like me has no use for a name," said the old man. "People call me He Tiao, the Basket Carrier."

Zi Lu hastened his steps and caught up with Confucius and repeated the old man's words to him.

Confucius said, "This is a recluse. Let's go back and find him."

They returned to where the old man had been but, to Confucius' disappointment, he had already disappeared. "Chang Ju, Jie Ni and He Tiao are all very learned men," said Confucius to his disciples.

"Unfortunately they chose to protect themselves from the evils in the world instead of taking office and working for a benevolent government. How can one shirk one's duties like this!" They turned back and resumed their journey. After traveling for some time, they heard a loud cry. A large band of troops emerged and surrounded them tightly.

Chapter Thirty-three

Confucius and His Disciples Starve
at the Chen-Cai Boundary;
The Magistrate of She Is Impressed
by Confucius' Teaching

Formerly, when they learned of Prince Zhao of Chu's intention to employ Confucius, many court officials of Chen became worried and went to advise Duke Min of Chen. According to them, Confucius was a very virtuous and capable man, who advocated the practice of ancient sage kings, criticized the defects in the various states, and opposed everything that went against the rites. Now the big state of Chu was sending an envoy to fetch him. Once he arrived in Chu and took up a high position, small states like Chen would have no choice but to submit and pay tribute to Chu. They hoped Duke Min would find a way to deal with this as soon as possible.

Duke Min of Chen regretted having let his own opportunity slip by and became aware of his ineptitude as a ruler of the state. "How stupid I was to allow a bright pearl to fall into someone else's hands!" he lamented to himself.

The court officials waited anxiously for him to make a decision.

The duke rested his chin on his hand and thought for a long time. Finally he said slowly, "At present we have no choice but to send people to invite Confucius and his disciples to return."

"That wouldn't do, Your Lordship!" cried one of the officials. "Confucius lived in our state for three years without obtaining any official post. If we send for him right after he left, people in other states would surely laugh at us."

Duke Min was at a loss. "I am at my wits' end!" he sighed.

A military official stepped out of the rank and suggested, "Your Lordship, in my opinion we could send some men to intercept Confucius and his disciples. We could conceal our identity and encircle them without doing them any actual harm until they can no longer bear the hunger and thirst. Then we would open up our encirclement and allow them to return to our state."

Duke Min clapped his hands in appreciation. "A marvelous plan indeed!" he exclaimed. "When Confucius returns, I will consider carefully how to make good use of him."

Thereupon a band of troops was dispatched forthwith.

The state of Cai had been ruled by Marquis Cheng for two years. He was a ruler who had neither experience nor ability. At the suggestion of his court officials, he also sent some men to intercept Confucius.

When the two bands of troops met they were at first very hostile, but after they learned each other's intention, they decided to coordinate their action. Together they surrounded Confucius and his disciples in the wilderness.

Confucius looked with surprise at the troops carrying no banners to identify themselves. Their intention was unknown, for they formed an encirclement but did not launch any attack. When he spoke to them, they acted as if they were both deaf and dumb. Confucius bade his disciples hoist the hoods of the chariots and made them temporary dwelling places. Luckily, beside the road there was an old house, where Confucius and a few of the weaker disciples could find shelter.

It was spring, and it was chilly in the morning but sultry at noon. Confucius and his disciples had to suffer both hunger and cold every day. After three days they all became haggard and listless.

Confucius kept up his talks about *The Book of Poetry*, *The Book of Rites* and *The Book of Changes* to his disciples. Sometimes he played the zither and sang aloud to cheer them up. On the fourth day he looked around at his disciples' distressed expressions and sat down with his zither. Licking his parched lips, he began to play and sing.

> Along the road damp with dew
> I travel in the morning and at night,
> To avoid the dew on the road.

As was common in *The Book of Poetry*, this poem also featured the ample use of metaphors. Confucius sang with deep emotion, though his voice was hoarse.

> Who said the sparrow has no horn?
> Why did it pass through my house?
> Who said you are not married?
> Why did you throw me into prison?
> Even if you throw me into prison,

You still have no reason to take me as your bride.

In the face of the present misfortune, Confucius had a deeper understanding of the heroine in the poem who defied brutal force.

Who said the mouse has no teeth?
Why did it pass through my wall?
Who said you are not married?
Why did you accuse me of breaking the law?
Even if you accuse me of breaking the law,
I will not be your bride!

The indignant, fiery outpourings of the heroine in the song were used by Confucius to scold his besiegers, who responded with simpering and snickering, for they were too stupid to grasp the meaning of the song.

As Confucius put down the zither, Zi Lu came up and said with irritation, "Master, we've been held up here for three days. Some of my fellow disciples are too hungry to sit up squarely. Why don't we find a way of escape instead of playing the zither and singing songs!"

Confucius turned to look at the soldiers all around them. "How can we get out of this tight encirclement?"

Zi Lu began to grow restless. He squared his shoulders and said, "Let me go and fight it out with them!"

"There you go again, Zi Lu. Though you are strong and brave, you have no hope of overpowering so many armed soldiers. Even if they were unarmed, they could overwhelm us by their sheer number."

"So we have no choice but to stay here and perish?"

"Heaven will always leave a door open. Perhaps we are fated to suffer through this difficult situation."

Zi Lu went off without being convinced.

On the fifth day Confucius felt weak and limp all over his body. At nightfall he sat on a pile of hay in the old house, his back against the earthen wall. Gazing at the crescent moon, he began to feel a bit lonely. "Zi Lu!" he called out.

Zi Lu answered his call and came into the house.

"In the *Book of Poetry*," said Confucius, "there are two lines: 'Not being fierce tigers or wild oxen/ Why should they roam in the wilderness?' I have always considered my propositions correct, but why should we suffer this infliction?"

"We haven't done anything evil, so we deserve no such infliction.

However, our good behavior has always brought us misfortune. Time and again we were besieged by evil people. Perhaps people do not believe you because you lack benevolence and virtue. Or maybe people fail to follow your advice because you lack wisdom."

"Why should you speak like that? Do you suppose a man will surely come to a good end if he is benevolent and virtuous? In your opinion, were Bo Yi and Shu Qi men of virtue?"

"Of course they were."

"In spite of that, they starved to death in Shouyang Mountain."

Zi Lu did not know what to say.

"And do you suppose," continued Confucius, "a man will surely be promoted if he is capable? In your opinion, was Bi Gan a capable man?"

"Yes, he surely was," replied Zi Lu.

"Yet King Zhou murdered him by plucking out his heart."

Aware of his mistake, Zi Lu fell silent, panting heavily.

"Do you suppose good advice will surely be followed? If that were the case, Wu Zixu would not have been killed. People like Bo Yi, Shu Qi, Bi Gan and Wu Zixu suffered misfortune because they were not in harmony with their time. Since the primeval past there have been numerous instances in which people of virtue and wisdom failed to achieve anything and died with deep regret; what's so strange about the adversity we are facing now? However, there is something you must bear in mind: The orchid growing in a remote mountain does not stop giving off fragrance even though there is no one to smell it. Neither will a man of benevolence and virtue relinquish his cause because of temporary setbacks."

At this Zi Lu retreated wordlessly.

Confucius then called Zi Gong into the house and repeated the words he had just spoken.

"Superior songs find few singers," said Zi Gong. "It is exactly because your propositions are too lofty and too unattainable that people object to you."

Confucius straightened his face with disapproval. "Zi Gong! A farmer may be skilled at ploughing the field and planting crops but he may not be good at harvesting. A craftsman may be able to produce superb handiwork, but it is impossible for him to master every craft. A man of virtue and benevolence strives to cultivate and improve himself constantly but may not seek to obtain others' understanding and support. At present you only want to obtain understanding and support from the others but make no efforts to enhance your virtue or improve your learning. In my opinion, you can not be said to have high aims and great foresight. You do not stand high enough."

At this Zi Gong retreated in silence.

Confucius then called Yan Hui into the house and repeated his conversations with Zi Lu and Zi Gong to him.

Yan Hui thought for a while, then said, "Your ideal has been widely rejected just because it is perfect. In spite of rejection, you endeavored to put it into practice and consequently brought prosperity to Zhongdu and strength to the state of Lu. His Lordship's failure to employ you is an irredeemable shame and regret for the state of Lu! Why should you worry over this, master? Your rejection by the world only testifies to the excellence of your teaching and virtue."

"Yan Hui," exclaimed Confucius, "you are a man of great intelligence and virtue! If you should become a powerful minister, I would be your head steward."

Yan Hui fell on his knees. "Master," he said uneasily, "you joke, for I do not deserve such praise!"

"Do get up quickly!" said Confucius. "So we can continue our conversation."

The two of them went on with their discussion and became so absorbed that they forgot all about hunger and fatigue.

At daybreak Zi Gong approached the house carrying two baskets of grain on a shoulder pole, his face covered in sweat.

Pleased, Confucius hurriedly went up to meet him. "Where did you get these, Zi Gong?"

"I bought them in a peasant's home nearby when the soldiers fell asleep at night."

Confucius broke into a smile.

Zi Lu and Yan Hui brought three rocks on which they set up their pot. The other disciples fetched water and gathered firewoods. Yan Hui was good at cooking for he came from a very poor family. He volunteered to light the fire and cook the rice.

Under the eaves of the thatched house there was a cobweb. Caught in the rising smoke and steam, the spider scurried into the cogongrass. As smoke and steam continued to rise, the cobweb drooped and hung low over Yan Hui's head.

Yan Hui, immersed in tending the fire, did not notice the cobweb.

When the rice was almost done, the cobweb suddenly dropped on it. Yan Hui hastily tried to grab the cobweb with his hand. He caught it with some rice grains stuck on it. Unwilling to throw the stained rice away, he picked out the grains one by one and ate them all.

When Zi Gong, who was fetching water from the well, saw Yan Hui moving his lips he thought he was eating rice on the sly, so he returned to the thatched house and asked Confucius, "Master, does a benevolent and virtuous man sometimes tarnish his integrity?"

Confucius was surprised by Zi Gong's question. "A man of virtue and benevolence never tarnishes his integrity," he replied. "Otherwise he can no longer be called a man of virtue and benevolence."

Zi Gong pulled a long face and said indignantly, "When I went to fetch water from the well, I saw Yan Hui eating rice stealthily. Wouldn't that be an instance of tarnishing one's integrity?"

Confucius started, then shook his head slowly. "Zi Gong," he said, "years ago I thought Yan Hui a benevolent man and I still think so. Though you claim to have seen him eating rice secretly, I can not believe he could have done such a thing. There must be some reason behind that."

Zi Gong was not convinced, thinking that Confucius was making excuses for Yan Hui, but before he could say anything Confucius waved him silent. "You don't have to argue, Zi Gong. I'll call Yan Hui over and ask him what happened." He walked out of the house.

"Master," Yan Hui said delightfully. "The rice is cooked. Let's have our meal!"

Confucius put on a stern expression. "Yan Hui, did you help yourself to rice when you were cooking it?"

Yan Hui stood respectfully with his hands at the sides when he replied, "When I was cooking the rice, a cobweb dropped on it. I took the cobweb out of the pot, but it carried some grains of rice on it. To put the stained rice back into the pot would stain the rest of the rice, but to throw them away would be too wasteful. So I ate them." He pointed to the rice in the pot. "Look, master! There is still some trace of the cobweb left there."

Confucius smiled. "If I had been cooking the rice, I would have done exactly the same." He turned to Zi Gong. "I have believed in Yan Hui's benevolence for a long time."

After that Zi Gong began to hold Yan Hui in respect.

Having gone without food for several days, the disciples felt their stomach churning and their mouths all watered at the smell of the cooked rice.

"My disciples," said Confucius, "we have not eaten for quite a few days. If an extremely hungry man eats a big meal, he will become sick. So let each of us take only a small bowl of rice."

After the meal they felt a little better, and Confucius decided to expound *The Book of Changes* to them.

Zi Lu was too preoccupied with their plight to study anything. "Master," he asked somewhat impatiently, "does a superior man also have worries?"

"What?" Confucius hesitated a little, then replied firmly, "A superior man has no worries." He thought for a while, then continued, "A superior man, when he has not yet attained benevolence, studies hard in order to attain it. After attaining benevolence, he strives to uphold and enhance it. He regards honor and wealth as floating clouds; since he does not strive for them, why should he worry about losing them? Therefore a superior man is always calm and well at ease. He rejoices all his life and does not worry for a single day."

"What about a petty man?" asked Zi Lu.

"The reverse is true of a petty man. A petty man strives for profits instead of righteousness. When he has not obtained profits, he worries all day for failing to obtain them. Having obtained profits, he worries all day for fear of losing them. Therefore a petty man is always anxious. He worries all his life and does not enjoy a single day of joy."

Zi Lu mused over Confucius' words and found them reasonable. His heart sank, however, when he turned to look at the soldiers all around them.

On the seventh day several disciples, including Yan Hui, Min Shun and Gao Chai, fell seriously ill. Confucius had them lie down in the thatched house and felt their foreheads. "You've got a fever!" He went out the house to the roadside, where he walked back and forth, unable to find a solution.

All the other disciples were very anxious and downcast. They sat on the ground and brooded in silence.

Zi Lu's eyes bulged with rage, and he clenched his fists tightly. He wanted to go and fight it out with their besiegers.

Gongliang Ru also lost his cool, stamping his feet and biting his teeth.

At noon they heard a loud shout. The soldiers fell into a

commotion and scattered in all directions.

Confucius felt puzzled at the sight. Just then a war chariot drove toward him, carrying a banner embroidered with the character "Chu."

The disciples, not knowing what was happening, gathered around Confucius protectively.

Zi Lu and Gongliang Ru drew their swords and went to meet the oncoming chariot.

Fearing that they would start a fight, Confucius followed them. "Zi Lu, Gongliang Ru, don't act rashly!" he called after them.

The chariot stopped, and out leapt a hefty man. He wore a suit of armor, a general's cap and a sword at his waist, its red tassels dangling to his knee.

Walking up to Confucius and his retinue, the man bowed with clasped hands. "May I ask who is Confucius from Lu?"

"Why are you looking for Confucius, general?" asked Zi Lu apprehensively.

"I have come at Prince Zhao of Chu's order to invite Confucius to come to our humble state."

Confucius felt greatly relieved. "I am Kong Qiu from Lu," he said.

The man made a deep bow. "Master, Prince Zhao respects you for your character and admires you for your ability. He has sent me to invite you to come to our humble state and help govern it well. Unfortunately I did not arrive in time to prevent you and your disciples from being ensnared by those villains."

Confucius was much moved by these words and a warm feeling rose in his heart. "May I learn your honorable name, general?" he asked with a smile.

The man stood at attention and replied modestly, "My family name is Shen, my given name Gong, and my styled name Zi Gong."

"I have done nothing for Chu," said Confucius, "yet Prince Zhao has bestowed me with this great favor, and General Shen has come such a long distance to receive me. Such kindness I will never forget!"

"You are too modest, master. Please have your luggage packed up. We will set out without delay."

Confucius bade Zi Lu, Gongliang Ru and a few other strong disciples help the sick ones get onto the chariots, and they started off for the state of Chu. Shen Gong led the way in his general's chariot, and his troops, riding in nearly a hundred chariots, brought up the rear.

When it began to grow dark they arrived at a small town. "Master," Shen Gong said to Confucius, "it is getting late. Let's stay the night here."

"Please take charge of everything, General Shen," said Confucius.

Shen Gong arranged for Confucius and his party to stay in an inn, where they had a meal. Then he ordered the troops to make camp outside the town.

After supper Confucius sent Zi Gong to find a local doctor, who examined the sick disciples, diagnosed cold and prescribed herbal medicine for them. It was not until midnight that the medicine was concocted and taken by the patients.

The next morning, Yan Hui, Min Shun and the other disciples who had been sick felt much relieved and expressed their wonder at the skill of the local doctor. After breakfast Shen Gong arrived and urged Confucius to mount the chariot to continue their journey. Confucius could not help smiling at his impulsiveness, so typical of a general.

As they continued on, a chariot met them head-on. Confucius took a close look and cried out, "Yang Jin!"

"Master!" Yang Jin also cried out in surprise.

Both of them had their chariots stop abruptly, got out and walked toward each other.

"What a blessing," said Yang Jin with a broad smile, "for me to meet you here so unexpectedly!"

Confucius gazed at Yang Jin's wrinkle-covered face. "Yang, how have you been since we last met?"

"Not too bad."

"Where have you been traveling all these years?"

Yang Jin frowned and said with a sigh, "Master, it would take a long time to describe what I've been through! After our meeting by the Yellow River that summer, I traveled to Qi, Lu, Wu, Yue and Chu." He sighed again. "People flaunt military strength and disregard rites and righteousness. The same is true wherever I go."

Prince Zhao of Chu's courteous invitation had raised Confucius' hope, but Yang Jin's words made his heart sink again.

"How did you spend the past few years?" asked Yang Jin.

"It's a long story. I've been to Wei, Song, Zheng and Chen, where I failed to find anyone to listen to my advice. Instead, on several occasions we were harassed by local villains."

"It seems that our dream will never come true," rejoined Yang Jin.

Confucius threw out his chest and said firmly, "I still believe the words of the ancient sages that someday the whole world will become one community."

"I don't doubt this, but I wonder how long we will have to wait for the day to come."

"The progress of the Great Way can be compared to the Yellow River. It has many twists and turns along the way and sometimes even goes backward, but it will finally flow into the East Sea."

"Where are you heading in such a grand style?" asked Yang Jin, looking at the Chu troops.

"Prince Zhao of Chu has sent General Shen to invite me. Why don't you come to Chu with me?"

"I am returning to my homeland," replied Yang Jin blandly. "Please forgive me!"

Confucius was disappointed. He gazed at Yang Jin for a long time and finally said sadly, "Please take care!"

"You too, master!" Yang Jin responded, his eyes glistening with tears.

They bade each other farewell and mounted their chariots to resume their respective journeys.

The contingent of Chu troops marched toward Chu. Shen Gong pointed to the city in the distance. "Master, that is the city of She."

"General Shen," said Confucius, "since we have arrived in She, I would like to pay a visit to the magistrate of She. You may lead the troops and return to the capital ahead of me."

Shen Gong hesitated. "Master, you were harassed by some evil people in Cai. Though we are already in Chu territory, I do not think it safe to leave you."

"You needn't worry. It is not far from the Chu capital. I will stay at the magistrate of She's residence for some three days, after which I will hasten to the capital to call on Prince Zhao. You may return to the capital and report this to the prince."

As Confucius would not change his mind, Shen Gong bade him good-bye and left with the troops.

Zi Lu looked at Confucius with puzzlement. "Master, what kind of a man is this magistrate of She? I don't think I have heard of him."

"His name is Shen Zhuliang, and his styled name is Zi Gao."

"Is he a man of virtue?"

"Haven't you heard that like attracts like? I am going to call on him. So what kind of a man do you suppose he is likely to be?"

Shen Zhuliang was overjoyed to learn that Confucius was coming to visit him. At the head of his subordinates, he went out to the gate of his office to receive Confucius. "Heaven has sent you to Chu, master," he said, "so that I am blessed with the opportunity to meet you."

"Your fame as a virtuous man has traveled far and wide," said Confucius. "It has been a long-time wish of mine to call on you."

The two of them walked into the office hand in hand. After they had taken their seats, Confucius introduced his disciples. "Master," asked the magistrate of She, "I have served in my present position for many years but failed to achieve much. Would you please tell me the most important thing for an official?"

Confucius looked at the magistrate's emaciated appearance and bright eyes, and thought for a while. "Those in office must first win people's support. You may be said to have achieved a great deal if you can make the people under your rule live in contentment and attract people to come from faraway places."

"For lack of talents, I dare not hope to achieve a great deal. However, I will try my best to follow your advice."

"I am so glad that you would say so."

"There's something I have been puzzling over for quite some time," said the magistrate. "I would like to hear your opinion."

"Please tell me about it."

"In my hometown there was an extremely straight and honest man. When his father stole a sheep, he went to inform the owner. As a result, his father suffered a lawsuit. Now tell me, master, wasn't this man being unfilial?"

"Of course he was being unfilial," replied Confucius without hesitation. "The relationship between father and son should not be taken so lightly. The father should conceal the son's mistakes, and the son should do the same for his father. That is what I call straightness and honesty."

Zi Lu, totally unconvinced, shook his head and was about to speak, but Zi Gong stopped him with a wink. However, his face was flushed with indignation.

After supper Zi Lu went to Confucius' room and asked bluntly, "Master, were you speaking your mind when you talked with the magistrate today?"

"Yes, I was."

"If the father conceals all the son's wrongdoings, and the son does the same for his father, how can we tell right from wrong, or black from white?"

Confucius was struck speechless by the question. After a while he said, "Zi Lu! It is you who can truly be called a straight and honest person! Whenever I make a mistake, you always point it out to me. Now I realize that what I said to the magistrate was not correct."

Zi Lu smiled happily. Two days later he called on the magistrate of She. "What my master said to you the other day was not right," said Zi Lu. "He has become aware of his mistake and sent me to tell you about it."

After hearing him out, the magistrate heaved a deep sigh. "Confucius is indeed a sage! Once he makes a mistake, he admits it and makes correction. A real sage indeed!" He turned to Zi Lu and asked, "You have followed Confucius for the past twenty or thirty years, so you must know your master very well. Please tell me, what kind of a man he is?"

Zi Lu, finding the question too difficult to answer, did not reply.

The magistrate of She looked at him attentively, waiting for him to say something. Zi Lu thought for a long time but still could not find an appropriate answer.

Chapter Thirty-four

Gao Chai Redresses a Wrong;
Confucius Explains the Importance
of Rectifying Names

Not knowing how to reply to the magistrate of She's question, Zi Lu returned and told Confucius about it.

"You could have answered the question," said Confucius, "by saying something like this: He is the kind of person who studies very hard to the point of forgetting his meals and sleep, never tires of teaching others what he has learned, and is always so happy as to forget his worries and the approach of old age. What else is there to say? I am just such a man."

Just then General Shen was announced.

Confucius quickly straightened his own robe and went out the door to receive the guest.

Shen Gong strode into the room and said in a sonorous voice, "Master, though Prince Zhao is ill, he thinks about you constantly and hopes you can teach him how to govern the state of Chu. Please set out as soon as possible!"

"Such kindness and sincerity is hard to resist," said Confucius. He turned to his disciples. "Get the chariots ready. We shall leave without delay."

When they arrived at the capital of Chu, they found it traversed by a river, and the streets were lined with flowers. Though he found the scenery attractive, Confucius was eager to meet with the ruler of Chu. He did not linger in the street but followed Shen Gong straight to the palace to call on Prince Zhao of Chu.

Prince Zhao had a haggard look due to illness and old age but his face lit up on seeing Confucius. "Master, it is most fortunate of me to have this chance to meet you!"

At that time language differed from state to state. When teaching *The Book of Poetry* and *The Book of Documents* and speaking on formal occasions, Confucius always used the standard language of Zhou instead of the Lu dialect. As the dialects of Lu and Chu were very much different, Confucius again used the standard Zhou language

when he addressed Prince Zhao. "Kong Qiu is greatly honored by your kind reception!"

"I have ruled this state for twenty-seven years," said the prince. "During all this time I managed to achieve a few things, which fall far short of my expectation. Now I am fatally ill and don't have much time left. I would die with everlasting regret if I leave Chu in such conditions. However, it seems that I am unequal to the task of restoring Chu to its former glory. What can I do?"

"Government is founded on the principle of uprightness," said Confucius. "If the ruler can formulate regulations and issue orders reasonably and his ministers take the lead in following them, the common people will offer their support. When he has the people's support, there will be harmony all across the land and the state will grow rich and strong."

Prince Zhao was delighted to hear these words. "Master, will you help me achieve this if I appoint you to high office?"

Confucius had gone through too many ups and downs in the various states to get excited at the offer. "Since you think so highly of me," he said, "how dare I not obey!"

"You may now return to your guesthouse to rest from your long journey," said the prince. "As soon as I get things ready, I will send for you."

As soon as Confucius had left Prince Zhao of Chu summoned his court officials for a counsel. "My honored ministers," he said, "thanks to the benefits of the Yangtze River, the state of Chu boasts fertile land, rich resources, and a large population. If well governed, it will surely become a great power. The arrival of Confucius is a precious opportunity bestowed by Heaven. He is a man of exceptional ability. When he was magistrate of Zhongdu, he made remarkable achievements in a single year. When he was chief of justice for Lu, he governed the state so well that people did not take any articles left by the wayside and did not have to bolt their doors at night. And when he accompanied Duke Ding of Lu to the Jiagu meeting, he won a splendid diplomatic victory for Lu against Qi." As he spoke, he forgot all about his illness, and his face was flushed with excitement. "Therefore I intend to use his service and enfeoff him with seven hundred li of land at Shushe."

The court officials reacted differently to the prince's words. Some cried out their approval, some were speechless with astonishment, and some would not say a word in comment. An official named Zi Xi said, "Your Highness, in the opinion of your humble servant, Confucius is indeed a man of remarkable ability. However, what he advocates is mostly things of the past. Nowadays when people rely on military strength to attain their ends he keeps canvassing for the restoration of ancient rites. That's why he has so far failed to obtain a high post in the many states he visited. Furthermore, one can not but wonder if he harbors some ulterior motive while traveling in the various states. Many of his disciples are no ordinary people. In the court of Chu, in diplomacy no one is equal to Duanmu Ci; in assisting the sovereign no one is equal to Yan Hui; in leading troops to go to war, no one is equal to Zi Lu; and in governing a reign, no one is equal to Zai Yu. If they serve Your Highness wholeheartedly, Chu will surely grow strong and prosperous. However, ..." He knitted his brows with apprehension. "Most of them are natives of Lu. If they should have some sinister designs against us, our beloved homeland would be ruined in their hands."

The sallow face of Prince Zhao turned gloomy. He heaved a deep sigh, not knowing what to do. He looked at his ministers expectantly, but none of them ventured to speak up again. The hall was silent as the grave. Finally he swayed his broad sleeves and said in a discontented tone, "We shall discuss the matter on another occasion. The audience is over!"

Confucius and his disciples stayed in the guesthouse for over half a year without receiving any message from Prince Zhao. They were in very low spirits. One day Confucius had just finished teaching his disciples when a palace messenger arrived with the news of Prince Zhao's demise. Confucius and his disciples went to the court to offer their condolences. After that, they bade Shen Gong farewell and left the Chu capital, traveling northward. Two days later they found themselves in a hilly area, where ripe crops and fruits signified a bumper year. Somewhat cheered up by the sight, Confucius suddenly heard someone singing and, turning his head, saw a middle-aged man in a ragged gown and straw sandals. The man was of eccentric appearance, and as he was walking past them he sang:

Phoenix! Phoenix!
Why are you so flustered?
Let sorrows be forgotten,

And look ahead into the future.
Give up! Give up!
Where can you ever find a ruler who is not corrupt!

The words sounded to Confucius like a knife stabbing his heart. He realized that the singer must be an unusual person, so he hastily dismounted the chariot and walked to the man, intending to have a conversation with him.

However, the man quickened his steps, turned to a narrow lane, and soon vanished out of sight.

Confucius heaved a sigh of regret. "This man understands me well," he said to his disciples. "He must be a recluse."

"Master," Zi Lu said quickly, "let me find him and bring him back!"

"He has already said what he wanted to say," said Confucius. "Since he avoided us, let's leave him alone!"

Zi Lu went off to inquire about the man and returned to report that he was called Jie Yu.

"Everyone has his own aspiration," said Confucius. "Let him roam about the world, as carefree as the clouds drifting in the sky!"

They traveled down the road for a while and came to a big river. A boat sailing by carried some red, round fruits that looked like melons.

One of the disciples was called Bu Shang, or Zi Xia by his styled name. He was taken on by Confucius during his stay in the state of Wei. Refined in manners and diligent in his studies, he was fond of asking questions. He took a good look at the fruits on the boat but failed to recognize them, so he turned to ask Confucius what they were.

"They are duckweed fruits."

"How can you tell, since we have never seen such things?"

"Didn't you remember?" said Confucius. "On our way to Chu in the spring, we met a small boy riding on a buffalo and singing these words: 'The Prince of Chu got a duckweed fruit when crossing the river/ Big as a measuring vessel, red as the sun, and sweet as honey when cut open and tasted.' That must refer to the fruits we see over there."

Bu Shang went over to ask the boatman, who confirmed Confucius' words.

Confucius gazed at the rushing stream and recalled the numerous hardships he had suffered. Finally he decided to go back to Wei.

At that time Wei was still under the rule of Zhe, or Duke Chu of Wei. His father, Kuai Kui, lacked the strength to launch another assault and stayed at Qidi, where he continued to recruit followers.

Duke Chu of Wei was not someone Confucius respected and wanted to offer his service to. Instead he went to call on his old friend, Qu Boyu.

The reunion of old friends was an exciting moment. After Confucius recounted his story, Qu Boyu sighed deeply. "Master, you have to admit that however hard one tries, his success depends on the will of Heaven."

Confucius was about to respond when the doorman came in to announce the arrival of Minister Gongsun. Confucius frowned with distaste on hearing Gongsun Yujia's name. However, he had no choice but to rise and receive him.

"Congratulations!" said Gongsun Yujia with a false smile.

Confucius returned his salute reluctantly. "What for?" he asked coolly.

"His Lordship is very happy to learn of your return and intends to make you an official."

Confucius felt ambivalent. He was only too glad to get a chance to take office and bring some order out of chaos in the world. However, he did not want to serve Duke Chu of Wei who, in his opinion, was an illegitimate ruler. After much consideration he finally said, "Kong Qiu is too old to take office."

"In that case," said Gongsun Yujia tentatively, "how about having some of your disciples serve His Lordship instead?"

Confucius thought this a good compromise and replied readily, "That would be fine."

"I will return to the palace and report to His Lordship at once."

After seeing Gongsun Yujia off, Confucius summoned his disciples and said to them, "The duke intends to appoint some of you officials. From now on you should pay more attention to affairs of the state to make yourselves qualified when appointments come."

Five days later Gongsun Yujia called again. "Minister Kong needs a magistrate for the city of Pu," he said to Confucius. "Could you recommend one of your disciples for the position?"

Confucius combed his beard with his fingers. "Zi Lu proved his ability as an official when he was steward in the house of Jisun Shi in

Lu. How about appointing him magistrate of Pu?"

"That would be excellent," said Gongsun Yujia, clasping his hands. "I'll return at once and report the matter to Minister Kong."

The "Minister Kong" mentioned by Gongsun Yujia was Kong Li, Kuai Kui's nephew. After Kuai Kui fled Wei, it was Kong Li who assisted Zhe in governing the state. He wanted to acquaint himself with famous personages with an eye to strengthening his position in the court and enhancing his own reputation. Therefore he was highly pleased when Confucius agreed to let Zi Lu take the office of magistrate of Pu.

Confucius called Zi Lu to him and informed him of the appointment.

Zi Lu pursed his lips with displeasure. "Master, since you won't take office in Wei, neither will I."

"I am advanced in years," said Confucius. "Even if I wanted to serve in an office, my strength would not be equal to my duties. As for you, it is an entirely different matter. You are strong and full of vitality. Thus you should not decline to shoulder such a responsibility. You must try your best to make a success of your official career."

Zi Lu agreed to do as his master said.

After packing up his luggage, he went to bid Confucius farewell.

"Now," said Confucius, "what shall I offer you as a gift? A chariot or a few words?"

Batting his eyes, Zi Lu said honestly, "I like to listen to your instruction, master. Please give me a few words!"

"When those in high posts adhere to the rites, the common people will be easy to govern. An official should make himself a worthy role model for the people."

"Can you explain this in detail?"

"Be diligent, modest, and cautious," admonished Confucius. "Never neglect your duties!"

Zi Lu looked at Confucius anxiously, waiting for him to continue.

"As a magistrate you are in a position to deal directly with the common people. If you fulfill your duties, the people under your jurisdiction will treat you with the same respect as they treat their parents. Therefore you should show concern over people's livelihood, take precautions against droughts and floods, teach the people the principles of righteousness and benevolence and the sense of honor and shame, so that both men and women fulfill their respective duties and behave properly. When there is no longer a single vagabond in the city, it can be said that you have achieved something remarkable. Once there is a lawsuit, you should investigate the case carefully and handle it impartially. Never must you show over-confidence in your judgement or mete out punishments indiscriminately."

Zi Lu knelt and kowtowed to Confucius. "Master, I will bear your words firmly in mind. I hope you will come to Pu to instruct me when you have the time."

"You may leave for Pu with full confidence. I will visit you sometime to see how well you have done."

Zi Lu saluted again. "Master, I will take my leave."

Not long afterward, Kong Li visited Confucius at Qu Boyu's house. After an exchange of greetings he said, "Master, since your disciple Zi Lu took office in Pu, he has eliminated the evil elements and given peace to the good people. He has made many improvements in the city already."

Confucius was delighted at the news.

"There is now a vacancy for a law official," continued Kong Li. "Would you recommend another of your disciples for the position?"

Confucius considered carefully before he replied, "To make a qualified law official one must be conversant with the law and ready to uphold it with all his efforts. He must not let himself be prejudiced because of personal interests."

"You have so many talented disciples. It should not be difficult to find a suitable candidate!"

Confucius smiled. "Actually there is a suitable candidate," he said, "but unfortunately he is very short in stature and far from handsome in appearance."

"Didn't the ancients say the worth of a man can not be judged by his appearance? Why should a capable man worry about how he looks! Which disciple are you talking about?"

"His family name is Gao, his given name Chai, and his styled name Zi Gao," replied Confucius. "He is a native of Qi." He sent someone to bring Gao Chai before him.

Kong Li's heart sank at the sight of Gao Chai, who had a sunken nose and small eyes and who was barely up to the shoulders of Confucius. This was definitely not what a law official should look like. Kong Li's disappointment showed all over his face.

"Gao Chai," Confucius said in a determined tone, paying no

attention to Kong Li's discomfiture. "I want to recommend you for a position of law official. What do you think?"

Gao Chai glanced at Kong Li's gloomy face and threw out his chest. "I will follow your instruction, master!" He turned to Kong Li. "I will be needing your guidance and support, minister!"

Kong Li started at Gao Chai's stentorian voice. "This dwarf must be shrewd and capable judging from his manners, " he said to himself. "When can you go to your post?" he asked.

"At your convenience, minister."

"Good! Will you be able to take office tomorrow?"

Gao Chai agreed.

After Kong Li left, Confucius summoned his disciples and said to them, "We are beginning to be offered official appointments in Wei. You must study hard and cultivate your virtues to prepare yourselves for an opportunity to restore the rites."

The disciples all expressed their willingness.

As soon as he assumed office Gao Chai toured the prison to inspect the inmates there. Suddenly a man shouted from behind the window. "Minister, I was wronged!"

Gao Chai walked up and took a close look at him. The man appeared to be in his twenties. He had big eyes with thick eyebrows and looked handsome and honest in spite of his dishevelled hair and unwashed face. "What's you name? How were you wronged? Tell me about it and stick strictly to the facts!"

The young man's nose twitched, and tears welled from his eyes. "My family name is Cheng and my given name Xin. In my childhood I was engaged with the daughter of Zhao Lai from the neighboring village. Later, my parents died before I attained adulthood, and my family became poverty-stricken. Zhao Lai tore up our marriage contract and promised his daughter to a wealthy old man. His daughter ran away from home to meet with me in secret. When Zhao Lai heard about this, he framed a case against me and charged me of abducting his daughter. So I was thrown into prison."

Gao Chai gazed at him with piercing eyes. "Cheng Xin, can you guarantee the truthfulness of what you just said?"

"Every word is true."

"I will look into the case." Gao Chai returned to his office and had Zhao Lai brought in. "Zhao Lai," he said sternly, "are you aware of your guilt?"

Zhao Lai fell on his knees. "Your humble subject does not know where his guilt could come from."

"Why was Cheng Xin imprisoned?"

Zhao Lai shuddered, then tried to look calm. "He was found guilty of abducting my daughter."

"Whom was your daughter betrothed to in the beginning?"

"Cheng Xin. Oh no, not him," said Zhao Lai confusedly. "She was betrothed to ..."

"Humph!" Gao Chai banged his fist on the table. "How dare you arrange your daughter's marriage in such a way!" He turned to the runners. "Drag him down and give him forty strokes of the birch!"

The runners responded with a loud shout and raised the birch canes.

Terribly frightened, Zhao Lai beat the ground with his forehead repeatedly. "Your humble subject deserves to die! Have mercy on me, minister!"

Gao Chai demanded severely, "Do you admit your guilt or not?"

"I plead guilty! I plead guilty!" Zhao Lai then recounted in detail how he had torn up the marriage agreement and falsely charged Cheng Xin of abducting his daughter.

Gao Chai had Zhao Lai sign his name on his confession recorded on a piece of white silk. "Take him to prison!" he ordered.

Zhao Lai started pleading piteously. "Minister, please pardon your humble subject! I am willing to marry my daughter to Cheng Xin!"

"Do you really mean it?"

"I will sign a contract."

Gao Cai had a marriage contract written by one of his runners and let Zhao Lai sign it. Then he summoned Cheng Xin and Zhao Lai's daughter to the hall. When the two of them knelt before him, Gao Cai asked, "Cheng Xin, Zhao Lai has agreed to marry his daughter to you. What do you think?"

Cheng Xin was so grateful that he broke into tears. "My parents engaged me to the daughter of the Zhao family when I was small, and we have always had mutual affection. Both of us think we are meant for each other."

Gao Cai turned to ask the girl, "Do you agree to this?"

The girl nodded her head repeatedly.

"Zhao Lai deserves to be imprisoned for breaking his promise and framing a case against Cheng Xin," declared Gao Chai. "However, since he sincerely admits his guilt and agrees to your marriage, his guilt is pardoned."

Zhao Lai knelt and kowtowed his gratitude.

"You can go home now," said Gao Chai to him, "and prepare for the marriage of your daughter!"

The three of them expressed their gratitude and left for home.

Thus Gao Chai won the people's admiration by redressing many wrong cases. Kong Li began to regard him with great respect, and Confucius was also very pleased.

One day in the spring of the seventh year of Duke Ai of Lu's reign (488 B.C.) Confucius called Yan Hui to him. "Yan Hui," he said, "there has been a serious drought this spring. The Qingming Festival is already behind us, and I wonder how Zi Lu is doing in Pu and if he is already guiding the people to till the land and sow the seeds. You can take a trip there on my behalf and return to tell me what you have seen."

Accordingly Yan Hui got on a chariot and made his way to Pu. Along the road he found the earth parched, with dust rising high into the sky. The sight worried him deeply. He looked ahead into the distance and saw to his surprise large tracts of well-irrigated land. He raised the whip to spur the horse on, eager to find out what was happening. Soon he came to a big river where a huge crowd was busily digging ditches to lead the river water to the land. Delighted, he got off the chariot and stood by the river to watch.

Just then a man came up from the embankment in long strides. He was tall and broad-shouldered, his face and clothes all covered in dirt. "What wind blows you here?" he said to Yan Hui with a happy smile. "Let us go to my office!"

Only then did Yan Hui recognize Zi Lu, and he cried out in astonishment. "What happened? You are so dirty!"

Zi Lu smiled good-naturedly. "We have a serious drought this spring, and the land is too dry to grow anything. I am leading the people to dig the river and irrigate the land."

"It has been common practice since ancient times to draw river water to the field in case of a drought and dig trenches to drain water off in case of a flood," remarked Yan Hui. "But how have you been able to gather so many people to work for the project?"

"Pu is the granary of Wei," said Zi Lu with a look of satisfaction. "If the land of Pu is not cultivated in time, the entire state will suffer a famine. Therefore I am spending my own salary to provide each laborer with a meal of cooked rice and a bowl of porridge every day. That's why they are willing to work hard digging the river."

Yan Hui frowned but did not say anything. He returned to the capital and told Confucius what he had seen and heard.

After hearing him out, Confucius grew worried. "There is something that Zi Lu is not aware of," he said, and called Zi Gong to him. "Zi Gong, you will go to Pu at once and stop Zi Lu from using his salary to feed the laborers digging the river."

Zi Gong looked at Confucius inquisitively. "But why, master?"

Confucius heaved a sigh. "Zi Gong! Why should a clever man like you fail to see the reason behind it? The city of Pu belongs to the duke of Wei, and the state of Wei belongs to the king of Zhou. As magistrate of Pu, Zi Lu has the duty to extol the virtue of the duke of Wei and that of the king of Zhou. Only in this way will the relationship between superiors and inferiors be properly maintained!"

Zi Gong only had a hazy notion of what Confucius was talking about, but as time was short he set out for Pu in haste.

Zi Lu was delighted to see Zi Gong and began to talk about his irrigation project. "I am leading the local people to dig the river," he said, "because we have suffered a very bad drought this spring."

Zi Gong said seriously, "I have been sent by the master to stop you from doing that."

Zi Lu widened his eyes in astonishment. "It is for the benefit of the people," he argued, "that I strive to be an honest and upright official. And it is for the benefit of the people that I am organizing them to dig the river and relieve the drought. Why should the master want to stop me?"

"Maybe there is something improper about the way you are dealing with the matter. If you don't believe me, you can go and ask the master yourself."

Zi Lu sprang to his feet. "I will go! At once! I'll go with you to the capital and talk it out with the master."

"It's getting dark outside. Let me stay the night here, and we can set out tomorrow morning."

Zi Lu grew impatient. "I can not wait to get it clear! How can I waste any time faced with these parched fields?"

"So you want to leave immediately?"

"You can stay here if you want to. You'll have a place to sleep and something to eat. As for me, I must go at once."

"Aren't you neglecting your guest in this way?"

Zi Lu parted his thick lips and said apologetically, "The irrigation project is an urgent matter. Once the fields are watered and the five grains planted, I will go to the capital specially to apologize to you."

"Well, in that case I'll go with you at once."

Zi Lu and Zi Gong set out for the capital in the same chariot. Dust rose in the wind, and the sky was covered in dark clouds. They looked up to the clouds and prayed, "Heaven, please bless the people with a rain!"

At nightfall the clouds grew thicker, and no star appeared in the sky. The only light came from the lamps and candles in the villages.

The two of them were chatting as the chariot rolled into the capital and stopped in front of Qu Boyu's house. Zi Lu leapt out of the chariot and went in to see Confucius. He did not even greet the master but went straight to ask his question. "Master, Pu is suffering a serious drought, and I am spending my own salary to feed the people digging the river. Why should you want to stop me doing it?"

Confucius assumed a serious expression. "It is commendable of you to show concern for the common people and organize them in building a water project," he said.

Zi Lu was pleased on hearing this.

"But," Confucius continued, "as the magistrate of Pu you have to conduct yourself in the best interests of your lord and the king of Zhou. Since some people are starving in Pu, you should report the matter to the lord and beseech him to show sympathy by opening the state granaries to relieve the hungry. Then the common people will be grateful to their sovereign and the king of Zhou and obey their edicts wholeheartedly in the future. Instead, by feeding the hungry with your own salary, you are trying to cultivate your own popularity by dispensing petty favors. The common people will be grateful to you, not to their lord and the king. Think carefully: What will happen in the long run if people cherish such sentiments?"

Zi Lu began to feel remorseful.

"In the long run," said Confucius, "people will forget all about the benefits bestowed on them by the sovereign and the king. And you shall be blamed for it. That's why I sent Zi Gong to stop you."

Zi Lu became fully aware of his mistake. "Now I understand," he said ashamedly. "All land under Heaven belongs to the king. An official must never neglect his duty to his superiors."

"People must tend to their respective duties," said Confucius, "if great harmony is to be achieved in the world. This can be compared to a magnificent pagoda, with the king of Zhou standing at the top supervising all important affairs under Heaven. Immediately below him are the vassal lords, who pay homage to the king and command their ministers, who in turn govern the scholars and the common people."

"A big mistake was made because of my thoughtlessness," said Zi Lu self-deprecatingly. "What shall I do?"

"The worst mistake is refusal to correct one's mistake," said Confucius. "Now that you have recognized your mistake, nothing can stop you from correcting it."

Zi Lu was much comforted by these words. "Tomorrow morning I will report the matter to His Lordship and ask him to open the state granaries to relieve the hungry."

Confucius smiled with satisfaction.

"Master," asked Zi Lu, "if the duke of Wei asks you to help him govern the state, what would you do first?"

"I would undertake to rectify the names."

"Aren't you being pedantic?" asked Zi Lu in surprise. "Why should it be necessary to do that?"

"Why are you so rash in speaking?" said Confucius, clearly displeased. "With regard to something he does not understand, a superior man remains silent and does not make irrelevant comments. If the name is not right, speech will not be proper. When speech is not proper, nothing worthwhile will be accomplished. In that case the rites will not be restored in the state, the law will not be carried out effectively, and people will live in panic and insecurity. A superior man must phrase his speech carefully and use each word with the utmost caution."

Zi Lu was fully convinced. He was about to ask the master to give him more instruction on how to be a good official when they heard Zi Gong cry out in the courtyard. His voice was filled with delight.

Confucius looked up and saw Zi Gong bursting into the room, his face covered with smiles.

Chapter Thirty-five

Zi Gong Defeats Bo Pi in a Verbal Battle; Confucius Praises Zi Lu for Being a Good Official

"Master, it is raining!" Zi Gong exclaimed.

Confucius sprang to his feet and went out into the courtyard. He opened his palm to feel the raindrops and cocked up his head to enjoy the sweet rain after the long drought. He listened to the patter of the light rain and envisaged the happy bustle among the peasants after the rain and, still later, the joyous harvest.

Though Zi Lu could not see Confucius' expression in the dark, he could feel the master's delight. He walked up to Confucius. "Master, please come into the room!"

"Zi Lu," said Confucius with pleasure, "the rain was not preceded by wind, and the clouds look thick and even all across the sky. Therefore rain must be falling all over the region. It is no longer necessary for you to make people dig ditches to fetch river water to the fields."

Zi Lu shook his head. "We don't have any handiwork mills in Pu," he said, "so people have to rely entirely on the land to make a living. However, the land is so rugged and the ditches and canals so dilapidated that drought and flooding remain a constant threat. I have made up my mind to ask His Lordship to open the state granaries to feed the hungry. After sowing in spring, I will order the people to resume digging ditches."

"One must never use peasant labor during the busy season," remarked Confucius. "It is most appropriate for you to schedule the digging of ditches after sowing in spring and before harvesting in summer."

Zi Lu smiled happily hearing the master's praise.

Confucius, however, began to think of other matters. After witnessing the achievements of Gao Chai and Zi Lu, he thought of the state of Lu and his disciple Ran Qiu.

In summer of the seventh year of Duke Ai of Lu's reign (488 B.C.) Fu Chai, the prince of Wu, sent a letter to Duke Ai proposing a

meeting at Zeng, a city of Lu. Duke Ai agreed and, when the appointed date drew near, set out with Jisun Fei, his chief minister, who was to be the master of ceremonies for Lu at the meeting.

Situated more than a hundred li south of the Lu capital, the city of Zeng bordered on the northern frontier of Wu. As Wu was superior to Lu in strength, Duke Ai could not help feeling a little apprehensive about the meeting. But he comforted himself with the thought that Zeng was a heavily guarded city on Lu territory.

Arriving at Zeng, Jisun Fei went to take a look at the platform and returned to inform Duke Ai of what he saw. The following days they practiced the rites to be performed at the meeting.

On the day of the meeting, Duke Ai arrived at the platform early in the morning. The platform was built with earth on a piece of level ground, with steps on the south. Pigs and lambs were laid out on the altar for sacrifice. Duke Ai had to wait for over an hour for the prince of Wu to arrive. Looking up, he was astonished by what he saw. Fu Chai walked in measured steps, wearing a gold crown and a brocade gown and was shaded by a yellow canopy. He was escorted by eight armored, sword-swinging attendants, who were followed by a guard of honor in four columns, each carrying a colorful banner. Taking a look at his own attendants, who were few in number and very plainly dressed, Duke Ai was embarrassed by a sense of inferiority. By this time Fu Chai had approached him, so he plucked up his courage and went up to offer his greetings. The two of them walked to the platform to the accompaniment of music. Duke Ai and Fu Chai ascended the steps and took their seats on the platform, with the host on the right and the guest on the left.

Bo Pi, the chief minister of Wu, and Jisun Fei, who had been chosen by the two states to preside over the ceremony, came forth, exchanged greetings in front of the platform, and also ascended the steps to join their sovereigns. "Bring the incense!" Jisun Fei called out.

A servant brought the joss sticks in both hands.

Jisun Fei took the joss sticks, bowed to the north, and planted them in three groups in a bronze incense burner. He turned and saluted to Fu Chai and Duke Ai. "Everything is ready. Please take the oath!"

Fu Chai and Duke Ai walked up to the incense burner to the rhythm of the music and stood facing north.

"Bring the wine vessels!" shouted Jisun Fei.

Two attendants carrying the vessels ascended the platform.

Fu Chai and Duke Ai each took a wine vessel in his hands and offered sacrifices to Heaven and earth, then chanted the words of their agreement, pledging to maintain everlasting friendship and peace.

When the two lords returned to their seats, Bo Pi pulled a long face. "Your Highness," he said to Fu Chai, "among the various states, Wu is strong and Lu weak. Thanks to the protection provided by Wu, Lu has been able to avoid the calamities of war. The ancients said that a superior man should always repay the kindness he has received. But Lu does not show any intention of returning the kindness of Wu. Is it not incompatible with the code of proper conduct for Lu to behave in that manner?"

"Well said!" responded Fu Chai peremptorily. "Your words are quite reasonable, my honored minister. Wu has indeed bestowed great favor upon Lu."

Bo Pi took a look at Duke Ai and Jisun Fei, both choked with silent fury, then continued. "As the manor of the Duke of Zhou, Lu has enjoyed the reputation of a state governed by rites. But nowadays its ruler does not abide by the rites in his conduct. Does that mean the rites of Zhou have been abandoned in Lu?"

Duke Ai became so furious that his face darkened, and he trembled uncontrollably. However, he did not know what to say to strike back.

Jisun Fei tweaked his ears and scratched his cheeks in misery but also failed to come up with a word in retort.

Bo Pi felt greatly pleased with himself. He stood there gazing up into the sky for a while, then assumed a milder tone. "Since Wu and Lu are brothers, Wu regards it its duty to protect Lu. Moreover, Lu is not very wealthy. I suggest that Lu pay the tribute of one hundred oxen and the same number of sheep and pigs to Wu just by way of showing its gratitude. Would that be all right, Your Highness?"

"I care not so much about the tribute itself as the principle of proper behavior it signifies," said Fu Chai nonchalantly. "Let the matter be settled in this way."

Enraged, Jisun Fei took a few steps forward, intending to argue with Fu Chai.

Afraid of provoking a serious confrontation, Duke Ai stopped him, saying, "Hold on, honored minister! A few hundred oxen, sheep and pigs is a small matter; it's not worth making a big fuss and possibly bringing more harm to us. Let's give in for the time being!"

"The meeting is over!" Jisun Fei cried in a hoarse voice, no longer paying attention to prearranged procedure. "Let the sovereigns descend the platform!"

Crestfallen, Duke Ai hurried down the steps with his head bowed, without matching his steps to the rhythm of the music.

Fu Chai looked straight ahead and walked deliberately down the platform, carefully adjusting his steps to the music.

What happened at the Lu-Wu meeting had not been expected by Duke Ai. On his return to the palace, he was overwhelmed with shame and regret. He realized that, at a time when the various states were contesting for supremacy, a weak state must seek to strengthen itself if it did not wish to be pushed around by other states. To expect the strong to take pity on the weak would be just as futile as to expect the wolf not to prey on the lamb. Suddenly he thought of Confucius. He began to consider how he could fetch Confucius back to Lu.

In autumn that year Bo Pi invited Jisun Fei to visit him in Wu. Jisun Fei shuddered with trepidation on receiving the letter, for what happened at the meeting in Zeng was still fresh in his memory. "If Bo Pi could be so overbearing in Lu territory," he muttered to himself, "what outrages will he stop at when I meet him in Wu?" Then he remembered his father's last words and decided to ask help from Zi Gong. He sat down and wrote a letter and had it taken to Wei.

On receiving Jisun Fei's letter, Zi Gong went and reported the matter to Confucius.

"Zi Gong," said Confucius, "you are an eloquent speaker. You may accompany the chief minister to Wu and try to exhort the chief minister of Wu to conform to principles of benevolence and righteousness."

"With Bo Pi's assistance, Fu Chai is trying to make himself an overlord. If I were to talk about benevolence and righteousness, how could I make him listen to me?"

"Fu Chai is a man amenable to reason. If you expound your views clearly, how will he remain unmoved?"

Zi Gong took Confucius' advice and returned post-haste to Lu, where he joined Jisun Fei on his mission to Wu.

After crossing the Yangtze River, they found the scenery entirely different from that of the north. Wherever they looked they saw a lively green: the crisscrossing rivers and canals, the willow trees along the dikes, and the wheat and rice fields. The capital of Wu was a picturesque city with ancient temples, neat residential houses, well-ordered streets and alleys and many streams cutting across the city. There were dikes and small bridges everywhere, making it truly a waterborne city. Riding in the chariot, Zi Gong could not help marveling at the wonderful sights.

Jisun Fei, however, was in no mood to enjoy those sights. He was preoccupied with the oncoming meeting with Bo Pi, wondering what the wily minister had in store for him.

At twilight they stopped in front of an inn, where they unsaddled the horses and planned to stay the night. Just then the sun's reflection in a nearby stream caught Zi Gong's eyes. A gentle breeze sent ripples in the stream and created a kaleidoscopic view of the evening glow on the water surface. Zi Gong stood by the stream, enchanted by the sight, until Jisun Fei called out his name from behind him.

That night Jisun Fei tossed and turned in his bed, wondering what Bo Pi would be up to this time and whether Zi Gong would be any match for the crafty Wu minister. He was afraid that he might return to Lu in shame and humiliation.

The next morning Jisun Fei got up looking haggard, with blood-shot eyes and black eye sockets. Though he noticed this, Zi Gong could not very well ask Jisun Fei about it but followed him without a word into a chariot and headed for Bo Pi's residence.

At the news of their arrival Bo Pi hurriedly groomed himself and came out to meet them. After they entered the house and took their seats, Jisun Fei was so nervous that he forgot to exchange greetings with Bo Pi but asked bluntly, "Chief Minister, what do you have to teach me by inviting me to your honorable state?"

Bo Pi bit his lips to suppress a chuckle. Pointing to the tangerines on a small table, he said to Jisun Fei and Zi Gong, "Would you like to taste the tangerines of Wu?"

Realizing his mistake, Jisun Fei blushed and lowered his head. "Thank you, Chief Minister!"

Zi Gong placed a piece of tangerine into his mouth and tasted it. "The tangerines in the south have such a unique flavor!" he said with approval.

Jisun Fei felt relieved. He took a tangerine from the table, peeled it and began to eat.

"Is the lord of your honorable state enjoying good health?" asked

Bo Pi with a big smile.

"Yes, yes!" replied Jisun Fei.

To ease up the awkward atmosphere, Zi Gong bowed slightly with clasped hands and inquired Bo Pi after the prince of Wu's health.

Impressed by Zi Gong's perfect accent of the standard Zhou language and impeccable manners, Bo Pi became aware that this was someone not to be taken lightly. He gave Zi Gong a close look. "May I have your honorable name?"

"My family name is Duanmu, and my given name Ci," replied Zi Gong.

"Oh!" Bo Pi exclaimed and bowed slightly in his seat. "A distinguished disciple of Confucius! I'm sorry I didn't recognize you."

"I do not deserve such high regards," said Zi Gong by way of modesty.

Faced with such an eloquent opponent, Bo Pi felt a little discouraged. He paused for a moment, then turned to Jisun Fei. "Chief Minister, at the meeting in Zeng last summer, it was agreed that Lu would pay Wu the annual tribute of a hundred oxen, sheep and pigs each. When will this year's tribute be paid?"

"Well, ..." Jisun Fei hesitated, unable to give a reply.

Zi Gong broke in, "Chief Minister, there is something wrong in what you just said."

"What?" Bo Pi widened his eyes with anger. "The lord of Lu made the promise himself. What's wrong with my words?"

Zi Gong's reply was calm and fluent. "According to the words of ancient sages, when the great Way prevails the whole world will live as one. Both Lu and Wu belong to Zhou, and the sovereigns of both Lu and Wu serve the king of Zhou. At the meeting in Zeng Lu and Wu signed an agreement to treat each other with courtesy and never resort to war, so the two states have since become brothers. As brothers they should share their weals and woes. Today Wu is rich and strong whereas Lu is poor and weak, so it would stand to reason for Wu to provide aid to Lu. Would it not be putting the cart before the horse for you to ask Lu to pay tribute to Wu instead of advising the prince of Wu to act in accordance with the rules of propriety?"

"What an eloquent talker!" Bo Pi thought to himself in dismay. "It is natural for the weak to pay tribute to the strong," he insisted. "This has always been the case since ancient times."

Unperturbed, Zi Gong retorted, "As the manor of the Duke of

Zhou, Lu is renowned for its adherence to the principles of benevolence and righteousness and its preservation of the ancient rites. When we look at the course of history, it is obvious that warlike states are always ridden with crises despite their powerful appearances and only those states that adhere to the rites can enjoy long-term peace and prosperity. Therefore it is states like Lu that are really strong. In that case isn't it natural for Wu to pay tribute to Lu?"

Bo Pi's face was flushed with shame and indignation. "Are you saying that the agreement between Wu and Lu has no validity at all?"

"Chief Minister, I have a question for you. When Lu and Wu met in Zeng, did they aim to enhance friendship or compel one state to pay tribute to the other?"

"To enhance friendship, of course."

"Then please advise the prince of Wu to keep this promise," said Zi Gong in a triumphant tone.

Bo Pi was about to speak again when Zi Gong stood up and turned to Jisun Fei. "The chief minister of Wu has agreed to maintain everlasting friendship between Lu and Wu. We may take our leave now."

Taking his cue from Zi Gong, Jisun Fei stood up and left the room.

Back in Lu, Jisun Fei reported what had happened to Duke Ding of Lu, who was deeply impressed by Zi Gong's outstanding talents.

Zi Gong returned to Wei and recounted his experience to Confucius. "You are indeed an invincible debater!" said Confucius. Gazing at the yellowing leaves of the scholartree in the courtyard, he continued, "It is autumn now. I intend to take a trip to Pu to find out how Zi Lu is doing there. Will you accompany me?"

"It is a great pleasure to drive the chariot for you, master," replied Zi Gong. "Of course I will go."

Early the next morning the two of them set out. Still relishing his success in his mission to Wu, Zi Gong was in a happy mood as he drove the chariot for the master with great adeptness. "Master," he said, "how would you describe Yan Hui, Zi Lu and myself?"

"Yan Hui is a man of virtue and benevolence and Zi Lu is a man of great bravery."

Zi Gong turned and looked at Confucius expectantly.

"You are a man of great intelligence."

Zi Gong thought for a moment, then asked again, "What are the characteristics of those three types of men?"

"An intelligent man is never deceived, a benevolent man is never worried, and a brave man is never afraid."

Delighted, Zi Gong said, "Master, you are endowed with all these attributes."

Confucius gave him a look of disapproval. "An intelligent man is never deceived, a benevolent man is never worried, and a brave man is never afraid. These are the attributes of a superior man, but unfortunately I have none of these. I am merely a man who is eager to learn, who is not ashamed of asking advice from people below himself in rank, and who is afraid of missing anything important. What else? I am just eager to learn."

Zi Gong fell silent and raised the whip to speed the horses on. After a while he felt bored and began to talk about his trip to Wu again. "The chief minister of Wu was such a half-witted man, yet he tried to show off his cleverness."

"Zi Gong!" Confucius admonished him in a serious tone. "Are you totally faultless? A superior man extols others for their goodness and does not speak unfavorably behind their backs. I don't enjoy listening to you speaking ill of others like that."

As soon as they entered the area of Pu, Confucius was delighted at what he saw. "Good!" he said. "Zi Lu has been able to win people's trust with a sincere and respectful attitude!" When they entered the city, Confucius was even more delighted. "Good! Zi Lu has been able to deal with the people with honesty and tolerance!" When they reached the magistrate's office, Confucius again exclaimed with joy, "Good! Zi Lu has been able to investigate the cases carefully and judge them resolutely!"

His hands grasping the rein, Zi Gong asked, "Master, you have not yet met Zi Lu and listened to him talk about what he has done, but you have already praised him three times. What makes him so praiseworthy?"

"I have already seen what he has done," replied Confucius in a delighted tone. "When we entered the outlying area of Pu, we saw irrigation ditches all over the fertile fields grown with luxuriant crops. Only when the people have faith in the authorities will they spare no efforts digging the ditches to irrigate the fields and tend the crops. When we entered the city, we saw row upon row of shops lining the streets. The fair was lively with throngs of people, the houses looked solid, and the trees were dense and luxuriant. Such a scene of peace and prosperity would be impossible unless the magistrate treats the people with honesty and tolerance so that the people also become simple and honest, and robbers and thieves vanish from the land. When we came to the magistrate's office, we found the house quiet and deserted, with only the runners standing there ready to take orders. From this we know the magistrate is well acquainted with the people's conditions, works in the public interests and judges the cases impartially, for only thus will we find no one at the office to voice his grievances or create trouble for the magistrate. Though I have uttered praise three times, the magistrate deserves even more!"

Zi Gong was totally convinced and nodded his head. He extended his hands to help Confucius dismount the chariot.

The guards hastened inside to report their arrival. As soon as Confucius descended the chariot, Zi Lu came out of the office in giant strides. He was still dressed in a coarse-cloth garment, and his dark, sun-tanned face was all smiles. "Master! Forgive me for not coming out to receive you earlier!"

"Not at all," said Confucius with a broad smile. "I am here only for a casual visit."

"Please come in!"

Confucius entered the office and found it simply furnished as to be almost squalid, just as he had expected. However, there was something he found strange. In the main hall and the side rooms were placed all kinds of weapons including spears, swords, broadswords, halberds, bows, arrows, and shields. Looking at the weapons he turned to Zi Lu, "Zi Lu, from what I have seen your achievement at your office is quite remarkable. However, your duty as the magistrate is to exhort the people to behave according to the rites and understand the sense of shame and honor. Why should you attach so much importance to martial arts and the use of wapons?"

Zi Lu knew that Confucius had misinterpreted his intention. "Though I am lacking in ability and learning, I understand that a magistrate should fulfill his duties to the king of Zhou and the lord above and the common people below."

"I have seen that Pu is enjoying prosperity thanks to your good administration," said Confucius.

At this Zi Gong recounted how Confucius had praised Zi Lu three times on their way to Pu.

A little embarrassed, Zi Lu said, "Master, you favor me with too much praise. Actually, Pu suffers from many problems. For example, there is not a single handicraft mill in the entire reign, so that people depend solely on the fields for their living. They are able to manage in ordinary times, but a drought or flood will endanger their very livelihood. Therefore I am trying to have the people trained in handicraft skills, so that they will open some mills and earn money to pay their daily expenses. If that can be done, people would not starve even when the place suffers from natural or manmade calamities. This has kept me busily occupied. In addition, I plan to set up a school and hire some teachers to educate the local children, and I have to think of ways to help the vagabonds settle down to earn a decent living. I would have no time for practicing martial arts even if I want to!"

"If you do not practice martial arts, why do you have so many weapons placed in your office?"

"I have put them there to guard against emergencies. If there is an alarm of bandits, I will distribute the weapons among the local people and have them ascend the city wall to show off our strength. Finding the city well-guarded, the robbers will surely run away without launching an attack. If we don't take such precautions, people in the city would fall into confusion when robbers come to besiege the city, and the result would be unthinkable."

Confucius smiled joyfully. "Zi Lu, I did not know you are capable of such careful planning." He turned to Zi Gong. "Did I tell you there is still more to praise after I have praised him three times?"

Zi Gong smiled and nodded his head.

Zi Lu lowered his head in abashment. "I used to be a sword-taunting man who knew nothing about officialdom. Thanks to your tireless instruction, master, I am beginning to know a little. Since I took office in Pu, you have not stopped giving me timely advice. That's why I have been able to achieve some success here."

"It was well said by the ancients that a worthy disciple will excel his master someday," said Confucius with a sigh. "The young are to be regarded with awe, for they will get ahead of their seniors." He pointed to the weapons leaning against the walls. "Didn't I fail to understand why you put them there?"

It was getting dark. "It is time for supper," said Zi Lu, and he ordered a meal to be prepared.

A moment later the servants returned with four dishes of vegetables, three bowls of rice and a saucer of ginger slices.

At the sight of this Zi Gong knitted his brows.

Confucius took up the bowl with pleasure and began to eat slowly. When eating he took his time and did not speak.

Zi Lu smiled happily when he saw Confucius was enjoying his meal.

After supper Zi Lu led Confucius and Zi Gong to the guest rooms. "You must be tired after the trip," he said. "I'll leave you now."

Confucius stopped him, saying, "Zi Lu, I have not seen you for over half a year. Sit down and let's have a good talk!"

The three of them sat down around a small table, on which stood a candle with flickering light. Zi Lu sat cross-legged to the right of Confucius, facing Zi Gong.

Zi Lu rubbed his hands. "Master, as the magistrate of Pu I work harder and worry more than I did as your disciple."

"A scholar should work untiringly for a great cause instead of seeking ease and comfort," said Confucius. "A man who hankers after ease and comfort does not deserve to be a scholar."

"Master," asked Zi Lu, "what's the relationship between reading and thinking?"

"One who reads without thinking is easily deceived; one who thinks without reading lacks the confidence to work for a great cause."

"What shall we do when we read about a viewpoint which is not correct?" asked Zi Gong.

"We should speak out against the incorrect viewpoint. If we can always act in this way, we will be free of perils."

Zi Lu took up the candlestick, snuffed the candles, and sat down again. "What should one do in order to be a superior man?" he asked.

"A superior man should be strict with himself and fulfill his duties seriously and earnestly."

"Can one be called a superior man if he does this?" asked Zi Lu with a little perplexity.

"He should keep making strict demands on himself so that people of virtue and benevolence are all pleased with his behavior."

"Can one be called a superior man then?"

"He should be so strict with himself," continued Confucius, "that the common people are all pleased with his behavior." He paused a little and combed his beard with his fingers. "However, where can we find a man since ancient times who can make the common people pleased with his behavior? Even the great sage kings Yao and Shun were not up to this standard."

"Yao and Shun are highly renowned for their virtue. Why do you diminish their worth in this way?"

"Yao and Shun are indeed universally respected," said Confucius. "However, what did they do all their lives? No more than sit through audiences all day with earnest and serenity."

"Are there many people in the world who understand virtue?" asked Zi Lu.

"According to my observation, very few people understand virtue."

As it was getting late, Zi Lu said, "Master, you may go to bed now. I will come and talk with you tomorrow morning."

After breakfast the following morning, Confucius told Zi Lu that he and Zi Gong would like to stay in Pu one more day and he should take them on a trip to the suburbs.

"I would be so happy," said Zi Lu. "Wait till I get the chariot ready." He went out the office in quick steps.

A short while later Zi Lu drove his chariot to the office. "Get on, master! It has been a long time since I last drove the chariot for you."

The three of them rode out of the city. The sights in the fields gave the promise of a good harvest, and Confucius began to chant the poem "The Seventh Month" from *The Book of Poetry*. He asked Zi Lu to stop before a tract of sorghum field and got down to take a close look. "The sorghums have thick stalks and plump ears," he said with delight. "Zi Lu, you have done well in governing Pu!" He walked to a piece of rice field nearby and was again pleased with what he saw. Suddenly his attention was attracted by the grave mounds of various sizes in the rice field, and the smile vanished from his face. "Zi Lu," he said. "Do you remember how I prohibited the building of graves in fertile land when I governed Zhongdu? Look at all these grave mounds: They take up too much room in the rice field. On the other hand, where should graves be built since this area has very few hills?"

"I will issue an announcement, and order the people to bury the coffins deep in the ground and prohibit them from building grave mounds. In this way we can save the fertile land for cultivation."

Confucius shook his head. "That would not be appropriate. People build graves for the dead so that they can offer sacrifices on festivals to express their cherished memories for their ancestors. You would provoke strong opposition if you forbid the people to build graves. Such an act, which will be strongly opposed by the common people, should never be taken." He lowered his head and thought for a while. "You may try to persuade people to choose barren, uncultivated land as the site for the graves. If they have to build graves in fertile land, they should keep the grave mounds small."

Zi Lu sighed. "Master, you once said that when a man dies, he is like a candle that has burned out. Why should we worry so much about dead people!"

"We should deal with such matters with caution, because people believe in the existence of ghosts and spirits."

"In that case, would you please tell us how to serve the ghosts and spirits?"

"You don't yet know how to serve living people," said Confucius, "how can you serve ghosts and spirits?"

Just then a horseman galloped toward them, and they all looked up in surprise.

Chapter Thirty-six

Confucius Misses His Sick Wife Back in Lu; You Ruo Leads the Lu Army to Defeat Invaders from Wu

W hen the horseman came near, Confucius and his disciples recognized him to be Gongliang Ru. They looked at him anxiously, not knowing what news he had brought.

Gongliang Ru rode up to Confucius, leapt down the horse and bowed deeply. "Master, your nephew Kong Zhong has come to Wei from Lu."

Confucius gave a start. "What business has brought him here?"

"He said your wife is seriously ill," replied Gongliang Ru in a muffled voice.

The news came as a terrible blow to Confucius. His head swirled, his knees felt weak, and his eyes became dazed. Gazing east, he muttered to himself, "For dozens of years she has cared for the family and worried for me while I wandered from place to place." He longed to return to her side and comfort her. His eyes dimmed as he remembered her voice and smiles, her gentleness toward him, her modesty and humility toward his mother, her loving care for their children, and her generosity and tolerance toward the neighbors. He had spent the prime of his life roaming the states with the aim to restore the rites of Zhou. If only he could return to her side in his old age to enjoy a peaceful life with the knowledge of a job well done, of a lifetime well spent! But frustrations were not followed by success, and he would not know what to tell her if he should return home now. For a short moment he was overcome with a sense of loss.

Zi Lu was deeply upset to find Confucius so grieved. He went up to him and said with a lump in his throat, "Master, you have been away from home for ten years. Your wife has worked very hard about the house all her life and she should obtain her deserts from you. Now that she is seriously ill, you'd better return and see her, master."

"I agree," said Zi Gong. "You should return home to see her, master."

Confucius looked at them with gratitude, but did not say a word.

He was torn by conflicting emotions. He missed his family dearly, his wife, Kong Li, Kong Zhong, Kong Wuwei and Kong Wujia, and his grandson, Kong Ji, whom he had never seen. He longed to return to Lu, his homeland, where the rites of Zhou were best preserved. However, it would compromise his honor and dignity to return like this. Though Duke Ding and Jisun Si had died, the calamities and shame they had brought to Lu remained. For many years Confucius had hoped that Duke Ding and Jisun Si would send an envoy to fetch him back and consult him on matters of the state, but it never happened. Combing his grey beard, he gazed up into the sky and looked down at the earth, as if saying, "Heaven is so impartial, but it does not allow an honest man to have a good end. Earth is so broad, but it does not have room for me." He lowered his head and held back his tears.

"Master," urged Gongliang Ru, 'let's return to the city!"

Confucius took another look at the ripe crops in the field and said to Zi Lu, "Since you took office less than a year ago, you have made some improvements in Pu and have made arrangements for the education of children, employment of the vagabonds and precautions against bandits. This shows that you have talents for an official career and you care for the common people. I hope you will try your best to fulfill your duties in your office so that people will be grateful to His Lordship and the king of Zhou."

Zi Lu broke into tears. "Master, all your life you have worked for the restoration of the rites of Zhou. But how many people in the whole world understand you? Please return to Lu!"

Confucius suppressed his sorrow. "Though I have been misunderstood, I get benevolence when I seek after it, and I get righteousness when I seek after it. What else do I want?"

Zi Lu looked at him with perplexity.

"Is benevolence far away?" said Confucius. "When I seek after it, it comes."

Zi Lu, Zi Gong and Gongliang Ru were much comforted by the master's determined voice. Together they helped him get on the chariot.

When they returned to Qu Boyu's house, Kong Zhong came out to meet them. "Uncle!" he said to Confucius with a deep bow, tears welling up in his eyes. "I missed you so much in all these years!"

"How is your aunt?" asked Confucius.

"She is suffering from partial paralysis of the body."

"Oh!" Confucius heaved a deep sigh. "This illness is difficult to treat. It must have brought her great sufferings! It must also have caused you and your brothers and sisters a great deal of trouble!"

The disciples gathered around Confucius and tried to persuade him to return home. Min Shun, a habitually reticent man, also spoke up. "Master," he said, "you have left home for ten years, and your wife has now fallen ill because of over-exertion. You should return and see her as soon as possible!"

The other disciples all agreed. Confucius walked back and forth in the courtyard for a long time. Finally he said, "You may go back to your studies! I can not return home now."

Knowing they could not make him change his mind, the disciples went away in low spirits.

Confucius called Kong Zhong into his room and asked him about what happened in Lu and in his family in the past few years. Confucius was pleased to find Kong Zhong a handsome young man with graceful manners and a refined style of conversation. His gloomy mood was a little lightened as he thought to himself, "Elder brother, your spirit in Heaven can be comforted because of your son!"

Kong Zhong was almost begging. "Uncle, the whole family miss you so much and want you to return. Please come back!"

"I was forced to leave Lu," said Confucius, "by the late lord of Lu and chief minister. Though both of them have passed away, their successors have not yet sent an envoy to invite me back, which shows they are not ready to pursue policies that will make Lu strong and prosperous. If I were to return without being invited, I would surely be laughed at by the people and looked down upon by the lord and the chief minister. I have to stay in Wei and wait for the right opportunity."

"My aunt longs so much to see you," pleaded Kong Zhong. "Please return for her sake, if not for the sake of the state."

"Don't I long to see her?" said Confucius. "But I have advocated the rites of Zhou all my life. Unless His Lordship and the chief minister want to govern the state by the rites and send an envoy to invite me back, I would not return to Lu."

Kong Zhong realized it would be in vain for him to argue further.

Just then the gate-keeper came in and announced, "Minister Wangsun is here!"

Confucius had always treated Wangsun Jia with respect, for he was one of the capable and honest ministers in the Wei court. On hearing of his visit, Confucius hastily went out the gate to meet him.

"I heard of your wife's illness," said Wangsun Jia with a bow, "and have come to see you lest you return home in a hurry."

Confucius saluted in return. "She has only a minor ailment and will recover soon. I do not plan to return."

Wangsun Jia frowned. "A sickness in old age should not be taken lightly, master. I think you'd better return and have a look."

"Thanks so much for your kind solicitation," said Confucius. "I can not return to my homeland for the time being."

Wangsun Jia was greatly puzzled by this reply.

At this juncture Qu Boyu came over and said to Wangsun Jia, "I understand the master's attitude. He will not return to Lu unless the lord of Lu and Chief Minister Jisun send someone to invite him back."

Wangsun Jia considered this and broke into a sad smile when he saw the point. He changed the subject. "Master, you have lived in Wei for many years and are therefore quite familiar with many happenings here. Today Kuai Kui is gathering forces at Qidi and recruiting rebels like Gongsun Shu and Gongshu Shi. He plans to fight his way back to the capital and set himself up as the lord of Wei. Suppose that should happen someday, whom should the ministers of Wei support?"

Confucius could not very well speak his mind on such a sensitive topic, so he said noncommittally, "Kuai Kui is the eldest son of Duke Ling and therefore his legitimate successor, but unfortunately he hurt his father by his assassination attempt against Nan Zi. Zhe is Kuai Kui's son and should rule after him, but it was Duke Ling who set him up as the new lord of Wei."

Unsatisfied with such an equivocal reply, Wangsun Jia did not press further.

At this moment a handsome lad came to the gate and bowed deeply to Confucius. "Your junior Xiang Tuo has a question for you, master!" he said in a clear voice.

Confucius looked him up and down and said in surprise, "Xiang Tuo, you have grown so much in just a few years! Come into the room and have a seat!"

Xiang Tuo saluted to Wangsun Jia, Qu Boyu and Kong Zhong and sat down opposite Kong Zhong.

Confucius had been deeply impressed when he first met Xiang

Tuo, and he was pleased to find him now a young man with refined manners. "You are a very intelligent person," he said. "What question could be too difficult for you?"

Batting his bright eyes, Xiang Tuo began to talk in a leisurely way. "Nowadays the vassal lords, in their contention for supremacy, resort to both deception and force. Though King Jing of Zhou wants to restore the authority of the royal house, the lords persist in their old ways. In my opinion, the situation is hopeless for the ruling house of Zhou, which only holds nominal power over the vassal states."

As Confucius listened, his face darkened.

Xiang Tuo continued relentlessly. "The rites and music formulated by the Duke of Zhou played a significant role in the early years of the Zhou Dynasty. Today, however, they seem quite unsuitable. The founders of Zhou governed the kingdom by rites and music, but nowadays the lords contend for power by military means. There have been innumerable instances in the past, but let's just look at those of this year. First Zhao Jianzi in the state of Jin sent an expedition against Yu, then Minister Chen Qi in the state of Qi murdered his sovereign Yan Ruzi and set up Yang Shen as the new lord. Almost everyone who achieved success did so by using force."

Confucius looked at Xiang Tuo with increasing astonishment, not knowing why he should think and talk in this way.

"Master," asked Xiang Tuo, "is there any chance of restoration for the rites of Zhou?"

Confucius had worked all his life to that end, and the question touched a sore spot. "The central idea of the rites of Zhou is benevolence," he began. "Benevolence means loving people. If a man does not love people or even intends to harm people, how can you tell him apart from an animal?" His face lit up when he talked about benevolence. "In order to live in harmony, people have to depend on benevolence. There would be no peace in the world unless people adhere to principles of benevolence in their daily life and in the way they treat one another. Men like Zhao Jianzi and Chen Qi, who ruthlessly murder and kill, can only be compared to wolves and jackals. Man's nature is good at birth, but education and other influences result in differences in people's character. There will be a time when, under a benevolent government, people all over the world have plenty to eat and wear, when all the children receive a good education, and when benevolence becomes the ultimate standard by which people talk, behave and deal with one another. When that day comes, there will be no more wars and therefore no sufferings and ruined families."

"The state of Wei is now ruled by Zhe," said Xiang Tuo. "His father, Kuai Kui, has fled to Qidi. The son refuses to fetch his father back, and the father plans to attack the son. Which of them do you think is not benevolent?"

Confucius repeated what he had just said to Wangsun Jia.

Unsatisfied with such a reply, Xiang Tuo lost interest in their conversation and took his leave.

After seeing Wangsun Jia and Xiang Tuo off, Confucius felt overwhelmed by a sense of perplexity. He was convinced, as he had told Xiang Tuo, that the day would come when people all over the world held benevolence in the highest esteem and carried it out in their daily life; but what could he say about what was actually happening? Almost every event he experienced or heard of went against the principle of benevolence. The image of a future society of harmony dimmed, replaced by a picture of confusion and chaos.

After breakfast the following morning, Kong Zhong bade Confucius farewell with tears in his eyes and returned to Lu.

For several days Confucius remained deeply perturbed. One day, he felt a little better and began to play the zither. After a while he beat the chime stone, which gave off a low, melancholy sound.

Just at this moment a man carrying two loads of firewood on a shoulder pole happened to pass in front of the gate. He stopped and said with a sigh, "This man seems to have a lot to get off his mind!" He listened for a while, then said, "The man seems to be complaining that he is not understood. What of that? If the river is deep, just swim across with your clothes on. If the river is shallow, you may lift your clothes and ford across it. Why should anyone try to seek after something beyond his reach!"

The gate-keeper recounted the man's words to Confucius.

"This man is determined in his ways," commented Confucius. "It would be in vain to persuade him."

After that, Confucius stayed on in the state of Wei.

Fu Chai, the prince of Wu, was not pleased when he learned news about the talented disciples of Confucius. One day in the spring of the eighth year of Duke Ai of Lu's reign (487 B.C.) he went to the rear garden to enjoy the flowers. Walking down the pebble lane, he was attracted by a bee busily gathering pollen in an open blossom. He was watching intently when a wasp flew overhead into a cluster of flowers. Sensing danger, the bee cowered to the side and made ready to fly away. The wasp, however, planted itself on a petal and fixed its gaze on the bee, waving its tentacles. The bee crawled for two steps and was just about to take off when the wasp leapt over and killed the bee instantly with a deadly sting.

A concubine who was accompanying Fu Chai broke off a twig and tried to beat the wasp with it.

Fu Chai took hold of her hand. "My beloved, it is natural for the strong to overcome the weak in this world."

"What about people?" asked the concubine.

"The strong will live on while the weak perish," replied Fu Chai without hesitation.

The concubine shuddered. "Your humble servant is also weak," she said anxiously.

"Well," said Fu Chai, comforting her. "I am strong, so you are also strong." He suddenly thought of Confucius and his disciple Zi Gong. "When I sent General Wuma Cheng to attack Chen, Confucius argued him into retreating. And it was his disciple Zi Gong who argued eloquently that Lu should not pay tribute to Wu." He began to worry. If the lord of Lu should employ such talented people, Lu would probably grow into a formidable power in the east. When that day came Wu would have to pay tribute to Lu. An idea occurred to him, and he sent someone to bring Bo Pi into the palace.

As soon as he received the summons Bo Pi hastened to the palace.

Fu Chai was waiting in the rear palace. "My honored minister," he said to Bo Pi, "Confucius and many of his disciples are very capable. If they should be employed by the lord of Lu, someday Wu would be destroyed by Lu. Therefore I plan to ..."

Bo Pi immediately understood what was on Fu Chai's mind. "Does Your Highness plan to send an expedition against Lu?"

"Exactly," said Fu Chai.

Thereupon the two of them decided to send General Liang He to invade Lu with a thousand war chariots.

The news filled Duke Ai of Lu with trepidation and regret. He blamed the invasion on Zi Gong, who he thought must have offended Wu by his denial of Lu's obligation to pay annual tributes to Wu. The duke hastily summoned his court officials to discuss the matter.

The entire court was overtaken with fright. Most of the officials voted in favor of the idea to send an envoy, who would carry Lu's tribute to Wu and apologize for the delay.

One of Confucius' disciples was You Ruo, also known by his styled name Zi You. As a native of Lu he did not accompany his master wandering from state to state but stayed on in Lu. He was born in the twenty-fourth year of Duke Zhao of Lu's reign (518 B.C.). He was a man of fortitude, and in spite of his young age he was already conversant with the six arts. Hearing of Wu's invasion, he went to the court and got an audience with Duke Ai. "Your Lordship," he said, "the ancients said that, unlike the birds that only fight for food, man should fight for his dignity. Relying on its superior strength, Wu has sent an army to invade Lu. We must put up a resistance. Though Lu can not compare with Wu in strength, it does have many advantages."

"Please explain," Duke Ai said, gazing at the strong, vigorous young man in front of him.

"First of all, the Wu army has to travel a long distance to attack us, so upon their arrival both men and horses will be tired out, and morale will not be high. An army with low morale loses nine-tenth of its combat strength. Second, the invading army of Wu will be fighting in unfamiliar terrain, which will put them at a great disadvantage. Third, the invasion from Wu will bring calamity to the people in Lu, who will therefore put up a desperate fight, so the Wu army is only outwardly strong but actually weak. Fourth, Wu attacks us without declaring war, for it can find no excuse for the invasion. Such behavior will surely provoke universal opposition. Therefore Lu will surely win the battle."

"Who will be able to command our troops then?" asked Duke Ai.

"I will!" replied You Ruo resolutely.

Duke Ai was surprised. "Have you ever commanded troops?" he asked.

"The art of war, like everything else, can be learned in practice."

Duke Ai was a bit disappointed. "This is a matter of life and death for the state. You must not take it lightly!"

"I have studied the matter thoroughly. By exploiting Wu's weakness and giving full play to Lu's strength, I can lead the Lu army to victory if Your Lordship puts five hundred war chariots under my command."

Duke Ai still felt a little uncertain. "How do you plan to defeat Wu?"

You Ruo recounted his battle plan in detail.

After hearing him out, Duke Ai nodded his head with satisfaction.

You Ruo first sent some mounted scouts to find out about the enemy's movement. Then he gathered five hundred war chariots and set out for the southern border of Lu. They stopped by a river and made camp in the forest about forty li south of the city of Zeng. It was an area of dense forest with few inhabitants. You Ruo and his officers surveyed the local terrain and decided to make use of the river and forest. The river was about one li wide and flowed in a leisurely pace from west to east, its bed covered in sands as fine as flour. Willows and bushes grew along both banks of the river. There was a big forest of poplars on the northern bank. About four to five li to the south flowed the boundary river between Wu and Lu.

It took You Ruo one day and one night to array the troops in accordance with his well-thought-out battle plan. Then a mounted scout returned and reported, "The Wu troops have made camp on the southern bank of the boundary river."

That evening You Ruo dispatched two chariots, each carrying a drum and several drummers, to the dense forest in the southern bank of the river.

The men of Wu, exhausted by several days' travel, went to sleep early in their tents.

At the third watch of the night the Lu drummers hidden in the forest suddenly started beating their drums vigorously. Greatly frightened, the birds in the wood uttered shrill cries and flew in all directions. Aroused from their sleep, the men of Wu scrambled to their feet and hurriedly put on their armor. The general, Liang He, did not know what action the Lu army would take, so he ordered the troops to stand by awaiting further instruction.

The vigorous drumming went on for two hours before it stopped.

Liang He realized that the enemy was merely trying to disturb his troops, so he ordered, "Return to the tents to rest!"

No sooner had the men of Wu lain down in their beds than the drumming started again. Even though he knew it to be a feint, Liang He still felt upset by the loud drumming. His officers and men also found it hard to go asleep and spent a restless night in their tents.

At daybreak You Ruo picked out fifty chariots, which he led to the northern bank of the river and arranged into a battle formation.

Liang He took a glance at the banner carried by You Ruo's chariot embroidered with the big character "Lu," and snorted in contempt. "You want to pull me into an ambush," he said to himself, "but your arrangement is too clumsy to fool anyone."

At this moment a scout came to report, "General, the Lu army has five hundred war chariots altogether."

Liang He took another look at You Ruo and said to himself, "Humph! Just another of those useless scholars! How can you gain any advantage with your puny force against my superior, well-trained troops?"

The boundary river was deep and narrow. When You Ruo looked ahead at the enemy troops, he found them in full battle array. The fury of war filled the air. The enemy general was a hefty man with a look of contempt in his piercing eyes. You Ruo bowed with clasped hands. "May I learn your honorable name, general?"

Liang He returned the salute with some reluctance. "My family name is Liang, my given name He, and my styled name Zi He."

"In observing the rites," said You Ruo, "the highest principle is to maintain peace and harmony. The ancient sage rulers abided strictly by this principle so that they were able to deal properly with both important and minor affairs. But you have come today to invade our land, general, without declaring war and without any excuse to justify your action. In doing so you not only go against the instructions of the ancient sage rulers but also grossly violate the essential moral principles. Are you not afraid of being condemned by posterity?"

"I am just a warrior who serves the prince and the state wholeheartedly. I am not interested in other matters. May I learn your honorable name, general?"

"My family name is You, my given name Ruo, and my styled name Zi You."

"You don't look like a general at all, instead you look like a scholar who spends his time reading books and practicing the rites."

"I admire you for your acute observation, general. I am a disciple of Confucius, and this is the first time I have ever commanded an army. I have come here mainly to persuade you to withdraw your troops and save people from misery and suffering."

Liang He was annoyed on hearing this. "The prince has a lifelong regret over the harm caused by your master, who once deceived General Wuma with his eloquence. Do you plan to play the same old trick again? You must realize that I am not as gullible as Wuma Cheng!"

"In that case, do whatever you please."

Liang He beat his chest with his palm. "I am a general of Wu. I will not order my men to charge at you now, otherwise I would be taking advantage of my superior strength, and you would not admit failure even after your defeat."

You Ruo tried to provoke him. "You are actually afraid to fight, because your troops are tired out after a long journey."

"What do you mean?"

"I am saying you are afraid to fight!"

Liang He stamped his foot madly. "I will never lead an army again," he roared, "if I can not wipe you out this time!" He looked back at his troops and found them fully prepared to attack. "Charge forth!" he ordered.

Uttering loud battle-cries, the men of Wu dashed onto the bridge.

You Ruo had his chariots arrayed in a line facing the bridge. When the Wu chariots approached the north end of the bridge, he cried loudly, "Shoot!"

In the shower of arrows the chariot at the head of the Wu army broke down as its driver was shot dead. The chariots behind it stopped abruptly, and the advance of the entire Wu army came to a halt. Caught in a line of immobile chariots midway across the bridge, Liang He yelled in exasperation, "Push the broken chariot down the bridge!"

At You Ruo's order the archers of Lu kept shooting arrows, destroying over ten enemy chariots. "Retreat!" You Ruo passed on the order in a whisper. The fifty Lu chariots turned and left the boundary river swiftly, without suffering any casualty.

Liang He fumed with rage at the sight of the retreating Lu army. "Cross the river quickly!" he shouted to his troops. As soon as they reached the other bank, he flourished his sword and ordered them to charge forth. Soon he came to the river by which the Lu army was camped. He stopped his chariot, dismounted and surveyed the enemy camps on the northern bank. As he thought of the humiliation he had just suffered, his first impulse was to charge forth and crash the enemy once and for all. However, he grew a little apprehensive at the sight of the dense forest. He turned and asked his subordinates, "Is there a roundabout route to get there?"

"There is none," replied one of them. "The forest is too dense for the troops to pass through."

Liang He went down to the river and stabbed the sand under the shallow water with his sword. He got on his chariot and ordered, "Ford across the river!"

The chariots rolled forward. Due to the obstruction of the dike, only two chariots could move abreast onto the northern bank at one time. After a dozen chariots had got across without meeting any resistance, Liang He also crossed the river in his chariot. Eager to catch up with the enemy, he ordered the troops to move forward at full speed. Then it occurred to him that You Ruo was unlikely not to make use of the forest. He was about to order the troops to stop when a cloud of dust rose ahead and two leading chariots were caught in the trap. Aware of his mistake, he ordered the troops to make an about face and withdraw, but there was not enough room to do it. The chariots bumped against one another and fell into confusion.

At this very moment they heard loud drum-beats. The Lu soldiers who had lain in ambush suddenly emerged from behind the trees and began shooting arrows. The Wu chariots that had crossed the river had no way of escape. The men of Lu uttered loud battle-cries while the men of Wu screamed and howled in misery. Many Wu soldiers were shot down, but a few lay beside the chariots, feigning death, and fled while the Lu army mounted the dike to shoot at the Wu chariots in the river. Shielding himself from the arrows by brandishing his sword, Liang He retreated along the abandoned chariots. When he reached the river, he found his troops scattering in all directions.

More and more Lu soldiers came to the dike to shoot arrows into the river. The men of Wu could not fight back but fled helter-skelter.

Liang He also fled as fast as his legs could carry him, shouting "Retreat! Retreat!" as he ran.

Suddenly You Ruo appeared on the dike and shouted, "Charge forth! Catch Liang He alive!"

Glancing back, Liang He found that the Lu soldiers had dismounted their chariots and were pursuing him hotly on foot. In his panic he tripped on a horse rein and fell into the water with a splash.

Chapter Thirty-seven

Zi Gong Successfully Reclaims
the Lost Land for Lu;
Lady Qiguan Longs in Vain
for Her Husband's Return

Seeing Liang He fall a soldier ran over and cut the rope with his sword. Liang He got up and scampered to the southern bank. The men of Wu suffered great casualties, with only less than two hundred war chariots managing to get away.

You Ruo wanted to pursue the enemy further, but unfortunately his chariots were stopped by the river. So he had the gong beaten to call back the troops, which had suffered only slight losses. They rested for a short while, cleaned up the battlefield and returned to the capital carrying all the booty.

Duke Ai of Lu was overjoyed at the news of the victory and treated You Ruo with special favor. At the same time he could not help thinking of Confucius.

When the news reached Confucius, he was filled with all sorts of feelings along with a flickering hope that Duke Ai and Jisun Fei would take this chance to invite him back. However, several months went by with no message from Lu.

In summer that year Duke Dao of Qi, a young, ambitious ruler who wanted to become an overlord just like his ancestor Duke Huan of Qi, launched a surprise attack against Lu, capturing Huan and Yangguan.

At the news Confucius called Zi Gong to him. "For the past few years Lu has suffered both natural and manmade calamities, and it just lost Huan and Yangguan to Qi," he said to Zi Gong. "What would happen if things develop in this way! Formerly you overwhelmed Duke Jing of Qi with your eloquence and won great fame in Qi. I want you to take another trip to Qi and try to persuade Duke Dao to return the occupied land to Lu."

"You may rest assured, master! I will argue Duke Dao of Qi into returning Huan and Yangguan to Lu!"

Confucius looked at him with great approval.

Zi Gong set out for Qi immediately. Riding in his chariot, he recalled his visit to Qi eight years before. In autumn of the fifteenth year of Duke Ding of Lu's reign (495 B.C.) Zi Gong went to Qi to traffic in horses and mules. Learning that Zi Gong was a disciple of Confucius, Duke Jing of Qi summoned him to the palace and asked deliberately, "According to what I have heard, you are very smart and have never lost money in business. May I ask who your master is?"

"My master is Confucius of Lu."

"Is Confucius a man of virtue?"

"Why should you ask that?" Zi Gong thought to himself. "You have met him and must know for yourself." He cleared his throat and announced proudly, "My master is not merely a man of virtue. He should be regarded as a sage!"

Duke Jing snorted derisively. "So what kind of a sage is he?"

Zi Gong thought for a while, then raised his head slowly. "I don't know."

Duke Jing was greatly annoyed, thinking Zi Gong was making fun of him. "What do you mean by saying you don't know?"

Unruffled, Zi Gong replied, "I have always lived with the sky above my head, yet I don't know how high it is. I have always lived with the earth under my feet, yet I don't know how thick it is. I have to use a comparison to explain my opinion concerning my master."

The duke nodded his consent.

"The master can be compared to a big river. When I feel thirsty I go to the river and drink my fill from it. But how could I possibly know the depth of the river?"

Duke Jing was impressed by Zi Gong's eloquence but still found his words hard to believe. "Are you not giving your master too much praise," he asked, "when you make such a comparison?"

"My only fear is that the comparison I use fails to convey my admiration for my master. In my opinion, he is like ..."

"What is he like?" the duke anticipated him impatiently.

Zi Gong paused meaningfully, then continued, "My master can be compared to Mount Tai. If I add a handful of earth to Mount Tai, it will not become any higher. If I take a handful of earth from Mount Tai, it will not become any lower. The fact is obvious: Mount Tai was not piled up by man. It towers over all other mountains whether I extol it or not."

Duke Jing was very satisfied with this reply. "Well said. Very well indeed!"

After that, Duke Jing of Qi began to look upon Zi Gong in a new light and regretted not having employed Confucius.

When Zi Gong returned to Wei and recounted the incident, Confucius said approvingly, "You are really an eloquent speaker!"

Zi Gong felt quite pleased with himself when he recalled how he had convinced Duke Jing with his eloquence and won Confucius' high praise. It took him less than half a month to arrive in the Qi capital. It was still early in the day, so he headed straight for the palace.

Duke Dao of Qi was much startled when he was informed of Zi Gong's visit, for he instantly recalled how Zi Gong had rendered the late duke speechless with his eloquence. After a while he said reluctantly, "Ask him to come in!"

At the age of thirty-three Zi Gong was in possession of great ability, rich experience and graceful manners. He walked unhurriedly into the rear palace and saluted duke Dao. "A native of Wei and a disciple of Confucius pays his respects to Your Lordship!"

Duke Dao looked at Zi Gong uneasily. "Please get up!"

Zi Gong thanked the duke and got on his feet.

"So you are a disciple of Confucius?" asked the duke conversationally, not knowing the purpose of Zi Gong's trip to Qi.

"Yes, I am," Zi Gong replied with a slight bow.

"How is your master?"

"Thanks so much for your concern! My master is very well."

"You have come to Qi this time ..."

"There is something that I don't understand, so I have come to ask Your Lordship's instruction."

Duke Dao sighed with relief. "Please let me hear about it."

"In the state of Wei there lived a rich man who stole the rice and wheat from his poor neighbor. The neighbor's family went hungry as a result. The rich man went on to enjoy the stolen food without feeling the least sense of shame. I wonder if the thief's behavior was right or wrong?"

Duke Dao looked at Zi Gong with surprise and covered his mouth with his sleeve to suppress a giggle. "This is not difficult to judge. The thief did two wrongs: First, he was rich and had enough to eat and wear, so he should not steal. Second, to steal rice and wheat from a neighbor whom he knew to be very poor would be like murdering for gain! The man was worse than a beast, for even a rabbit does not eat the grass by its own burrow!"

"If such a thief fell into your hands, how would you deal with him?"

Duke Dao assumed a serious tone. "If such a thief fell into my hands, I would confiscate his property and distribute it among the poor, and throw him into prison so that he would not get another chance to harm others!"

"You are such a wise sovereign!" Zi Gong exclaimed with assumed admiration. "However, there is something else I don't quite understand," he said gravely.

"You may speak freely," said Duke Dao with a smile.

"It is common knowledge that Qi is a wealthy and powerful state, whereas Lu is a poor and small one. However, in spite of universal condemnation, Qi sent troops to attack Lu and occupied Huan and Yangguan by force. Would Your Lordship please tell me if there is any difference between Qi and that rich thief from Wei?"

Duke Dao was struck speechless, and his face turned pale.

Zi Gong went on relentlessly, "In the state of Lu there are many barren hills and turbulent waters, but very few places with fertile land such as Huan and Yangguan. The loss of Huan and Yangguan has deprived Lu of two major crop producers. How will the people of Lu be able to save themselves from starvation?"

Duke Dao's face was now ghastly pale, beads of perspiration standing on his forehead, and his lips quivering. After a long pause he muttered, "Some treacherous ministers did that behind my back."

"In that case," Zi Gong beamed, "I hope Your Lordship would be kind enough to issue an order to recall the Qi troops garrisoned in Lu territory and return Huan and Yangguan to Lu."

Duke Dao knew he was no match for Zi Gong in a verbal battle. He thought for a while, then raised his head. "You can rest assured that I will withdraw the troops as soon as possible and return the two places to Lu."

Zi Gong got up from his seat. "A promise made in the palace is no joke, Your Lordship."

Duke Dao nodded with a forced smile and also got up. "It has been a long time since I first heard of you as a man of extraordinary ability. Now I have found out for myself that your reputation is well-deserved. Why doesn't a capable man like you serve in the government?"

Zi Gong sighed lightly. "Every man wants to achieve something great in his lifetime, but he may have to do that against great odds. Even my master, a man with the height of Mount Tai and the depth of a great river, has met numerous setbacks and frustrations, let alone someone like myself."

"From what I have heard, both Zi Lu and Gao Chai serve as officials under the lord of Wei and have done quite well. Is that true?"

"Yes."

"I see. Zi Lu comes from Lu and Gao Chai from Qi, but you are a native of Wei. Now that both of them serve the lord of Wei, why don't you follow suit?"

"The entire world is under the rule of the king of Zhou. Though Zi Lu and Gao Chai are not natives of Wei, they are both subjects of the king of Zhou. Whichever state they choose to serve in, they are actually serving His Majesty the king of Zhou. As for me, I am not yet an official, perhaps because I am not qualified in terms of virtue and ability."

"If I ask you to stay in Qi, would you condescend to take up a position unworthy of your great talents?"

Zi Gong smiled blandly. "If I were to take office, I would care more about what I can achieve than what status it will bring to me." With this he took his leave. Duke Dao showed his courtesy by accompanying Zi Gong to the gate of the rear palace.

Soon afterward, Huan and Yangguan were returned to Lu.

When Zi Gong came back with the news, Confucius was much delighted. "The lord of Qi was impressed by your talents. You may prepare to receive an appointment in Qi."

"The lord of Qi must be joking. Why should he want to employ someone who has twice created trouble for them?"

Confucius was about to speak when Qidiao Kai came up and said, "Master, I have just heard that Kuai Kui was planning another assault against the capital."

"The discord was sowed," said Confucius, "when Duke Ling let his grandson, Zhe, succeed him. An outbreak of war will be unavoidable unless Zhe invites his father back to rule Wei."

"When that day comes, it would be inconvenient for us to stay on in Wei. What shall we do?"

Confucius gazed up at the ceiling and thought for a long time.

"Qidiao Kai," he said, "whatever happens, we must have faith in our cause and be eager to learn and ready to die for it. Haven't you noticed already? I never enter a state full of instability or stay in a state with internal turmoil. We may have to leave Wei for another state some-day."

"What about Zi Lu and Gao Chai?"

"When the world is at peace, one should come out to take office; when the world is in turmoil, one should conceal oneself and not take office. When that day comes Zi Lu and Gao Chai will have to resign from their posts and move away."

"Wouldn't they be widely criticized for such behavior?"

"Why should they be criticized? When the ruler is wise and benign, it would be shameful for a man with wide vision not to take office and remain humble and poor. It is also a shame for him to obtain wealth and honors when the ruler is fatuous and malevolent."

Qidiao Kai smiled his understanding and turned to leave.

Confucius called him back. "Qidiao Kai," he said, "both Zi Lu and Gao Chai have done well in their office. I intend to recommend you to a position. What do you think?"

Qidiao Kai declined, saying, "Master, I am slow-witted and lacking in ability. I do not have the confidence for an official career and have not even thought about it."

Confucius gave him an approving smile.

"Master," Zi Gong asked, "as far as I know there will not be any war in Wei in the near future. Why don't you seek an official position in Wei?"

Confucius sighed, "Ten years ago I left Lu for Wei with the intention to assist Duke Ling of Wei in governing the state. However, though the duke was very generous to us, he never offered me any official position. Today, Kuai Kui and Zhe are at daggers drawn, and the state will be plunged into chaos sooner or later. When the ruler of the state is facing an uncertain future, how can I go and serve him?"

"Suppose there is a fine piece of jade, should it be locked up in a casket or should it be for sale?"

"For sale! For sale!" replied Confucius bluntly. "I have been waiting for a buyer who truly appreciates its value." Then he sighed as he remembered what they had gone through in the past ten years. "Where can I find such a buyer?" His thoughts drifted from the many states he had visited, and finally to Lu and to his family.

Back in Lu Lady Qiguan had become bedridden. Her face was sallow, her body weak, and she lay in bed all day staring vacantly at the ceiling. She had spent all her life in this courtyard and the few thatched houses, sharing weals and woes with her husband. Looking back, she found to her regret that their happy moments together were too few. The family had rejoiced with him when he distinguished himself as magistrate of Zhongdu, served in the court as minister of justice and won a diplomatic victory for Lu at the Jiagu meeting. They had also shared his distress over the rampant corruption among officials, the power struggle in the palace, and above all, the shame brought on Lu by its fatuous sovereign and chief minister. She made herself think of the happy moments and relived them again and again in her mind. Through the window she could always see the old scholartree, its leaves turning yellow in autumn and green again in spring. At night she closed her eyes and prayed for her husband, wishing for his stars to smile upon him.

Confined to bed for a long time, she had developed bedsores in many parts of her body. Kong Li and his wife sent for a physician, who prescribed ointment for her, but it produced little effect. Wuwei often returned from her husband's home to take care of her mother, helping her to turn over in bed, comb her hair and wash her face. Kong Zhong, his wife and Kong Wujia also came to look after her very often, treating her as their own mother, and even the little grandson Kong Ji came to give a helping hand. However, Lady Qiguan's condition continued to deteriorate.

On a spring day in the ninth year of Duke Ai of Lu's reign (486 B.C.) Lady Qiguan gazed at the old scholartree outside the window. New leaves were sprouting in the twigs, and some sparrows were leaping and chirping merrily. She shifted her gaze to the gate, through which Confucius used to enter every day. When she heard the sound of opening the gate she would put down her needlework and went out to the courtyard to meet him. Every time he left home, she would stand in the courtyard and gazed after him, wishing him good fortune. Just at this moment the gate was pushed open by a gust of wind. She widened her eyes as she seemed to catch a glimpse of her husband entering the gate. She wanted to leap out of the bed into his arms and tell him how much she missed him. However, she could only raise her hands a little.

"Mother," asked Wuwei, who was sitting by her side. "What do you want?"

The voice brought Lady Qiguan back to reality. She shook her head slightly, and tears rolled down her cheeks.

"Mother!" Wuwei pressed her head against Lady Qiguan's bosom. "What do you want to say?"

Lady Qiguan slowly raised her hand and wiped the tears off Wuwei's face. "I am fine, my dear daughter. Don't worry. I will get better."

Wuwei knew that her mother was only trying to comfort her, and wept more sadly.

In the increasingly strong wind the gate kept making thumping noises. Wuwei could not help looking back at the gate, hoping against hope that it would be her father returning home.

Kong Ji ran over to the bed and asked, as his mother had taught him to, "Grandma, are you feeling better?"

Lady Qiguan stroked him on the head and smiled. "I am feeling much better, much better."

The wind blew fiercely all day, and dark clouds gathered in the sky at nightfall. At the third watch of the night the wind stopped, and it started to rain.

"Rain in spring is as precious as oil," as the saying goes. Every household rejoiced and prayed for a good year.

It grew dark in the room as the lamp had almost run out of oil. Lady Qiguan coughed in a barely audible voice, pointing her hands to the courtyard. She gazed out the window with widened eyes but could not utter any sound.

The family gathered around her waiting for her to speak. They had stayed up for forty-eight hours without sleeping a wink.

Her lips trembling with effort, Lady Qiguan finally said, "Ask him to return ..."

"Mother," asked Kong Li anxiously, "please tell us what you want!"

She rolled her eyes and looked at her children one by one, then slowly shook her head.

Kong Li did not know what to do. His wife suddenly caught on and went to the west room. She returned with Kong Ji, who was still fast asleep, in her arms and held him to Lady Qiguan's bed.

Lady Qiguan's lips parted in a smile. Her head slipped sideways, and she breathed her last.

At daybreak the rain stopped. Kong Li invited some of Confucius' disciples in Lu and asked their advice on how to arrange the funeral for his mother.

Ran Qiu said, "When the master toured the Sihe River he noticed a piece of high ground outside the north city gate. How about bury Lady Qiguan there?"

The other disciples all expressed their consent, and Kong Li also agreed. With the disciples' help Kong Li buried his mother.

On a sunny day Confucius and his disciples paid a long-expected visit to the city of Tang, a place mentioned in one of his favorite poems from *The Book of Poetry*. They were delighted to see large tracts of well-cultivated field and luxuriant mulberry trees. Bees and butterflies danced among the flowers and birds sang merrily. Confucius walked up a high mound to look around. Pleased with the lively scene, he began to sing the poem.

Just then a chariot rushed toward them at full speed, leaving clouds of dust behind it.

Confucius stopped singing and looked apprehensively at the chariot.

The driver came up to them. It was Gao Chai.

"What has happened?" asked Confucius, looking at Gao Chai's anxious expression.

Gao Chai was nearly out of breath. "I just heard that Kong Li's mother, Kong Boji, and her lover, Hun Liangfu, are plotting with Kuai Kui against Zhe. Wei will soon fall into chaos, so I no longer want to be an official here. Master, let's leave for another place!"

"Where can we find a peaceful place? As long as the rites of Zhou are not restored, people will not stop using force against one another, and there will be no peace in this world."

"Master, it is true that all the other states have their problems, but here in Wei there is going to be a fight between father and son. It would be most inconvenient for us to stay on and probably get involved."

"We have already been to Song, Chen, Cai and Chu," said Confucius. "Wherever we went, there was no opportunity for us to realize our aspirations." He was no longer in the mood to enjoy the scenery and decided to call it a day.

As soon as they entered the gate of their house they found Kong Zhong stand waiting in the courtyard, dressed in mourning.

Confucius immediately knew what had happened.

"My aunt passed away," said Kong Zhong tearfully, "and was buried outside the north gate of the capital."

Confucius felt a pang in his chest, and tears rolled down his face. He imagined how she had spent the last minute of her life still longing to see him, and for a short moment he almost regretted not having returned home. But quickly he brushed the thought aside. "How could I compromise my integrity because of that?" he said to himself.

That night Confucius tossed and turned in bed, unable to go to sleep. He had nearly lost hope in the lords of the various states because of their fatuity, ineptitude and corruption. The past was full of frustrations, and the future looked rather grim. He closed his eyes and tried to envisage the shining pagoda, the symbol of an ideal kingdom, but failed to see any light. He felt as if he were standing at crossroads, not knowing which way to take.

The next day the disciples found him in a bad mood, so they either went away reading or sat around in the house chatting. Annoyed, Confucius said with disapproval, "Why should one eat three meals a day and yet do nothing worthwhile? If one does not want to study, why not play chess to improve his mind? That would be better than idling his time away."

Just as he finished these words, it was announced that Gongsun Yujia was at the gate. Confucius was not in the least pleased to hear that. "Invite him to come in!" he said with great reluctance.

Gongsun Yujia bowed deeply, saying, "His Lordship has heard of your wife's death and sent me to offer his condolences!"

"I am grateful to His Lordship for his kind solicitation!"

After an exchange of greetings the two of them had no more to say, and Gongsun Yujia took his leave.

In order to comfort Confucius and take his mind off his grief, Fan Chi deliberately asked an irrelevant question. "Master," he said, "I eat grain every day but know nothing about farmwork. Can you tell us how to plant crops?"

"I have studied books and practiced rites since my early childhood, but when it comes to growing crops, I know less than an experienced peasant."

"I eat vegetables every day, but I don't know the first thing about vegetable-growing. Can you tell us how to grow vegetables?"

"I have never learned to grow vegetables," replied Confucius with increasing annoyance. "You'd better ask an old vegetable grower."

The look of displeasure on Confucius' face told Fan Chi that he was misunderstood. So he went away without venturing to say more.

"Fan Chi is so ignorant!" said Confucius irritably. "He has not understood my teachings about benevolence. If the sovereign and his ministers observe the rites, the common people will not dare to show disrespect; when the sovereign and his ministers act properly, the common people will not dare to disobey; if the sovereign and his ministers are honest and sincere in their attitude, the common people will not dare to tell lies. If the sovereign and his ministers can achieve all these things, people will come from all directions to submit to their authority. Why should there be any need to learn to grow crops oneself?"

Just then Zi Lu arrived from Pu. "Master," he said as soon as he entered the gate. "I just heard the sad news and have come to keep you company for a few days."

Deeply moved, Confucius asked, "How are the crops in Pu this year?"

"Pu suffers from drought almost every spring, and it is especially serious this year. Fortunately we've been able to plant the crops in time thanks to the canals we dug last year."

Confucius looked at Zi Lu and found he was still wearing his old gown of coarse cloth. He was about to express his approval when he suddenly felt dizzy. He staggered back a few steps and leaned against the wall.

"Master is ill!" cried Zi Lu anxiously. "Help him onto the bed and I'll go find a doctor!"

After having been helped onto the bed, Confucius sighed, "Zi Lu has made a lot of improvements in Pu, but he is still wearing his old clothes. He might be the only one among you who can stand in a worn-out gown alongside well-clad people without feeling in the least uneasy. This reminds me of some words from *The Book of Poetry*: 'To be free of jealousy and greed, is this not good?'"

Soon Zi Lu returned with the doctor, who felt Confucius' pulse and prescribed some medicine. After Confucius had taken the medicine, Zi Gong repeated to him what Confucius had just said about him.

That night Zi Lu stayed by Confucius' bed to take care of him. "To be free of jealousy and greed, is this not good?" he began to chant the words.

When Zi Lu would not stop chanting the words, Confucius stopped him by saying, "Is it good enough just to do that?"

Zi Lu blushed and changed the topic. "Master, let me pray to Heaven to make you recover soon!"

Confucius sighed and did not reply.

Chapter Thirty-eight

You Ruo Defeats the Qi Army by Strategy; Zi Gong Uses His Eloquence to Convince the Prince of Wu

At Zi Lu's offer Confucius said, "I have already prayed. But where is Heaven? And what's the use of praying?"

Zi Lu knew that Confucius must have caught cold due to mental exhaustion, so he prepared the herbal medicine carefully. Three days later Confucius was on his feet again. After seeing Kong Zhong off, he continued to teach his disciples.

The conflicts among the vassal states grew increasingly fierce. In spring of the ninth year of Duke Ai of Lu's reign (486 B.C.) Song defeated Zheng at Yongqiu. That autumn Fu Chai ordered vast dredging work to be executed to connect the Yangtze River with the Huai. This facilitated transportation in Wu and strengthened it militarily, placing it in a more advantageous position in its contention for supremacy with its rival states in the north.

In spring of the tenth year of Duke Ai's reign (485 B.C.) Fu Chai joined forces with Lu, Zhu and Tan to attack Qi. The expedition, led by the Wu general Xu Cheng, headed north by boats. Suffering a defeat, they returned. Soon afterward, a Qi minister named Bao Mu murdered Duke Dao of Qi and set up his son Ren as the new duke, who became known as Duke Jian. In summer that year Zhao Jianzi of Jin led troops to attack Qi; in the subsequent battle both sides suffered heavy casualties. In that winter when Prince Hui of Chu sent an expedition against Chen, Duke Min of Chen turned to Fu Chai for help. The force sent by Fu Chai to rescue Chen inflicted a crushing defeat on the invading troops of Chu.

In spring of the eleventh year of Duke Ai's reign (484 B.C.) Duke Jian of Qi put Bao Mu in command of a crack force to attack Lu. The Qi army smashed all resistance as it swept across Lu territory, soon reaching the suburbs of the Lu capital.

Duke Ai and his ministers became panic-stricken, and most of the officials were in favor of sueing Qi for peace.

Confucius was deeply disturbed by the news. "The Lu capital has

a history of over six hundred years," he said. "It is home to many classics and ancient buildings, including the Temple of the Duke of Zhou. If the men of Qi should capture it, they would surely rob it of everything." He walked to and fro in the courtyard, wishing he could sprout wings and fly back to his homeland to lead a Lu force to ward off the invading troops.

"Master," said Zi Lu, "let me return to Lu and command a thousand chariots to dispel the Qi army."

"The Lu capital is in imminent danger," said Confucius with a frown. "By the time you get there it would already be too late. Moreover, how can you be sure you could defeat the Qi army?"

Zi Lu stamped his foot in great distress. "We can't let the men of Qi capture our capital without doing anything about it!"

"You are right. We must find a way to stop them."

"Master," said Zi Gong, "it is true that the Qi army has approached the Lu capital, but whether they can capture the city is entirely another matter. Both You Ruo and Ran Qiu are staying in Lu, and they will surely rise to the occasion and do their best to protect Lu against the invaders."

"Right!" said Confucius. "But I have received no news about them."

"Don't worry. Let me go to Lu to find out."

"That will be great. You may take the trip immediately!"

Zi Gong set out for Lu without further delay.

The atmosphere was tense in the Lu court. Duke Ai looked very pale, and his voice trembled when he spoke. "My honored ministers, the Qi army is bearing down on us with overwhelming force, and our troops have failed so far to stop them. The capital is in great danger. What shall we do about it?"

Mengsun Heji and Shusun Zhouchou were both old men over sixty. They looked appealingly to Jisun Fei.

"Your Lordship," Jisun Fei said, "Ran Qiu is well versed in the six arts. Shall we let him lead the troops?"

Duke Ai's face lit up with delight. "Yes! Why not let him lead our troops? It was You Ruo, another of Confucius' disciples, who defeated the Wu army not long ago." Feeling reassured, he sat down in his chair. "Summon Ran Qiu and You Ruo to the palace immediately!"

No sooner had he finished these words than a guard entered.

"Your Lordship," he said, "Ran Qiu and You Ruo are outside the palace gate asking for an audience!"

Duke Ai almost leapt from his seat with joy. "Quick! Invite them to come in!"

"Ran Qiu and You Ruo, enter the palace!" the guard went out and announced in a loud voice.

Ran Qiu and You Ruo walked in side by side and dropped on their knees before the duke.

Forgetting all about formalities, Duke Ai stood up and waved his hands to them. "Stand up! Stand up!" They had barely got on their feet when the Duke asked anxiously, "The Qi army will arrive soon to besiege the capital. I intend to have you lead the troops and go out the city to dispel the enemy. What do you think?"

"As a native of Lu, I am willing to risk my life fighting against invaders," said Ran Qiu. "But I have a request."

"Please speak!"

Ran Qiu took a look at Jisun Fei, Mengsun Heji and Shusun Zhouchou, then went on, "Your Lordship, the Qi army is strong and high-spirited after successive victories, whereas the Lu army is weak and low-spirited after successive defeats. In order to reverse the course of events we have to mobilize the armed forces of the entire state. Ministers Jisun, Mengsun and Shusun have thousands of soldiers each in their manors. If all these troops can be put into action, there is no doubt that we can drive the Qi invaders from Lu territory."

"When the nation is in danger," said You Ruo, "everyone shares a responsibility to save his homeland. I hope the three ministers will rise up to the crisis!"

Jisun Fei pulled a long face. "Your Lordship, it isn't that we did not want to use the forces in our manors. The Qi army moved in so fast that before we could react, they were already at the gates of our capital. It would be too late to send for the forces in those outlying reigns."

"That's right!" agreed Mengsun Heji and Shusun Zhouchou in a mumbled voice. "That would surely be too late."

"The Qi army launched a surprise attack and met with little resistance," said You Ruo. "That's why they were able to move in so fast. Though this has put us at a disadvantage, there is still a chance that we can save the situation. First, when the fate of out state is at stake, our people must be willing to fight the enemy to death. Second, the men of Qi have marched at full speed for a long distance, so they must be exhausted, and their fighting capacity greatly reduced. Third, Minister Jisun has seven thousand crack forces at Fei, Minister Mengsun has three thousand crack forces at Cheng, and Minister Shusun has four thousand crack forces at Hou. We can gather these forces and order them to close in on the enemy from the rear, while we venture out of the capital to launch a frontal assault. Attacked on both sides, the men of Qi will panic and fall into confusion. We will then be able to wipe them out. Failing that, we can at least drive them out of Lu territory."

Duke Ai stood up abruptly and said in a firm voice, "Ministers Jisun, Mengsun and Shusun, order your forces to set out at once!" Turning to Ran Qiu and You Ruo, he asked, "I intend to put you in command of the troops in the capital to fight the enemy. What do you think?"

"It is our duty to fight for our homeland!" replied Ran Qiu and You Ruo with one voice.

"You must exercise the utmost caution," admonished the duke. "The fate of our state lies in your hands!"

"We will carry out your order!" responded Ran Qiu and You Ruo. They saluted the duke and left the palace. The three ministers sent mounted messengers to Fei, Hou and Cheng to order the troops there to proceed to the suburbs of the capital.

Ran Qiu and You Ruo climbed up the watchtower at the east city gate to gaze into the distance. They saw nothing but mist and dust.

"There are only four hundred war chariots in the capital," said Ran Qiu. "Let us take one hundred each and leave two hundred to defend the city. In this way we can guard against emergencies and reassure His Lordship and the city residents."

"It's quality, rather than quantity, that counts for an army," agreed You Ruo. "We will be able to regain the initiative by using the right strategy."

Reaching an agreement, they sent a message to the troops outside the city ordering them to hold their ground. A counterattack was scheduled after dark.

The stars shone brightly that night. Ran Qiu and You Ruo, each leading a hundred war chariots, went out the east and south gates respectively. To intimidate the enemy, they gathered many able-bodied city residents, who were made to accompany the chariots carrying lanterns and torches.

The men of Qi had hoped to overcome the Lu capital very quickly, but the Lu soldiers entrenched themselves outside the city and put up a stubborn resistance. Having failed to make any progress for several days, the Qi generals held a meeting to discuss the matter. Just then a soldier came into the tent and reported, "Many Lu troops are coming out of the city!" When the Qi generals went out of the tent, they were amazed by the sight.

Ran Qiu and You Ruo met with the officers in charge of defense outside the city. They ordered the city residents to extinguish the lanterns and torches and return to the city quietly.

The Qi generals were deeply puzzled by what they saw. They wondered how many Lu troops had arrived and what action they would take to fight back.

After daybreak Ran Qiu and You Ruo ordered the soldiers to keep on digging trenches and building defense works. Many archers were arrayed behind the rampart, each with a large stack of arrows by his side.

When the Qi generals climbed up a mound to take a look, they saw only a small number of enemy chariots and realized that they had been the victim of a false alarm the night before. Greatly annoyed, Bao Mu ordered his men to charge forth in their chariots.

About fifty chariots rushed forward. Arriving before the trench, some did not stop in time and dropped into it. Some soldiers managed to rein in their horses, but they were instantly shot down by the Lu archers who emerged from behind the rampart.

Bao Mu was furious and ordered another assault.

Another fifty chariots charged forward, but they suffered the same fate as their predecessors.

Bao Mu came to his senses and told his men to take no more action.

At this You Ruo said to Ran Qiu, "The enemy has failed twice in his assault and will not take any more action for some time. You stay here to defend this position, and I will lead a hundred archers to storm the enemy camp at night to destroy the Qi soldiers' morale."

"That's a good idea, but we may suffer some casualties as a result."

"The surprise attack only aims to upset the Qi troops. We don't need to engage the enemy in fierce combat. So long as we can send a wave of panic among the enemy troops, we will have achieved our purpose."

"In that case, you don't have to take the risk yourself."

"Morale is still low among our troops. If the chief commander did not go, the soldiers would lack confidence and be unable to fight bravely. Led by the chief commander, the soldiers will feel confident and eager to gain victory."

"Be careful!" said Ran Qiu with concern.

"Just wait for good news!" responded You Ruo confidently.

"I will deploy the archers to coordinate your action and beat off the men of Qi if they should pursue you."

"Many thanks, brother!"

Thwarted twice, the Qi troops were no longer in high spirits. After dark most soldiers went into their tents to sleep.

Sword in hand and bow and arrows slumped over their backs, You Ruo and a hundred selected soldiers approached the enemy camp in the dead of the night. After dispatching the sentries, they stormed into the tents, hacking and stabbing in all directions.

The injured Qi soldiers howled in agony as the entire camp-site was plunged into commotion. Some soldiers stumbled out of the tents and began running wildly, and some picked up their weapons and fought among themselves in the dark. When the men of Qi finally came to their senses, You Ruo had already returned safely to his own camp with his soldiers.

The next morning Bao Mu advanced with a hundred chariots and stopped at an arrow's shot from the Lu army. "General Ran!" he shouted. "If you are a real man, why don't you come out and fight a decent battle with me? To hide yourself behind the rampart and gain advantage by petty tricks is unworthy of a chief general!"

Ran Qiu summoned a hundred chariots and advanced to meet the enemy. "General Bao," he sneered, "Lu and Qi enjoyed friendly relations for a long time. Now Qi has invaded Lu in total disregard of honor and faith, yet you seem to take pride in such a base act instead of feeling deeply ashamed. Is such behavior worthy of a chief general?"

Bao Mu pointed to his general's banner and declared, "As a general of Qi I must protect the interests of my homeland. If you can persuade your lord to pay annual tribute to my lord, I will withdraw my troops immediately."

"Lu and Qi are both vassal states under the king of Zhou, why should Lu pay tribute to Qi? It is not clear yet who will win. If Lu should inflict a crushing defeat on Qi, would you persuade the lord of Qi to pay tribute to Lu?"

"Victory will definitely belong to Qi. It won't take me more than a few days to capture the capital of Lu."

Ran Qiu let out a roar of laughter. "How lamentable! What a pity! A chief general like you doesn't even know the simple truth that an army swelling with self-conceit is bound to lose!"

Bao Mu was so enraged that even his beard trembled uncontrollably. He pointed to the trench in front of him. "You are so scared of the great Qi army that you have dug ditches and holes just like rats and ants. That is indeed lamentable!"

"A hedge is needed to keep off pigs and dogs, not to mention wolves and jackals."

Bao Mu's face turned livid with rage. He drove his chariot forward and shot an arrow toward Ran Qiu's banner. The arrow cut through the character "Ran" and landed on the pole of the banner.

Ran Qiu picked up his bow and shot back. The arrow broke the rope of Bao Mu's banner, which fell squarely on Bao Mu's head.

Bao Mu screamed furiously and started shooting nonstop at Ran Qiu, who dodged nimbly.

Just then Ran Qiu saw some banners rise in the low hills in the east and knew to his joy that reinforcements had arrived from Fei. "Bao Mu," he shouted, "you are doomed! Come forth in your chariot and meet your death!"

Bao Mu stared blankly, not knowing what was happening. Then his soldiers began to cry, "General Bao, we are surrounded!" He turned and was stupefied by the enemy troops that seemed to have come out of nowhere. "Retreat!" he shouted madly. "Retreat!"

As the men of Qi turned to flee, You Ruo ordered the soldiers to fill up the trench. Then he and Ran Qiu led the troops east to pursue the enemy.

Reaching the Sihe River, the Qi troops prepared to cross it. However, a band of Lu troops, which had come from Hou and Cheng, emerged on the northern bank to form a pincer with the troops from Fei. Having no alternative, the men of Qi drove their chariots into the river and traveled upstream to the east.

Soon after, Ran Qiu and You Ruo also reached the river. Ran Qiu stayed on the southern bank while You Ruo crossed the river. They ordered the Lu troops to shoot arrows at the Qi soldiers in the river.

The Qi army suffered such heavy casualties that water in the Sihe River turned red. The remnants got on the northern bank and fled as fast as they could.

Ran Qiu and You Ruo sent a mounted messenger to report to Duke Ai while they led the troops in a hot pursuit.

The Qi troops fled helter-skelter, leaving many chariots and corpses behind.

The chase lasted an entire day and night when the two armies, both exhausted, reached Jiagu.

Coming to a big river, both soldiers and horses began drinking from it.

Having drunk his fill, Bao Mu leapt back onto his chariot. Just then he caught sight of Ran Qiu coming after him. He tried to get away in his chariot, but the horses, having not drunk enough, refused to move.

Riding along the southern bank, Ran Qiu approached Bao Mu and aimed an arrow at his bosom.

Bao Mu dodged hurriedly, and the arrow landed on his left shoulder. He drew his sword and stabbed the rumps of the horses, which neighed in pain and bolted, drawing the chariot out of the river unto the northern bank.

Ran Qiu and You Ruo engaged in a hot pursuit until they drove the remnants of the Qi army out of Lu territory. Arriving at Ailing of Qi, they encountered reinforcements from Qi and stopped to make camp. The two armies confronted each other across a river.

Traveling at double speed, Zi Gong arrived in Lu and learned to his joy that the invading army of Qi had already been beaten by Ran Qiu and You Ruo. He immediately wrote a letter and asked Kong Zhong to take it to Confucius. As Bao Mu had obtained reinforcements and made camp at Ailing, Zi Gong worried that the Qi army might launch another attack, so he went to the palace to see Duke Ai. "Your Lordship," he said, "the Qi army has suffered a grave defeat, but it has now stationed itself at Ailing close to the Qi-Lu boundary. If we don't take the opportunity to wipe it out but allow it to recuperate, there will be no end of trouble in the future."

"For several years our state has suffered natural disasters and foreign invasions," said Duke Ai, "and our resources have been exhausted as a result. Since Ran Qiu and You Ruo have already driven the Qi invaders out of our land, we can call back the troops, so we can take a rest and build up our strength."

Zi Gong disagreed. "Your Lordship, a snake must be struck at its most vulnerable point, and a weed must be torn out by the roots. As the greatest power in the east Qi has always intended to lord it over the other states. As Qi's close neighbor, Lu can be compared to a high wall that obstructs its expansion. In order to conquer the other states, Qi has to bring Lu to submission first. That's why Qi has invaded Lu time and again. To eliminate the threat from Qi and secure lasting peace, Lu has to join forces with some powerful states in an expedition against Qi and defeat it summarily until it no longer has the strength to fight back."

"Your words are very reasonable," said Duke Ai with a sad smile. "However, where can we find our allies?"

Zi Gong was well prepared to answer the question. "The state of Wu is powerful and prosperous. We can try to form an alliance with it."

"That won't be possible. Not long ago Wu was gravely defeated by Lu. With this injury still fresh in its mind, why should it agree to cooperate with us?"

"Because the situation has changed. Relying on the fertile land and vast resources, the prince of Wu has the ambition to make himself an overlord among the vassal states. If Your Lordship writes a letter to him explaining Qi's potential threat to him, he will surely agree to send troops to assist us. What's more, he will even believe that Lu is doing him a favor."

Duke Ai nodded his agreement. "But who is suitable to be the envoy to Wu?"

"If given the chance, I will carry out the task."

Duke Ai smiled, "No one else could be more suitable. So I would ask you to take the trouble to fulfill this mission."

"My master, Confucius, has been traveling from state to state all his life in order to restore the rites of Zhou and bring the world under the rule of virtue and benevolence," said Zi Gong. "I am only too glad to contribute a little in protecting peace against violence."

"Well said! I am so happy that you are willing to take on this important task. I will write a letter at once."

Duke Ai wrote a letter and gave it to Zi Gong. "The outcome of your mission will decide the fate of our state. Please be careful!"

"Please have trust in me and wait for me to bring back good

news." With this Zi Gong took leave and started off for Wu.

As soon as Zi Gong arrived in the Wu capital he went straight to the palace.

A guard recognized him."Aren't you a disciple of Confucius?"

"Yes, I am. Please inform the prince that I need to see him on an important and urgent matter."

"Please wait a moment." The guard turned and went into the palace to report.

Zi Gong stood at the palace gate, relishing the beautiful sight around him. "The south has everything—beauty, resources and wealth," he thought to himself. "Yet the prince of Wu is by no means satisfied and wants to rule the entire world. There is truly no limit to man's greed. After a victory over Qi, Wu would surely grow more domineering and aggressive. And when that day comes, I will have no choice but to foster another alliance among some states to fight against Wu."

In the rear palace Fu Chai was working on a plan to line up with Yue, Lu and Chu to fight against Qi and Jin.

Informed by the guard of Zi Gong's arrival Fu Chai frowned and hesitated for a moment, then swept his hand. "Tell him I am sick and can not see him!"

The guard went out to the palace gate. "His Highness is not feeling well and can not see you. Please do not be offended!"

Zi Gong strolled for a few steps, then stopped. "I have come especially to inquire after your lord's health; how can I leave without meeting him? Please report for me once more."

Puzzled, the guard went back into the palace and repeated what Zi Gong had just said to the prince.

"That's ridiculous!" Fu Chai sprang to his feet. "I could not be feeling better. What illness is he talking about?"

The guard stood waiting, holding his breath.

"Well, let him enter," said Fu Chai finally. "I want to find out what trick he is up to."

The guard came to the palace gate to pass on the order. Zi Gong was pleased with his success, and a faint smile flickered across his lips. He walked slowly into the palace and knelt in obeisance. "I was dismayed to learn of Your Highness's illness and has come to offer my solicitude."

Fu Chai wondered what trick Zi Gong was playing. "You may get up," he said coldly.

Zi Gong got on his feet.

"Please take a seat!"

Expressing his thanks, Zi Gong sat down.

Fu Chai looked at Zi Gong from head to toe and shook his head slightly. "When did you arrive in Wu?" he asked.

"I have just arrived."

"Lu is one thousand li from here, and I only began to feel ill this morning. How could you have learned it many days ago?"

"I have been aware of your illness for a long time," said Zi Gong with emphasis.

Fu Chai was dismayed. "I have always enjoyed the best of health. What illness could you be talking about?"

"An illness of the heart, Your Highness."

"Please go on!"

"Nowadays the various states are contending for control of the world. Victors will be masters, and losers will be slaves. The rule of the king of Zhou has become purely nominal, and it is beyond his power to redeem the situation. Under the circumstances, anyone who has high aspirations will be eager to grasp this opportunity to achieve something truly great." Zi Gong saw the eagerness in Fu Chai's eyes and stopped abruptly.

"Please go on!" urged Fu Chai.

"The state of Wu is located in the lower reaches of the Yangtze River. Its land is fertile, its climate temperate, and its resources plentiful. The people enjoy great wealth and the state is strong and prosperous."

"You are right!" said Fu Chai in a contented tone. "It is true that Wu enjoys great power and wealth."

"Don't you know that famous saying?" asked Zi Gong. "Pearls and precious stones must be concealed, otherwise they will attract robbers' attention. The great powers can not but have a craving for the fertile land of Wu. In my opinion, the illness on your heart is caused by fear of losing your treasure."

Fu Chai stared dazedly and did not speak.

"Suppose a large, luminous pearl is placed on the table surrounded by several robbers. Will they decline to take the pearl out of modesty, or will they fight one another to seize it?"

"Of course they will fight for it!"

"Wu can be compared to such a luminous pearl, so you must do your best to protect it from the robbers."

"How can I ensure the utmost safety of my treasure then?"

"When there is a treasure in the house, the owner must have the house fortified and its wall strengthened. When there is a treasure in the state, the ruler must build up the troops and find capable generals to command them. Only thus will he be able to send the troops to eliminate the robbers and ensure the safety of his treasure." Zi Gong thought that the time was ripe to come to his point. "At present Duke Jian of Qi, an impetuous youth, is longing to follow the example of his ancestor Duke Huan and ride roughshod over the other states. Several times in the past he launched expeditions against neighboring states, and in the third month this year he sent his chief general Bao Mu to attack Lu. Though Bao Mu lost the battle, he has not yet given up. He has stationed his troops at Ailing and declared he will conquer Lu first, after which he will storm into Wu."

"Really?" asked Fu Chai dubiously.

"If a poor and weak state like Lu has aroused Qi's greed, what about a wealthy state like Wu?"

"You are right!" exclaimed Fu Chai, whose ambition was aroused. "As long as I am alive, I will not let that callow youth have his way!" Then, looking Zi Gong squarely in the eye, he asked, "If Wu sends an expedition against Qi, will Lu take concerted action?"

"Qi has invaded Lu on many occasions," said Zi Gong. "The lord of Lu will be greatly satisfied if you can send an expedition against Qi and will only be too glad to do what he can to help." He slipped his hand into his sleeve.

Fu Chai looked at him in surprise.

Chapter Thirty-nine

Bao Mu's Army Is Routed by the Joint Forces of Lu and Wu; Confucius Returns to His Homeland to Meet with Duke Ai of Lu

As Fu Chai looked on in surprise, Zi Gong slowly produced a piece of white silk from his sleeve and handed it to him. "This is a letter from the lord of Lu. Please read it!"

Fu Chai spread out the silk and read carefully. He thought for a long time, then said, "Please return and tell the lord of Lu that his troops at Ailing will soon be joined by five hundred chariots from Wu. We will fight Qi together."

"Many thanks, Your Lordship! I will take my leave then." Zi Gong left the Wu palace and returned to Lu.

Fu Chai sent for a general named Xu Cheng and said to him in a severe voice, "Last year you were ordered to sail north to attack Qi but suffered a grave defeat. Now the troops of Lu and Qi are engaged at Ailing. I want you to command five hundred war chariots to help Lu against Qi. What do you think?"

"Though I lost the battle last year," said Xu Cheng nervously, "this time I will have a chance to amend for my incompetence!"

"Then gather your troops and set out tomorrow!"

"I will carry out your order!" responded Xu Cheng.

At Ailing the Lu army made camp on the plain by the Dasha River, while the Qi army stationed itself among the low hills on the other bank. The two armies challenged each other and fought a series of battles. Each sustained some casualties but neither could gain the advantage. A month passed like this. In early summer the weather grew increasingly warm. Ran Qiu and You Ruo were worried that they had failed so far to overcome the enemy. Just then a mounted scout returned to report, "General Xu Cheng from Wu has arrived with five hundred chariots."

Delighted, Ran Qiu and You Ruo went out to take a look. They climbed up a mound to gaze into the distance and found the Wu army

494

was approaching them at full speed. They immediately ordered pigs and sheep to be slaughtered and treated the officers and men of Wu to a grand feast.

The following day the men of Qi looked to the southern bank of the river and saw to their dismay the banners of Wu together with those of Lu. In a subsequent battle the Qi troops found it hard to stand their ground. At the end of three days Bao Mu realized he could not hold out any longer, so he wrote a letter to Duke Jian of Qi asking for reinforcements; in the meantime he ordered the troops to prepare for withdrawal. That night he ordered lamps to be lit in the camp as usual. At the third watch the troops left the camp-site in secret, leaving the banners and tents behind. As they climbed over a hill, a band of forces suddenly emerged from a nearby forest and charged at them, then scattered into the forest as abruptly as they had come. Bao Mu had no intention to linger and pursue the enemy. "Retreat!" he ordered. After this surprise the Qi troops grew fearful and sped on in a headlong flight. They traveled for only a short distance when another band of soldiers rushed out of the woods, letting loose hail after hail of arrows. The Qi troops fled as fast as they could, leaving many corpses and chariots behind.

At daybreak Bao Mu made a head-count and found to his distress that he had lost sixty chariots and two hundred soldiers. He still did not know where the two bands of troops had come from.

The night before, Ran Qiu, You Ruo and Xu Cheng were talking in the tent when a soldier came in to report, "The lamps are lit as usual in the Qi camp."

"In the past three days the enemy soldiers have become greatly demoralized by successive defeats," said You Ruo. "It is strange that they should have lit all the lamps tonight just as usual."

"Maybe they are trying to put up a false front so they can get away stealthily," said Xu Cheng.

"Yes," Ran Qiu agreed. "That's very likely."

You Ruo said, "In that case we can have two generals, each leading two hundred soldiers, take a roundabout route and lie in ambush in the woods along the escape route of the enemy. When the men of Qi arrive, we can attack by shooting arrows, which will throw them into confusion."

Thus Ran Qiu and Xu Cheng carried out the plan with satisfactory results.

After cleaning up the battlefield and collecting the booty, the Lu and Wu troops returned to Lu triumphantly.

Duke Ai of Lu, overjoyed at the news, declared a state-wide holiday to celebrate the victory and ordered Jisun Fei to personally reward the troops.

Having rewarded the troops, Jisun Fei saw Xu Cheng off at the south gate of the capital. Then he turned to Ran Qiu and You Ruo, "Both of you are military geniuses!"

"We have learned all we know from our master," replied You Ruo earnestly.

"Yes," Ran Qiu agreed. "Our master is conversant with the six arts and understands things both ancient and modern, in heaven and on earth. Unfortunately, his outstanding ability has not been fully recognized."

"As far as I know, Confucius is an erudite scholar and an excellent teacher," said Jisun Fei. "But he must be a laymen when it comes to military affairs."

"You are wrong there, Chief Minister," said You Ruo. "It was our master who commanded the Lu army to subdue the revolts of Yang Hu and Hou Fan and pacify Shusun Zhe and Gongshan Buniu. The rebels trembled with fear whenever his name was mentioned."

"So Confucius is proficient in dealing with both civil and military affairs," said Jisun Fei, smiling through half-closed eyes.

"Yes," said Ran Qiu and You Ruo with one voice.

"What do you say if I send someone to fetch him back to Lu?" asked Jisun Fei.

Ran Qiu was delighted. "I should say this should have been done long ago."

"Chief Minister," said You Ruo, "our master was compelled to leave Lu many years ago. If he comes back this time, please trust him completely and do not allow petty men to harm him."

"Lu is in great need of capable men, how can I neglect a man of exceptional talents like Confucius?" Returning home, Jisun Fei immediately ordered Gong Hua, Gong Bing and Gong Lin to set out for Diqiu, the Wei capital, in ten chariots and invite Confucius back with a gift of three thousand taels of silver.

One day Confucius had just finished teaching his disciples when he saw Zi Gong, Qidiao Kai and Gongliang Ru coming toward them while talking excitedly.

"Master," said Zi Gong cheerfully, "I persuaded the prince of Wu into agreeing to aid Lu. The joint forces inflicted a crushing defeat on Qi at Ailing. The victorious Lu army has already returned to the capital."

Confucius was immensely pleased. "Zi Gong, you have achieved great merits for your homeland! Once I return to Lu I will ask His Lordship to reward you amply for this."

Zi Gong smiled broadly. "That was nothing at all. I only played a little trick, that was all."

Confucius was not pleased on hearing this. "Zi Gong, your ingenuity is truly exceptional, but you must not take pride in petty shrewdness!"

Zi Gong realized his mistake and lowered his head, not saying anything.

Two days later Gong Hua, Gong Bing and Gong Lin arrived in Wei and called on Confucius, who could hardly contain his joy on learning the news. "After fourteen years, I am going home at last!" He said to himself and invited the three envoys into the house and asked them about things in Lu. In the meantime he sent someone to inform Zi Lu and Gao Chai.

When Zi Lu and Gao Chai arrived, Confucius was talking to the other disciples. "Gong Hua, Gong Bing and Gong Lin have come with the chief minister's letter to invite me to return home. You may go and pack up so we can set out tomorrow morning." He turned to Zi Lu and Gao Chai. "You don't have to follow me to Lu since both of you have your own official career here."

"Master," said Zi Lu, "I don't want to leave you even though I am an official. Let me accompany you to Lu."

"I know you have done quite well in your present position, and you can stay on to make full use of your talent here. Moreover, the lord of Wei would be disappointed if you should leave."

"Lu is my homeland. If I return to Lu I will be able to make my contribution to it."

"Since you have made up your mind, I won't insist."

"I will also return to Lu with you, master," said Gao Chai.

Surprised, Confucius asked, "You are a native of Qi, aren't you?"

"But I want to stay by your side, master."

Confucius nodded his consent.

When all was ready, Confucius went to bid farewell to Qu Boyu.

Qu Boyu was then a shaky old man in his eighties. When he learned Confucius was leaving, his eyes brimmed with tears and he choked with emotion when he spoke. "Master, please make allowance for my lack of consideration in the many years you and your disciples stayed in my humble place!"

"My disciples and I have stayed in your house for over ten years and have caused you innumerable inconveniences. I hope there will be a chance for us to repay your great kindness!"

"Friendship between superior men appears indifferent but will last long," said Qu Boyu, "whereas friendship between petty men appears intimate but will soon break down. As long as we cherish one another in our mind, there is no need to mention the give and take of favors. If I have favored you by putting you up, how much have you favored me with your invaluable instructions?" Thereupon he had a farewell banquet prepared for Confucius and his disciples.

The next morning Confucius took leave of Qu Boyu and set out for Lu.

Several days later they came to the Lu-Wei boundary. On the hillside some pheasants were chirping merrily and running hither and thither in search of food. All of a sudden a hawk appeared in the sky over the hill. The pheasants scurried into the caves and dense woods, vanishing out of sight in an instant.

At the sight of this Confucius was seized by a wave of sadness. He heaved a deep sigh and continued the journey in silence. He could not help thinking what would have happened if he had not been forced to leave Lu many years before. "If I had stayed in the court of Lu, it would probably have become strong and prosperous, with the rites of Zhou fully restored. Envoys from other states would have kept coming to Lu to learn the rites, and there would have been no more warfare in the world." He looked at the uneven fields of Lu where the canals seemed to have been neglected for years, and frowned with dissatisfaction. On reaching the west gate of the Lu capital he found many holes and breaches in the city wall, and the gate tower was in a state of disrepair. The sight filled him with sorrow. He felt as if he had achieved nothing wandering from state to state for fourteen years. Entering the city, Confucius and his disciples attracted many onlookers, who stared at their chariots in surprise.

When Confucius returned home, the family was overjoyed. He took Kong Ji into his arms and gazed at him with tearful eyes. "You are such a big boy now, Kong Ji," he finally said with a smile.

Kong Ji stretched out his hand to pull Confucius' beard. "Grandpa, why are you crying and smiling at the same time?"

"I am smiling because I am so happy to see you."

"Then why are you crying, grandpa? Are you thinking of grandma?"

Confucius could no longer contain his tears. "Yes," he said, sobbing. "I have let her down. I have let all of you down."

"Father," said Wuwei, "you should be glad that you have returned home at last."

Confucius wiped off his tears and nodded. "Yes, I should be glad of that."

The family had dinner together. As it was still early, Confucius changed into formal clothes and said to Zi Lu, "I want to pay a visit to the chief minister. Will you drive the chariot for me as usual?"

Zi Lu smiled. "Master, I am willing to drive the chariot for you all my life."

The two of them came to the chief minister's residence, where they learned from the guard that Jisun Fei was in the palace discussing state affairs with the duke. So they headed for the palace.

"Let them come in!" Duke Ai ordered on hearing of their arrival.

Confucius groomed himself and walked into the palace in small, quick steps. He knelt to salute the duke. "Kong Qiu pays respects to Your Lordship!"

Duke Ai felt both joy and sadness on seeing Confucius. He had intended to make use of Confucius' great talent, but he was disappointed to find an old and shaky man in Confucius. "Please get up," he said.

Confucius got on his feet and greeted Jisun Fei with a bow.

"Please sit down, master," said Jisun Fei.

Confucius sat down to the right of the duke.

The duke said, "According to what I have heard, you have many talented disciples. Some of them have mastered all the six arts."

"Since I started teaching, I have made no distinction of social status," said Confucius. "That's why I have taught so many disciples so far."

"At present the state of Lu is very weak and I intend to rebuild its former glory with the help of your talented disciples. Can you recommend some to me?"

"Though I have many disciples, few of them are really exceptional," said Confucius. "Let me see. Yan Hui, Min Shun, Ran Geng and Ran Yong are noted for their virtue and proper conduct; Zai Yu and Zi Gong excel in eloquence; Ran Qiu and Yan Lu are good at administering office; Yan Yan and Bu Shang have special literary talents."

"Can you write a name list of your most outstanding disciples for me?"

"I will have to think carefully, but I will finish it as soon as possible."

Duke Ai smiled with satisfaction, then he changed the subject. "You are widely known for your rich knowledge. Can you tell me what a ruler should do as his first priority?"

Confucius thought carefully before he replied, "The ruler must select suitable officials."

"Please explain."

Confucius sighed when he called to mind the many instances in which the ruler determined the fate of a nation by employing either virtuous or corrupt officials. "People are the dominant factor in everything," he said. "The same affair executed by different people will produce different results. The sage ruler Shun, by relying on five virtuous ministers, achieved prosperity in the entire world. King Wu of Zhou once remarked that he had ten capable ministers to help him govern the kingdom. However, people of great talent are always hard to find. In the time of Yao, Shun, King Wen and King Wu, there were relatively large numbers of capable people. Even so, King Wu had only nine capable ministers if we exclude the one woman official he employed. Therefore, when selecting officials, a ruler should pay attention to quality instead of number."

"What kind of men should I choose to assist me then?"

"They should be endowed with both virtue and ability. You can only rely on people who are highly respected for their virtue, who can not be corrupted in high office, who are accomplished in both the letters and martial arts, and who devote themselves to the restoration of rites in the state. In order to bring our state back to prosperity, you must select and promote people in possession of such qualities."

Duke Ai found the words very reasonable. "What kind of men should I avoid?"

"Avoid three types of men."

"Who are these?"

"Those who are excessively greedy, those who are arrogant and unscrupulous, and those who are hypocritical and deceptive."

Duke Ai nodded his head. "You are right. I can not use people like that."

"You have to adjust a bow before you will know whether it is strong," added Confucius. "You have to harness a horse to a chariot before you will know whether it is a fine horse. As regards a man, you have to make sure he is honest and virtuous before you go on to test his ability, for the more capable a dishonest and corrupt man is, the greater harm he will do. Such a man can be compared to a wolf or jackal. Yang Hu, Hou Fan, Gongshan Buniu and Shusun Zhe all belong to this category."

Both Duke Ai and Jisun Fei shuddered on hearing the names of Yan Hu and other rebels, which reminded them of the turmoils these people had caused in Lu. After a long pause Duke Ai asked, "I intend to select several men to help me rule the state. How can I find suitable candidates?"

"I have looked into history," said Confucius, "and found the rites and music of Zhou to be the most complete. To select people to help you rule the state, you should start with men who observe the rites of Zhou."

"If I see someone who wears a Zhou-style garment, and even the pattern and adornments on his shoes are of the same style, shall I make him an official?"

"That is not what I mean. A man should be judged not by the style of his dress but by his code of conduct."

"Please explain!"

"In my opinion, people of the upper class can be divided into five types: the ordinary man, the gentleman, the superior man, the virtuous man and the sage. An ordinary man has no lifelong goal. He neither follows the teachings of the ancients in his speech nor adheres to any moral principles in his conduct. He does not make friends with people of virtue and forgets righteousness at the prospect of gain. Therefore he has no destination in life but simply drifts with the tide. A gentleman has a certain goal that he strives after in his lifetime. He will finally reach the goal despite many setbacks. What he seeks after is not broad knowledge but deep understanding, not great eloquence but speech that is suitable and to the point, not numerous achievements but the completion of every single task he chooses to undertake.

Wealth and honor can not make him indolent and indulge in luxury, nor can poverty induce him to give up his aspirations. A superior man is loyal and honest in speech and benevolent and righteous in conduct. His mind is clear, and his work diligent and persistent. However, he also fails by a thread to reach his goal. A virtuous man does not break the rules of propriety in his behavior. He can make people listen to him and mend their ways in imitation of his virtue. Under his influence the rich become kindhearted and use their property to help the poor. As for a sage, his virtue can be compared to Heaven and earth, and the great Way he seeks for can be compared to the sun and moon. He understands the roots of all things and conducts himself in accordance with the will of Heaven. Therefore he can penetrate deeply into the universe and deal with everything effectively."

"Excellent!" exclaimed Duke Ai. "Where could I have learned all this if you had not taught me! I grew up behind palace walls and have no experience of sorrow, worry, fatigue, fear or danger. Therefore I failed to gain a deep understanding of your instruction."

"From what you just said," remarked Confucius, "it is clear that you have already understood my words."

Duke Ai had a blank look on his face.

Confucius explained, "When you climb up the steps and enter the temple of the late dukes, you will see the beams by looking up and the tables by looking ahead, but you will not see your ancestors who have long passed away. By pondering on this you will obtain an experience of sorrow. When you get up in the morning, adjust your garment and sit down facing the wall, you can consider the presence of peril and experience worry. When you preside over the audience in the morning, busying yourself with affairs of the state and receiving guests from far and near, you will know the meaning of diligence. If you gaze into the distance and see the ruins of ancient kingdoms, you will became aware of the vicissitudes of the mundane world and therefore understand fear. Then you will know the key to governing the state well."

"What is that?" asked Duke Ai and Jisun Fei simultaneously.

"First and foremost, the ruler must enable the common people to grow wealthy."

"How can I make the people wealthy?" asked the duke.

"Reduce taxes and labor conscription, and the people will gradually grow wealthy."

"The people would indeed grow wealthy in that way, but the state would become impoverished in the process."

"*The Book of Poetry* compares the benevolent ruler to the parent of his subjects. How is it possible for the parent to remain poor while his children are wealthy?"

"If I set out to make all people in Lu wealthy, can I achieve my goal?"

"You can if you treat men of virtue and talents with courtesy and show your loving kindness to the people," said Confucius. "How can you fail to gain respect when you treat people with courtesy in spite of your wealth and power? How can you fail to gain devotion when you help people grow wealthy by means of your wealth and power? If you succeed in making others wealthy, you would not become poor yourself even if you wanted to; if you succeed in giving others honor and prestige, you would not get humility for yourself even if you wanted it."

"I have heard there are many evils in the world. What are those?"

"According to what I have learned, there are five evils in the world. First, to satisfy oneself at the expense of others is called the evil in the person. Second, to discard the old in favor of the young is called the evil in the household. Third, to employ faithless men instead of the virtuous is called the evil in the state. Fourth, the old do not instruct and the young do not learn—this is called the evil in habit. Fifth, the sage conceals himself while fatuous men monopolize power —this is called the evil under the heavens."

Duke Ai was getting a little tired listening to all this and wanted to enjoy song and dance for a change. He yawned. "Master, do you also enjoy pleasure in your life?" he asked.

"There are three kinds of beneficial pleasure: to cultivate oneself by the rites and music, to recommend others for their good qualities, and to make good friends with men of virtue. I have taken pleasure in things like that all my life. There are also three kinds of harmful pleasure: to take pride in one's position, to take pleasure trips to one's heart's content, and to show excessive interest in food and wine. It is improper for one to take pleasure in things like that."

Duke Ai's face reddened as he thought Confucius was alluding to his behavior, so he changed the topic abruptly. "I once heard a story," he said, "about a man with so poor a memory that he forgot he had a wife." He placed his hands on his stomach and broke into a fit of laughter.

"That is not the most forgetful man in the world," said Confucius gravely. "The most forgetful man can even forget himself."

"Really?"

"We can find such an example in King Jie of the Xia Dynasty. He abandoned the principles and institution established by his ancestors and gave himself up to sensual pleasures. Treacherous officials ingratiated themselves with him while honest officials either fell silent or ran away. When the common people finally rose up against him, he not only lost his own life but also brought about the downfall of the Xia Dynasty. Can't we say he was a man who forgot all about himself?"

Duke Ai drew in a deep breath in dismay and took a good look at Confucius. "What a sharp-minded man!" he thought. "With you as a high official in the court, I would feel constantly watched!" He stood up. "Master," he said, "I am greatly impressed by your outstanding talent and have learned a lot from what you said today. It is now getting dark. Shall we resume our talk some other time?"

Confucius was filled with disappointment at the sight of the duke's expression. "I was away from my homeland for many years," he said, "and am so glad to return at last!" He took leave of the duke and left the palace with Jisun Fei.

"Master," Jisun Fei asked, "as the chief minister, how can I best help His Lordship?"

"Fairness is the foundation of political leadership. If you stick to fairness in your office, how dare the other officials do otherwise?"

On his return home Confucius found the courtyard filled with his disciples. "How are you, master?" asked Yan Lu, his eyes moist. "We have not seen you for so many years."

Confucius remembered his longtime friendship with Yan Lu and also felt a lump in his throat.

The other disciples came up to greet Confucius and ask about his experiences in the various states.

The following day Confucius continued to teach his disciples.

When several days passed without any message from Duke Ai, Confucius realized that his chance of getting a high position in the Lu court was pretty slim. So he devoted himself to teaching and in the meantime continued his work of sorting out the ancient classics, including *The Book of Poetry*, *The Book of Documents*, *The Book of Rites*, *The Book of Changes*, and *The Book of Music*.

The disciples were dissatisfied that their master was not given an important position by Duke Ai. Zi Gong suspected that Jisun Fei must have obstructed his master's appointment out of jealousy. He came to Confucius and asked, "Master, who is the most virtuous among the court ministers?"

Confucius considered, running over the names of the ministers in the various states in his mind. "I can find no virtuous one," he said. "Formerly there were Bao Shu in Qi and Zi Pi in Zheng. They were both virtuous."

"Was there anyone else?"

"No."

Zi Gong was puzzled. "But the state of Qi also had Guan Zhong, and the state of Zheng had Zi Can."

"Zi Gong," said Confucius, "you have not penetrated into the essence of the matter. Who would you consider as more virtuous: the one who is talented and makes use of his talent, or the one who is virtuous and recommends other people of virtue?"

"The virtuous man who recommends others," replied Zi Gong.

"Right! A minister is valued more for his virtue than for his talent. Bao Shu praised Guan Zhong for his talent, and Zi Pi praised Zi Can for his talent. But Bao Shu and Zi Pi never praised themselves."

Zi Gong felt downhearted when he remembered how the three successive rulers of Lu had treated his master. "Master," he asked, looking up at Confucius. "Can one who repays resentment with kindness be called a man of virtue?"

"What, then, should he repay kindness with?" responded Confucius. "A man of virtue repays resentment with fairness and repays kindness with kindness."

"Even that is no easy thing to do," remarked Zi Gong.

"One should be loyal and tolerant when dealing with others," said Confucius. "Bo Yi and Shu Qi did not bear old grudges so that few people bore resentment against them."

"Is there anything a superior man detests?"

"Yes. A superior man detests those who publicize the faults of others, those who are low in rank but slander their superiors, those who are brave but neglect the rites, those who are not modest but think themselves brave and those who are impetuous and obstinate."

Zi Gong considered the words carefully.

"Zi Gong," asked Confucius, "what do you detest?"

"I detest those who consider themselves clever while passing off other's achievements as their own, those who take insolence for bravery, and those who are fond of exposing others' secrets and consider themselves upright."

As they were talking in this fashion two men entered the courtyard.

Chapter Forty

Confucius and His Disciples Discuss
Their Political Ideals;
Min Shun Declines to Take Office to
Preserve His Purity

The old man was Zeng Dian, now white-haired and full of wrinkles. He was followed by a young man of medium height. He had a round face, a high nose and bright eyes. His expression was calm and his manners graceful.

"Master, this is my son," said Zeng Dian. "His given name is Shen, and his styled name Zi Yu. He is twenty-one. I have brought him here today to study with you." As he said this, both he and his son knelt in obeisance.

"Your disciple Zeng Shen pays respects to you, master," said the youth.

"About ten years ago," Confucius said to Zeng Dian with a smile, "Yan Hui became my disciple after his father. Today I receive your son. Yan Hui is so intelligent and eager to learn that he has surpassed his father in his learning. Zeng Shen, I hope you will follow Yan Hui's example!"

"Master," said Zeng Dian, "you remarked on Yan Hui's diligence many years ago. Does he have any weakness then?"

"Yes, he has. He agrees to whatever I say. That is of no help to me."

Zeng Dian opened a parcel and took out some dried meat, which he offered to Confucius in both hands. "Master, this is a tributary gift from Zeng Shen."

"It was with you that I began the practice of accepting dried meat as remuneration. You have proved yourself meticulous in observing the rites by adhering to this old custom."

"I dare not forget your instruction."

"Zeng Shen, you may go and meet your peers. You will begin studying with them tomorrow!"

When he taught the disciples the following day, Confucius found

to his delight that Zeng Shen not only listened attentively but was also capable of making inferences on his own. So he often conversed with Zeng Shen.

Zeng Shen made rapid progress in his study in half a year. One day he was discussing poetry and rites with Gongsun Long and a few other young disciples when Confucius walked over and said to him, "Zeng Shen! There is one essential idea underlying my teaching."

"Yes, I understand!"

Confucius walked away, pleased with Zeng Shen's reply.

"What did the master refer to?" asked Gongsun Long.

"The essential idea underlying the master's teaching is loyalty and forgiveness."

Gongsun Long went to Confucius and asked, "Master, did you refer to loyalty and forgiveness by your remark just now?"

Confucius nodded. After that he grew even more fond of Zeng Shen.

It was in spring of the twelfth year of Duke Ai of Lu's reign (483 B.C.). More than six months had passed since Confucius returned to Lu, and still Duke Ai had not offered him a position. He was staying home disconsolately playing the zither after teaching his disciples, when Zi Lu and other disciples, Zeng Dian, Ran Qiu and Gongxi Chi, entered the room. Confucius looked up at them. "I am old and will not be given a high position in the government. You often complain that few can understand you and appreciate your talent."

"Master," said Zi Lu, "don't you feel the same way?"

"I am not worried that others do not understand me. Instead, I am worried that I may not understand others."

Zi Lu fell silent.

"Suppose there is a ruler who understands you and wants to put you in an important position, what would you do?"

Without the least hesitation, Zi Lu answered, "If I were to govern a small state such as Chen and Cai, which suffers from invasion by its powerful neighbors and various natural calamities, it would only take me three years to make its people both brave and amenable to reason."

Confucius smiled without making any comment. After a while he asked, "Ran Qiu, how about you?"

"If I were to govern a small state a hundred square li in area, it would take me three years to make the people prosperous. As for the rites and music, I am lacking in ability in that respect and must leave it to other superior men."

Confucius did not make any comment, but turned to Gongxi Chi. "How about you?"

Gongxi Chi was a young man of twenty-six. He was as shy and demure as a young maiden. "I dare not say I am already qualified to take office," he said, blushing a little, "but I am willing to learn. When there is a sacrificial ceremony at the ancestral temple or at a meeting among the lords, I would like to be a subordinate official to assist in the performance of the rites."

"Zeng Dian, how about you?"

Zeng Dian had been playing the zither. On hearing Confucius' question he stopped playing. "My ideal is somewhat different from theirs, master."

"That doesn't matter. I only want to hear about your respective wishes."

"I would like to take an outing with a few friends and some children on a sunny day in late spring. We would bathe in the Yishui River, dry ourselves in a gentle breeze on the Praying for Rain Platform, and return home singing."

Confucius sighed deeply. "I am for Zeng Dian!"

When Zi Lu, Ran Qiu and Gongxi Chi had left, Zeng Dian stayed behind and asked Confucius, "What do you think of what they just said?"

Confucius smiled. "They were just expressing their respective wishes."

"Why did you laugh at Zi Lu's words?"

"Governing a state needs modesty, but Zi Lu was far from modest in his words. That's why I laughed at him."

"Didn't Ran Qiu and Gongxi Chi also say they could govern a state?"

"I laughed at Zi Lu not because he could not govern a state, but because he was not modest. Unlike Zi Lu, Gongxi Chi said he would like to be a subordinate official at a ceremony, though he is quite conversant with the rites and music. If he could be only a subordinate official, who could be the master of ceremonies?"

"It is still early in the day. Why don't we take a trip to the Yishui River to enjoy the spring sights?"

Confucius went into the courtyard and looked at the afternoon sun. "Well, let's go then."

Zeng Dian went at once to prepare the chariot.

Accompanied by Zeng Dian, Zi Lu and Min Shun, Confucius rode out of the south gate and arrived at the northern bank of the Yishui River. In the shallows of the river cranes were strolling in search of food, and swallows were busily building their new nests among the trees. Confucius was pleased with the lively scene. "Spring is the time of revival," he remarked. "It makes people feel uplifted in spirit."

Enchanted with the lovely sight, Zeng Dian began to sing:

> The sound of the chariot came near,
> The horses' heads flashing.
> The lord did not show himself,
> For he had attendants to pass on his order.

Confucius gazed at the undulating hills of Jiulong Mountain in the south, then looked east at Mount Ni. The glow of the setting sun reminded him of his old age, and he felt a pang in his heart.

Zeng Dian was not happy to find his master in such a mood. He walked up to Confucius. "Master, let's return, shall we?"

"What?" Confucius was awakened from his reverie. "Yes, let's return!"

On entering the south gate they encountered a large crowd in the road and heard the sound of quarreling.

Confucius stood up in his chariot and looked ahead. Encircled by a huge crowd of onlookers, two men were engaged in a tangled fight, grabbing at each other's clothes and hair.

The onlookers pointed at the two men and commented. Some tried to stop the fight, while others shouted encouragement to the two men to fight on.

Confucius dismounted. "Zi Lu, let's go and take a look."

When they saw Confucius, the onlookers bowed and made way for him. Confucius returned their greetings as he walked toward the two men.

The two men were fighting on a pile of vegetables. Their clothes were torn, their hair dishevelled, and their faces covered in dust. A basket lay overturned on the ground with a shoulder pole stretched across it. The man at the east seemed to have gained the upper hand, pushing his opponent to the roadside. The man at the west, feeling the shoulder pole touch his leg, suddenly shook himself free and picked up the pole. "I'll beat you to death!" he shouted, raising the pole into the air with both hands.

The other man panicked and hid himself in the crowd, trying to escape.

The other man ran after him, poking at him with the pole.

"Stop!" shouted Confucius.

The man holding the shoulder pole started and turned to look. At the sight of Confucius he shuddered and dropped the pole.

"Why were the two of you fighting in the road?" demanded Confucius.

"I was selling vegetables by the road," said the man hiding in the crowd. "He came up to buy some, but he claimed he had paid me when he hadn't. I tried to reason with him, but he knocked over my vegetable basket and tried to beat me."

Confucius took a close look at him. This was a hefty man in his forties, with big eyes and thick eyebrows. He had a modest, bland expression in his face and did not look like a bully.

"What's your name?" asked Confucius.

"I am Cheng Cheng," the man replied as he walked out from the crowd. "I live at Lihuadian in the west part of the city."

Confucius turned to look at the other man, who looked in his sixties and had a lean face and pointed mouth. His long beard and hair were entangled.

The man lowered his head, not daring to look Confucius in the face.

"What's your name?" demanded Confucius.

"I ... I ..." the man lowered his head further.

Zi Lu came up to Confucius and whispered, "This is Ran Yong's father."

Just then Ran Yong rushed over. "Master, he is my father!"

"Ran Yong, your father has damaged Cheng Cheng's vegetables. What should be done about it?"

"I will pay for the vegetables damaged by my father. Would that be all right, master?"

Confucius looked at Ran Yong sympathetically. "All right, you can take care of that."

Confucius returned home with a heavy heart, disconcerted that one of his disciples should have such a man for his father. He asked Zi Lu, "Does Ran Yong's father always behave like that?"

"Yes."

"Why didn't you ever mention it to me?"

"Because ..."

"Well?"

Zi Lu stood up in front of Confucius. "I think one should publicize others' merits rather than expose their faults."

Confucius smiled approvingly. "Yes, you are quite right." Then he sighed, "It is so unfortunate for Ran Yong to have such a father."

"Master," said Zi Lu, "I did not tell you about this though I had known it all along. Does it mean that I was keeping something back from you?"

"No, it doesn't. From my observation, you have nothing to hide from me."

Zi Lu smiled good-naturedlly.

It was getting dark. The other disciples gathered around to join in the discussion.

"My disciples," said Confucius, "do you think there is anything I keep from you?" He looked at them one by one, then said, "I do not conceal anything from you. This is the kind of man I am."

"When we go out to make friends," asked Zi Lu, "what people should we seek after and what should we avoid?"

"There are three kinds of people one should make friends with," replied Confucius. "There are also three kinds of people one should avoid. It is beneficial for one to make friends with those who are upright, those who are true to their word, and those who have rich knowledge and great learning. It is harmful for one to make friends with those who are insincere in speech, those who flatter people but slander them behind their backs, and those who are boastful but ignorant."

"Master," asked Min Shun, "how should we deal with all kinds of people we encounter?"

"When you meet a virtuous man, you should try to emulate him to improve yourself; when you meet an unrighteous man, you will know what to avoid in yourself."

"Master," asked Ran Geng, "can one be called a superior man if he thinks thrice before taking an action?"

"Yes. Thinking thrice is enough when dealing with a specific matter. On the other hand, a superior man pays attention to nine things in his daily life. When looking at something, he must try to see clearly; when listening to something, he must try to hear accurately;

in facial expression he must look gentle and mild; in manners he must be courteous; when speaking he must be honest; when carrying out official duties he must be conscientious; in the face of difficulty he must ask others for advice; when enraged, he must consider the consequences; at the prospect of gain, he must ask himself whether it is righteous."

Zeng Dian found the words very instructive. "Master, can you explain further?" he asked.

"If you do not see clearly, you will be deceived by falsehood. If you do not hear accurately, you will get things confused; if you do not look gentle and mild in your facial expression, you will find it hard to get along with others; if you are not courteous in your manners, you will grow shallow and frivolous; if you are not honest in speech, you will be given to flowery words and cunning statements; if you are not conscientious in work, you will evade your responsibility and do things perfunctorily; if you do not seek advice from others, you will become arrogant and self-willed; if you get angry easily, you will be punishing yourself for others' faults; if you take ill-gotten gains, you will feel sorry for it someday."

"Master!" Ran Yong called out, coming into the courtyard.

All the disciples turned to look at him.

Feeling embarrassed, Ran Yong came up to Confucius with his head lowered. "Master, I paid Cheng Cheng for his loss and apologized to him for what had happened."

"I knew you would handle the matter well," said Confucius approvingly.

Just then Nangong Jingshu arrived. "Master, His Lordship urges you to recommend some of your talented disciples to him."

"All right," said Confucius, pleased. "I will write a list this evening and take it into the palace tomorrow."

After supper, Confucius took a bundle of bamboo slips and, under the candlelight, began to write down the names of the disciples he would recommend to Duke Ai.

Name List

Yan Hui, styled name Zi Yuan, a native of Lu. He does not complain even though his family is poor, and he studies diligently and tirelessly. He is of outstanding moral integrity.

Zeng Shen, styled name Zi Yu, a native of Nanwu of Lu. He is intelligent, eager to learn, and sedate in conduct.

Min Shun, styled name Zi Qian, a native of Lu. Well-known for his filial piety, he is experienced and prudent in conduct. He is of outstanding moral integrity.

Ran Geng, styled name Bo Niu, a native of Lu. He is honest and upright in conduct and of outstanding moral integrity.

Ran Yong, styled name Zhong Gong, a native of Lu, belonging to the same clan as Ran Geng. He is of outstanding moral integrity.

Zai Yu, styled name Zi Wo, a native of Lu. He is gifted with a silver tongue.

Duanmu Ci, styled name Zi Gong, a native of Wei. He is eloquent in speech and well versed in the letters.

Ran Qiu, styled name Zi You, a native of Lu. He is skilled at administration.

Zhong You, styled name Zi Lu or Ji Lu, a native of Biandi in Lu. He is forthright, brave, and highly talented.

Yan Yan, styled name Zi You, a native of Wu. He is conversant with the letters.

Bu Shang, styled name Zi Xia, a native of Wei. He is conversant with the letters.

Zhuansun Shi, styled name Zi Zhang, a native of Chen. He is good at making friends.

You Ruo, styled name Zi You, a native of Lu. He is intelligent, assiduous, and conversant with both the letters and martial arts.

Mi Buqi, styled name Zi Jian, a native of Lu. He is benignant in character and has a resourceful mind.

Qidiao Kai, styled name Zi Ruo, a native of Cai.

Gao Chai, styled name Zi Gao, a native of Qi.

Gongliang Ru, styled name Zi Zheng, a native of Chen. He is both virtuous and courageous.

Kong Zhong, styled name Zi Mie, a native of Lu.

The next morning Confucius entered the palace and submitted the name list to Duke Ai. "Your Lordship," he said, "among my numerous disciples only a few are qualified to take office. I have included all the suitable ones in this list."

Duke Ai took the list, spread it over the table and read the names carefully. He turned to Jisun Fei. "Honored minister, you may choose some of these and appoint them to appropriate positions!"

"I will carry out Your Lordship's order," responded Jisun Fei. He took up the name list and began to study it. "Your Lordship," he said, "we need to appoint magistrates in the following cities: Jufu, Fei, Zou, Wucheng, and Shanfu. I suggest that Bu Shang be appointed magistrate of Jufu; Min Shun, magistrate of Fei; Kong Zhong, magistrate of Zou; Yan Yan, magistrate of Wucheng, and Mi Buqi, magistrate of Shanfu. Would that be all right?"

"Since all the master's disciples are conversant with both the letters and martial arts," said Duke Ai, "you may appoint them as you have suggested." He turned to Confucius. "Master, you can inform them to take office as soon as possible."

Confucius returned home in high spirits and immediately sent for Bu Shang, Min Shun, Kong Zhong, Yan Yan and Mi Buqi and told them Duke Ai and the chief minister had invited them to take office. "An official has to fulfill his duties to the king and the lord above and to the common people below. You must practice diligence, frugality, and fairness, and act as a good role model for your subordinates. You will encounter different problems in different cities and should solve them in order of importance and urgency."

"Master," said Bu Shang, "I do not know how to be a good official. Can you give me some more advice?"

"Don't make haste and don't covet small gains. The more you make haste, the slower your progress will become. The more you covet small gains, the less chance there will be for you to achieve great things."

"I would be content enough if I could be an erudite scholar," said Bu Shang. "I did not plan for an official career."

Confucius assumed a serious expression. "I have taught you various fields of knowledge in order that you can do something for the state. What's the use of studying all those classics when you do not serve in the government and put into practice what you have learned? I want you to be a great scholar who cherishes high aspirations, not a petty scholar who spends his time without doing anything constructive."

"I see," said Bu Shang.

"Master," said Min Shun, "I am accomplished in neither the letters nor the martial arts and is not yet qualified to be a magistrate. Please decline the appointment for me!"

"Min Shun, you are modest and cautious in conduct and show great earnestness in fulfilling your filial duties. If you become the magistrate of Fei, you will be able to improve the morals of the local populace. You would make a great achievement if you could only make all the people in the city fulfill their duties to their parents and superiors. Why should you decline the post?"

"I vowed to stay with you all my life," said Min Shun. "If pressed to take office in Fei, I would have no choice but to run away to the north bank of the Wenshui River and hide myself in a secluded place there."

"In that case, I will not force you to take office. I will report to the chief minister and ask him to choose someone else to fill the post."

"Many thanks, master!" said Min Shun with great relief.

"How should I conduct myself after I take office?" asked Kong Zhong.

"Spare no efforts in learning what you do not know and making up for what you lack. Do not take excessive pride in yourself and doubt others' sincerity or underestimate their ability. In the face of success, rejoice without growing arrogant; in the face of danger, think hard without falling into anxiety. Speak and act with caution so that at the end of the day you will leave no cause for worry."

"I see." said Kong Zhong.

Confucius was pleased when he looked at the confident expressions of Bu Shang, Yan Yan, Kong Zhong and Mi Buqi. "I have not labored in vain," he said to himself. After seeing them off, he went to call on Jisun Fei. "Chief Minister," he said, "Min Shun declines to take office, saying that he is not fit for an official career. I hope you can find another suitable man to fill the post."

"No one knows your disciples better than you," said Jisun Fei. "So I would like you to recommend another one."

Confucius thought for a while. "Gao Chai, a native of Qi, is quite proficient at administration. Unfortunately he can not be described as handsome."

"That's no problem. Let him be the magistrate of Fei then!"

Confucius nodded his agreement.

"Ran Qiu is a very talented man," added Jisun Fei. "When acting as the head steward in my house, he did everything to my perfect satisfaction. When leading the Lu army to fight invaders from Qi, he achieved great merits together with You Ruo. I would like you to recommend another of your disciples to be my head steward."

"Ran Yong is both talented and virtuous," said Confucius. "He would make an ideal candidate. However, his father is a worthless man."

"That doesn't matter, as long as Ran Yong himself is a man of virtue and talent."

"I will return and inform Gao Chai and Ran Yong then."

"Thank you, master!"

Confucius immediately returned home and called Gao Chai and Ran Yong to him. "His Lordship and the chief minister are looking for talents, and both of you have been chosen. Gao Chai, you won high praise for your accomplishments when you were an official in Wei. You are now appointed magistrate of Fei, so you must double your efforts to fulfill your duties. Fei is the manor of the chief minister. It is a troublesome place where several revolts broke out, and its people are poor due to its arid, mountainous land. You must try hard to improve people's livelihood there!"

"I will do my best to follow your instruction."

"Ran Yong," continued Confucius, "when you enter the chief minister's residence, you should coordinate your work with Ran Qiu, who has already won the chief minister's trust and approval."

"How should I conduct myself in the chief minister's house?" asked Ran Yong.

"Be a good role model for your subordinates. In dealing with others, pay attention to their general behavior and overlook their minor faults. Search for and promote men of ability."

"How can I practice benevolence and virtue in my daily work?"

"Be devoted to your duty and diligent in administering daily affairs. When going out on a mission, be joyful as if you were receiving an honored guest. When conscripting laborers for public projects, avoid the busy seasons. Do not impose on others what you do not want for yourself. Be consistent in your words and deeds and do not complain when you run into difficulties."

"Faced with something I don't understand, should I think about it carefully or put more efforts into my study?"

"I once thought so hard that I forgot to eat and sleep," said

Confucius, "but I gained very little as a result. It is better to study!"

Fully satisfied, Gao Chai and Ran Yong took leave of Confucius.

When Zhuansun Shi learned that some of his fellow disciples had been appointed officials, he wondered if he should return to his homeland, Chen, to take office. He came to see Confucius and asked, "Master, what's the proper way of seeking an official position?"

"First you must listen to all kinds of opinions," said Confucius. "Set aside those that you find dubious and put forward those that you feel assured of. In this way you will make few mistakes. Secondly, you must pay attention to all kinds of practices. Set aside those that you find dubious and adopt those that you feel assured of. In this way you will have few regrets. When you make few mistakes in speech and have few regrets in action, an official position will come naturally to you."

Zhuansun Shi was greatly inspired by these words. After a while he asked again, "I heard that Zi Wen of the state of Chu served as chief minister for three times, yet he did not show any self-satisfaction. He was also deprived of his post three times, yet he did not show any resentment. On leaving his post he would always explain to his successor in detail the statutes of the state. What kind of a man is Zi Wen?"

"He is very loyal to the state," said Confucius.

"Can he be called benevolent?"

"I don't know, but how can this be called benevolence?"

"When Duke Zhuang of Qi was murdered by a minister named Cui Zhu, Chen Wenzi, another minister, left Qi for another state, giving up his post and forty horses in his possession. Then he said, 'The ruler of this state is not much different from Cui Zhu in my homeland,' and left for another state. There, again, he said, 'The ruler of this state is not much different from Cui Zhu in my homeland,' and left this state for another one. What kind of a man is Chen Wenzi?"

"I would say he is very honest and pure," replied Confucius.

"Can he be called benevolent for his behavior?"

"I don't know, but how can this be called benevolence?"

Zi Gong, who had been waiting for some time at the door, burst into the room.

Chapter Forty-one

Zi Gong Is Advised to Accept His Appointment to Magistrate of Wenyang; Confucius Dreams of King Jing of Zhou

Zi Gong came into the room. "Master, the duke of Qi has sent someone to invite me to be magistrate of Wenyang."

"Just as I told you!" Confucius stood up and smiled broadly. "Zi Gong, the lord of Qi must have been greatly impressed by your talent. If you prove to be a good official, you may get promoted to senior minister in charge of diplomatic affairs."

"I am good at doing business," said Zi Gong. "But I can't say I am enthusiastic about an official career."

"Why not?" asked Confucius in surprise.

"Because there are many pitfalls in official circles. First, it is no safer to keep the lord's company than to live side by side with a fierce tiger. The lord has supreme authority in his state, and the life and death of his subjects lie in his very hands. An official who enjoys his favor will get rapid promotion and lead a happy life, whereas an official who offends him will be demoted, banished or even put to death. Second, the official circles can be compared to a lion's den where danger lurks around every corner. Those who venture into officialdom will get involved in a tangled fight. A lucky few will survive, but many will lose the fight and come to a bitter end. Third, a magistrate has to bring order and justice to all the people under his jurisdiction. Nowadays, local bullies throw their weight about, but law-abiding people have to hold back their indignation. It will be no easy thing to bring the neighborhoods back to peace and tranquility. Furthermore, there are quite a few people who lack ability themselves but who are intensely jealous of real talents. They will stir up trouble by rumor-mongering and bring up false charges against the loyal and upright officials. For all these reasons, I am not inclined to take office."

Confucius heaved a deep sigh and knitted his brows. "Zi Gong, your words are somewhat reasonable. However, you have studied the six arts with me for so many years. Don't you think it regrettable not to put what you have learned into practice and do something for the

restoration of the rites in this world?"

Zi Gong clasped his hands and was about to say something when Confucius stopped him. "How could you know the danger of falling if you do not ascend the peak? How could you know the danger of drowning if you do not come before deep water? How could you know the danger of great waves if you do not sail the ocean? To know any of these you have to gain experience first. If you get to know the various dangers in an official career through experience, you will understand how to practice caution and protect yourself from harm."

"I still consider myself unsuitable for an official career."

Confucius was becoming a little annoyed. "What would be the use for one to know the three hundred poems from *The Book of Poetry* if he can neither take up administrative responsibilities nor fulfill diplomatic missions for the state?"

"If you really think I should accept the appointment, master, I will accept it then."

"I am sure you will be able to govern Wenyang well."

"What should I do first when I arrive in Wenyang?"

"Increase grain reserves and strengthen the troops."

Zi Gong was puzzled. "Master, you have always regarded adherence to the rites as the primary duty of the government. Why do you advise me to build up military strength?"

"To restore the rites is the long-term goal," explained Confucius. "Amid the turmoils in today's world, if you lack the military strength to guard against external threats, you will have no ground on which to plant your feet, much less the chance to restore the rites. Only by ensuring local security will the common people have faith in you."

"Since I am to take office, I would like to be an official loyal to the lord and sincere to the people. How can I achieve that?"

"Be diligent in fulfilling your duties and cautious in your action. A good official is widely admired for obeying the law and bringing benefits to the people. An evil official is widely despised for disobeying the law and seeking personal gains at the people's expense."

"How should I deal with scholars?"

"Publicize their good points and refrain from talking about their weaknesses. To conceal others' virtue would prevent capable people from obtaining office. To publicize others' faults would be unworthy of a superior man."

"I learned from my fellow disciples that you were asked how to rule the state on three separate occasions. To Duke Jing of Qi you mentioned frugality, to the lord of Lu you mentioned employment of men of ability, and to the magistrate of She you said a ruler should please the people nearby and attract people to come from afar. Why did you give different answers to the same question?"

"Because the question was put under different conditions," replied Confucius. "The state of Qi was very powerful, and its ruler gave himself up to excessive debauchery and dissipation. That's why I advised him to be frugal. The lord of Lu relied heavily on Jisun, Mengsun and Shusun, who were jealous of capable people and did not always serve their lord wholeheartedly. That's why I emphasized the importance of selecting the right people to fill the government. The magistrate of She governed a vast, sparsely populated region, where people had a tendency to drift away. That's why I advised him to please people nearby and attract those from afar."

Zi Gong thought for a while, then asked, "What man can be called a scholar?"

"One can be called a scholar who understands the principle of righteousness and the sense of shame, and is able to carry out diplomatic missions to the satisfaction of his sovereign."

"What about the grade below?"

"One who is praised by his neighbors for being filial to his parents and by his fellow villagers for treating his elders with respect."

"What about the grade below?"

"One who keeps his word and is resolute in his action."

"What do you think of those at the helm of the various states today?" asked Zi Gong.

"Oh," Confucius replied angrily, "they are so narrow-minded that they are not worth mentioning at all."

"If there is someone who is liked by everyone in a village, what would you think of him?"

"It is hard to tell."

"If someone is disliked by everyone in a village, what would you think of him?"

"It is hard to tell."

"Then how do you tell good people from bad?"

"Only if all the good people in the village like him and all the bad people in the village dislike him can a man be called good. Likewise, only if all the bad people in the village like him and all the good people in the village dislike him can a man be called bad."

The following day Confucius summoned Bu Shang, Yan Yan, Mi Buqi, Gao Chai, Kong Zhong and Zi Gong and said to them, "There were all sorts of officials in history. Some were pure and just whereas others were vile and corrupt. Some achieved great merits whereas others did practically nothing worthwhile all their lives. Some served their rulers with devotion and brought benefits to the people, whereas others were disloyal to their rulers and rode roughshod over the people. What happened in the past may serve as a lesson to people today. You should follow the example of the ancient men of virtue and govern people with benevolence and righteousness. Increase grain reserves, consolidate military strength, and obtain people's trust and respect."

The disciples received his instruction and saluted in farewell.

After seeing them to the gate, Confucius felt a surge of relief and returned to the classroom, where many disciples were gathered. The thatched house was first built many years ago, and now it had become rather dilapidated with the walls peeling off and weeds growing on the roof. Pleased with the attentiveness of the disciples, he began to deliver a discourse on *The Book of Changes*.

Having finished teaching, Confucius returned to his room. "It's unlikely for me to take office," he said to himself, "so I will devote myself to editing ancient documents." He looked at the stacks of bamboo slips on the shelf, carefully covered with cloth, and felt a great comfort in his heart. His wife and children had shown their understanding and support by taking good care of his books. When he thought of Lady Qiguan, he could still remember her voice and countenance vividly as if she were standing there right before him. He went to the shelf, lifted the covering cloth, and looked through the bamboo slips. He started to edit *The Book of Poetry* and spent the whole day collating its classification and titles.

That evening he found it hard to fall asleep, as his mind kept envisaging what his disciples would achieve in their career and what he would do himself in his old age. He felt dizzy in the head and finally drifted into a dream.

He found himself riding in his chariot along a wide boulevard. The clouds were painted rosy by the glow of the morning sun. The trees lining the road were mixed: willows, poplars and apricots.

When the chariot came to a hill, he went down to take a look. Two phoenixes, green-feathered and red-tailed, emerged from the morning mist that hung low over the wilderness. Two giant dragons also leapt out of the mist, their scales reflecting the golden sunlight, and began frolicking among the colored clouds.

"Dragons and phoenixes!" exclaimed Confucius. "What an auspicious omen!"

The melodious music of certain instruments came floating into his ears. Turning to the west, he was stupefied to see a shining pagoda towering into the sky. Enchanted, Confucius left his chariot behind and walked swiftly toward the pagoda. He crossed a hill and forded a river, but the pagoda still looked out of reach. By this time he was gasping for breath and sweating profusely, and he wished he could fly over to take a close look. As soon as the idea occurred to him, he drew in his legs, waved his arms, and actually began to fly. Soaring over numerous mountains and streams, he finally alighted in front of a stone archway bearing the words "Royal Palace of the Zhou Dynasty." He looked up to see some marble steps. He dusted his clothes and, lifting the hem of his robe, began ascending the steps until he reached a platform. Suddenly he was intercepted by two guards holding long halberds. Startled, he looked back and found a dozen halberd-carrying warriors stand in the way fixing their gaze on him.

Taken by surprise, he was at a loss what to do.

"Who are you?" demanded a red-haired and red-bearded guard. "How dare you break into the forbidden palace of His Majesty?"

Confucius made a deep bow before he replied, "I am Kong Qiu from the state of Lu."

The guard burst into a fit of laughter. "How dare you pretend to be Confucius?"

"I am indeed Kong Qiu," said Confucius.

The guard put down his halberd and asked in a mild tone, "Why do you come to the palace then?"

"Some of my disciples have taken office in the states of Lu, Wei and Qi. I have come to offer His Majesty the king my advice on employing men of ability to bring prosperity to the whole kingdom."

"This is something very praiseworthy," said the guard with a smile. "You may proceed!"

Confucius thanked the guards and continued to walk up the steps. He arrived at a pavilion with a thatched roof, where he stopped to rest for a while. When he was about to set off again, two guards emerged and reached out their broadswords to stop him.

Before Confucius could say anything, the guards widened their eyes in anger and demanded in a stern voice, "Who are you?"

"Kong Qiu."

"Which Kong Qiu?"

"Kong Qiu from the state of Lu."

"Why have you come to the royal capital?"

"I have something important to report to His Majesty."

The guards hesitated, then said in a mild voice, "Wait till we report this to the king." They turned and shouted to the guards standing above, "Kong Qiu from Lu asks for an audience with His Majesty!" The message was repeated several times as it passed among the guards stationed along the steps.

Confucius held his breath as he waited for a response.

Finally a magnificently dressed palace attendant came out and announced, "His Majesty has ordered Kong Qiu to enter the palace!"

Overjoyed, Confucius finished the last few dozen steps at one stretch. He found himself before a sea of flowers of all seasons. Among the flowers stood a majestic palace. A gentle breeze brought forth the fragrance of the flowers. He drew in a deep breath and felt totally refreshed in his mind.

Guided by the palace attendant, Confucius walked toward the palace. He was struck with wonder when, at his approach, the flowers automatically moved aside to reveal a pebbled path leading to the palace gate.

At the palace gate stood two ranks of armored guards holding spears, broadswords, swords or halberds in their hands.

Entering the gate, Confucius found himself in a great hall paved with white marble. He stamped his feet to shake the dust off his shoes.

Leaving the hall, they came to a two-story building, which was not large but very exquisitely constructed. Confucius frowned at the sight of the silver-paved path.

Passing through the two-story building, they came before an imposing palace. Three flights of stairs led to the palace, each flight consisting of three steps. The steps and the path were paved with gold. Confucius drew in a breath with dismay. He thought to himself, "With the king throwing gold about like dirt it is no wonder that the kingdom should have been brought to the verge of collapse!"

Suddenly the two ranks of palace guards raised their weapons and interlocked them over his head. Confucius realized to his indignation that he had to walk under the weapons to reach the palace gate.

The palace was richly decorated. King Jing of Zhou was sitting in his dragon-design chair wearing his crown. The court officials, all formally dressed, stood in two ranks. The palace attendant entered and announced, "Kong Qiu from Lu is here to see Your Majesty."

"Show him in!" said King Jing with pleasure.

Confucius entered the palace in small, quick steps and walked past the two ranks of civil and military officials. He knelt in obeisance and kowtowed. "Kong Qiu from Lu pays respects to Your Majesty."

"Stand up," said King Jing.

Confucius got on his feet and was about to join the rank of civil officials when someone called out his name. "Kong Qiu, come here!"

Confucius turned and found the Duke of Zhou smiling and waving at him. He walked over and stood by his side.

"For what purpose have you come to see the king?" asked the duke.

"I have come with the aim to restore the rites of Zhou."

"Let me report to His Majesty on your behalf." The duke stepped forward to address the king, "Your Majesty, Kong Qiu from the state of Lu has worked all his life for the propagation of the rites of Zhou. I beseech you to reward him with wealth and honor!"

"Well ..." King Jing looked around with a dazed expression.

The duke hastily changed topic. "I beseech Your Majesty to listen to Kong Qiu's idea about ruling the kingdom."

"Your request is granted. Kong Qiu, you may explain your viewpoints to all the court officials."

"I will obey your order!" Confucius said, kowtowing in obeisance.

"Stand up."

"Thank you, Your Majesty!" Confucius rose and took his place beside the Duke of Zhou.

"Kong Qiu," said the king, "the world has been plunged into chaos by the constant wars among the vassal lords. I intend to restore Zhou to its former glory as in the days of my ancestors, but the task seems to be beyond my capacity. Can you give me some advice?"

Confucius thought this a good opportunity to explain his views. "Your Majesty," he said, "many of the evils in the world have originated from ignorance."

"You are right," the king nodded. "What shall we do about it then?"

"Set up schools and promote education. Provide everyone under the sun the education he deserves. People should be taught the six arts of rites, music, archery, chariot driving, writing, and arithmetic and made to understand the five moral principles of benevolence, righteousness, courtesy, wisdom and sincerity. When everyone has become well-cultivated, the king's edict will be carried out without a hitch."

King Jing listened attentively, his eyes wide with admiration.

"War will be stopped and contention avoided when everyone becomes well-cultivated and understands moral principles," continued Confucius.

King Jing beckoned Confucius to stop. "Kong Qiu," he asked, "explain this point in detail. How can war be stopped and contention avoided in this way?"

"When people are well-educated, they will know why precedence should be maintained between seniors and juniors. They will be loyal to the king and cherish the people, show respect for the elderly and loving kindness for the young. When people are well-educated, they will know the benefits of courtesy, and the vassal states will be governed according to the rites. When rites and courtesy become the norm in interpersonal and interstate relationships, rulers will act like rulers, subjects like subjects, fathers like fathers, and sons like sons. Wars and contentions will naturally vanish from the world."

King Jing nodded thoughtfully.

"I have heard that many of your disciples have taken office," the Duke of Zhou chipped in.

"Yes," said Confucius with pleasure. "Among my disciples Zi Lu, Gao Chai and Ran Qiu had served as officials before. Recently Bu Shang, Yan Yan, Mi Buqi, Kong Zhong and Zi Gong were appointed magistrates."

"And they have done well at their offices?" asked the Duke of Zhou.

"Yes, they have all made remarkable achievements."

King Jing was pleased. "I hear that you have taught three thousand disciples, and seventy-two of them are well-versed in the six arts. If I employ you and your disciples in my court, will I be able to govern the kingdom well?"

Confucius decided this was no time for modesty. "If my disciples and I are given the chance to help govern the kingdom, it will take no more than a few years to achieve universal peace and prosperity."

"In that case, listen to your appointment!"

"I am all attention," answered Confucius, falling on his knees.

An immense stir ensued among the court officials.

"Your Majesty," one official said, "Kong Qiu is merely a pedant with a glib tongue. How can he have the ability to govern the kingdom?"

"Your Majesty," another said, "it would be unsuitable to appoint such a man to high office!"

"Your Majesty," still another said, "please don't listen to his flowery words!"

Confucius got up and glanced at the indignant faces around him. Unwilling to make himself a target of attack, he remained silent.

King Jing slapped the table in great anger. "How dare you make such a racket in the court! Shut up, all of you! I have made up my mind. Confucius and all his disciples will be given official posts."

The officials lowered their heads and held their tongue.

King Jing stood up and scolded them. "You can neither pacify the kingdom nor fulfill your administrative duties. What else can you do apart from enjoying high salaries? How can an ill-bred, worthless bunch like you be compared with Kong Qiu, a man of wide knowledge and great learning!"

Confucius felt ashamed for the officials. He bowed deeply to King Jing, intending to dissuade him from reprimanding the officials.

King Jing was still fuming with rage. "Get out, all of you. Don't stay here to annoy me!"

The officials saluted the king and retreated.

King Jing left his seat and came over to Confucius. "Honored minister," he said amiably, "these narrow-minded people did not know how to treat a man of worth. Please do not be offended!"

"Kong Qiu is a humble commoner," said Confucius. "I am to blame for causing displeasure among the court officials."

"Why should you be blamed for it?" said King Jing. "Come, let me show you some lovely sights." He took Confucius by the hand and walked out of the palace.

Confucius followed the king out. Looking around, he was astonished to find himself standing right at the top of the shining pagoda he had been dreaming of all his life. Golden rays were radiating from the pagoda toward the entire land under heaven. When he walked to the railings and looked down, he found the pagoda consisting of several levels. On the first level below the top stood a dozen civil and military officials. Dressed in official gowns and holding jade tablets in their hands, they stood at attention waiting for the king to issue his edict. On the second level stood about a hundred officials with similar manners and postures, but they belonged to a lower rank judging by the style of their gowns. On the third level stood thousands of people. Dressed in scholar's gowns and caps, they looked modest in attitude and graceful in manners. On the fourth level there stood countless people with different expressions and clothing styles. When King Jing and the Duke of Zhou came to the balustrades, the people below began to hail, "Long live the king!" The cheering started from the first level to the last.

Moved to tears Confucius thought, "The Great Harmony must have already been achieved in the whole world, otherwise I would not be witnessing this wonderful sight."

He looked into the distance and found the pagoda surrounded by mountains festooned with flowers. In the mountains he could see deer, cranes and other auspicious animals. Towers and pavilions were built beside waterfalls, and there were several great rivers flowing eastward. Music seemed to be coming from the mountains to accompany the loud cries of worship uttered by the multitudes. Confucius was almost carried away by the feelings the scene excited in him.

"Kong Qiu," asked King Jing with a smile, "do you have anything to say to these people?"

"Your Majesty," said Confucius uneasily, "this is not the place where I can speak."

"If you have anything to say, just say it!" encouraged the Duke of Zhou.

An idea came to Confucius' mind. "Your Majesty," he said bluntly, "the royal palace seems to be too luxurious."

King Jing flew into a rage on hearing this. "What?" he retorted. "Are you implying I should live like an ordinary man? Didn't you say just now that rulers should be like rulers, subjects like subjects, fathers like fathers and sons like sons?"

Confucius realized he had made an inappropriate remark and was at a loss what to say.

King Jing brought his hand down on the balustrades. "No one else has ever dared to speak irreverently in front of me. Do you think you can criticize me just because you have read a few books? Guards!"

"Here!" a few dozen guards instantly appeared, sword in hand.

"Off with his head!"

The guards instantly raised their swords to strike at Confucius.

Confucius fell on his back with a scream, and the pagoda also toppled.

He opened his eyes, and found Kong Ji standing beside the bed. "Grandpa, why were you shouting in sleep?"

"Grandpa just had a bad dream," said Confucius with an awkward smile.

"A dream?" repeated Kong Ji, his eyes large with puzzlement.

"Yes, just a dream," said Confucius. He wiped the sweat from his forehead and got dressed.

Kong Li entered the room to offer his greetings. "Father," he said, "the weather is warm and flowers are blooming. Some of your disciples want to go for an outing to enjoy the spring sights, and I'd like to go with them."

"Go with them then," agreed Confucius readily.

Chapter Forty-two

Confucius Talks About Filial Duties;
Master and Disciples Plant Junipers
in the Courtyard

"But," Confucius added, as an afterthought, "you must not neglect your study. His Lordship has begun to employ men of ability and integrity to fill offices. You should try to enhance your learning and get prepared to serve the state."

"I understand," Kong Li replied, then went out to find his fellow disciples.

The disciples left the city in threes and fours. Among them was a young man, Chen Kang, whose styled name was Zi Qin. He was born in the state of Chen in the thirty-first year of Duke Zhao of Lu's reign (511 B.C.). He said to Kong Li, "We have accompanied our master to the outskirts of the capital many times. It is a fine day today. Let's go to the Daqing Mountain in Wucheng for a change!"

Kong Li's face lit up. "Daqing Mountain is famous for its ancient temples, springs and grotesque trees. But it is over sixty li away. It would not be possible for us to return on the same day."

"Zeng Dian and Zeng Shen live near the mountain," said Chen Kang. "If it's too late for us to return, we can stay the night in their house."

Kong Li hesitated.

Chen Kang grabbed him by the hand and dragged him along. "What's there to worry about? Let's go!"

By the time they reached Daqing Mountain, the two of them were sweating all over and very thirsty. They climbed halfway up the mountain when they came to an ancient temple, beside which a clear spring was flowing from a fissure in the rock. Chen Kang ran over to it, drank his fill and cupped water with both hands to wash his face.

Kong Li stood waiting until Chen Kang finished washing, then went over to drink.

Daqing Mountain consisted of great black rocks. Many elm trees grew out of fissures in the rock. Their tangled roots were exposed in the air, and along the trunks were many bumps.

Chen Kang pulled at a small cypress tree. "Kong Li, come and look at this! This tree grows out of a hole in the rock!"

Kong Li went to take a close look. This was a smooth, cone-shaped rock, and out of a narrow fissure grew the cypress tree, already as thick as the grasp of one's palm.

"Everything grows out of the soil, so the saying goes," said Chen Kang. "But this tree grows out of a rock. Isn't it strange?"

"Very curious!" agreed Kong Li.

Reaching the mountaintop, they looked around and saw many hills spread all across the vast plain. Some were totally naked while others were covered in grass or dense woods.

They went around enjoying the scenery, oblivious to hunger. When the sun began setting, they entered a temple. The courtyard was empty except for two turtledoves leaping about feeding on pine nuts. Looking ahead at the main hall, they could vaguely see a statue in the shrine.

Chen Kang walked into the hall and examined the statue careful-ly, but he could not recognize it. He turned to Kong Li, "Do you know whom is this temple dedicated to?"

Kong Li looked the statue up and down and murmured, "It might be the Jade Emperor or the legnedary sage king Fu Xi."

"Could it be Lao Zi?"

Kong Li could not be sure. He went out of the temple and said, "It's getting late. Shall we go and find Zeng Dian by Nanwu Moun-tain?"

Chen Kang began to feel hungry, so he agreed.

At dusk they reached Nanwu Mountain, totally exhausted. They found out the location of Zeng Dian's house from the locals and made their way to it.

It was a thatched house at the foot of the mountain. The entire courtyard was shaded by poplar and elm trees.

Chen Kang was about to knock at the gate when he heard the sound of someone playing a zither. He listened for a moment before he knocked on the gate.

The sound of music stopped. A moment later Zeng Shen came out to open the gate. Chen Kang and Kong Li were surprised to find Zeng Shen covered in mud. "What did you do to get your clothes so dirty?" asked Chen Kang.

Blushing up to the temples, Zeng Shen murmured, "My father had someone bring back a few white gourd seeds from the state of Wu and planted them in the backyard. When I was weeding the yard today, I accidentally broke two white gourd seedlings."

"What did all that have to do with your dirty clothes?" asked Chen Kang.

Zeng Shen was greatly embarrassed. "When my father scolded me severely, I tried to explain. My father got so angry that he beat me."

Chen Kang became even more puzzled. "If your father beat you, you should be feeling sad. Why were you playing the zither as if you were happy?"

Zeng Shen produced a forced smile. "I feared that my father may regret having beaten me and feel sad, so I played the zither to tell him that I was all right."

"Isn't it remarkable," said Kong Li, "for an unkind father like him to have a filial son like you!"

Just then Zeng Dian emerged from the backyard, still looking angry. At the sight of Kong Li and Chen Kang he smiled apologetically. "Sorry for not coming out to meet you!"

Kong Li and Chen Kang greeted him. "We are a couple of uninvited guests. Please don't close the gate to us!"

Zeng Shen smiled. "We were talking outside, and I forgot to invite you to come in. Please enter the house!"

They entered the house and took their seats. "Where did the two of you have lunch?" asked Zeng Dian.

Kong Li swallowed and said, "Actually we haven't had our lunch yet."

Zeng Dian looked out the window and found the sun had already set. "It's time for supper," he said with a smile.

"Father," said Zeng Shen, "please keep the guests company while I prepare the supper."

After supper Kong Li and Chen Kang were put up in the same room. They could not fall asleep, so they started chatting.

"Did your father ever beat you?" asked Chen Kang.

"No," replied Kong Li. "He never beat me."

"You are lucky to have such a great man as your father."

"Did your father ever beat you then?"

"No, he didn't."

"Aren't you lucky too?"

"Though he never beat me, he taught me nothing because he is not a learned man."

Kong Li did not know what to say.

"Did you get any special instruction from your father?" asked Chen Kang.

"No," said Kong Li. "My father never gave me any special instruction. But I do remember two incidents."

"What incidents?" asked Chen Kang with interest.

"One day my father was standing by himself in the courtyard. When I walked past he stopped me and asked, 'Have you studied *The Book of Poetry?*' 'Not yet,' I replied. He said, 'Until you have studied it, you won't know how to speak properly.' After that I began to study the book."

"And the other incident?"

"Another day, I again walked past my father when he was standing by himself in the courtyard. He stopped me and asked, 'Have you studied *The Book of Rites?*' 'Not yet,' I replied. He said, 'Until you have studied *The Book of Rites*, you won't know how to conduct yourself properly.' After that I began to study the book. These two incidents can be regarded as the special instruction I received from my father."

Chen Kang was delighted. "I asked you only one question, but I learned three things. First, I learned the essence of *The Book of Poetry*; second, I learned the essence of *The Book of Rites*; third, I learned that a superior man does not show special favor toward his own son."

When they returned to the capital the following day, Chen Kang told Confucius how Zeng Shen was beaten by his father, Zeng Dian.

"A man of virtue should not go about spreading hearsays," said Confucius. "Why should you come to me and talk ill of the Zengs in this way?"

"But I learned of it from Zeng Shen himself," said Chen Kang. "And Kong Li was also present."

Confucius was highly displeased. "To destroy two white gourd seedlings was a trivial matter," he said. "To beat his son because of this shows that Zeng Dian was neither kind nor benevolent. When Zeng Shen played the zither after he was beaten to comfort his father it shows that he was neither filial nor benevolent." He called Kong Li to him and said, "Tell the gate-keeper not to allow Zeng Dian and Zeng Shen to enter the classroom!"

Kong Li was caught in a dilemma. He did not want to disobey his father, but he didn't want to have Zeng Dian and Zeng Shen kept out either. He silently blamed Chen Kang for not telling the story of the Zengs to Confucius.

The gate-keeper was an honest man in his fifties. When he saw Kong Li's worried look, he came up to inquire what was wrong.

"My father said you must not allow Zeng Dian and Zeng Shen to enter the classroom," said Kong Li.

The gate-keeper's eyes widened in surprise. "Why?"

Kong Li recounted what had happened.

"What shall I do when they come?" asked the gate-keeper.

"Try to think of some way out," urged Kong Li.

Two days later, when Zeng Dian and Zeng Shen came, they were stopped by the gate-keeper. "The master has instructed me not to allow the two of you to enter."

"We are the master's disciples," said Zeng Dian. "Why can't we enter?"

"Did you beat your son two days ago?" asked the gate-keeper.

Zeng Dian realized what had happened. He was filled with regret, not knowing what to do.

Zeng Shen walked to and fro in front of the gate but could not come up with a solution either.

"Nangong and Gongye are the master's honored guests as well as favorite disciples," said the gate-keeper. "Why not ask them for help?"

Zeng Dian thought it a good idea. They thanked the gate-keeper and went to Gongye Chang's house, where they learned that Gongye Chang had gone to the classroom. So they went to call on Nangong Shi.

"What business has brought both of you here?" asked Nangong Shi with a smile.

"I did something preposterous," said Zeng Dian, "and the master would not allow us to enter the classroom."

"Something preposterous?" muttered Nangong Shi in astonishment. "How could a distinguished man like you have done something preposterous?"

Zeng Dian then described to him what had happened.

Nangong Shi found the problem difficult to solve. "The master has always attached great importance to father-son relationship," he murmured to himself. "So he must be much offended by what happened between the two of you."

"For old time's sake," pleaded Zeng Dian, "help me out of this!"

Nangong Shi thought for a while, then his face brightened. "Today is the fifteenth of the fourth month," he said, "so the master will be enjoying the moon with some of the disciples in the courtyard this evening. The two of you can wait by the side gate to the east. When the master is talking congenially, go in and admit your mistake. If your attitude is sincere, he would not drive you out."

"A good idea!" exclaimed Zeng Dian. "Thanks so much."

"Don't mention it."

Zeng Dian still felt a little apprehensive. "Please go there yourself this evening and give us a sign!"

Nangong Shi agreed. "When I cough three times, you may enter by the side gate."

Zeng Dian and Zeng Shen expressed their gratitude and took their leave.

Soon after dark the moon rose above the roof of the eastern chamber and peeked through the dense leaves of the old scholartree.

Confucius and some of his disciples sat chatting in the courtyard.

The disciples began asking questions. Zai Yu said, "Master, it is common practice to observe a three-year mourning after the death of one's parent. I think three years is too long. The rites will be abandoned if the superior man does not practice them for three years; the music will be forgotten if the superior man does not play it for three years. In my opinion, one year is already long enough, for even during that period the old grain will have been used up and new grain will have been harvested. Why should one mourn for as long as three years?"

"Because the parents took great pains to bring up their children," said Confucius. "Would you be at ease enjoying rice and wearing finery before three years' mourning is over?"

"Yes, I would," said Zai Yu.

Confucius was highly displeased. "If you feel at ease doing it, do as you please! A superior man in mourning finds no taste for delicious food and no pleasure in melodious music. Let me repeat: if you feel at ease doing it, do as you please."

Zhuansun Shi, who had often dreamed of returning to the state of Chen to seek officialdom, asked, "What must a man do in order to make a good official?"

"Cultivate the five virtues and avoid the four defects," replied Confucius.

"What are the five virtues?"

"A superior man should benefit the common people without depleting himself. He should use the labor of the common people without arousing their complaints. He should pursue benevolence and justice but not be greedy. He should look solemn but not arrogant. He should inspire awe but not terror."

"How can I achieve all that?" asked Zhuansun Shi.

"If you adapt your policies to local conditions, you can bring benefits to the people without depleting yourself. If you use the labor of farmers in the slack seasons, they will have no complaints. If you pursue benevolence and justice, you will be satisfied when you obtain them. If you treat people with courtesy regardless of their social status or the size of their clans, you will achieve a solemn, but not arrogant, mien. If you are dressed properly and conduct yourself with dignity, you will surely inspire awe but not terror."

"What are the four defects?"

"To impose death penalty without instructing the people is called cruelty; to seek quick success and instant benefits is called impetuosity; to change policy without notice is called wreaking havoc, and to refuse to give what should be given is called avarice."

"What man can be called benevolent?"

"To practice the five qualities at all times and all places can be called benevolent."

"What are the five qualities?"

"Solemnity, tolerance, honesty, diligence and generosity."

"Could you explain them in detail?"

"With solemnity you will not suffer humiliation; with tolerance you will gain the support of the common people; with honesty you will win the trust of others; with diligence you will achieve merits in your official career; and with generosity you will receive the service from others."

"How can I make myself accepted wherever I go?"

"If you are frank and sincere in speech and honest and solemn in conduct, you will be accepted even in a foreign state. If you are insincere and deceitful in speech and crude and unconstrained in conduct, you will not be accepted even in your own neighborhood. Thus a superior man always bears in mind the qualities of frankness, sincerity, honesty and gravity. When standing, he feels as if he could see these words in front of him; when riding in a chariot, he feels as if he could see these words inscribed on the armrest. By always remembering these words, you will be able to make yourself accepted wherever you go."

"Wonderful!" exclaimed Zhuansun Shi. "Master, I'll make these words my motto and write them on my sash."

Confucius looked up at the clear, blue sky and sighed with satisfaction. "Zhuansun Shi, I can see that you are a very sincere person!"

"I will follow your instruction!" pledged Zhuansun Shi.

"Master," asked Min Shun, "what man can be called filial?"

"You can be called a filial son, Min Shun," replied Confucius. "Your stepmother mistreated you, but you pleaded for her rather than trying to get even. Don't you deserve to be called a filial son?"

While Confucius was conversing with his disciples in the courtyard, Zeng Dian and Zeng Shen waited anxiously outside the east wall. Nangong Shi thought it was time to let them in, so he coughed deliberately.

Hearing the signal, Zeng Dian and Zeng Shen entered by the side gate and knelt before Confucius. "Your disciple pays respects to you, master!" they said at the same time.

"You may get up!" said Confucius.

Zeng Dian and Zeng Shen got on their feet and stood by Confucius' side.

"Have you become aware of your mistake?" asked Confucius gravely.

"Yes," replied Zeng Dian.

"What's your mistake?"

"I should not have beaten my son for a trivial matter."

"Zeng Shen, what's your mistake?" asked Confucius.

"I ..." Zeng Shen did not know what to say.

Confucius raised his voice. "What's so important about destroying a couple of white gourd seedlings? Zeng Dian lacked the loving kindness of a father when he gave his son a heavy beating for something so insignificant. Furthermore, Zeng Shen is also a subject of the king of Zhou. By beating your son without a good cause, Zeng Dian, you compromised your loyalty to the king."

Zeng Dian shook with fear and knelt again. "I am aware of the seriousness of my mistake!"

"Zeng Shen," continued Confucius, "you should have dodged

when your father beat you. Instead, you submitted willingly to the beating and played the zither afterward. Weren't you not abetting your father to commit his mistake?"

Zeng Shen also dropped on his knees. "I was wrong, master."

"Get up, the two of you!"

Zeng Dian and Zeng Shen got up and took their seats.

"One must adhere to the principles of benevolence, righteousness, loyalty and filial piety," admonished Confucius to his disciples.

"We will remember it!" responded the disciples.

"Do you know why it should be so?" asked Confucius.

"Benevolence has its roots in filial piety," answered You Ruo, "and filial piety finds broader expression in benevolence. A man who fulfills his filial duties to his parents and treats his seniors with respect will not commit insubordination and rebellion."

"Min Shun," asked Confucius, "why don't you say something?"

"I only know how to do my share," said Min Shun, looking a little bashful. "But I don't know how to talk about it."

"Good! To be able to do one's share is just fine. It is unnecessary to be eloquent. Someone who puts up a false front and talks without sincerity has no benevolence or virtue to speak of."

The moon was high in the sky, surrounded by a few clouds. There was a nip in the night air. Confucius did not feel tired. He gazed into the sky for a while, then turned to Zeng Shen. "Zeng Shen, do you also have your motto?"

"No," replied Zeng Shen. "But I do have a few guidelines."

"Tell me about them!"

"At the end of every day I examine what I did in three respects: whether I tried my best to help others, whether I was sincere and honest with my friends, and whether I reviewed what I learned from you."

Confucius smiled approvingly. "The three guidelines of yours are very sound. If you follow them every day, you will surely become a superior man."

"Can these guidelines be called a motto?" asked Zhuansun Shi.

"Yes," replied Confucius, "as long as one can really follow them."

The other disciples fell silent as they examined themselves with the three guidelines.

After a while Confucius remarked, "My disciples, remember this: Be filial to your parents when at home, and be respectful to your seniors when outside. Be cautious in both speech and conduct. Be as good as your word. Be kind to the multitudes and associate with people of virtue. After you have achieved all this, you may devote the rest of your time studying ancient documents."

Kong Li walked up and said in a low voice, "Father, it's getting late. It's time you retired for the night!"

Confucius looked up at the evening sky. Just at this moment a meteorite dashed across the sky and vanished in an instant. Confucius and his disciples witnessed the sight with wonder. Then they bade one another good night.

The next morning, after giving a lecture on *The Book of Changes*, Confucius walked into the courtyard to enjoy the sun and the magpies chirping overhead in the old scholartree. He looked around and felt the yard to be a little empty. "I should have a few more trees planted here," he muttered to himself. "But what type shall I choose?"

Zhuansun Shi walked up to him with a question. "Master, how can a scholar be called knowledgeable?"

"What do you mean by 'knowledgeable?'"

"I mean achieving a good reputation whether one serves as an official in the court or a steward in a minister's house."

"This is called being known, not being knowledgeable."

"What can be called knowledgeable then?"

"In order to be knowledgeable," said Confucius, "one must be upright in nature and always uphold righteousness in his conduct. One must be careful in listening to people's words and in watching their expressions, and willing to allow others to take precedence over himself. Such a man will surely be knowledgeable when he serves as a court official. As for a man being known, he only pays lip service to benevolence and goes against it in his conduct. In spite of all that he thinks of himself as a benevolent man. Such a man will obtain fame by deceptive means whether he serves as a court official or a steward."

"Now I understand," said Zhuansun Shi, nodding his head.

"I want to plant some trees in this courtyard," said Confucius. "What type of trees do you think would be suitable?"

"I like fruit trees," said Zhuansun Shi. "It's so delightful when they blossom in spring and bear fruits in autumn."

Zi Lu came over and declared in a loud voice, "I like poplars because they are tall and upright."

Yan Hui also came up to express his view. "I like cypresses.

Master, cypresses would suit this place well."

"I agree," said Confucius with a smile. "When it turns cold in winter, pines and cypresses are the last to lose their leaves. However, I think I like junipers better. Their trunk is tall and straight, their canopy large and round, their leaves thick and luxuriant, and their fruits full but inconspicuous."

"Let's plant junipers then," said Zi Lu.

"Unfortunately we've just missed the tree-planting season," said Confucius regrettably. "We'll have to wait till next year."

"Master, at your age it's never too early ..." Zi Lu blurted out, then checked himself.

"Master," said Yan Hui, "a sapling will survive if its roots are well protected. Let me get some saplings with intact roots. We will be able to make them grow."

"Let me go get some," volunteered Zi Lu.

"The two of you may go together," said Confucius.

After seeing the two disciples off, Confucius walked back to the classroom and continued to teach *The Book of Changes*.

At noon Zi Lu and Yan Hui returned, each carrying a juniper sapling on his shoulder. The roots of the saplings were covered with mud and wrapped up in hemp cloth. This made the saplings very heavy, and both Zi Lu and Yan Hui had sweat on their forehead.

Confucius was delighted. Bringing his lecture to an end, he went out of the classroom and pointed to the south wall of the courtyard. "Let's plant the two junipers there."

Kong Li came out with some pickaxes and hoes. The disciples rushed over and finished digging two deep pits in a short time.

"As a common saying goes, it takes ten years to grow trees but a hundred years to educate people," said Zi Lu. "Master, you have taught us for dozens of years but have never planted trees. Please plant these two junipers yourself."

"It does not make much difference who plants them," said Confucius. But when Yan Hui also urged him, Confucius assented. He rolled up his sleeves and placed one of the saplings in the pit.

The disciples came over and dumped earth into the pit, then watered it.

No sooner had they finished planting the two junipers than Nangong Jingshu came in from the side door. "Master," he said, "His Lordship wants to see you."

Chapter Forty-three

Yan Yan Is Highly Praised for High Performance in Office; Confucius Loses His Son and His Favorite Disciple

It was already past noon. Without stopping to eat lunch, Confucius changed into ceremonial clothes and went to the palace.

Duke Ai of Lu asked, "Master, what's the most important thing for me to govern the state well?"

Confucius was pleased to hear such a question from Duke Ai. "In governing a state, Your Highness must, first and foremost, be upright. If you adopt rational policies, the people will rectify their behavior accordingly. If you set a good example, the people will follow suit. Should you fail to conduct yourself properly, how could you expect the people to listen to you?"

Duke Ai asked with great concern, "How should I rule the state properly then?"

"Ancient sage rulers based their rule on their love for the people. Love for the people is in turn based on rites, and rites, on respect. Rites and respect are the foundations of government. Therefore a superior man never neglects to cultivate himself, for self-cultivation is the starting point for the attainment of the right way. If a man treats people of virtue with respect, he will not get easily confused. If a son treats his parents with filial piety, there will be no discord among the siblings. If a ruler treats his officials with respect, he will not be deceived. If he treats his officials with tolerance, they will give him their loyalty. If he treats the common people with love, they will be diligent in carrying out his edicts. If he pays attention to agricultural production, the state will grow strong. If he treats people from other states with kindness, people will come from distant quarters to submit to his rule."

"If I am to follow your instruction," asked Duke Ai, "where shall I begin?"

"Take a bath, fast, and put on ceremonial clothes," answered Confucius. "Make sure that you don't do anything that goes against the rites. Keep away from treacherous officials, extinguish slanderous talk,

and place virtue above wealth. Firstly, treat your subjects with impartiality and promote people according to their ability. Secondly, reduce taxes and bestow favor on the multitudes. Thirdly, mete out reward or punishment to those who deserve it. Fourthly, spare no effort in promoting education. Fifthly, increase grain reserves and strengthen the military forces."

Duke Ai of Lu was a little surprised. "Master, you have always talked in favor of the state being governed by rites. Why do you advise me now to build up military strength?"

"Because of the change in situation," replied Confucius. "The rites formulated by the Duke of Zhou were complete and perfect. If all rulers had adhered to the rites, universal peace and prosperity would have already been attained. Unfortunately, contention often arises among the states, sometimes leading to armed conflicts. Under such circumstances, a state must have enough grain reserves and adequate military strength. Otherwise it will suffer great instability in case of famine, or be brought to submission in case of invasion from other states."

Duke Ai nodded his approval.

Confucius added, "It is easy for us to refrain from invading another state, but it is not so easy for us to prevent others from invading us."

"I admire you deeply for your learning!" said Duke Ai. "By the way, what kind of hat did Shun wear in his time?"

Displeased with the question, Confucius fell silent.

"I asked you what kind of hat Shun wore in his time," said Duke Ai after a while. "Why don't you answer me?"

Confucius assumed a serious expression. "You asked me a question about a trivial matter instead of essentials. Therefore I find it hard to answer."

Duke Ai widened his eyes. "What are the essentials then?"

"When Shun ruled the world, he did everything he could to improve people's livelihood. He was aversive to men who were mean, treacherous, or bloodthirsty and sought out men of virtue and talent to replace them. He bestowed his favor upon the populace just as the sun nourishes every living thing all across the land, and he adjusted his policy in a natural way similar to the rotation of the four seasons. People all over the world benefited from his benevolent rule and rejoiced in their good fortune. However...." He cast a glance at Duke

Ai and paused.

"You may speak without restraint!" said Duke Ai.

"However," said Confucius, "you were not so much interested in the essence of Shun's rule as in the style of his hat. That was an instance of attending to trifles and neglecting essentials. I really don't know how to answer that question."

Duke Ai found these words reasonable, but he still felt piqued. "You are right, master!" he murmured. "You are absolutely right!"

Confucius knew he'd better take his leave, and he returned home with a heavy heart. "What a ruler!" he thought to himself. "What will be the future of Lu?" He forced himself not to think of this and devoted himself to editing the ancient documents.

First he collated and expunged *The Book of Poetry* and went on to work on *The Book of Documents*, *The Book of Rites*, *The Book of Changes*, and *The Book of Music*, till huge quantities of bamboo slips piled up in his room.

To ensure the reliability of the texts he checked them time and again. On one occasion he was collating *The Book of Rites* when the string linking the bamboo slips broke, and he had to find another string to tie them up. He worked on and on like this for half a year until one day, completely done up, he decided to take an outing to relax.

It was late autumn. Confucius and some disciples rode to Wu-cheng in a chariot. Coming to a mountain north of the city, they found it covered in red leaves and stopped to enjoy the lovely sight. Confucius asked, "What is this mountain called?"

"Phoenix Mountain," replied Yan Hui.

"But why?" asked Confucius. "It doesn't look like a bird at all."

"According to what I have heard, some phoenixes presumably alighted on this mountain in the past," said Yan Hui. "That's how it got its name."

"There are many small holes in the rock of this mountain," said Zai Yu. "When winter comes, many pheasants spend the night by sticking their heads into the holes. The locals call this 'the birds paying homage to the phoenix.'"

Confucius could not help smiling. "That would be interesting to see. Unluckily it is not winter yet. Otherwise we could wait till dark to enjoy the sight."

"It's only half a day's journey from the capital," said Zai Yu. "You can come back here in winter, master."

"I am getting old," Confucius sighed. "It becomes more and more difficult for me to move around."

They left the mountain and moved on, then came to a small hill. "Yan Hui, what's this called?" asked Confucius.

"Plum Blossom Hill."

"That's strange. I see only pines and cypresses, but not a single plum tree."

"Master," said Yan Hui, "the hill got its name because of something peculiar about its rocks. If one climbs the hill right after rain, he will find patterns of plum blossoms on the surface of the rocks."

"The world is indeed full of wonders," said Confucius. "What a pity we don't have rain today."

They headed south and traveled for about ten li, when the city of Wucheng came into sight. Just then they heard someone singing to the accompaniment of a zither:

The man comes joyfully.
In the left hand he holds a flute,
With the right hand beckoning me to join the ride.
What a joy! What a joy!

The man comes joyfully.
In the left hand he holds a feather,
With the right hand beckoning me to join the ride.
What a joy! What a joy!

As they listened to the song, Confucius and his disciples felt as if a fresh spring breeze were puffing across their faces.

Learning of Confucius' arrival, Yan Yan hotfooted it to the north gate, without waiting to have his chariot prepared.

Confucius was delighted to see him. "What a cheerful song and beautiful tune we just heard! But why do you need the rites and music when governing a small city like this? Aren't you killing a chicken with a knife meant for oxen?"

"Master," said Yan Yan, "I once heard you remark that an official, by practicing the rites and music, will develop benevolence toward the people and that the people, by practicing the rites and music, will be willing to follow orders. I have been acting upon your instruction in my office here, but I can't say I have done very well."

Confucius smiled and said to the other disciples, "Yan Yan is right. An official should attach great importance to education in the rites and music regardless of the size of the place that he governs. What I said just now was only a joke."

Led by Yan Yan, the company entered the city and went to his office.

Confucius was pleased when he did not see a crowd of visitors in front of the office. He got down from the chariot and walked into the house. In the courtyard there was a scholartree to the right and a persimmon tree to the left. The scholartree was already shedding its leaves, whereas the persimmon tree was luxuriant with reddening leaves and plump fruits.

A zither was placed on the table in the main hall.

"No wonder people in Wucheng are good at music and songs," said Confucius. "Yan Yan has been setting an example for them!"

Yan Yan lowered his head, smiling.

After they had taken their seats, Confucius asked, "Yan Yan, you have governed the city for almost a year. The office has few visitors, so that there must be few lawsuits. This indicates that you are quite successful in educating the people in the rites. But have you discovered any man of virtue in Wucheng?"

"Yes," said Yan Yan. "I made a friend shortly after I came to Wucheng. His family name is Tantai, his given name Mieming, and his styled name Zi Yu. He is only nineteen years old. Though we have become close friends, he never calls on me at the office except for official business. In my opinion, he not only has good manners but is also an impartial and unselfish man."

"In that case, you may take me to visit him tomorrow."

Yan Yan left his seat and said to Confucius, "Master, there is something I meant to tell you. He wants to be your disciple and study with you."

At this moment a youth came into the hall. He was handsome, fair-skinned, and of middle stature. He wore a garment of coarse cloth and a pair of cloth boots.

"Brother Tantai, this is my master," said Yan Yan.

Tantai Mieming knelt and kowtowed in obeisance. "Master, Tantai Mieming has come to learn from and pay respects to you!"

"Get up, please," said Confucius.

Tantai got on his feet and took a seat.

Confucius introduced Tantai to his disciples, then asked, "What books have you read?"

"I've read *The Book of Poetry*, *The Book of Documents*, and *The Book of Rites*."

"What about *The Book of Music*?"

"I've read it also."

"Are you good at singing and playing the zither?"

"I can't say I am good at it," replied Tantai. "I can do it after a fashion."

Confucius could hardly contain his delight. "Have you read *The Book of Changes*?"

"Yes," Tantai took a look at the other disciples. "However, the principles expounded in *The Book of Changes* are so profound that I don't yet have a thorough understanding of them."

"What's the relationship between yin and yang?" asked Confucius.

"They both contradict and complement each other."

"Good," said Confucius. "Which of the six arts have you mastered?"

Tantai Mieming stood up, placed his hands on the sides, and replied respectfully, "I have mastered none of the six arts. However, I have obtained a cursory knowledge of them."

Confucius was very pleased. "Please sit down."

Confucius and his disciples talked for a long time. Yan Yan bade servants prepare a simple supper.

The following day Yan Yan escorted Confucius on a tour in the city of Wucheng. The shops along the street looked well-stocked. Confucius smiled with satisfaction as he walked along.

Yan Yan said, "Master, we've walked quite a distance. Shall we return to my office?"

"First I want to climb up the gate tower to view the entire city," said Confucius.

With Yan Yan leading the way, they went to the south gate.

Ascending the gate tower, they commanded a bird's-eye view of the whole city. They saw the thatched houses surrounded by trees and heard the barking of dogs and neighing of horses. It was a peaceful, prosperous scene.

"Wucheng is more prosperous than I expected," said Confucius. "Is this not a manifestation of the power of rites?" He turned to Yan Yan. "Do you think it possible to govern the world with your method?"

"I can only carry a hundred catties," said Yan Yan. "How can I bear ten thousand?"

"Do you think it possible to govern Lu with your method?"

"I can only carry a hundred catties. How can I take up one thousand?"

"The wisdom of knowing oneself is worth ten thousand pieces of gold," Confucius remarked. "Apparently Yan Yan has already acquired this wisdom."

When Confucius returned to the capital, some disciples brought him the news that Kong Li was seriously ill.

It was like a bolt from the blue. Confucius hastened home, only to find the entire family weeping over Kong Li's body.

Confucius was overwhelmed with grief. He gazed tearfully at the pallid visage of his deceased son. "The injustice of Heaven!" he exclaimed. To lose one's parent in childhood, one's spouse in middle age and one's son in old age were the greatest inflictions in life, and Confucius suffered all three of them. "What disease did he catch?" he finally asked.

"Two hours ago he was perfectly all right," said Nangong Jingshu, pointing to a pair of wooden pails. "He carried two pails of water from the well and cleft some firewood, then sat down to read a book. Suddenly he said he had a headache and passed out at once. He stopped breathing before the doctor arrived."

"Was this fate?" Confucius sighed. He stroked Kong Li's cheeks, which were already turning cold, and again tears welled up in his eyes.

Except for Kong Ji, the family spent a sleepless night. The following morning a coffin was bought and Kong Li's body placed inside.

"Kong Li has no outer coffin," said Nangong Jingshu. "Shall we buy one for him?"

Confucius objected. "Why should someone who lived a simple life have an ostentatious funeral?"

"Where shall we bury him?"

"By his mother's side."

After that Confucius resumed the collation of ancient documents and the writing of The Spring and Autumn Annals, a chronological history record starting from the first year of Duke Yin of Lu's reign (722 B.C.). In the meantime he continued to teach his disciples and his grandson, Kong Ji. Exceptionally endowed, Kong Ji was also a very sensible child. Confucius placed high hopes on his grandson and devoted all his love to the boy to compensate for what he had failed to do for his wife and son.

In the thirteenth year of Duke Ai of Lu's reign (486 B.C.) Confucius finished the first three tomes of *The Spring and Autumn Annals*. One day, accompanied by Kong Ji, Yan Hui, Zi Lu and Zeng Shen, he went out of the north city gate to tour the Sihe River. As he gazed at the green, clear rushing water, he felt a sense of urgency and wondered if he could finish *The Spring and Autumn Annals* in his remaining years.

On their way back to the city Confucius stopped at the grave site he had chosen for himself and his family. He went up to the graves of his wife and son, walked around, and stared at the grass growing there.

"Master, let's return home," urged Zi Lu.

Confucius turned slowly to face south. "When I die, I want to be buried here with my wife and son. When Kong Ji dies, he will be buried by my side. Look!" He made a gesture with his hand. "In this way I will be taking my son in one hand and my grandson in the other."

On their return they found Ran Qiu waiting anxiously in the house. "Master, Ran Geng has fallen ill," he said.

"Why should you get so flustered about it?" asked Confucius.

"The illness seems to be very serious," said Ran Qiu. "He has distension of the hands and feet and his skin is peeling off."

"What?" Confucius was flabbergasted. "Could it be leprosy?"

At that time leprosy was incurable. It was regarded with horror because of its gruesome symptoms and its being highly contagious. After a moment Confucius asked, "Where is he?"

"At home."

"Get the chariot ready!"

Yan Ke immediately went to harness the horse to the chariot, and they set out for Ran Geng's home.

The chariot stopped in front of a lone thatched house. Confucius alighted and found Ran Geng staring out of the window in the west room. At the sight of Confucius, Ran Geng broke into tears. "Master," he sobbed, "I have received your instruction for so many years but have never got a chance to repay your kindness. Now that I have caught this foul disease, I will return your kindness only in the life to come."

Confucius wept bitterly. "Why should a person of virtue like you be inflicted with such an illness? Could it be fate?"

"Master," said Ran Geng, "don't worry for me. You have much work to do—editing the ancient classics to be passed down to future generations."

Confucius was deeply grieved but could find no words to comfort Ran Geng. Finally he said, "Ran Geng, I'll send the other disciples to find famous doctors to cure your illness." With this he took his leave.

Back home, Confucius told his disciples to go out and look for doctors capable of treating leprosy. Many days later they returned one after another without any good news. Bitterly disappointed, Confucius went to call on Ran Geng again.

Ran Geng looked at Confucius expectantly, but his heart sank at the sight of his worried look.

Standing by the window, Confucius took Ran Geng by the hand and said woefully, "Ran Geng, I have sent people to look for doctors who might have secret cures, but they all returned empty-handed. It seemed that...." His voice trailed off.

"Master, you have done all you can for me. I will remember your kindness even if I die today. My only regret is that I no longer have a chance to repay you for what you have done for me."

"Take care of yourself!" Confucius said. "I will go now." He let go of Ran Geng's hand and stepped back.

Ran Geng extended both hands out of the window. "Master, take care of yourself!"

Confucius walked up to him and took him by both hands. "Ran Geng," he said sadly, "there is really nothing more I can do."

Ran Geng grasped Confucius' hands firmly and wept uncontrollably. Finally he loosened his grip and placed his hands on the latticework of the window. "Master, please go home!"

Confucius stumbled his way back to the chariot. When he looked back, Ran Geng had passed out because of over-exertion. His hands were still placed on the window lattice, but his head had turned away. Thinking that Ran Geng was deliberately looking away, Confucius gazed at him for a long moment before mounting the chariot to leave.

For the next few days Confucius did not go to teach his disciples. Kong Li's death and Rang Geng's illness weighed heavily on his heart. He looked at his gray hair and said to himself that he must finish *The Spring and Autumn Annals* in his remaining years. He was about to resume working on it when Nangong Jingshu arrived. Confucius looked at him inquisitively.

"Yuan Rang's mother just died," said Nangong Jingshu. "He invites you to help him arrange the funeral."

Confucius was hesitant. Yuan Rang and he were friends when young, so it was proper for him to help on such an occasion. However, he bore a strong aversion to Yuan Rang, who showed no respect for the rites in his daily behavior. After much deliberation Confucius finally agreed to go.

Weak in health and low in spirits, Confucius had to walk with a stick.

The coffin was laid in the central room, draped over with a piece of cloth bearing a large character: "Mourning." The courtyard was strewn with earthen ware meant for burial. Confucius frowned with disapproval at the sight of this.

Just then a man dressed in mourning leapt onto the coffin, where he began to sing and dance.

Confucius started and recognized it was Yuan Rang himself. Acting as if he had not seen him, Confucius went up to the coffin and made a deep bow.

Expecting an outburst from Confucius, Yuan Rang felt at a loss when Confucius paid him no attention. He jumped down from the coffin and sat onto the ground, with his legs spread wide.

Unable to contain his anger, Confucius went up to Yuan Rang and tapped him on the leg with the stick. "When young you did not study and had no respect for the rites, and when grown up you did nothing worthwhile. Now old you just eat food. You are a real good-for-nothing!"

Yuan Rang protested, "There are all kinds of people in the world. Why should everyone conform to the same rules?"

"How can you tell a man from a beast if he does not learn the rites?" demanded Confucius. "Your mother took great pains to bring you up, but how did you treat her? At her death, you dance and sing happily instead of weeping with grief. What makes you behave like that?"

Yuan Rang grinned, "I hear that death at old age is a blessing. My mother was over eighty at her death; isn't that something worth celebrating?"

Confucius stamped his feet. "There is no common language between a man and a beast. What can I do with someone who is dead

to all sense of shame?" He made another bow to the coffin and turned
to leave. As soon as he came out the gate of Yuan Rang's house, he
saw Yan Hui running toward him.

Chapter Forty-four

Gao Chai Tries Cases Justly;
Kong Zhong Places Trivialities over Essentials

When Yan Hui saw Confucius, he told him that an envoy from the lord of Wei had come to invite Gao Chai to take office in Wei.

"Where is the envoy?"

"He is waiting for you in the classroom."

"I'll go there to meet him."

When they entered the classroom the envoy from Wei saluted Confucius. "Master, His Lordship the duke of Wei has sent me to invite your disciple Gao Chai to return to Wei to take office."

"Gao Chai has been working for Lu's chief minister as magistrate of Fei," said Confucius. "If he is to return to Wei, the duke of Lu and the chief minister must be informed beforehand."

"Please take the trouble to speak to your lord and the chief minister about it!" said the envoy, bowing with clasped hands.

"I will do what I can," said Confucius. He told Yan Hui to take the Wei envoy to the guesthouse while he set out for the chief minister's residence.

"You have many talented disciples, master," said Jisun Fei. "After Gao Chai's return to Wei, we only have to find another one to replace him as the magistrate of Fei."

"Since you have given your permission, Chief Minister, I'll return and tell the Wei envoy."

When Confucius informed him of the chief minister's permission, the Wei envoy expressed his thanks, then said, "Master, please tell Gao Chai to leave for Wei as soon as possible. I will return and report to my lord."

After the departure of the envoy, Confucius returned home. He called Zi Lu to him, saying, "The chief minister agreed to let Gao Chai return to Wei to take office. Tomorrow I will take a trip to the city of Fei. I will persuade Gao Chai to accept the invitation from the duke of Wei; in the meantime I will see for myself how he has been doing in Fei."

"Let me drive the chariot for you," volunteered Zi Lu.

"No, you are also getting on in years. I can have Yan Ke drive for me."

Zeng Shen came over. "Master, I learned driving when I was only a child. Let me drive you to Fei tomorrow!"

Early the following morning Confucius and Zeng Shen set out for Fei, enjoying the scenery as they journeyed down the road.

Upon setting foot on Fei, they found themselves in a hilly land with tracts of terraced fields. The peasants were weeding the fields to prepare for cultivation. Some of them were taking a rest, singing and chatting merrily.

At twilight they arrived before the magistrate's office. Zeng Shen stopped the chariot and was about to go and speak to the gate-keeper when he heard Gao Chai's stern voice. "There is ample evidence that you robbed and pillaged. How can you deny your guilt?"

Confucius remained seated in the chariot and listened attentively.

"Honored sir," came the voice of an accused, "people all say you are a just and wise official. But it seems to me you are just as muddle-headed as the rest of them!"

"Stop shooting off your mouth, you maniac!" yelled the runners.

Gao Chai remained unruffled. "I'll give you a chance to speak your mind." He pointed to the four men kneeling before him. "If you think you are wronged, you may tell me the truth!"

A tall, hefty man spoke up. "The four of us were employed by Wu Xinqian, a wealthy man of this city, to make copperware. We worked hard for a whole year, enabling him to gain huge profits, but he refused to pay us. We tried to reason with him, but he turned a deaf ear to us. When we pressed him further, he brought a false charge against us."

"Can you guarantee the truth of your words?"

"Every single word is true."

"What's your name?"

"Shen Cheng."

When Gao Chai asked the others of their names they gave them as Shen Shi, Shen Ren and Shen Yi.

"Good!" said Gao Chai. "Are you brothers?"

"We are cousins," replied Shen Shi.

"Did Shen Cheng speak the truth?"

"Yes!" responded the three in unison.

"So you were all falsely charged," said Gao Chai.

"Yes, we are all innocent."

Gao Chai thought for a while, then said abruptly, "If you did raid homes and plunder houses, what should I do with you?"

The four men replied without hesitation, "If we indeed committed such a crime, we would accept whatever punishment we should deserve!"

"However the case turns out," said Gao Chai, "today you have to put up with some inconvenience."

The four men looked at him in puzzlement.

Gao Chai turned to the runners. "Give them a hot meal and let them stay in prison."

The runners answered and took the men out of the hall.

Gao Chai heaved a sigh of relief. Just then the gate-keeper came in and announced, "Your master has come!"

Gao Chai hurried out of the gate and saluted Confucius. "Master, forgive me for not coming out to meet you earlier!"

"You have your official duty and were not informed of our visit," said Confucius. "There is no reason why you should have come out to receive us."

They entered the office and took their seats. "Master," asked Gao Chai, "have you come especially to supervise my work, or is there something else?"

"The lord of Wei sent an envoy to invite you to return and take office in Wei. The chief minister agreed and asked me to inform you of this."

"I have governed Fei for only one year and have barely made any progress. I do not want to leave just now."

"Both the lord of Wei and Kong Li, the chief minister of Wei, admire you for your talent and place high hopes on you. You must not let them down. Furthermore, Chief Minister Jisun has already given his consent."

"In that case I will leave for Wei," agreed Gao Chai. "However, there is something I must deal with before I leave. A difficult case just turned up today; it will take me some three to five days to tackle it."

"I overheard something about it outside the gate," said Confucius. "Of course you must finish the case before you leave. How do you plan to go about it?"

"I have known Wu Xinqian to be a rich, heartless man. But to deny four workmen one year's pay is really outrageous. It won't be difficult to clear this up. However, in the past few days over a dozen houses were reportedly looted. It will take some time to find out the truth about that."

"Since Wu Xinqian insisted that it was the Shens who did the looting, he must have something to do with it. Why don't you begin by investigating him?"

"Yes, I will start tomorrow. I won't stop until I get to the bottom of the matter!"

The following day Gao Chai changed into plainclothes and went around inquiring about Wu Xinqian. People, however, turned pale at the mere mention of Wu's name. Knowing where he was now, Gao Chai returned to his office and ordered the runners to arrest Wu Xinqian.

When he was brought to the hall, Wu Xinqian refused to kneel. "Why do you arrest the plaintiff?" he demanded in a loud voice.

Gao Chai paid no attention to him. "Take him to prison!" he ordered the runners.

Wu Xinqian began cursing loudly. "You corrupt official! What benefit did you get from those workmen to make you treat me like this?"

Gao Chai said quietly, "You deserve severe punishment because first, you denied those workmen their pay and second, you brought a false charge against them!"

When Wu Xinqian heard this, his lips trembled and his knees grew weak.

Gao Chai waved his hand, and the runners took Wu Xinqian out of the hall.

When Gao Chai went out again to the neighborhood where Wu Xinqian lived to inquire about him, people became willing to talk about the many misdeeds Wu had committed.

An old man in his sixties said, "For many years Wu Xinqian threw his weight about in this neighborhood. He often extorted money from others and deprived workmen of their pay."

"Why didn't those workmen sue him?" asked Gao Chai.

"It seems, young man, that you have never been in a lawsuit," said the old man. "Though the magistrate's office is open to everyone, you will have no chance of winning the case if you are poor. The four Shens worked for him a whole year, but he refused to pay them. What's more, he accused them of looting. The magistrate is reputed to be a wise man, but he threw the Shens into prison. Then Wu Xinqian was also arrested; that's something to celebrate! But the Shens have not yet been released, and no one can tell what will happen in the end!"

"Since Wu Xinqian acted so unscrupulously," asked Gao Chai, "why didn't someone stand out to reason with him?"

"Who would dare challenge him!" a young man chipped in. "He not only has high connections but also has local bullies to help him."

"Local bullies?" asked Gao Chai.

"To extort money from the local people, Wu Xinqian has gathered a group of local ruffians to work for him." The young man suddenly stopped speaking, and the onlookers scattered in a hurry.

Gao Chai looked up in surprise and saw a heavy man coming to him ferociously. The man was wearing a wide silk belt across his waist, a pair of warrior's boots and a sword with a worn sheath. Thumping his way to Gao Chai, he yelled in a stern voice, "Who are you? How dare you create trouble here!"

"Why do you think I am creating trouble here?"

"Well ..." the man scratched his head. "You are a stranger here. Why should so many people be speaking to you if you did not intend to create trouble?"

Gao Chai burst out laughing. "Just as anyone else, I am a subject of His Majesty the king of Zhou," he said. "Don't I have the right to talk?"

The man was struck speechless, and his face turned crimson with rage.

"I don't suppose you are a well-behaved person," continued Gao Chai. "Otherwise why should you ride the high horse like this?"

Furious, the man drew his sword and roared, "Who are you anyway? Speak! Or I'll kill you!"

Gao Chai was not the least intimidated but smiled contemptuously. "It seems that you are in the habit of bullying others. I'll have to teach you a lesson today!"

The man thrusted his sword toward Gao Chai.

Gao Chai leapt sideways nimbly.

The man pursued him, brandishing the sword.

Gao Chai suddenly closed in on the man and struck his wrist with the palm. The man dropped the sword. "Runners!" shouted Gao Chai.

Two runners waiting in the distance came over running. "Here!"

"Tie him up and bring him back to the office!"

"Yes!"

Back in his office, Gao Chai began interrogating the man. "What's your name?"

Finding Gao Chai to be the magistrate, the man realized he was in real trouble. Lowering his head, he replied, "My name is Wu Nai."

"Are you aware of your guilt?"

"Yes."

"What's your guilt?"

"I should not have offended you, honored sir."

"What else?"

"I don't know."

"What's your relationship with Wu Xinqian?"

"I am his ... his ..."

"His bodyguard? Or his hatchet man?"

Wu Nai became paralyzed with fright.

"How did Wu Xinqian deny the Shens their pay?" demanded Gao Chai, raising his voice. "How did he frame a charge against them?"

"I really don't know," replied Wu Nai in a trembling voice.

"Maybe you will change your mind if you are put on the rack," said Gao Chai. "Runners!"

"Here!" came the thunderous response.

"Get the rack ready!"

"Yes!"

Badly frightened, Wu Nai beat his head on the floor. "I will confess! I will confess!"

"The rack can wait," said Gao Chai, "but you must tell the truth!"

"I will tell the truth!" said Wu Nai. "Master Wu ..."

Gao Chai sneered with annoyance.

Wu Nai hastily dropped the epithet. "Wu Xinqian is truly a rich but cruel man. Many years ago he opened a copperware mill and recruited workmen from surrounding areas. He promised each workman an annual pay of twenty taels of silver, but at the end of the year he always found an excuse to deny them their pay. The workmen dared not oppose him and left empty-handed. The Shens were the first ones to dare say no to him. Wu Xinqian then devised a vicious plot against them."

"What was his plot?"

Wu Nai could not bring himself to say anything.

"Put him on the rack!" ordered Gao Chai.

"No! Please!" Wu Nai cried out. He finally decided to make a clean breast of it. "Wu Xinqian learned that you are an honest official who tries cases with justice and impartiality, so he feared that the Shens might come to you to charge him. Therefore he told some of us to damage the doors of our houses, so that he could accuse the Shens of breaking into houses and looting."

"Can you guarantee the truth of your words?"

"Every single word is true."

"Will you testify in front of Wu?"

"Erh ..."

"Well?"

"Yes!" Wu Nai had no choice but to agree.

"Bring Wu Xinqian here!" ordered Gao Chai.

The runners went and returned with Wu Xinqian.

Wu Xinqian entered the hall with a defiant look on his face. At the sight of Wu Nai, however, he withered like a cucumber caught in frost. With a thump he fell on his knees.

"Wu Xinqian!"

"Here," answered Wu Xinqian.

"Are you aware of your guilt?"

"Yes, I am."

"All right!" Gao Chai stood up. "Describe your unlawful deed!"

Aware that there was no escape for him, Wu Xinqian decided to play smart and recounted in detail what he had done.

"Wu Xinqian," announced Gao Chai, "you have habitually cheated your workmen. For this you deserve severe punishment."

"Spare me!" Wu Xinqian pleaded, trembling and beating his head on the floor. "Spare me!"

"Do you want a death sentence, or a forfeit?"

"A forfeit!"

"How much is the worth of your household property?"

"No more than three thousand taels of silver."

"How many workmen have you cheated?"

"Forty-five."

"To everyone of them you must pay forty taels in forfeit in addition to the twenty taels due. That will be two thousand seven hundred taels altogether. You will still have three hundred taels left, enough to make a reasonable living."

"But, honored sir, I owe each workman only twenty taels," pleaded Wu Xinqian. "Please be merciful!"

"For all these years you have defied the law and ridden on the back of the local people," said Gao Chai. "I imposed a forfeit on you because you were quick in admitting your guilt. However, if you dare disobey, you will suffer heavy penalty, and all your property will be confiscated!"

"Spare me! I am willing to pay each workman sixty taels."

"You are allowed three days to pay the forfeit!"

"Yes!"

"From now on you should behave yourself and stop bullying your neighbors!"

"I understand!"

"If you slip back into your old ways, you will be penalized with interest."

"I dare not do evil again."

Gao Chai turned to Wu Nai. "As an accomplice you deserve forty strokes of the birch. However, on account of your repentance, you are spared."

"Thank you, honored sir, for your great mercy!"

"From now on you should have a sense of right and wrong," said Gao Chai, "and stop abetting evil people to do evil deeds!"

"I understand!" answered Wu Nai.

After dismissing the two men, Gao Chai told the runners to bring the four Shens.

"I have looked into the case," said Gao Chai, "and found out that Wu Xinqian had tried to frame you. I ordered him to pay each of you a forfeit of sixty taels of silver. You may go to his house and collect your money tomorrow." He paused, then said apologetically, "I have detained the four of you here in order to find out the truth of the matter. Please do not take it to heart!"

Shen Cheng said hastily, "Honored sir, why should we take it to heart? You have settled the case justly and redressed the wrong. We don't know how to express our gratitude!"

The four Shens kowtowed their thanks and left.

After that, Gao Chai hastened to report to Confucius what had taken place.

Delighted, Confucius said, "I did not place high hope on you in vain, nor did the lord of Wei. You are truly suitable for an official career!"

"I don't really deserve such praise," said Gao Chai.

"Now that you have finished your business here, when will you leave?"

"I will stay for three days to make sure that Wu Xinqian behaves himself this time."

"You are right," said Confucius. "Zeng Shen and I will return to the capital then."

On their way back to the capital, Confucius was feeling greatly pleased with Gao Chai's ability and honesty. Then an idea occurred to him. "It is not far from Zou," he said to Zeng Shen. "Why don't we go there and visit Kong Zhong?"

Zeng Shen thought it a good idea. "Some of your disciples have left the capital to take office in various places. They must miss you a lot and will be only too happy to have you visit them."

"We will visit Zou then. Someday we can go to Shanfu. As for Zi Gong, who is magistrate of Wenyang in Qi, I'm afraid it is too far away for me to go at such an old age."

"We will ask him to return to visit you when he has time," said Zeng Shen.

The city of Zou was located south of the Lu capital. Hearing Confucius' arrival, Kong Zhong hurried out of his office.

Confucius gazed at Kong Zhong and thought of his elder brother, Meng Pi, and a wave of pride for his nephew arose in his mind. However, when he entered the office and found it lavishly decorated, a look of displeasure flit across his face. After taking his seat he asked, "Kong Zhong, what have you gained and what have you lost since you took office here?"

"It seems that I have gained little but lost a lot," replied Kong Zhong. "Firstly, heavy official duties have made me unable to continue my study, so that I have learned nothing new but have begun to forget what I learned. Secondly, with a low position and a low pay I can barely support myself and find it beyond my power to help my relatives. Thirdly, I have been too busy to visit my friends even when they are ill or lose a parent."

"These three losses are not difficult to make up for," said Confucius. "Firstly, the ancients said that whenever you open a book, you will benefit from it. As long as you persevere in your study, you will make progress. Secondly, though your pay is low, you will be able to support yourself if you practice frugality and guard against extravagance. Thirdly, by handling administrative affairs diligently and educating the local people in the rules of proper behavior, the number of lawsuits will dwindle, and you will achieve twice the result with half the effort."

"This is the first post I have been given," said Kong Zhong, "and I find myself so inexperienced and ignorant. Your instruction is of great help to me."

"You have talked about your losses," said Confucius. "How about your gains? Haven't you made any achievement that you are proud of?"

"Yes, I have," replied Kong Zhong. "Soon after I took office, I set up a school and ordered parents to send boys under fifteen to the school. Those who disobeyed were punished severely. As a result most boys are now in school. This is the first thing I am proud of. The second thing concerns tax collection. When some unlawful person refused to pay tax, I had his land confiscated and reallocated to others. Thus no one dare evade tax anymore. The third thing is that when robberies occured, I had the offenders arrested and punished severely. Thus the number of robbers has been effectively reduced. The fourth thing is that I settled each and every case in strict accordance with the law. I have never taken any bribe or shown partiality toward anyone. Thus the number of lawsuits has also been reduced."

"Do the common people praise you for what you have done?"

"It is puzzling," said Kong Zhong with a frown. "I think I have handled affairs justly and fulfilled my duties conscientiously, but I fail to receive any praise from the common people. Is it because they doubt my sincerity?"

"The things you just described are indeed good deeds," said Confucius. "However, in dealing with each of these problems you chose to treat the symptom instead of the cause. That's why you only achieved half the result with twice the effort."

Kong Zhong looked at Confucius with perplexity.

"Let me explain," said Confucius. "It is good to encourage young boys to study. However, it is unsuitable for you to force parents to send their children to school and punish those who don't. Instead, you should select men of great learning and outstanding virtue to teach in school and act as role models for the students. Then you will have young people from all parts of the area coming to schools of their own accord. When collecting land tax, it is unsuitable to mete out severe

punishment to those who are late in payment. Instead, you should
show sympathy for the peasants and understand their difficulties.
Canals and ditches should be dug to enable the peasants to fight
against flood and drought. In case of natural calamities you should
report to His Lordship requesting a tax reduction or exemption for the
year. As for robbers, it is hunger and cold that give rise to such people.
You should find work for the vagabonds and exhort them against
lavishness. If everyone has enough to eat and wear and does not crave
for luxury, why should anyone turn to robbery? To settle cases justly
is also not the best strategy. You should educate the people so that they
understand the difference between right and wrong and observe the
rites. When the old are respected, the young are well cared for, and
everyone lives in peace and harmony with everyone else, then there
will no longer be any lawsuits."

"I see the light," said Kong Zhong, "after listening to your
instruction. I thought myself a good, responsible official, but now I
realize my conduct left much to be desired. I will follow your instruction in the future!"

Confucius nodded with satisfaction.

Kong Zhong had dinner served and invited Confucius and Zeng
Shen to sit down at the table.

At the sight of the dishes Confucius became highly displeased.
"Didn't you tell me your pay is low?" he asked. "Why have you
prepared such a sumptuous meal?"

"On ordinary days I eat coarse meals," said Kong Zhong.
"But since you and Zeng Shen have come, I told the cook to prepare
a good meal."

"As a magistrate you must be cautious in your daily conduct,"
admonished Confucius, "and guard against extravagance. Many of the
evils in the world originate from extravagance. For example, people
used to an extravagant lifestyle will throw money around when rich.
When poor, they will resort to robbery."

"I understand!" responded Kong Zhong.

After the meal Kong Zhong said, "Uncle, my sister, Wujia, came
to Zou yesterday. Would you please go to the rear room to meet her?"

"Yes, I'd like to,'" said Confucius.

Kong Zhong's wife and Kong Wujia were delighted to see Confucius. They greeted him and let him take the seat of honor in the room.
Confucius combed his beard with his fingers and was about to

speak when he caught sight of Wujia's high topknot and jade hairpin. His expression grew serious. "Wujia, you are still in mourning and should neither tie your hair so high nor wear a jade hairpin."

"Back home I didn't tie my hair above and wore a wooden hairpin. It was after I came to Zou yesterday that I tied my hair high and borrowed this hairpin from my sister-in-law."

"Honesty is an essential virtue," said Confucius. "No matter where you are, you should conduct yourself properly."

"It was my fault, uncle," said Kong Zhong's wife. "I combed hair for her and lent her the hairpin."

"She can change it back tomorrow," said Confucius. "A mistake will no longer be a mistake when it is recognized and corrected."

They talked for a while on family matters, then Confucius and Zeng Shen were taken to the guest room to rest.

The following day, when they returned to the Lu capital, Confucius went to see Jisun Fei and informed him of Gao Chai's agreement to go to Wei.

"The position of magistrate will be vacant when Gao Chai leaves," said Jisun Fei. "Please recommend someone else to fill it."

"Zi Lu would be a suitable candidate," said Confucius. "He did pretty well when he served as magistrate of Pu in Wei. However, he is advanced in years and may not have the energy to take office again."

"You have a lot of talented disciples," said Jisun Fei. "No doubt you can find another one."

"Let me think carefully, then I will give you an answer."

"I will wait for your good news then."

Confucius took his leave and returned home. When he entered the classroom, he was startled by Yan Hui's haggard appearance.

Chapter Forty-five

Confucius Finds His Favorite Disciple
in Poor Health;
Gao Chai Deals with a Difficult Case
Involving the Duke's Consort

Finding Yan Hui looking thinner and more fragile than ever Confucius asked, "Why are you looking so thin and pale? Are you ill?"

Yan Hui smiled quietly. "I have always been small and thin, master. You find me unusually thin today because you just took a trip to Fei and didn't see me for a few days."

Confucius produced a forced smile and did not pursue the subject, but secretly he felt very worried over Yan Hui's cadaverous look. Later he found Yan Hui often went hungry and his wife and children often had to go out gathering wild vegetables to fill their stomachs, whereas his father often had to leave home to borrow grain or money from their relatives. His heart gnawed at by sympathy for Yan Hui, Confucius often sat alone racking his brains for ways to change the world so that the poor and wretched on earth could all enjoy a well-fed and well-clad life.

One day Confucius was sitting in his room when Zeng Shen arrived to ask some questions. "Master, what's the relationship between the great Way and virtue?"

"Sit down and let me explain," said Confucius. "The great Way makes people cultivate their virtue, and with their virtue cultivated people can follow the great Way unswervingly. The ancients held that a man without virtue will not follow the Way, and a man who does not follow the Way will not acquire virtue. Given a fine horse capable of covering a thousand li a day, if you do not ride it in the right way, it will not obey your call. If a ruler who has thousands upon thousands of subjects does not govern them in the right way, they will not submit to his commands. Therefore a sage ruler always attempts to cultivate the seven virtues and attain the three ultimates. With the seven virtues cultivated, he will govern the nation well

without much effort; with the three ultimates attained, he will enable the people to live in wealth without spending money himself. Nowadays the rulers act just in the opposite way. They attempt to achieve their goals by force and violence and indulge in extravagance at the expense of the common people."

"Master," asked Zeng Shen, "please tell me how a sage ruler can give the people a good life without much effort or expense."

"In the old days, Yao, Shun and Yu were able to rule the world without leaving their home. If the government is unjust, the ruler is to blame; if edicts can not be carried out, the officials are to blame. If the government is just and edicts are carried out without fail, the common people will enjoy peace and wealth. In their gratitude to the ruler they will be eager to pay their tax and offer their service. In this way the ruler will make the nation grow strong and prosperous with little effort or expense."

"What are the seven virtues?"

"The seven virtues refer to filial piety, respect for the elderly, generosity, attachment to virtuous men, love of virtue, aversion to greed, and modesty. If the ruler displays filial piety toward his parents, his subjects will follow his example. If the ruler treats the elderly with respect, his subjects will treat one another with courtesy. If the ruler is generous in helping others, his subjects will also be kind and generous. If the ruler stays close to virtuous men, his subjects will also seek out virtuous people as his friends. If the ruler cultivates his own virtue, his subjects will learn to be honest and sincere. If the ruler is aversive to greedy people, his subjects will think it shameful to fight for power and private gains. If the ruler is modest and devoted to his duties, his subjects will serve him wholeheartedly."

Zeng Shen listened in rapt attention.

"The seven virtues are the foundation of a good government," Confucius went on. "The ruler is the role model for his subjects. If he is upright in his behavior, who else would dare to be crooked? Therefore a sage ruler first achieves benevolence himself, then proceeds to make the ministers loyal, the scholars sincere, the common people forthright, the men honest and the women chaste. When all these have been achieved, the ruler's edicts will spread all over the nation and be followed by every household. People will stay away from the wicked and seek after the pure, evade petty men and respect superior men. All evil men and evil practices will be wiped out like the snow under the sun."

Zeng Shen was enthralled.

Confucius continued, "The ancient sage rulers promoted virtuous men and demoted treacherous men, so that virtuous men could give full play to their talent whereas treacherous men could find no chance to do evil. If the ruler takes pity on the widowed, cares for orphans and the sonless, helps the poor, educates the filial, and employs the talented, there will be no lawbreakers within the four seas. If the ruler treats his subjects the way he treats his brothers, his subjects will respect and serve him as if he were a parent to them. With such a relationship between ruler and the ruled established, people will obey orders with gladness, and even barbarians from remote areas will come to submit themselves to the sage ruler. The ancients said that people will stop complaining when oppressive policies are done away with and stop breaking the law if severe penalties are done away with. Therefore the sage ruler is able to subdue the barbarians without resorting to military forces and establish order without resorting to punishment. People will cherish intense gratitude to the ruler, and even those who live in distant quarters will feel close to him because they have benefited from his favor."

"What are the three ultimates?" asked Zeng Shen.

"These refer to the ultimate rites, the ultimate reward, and the ultimate joy. The ultimate rites enable the ruler to attain universal harmony without resorting to modesty and courtesy. The ultimate reward makes the people happy and joyful without incurring any expense. The ultimate music has no sound, but it makes the people join in the chorus. With the three ultimates attained, harmony will be achieved all over the world, whereby the ruler will govern the state well, the scholars under Heaven will become his loyal subjects and the people across the land will serve him heart and soul. Therefore, the most benevolent man will have the closest followers, and the wisest man will recommend the most virtuous people. A benevolent man is one who loves people, a wise man is one who recognizes people of virtue, and a good administrator is one who knows the need to select the worthy and capable and call them to office. The benevolent rule of a sage ruler benefits the people like the rain after a long drought, giving them great happiness. For this reason, the more a ruler exercises government by means of benevolence, the greater popularity he will enjoy among the people."

Just then Zhuansun Shi also came to ask how to serve in the government.

"Sit down and let me explain to you carefully," said Confucius. Zhuansun Shi sat down opposite to Zeng Shen.

"An official," said Confucius, "should guard against the following: rejection of advice, discourtesy, laziness, luxury, and imperiousness. Rejection of advice will make him isolated and ignorant; discourtesy will make him think highly of himself and look down on others; laziness will make him neglect his duties and fail to have things done in time; luxury will make him spend all he has without thinking about the future; and imperiousness will make him act in total disregard of others and achieve nothing in the end. A high official can be compared to a rafter of the house. He stays high above the others, who look up to him and pay close attention to his conduct. If he conducts himself properly, people will follow his example and hold him in high esteem; if he conducts himself improperly, people will hold him in contempt and turn their back to him."

"How can one induce the common people to serve the nation willingly?" asked Zhuansun Shi.

"Don't force them to do what they are unwilling or unable to do. To force them to do what they cannot do will provoke their resistance. Do you know why the ancient sage kings had jade tassels on their crowns?"

"No, I don't."

"These were used to blur the king's sight," said Confucius. "Do you know why there were silk ribbons on the sides of the crowns?"

"No, I don't."

"These were used to muffle the king's hearing."

Zhuansun Shi was suddenly enlightened.

Confucius went on, "When the water is too clear there is no fish; when a man is too clever he has no friends. Therefore a sage ruler limits his own sight and hearing and treats his subjects with tolerance. To those who act improperly he offers guidance and leads them onto the path of righteousness. To those who commit minor offenses he offers forgiveness, and to those who commit serious offenses he tries to find out the cause and make them change by persuasion. In this way people will dedicate themselves wholeheart-edly to the ruler, whose orders will be carried out without obstruc-tion. Tolerance is therefore the starting point for the establishment of a benign government. In order to have government decrees carried out all across the nation, the ruler must first of all follow them himself and in order that the people obey those decrees he must educate them in moral principles."

"Master," asked Zeng Shen, "aren't the penal codes in the various states too severe?"

"Yes, they are!" agreed Confucius. "The ancient sage rulers obtained people's willing submission by educating them in the codes of proper conduct, but nowadays rulers tend to force the people into submission with harsh penal codes. As a result, people become estranged from their rulers. Just as a skilled weaver will select fine silk or hemp to work on and a skilled craftsman will select fine material with which to make his wares, a virtuous man will select a sage ruler to offer his service to. Rulers who have lost the trust of their subjects will suffer sooner or later."

After taking leave of Confucius and fellow disciples, Gao Chai left Lu for Wei. Kong Li was pleased to have him back and put him in charge of justice and penalty in Wei.

Soon after he took office Gao Chai successfully tried a series of difficult cases. One day he was reading a book in his office when a prison warden came in and whispered, "Honored sir, I heard a rumor concerning Lady Zuo, the duke's consort, and Hou Biao, a handsome palace guard. They are said to be having an illicit affair."

"Hasn't His Lordship the duke noticed anything?"

"I don't know. I think he hasn't, otherwise Hou Biao would not be alive now."

"You are right. Keep your mouth shut and don't mention it to anyone else."

"I understand!"

"You will be severely punished if you tell others about it."

"You may rest assured, sir, that I will not tell others about it."

After that Gao Chai entered the palace several times in order to observe Hou Biao's behavior.

One summer evening, after downing several cups of wine, Duke Chu of Wei felt on top of the world and went to the rear garden to enjoy song and dance. Gao Chai also went there to have a look.

While Duke Chu became enthralled in the voluptuous dance, Lady Zuo sitting by his side had something else on her mind. She looked all around and, catching sight of Hou Biao, gave him a most alluring smile.

As he watched the exchange of amorous glances between Lady Zuo and Hou Biao, Gao Chai became convinced that there must have been something between the two. He returned home and began to think how to deal with the problem. He was unwilling to report the matter to Duke Chu, who would doubtlessly put Hou Biao to death. Instead, he wanted to deal with the case leniently and save Hou Biao's life. He thought for a long time but failed to come up with a solution. The lamp on the table grew dim as the oil was nearly used up. A mouse slipped onto the table and made its way stealthily to a bowl of steamed bread. It nibbled at a piece of bread, then shoved it off the table. However, the sound of the bread landing on the ground frightened it away.

"I can charge him of theft!" Gao Chai hit upon an idea watching the mouse stealing the bread. "I will charge Hou Biao of stealing a jade ware from the palace."

The following day Gao Chai had Hou Biao brought to him in his office. "Hou Biao," he demanded sternly, "are you aware of your guilt?"

Hou Biao was struck speechless. He paused for a long moment and finally muttered, "What am I guilty of?"

"Are you trying to deny your guilt?"

"I don't really know what my guilt could be."

"Do I have to tell you?"

Hou Biao thought that his affair with Lady Zuo could not have been discovered, so he insisted, "I am upright and honest in my conduct. I don't know what my guilt could be."

"You have betrayed His Lordship!" said Gao Chai. "Do you deny this?"

Hou Biao shuddered, perspiration streaming from his forehead. Falling on his knees, he pleaded, "I committed a most heinous crime for lack of judgement. Please spare me!"

"If you are a real man, you should not be afraid to admit what you have done. Why don't you go to His Lordship and ask his forgiveness?"

"No!" Hou Biao broke into tears. "If His Lordship should learn about this, I would surely be put to death. My mother is now advanced in years. If I should die, who would be there to take care of her? Please have mercy and spare my life!"

"You may get up," said Gao Biao. "If you want me to save your life, you must leave the palace."

Hou Biao felt a great sense of relief. "That's easy," he said. "I can just run away."

"No," said Gao Chai, "that wouldn't do. You have brought shame to the lord of Wei. If you simply run away, all kinds of rumors will arise. His Lordship will then send men to capture you no matter where you choose to hide yourself."

"What should I do then?"

"Under the circumstances, only you can save your own life."

Hou Biao looked at Gao Chai, uncomprehending. "I don't understand."

"If what you did became known to His Lordship, he will surely put you to death. The only solution is for you to be punished for some minor offense. I have an idea, but I don't know if you will agree to it."

"So long as I can escape death, I will do whatever you tell me."

Gao Chai explained his plan to Hou Biao, who looked reluctant at first. After some consideration, however, he agreed.

That evening Hou Biao stole a piece of jade from the palace.

The following day Duke Chu of Wei discovered the theft and was flabbergasted. "That jade is our state treasure handed down to me by the late duke," he said to the court officials at the morning audience. "The thief must be caught, and the jade brought back intact!"

An investigation was launched. Palace attendants became the chief suspects and underwent interrogation one by one. When it was Hou Biao's turn, his abnormal response betrayed him, and he was arrested and thrown into prison.

Gao Chai was deeply vexed on hearing the news. He had expected Hou Biao to steal an ordinary jade object from the palace, not something so precious. Now Duke Chu would not be satisfied if Hou Biao were not punished severely. He ordered Hou Biao to be brought to the main hall.

In front of the runners, Hou Biao first put up a feigned denial, then admitted his guilt.

"Where is the jade?" asked Gao Chai.

"It is in my house," replied Hou Biao in a trembling voice.

Gao Chai then had two runners escort Hou Biao to his house to fetch the jade.

"Hou Biao," said Gao Chai, "as a palace attendant you have received great favor and reward from His Lordship. Instead of showing your gratitude by wholehearted service, you stole the most precious treasure from the palace. Such a monstrous crime is unpardonable! You will be put into the death house awaiting your death sentence!"

The runners took Hou Biao to the death house.

Gao Chai went into the palace, returned the jade to Duke Chu and reported the case to him.

Immensely pleased, Duke Chu took the jade in his hands and examined it carefully. "Honored minister," he said, "people have told me repeatedly that you are very capable, and now I find that your reputation is well-deserved." He placed the jade on the table. "How do you plan to deal with Hou Biao?"

"Your Lordship," replied Gao Chai carefully, "as a palace attendant Hou Biao must know the law perfectly, so his theft of a palace treasure was therefore a willful offense. He should be given the most severe punishment."

"Yes!" agreed Duke Chu. "Only the most severe punishment will vent my hatred against him."

"On the other hand," continued Gao Chai, "he did render his service faithfully for many years. Your Lordship would be showing magnanimity by sparing his life."

"A treacherous man like this one must be eliminated," said Duke Chu. "Otherwise he would create more trouble in the future."

"Maybe we could find a middle way."

"Tell me your idea, honored minister!"

"Though Hou Biao is guilty, he has admitted his guilt readily and returned the jade intact, therefore his life should be spared. To prevent him from creating trouble in the future, we can have his left foot cut off. Thus incapacitated, he will no longer be able to commit unlawful activities."

"Won't this be letting him off too lightly?"

"Severe punishment should be meted out as a warning to others. Now that Hou Biao has admitted his guilt, a lenient sentence will make him repent his past and be deeply grateful to Your Lordship."

Duke Chu considered for a long time, then finally agreed. "Well, you may proceed with your suggestion and have Hou Biao's left foot cut off. Carry this out without delay!"

Thereupon Gao Chai left the palace and returned to his office. He ordered Hou Biao to be brought to him.

Hou Biao knelt and broke into tears on seeing Gao Chai.

"Hou Biao, you don't have to worry," said Gao Chai. "His Lordship has consented to exempt you from death."

Hou Biao kowtowed repeatedly. "Thanks to His Lordship for his mercy!"

"However," continued Gao Chai emphatically, "you must be punished for your crime and have your left foot cut off."

Hou Biao turned pale with fright on hearing this.

"What do you have to say?" asked Gao Chai.

Hou Biao wept bitterly. "I committed a grave crime and deserve the punishment!"

Gao Chai called the runners and ordered, "Take him away and cut off his left foot!"

The runners took Hou Biao to the torture room, tied him onto a board, cut off his left foot, and brought it to Gao Chai for verification.

"Find a doctor to treat his injury," ordered Gao Chai.

Hou Biao was treated and carried into another room to recuperate.

Lady Zuo was deeply puzzled by the news of Hou Biao's arrest for theft. When Hou Biao had his foot cut off, she finally realized what had happened. She felt grateful to Gao Chai for keeping her affair from the duke, but in the meantime she also blamed him for making Hou Biao, her handsome lover, handicapped. She recalled her rendezvous with Hou Biao and regretted having been the cause of his misfortune.

While she was thus overcome by grief and sorrow, Duke Chu entered her room with a bright smile. "My beloved," he said, "it is good that the jade treasure has been recovered. Why do you look so unhappy?" He sat down by her side and began combing her hair with his hand.

Unable to contain her grief, she broke into tears.

Greatly surprised, Duke Chu held her face in both hands and asked, "My beloved, why are you so tearful? Aren't you feeling well?"

"I caught a cold yesterday evening," said Lady Zuo. "Just then I had such a splitting headache that I wept."

"Guards!" shouted the duke.

"Here!" a palace attendant came in running.

"Find the court physician and bring him here!"

The attendant left without delay. Soon afterward the physician arrived.

"Lady Zuo has a headache resulting from a cold," said Duke Chu. "Feel her pulse and prescribe some medicine!"

The physician felt her pulse and, failing to find any symptom, prescribed some tonics.

Gao Chai sent men to look after Hou Biao, whose wound healed a month later. It took him another two months to get out of bed and learn to walk with a crutch.

"You can now move by yourself," said Gao Chai. "Do you plan to go home or find a post in the city?"

Hou Biao was tearful with gratitude. "Sir, you are my savior! I have become a disabled man and would find it difficult to support myself back at home. Please find me something to do in the city!"

"I have already found a post for you," said Gao Chai. "I don't know if you want it."

"If you think it suitable, I will take it."

"There is a vacancy for a gate-keeper at the east city gate. Your only duty would be opening and closing the gate. It wouldn't be very laborious, and you wouldn't have to walk a lot. The only setback is its low pay."

"I will be content to have something to do for a living."

"In that case you may go and take the job. However, you must draw a lesson from this incident. Don't forget the pain after the wound is healed!"

"I went astray and almost lost my life. How dare I do wrong again?"

After Hou Biao left, a runner came in. "Sir, Mr. Bu asks to see you."

"Where is he?" asked Gao Chai eagerly.

"Outside the gate."

Gao Chai immediately went out. He saluted Bu Shang and

asked, "When did you arrive?"

"Only yesterday."

"How is our master?"

"He is well. But Ran Geng just died of illness."

Gao Chai felt much grieved, and tears welled up in his eyes. "Ran Geng is one of our master's favorite students. His death must have been a severe blow to him."

"Yes!" Bu Shang said, on the verge of tears. "Master has been overwhelmed with sadness all these days."

Gao Chai invited Bu Shang into his office, and they exchanged news.

"When I arrived in Wei yesterday, I heard someone make a funny remark," said Bu Shang.

Chapter Forty-six

Mi Buqi Reports to Confucius His Achievements in Office;
Yan Hui Dies of Illness in the Prime of Life

Bu Shang continued, "On entering the capital I heard someone quoting from a history book, 'The Jin army crossed the river with three pigs.'"

"Did you correct him?" asked Gao Chai.

"Yes. I told him that he mispronounced and misinterpreted the text. The 'three pigs' he had mentioned actually designated a certain date."

"The incident shows that you are indeed a very observant person," said Gao Chai.

"It also shows that someone studying history may understand neither history nor the calendar."

The loss of his only son, followed by the death of Ran Geng, made Confucius very gloomy. One day after lunch he walked into the classroom and saw Yan Hui pushing a piece of cloth into his sleeve. "Yan Hui, what were you hiding?"

Yan Hui stood up and replied, "Nothing, master."

Confucius fixed his stare on Yan Hui's sleeve.

Just then Yan Hui broke into a fit of severe cough. He took the piece of cloth from his sleeve and spit into it.

Confucius noticed to his dismay that Yan Hui was spitting blood. He watched Yan Hui's face closely and found him unusually thin and sallow, his eye sockets sunken deeply.

Yan Hui pushed the cloth back into his sleeve and said with a mirthless smile, "Master, I only have a cold. Don't worry about me." Then he broke into another fit of coughing.

Confucius was so distressed that his eyes became blurred, and his legs went limp. He staggered.

Yan Hui hastily supported him. "Master, please go home to take a rest!"

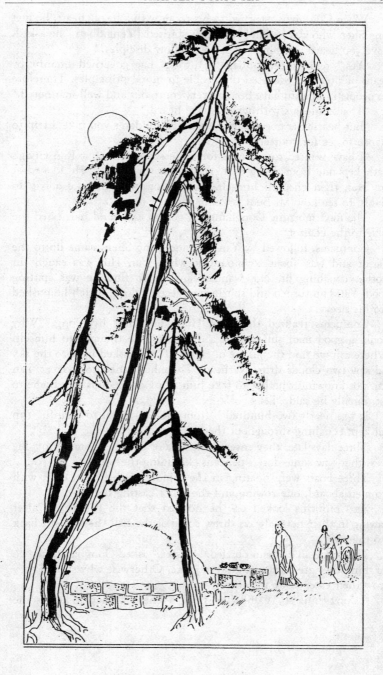

When Confucius returned to his room with a heavy heart, he met Zeng Shen who was looking very high-spirited. "Zeng Shen," he asked, "have you heard anything about your fellow disciples?"

"Yes," replied Zeng Shen. "Mi Buqi has governed Shanfu by means of rites and educated the people in moral principles. Therefore the people in Shanfu have become very courteous and well-mannered."

"That conforms with what I have heard."

"But hearsay is not always reliable. Why don't you take a trip to Shanfu to see for yourself?"

"I have wanted to go there for quite some time, but Ran Geng's death kept me from doing that. And then there is ..." He looked at Yan Hui, then checked himself. "Tomorrow we will take a trip to Shanfu to see how Mi Buqi is doing there."

The next morning Gongliang Ru got up early and harnessed the horse to the chariot.

Confucius, followed by Yan Hui and Zeng Shen, came up to the chariot and was about to mount it when Yan Hui was caught in another coughing fit. Not wanting anyone to find he was spitting blood, Yan Hui turned and spit into a piece of cloth, which he pushed into his sleeve.

Confucius realized that Yan Hui would not live long. "Why should a good man suffer such a dire fate?" he thought to himself. "Where can we find the justice of Heaven?" He looked up into the sky and saw two clouds drift overhead. Then he turned to look at Yan Hui, not knowing whether to take him along or let him stay home to rest. Finally he said, "Let's go!"

It was nearly two hundred li from the Lu capital to Shanfu. Yan Hui kept coughing throughout the journey.

Three days later they entered the area of Shanfu. Coming to a big river, they saw some dozen pelicans skimming the water.

Three boats were floating in the middle of the river, each with two men aboard, one rowing and the other casting net.

As Confucius looked on, he noticed that the fishermen, after drawing in their nets, always threw some of the fish they caught back into the river.

This made all of them puzzled. "Master," asked Gongliang Ru, "do you think they are playing a kind of game? Otherwise why should they throw their catch back into the river?"

"I don't think so," Confucius shook his head. "They do keep some of the fish they caught."

When they moved onto the bridge, Confucius told Gongliang Ru to stop the chariot, and they all dismounted to take a good look at the fishermen. Unable to make head or tail of it, Confucius waved his hand at them.

A fisherman rowed his boat ashore, and Confucius walked over to speak with him. "When I watched you from the bridge, I noticed that you kept some of the fish you caught and threw the rest back into the river. Could you tell me why?"

The fisherman explained patiently, "It is Magistrate Mi who taught us to do that. He exhorted us that since we live by the water, we can make a living off it. At the same time, however, we should protect it from overuse. Since it is the spawning season, we only pick out and keep large male fish from our catch and throw small or female fish back into the river. In this way we can protect the resources of this river."

"You are absolutely right!" Confucius smiled with great satisfaction. "People who live by the river should rely on it and also protect it." He thanked the fisherman and returned to the chariot. "Mi Buqi is obviously doing well," he remarked to the disciples. "Otherwise the fishermen would not have acted that way!"

Yan Hui, Zeng Shen and Gongliang Ru all expressed their admiration.

Coming to the east gate of Shanfu, they saw an old blindman carrying a zither on his back and probing his way along the city wall with a stick. As he made a turn into the city, a youth ran over to him and asked in an affectionate voice, "Uncle, are you entering or leaving the city?"

"I am leaving the city."

"You are going in the wrong direction," said the youth. "Come, let me show you the way." He took hold of the stick and led the blindman out of the city onto the main road, then returned.

Confucius was greatly delighted to witness the scene.

As the chariot drove along the street, Confucius was pleased to see that people were behaving politely to one another. "Drive slowly," he told Gongliang Ru. "I want to take a good look at Shanfu.

Gongliang Ru drew in the rein, and the chariot slowed down.

As he looked on with satisfaction, Confucius combed his gray beard with his fingers.

A young boy some eleven to twelve years old caught his attention. The boy stood weeping by the road with an empty basket by his side.

Confucius bade the chariot to be stopped, and he dismounted. "Why are you crying?" he asked the boy.

The boy looked up, removing his hand from his tear-stained face. "My mother is ill," he said, "and I went to the drugstore to buy some medicine. On my way back I was scared by a large yellow dog and began to run. But I tripped and fell, and lost the medicine and the change."

Confucius was about to ask Gongliang Ru to give the boy some money when an old man came up. He greeted Confucius politely, then turned to the boy, handing him a parcel. "This is your medicine."

The boy broke into a smile. He took the medicine in both hands and bowed deeply. "Thank you, grandpa!"

"Not at all," said the old man. Then he took a piece of silver from his sleeve. "This is also for you."

The boy waved his hands. "No, grandpa, this is not mine."

"Listen," said the old man. "The doctor discovered your family is very poor, so he came to my drugstore and gave me two taels of silver to pay for your medicine. As you had already paid for the medicine out of your pocket, so I put the silver into the medicine packet."

The boy was moved to tears. "I am so grateful to you, grandpa, and to the kindhearted doctor, but I can not accept the money."

"But the money was given to me by the doctor to pay for your medicine," said the old man. "If you don't take it, what can I do with it?"

"Well..." the boy batted his eyes and stroked his head. "Grandpa, I will take the money and return it to the doctor later."

"You needn't do that!" said the old man. "Your mother is ill, and your family must be in financial difficulty now. The doctor offered his help with sincerity, so you'd better accept it!" Then he took another piece of silver from his sleeve. "Since your family is so poor, these five taels are a gift from me."

The boy stood there, tearful with gratitude, not knowing what to do.

Greatly touched by the scene, Confucius said to the boy, "The doctor and this gentleman have both offered their generous help, so you might as well accept it. It is natural for people of the same neighborhood to help one another out. Take the money and go home to take care of your mother!"

The boy made a deep bow, took the silver in both hands, and went away.

Confucius expressed his admiration for the old man and returned to the chariot.

When they arrived at the magistrate's office, Confucius found to his delight that it was almost deserted with no one in sight. He got off the chariot and saw Mi Buqi come running out. Mi Buqi saluted and said, "Master, please forgive me for not coming out to receive you!"

Confucius smiled. "There is no need to apologize. As long as you are doing well in your office, I shall be quite contented."

As it was getting dark, Mi Buqi ushered Confucius into the drawing room. After taking his seat, Confucius looked around and found the room simply furnished.

After they had chatted for a while, Mi Buqi said, "Master, I haven't hired a cook in my office. Usually it is my wife who cooks the meals, and I'll ask her to prepare us some simple dishes tonight, since it's too late to find a cook. Tomorrow I'll send for a cook and have him prepare some good dishes."

"It is highly commendable that you educate the people in benevolence and practice frugality in your own office. A simple meal will be quite all right with me."

Mi Buqi bade his wife prepare the meal.

A short while later the servants brought in four dishes.

When he saw the dishes, Mi Buqi got up hastily, went into the kitchen, and soon returned with a saucer of ginger slices.

Confucius looked at the dishes on the table with approval. "These dishes consist mainly of vegetables, but they are so finely prepared! This is what I would call a well prepared meal!"

Mi Buqi took up the wine pot and poured some wine for Confucius and the other disciples.

Much pleased with what he had seen, Confucius drank three cups of wine before he started eating. As usual he refrained from speaking while having his meal.

It was already nightfall after they had supper. Confucius chatted with his disciples under the oil-lamp. He asked Mi Buqi the same question he had put up to Kong Zhong, "Since you took office here, what have you gained and what have you lost?"

Mi Buqi thought carefully before replying. "I have lost nothing since I became magistrate of Shanfu, but I have gained a lot, mainly in three aspects. First, I have put what I have learned into practice and in the process improved my learning. Second, with my salary I have not only been able to support myself and my family but also help some poor relatives. Third, as my official duties do not take up much time, I have been able to meet my friends frequently and visit them to offer my congratulations or condolences when necessary."

"Excellent!" said Confucius. "As the magistrate you have set up a good example for the people to follow. That's why you are widely respected here. On our way here we were really excited by what we saw. I think you have grasped the essence of good officialdom: educating the people in benevolence."

"I don't really deserve such high praise," said Mi Buqi bashfully.

"You have managed to achieve remarkable results and gained the support of the people in Shanfu in quite a short time. Tell me how you are able to do it."

"I set up an example by respecting the old and loving the young. I treat others' fathers as my own fathers and others' sons as my own sons. I provide financial assistance to all orphans in the city and take pity on all those who have suffered misfortunes."

"This is only a minor virtue," responded Confucius.

"I have a lot of friends to help me," continued Mi Buqi. "Three of them teach me how to treat elders, five of them teach me how to deal with my brothers, and eleven of them teach me how to build and develop friendship."

Confucius smiled. "With help from those three friends you will be able to teach the people the principle of filial piety. With help from those five friends you will be able to teach the people the principle of harmonious relationship among brothers. With help from those eleven friends you will be able to teach the people the way to live in mutual respect. However, all this only constitutes a virtue on the intermediary level."

"There are five people in Shanfu who exceed me in virtue and talent. Whenever I ask their advice, they will offer it earnestly, telling me how to govern Shanfu in the proper manner."

"This is virtue at its highest level!" exclaimed Confucius with pleasure. "Both Yao and Shun traveled incognito in search of talented men. They became sage kings just because they were able to find and promote talented men to help them govern the kingdom. It is a pity that Shanfu only covers a small area; otherwise you would be able to bring benefit to more people!"

After spending three days in Shanfu, Confucius took leave of Mi Buqi and returned contentedly to the capital to resume his writing of *The Spring and Autumn Annals*. Mi Buqi's achievements in Shanfu gave him renewed hope in the restoration of the rites of Zhou, and he ardently wished that more of his disciples would be like this one.

He had always had a keen interest in ancient history and cultural traditions and had accumulated an ample collection of historical materials, which he was now utilizing to write his own history book. One day he was working on his book when Bu Shang came. "Master, when you finish *The Spring and Autumn Annals* someday, it will surely be a great creative work."

"I haven't created anything," said Confucius. "I merely transmit what was said by the ancient sages. I am fond of ancient culture and find pleasure in expounding it."

"How much have you written?"

"I have just begun!"

Bu Shang felt worried for Confucius' health and frowned slightly.

Confucius went on, "It is not easy to pass down something worthwhile to future generations! You have to be very serious and diligent. Some people are not like this. They write about things they hardly understand and make numerous mistakes. As for me, I read ancient texts extensively and try to grasp their essence. On the other hand, I often ask help and guidance from learned people."

"You are very learned yourself, master. When you seek advice from others, are they ready to give it?"

"If I am eager to learn and sincere when seeking advice, why should the others refuse to instruct me? If I should put on airs and act like a know-it-all, who would be willing to talk to me?"

Bu Shang pointed to the great pile of bamboo slips on the table. "Master, these books are old and must have lots of missing parts. Isn't it very time-consuming to collate them?"

"That's what I've been worrying about!" said Confucius. "When I was young, many fragments of ancient texts were still available. After dozens of years they have become scarce due to destruction by war and damage by worms. A few years from now they may disappear completely. Therefore I must complete *The Spring and Autumn Annals* in my lifetime. Posterity will learn of my name because of this book. The same book may also cause some people to curse me."

After Bu Shang left, Confucius went back to work. His plan was to record all major events in the over two hundred years from Duke Yin to Duke Ai of Lu. He had to refer to materials scattered in various documents to ensure the authenticity and accuracy of his writing, which was to cover internal turmoils and interstate warfare as well as eclipses of the sun and moon.

One day Confucius was writing in his room when Bu Shang, Zhuansun Shi and Shang Qu came to seek instruction.

Bu Shang asked, "Master, your book will cover both past events and what is happening in the world today. Can you forecast what will happen ten generations from now?"

"The culture of Shang was derived from that of Xia with a few alterations," said Confucius, "and the culture of Zhou was derived from that of Shang with a few alterations. Thus by making deductions we can predict what will happen a hundred generations from now."

"Master," said Shang Qu, "I am very interested in *The Book of Changes*, but there are many things in it that I find hard to understand."

"Yin and yang are a pair of opposing and complementing forces in nature," said Confucius. "The yin-yang relationship, which underlies all processes in the world, is the focus of *The Book of Changes*. The book is so profound that even I have only a partial understanding of many topics discussed in it." He paused for a while, then went on, "At fifteen, I set my mind on learning. At thirty, with some knowledge of the rites, I learned how to conduct myself. At forty, having mastered the six arts, I was no longer confused. At fifty, I understood the way of Heaven. At sixty, I could distinguish between right and wrong in other people's words. At seventy, I could do what my heart desired without going against the rites. I am old now. If Heaven endows me with a few more years, I will probably be able to attain a thorough understanding of *The Book of Changes*."

Zhuansun Shi asked, "Dynastic changes have occurred since the remotest antiquity. Is it possible to establish peace and prosperity in the world and maintain it forever?"

"That can probably only remain a dream," said Confucius. "Good medicine tastes bitter to the mouth, and good advice sounds unpleasant to the ear. Cheng Tang and King Wu were able to govern the kingdom well because they listened to unpleasant advice. In contrast, King Jie of Xia and King Zhou of Shang ruled arbitrarily and turned a deaf ear to others, thus they brought the kingdom to its downfall. It is impossible for a ruler never to make mistakes, so he always needs a few ministers who are not afraid to correct him. A lucid exposition of the relationship between loss and gain can be found in *The Book of Changes*. When a man gains a position of honor, he is apt to act domineeringly and grow intolerant of opposing views. But a haughty and imperious man will not retain his position of honor for long."

The four of them were chatting away when Zi Lu burst into the room. "Master, Yan Hui's illness is getting worse. He is on the point of dying!"

Confucius was flabbergasted. He got up hastily. "I must go and see him."

Yan Hui's house was crowded with people, including both his fellow disciples and some neighbors. When Confucius arrived they made way for him.

Confucius went up to Yan Hui's bed and took him by both hands. Overwhelmed with grief, he could not say a single word.

Yan Hui had tears in his eyes, and his voice was weak and trembling. "Master, you have taught me for so many years, and I have learned the rites and the six arts. Unfortunately I am not able to repay your kindness. It seems that ... I won't recover from this illness. Please forgive me for not fulfilling my duties!"

Confucius grasped his hands tightly and tried to comfort him. "You look fine. You must not think about death!"

Yan Hui felt so choked by phlegm that his lips turned dark purple. Supporting himself by both hands, he made a futile attempt to sit up in bed. Confucius stopped him.

Suddenly Yan Hui opened his eyes wide and stared at Confucius without blinking.

"Yan Hui, what do you want to say?" asked Confucius in a hoarse voice.

Yan Hui's lips trembled slightly as if trying to say something, then abruptly he stopped breathing, his eyes still open.

"Yan Hui! Yan Hui!" wailed Confucius.

People around began to weep.

Confucius raised his head and said woefully, "Heaven has bereaved me! Heaven has bereaved me!" Then he cried bitterly.

Zi Lu took him by the arm and tried to console him. "Master, you are grieving too much. You should mind your health!"

Confucius beat his chest and stamped his feet. "Am I grieving too much? If I don't grieve for such a person, whom should I grieve for?"

Zi Lu and Gongliang Ru helped Confucius out of the room into the courtyard.

Yan Lu said, "Master, a dead man can not be brought back to life whatever we do. This is fate! Please go home to rest!"

"How do you plan to bury him?" asked Confucius.

"My family is very poor, so I have only prepared an inner coffin for him. I can not afford to buy an outer coffin. What shall I do?"

Confucius brushed the question aside. "An inner coffin will be sufficient," he said.

"He was your favorite disciple," said Yan Lu. "Could you sell your chariot to buy an outer coffin for him?"

Confucius changed countenance on hearing this. "I was once a minister of Lu. I can not do without a chariot."

"You used to praise him so often," pleaded Yan Lu. "Shall we let him leave us in such a humble fashion?"

Confucius heaved a deep sigh. "He endured poverty and hardships all his life. Why should we spend lavishly for him when he is dead?"

"But he was your favorite disciple!"

"When my son, Kong Li, died, he too had only an inner coffin."

"But ..."

Confucius stopped Yan Lu. "Though people are different in intelligence, Kong Li was after all my own son. Since he was buried without an outer coffin, Yan Hui can also do without one."

After Zi Lu and Gongliang Ru had escorted Confucius home Zhuansun Shi, Bu Shang and a few others talked it out among themselves and donated some money, with which they bought an outer coffin for Yan Hui.

On the day of the funeral, Confucius was annoyed at the sight of the outer coffin. "Yan Hui!" he announced loudly in front of the coffin, "you treated me as your father, but I failed to treat you as my son. You must understand that this was not my idea. A few of your fellow disciples did this without my knowledge."

Overwhelmed by grief, Confucius fell ill. His heartbeat grew irregular and he often felt tight in his chest. Realizing that he had not much time left, he worked day and night to write *The Spring and Autumn Annals*.

One day in the spring of the fourteenth year of Duke Ai of Lu's reign (481 B.C.) Confucius felt a pang in his heart when he thought of Yan Hui. He said to Gongliang Ru, "Get the chariot ready. I want to go out of the city to visit Yan Hui's grave."

Gongliang Ru went out and harnessed the horse to the chariot. They mounted the chariot and set out.

Yan Hui's grave lay by a small river outside the east city gate, surrounded by a few young cypresses.

Confucius got down from the chariot by the road and walked up to Yan Hui's grave. He stood there for a long time until his legs grew numb and his eyes became blurred. He fell into a trance and saw Yan Hui stand before him, looking poor in health but high in spirit. "Yan Hui!" He called out and was jostled out of his trance by his own voice.

Gongliang Ru started and came up to support Confucius with his hand. "Master, don't grieve too much. Let's return to the city!"

Confucius did not move but kept his gaze on a piece of newly sprouting grass on Yan Hui's grave, a train of memories crowding into his mind.

Just then they heard the sound of many chariots traveling toward them.

Chapter Forty-seven

Confucius Despairs of Realizing His Ideal on Seeing an Auspicious Animal Shot Dead in Lu; Kuai Kui Celebrates the Success of His Southern Expedition with Jubilation

Brought back to earth by the sound of approaching chariots, Confucius turned and saw Jisun Fei and his retinue, apparently on a spring outing. Jisun Fei leapt out of his chariot and came up to him. "Master," he beamed, "why do you look so sad? Whose grave is this?"

"It's Yan Hui's. He was one of my disciples."

"Why should you feel so grieved at the loss of a disciple?"

Confucius did not know how to reply.

Jisun Fei seemed to become aware of something. "Among your three thousand disciples, who is the most diligent?"

"Yan Hui was the most diligent of my disciples. Unfortunately he died early, and there is no one like him today."

When Jisun Fei recounted the incident to Duke Ai of Lu, the latter did not quite believed him. "Confucius has numerous talented disciples. How could Yan Hui have been the only diligent one?"

One day Duke Ai summoned Confucius into the palace and asked, "Among your disciples, who is the most diligent?"

Confucius assumed a grave expression. "A disciple named Yan Hui was very diligent. He never blamed others for his own mistake and never made the same mistake twice. Unfortunately he died prematurely. Today there is no one as diligent as he."

Duke Ai was puzzled. "I heard that you have taught three thousand disciples. Is there no one among them who can compare with Yan Hui?"

"No, there is none."

Somehow Duke Ai found this hard to believe.

"Yan Hui set his mind on benevolence and righteousness," said Confucius by way of explanation. "As for the other disciples, they think of benevolence and righteousness only occasionally. Yan Hui listened to me attentively and never slackened his efforts. He kept

594

making progress and never halted even once."

"What are your lifelong strivings?"

Confucius had mixed emotions on hearing this question. Many years before he would have given a full, hearty expression to his feelings. However, he was now too old to get excited, so he replied simply, "I strive after the Way, virtue and benevolence, and spend all my life studying the six arts."

"What's your greatest pleasure in life?"

"To practice what I have learned, and to have friends coming from afar to visit me."

"Is there anything that worries you?"

"Failure to cultivate one's virtue, to upgrade one's learning, or to act upon the principle of righteousness and correct one's errors—these are what I worry about."

Just then Nangong Jingshu came in and said to Duke Ai, "Your Lordship, Shusun's chariot driver, Ju Shang, caught a strange beast while hunting in Wucheng. No one can tell what it is, so we would like the master to come over and have a look."

"We'll continue our talk on another occasion then," said Duke Ai to Confucius. "Let's go and take a look at the strange animal."

"Where is Ju Shang?" asked Confucius.

"He is waiting in your residence," replied Nangong Jingshu.

Duke Ai got on his chariot and, accompanied by Nangong Jingshu and Confucius, went to Confucius' house.

The onlookers hastily made way for the duke upon his arrival.

At the sight of the dead animal, Confucius cried out in astonishment. "It's a kylin! This auspicious animal looks both like a horse and a deer, and it only makes its appearance when the state has a wise ruler. But this one got killed as soon as it appeared. What a bad omen!" He bent down and stroked the kylin on its head and horns. He covered the arrow wound on its body with his hand, wishing he could bring it back to life.

Gongliang Ru went up and helped Confucius up to his feet. "Master, the kylin's dead. Don't be too sad over this!"

Staring at the kylin with glazed eyes, Confucius let out a deep sigh. "The kylin is a benevolent animal! It was killed right after it appeared. It seems that there is no longer any hope for me to realize my ideal in this world!"

Duke Ai also felt very sad and despondent. He got on his chariot and left with a heavy heart.

Having seen the duke off, Confucius went into his room and saw on the table *The Spring and Autumn Annals* he had been writing, to which he added the following words: "In spring of the fourteenth year of Duke Ai of Lu's reign, a kylin was caught in a hunting trip west of the capital." He dropped his brush, being in no mood to write on. *The Spring and Autumn Annals* was thus brought to an abrupt end.

In the sixth month that year Chen Heng, a minister of Qi, staged a palace coup, killing Duke Jian of Qi and erecting Duke Jian's younger brother Ao as Duke Ping of Qi. Chen Heng himself took overall control of the Qi court.

On hearing the news Confucius was very indignant and went to the court to call on Duke Ai. "Your Lordship," he said, "Lu and Qi are close neighbors. When something untoward happens in Qi it is bound to affect Lu in some way. Furthermore, the ruling houses of the two states are related by marriage. Now that Chen Heng has murdered his lord and set up a new duke, Your Lordship should send an expedition to punish him."

Duke Ai's face turned pale and his lips trembled. "You must be quite familiar with the situation in Lu," he said. "All the troops are controlled by the three big houses. If you really think an expedition should be dispatched, you have to go and talk with Jisun, Mengsun and Shusun."

Confucius was sorely disappointed. "I was once a minister of Lu," he said, "so I did not dare not to report the case to Your Lordship. I will call on the three houses as Your Lordship has told me." He left the court and went post-haste to Jisun Fei's residence.

After hearing him out, Jisun Fei said, "Lu is now barely strong enough to protect itself. How can we intervene in the affairs of Qi?"

Confucius left the chief minister's residence and went on to visit Mengsun Heji and Shusun Zhouchou, who gave him the same reply. He returned home in bitter disappointment.

Just then someone knocked at the gate, and Kong Ji hurried out to open it. It was Zi Gong.

"Is master at home?" he asked.

Confucius recognized his voice and walked out into the courtyard.

Zi Gong knelt in salute. "Your disciple pays respects to you, master!"

"Get up, please!" said Confucius. "Come in and we can talk."

When Zi Gong got on his feet, Confucius looked at him closely. "How have you been doing in Wenyang?"

Zi Gong smiled with self-satisfaction. "I have governed Wenyang according to your instruction with remarkable success. The common people even donated money to build a temple in my honor."

Confucius was greatly pleased. "You must have done a lot for the people. With disciples like you I don't have to worry that my cause will cease upon my death."

"Not long ago," said Zi Gong, "Chen Heng murdered Duke Jian of Qi and set up a new ruler."

"I have heard of it," Confucius sighed. "Have you come to inform me of this, or are you on a trip to visit your family in Wei?"

"I suspected Qi will soon fall into great turmoils, so I resigned the post of magistrate of Wenyang."

Confucius was taken aback and remained speechless for a moment. "What do you plan to do now?" he asked finally.

"I will be a trader," replied Zi Gong with self-assurance.

Confucius shook his head with regret. "Why don't you make use of your administrative talent to improve the ways of the world?"

"I am lacking in learning and ability. It is beyond my power to achieve anything worthwhile in this turbulent age. Since I can not change the world, I might as well preserve my own purity."

"What a waste!"

"Master, it is futile to attempt to restore the rites in a world beset with war and violence. Hasn't your experience testified to this? For all your learning and ability, you have been unable ..."

"Zi Gong," said Confucius, "do you think I have acquired my knowledge by diligent study?"

"Yes. Isn't that the case?"

Confucius straightened his back and thumped his walking stick on the floor. "No. I have an essential idea that guides all my action."

Zi Gong nodded his understanding.

"If you only seek after personal gains, you will have a lot of grudges and regrets," said Confucius.

"I understand," said Zi Gong. After a while he asked, "Master, what do you plan to do?"

Confucius recounted how he had witnessed the slaughtered kylin, and how he had tried in vain to persuade the duke to send a punitive expedition against Qi. "The kylin emerges only in a prosperous age.

But no sooner had it appeared than it was shot dead. This indicates that my teaching will not prevail in the world. Chen Heng murdered his lord, yet there is no one to punish him for it. The moral principles have all been discarded."

"Under the circumstances," said Zi Gong, "what is there for us to do?"

"I won't swerve from my goal to restore the rites of Zhou," said Confucius determinedly. "I will persevere to the end despite all these difficulties and setbacks!"

For the next few days Zi Gong stayed on to keep his master company. One day he asked, "Master, how should one deal with his friends?"

"Advise them earnestly and guide them properly. If they don't listen to you, do not persist. Otherwise you would only bring shame and worry upon yourself."

Just then Jisun Fei was announced. Confucius hurried out to meet him. "What do you have to teach me, Chief Minister?" he asked.

"Recently there are too many thieves in our land," said Jisun Fei. "I would like to hear your advice on how to prevent this."

"People become thieves because of poverty. If you enable the common people to enjoy a good life, no one would resort to theft even if you should set a reward for it."

Jisun Fei blushed and changed the topic. "Do you think it appropriate if I govern the state by eliminating the villains and promoting people of virtue?"

"Why should you resort to killing in governing the state?" Confucius retorted. "To govern well, you must first be upright. When you are upright, who dares not to be upright? The ruler can be compared to the wind, and the common people to grass. Whichever way the wind blows, the grass will bend in that direction. It is, therefore, no exaggeration to say that, if you are upright, people will carry things out without your ordering them to, and if you are not upright, people will not carry things out even when ordered to."

"How can I make the people carry out my orders earnestly, fulfill their duties to me wholeheartedly, and encourage one another in the right way?"

"If you attend to the affairs of the people earnestly, they will carry out your orders earnestly. If you are filial to your parents and kind and loving to your children, the people will serve you wholeheartedly. If you promote men of virtue and educate the ignorant, they will encourage one another in the right way."

"You have lived in Wei for many years and must know Duke Ling quite well. What kind of a ruler was he?"

"He was an immoral ruler," replied Confucius without hesitation.

"If Duke Ling of Wei was immoral, why didn't the state of Wei decline and collapse?"

"Duke Ling had Zhong Shuyu in charge of receiving guests from other states, Zhu Tuo in charge of ancestral worship, and Wangsun Jia in charge of the military forces. These learned, brave, and upright ministers fulfilled their respective duties conscientiously. How could such a state have declined and collapsed even though the ruler was immoral?"

Jisun Fei could find no fault with this argument.

Confucius went on, "What pomp and splendor when Duke Jing of Qi owned more than a thousand war chariots! However, after his death people can find no reason at all to admire him. On the other hand, Bo Yi and Shu Qi starved to death under Shouyang Mountain, yet even people today hold them in high esteem because of their virtue."

Jisun Fei blushed to the roots of his hair, for he regarded Confucius' remark as a veiled invective against him. But he could not express his dissatisfaction, for Confucius had made the remark in answer to his question. "Your words are very instructive," he murmured. "I have benefited a lot." With this he left.

Confucius had just seen Jisun Fei off when Zi Lu rushed into the room. "Master, I just heard that Kuai Kui is gathering forces at Qidi. He is planning another assault to overthrow his son."

Confucius was not surprised at the news. "This should not have happened," he said. "If Duke Ling of Wei had not been so old and benighted, Nan Zi would not have been so licentious, and Kuai Kui would not have attempted to assassinate her. The internecine strife would not have taken place at all."

"I once served Duke Chu as magistrate of Pu, so I want to return to Wei to help him," said Zi Lu.

"Zi Lu," said Confucius, "you must think twice before you act. Intrepidity is one of your weaknesses, and it may bring harm upon yourself."

"I served in office in Wei and received salary from the duke of

Wei. How can I stand by doing nothing when the duke of Wei is in trouble?"

"It was several years ago when you were a magistrate in Wei. Why should you get involved in the strife between father and son?"

Zi Lu was not convinced. "Though Kuai Kui is Duke Chu's father, he is also a treacherous subject of Wei."

"When you are no longer in office, you should not concern yourself with official affairs. Stay in Lu and do not seek trouble. You are already over sixty and must not overreach yourself. I can still remember the inscription on the bronze statue in front of the Duke of Zhou Temple: 'An overbearing man will come to a sorry end, and a proud man will one day meet his rival.' Bear this firmly in mind!"

Zi Lu did not venture to say anything again.

By this time Kuai Kui had stationed himself in Qidi for over ten years. He never gave up the hope of capturing the capital, but he grew cautious after his aborted attempt. This time, apart from Zhao Jianzi's assistance, he was counting on Kong Li to collaborate with him. Kong Li was his elder sister's son. After his brother-in-law died of illness, his sister fell in love with her servant Hun Liangfu. This created a scandal in the state of Wei. Many people thought a woman of her status should guard her chastity after her husband's death. For her to marry again would be inconceivable, and for her to marry a servant would be entirely out of the question. Kong Li also objected strongly to his mother's marrying again, but Kuai Kui encouraged her to do it.

One day Kuai Kui sent a messenger to inform his sister of his plan. His sister talked it over with Hun Liangfu, and they decided to coordinate with Kuai Kui.

Kuai Kui was overjoyed by this reply. He immediately went to visit Zhao Jianzi in the state of Jin and borrowed two hundred war chariots from him.

After long-term preparation, Kuai Kui set out with his troops in a winter evening in the fifteenth year of Duke Ai of Lu's reign (480 B.C.). Forty li from the capital he stopped and made camp.

Duke Chu of Wei was panic-stricken and hastily gathered all his military forces to defend the capital.

Kuai Kui was in no hurry to attack. Each day he had a few pigs and sheep slaughtered to feast his men, while he waited for a message to come from his sister.

One day at noon Kuai Kui was sitting listlessly in his commander's tent when a soldier came in to report, "Someone asks to see you."

Kuai Kui instantly became alert. "Show him in!"

The visitor was a young man dressed like a peasant. He knelt in obeisance. "Your Highness, I was ordered by your sister to bring a message to you."

"Where is the letter?"

"Your sister did not write any letter in case something wrong happens to me. She told me to pass on an oral message."

"Speak then!"

The young man came up to Kuai Kui and whispered in his ear.

Kuai Kui nodded repeatedly with a look of satisfaction on his face.

That evening three people carrying stacks of firewood on shoulder poles arrived at the city gate. The guards searched them thoroughly and, finding nothing suspicious, allowed them to enter.

They took a couple of turns and arrived at the street where Hun Liangfu lived. Making sure that they were not being followed, they slipped into the house.

The sister and brother met, exchanging greetings. "A long night brings many dreams," said Lady Kuai, "and undue delay brings trouble. Let's act at once."

"Your son, Kong Li, is the chief minister. If we obtain his help, success will lie in our hands. If he should choose to help Zhe, that would mean great difficulties for us."

Lady Kuai drew in a deep breath. "Kong Li has stopped visiting me because of his objection to my getting married again. It would be no easy thing to win him over to our side."

Hun Liangfu was an accomplished fighter. He clenched his fists, saying, "I'll take a few men with me and abduct him here. Then he has no choice but to cooperate with us."

Kuai Kui hesitated for a while, unable to come to a decision, and turned to look at his sister.

Lady Kuai did not speak but fixed her gaze on the flickering oil-lamp.

Hun Liangfu grew impatient. "When two tigers fight, one is sure to get killed. If you don't kill your opponent, he will kill you. Why should we wait passively until the situation turns against us?"

Kuai Kui shuddered. He turned to his sister. "Since Kong Li is unwilling to help us, we will have to force him."

Lady Kuai bit her teeth, making up her mind. "All right, let's do it! However," she turned to Hun Liangfu, "you must act with caution. Do not wound him, or get wounded by his guards!"

"You can trust me!" shouted Hun Liangfu. He set out for the chief minister's house with four soldiers.

When Hun Liangfu was announced, Kong Li decided he did not want to see him. Failing to think up of anything to cope with the situation, he went and hid himself in the toilet.

Hun Liangfu broke into the house and searched everywhere for Kong Li, finally finding him in the toilet. "I have come at the order of your uncle and your mother," he said to Kong Li, "to invite you to come over to discuss something important."

"I won't go, until you tell me what is to be discussed there."

"I'm afraid I don't know."

"What if I refuse to go?"

The four soldiers standing behind Hun Liangfu drew out their daggers at the same time. "It's not for you to decide, Chief Minister." They escorted him out of the house, pushed him into a waiting chariot, and brought him back to Hun Liangfu's residence.

Kuai Kui and his sister were delighted. "Let's find a place where we can take an oath," said Kuai Kui at last.

"Oh yes!" exclaimed Lady Kuai. "I almost forgot. Where can we go?"

"Let's build an earthen platform in the vegetable garden," suggested Hun Liangfu.

Kuai Kui was too eager to become the lord of Wei to be fastidious about such formalities. "That's a good idea!" he said, nodding his head repeatedly.

They brought Kong Li to the vegetable garden.

Holding a torch in his hand, Hun Liangfu ordered the soldiers to build an earthen platform. He jumped onto it and announced in a low voice, "Zhe usurped the dukedom and banished his father from the court. However, with Heaven's blessing, his father has returned to the capital to reclaim Wei. No one can act against Heaven's will!"

Kuai Kui also climbed up the platform, torch in hand. "How can the son rule the state when his father is still alive?" he said. "My son has committed unpardonable crime by going against Heaven's will and betraying his father! I will kill him with my own hands!"

Lady Kuai went up to Kong Li, who was shaking in his shoes. "From now on, those who cooperate with Kuai Kui will be amply rewarded, and those who dare oppose him will meet their deaths!"

"Bring the bull!" ordered Hun Liangfu.

A soldier ran up to him and reported, "We failed to find a bull. We only managed to get a pig."

"We will use the pig then!" said Hun Liangfu.

The soldiers brought the pig to the platform. Kuai Kui burnt incense and laid out four bowls.

At Hun Liangfu's beckoning, a soldier plunged his dagger deep into the pig's neck and brought over a bowl of blood, which he poured into the four bowls.

Kuai Kui handed one bowl to his sister, and Hun Liangfu handed one to Kong Li, who refused to take it. At this the soldiers approached him, swords in hand. Reluctantly, Kong Li took the bowl.

"To return Wei to its legitimate ruler ..." said Hun Liangfu.

"To kill Zhe or drive him out of Wei ..." said Lady Kuai.

"To ensure peace and prosperity in Wei ..." said Kuai Kui.

"Let's make this oath of blood!" The three of them chanted in unison and drained the bowls at one gulp.

Kong Li's hand trembled so much that he almost spilled the blood in the bowl.

Taking a hint from Kuai Kui, one of the soldiers grabbed Kong Li's head and poured the bowl of blood down his throat.

Seeing that everything was ready, Kuai Kui mounted the platform and announced, "Tell the guards to open the city gates and welcome my troops into the capital!"

"The order has already been issued!" said Hun Liangfu.

Kuai Kui laughed boisterously. "We made it!" At this moment someone suddenly shouted, "It's too early for you to celebrate your success! I am here to stop you!"

They turned to look and found it was Zi Lu. Formerly, when news reached Zi Lu that Kuai Kui had borrowed troops from Jin and planned to invade the Wei capital, he left Lu for Wei in haste without informing Confucius. About thirty li from the Wei capital, Diqiu, he saw a flock of crows hovering over the bank of a river. Curious, he went there to look and found a stinking corpse. To his great joy, he recognized it was Yang Hu. "This is indeed an excellent example of the saying 'Good will be rewarded with good and evil with evil'," he said to himself. Then he hesitated. "Shall I dig a hole to bury him, or leave him here to be devoured by the crows?" He circled around Yang

Hu's body and stabbed the ground with his sword. The ground was frozen and as hard as stone. He decided it would be too much trouble to bury the body, so he left Yang Hu's body and hurried on to Diqiu. It was dark when he reached the capital, and the east gate was already closed. He had supper at an eating house, then returned to the gate.

At the same time Gao Chai, having learned of the kidnapping of Kong Li by Kuai Kui and Hun Liangfu, decided to leave Wei and not get involved in the oncoming tumult. He went to the east gate by himself.

Kuai Kui's men had already taken over the four gates of the city, and Gao Chai could find no way to get out.

Suddenly he heard someone calling him. He went over and saw Hou Biao.

"Sir, Kuai Kui's men were searching and arresting Minister Kong's subordinates. There is an opening in the wall over there. You can escape by that opening."

"A superior man does not climb walls," said Gao Chai. "I can not bring myself to do it."

"Then hide yourself in the small room here."

Gao Chai agreed with reluctance.

Some of Kuai Kui's soldiers came and, failing to find anyone, left. "Sir," said Hou Biao, "there's no one else here at this moment. Let me open the city gate for you."

"It was at my order that you lost your foot and became a handicap. Why should you save my life instead of taking revenge on me?"

"You gave me the punishment that I fully deserved. Without your careful arrangement and magnanimous help, I would have died long ago!"

"Despite all that," said Gao Chai, "you have saved my life. Please accept my gratitude!" He knelt.

"Please," Hou Biao also fell on his knees. "I don't deserve such honor."

The two of them got up. Hou Biao said, "I'll open the city gate now, Sir. Leave here as fast as you can!"

Stepping out of the gate, Gao Chai ran into Zi Lu. He grabbed Zi Lu by the hand and dragged him along.

"I want to enter the city," protested Zi Lu. "Why are you in such fluster?"

"Kuai Kui has kidnapped Minister Kong. The situation looks

really bad."

"How can you run away like this, when you have been receiving salary from Minister Kong?"

"Kuai Kui and Kong Li are blood relations. It is unsuitable for outsiders like us to get involved in their contention. You must not throw yourself into danger for nothing!"

"You can flee if you want to," said Zi Lu. "As for me, I will go and rescue Minister Kong!" With this he burst into the city gate and ran all the way to Hun Liangfu's house.

Chapter Forty-eight

Zi Lu Dies a Cruel Death in the State of Wei;
On His Deathbed Confucius Finds
a Successor for Himself

Zi Lu suddenly burst into the vegetable garden in Hun Liangfu's
house. "It's too early to celebrate your success!" he shouted. "I am here
to stop you!"

Hun Liangfu yelled, "You are a native of Lu. What's happening
here in Wei has nothing to do with you!"

"You can do whatever you want," said Zi Lu, "but you should not
have abducted Minister Kong and forced him to take an oath with you.
I once served under Minister Kong, and I demand you to let him go!"

Kuai Kui roared with laughter. "I thought you would know better
after reading so many books. Kong Li is my elder sister's son. It is
fitting and proper for him to assist us. There is no reason for an
outsider like you to interfere."

Zi Lu realized it was impossible for him to stop them. He beat his
chest and stamped his feet in frustration. Just then a pile of firewood
in the garden caught his eye. "If you don't free Minister Kong, I'll set
this house on fire." He ran over to the pile of firewood and set fire to
it.

"Kill him!" Kuai Kui ordered his soldiers. "Or at least drive him
away!"

Two soldiers came running toward Zi Lu, brandishing their long
halberds. Zi Lu hastily drew his sword to fight back. After a few dozen
rounds he began to feel weak and could barely stall the thrusts of his
two opponents. When one soldier thrusted forth his halberd, Zi Lu
did not dodge fast enough, and the tassel of his hat was cut off. The
other soldier struck down and hit him in the left arm. Zi Lu warded
off their attack with all his might and said in a loud voice, "The
ancients said that a hero must wear his hat squarely when he meets
his death. Allow me to adjust my hat properly." He put his sword onto
the ground, picked up the tassel and tied it onto his hat. When he
bent down to pick up his sword, the two soldiers raised their halberds
and drove them into his chest. Other soldiers swarmed over and cut

Zi Lu to pieces.

Overcome with excitement, Kuai Kui shouted in a shrill voice, "Soldiers! Storm into the palace and kill Zhe, that treacherous son of mine!"

When Kong Li was abducted, his steward Luan Ning was enjoying a supper of wine and roast meat. He grabbed a piece of half-cooked meat and fled the house in a chariot. He went into the palace, where he found Duke Chu of Wei, and together they left for Qi via Lu.

The soldiers searched the palace up and down and, failing to find Zhe, returned to report to Kuai Kui.

"Since my treacherous son has fled, we won't worry about him now," said Kuai Kui. "Honored ministers, let's enter the palace and bring the state back to order!" In this way Kuai Kui took over Wei and ruled as Duke Zhuang of Wei.

On hearing of the coup in Wei, Confucius immediately sent for Zi Lu. It was only then that he learned Zi Lu had left secretly. Confucius sensed that something untoward will happen to Zi Lu. "To fight a fierce tiger with bare fists, and to ford a great river without a boat—these are acts I do not approve of," he remarked. "Gao Chai will extricate himself from the unfortunate situation in Wei. As for Zi Lu, I'm afraid he won't be able to return alive!"

Soon afterward they received the news of Zi Lu's death. Confucius went out to the courtyard and wept bitterly. Then he asked the man who had brought the news how Zi Lu was killed.

"He was cut to pieces by Kuai Kui's men."

Confucius was gripped with grief on hearing this. He had the jug of soya paste covered and never touched it again.

After a spate of violent wind, dark clouds covered the sky. At dusk it began to snow heavily. Confucius sat in a daze before an oil-lamp. He felt as if he had caught a glimpse of someone. "Zi Lu!" he called out involuntarily.

At nightfall the wind grew more fierce. The shadowy figure of Zi Lu kept drifting into Confucius' mind, as he remembered many joys, comforts and sorrows he had shared with this long-time disciple. His head reeling and his legs limp, he got into bed and covered himself with a cotton-padded quilt.

The sound of wind and snow outside somewhat comforted him. "Let Zi Lu's remains be covered in snow," he said to himself. The faces of some of his favorite disciples emerged before him: Gao Chai, who was very astute; Zeng Shen, who was slow but wise; Zhuansun Shi, who was stubborn but at the same time broadminded, and Zi Lu, who was intrepid and unyielding. "Ai!" Confucius heaved a deep sigh. "He came to a miserable end because of his intrepidity!"

He forced himself not to think about it any longer and closed his eyes to get some sleep. However, his eyes hurt badly as if being constantly pricked by needles. He did not fall asleep until it was nearly dawn.

The following morning the wind let up, but it was still snowing. When Confucius got up, Zeng Shen came to greet him. "Master," he said, "it was very cold and windy last night. Did you sleep well?"

"After hearing of Zi Lu's death," replied Confucius, "I felt tightness in my chest and hardly got any sleep last night."

"A dead man will not come back to life whatever we do," said Zeng Shen. "Please take good care of yourself, master!"

Confucius' eyes brimmed with tears, and his voice broke. "Zi Lu was one of my earliest disciples, who had accompanied me all his life. I can not help feeling grieved at his death."

Zeng Shen rubbed his hands and could not find any words to comfort Confucius.

Just then Kong Ji came into the room and began to ask a lot of questions. "Grandpa, why doesn't it snow in summer? We would be able to play in the snow then."

Confucius looked at his grandson and did not know how to answer him.

The sparrows in the old scholar tree in the courtyard chirped a couple of times.

"Grandpa," asked Kong Ji, "why don't these sparrows feel cold sitting outside in the snow?" Getting no answer, he asked again, "Grandpa, who is pouring all this snow from the sky?"

Confucius finally broke into a smile.

Zeng Shen sighed with relief and went to read in the classroom.

Confucius spent that winter in sorrow and dejection. One day in the spring of the sixteenth year of Duke Ai of Lu's reign (479 B.C.) he remarked to Zi Gong, "I spent the best time of my life wandering from state to state, seeking in vain for an important official post at which to put my knowledge to good use. What an age we live in!"

"Yes!" agreed Zi Gong. "This is an age of confusion and injustice. You can not find a chance to put your learning into practice, yet there are all those rulers issuing orders to the people out of ignorance and stupidity."

"I have grown accustomed to it though," said Confucius. "It is useless to complain. I find comfort in what I have already achieved, and especially in the achievements of all my disciples."

"Yes," said Zi Gong. "You have taught three thousand disciples altogether. This must be unprecedented in history."

Confucius walked into the courtyard and gazed speechlessly at the juniper trees.

"Master," asked Zi Gong, trying to keep Confucius' mind away from sad thoughts. "I heard that Kong Yu, a minister of Wei, received the title Wen upon his death. Why?"

"Kong Yu was eager to learn and not ashamed to seek advice from his subordinates. That's why he got the posthumous title Wen."

"I have never heard your teaching about Heaven," said Zi Gong.

"The way of Heaven is open for all to see. It is unnecessary for me to talk about it."

After breakfast Confucius walked into the classroom with a stick. When he saw the young faces of the disciples there, he sighed, "All those who suffered with me in Chen and Cai are not here." He was about to begin his lecture when he suddenly felt dizzy. He staggered back a few steps and leaned on the wall to rest a while, then he went to the table and supported himself with both hands. "It has been a long time since the phoenix appeared and the divine chart was found in the Yellow River. And it has been a long time since I last dreamed of the Duke of Zhou. It looks as if my life is coming to an end!"

Zeng Shen came up and supported Confucius with his hands. "Master," he said, "why should you say something like that? You have not yet taught us everything you know."

"Do I have knowledge?" said Confucius. "I have none. One day a villager asked me a question. I was at a loss to understand. I had to ask him to explain the question thoroughly before I managed to understand a little and gave him what advice I could think of."

The disciples wanted to ask more questions, but Confucius suddenly felt palpitations in his heart, and his forehead was covered with perspiration.

"Are you not feeling well, master?" asked Zeng Shen.

Confucius began gasping for breath, and his face turned sallow. "My heart sometimes beats too fast, sometimes too slowly. I am not long for this world."

Startled, the disciples came up and carried the master back to his room.

Confucius stayed in bed for the next few days without eating anything. The disciples went out to find doctors. But when the doctors learned Confucius' age and symptoms, they all said there was nothing they could do.

Confucius lay quietly in bed, drifting in and out of consciousness. Past events thronged into his mind, causing emotions of both joy and sorrow: studying together with his elder brother, receiving instructions from his grandfather, serving as petty officials, achieving widespread fame at his post of minister of justice, traveling from state to state in search of a sage ruler, and returning to his homeland in old age....

The disciples often came to visit and take care of him. When he felt a little better, he would talk with them.

One day Confucius felt a lot better and sat up in his bed. Just then Gao Chai burst into the room and knelt before the bed. "Master, please forgive me for not coming earlier!"

Confucius stretched out his hand to pat Gao Chai on the shoulder. "Gao Chai, I am much better. I was hoping that you would come. Where have you been all these days, after the court coup in Wei?"

"I left Wei and came back to Lu, where I learned of Zi Lu's death. I was responsible for his death, for I had not stopped him from going into danger. I felt too ashamed to come to see you, so I returned to Qi. But I did not know you were so ill." Tears rolled down Gao Chai's cheeks.

"Zi Lu died such a cruel death because he was too intrepid and thought he could save the situation all by himself. Of course you were not responsible for what had happened to him."

Gao Chai felt a great sense of relief on hearing this. He got on his feet and began asking some questions. "Master, how should a man conduct himself in office?"

"You were able to achieve a lot when you took office in Wei and Lu. Why are you asking me this question?"

"I barely know enough to govern a county. I would like to learn the way to govern a state and bring peace and prosperity to all its people."

Confucius did not answer right away.

"Should an official rely mainly on moral instruction or should he use law enforcement?" asked Gao Chai.

"If the people are guided by administrative orders and legal punishment, they will try to avoid breaking the law but have no sense of shame. If the people are educated in moral principles and guided by rites, they will know the sense of shame and become devoted to the government."

Gao Chai recalled to his embarrassment what he had done while serving as an official.

"Master," asked Zeng Shen, "you have grasped the teachings of all the ancient sages. In your opinion, what's the relationship between man and truth?"

"A man of ability can enhance the truth, but truth can not enhance the man's ability."

"Master," asked Zhuansun Shi, "how should I treat someone who is disliked by everyone around him? And how should I treat someone who is liked by everyone around him?"

"When a man is widely disliked, you must look into the case yourself to find out the truth about him. When a man is widely liked, you must also look into the case yourself to find out the truth about him. In neither case can you agree with the others without further investigation."

As it was getting late, the disciples took their leave, but Gao Chai decided to stay and keep Confucius company.

That night Confucius tossed in bed and did not fall asleep until the third watch. Gao Chai wrapped himself in a sheepskin and slept beside the bed.

It was broad daylight when Confucius woke up the next morning.

"Master," asked Gao Chai anxiously, "did you sleep well last night? Was it cold?"

Confucius replied with a frown, "In the Xia Dynasty the coffin was laid on the east terrace. In the Zhou Dynasty the coffin should be laid on the west terrace. In the Shang Dynasty, the coffin was placed in between two pillars. In a dream last night I sat between two pillars to receive sacrifice. My ancestors, you know, were Shang people. It seems that I won't live for long."

Gao Chai was dumbfounded. He went to the classroom and said to his fellow disciples, "The master is very sick. He was even delirious just now."

The disciples all hurried into Confucius' room. Surprised, Confucius asked, "Is there anything wrong?"

The disciples lowered their heads, not knowing how to reply.

Confucius got out of bed and, leaning on his stick, walked into the courtyard. When he did not see Zi Gong, he asked, "Where is Zi Gong?"

"I have sent someone to Wei to look for him," said Yan Lu. "He will be here in a few days."

At this moment someone came in through the main gate.

Confucius was glad when he found it was Zi Gong. "Zi Gong!" he called out. "Why are you so late? Why are you so late?"

Zi Gong knelt in obeisance. "Master," he said, "I did not know your illness was so serious."

"Do get up!" Confucius said. "Get up!" He turned and asked Yan Lu, "Who else is missing?"

"I have sent for all who are absent," said Yan Lu. "They will be here in a few days."

Confucius looked around at his disciples and raised his voice. "My disciples, six hundred years ago King Wu established the Zhou Dynasty, for which the foundation had already been laid by King Wen. Since that time the kingdom has gradually declined. All my life I have attempted to help the rulers of the various states to restore the rites of Zhou and bring the Zhou kingdom to its former glory. For many years some of you accompanied me on a long, arduous but fruitless journey from state to state. Is that what people call the will of Heaven?" He paused, then chanted the following:

> Mount Tai is toppling,
> The beam of the house is breaking.
> Like broken twigs and fallen leaves,
> The philosopher is withering!

Zi Gong and Yan Lu helped Confucius get back to his room and lie down in bed. That was the fourth day of the second month in the year 479 B.C.

The disciples waited on him day and night. One day when Yan Lu was sitting by his bed, Confucius said, "In my lifetime I have taught three thousand disciples. Some of them are very talented and have a very bright future ahead of them. Apart from The Spring and Autumn Annals, I will be known to posterity because of my disciples. If I have done something worthwhile in that respect, you should be the first to be praised."

Yan Lu looked at him with query in his eyes.

"My teaching career had much to do with you," Confucius went on. "Had it not been for your insistence, I would not have started teaching."

"Even if I had not asked you to take me as your disciple, someone else would have done so sooner or later. A man of true worth will always attract admiration."

"It seems that I am not long for this world," said Confucius. "Which one among you is willing to carry on my cause and start taking disciples?"

"By my observation, Zeng Shen is the most suitable one," replied Yan Lu. "He studies hard and has a deep understanding of the classics. Furthermore, he conducts himself with prudence worthy of a teacher."

Confucius was considering Yan Lu's words when Zeng Shen came into the room to greet him. "What's your aim in life?" Confucius asked.

Zeng Shen hesitated a little, then replied, "Since I became your disciple, I have learned a great deal. It is my hope that ..." He paused and looked at Confucius, then continued slowly, "that I will start teaching others someday just as I have been taught by you."

"Excellent!" Confucius was so delighted that he felt as if his illness had gone. "With you to carry on my cause, I will die with a contented heart."

"Master," said Zeng Shen, "your learning is as lofty as the sun and moon. In following your example I would be content if I could grasp one or two-tenths of it."

"You shouldn't put it that way," said Confucius, shaking his head. "If you are insatiable in learning and tireless in teaching, you will be able to achieve something great."

Zeng Shen lowered his head bashfully.

"The ancients said that in the face of benevolence you don't give precedence even to your teacher. Since you cherish such a lofty aim, you should do your best to achieve it."

"I will do my best and not let you down, master."

Confucius heaved a deep sigh of relief. "I can set my mind at ease now!" After a while he called out, "Kong Ji!"

"Here!" Kong Ji ran over very nimbly.

"Grandpa will not live for very long," said Confucius. "I want you to acknowledge Zeng Shen as your teacher and take pleasure in learning. Someday, I hope, you will make great progress in your learning and put your knowledge to practical use!"

"Yes!" Kong Ji answered in a clear voice.

"Salute your teacher!"

Kong Ji knelt before Zeng Shen and kowtowed. "Your disciple Kong Ji pays respects to you, sir!"

Zeng Shen helped Kong Ji up with both hands. When he turned, he saw Confucius frowning and covering his chest with both hands as if enduring great pain.

The disciples stood by Confucius' bed, praying that he would soon recover his health.

Confucius suffered spasmodic attacks of acute pain. Sometimes he felt such pain that his teeth were clenched, and his forehead was covered in perspiration. When he got a little better, he would talk with his disciples on various subjects. One day, when his condition improved a little, Duke Ai of Lu suddenly visited him. Greatly moved, he struggled to get up from his bed to receive the duke.

Duke Ai hurried over and placed his hands on Confucius. "Master, please don't move!"

"Your Lordship!" Confucius' eyes were filled with tears. "You have to attend to numerous affairs of the state, yet you have taken the trouble to visit me. How do I deserve such a great honor!"

"For many generations the Kong family has served Lu with great devotion and achieved outstanding merits," said Duke Ai. "Why shouldn't I pay a visit to you when you are so seriously ill?" He paused for a while, then went on, "Master, you are conversant with things ancient and modern and understand both civil and military affairs. I intend to put the court in good order and make Lu prosperous, but I don't know where to begin."

Pleased with the question, Confucius answered in a low but determined voice, "In my opinion, of the Xia, Shang and Zhou dynasties, Zhou has the most complete system of rites. Therefore I have always advocated that people should make their speech and conduct conform with the rites of Zhou."

"You seldom talk with others without mentioning the importance of rites. Can you explain the rites to me in detail?"

"The rites are of primary significance in people's lives," said Confucius. "Without rites, people would not know how to worship the gods properly, would not know the relationship between rulers and subjects, superiors and inferiors, seniors and juniors, and would not know the proper rules of conduct between male and female, father and son, and elder and younger brothers. Therefore a superior man in ancient times always conducted himself in strict accordance with the rites."

"Why don't people nowadays observe the ancient rites?" asked Duke Ai.

"Nowadays people become blinded by inordinate greed and ambition," said Confucius. "They lead a life of extravagance and dissipation and do not hesitate to resort to violence and murder to achieve their aims. How can such people observe the ancient rites?" As he said this, he felt his heart thumping violently and began gasping for breath.

Duke Ai bade Confucius good-bye and took his leave in haste.

After a while Confucius calmed down but felt very weak. He called out, "Kong Ji!"

Kong Ji ran over, cuddling himself against Confucius.

"You are the only descendent of the Kong family. You must study hard to master the six arts so that when the opportunity comes, you can apply your knowledge to serve the state."

"I understand," said Kong Ji.

"I have failed to find practical use for my knowledge," Confucius sighed, two teardrops coursing down his cheeks.

The disciples crowded round him and listened quietly.

With the help of some of the disciples, Confucius turned in bed. He stretched out his hand. "All of you must do your best to serve the state and restore the rites of Zhou."

Some of the disciples began to weep.

"You shouldn't be crying," said Confucius. "You should smile. Look!" He pointed to the wall. "The Duke of Zhou has come. He's smiling at me. Tidy up your clothes and stand at attention to receive him!"

Min Shun shuddered and pulled Ran Qiu and Yan Lu aside. "The master is delirious. We should prepare for the worst."

"The coffin is ready," said Yan Lu.

"I'll take care of subsequent proceedings," offered Ran Qiu.

When the three of them returned to the room, Confucius was pointing with his finger to the ceiling. "A shining pagoda!" he muttered. "Yao...Shun...Cheng Tang...King Wen...King Wu...the

Duke of Zhou..." He murmured in this way all night. The following morning, when the sun was shining through the window, Confucius again said excitedly, "A shining pagoda!"

The disciples looked at one another, not knowing what Confucius was talking about.

Confucius no longer felt pain. He beckoned the disciples to help him lie on his back, then he said with a smile, "When the great harmony is achieved, the whole world will become one." After saying these words, he closed his eyes and stopped breathing. It was early morning on the eleventh day of the second month in the sixteenth year of Duke Ai of Lu's reign (479 B.C.).

A memorial tablet was set up in the main hall of the house. The disciples, dressed in deep mourning, stood beside the coffin or in the courtyard, weeping.

Zeng Shen wiped off his tears. "Fellow disciples, our master is a great sage of our time. We need a person of high standing to write an elegy for him."

No sooner had he said this than someone responded outside the gate, "An elegy has already been composed."

Chapter Forty-nine

Yan Hui Ranks First Among Confucian Disciples in Virtue; Zi Gong Stays by Confucius' Grave in Mourning for Six Years

The visitor was Jisun Fei. He walked quickly to the coffin and made a deep bow. Then he turned to the disciples. "His Lordship has written an elegy for the master. He has left the palace and will arrive here soon."

Hearing this, the eldest disciples, including Min Shun, Ran Yong, Ran Qiu, Yan Lu, Zeng Dian and Qidiao Kai, lined up outside the gate in sequence of seniority to wait for Duke Ai's arrival.

When Duke Ai arrived he stopped his chariot about fifty steps from the house as a gesture of deep respect for the deceased master. He dismounted the chariot and walked slowly into the house. Making a deep bow to the coffin, he took out from his sleeve a piece of white silk on which the elegy was written and unfolded it slowly with both hands. "Oh Heaven! Why are you so cruel as to deprive me of the great master! From now on I will be totally alone to rule the state and bear the heavy burden of responsibilities. Oh Father Ni! Whom can I turn to for instruction now?" He was torn with grief and regret, deploring that he had not made use of Confucius' service. The sight of the tear-stained faces of the disciples added to his sadness. With tears in his eyes he prayed in silence in front of the coffin, then returned to the palace.

After the duke had left, the disciples buried their master, according to his wish, to the left of Lady Qiguan's grave by the Sihe River. The two coffins lay side by side, and a high grave mound was constructed above. About thirty steps to the left was the grave of Kong Li.

After the burial the helpers left one by one, but the disciples, deeply grieved as if they had lost a parent, were all unwilling to go. They wept bitterly and kowtowed to the grave again and again. It was getting dark, but none of them wanted to leave.

"It is customary for a son to guard the grave for three years after his father's death," said Min Shun. "Our master was like a father to all of us. Since we do not want to leave, let's stay here and guard our master's grave for three years!"

"Good idea!" The disciples responded unanimously.

"It is very cold here," said Zeng Shen with a frown. "If we want to guard the grave, we have to build some grass sheds at least to keep us warm."

"It is too late to build sheds today," said Min Shun. "Let's go and find some firewood and light a bonfire by the grave. The fire will not only keep us warm but may also light up the road to Heaven for our master's spirit."

The disciples went away and returned with a lot of firewood. They built a large bonfire which lasted the whole night.

The next day the disciples built a few sheds and stayed in there to guard the grave. Apart from reading and conversing among themselves, they spent much time fortifying the grave and planting flowers and grass around it. They even built a wide passageway leading to the grave.

Spring arrived about half a month later, bringing new life to the land. Min Shun suggested to the other disciples, "Let's plant some trees around the master's grave."

His suggestion won instant approval among the others.

"What kind of trees shall we plant?" asked Min Shun.

"Pines and cypresses," said You Ruo firmly. "Our master once said that only when it grows cold in winter do we recognize the pines and cypresses are the last to lose their leaves. There is no doubt that our master liked these trees a lot."

"We can plant junipers," suggested Gongliang Ru. "Junipers not only remain green all the year round but are very tall and upright and have luxuriant leaves. They can be a symbol of the perseverance of our late master."

"You are right!" agreed Yan Yan, Bu Shang and Zhuansun Shi. "Let's plant junipers."

"We can plant many kinds of trees," said Zi Gong.

The others turned to look at him.

"Each of us has his own distinctive appearance and disposition," explained Zi Gong. "We have different opinions not only about trees but about a lot of other things in the world. In spite of this, our master liked everyone of us. Therefore I think we should go and collect our favorite trees and return here to plant them."

"An excellent idea!" said Zeng Shen. "Various trees growing around the master's grave can signify his love and concern for us and our deep respect for him. After we leave at the end of three years, the trees will remain here to keep the master company."

"Are we all agreed?" Zi Gong turned to the others and asked.

"Yes, we are."

"In that case," said Zeng Shen, "let's set out to collect the saplings!"

"Some of us can go first," suggested Min Shun, "while others stay here to guard the grave."

"Yes," agreed Zi Gong. "Let the eldest ones go first."

About thirty disciples left. These included Min Shun, Ran Yong, Ran Qiu, Zeng Dian, Yan Lu, Qidiao Kai and Shang Qu. They returned one after another three days later, each carrying two saplings, mostly cypress or juniper.

"Why has each of you brought back two saplings?" asked Zi Gong.

"We fear that some saplings may not survive in case of natural or man-made calamities," said Min Shun. "So each of us will plant two to ensure that at least one will survive."

"How shall we arrange the right sequence?" asked Zi Gong.

Almost all had a blank look, not knowing what he was driving at.

Zeng Shen immediately understood what Zi Gong meant. "The master always placed great emphasis on the right sequence," he said. "Two proper sequences must be observed here: First, the trees should be arranged according to their variety. Second, we should plant our trees according to seniority."

You Ruo shook his head. "It would be natural to group trees by variety, so that they may appear well-ordered and pleasing to the eye. But it would not be suitable for us to plant trees according to seniority."

"What's your opinion then?" asked Zeng Shen.

"The sequence should be decided by learning and virtue."

"The master's favorite disciple was Yan Hui," said Zeng Shen. "Unfortunately he is no longer with us."

"That's no problem," said You Ruo. "Let Yan Lu plant trees first on Yan Hui's behalf."

Yan Lu, embarrassed on hearing this, declined. "No," he said, "that would not be appropriate."

Min Shun thought for a while and suddenly said, "It is appropriate!"

The others looked at him in surprise.

"First of all, Yan Lu is Yan Hui's father. Secondly, Yan Lu was the first disciple our master ever taught. It is therefore most appropriate for him to plant trees first."

Yan Lu opened his mouth intending to decline further, but Min Shun stopped him. "Since we all agree you are the suitable one to plant trees on Yan Hui's behalf, just do it!"

"Where shall I plant them?" asked Yan Lu.

"In my opinion," said Zi Gong, "we can plant junipers in the first row along the passageway, cypresses in the second row, and the other varieties subsequently."

"That's a good idea!" said Min Shun. "If the trees are arranged in this way, they will look neat and orderly when they grow up. Are we all agreed then?"

"Agreed!" responded the others.

They marked out the positions for digging pits, and Yan Lu began to dig.

After Yan Lu had planted the first two junipers, Min Shun asked, "Who will be the next?"

"Zeng Shen," said Zi Gong assuredly.

Zeng Shen blushed with embarrassment. "Don't poke fun at me, brother! I am not the one!"

"Why not?" asked Zi Gong earnestly. "I made the suggestion after careful consideration. First, though you began to study with the master quite late, you excelled among us by grasping the essence of his teaching. Second, you have made up your mind to become a teacher and carry on the work of the master. You will be the one to pass on the master's teaching to later generations."

All others agreed with him, so Zi Gong placed the pickax into Zeng Shen's hands.

Urged by the others, Zeng Shen took the pickax and dug two pits. "But I have no saplings to plant!" he said helplessly.

"That's no problem," said Zi Gong. "You can plant your father's saplings first."

On hearing this, Zeng Dian hastily brought forth the two junipers he had gathered.

"Who will be the next?" murmured Zi Gong to himself.

"Min Shun!" suggested Qidiao Kai.

"I don't deserve the honor," said Min Shun.

But the other disciples all agreed he should be the next to plant trees.

"But I have chosen the cypress," said Min Shun.

"You can plant them at the head of the second row," said Zi Gong.

After Min Shun had planted his two cypresses, Qidiao Kai asked Zi Gong, "What kind of trees do you plan to plant?"

Zi Gong thought for a while, then replied, "Only pines, cypresses and junipers have been chosen. These trees remain green and luxuriant all the year round and stand for purity and steadfastness. However, we don't have to plant trees of the same color. In my homeland we have the pistache, a beautiful tree whose wood is hard and fine-grained, and whose leaves turn red after frost. I intend to go and buy two pistache saplings."

"That would be fine. When will you go?"

"I will go tomorrow."

There were some disciples who preferred oaks and poplars. Altogether, several hundred trees were planted beside Confucius' grave.

About a dozen days later Zi Gong returned with two pistache saplings. To prevent the roots from drying up he had wrapped them with mud and kept watering on them, so that when he arrived at Confucius' grave the roots were still wet. Without waiting to take a rest, he immediately planted the two saplings on both sides of the passageway.

After that, the disciples stayed in the sheds to guard the grave. Apart from studying they also tended after the saplings, watering them and killing insects.

They held a ritual of sacrifice every seven days in accordance with local custom. After forty-nine days, a ritual would be held only on major festivals. One morning they were watering the flowers around the grave when Gongliang Ru said, "You Ruo looks very much like the master in appearance and manners. Why don't we treat him as our master and wait on him?"

"That's a good idea!" Yan Yan, Bu Shang and Zhuansun Shi responded in unison.

"We can't do that!" exclaimed Zeng Shen indignantly. "Our

master was pure and bright as if washed by the great river and shone by the sun. There is no one among us who can compare with him."

Aware of their mistake, Yan Yan and the others fell silent.

At the morning audience one day in the first month of the seventeenth year of Duke Ai of Lu's reign (478 B.C.), the duke said to his court officials, "It has been almost a year since Confucius died. The eleventh day next month will be the first anniversary of his death. I have often thought of him. It is an honor of our homeland to have produced such a great sage. I intend to do something to commemorate this first anniversary of his. What do you think?"

"Your Lordship," said Mengsun Heji emphatically, "Confucius is unparalleled in his virtue and talents. It would be most proper for us to commemorate him."

"Many things can be done to commemorate the dead," said Jisun Fei. "The offering of sacrifice is the most solemn and respectful. Why don't we hold a public sacrificial ritual in the master's honor to express Your Lordship's deep feelings for him?"

"That's not a bad idea," said Duke Ai, placing his hands on the table. "But where can the ritual be held, since there is no temple so far erected in his memory?"

An idea occurred to Mengsun Heji, and he said with excitement, "The master started teaching disciples in his residence. I think we could transform his residence into a temple and have sacrifice conducted there."

Duke Ai of Lu hesitated and turned to look at the other officials.

"In my opinion, Minister Mengsun's suggestion is very practical," said Jisun Fei.

"You really think so?" asked Duke Ai with great relief.

"Yes, I do think so!" replied Jisun Fei.

"What do you all think?" Duke Ai turned and asked the other officials, who all expressed their agreement.

Then Duke Ai thought of something and frowned. "A statue is needed at the sacrificial ceremony. But how can a statue be made in such a short time?"

"The statue can be made on a later occasion," said Mengsun Heji. "Confucius spent all his life practicing and teaching the six arts. In my opinion, we can clear up his house and put his books, his bow and arrows, and his chariot and tallies on display there in his memory."

Duke Ai smiled with satisfaction. "You have proved yourself a real disciple of Confucius by working out such a perfect solution." He got up from his seat and said decisively, "Good! Now you may go and get everything ready!"

"I'll carry out your order!" responded Mengsun Heji.

"You must arrange for a new residence for the Kong family!" said Duke Ai.

"I understand," replied Mengsun Heji. "I will have it arranged properly." With this he left the palace and began to work with Nangong Jingshu to prepare for the sacrifice.

In the meantime Zeng Shen, Min Shun and some other disciples were discussing how to offer sacrifice to Confucius to commemorate the first anniversary of his death.

"It would be nice to build a temple for the master," said Gongliang Ru and Yan Ke.

"Yes," agreed Yan Lu. "Let's send a petition to His Lordship asking him to have a temple constructed for our master."

"We have to deal with the matter carefully," said Min Shun. "It can be achieved only if the duke is willing to do so."

The disciples were engaged in animated discussion when Nangong Jingshu arrived. "Fellow disciples," he announced excitedly, "His Lordship has agreed to convert the master's residence into a temple. He even plans to go there in person to offer sacrifice on the eleventh of the second month."

The disciples were overjoyed on hearing this.

"His Lordship has also ordered a new residence to be prepared for Kong Ji. Soon the old residence can be transformed into a temple."

Thereupon the disciples began to gather various objects Confucius had used in order to exhibit them in the temple in time for the sacrificial ceremony.

On the eighth day of the second month Duke Ai, accompanied by Jisun Fei, paid a visit to Confucius' residence, which had been completely refurnished. The walls had been repainted, and trees and flowers in the court trimmed. Entering the main room, they saw the old chariot of Confucius by the east wall, a bow with some arrows on the west wall, and a scroll of bamboo slips and counting tallies on the table in the center of the room. Beside the chariot there were also some bamboo slips, pieces of silk, bows and arrows, all collected by the disciples. Duke Ai combed his beard with his fingers and nodded in satisfaction.

The duke returned to the palace, where he bathed and fasted for three days. At midnight of the eleventh, Duke Ai put on his ceremonial gown and, escorted by Jisun Fei, went to Confucius' residence to conduct the first sacrifice in the master's honor.

Lamps were lit everywhere in the residence, shining as bright as day.

Jisun Fei was made to preside over the ceremony. At the appointed hour he announced in a loud voice, "Let music be played and dance performed!"

Immediately melodious music arose as thirty-two dancers in four rows walked in an orderly pace to the front gate, where they began to perform a ritual dance, waving bamboo tubes and pheasant feathers.

The sacrificial music had three movements. At the conclusion of the first movement, Duke Ai took three stacks of incense handed to him by Jisun Fei, walked to the main hall of the house, and planted the incense in the burner. Then he took a copper cup from Jisun Fei and poured wine to offer sacrifice. After that, the main ceremony was conducted.

At the end of three movements of music the dancers retreated in good order.

"To extol the virtue and benevolence of the master," announced Duke Ai in a low voice, "a memorial ceremony will be conducted here on each major festival!"

The disciples were filled with gratitude on hearing this.

The lamps grew dim as Duke Ai mounted his chariot and left for the palace, and he disciples returned to guard their master's grave.

That summer it did not rain for a long time, and grain seedlings began to wither in the field. The young trees planted around the grave were also threatened by the drought. The disciples had to carry water from the river to water the trees and the flowers on the grave mound.

One evening a violent wind arose all of a sudden. Most of the straw sheds were torn apart and blown away. The disciples, taking the bamboo slips with them, gathered in the few sheds that remained standing.

The sky was pierced by thunder and lightning, which were followed by a torrential rain. The disciples were all soaked through.

About an hour later the wind abated, but it continued to rain heavily.

The rain stopped at daybreak. When the sun rose over the

mountain the land was brimming with life.

Zeng Shen looked at the other disciples. "Let's go out and air our books!" he suggested.

They took out the bamboo slips from the sheds and spread them in the sun. Then they rebuilt the sheds destroyed by the storm.

In this way the disciples spent three years of mourning beside Confucius' grave, dressed in white and abstaining from meat. They had to endure mosquitoes in hot summer and wind and snow in winter.

In the second month of the eighteenth year of Duke Ai of Lu's reign (476 B.C.) Duke Ai conducted a grand sacrificial ceremony to commemorate Confucius just as in the previous years. For the disciples, the three years' mourning was over, and it was time for them to part with each other.

Min Shun said to Zeng Shen, "In his lifetime our master taught three thousand disciples, but Yan Hui and you are the most diligent among us. Unfortunately Yan Hui died many years ago, leaving you as the only one to carry on the teaching cause of the master. This is no easy task! From now on you have to start preparing for your school. Don't fall short of our master's expectations!"

"Please trust me," said Zeng Shen. "I will keep the promise that I made to the master."

Min Shun smiled satisfactorily. When he turned and caught sight of Kong Ji, he said to Zeng Shen, "Kong Ji is the master's only grandson. He is well-endowed and has high aspirations in spite of his young age. By receiving a good education, he will surely become a great scholar. Please spare no efforts in teaching him!"

"I will of course do that," said Zeng Shen. He turned to the other disciples and raised his voice. "The teaching of our master is so high, deep and broad that it is beyond my power to pass it on all by myself. I hope some of you will volunteer to join me in carrying on the teaching cause of our master."

All fell silent.

"By my observation," continued Zeng Shen, "Bu Shang has been studying carefully and meticulously. He is fit to be a teacher."

The others all turned to look at Bu Shang, who blushed and said in a low voice, "Frankly speaking, I would very much like to do that, but I am worried that my learning is too shallow and limited for such a heavy task!"

"You will succeed in what you do if you really put your mind into it," said the other disciples in encouragement.

Bu Shang looked at them gratefully and acquiesced.

One after another the disciples left Confucius' grave for home.

"I do not intend to leave now," said Zi Gong to Ran Yong.

"Why not?" asked Ran Yong. "We have already expressed our respect for the master by watching his grave for a whole three years in accordance with the rites."

"The master taught me for dozens of years," said Zi Gong. "Only thus did I manage to obtain a little learning. I want to stay by his grave for another three years."

"A dead man can not come back to life," said You Ruo. "Our master would feel nothing if we should stay by his grave the rest of our lives. Why don't you leave with us?"

"In the past three years," said Zi Gong, "whenever I closed my eyes to think of the master, his face appeared before me, full of kindness, grace and tranquility, and I felt as if I could still hear his tireless instruction. To me the master is very much alive!"

The three disciples bade each other a tearful farewell.

After that Zi Gong stayed in the only shed by the grave. He got up early in the morning and went to bed late at night, studying diligently and tending after the grave.

The other disciples often came to visit. One day Ran Qiu came. The two of them took a walk around Confucius' grave. Ran Qiu said, "Nowadays, the authority of the king of Zhou keeps diminishing, and our lord seems helpless to rebuild Lu into a prosperous state. The condition in the world is going from bad to worse. What is there to be done?"

"Our master was unparalleled in his learning and ability," said Zi Gong, "yet he could achieve nothing when no ruler would use his service. As for us, we can do little to save the world with our insignificant skills. Let's simply be contented with preserving our own purity!"

Ran Qiu smiled bitterly. "You are not going to be a recluse, are you?"

Zi Gong sighed. "When those in power are inept, people of moral integrity go away and conceal themselves. When those in power are unrighteous, people of great virtue go away and hide themselves. Moreover, the old dynasty will eventually be replaced by a new one; this has been the case since ancient times. No one will be able to stop it."

Ran Qiu looked at Zi Gong in astonishment.

"The king of Zhou lives in the secluded inner quarters of the royal palace," Zi Gong went on in an agitated voice. "He knows neither the will of Heaven nor the sufferings of the common people, yet he continues to regard himself as the supreme ruler of the world. Isn't that deplorable! As a result, the world has been plunged into turbulence as the vassal lords keep fighting among themselves."

"What, then," asked Ran Qiu, "do you think the world will be like in the future?"

Zi Gong's reply was unequivocal. "Conflicts will intensify, and weak states will be annexed by the strong. The world will get unified, split up, then get reunified."

"When will the world truly become one community?"

"That is merely a picture of the ideal society envisaged by the ancients," said Zi Gong. "I am not sure if it would come true in a thousand years."

Ran Qiu shook his head with resignation. He took leave of Zi Gong with a heavy heart.

On the eleventh day of the second month of the twenty-first year of Duke Ai of Lu's reign (473 B.C.) Zi Gong attended the sacrifice to Confucius along with some other disciples, then prepared to leave his shed by Confucius' grave. Having put his books into the chariot, he went to pay homage to the grave for the last time. He burned incense and poured some wine, then knelt before the grave. "Master, please forgive me for leaving you. From now on you will only have these young trees for your company." He got up and stroked the trees planted by him and fellow disciples. Then he knelt again as tears rolled down his cheeks. "Master, please rest in peace. I am leaving at last!" He slowly rose and looked at the trees around the grave, taking them all in. He walked to his chariot, but stopped several times to look back. He could not help worrying that something untoward might happen to Confucius' grave, or that someone would try to defame the master.

With his heart filled with sorrow and concern, Zi Gong left Confucius' grave and set out for Wei.

Chapter Fifty

Confucius Receives Various Titles from Subsequent Kings and Emperors; The Confucian Descendants Enjoy Honor and Position in Successive Dynasties

Zi Gong's worry proved to be well-founded. In 221 B.C. Yin Zheng, the prince of the state of Qin, destroyed all rivaling states and unified China under the Qin Dynasty. To consolidate his rule, he not only ordered all weapons to be gathered and destroyed, but also had all the books of various schools of thought to be burned. More than four hundred and sixty Confucian scholars were buried alive, and the books handed down by Confucius and his disciples were almost completely destroyed. Fortunately Kong Fu, Confucius' grandson of the ninth grade, had a double wall built in the former residence of Confucius and hid some classics inside. The books thus preserved included *The Book of Documents*, *The Book of Rites*, *The Analects of Confucius* and *The Book of Filiality*.

After that, the situation took on a drastic change. In the twelfth month of 195 B.C. Liu Bang, first emperor of the Han Dynasty, conducted a grand ceremony in the Confucius Temple, offering the sacrifice of an ox, a sheep and a pig. Afterward, emperors of successive dynasties kept conferring various honors on Confucius.

In the fifth year of the Jianwu reign (A.D. 29) Liu Xiu, Emperor Guangwu of the Eastern Han Dynasty, while traveling past Queli, ordered his minister Song Hong to offer sacrifice to Confucius.

In the fifteenth year of the Yongping reign (A.D. 72) Liu Zhuang, Emperor Mingdi of Han, went personally to Qufu to worship Confucius and his seventy-two most illustrious disciples. He ordered the crown prince to give a lecture about the Confucian classics, to which he also attended in person.

In the second year of the Yuanhe reign (A.D. 85) Liu Da, Emperor Zhang of Han, went to Qufu to worship Confucius and his seventy-two disciples.

In the third year of the Yanguang reign (A.D. 124) Liu Hu,

Emperor Andi of Han, went to Qufu to worship Confucius and his seventy-two disciples.

In the nineteenth year of the Taihe reign (A.D. 495) Yuan Hong, Emperor Xiaowen of Northern Wei in the Southern and Northern Dynasties Period, went to Qufu to worship Confucius.

In the first year of the Qianfeng reign (A.D. 666) Li Zhi, Emperor Gaozong of Tang, went to offer sacrifice to Confucius while passing Qufu. Li Longji, Emperor Xuanzong of Tang, did the same in the thirteenth year of the Kaiyuan reign (A.D. 725). He also sent Su Ting, the Minister of Rites, to worship Confucius with the sacrifice of an ox, a sheep and a pig.

In the second year of the Guangshun reign (A.D. 952) Guo Wei, Emperor Taizu of Northern Zhou in the Five Dynasties Period, went to Qufu to worship Confucius in both the temple and the forest in front of Confucius' grave.

In the first year of the Dazhong Xiangfu reign (1008) Zhao Huan, Emepror Zhenzong of the Song Dynasty, stopped at Qufu on his journey and went to the Confucius Temple and Confucius Forest to offer sacrifice.

In the twenty-third year of his reign (1684) Emperor Kangxi of Qing prostrated himself three times and kowtowed nine times while worshiping Confucius at the temple. He prostrated himself once and kowtowed three times when worshiping in the Confucius Forest.

Emperor Qianlong of Qing visited Qufu nine times during his reign (in the years 1748, 1756, 1757, 1762, 1771, 1776, 1784 and 1790). Each time he went to the Confucius Temple and Confucius Forest to worship the master, prostrating himself three times and kowtowing nine times, or prostrating himself twice and kowtowing six times, or prostrating himself once and kowtowing three times to express his deepest respect.

Emperors of successive dyansties not only went personally to Qufu to worship Confucius but also conferred many honors and titles on him.

When Duke Ai of Lu made his elegiac speech after the death of Confucius, he addressed him as "Father Ni." Though not a formal title, it was nevertheless a very respectful epithet.

Confucius received his first title in A.D. 1, when Empeor Pingdi of Han conferred on him the title Baocheng Xuannigong, or "Praised for Attainment, Illustrious Duke Ni."

In the sixteenth year of the Taihe reign (492) Emperor Xiaowen of Northern Wei canonized Confucius as Wensheng Nifu, or "Cultural Sage, Father Ni."

In the second year of the Daxiang reign (580) Emperor Jingdi of Northern Zhou honored Confucius as Zouguogong, or "Duke of Zou."

In the first year of the Kaihuang reign (581) Emperor Wendi of Sui gave Confucius the title Xianshi Nifu, or "Foremost Teacher, Father Ni."

In the second year of the Zhenguan reign (628) Emperor Taizong of Tang honored Confucius with the title Xiansheng, or "Foremost Sage." The title was changed to Xuanfu, or "Illustrious Father" in the eleventh year of the Zhenguan reign (637).

Emperor Gaozong of Tang conferred on Confucius the title Taishi, or "Grand Teacher," in the first year of the Qianfeng reign (666).

The empress Wu Zetian called Confucius Longdaogong, or "Truth-Upholding Duke" in the first year of the Tianshou reign (690).

In the twenty-seventh year of the Kaiyuan reign Confucius' status was elevated by Emperor Xuanzong of Tang, who canonized him as Wenxuan Wang, or "Culture-Propagating King."

In the first year of the Dazhong Xiangfu reign (1008) Emperor Zhenzong of Song honored Confucius as Xuansheng Wenxuan Wang, or "Profound Sage, Culture-Propagating King," and in 1029 changed the title to Zhisheng Wenxuan Wang, or "Ultimate Sage, Culture-Propagating King."

In the eleventh year of the Dade reign (1307) Emperor Chengzong of Yuan honored Confucius as Dacheng Zhisheng Wenxuan Wang," or "Great Perfection, Ultimate Sage, Culture-Propagating King."

In the ninth year of the Jiajing reign (1530) Emperor Shizong of Ming honored Confucius as Zhisheng Xianshi, or "Ultimate Sage, Foremost Teacher."

In the second year of the Shunzhi reign (1654) Emperor Shizu of Qing conferred on Confucius the title Dacheng Zhisheng Wenxuan Xianshi, or "Great Perfection, Ultimate Sage, Foremost Culture-Propagating Teacher," and in 1657 changed the title to Zhisheng Xianshi, or "Ultimate Sage, Foremost Teacher."

While Confucius was given numerous posthumous titles and honored in successive dynasties, his temple in Qufu also underwent continuous expansion. By the beginning of the Ming Dynasty the temple had been extended to include three courtyards and nine gates. The Confucian forest, the grave site of Confucius and his descendants, had also been enlarged to more than two hundred hectares. The residence of the Kong family also had three courtyards and nine gates, the most prestigious style in traditional Chinese architecture.

The Confucian descendants also received many titles and honors.

Confucius had an only son, Kong Li, whose styled name was Bo Yu. He was given the posthumous title Marquis of Sishui by Emperor Huizong of Song in the first year of the Chongning reign (1102).

Kong Li also had an only son, Kong Ji, whose styled name was Zi Si. He received the posthumous title Marquis of Yishui in the first year of the Chongning reign (1102). Emperor Wenzong of Yuan gave him the title Duke Susheng of Yi in the first year of the Zhishun reign (1330). He is believed to be the author of the Confucian classic *Doctrine of the Mean.*

Kong Bai, of the fourth generation, had Zi Shang as his styled name.

Kong Qiu, of the fifth generation, had Zi Jia as his styled name.

Kong Ji, of the sixth generation, had Zi Jing as his styled name. He wrote a twelve-chapter book titled *Lan Yan (Old Tales and Anecdotes).*

Kong Chuan, of the seventh generation, had Zi Gao as his styled name.

Kong Qian, of the eighth generation, had Zi Shun as his styled name.

Kong Qian had two sons. The elder one was Kong Fu, and the younger one Kong Teng. Kong Teng, whose styled name was Zi Xiang, was entitled Lord of Fengsi by Emperor Gaozu of Han in the twelfth year of his reign (195 B.C.) and put in charge of sacrificial activities in honor of Confucius.

Kong Zhong, of the tenth generation, had Zi Zhen as his styled name. He received the title Learned Scholar from Emperor Wendi of Han.

Kong Wu, of the eleventh generation, had Zi Wei as his styled name. He was also titled Learned Scholar by Emperor Wendi of Han.

Kong Yannian, of the twelfth generation, was again titled Learned Scholar by Emperor Wendi of Han.

Kong Shuang, of the thirteenth generation, had Ci Ru as his

styled name. He received the title Marquis Baocheng from Emperor Yuandi of Han in the first year of the Yongguang reign (43 B.C.).

Kong Fu (also named Kong Ji), of the fourteenth generation, was titled Adept Marquis of Yinshao by Emperor Chengdi of Han in the first year of the Suihe reign (8 B.C.).

Kong Fang, of the fifteenth generation, inherited the title Marquis Baocheng in the second year of the Jianping reign (5 B.C.) under Emperor Aidi of Han.

Kong Jun, of the sixteenth generation, had Chang Ping as his styled name. He inherited the title Marquis Baocheng in the first year of the Yuanshi reign (A.D. 1) under Emperor Pingdi of Han.

Kong Zhi, of the seventeenth generation, inherited the title Marquis of Baocheng in the fourteenth year of the Jianwu reign under Emperor Guangwu of Han (A.D.38).

Kong Shun, of the eighteenth generation, had Jun Yi as his styled name. He inherited the title Marquis of Baocheng in the fifteenth year of the Yongping reign under Emperor Mingdi of Han (A.D. 72). He was given the title Marquis of Baoting in the fourth year of the Yongyuan reign under Emperor Hedi of Han (A.D. 92).

Kong Yao, of the nineteenth generation, had Jun Yao as his styled name. He was entitled Marquis of Fengshengting in the third year of the Yanguang reign under Emperor Andi of Han (A.D. 124).

Kong Wan, of the twentieth generation, inherited the title Marquis of Baoting in the second year of the Jianning reign under Emperor Lingdi of Han (A.D. 169).

Kong Wan died prematurely leaving no offspring. His brother Kong Zan's eldest son, Kong Xian, inherited the title of marquis. Kong Xian, whose styled name was Zi Yu, received the title Marquis of Zongsheng in the second year of the Huangchu reign under Emperor Wendi of Wei (A.D. 221). He belonged to the twenty-first generation.

Kong Zhen, of the twenty-second generation, had Bo Qi as his styled name. He inherited the title Marquis of Fengshengting in the third year of the Taishi reign under Emepror Wudi of Western Jin (A.D. 267).

Kong Yi (also named Kong Ting), of the twenty-third generation, had Cheng Gong as his styled name. He inherited the title Marquis of Fengshengting in the third year of the Taining reign under Emperor Mingdi of Eastern Jin (A.D. 325).

Kong Fu, of the twenty-fourth generation, inherited the title

Marquis of Fengshengting.

Kong Yi, of the twenty-fifth generation, inherited the title Marquis of Fengshengting.

Kong Xian, of the twenty-sixth generation, whose styled name was Yin Zhi, inherited the title Marquis of Fengshengting in the nineteenth year of the Yuanjia reign under Emperor Wendi of Song (A.D. 442).

Kong Cheng, of the twenty-seventh generation, whose styled name was Jing Shan, received the title Minister of Chongsheng in the third year of the Yanxing reign under Emperor Xiaowen of Northern Wei (A.D. 473).

Kong Lingzhen, of the twenty-eighth generation, was entitled Marquis of Chongsheng in the nineteenth year of the Taihe reign under Emperor Xiaowen of Northern Wei (A.D. 495).

Kong Wentai, of the twenty-ninth generation, inherited the title Marquis Chongsheng.

Kong Qu, of the thirtieth generation, inherited the title Marquis Chongsheng.

Kong Changsun, of the thirty-first generation, was entitled Marquis Gongsheng in the first year of the Tianbao reign under Emperor Wenxuan of Northern Qi (A.D. 550), and Duke of Zou in the second year of the Daxiang reign of Emperor Jingdi of Northern Zhou (A.D. 580).

Kong Sizhe, of the thirty-second generation, was entitled Marquis Shaosheng in the fourth year of the Daye reign under Emperor Yangdi of Sui (A.D. 608).

Kong Delun, of the thirty-third generation, was entitled Marquis Baosheng in the ninth year of the Wude reign under Emperor Gaozu of Tang (A.D. 626).

Kong Chongji, of the thirty-fourth generation, inherited the title Marquis Baosheng in the first year of the Zhensheng reign under Empress Wu Zetian of Tang (A.D. 695).

Kong Suzhi, of the thirty-fifth generation, had Chang Hui as his styled name. He inherited the title Marquis Baosheng in the fifth year of the Kaiyuan reign under Emperor Xuanzong of Tang (A.D. 717). He was entitled Duke Wenxuan and Magistrate of Yanzhou in the twenty-seventh year of the Kaiyuan reign under Emepror Xuanzong of Tang (A.D. 739).

Kong Xuan, of the thirty-sixth generation, inherited the title

Duke Wenxuan.

Kong Qiqing, of the thirty-seventh generation, inherited the title Duke Wenxuan in the third year of the Jianzhong reign under Emperor Dezong of Tang (A.D. 782).

Kong Weizhi, of the thirty-eighth generation, inherited the title Duke Wenxuan in the thirteenth year of the Yuanhe reign under Emperor Xianzong of Tang (A.D. 818).

Kong Ce, of the thirty-ninth generation, inherited the title Duke Wenxuan in the second year of the Huichang reign under Emperor Wuzong of Tang (A.D. 842).

Kong Zhen, of the fortieth generation, had Guo Wen as his styled name. He inherited the title Duke Wenxuan in the fourth year of the Xiantong reign under Emperor Yizong of Tang (A.D. 863).

Kong Zhaojian, of the forty-first generation, inherited the title Duke Wenxuan.

Kong Guangsi, of the forty-second generation, had Zhai Lang as his styled name. He was appointed an official of Sishui County in A.D. 905 and lost the hereditary title Duke Wenxuan. Soon after the birth of his son, Kong Renyu, Kong Guangsi was murdered by his tenant Kong Mo in A.D. 933. Kong Renyu's mother brought him to take refuge in the house of her father, Zhang Wen. When Kong Mo arrived, Zhang Wen saved Kong Renyu by submitting another grandson (by his son), who was killed by Kong Mo. Kong Renyu grew up in Zhang Wen's house. When Kong Renyu grew to the age of nineteen in the first year of the Changxing reign of Later Tang (A.D. 930), Emperor Mingzong was informed of what had happened in the Confucian house. The emperor looked into the case and ordered Kong Mo to be executed. Kong Renyu was put in charge of the Confucius Temple and appointed an official of Qufu County. In the third year of the Changxing reign (A.D. 932) Emperor Mingzong conferred on Kong Renyu the hereditary title Duke Wenxuan. Kong Renyu was appointed magistrate of Qufu County in the first year of the Jianlong reign under Emperor Taizu of Song (A.D. 960). Kong Renyu, styled name Wen Ru, was a Confucian offspring of the forty-third generation. He regained the hereditary title lost by his father and inherited the family fortune and later became known as the "resurgent ancestor."

Kong Renyu had four sons. The eldest son, Kong Yi, whose styled name was Bu Yi, was appointed an official of Qufu County in the fourth year of the Qiande reign under Emperor Taizu of Song (A.D.

966). He was entitled Minister Zanshan in the third year of the Taiping Xingguo reign under Emperor Taizong of Song (A.D. 978) and inherited the title Duke Wenxuan. Kong Yi was a Confucian offspring of the forty-fourth generation.

Kong Yanshi, of the forty-fifth generation, had Mao Xian as his styled name. He inherited the title Duke Wenxuan in the third year of the Zhidao reign under Emperor Taizong of Song (A.D. 997). He was also appointed an official of Qufu County.

Kong Shengyou, of the forty-sixth generation, inherited the title Duke Wenxuan and was appointed a magistrate's assistant of Qufu County in the fifth year of the Tianxi reign under Emperor Zhenzong of Song (1021). As Kong Shengyou had no offspring, his younger cousin Kong Zongyuan inherited the title Duke Wenxuan and was appointed magistrate's assistant of Qufu County in the second year of the Baoyuan reign under Emperor Renzong (1039). Kong Zongyuan, whose styled name was Zi Zhuang, received the title Duke Yansheng in the second year of the Zhihe reign under Emperor Renzong (1055). After that, the title Duke Yansheng was passed down in the Kong family from generation to generation.

Kong Ruomeng, of the forty-seventh generation, had Gong Ming as his styled name. He inherited the title Duke Yansheng in the first year of the Xining reign under Emperor Shenzong of Song (1068). In the first year of the Yuanfu reign under Emperor Zhezong of Song (1098) Kong Ruomeng was deprived of his title, which was then given to his younger brother, Kong Ruoxu, whose styled name was Gong Shi. Upon Kong Ruoxu's death, Kong Ruomeng's son Kong Duanyou inherited the title.

Kong Duanyou, of the forty-eighth generation, had Zi Jiao as his styled name. He inherited the title Duke Yansheng in the first year of the Chongning reign under Emperor Huizong of Song (1102).

Kong Duanyou had no offspring. His younger brother, Kong Duancao, had two sons: the elder son was named Kong Jie, and the younger one, Kong Fan.

Kong Fan, of the forty-ninth generation, had Wen Lao as his styled name. He twice received the hereditary title Duke Yansheng, in the twelfth year of the Tianhui reign under Emperor Taizong of Jin (1134) and in the third year of the Tianjuan reign under Emperor Xizong of Jin (1140).

Kong Zheng, of the fiftieth generation, had Yuan Ji as his styled name. He inherited the title Duke Yansheng in the second year of the Huangtong reign under Emperor Xizong (1142). Kong Zheng died prematurely, leaving no offspring. His younger brother Kong Zong inherited the title Duke Yansheng in the third year of the Dading reign under Emperor Shizong of Jin (1163). Kong Zong gave birth to a son, Kong Yuancuo, whose styled name was Meng De.

Kong Yuancuo, of the fifty-first generation, received the hereditary title Duke Yansheng twice, in the second year of the Mingchang reign under Emperor Zhangzong of Jin (1191) and in the fifth year under the reign of Emperor Taizong of Yuan (1233). Kong Yuancuo had no offspirng, and the hereditary title was passed on to his younger brother Kong Yuanhong's son, Kong Zhen.

Kong Zhen, of the fifty-second generation, had Zhao Du as his styled name. He inherited the title Duke Yansheng in the first year of the reign of Emperor Xianzong of Yuan (1251). The following year he was deprived of this title, as he was said to be the son of someone named Li.

For forty-three years after that, no one held the title Duke Yansheng in the Kong family. In the first year of the Yuanzhen reign of Emperor Chengzong of Yuan (1295), Kong Zhi received the title Duke Yansheng. Kong Zhi, of the fifty-third generation, whose styled name was Shi An, was the grandson of the sixth degree of Kong Ruoyu, Kong Zongyuan's third son. Kong Ruoyu had one son, Kong Duanli, who had Zi Zhi as his styled name. Kong Duandi had one son, Kong Hu, who had Xi Lao as his styled name. Kong Hu had one son, Kong Fo, who had Wen Tong as his styled name. Kong Fo had one son, Kong Yuanyong, who had Jun Qing as his styled name.

Kong Zhi's son, Kong Sicheng, of the fifty-fourth generation, inherited the title Duke Yansheng. As Kong Sicheng did not belong to the direct line of descent, the conferment caused much controversy among the Kong family and was later canceled, and the title was passed on to Kong Sihui, an offspring of Kong Ruoyu. Kong Sihui, whose styled name was Ming Dao, inherited the title Duke Yansheng in the third year of the Yanyou reign under Emperor Renzong of Yuan (1316). Kong Sihui gave birth to a son, Kong Kejian, whose styled name was Jing Fu.

Kong Kejian, of the fifty-fifth generation, inherited the title Duke Yansheng in the sixth year of the Zhiyuan reign under Emperor Shundi of Yuan (1340).

Kong Xixue, of the fifty-sixth generation, had Shi Xing as his styled name. He inherited the title Duke Yansheng in the fifteenth year of the Zhizheng reign under Emperor Shundi of Yuan (1355). He again received the title in the first year of the Hongwu reign under Emperor Taizu of Ming (1368). In the thirteenth year of the Hongwu reign (1380) Emperor Taizu of Ming issued a decree that made Duke Yansheng head of all civil officials.

Kong Na, of the fifty-seventh generation, had Yan Bo as his styled name. He inherited the title Duke Yansheng in the seventeenth year of the Hongwu reign under Emperor Taizu of Ming (1384).

Kong Gongjian, of the fifty-eighth generation, whose styled name was Zhao Wen, inherited the title Duke Yansheng in the second year of the Jianwen reign under Emperor Huidi of Ming (1400).

Kong Yanjin, of the fifty-ninth generation, had Chao Shen as his styled name. He inherited the title Duke Yansheng in the eighth year of the Yongle reign under Emperor Chengzu of Ming (1410).

Kong Chengqing, of the sixtieth generation, whose styled name was Yong Zuo, died prematurely and received the title Duke Yansheng posthumously. Kong Chengqing had two sons. The elder one, Kong Hongxu, had Yi Jing as his styled name and Nan Xi as an alternative name. The younger son, Kong Hongtai, had Yi He as his styled name.

Kong Hongxu, of the sixty-first generation, inherited the title Duke Yansheng in the first year of the Jingtai reign under Emperor Daizong of Ming (1450). He was impeached for the overstandard scale of his residence and deprived of his title. His younger brother, Kong Hongtai, inherited the title Duke Yansheng in the fifth year of the Chenghua reign under Emperor Xianzong of Ming (1469). After that, the title was passed on to Kong Hongxu's son, Kong Wenshao.

Kong Wenshao, of the sixty-second generation, had Zhi De as his styled name and Chang An as an alternative name. He inherited the title Duke Yansheng in the sixteenth year of the Hongzhi reign under Emperor Xiaozong of Ming (1503).

Kong Zhengan, of the sixty-third generation, had Yong Ji as his styled name and Ke Ting as an alternative name. He inherited the title Duke Yansheng in the twenty-fifth year of the Jiajing reign under Emperor Shizong (1546).

Kong Shangxian, of the sixty-fourth generation, had Xiang Zhi as his styled name and Xi An as an alternative name. He inherited the title Duke Yansheng in the thirty-fifth year of the Jiajing reign under

Emperor Shizong of Ming (1556). Kong Shangxian's two sons, Yin-chun and Yingui, both died prematurely and left no offspring. The title was passed on to Kong Yinzhi, the son of Kong Shangxian's younger cousin, Kong Shangyuan. As Emperor Yongzheng was named Yinzhen, the character "Yin" became a taboo for his subjects, who had to use Yan in its place. Thus in some history books Yinchun became Yanchun; Yingui, Yangui, and Yinzhi, Yanzhi.

Kong Yinzhi, of the sixty-fifth generation, had Mao Jia as his styled name and Dui Huan as an alternative name. He inherited the title Duke Yansheng in the first year of the Tianqi reign under Emperor Xizong of Ming (1621).

Kong Xingxie, of the sixty-sixth generation, had Qi Lu as his styled name and Fu Yuan as an alternative name. He inherited the title Duke Yansheng in the fifth year of the Shunzhi reign in the Qing Dynasty (1648).

Kong Yuqi, of the sixty-seventh generation, had Zhong Zhai as his styled name and Lan Tang as an alternative name. He inherited the title Duke Yansheng in the sixth year of the Kangxi reign in the Qing Dynasty (1667).

Kong Chuanduo, of the sixty-eighth generation, had Zhen Lu as his styled name and Yong Min as an alternative name. He inherited the title Duke Yansheng in the first year of the Yongzheng reign in the Qing Dynasty (1723).

Kong Jihu, of the sixty-ninth generation, had Ti He as his styled name and Chun Zhai as an alternative name. He died of illness and received the title Duke Yansheng posthumously.

Kong Guangqi, of the seventieth generation, had Jing Li as his styled name and Shi Men as an alternative name. He inherited the title Duke Yansheng in the ninth year of the Yongzheng reign in the Qing Dynasty (1731).

Kong Zhaohuan, of the seventy-first generation, had Xian Wen as his styled name and Yao Yi as an alternative name. He inherited the title Duke Yansheng in the ninth year of the Qianlong reign in the Qing Dynasty (1744).

Kong Xianpei, of the seventy-second generation, had Yang Yuan as his styled name and Du Zhai as an alternative name. He inherited the title Duke Yansheng in the forty-eighth year of the Qianlong reign in the Qing Dynasty (1783). Kong Xianpei, formerly named Kong Xianyun, had his name changed by Emperor Qianlong. He married

Emperor Qianlong's daughter, but the couple was childless. The hereditary title of the family was passed on to Kong Qingrong, son of Kong Xianpei's younger brother Kong Xianzeng.

Kong Qingrong, of the seventy-third generation, had Tao Fu as his styled name and Ye Shan as an alternative name. He inherited the title Duke Yansheng in the fifty-ninth year of the Qianlong reign in the Qing Dynasty (1794).

Kong Fanhao, of the seventy-fourth generation, had Wen Yuan as his styled name and Bo Hai as an alternative name. He inherited the title Duke Yansheng in the twenty-first year of the Daoguang reign in the Qing Dynasty (1841).

Kong Xiangke, of the seventy-fifth generation, had Guan Tang as his styled name. He inherited the title Duke Yansheng in the second year of the Tongzhi reign in the Qing Dynasty (1863).

Kong Lingyi, of the seventy-sixth generation, had Yan Ting as his styled name. He inherited the title Duke Yansheng in the third year of the Guangxu reign in the Qing Dynasty (1877). He also received the title Duke Yansheng from President Yuan Shikai in the fourth year of the Republic (1915).

Kong Decheng, of the seventy-seventh generation, had Da Sheng as his styled name. He was given the title Duke Yansheng in the ninth year of the Republic (1920) by President Xu Shichang. He was appointed master of ceremonies in charge of ceremonial sacrifices in honor of Confucius by Chiang Kai-shek in the twenty-fourth year of the Republic (1935). Kong Decheng was the last one in the Kong family to receive the title Duke Yansheng, which was subsequently abolished by the Republic. Therefore he became known as the "last sage."

After "De" the succeeding generations were named Wei, Cui, You, Qin, Shao, Nian, Xian, and Yang.

Kong Lingyi also chose the first part of the given name to be used for twenty generations after "Yang": Jian, Dao, Dun, An, Ding, Mao, Xiu, Zhao, Yi, Chang, Yu, Wen, Huan, Jing, Rui, Yong, Xi, Shi, Xu and Chang.

Afterword

Confucius is a great historical figure. His contribution and influence in thinking, culture and politics have spread far beyond the national boundary. However, few people in the past wrote biographical or literary works to depict such an important figure. Apart from a chapter in Sima Qian's *Records of the Historian* and the *Trails of the Sage* of the Song Dynasty, there was virtually no literary or artistic work about Confucius before the Qing Dynasty. Dramas about Confucius began to be written in the twentieth century, and in recent years biographies, dramas, films, and television programs kept appearing. The authors included both Chinese and foreigners, both elderly and middle-aged people. This is certainly something to be rejoiced at. It is my hope that more and better literary works about Confucius will emerge in the future.

My career in creative writing is not long, but the wish to write a historical novel about Confucius has been on my mind for many years. The idea first occurred to me when I visited the Confucius Temple, Confucius Residence and Confucius Forest for the first time in 1964. In 1966, when I was transferred from Jinan to work in Jining, the idea began to take root. Jining is a beautiful and fertile land which has given birth to Confucius and many other great men: Mencius, Yan Hui, Zeng Shen, and Kong Ji. After I was made a foreign affairs official in 1980, I made frequent visits to Qufu, Zou County, Jiaxiang and Weishan and began to acquire a better understanding of Confucius, Mencius, Yan Hui and Zeng Shen. Such experience proved very helpful to my writing the story of Confucius. It was convenient for me to find relevant materials and gave me the opportunity to become familiar with the geography of the area. In addition, I came into contact with many people who knew legends about Confucius. Starting from spring 1987 I spent all my spare time writing the story of Confucius and completed the book in May this year.

In writing this book I received help from several people. Kuang Yaming wrote the preface, Cai Ruohong and Liu Kaiqu wrote the calligraphy for the title, and Sun Molong painted the picture of Confucius. I am grateful for their generous help.

In May 1988 I met Inoue Yasushi, a well-known Japanese writer and vice-chairman of P.E.N., when he visited Qufu. At the age of eighty-one, he was tirelessly working on his book about Confucius. I was moved by his high reverence for Confucius and love for the hometown of Confucius and inspired by his perseverance.

Wang Jinzhi volunteered to transcribe the manuscript for me, which cost him a lot of time and effort. His handsome and neat handwriting was admired by all who read it, including editors, proof-readers and typesetters. I can not thank him enough for this.

When I was busily writing the book, my wife, Sun Yunhua, took up the burden of doing household chores while not giving up her full-time job. She ran the house in good order and sent our two sons, Qu Xiaoqian and Qu Xiaojin, to college. I had nothing to worry about and therefore was able to complete the book in good time.

The publication of this book is therefore made possible by many people. Hereby I express my gratitude and respect for all those who have shown their concern and given their help.

I was asked what I planned to do next. Mencius was the greatest Confucian scholar after Confucius, and he was also born in the area of Jining. My next plan is therefore to write the story of Mencius.

Qu Chunli
October 1989

图书在版编目(CIP)数据

孔子传:英文 /曲春礼著. 一北京:外文出版社,1996
ISBN 7 - 119 - 01863 - 9
ISBN 7 - 119 - 01909 - 0

Ⅰ.孔… Ⅱ.曲… Ⅲ.①长篇小说－中国－现代－英文②
传记小说－中国－现代－英文Ⅳ.Ⅰ247.5

中国版本图书馆 CIP 数据核字(96)第 02967 号
中国版本图书馆 CIP 数据核字(96)第 12864 号

责任编辑 吴灿飞
封面设计 唐 宇
插图绘制 马 骥

孔 子 传

曲春礼 著
孙海晨 译

✕

ⓒ外文出版社
外文出版社出版
(中国北京百万庄大街 24 号)
邮政编码 100037
北京外文印刷厂印刷
中国国际图书贸易总公司发行
(中国北京车公庄西路 35 号)
北京邮政信箱第 399 号 邮政编码 100044
1996 年(28 开)第 1 版
(英)
ISBN 7 - 119 - 01863 - 9 / G·95(外)
04600(精)
ISBN 7 - 119 - 01909 - 0 / G·100(外)
03800(平)
7 - E - 3091